Lecture Notes in Computer Science   12769

More information about this subseries at http://www.springer.com/series/7409

Margherita Antona · Constantine Stephanidis (Eds.)

Universal Access in Human-Computer Interaction

Access to Media, Learning and Assistive Environments

15th International Conference, UAHCI 2021
Held as Part of the 23rd HCI International Conference, HCII 2021
Virtual Event, July 24–29, 2021
Proceedings, Part II

 Springer

Editors
Margherita Antona
Foundation for Research and Technology –
Hellas (FORTH)
Heraklion, Crete, Greece

Constantine Stephanidis
University of Crete and Foundation
for Research and Technology – Hellas
(FORTH)
Heraklion, Crete, Greece

ISSN 0302-9743   ISSN 1611-3349   (electronic)
Lecture Notes in Computer Science
ISBN 978-3-030-78094-4   ISBN 978-3-030-78095-1   (eBook)
https://doi.org/10.1007/978-3-030-78095-1

LNCS Sublibrary: SL3 – Information Systems and Applications, incl. Internet/Web, and HCI

This Springer imprint is published by the registered company Springer Nature Switzerland AG
The registered company address is: Gewerbestrasse 11, 6330 Cham, Switzerland

Foreword

Human-Computer Interaction (HCI) is acquiring an ever-increasing scientific and industrial importance, and having more impact on people's everyday life, as an ever-growing number of human activities are progressively moving from the physical to the digital world. This process, which has been ongoing for some time now, has been dramatically accelerated by the COVID-19 pandemic. The HCI International (HCII) conference series, held yearly, aims to respond to the compelling need to advance the exchange of knowledge and research and development efforts on the human aspects of design and use of computing systems.

The 23rd International Conference on Human-Computer Interaction, HCI International 2021 (HCII 2021), was planned to be held at the Washington Hilton Hotel, Washington DC, USA, during July 24–29, 2021. Due to the COVID-19 pandemic and with everyone's health and safety in mind, HCII 2021 was organized and run as a virtual conference. It incorporated the 21 thematic areas and affiliated conferences listed on the following page.

A total of 5222 individuals from academia, research institutes, industry, and governmental agencies from 81 countries submitted contributions, and 1276 papers and 241 posters were included in the proceedings to appear just before the start of the conference. The contributions thoroughly cover the entire field of HCI, addressing major advances in knowledge and effective use of computers in a variety of application areas. These papers provide academics, researchers, engineers, scientists, practitioners, and students with state-of-the-art information on the most recent advances in HCI. The volumes constituting the set of proceedings to appear before the start of the conference are listed in the following pages.

The HCI International (HCII) conference also offers the option of 'Late Breaking Work' which applies both for papers and posters, and the corresponding volume(s) of the proceedings will appear after the conference. Full papers will be included in the 'HCII 2021 - Late Breaking Papers' volumes of the proceedings to be published in the Springer LNCS series, while 'Poster Extended Abstracts' will be included as short research papers in the 'HCII 2021 - Late Breaking Posters' volumes to be published in the Springer CCIS series.

The present volume contains papers submitted and presented in the context of the 15th International Conference on Universal Access in Human-Computer Interaction (UAHCI 2021), an affiliated conference to HCII 2021. I would like to thank Margherita Antona for her invaluable contribution to its organization and the preparation of the proceedings, as well as the members of the Program Board for their contributions and support. This year, the UAHCI affiliated conference has focused on topics related to universal access methods, techniques and practices, studies on accessibility, Design for All, usability, UX and technology acceptance, emotion and behavior recognition for universal access, accessible media, and access to learning and education, as well universal access to virtual and intelligent assistive environments.

I would also like to thank the Program Board Chairs and the members of the Program Boards of all thematic areas and affiliated conferences for their contribution towards the highest scientific quality and overall success of the HCI International 2021 conference.

This conference would not have been possible without the continuous and unwavering support and advice of Gavriel Salvendy, founder, General Chair Emeritus, and Scientific Advisor. For his outstanding efforts, I would like to express my appreciation to Abbas Moallem, Communications Chair and Editor of HCI International News.

July 2021   Constantine Stephanidis

HCI International 2021 Thematic Areas and Affiliated Conferences

Thematic Areas

- HCI: Human-Computer Interaction
- HIMI: Human Interface and the Management of Information

Affiliated Conferences

- EPCE: 18th International Conference on Engineering Psychology and Cognitive Ergonomics
- UAHCI: 15th International Conference on Universal Access in Human-Computer Interaction
- VAMR: 13th International Conference on Virtual, Augmented and Mixed Reality
- CCD: 13th International Conference on Cross-Cultural Design
- SCSM: 13th International Conference on Social Computing and Social Media
- AC: 15th International Conference on Augmented Cognition
- DHM: 12th International Conference on Digital Human Modeling and Applications in Health, Safety, Ergonomics and Risk Management
- DUXU: 10th International Conference on Design, User Experience, and Usability
- DAPI: 9th International Conference on Distributed, Ambient and Pervasive Interactions
- HCIBGO: 8th International Conference on HCI in Business, Government and Organizations
- LCT: 8th International Conference on Learning and Collaboration Technologies
- ITAP: 7th International Conference on Human Aspects of IT for the Aged Population
- HCI-CPT: 3rd International Conference on HCI for Cybersecurity, Privacy and Trust
- HCI-Games: 3rd International Conference on HCI in Games
- MobiTAS: 3rd International Conference on HCI in Mobility, Transport and Automotive Systems
- AIS: 3rd International Conference on Adaptive Instructional Systems
- C&C: 9th International Conference on Culture and Computing
- MOBILE: 2nd International Conference on Design, Operation and Evaluation of Mobile Communications
- AI-HCI: 2nd International Conference on Artificial Intelligence in HCI

List of Conference Proceedings Volumes Appearing Before the Conference

1. LNCS 12762, Human-Computer Interaction: Theory, Methods and Tools (Part I), edited by Masaaki Kurosu
2. LNCS 12763, Human-Computer Interaction: Interaction Techniques and Novel Applications (Part II), edited by Masaaki Kurosu
3. LNCS 12764, Human-Computer Interaction: Design and User Experience Case Studies (Part III), edited by Masaaki Kurosu
4. LNCS 12765, Human Interface and the Management of Information: Information Presentation and Visualization (Part I), edited by Sakae Yamamoto and Hirohiko Mori
5. LNCS 12766, Human Interface and the Management of Information: Information-rich and Intelligent Environments (Part II), edited by Sakae Yamamoto and Hirohiko Mori
6. LNAI 12767, Engineering Psychology and Cognitive Ergonomics, edited by Don Harris and Wen-Chin Li
7. LNCS 12768, Universal Access in Human-Computer Interaction: Design Methods and User Experience (Part I), edited by Margherita Antona and Constantine Stephanidis
8. LNCS 12769, Universal Access in Human-Computer Interaction: Access to Media, Learning and Assistive Environments (Part II), edited by Margherita Antona and Constantine Stephanidis
9. LNCS 12770, Virtual, Augmented and Mixed Reality, edited by Jessie Y. C. Chen and Gino Fragomeni
10. LNCS 12771, Cross-Cultural Design: Experience and Product Design Across Cultures (Part I), edited by P. L. Patrick Rau
11. LNCS 12772, Cross-Cultural Design: Applications in Arts, Learning, Well-being, and Social Development (Part II), edited by P. L. Patrick Rau
12. LNCS 12773, Cross-Cultural Design: Applications in Cultural Heritage, Tourism, Autonomous Vehicles, and Intelligent Agents (Part III), edited by P. L. Patrick Rau
13. LNCS 12774, Social Computing and Social Media: Experience Design and Social Network Analysis (Part I), edited by Gabriele Meiselwitz
14. LNCS 12775, Social Computing and Social Media: Applications in Marketing, Learning, and Health (Part II), edited by Gabriele Meiselwitz
15. LNAI 12776, Augmented Cognition, edited by Dylan D. Schmorrow and Cali M. Fidopiastis
16. LNCS 12777, Digital Human Modeling and Applications in Health, Safety, Ergonomics and Risk Management: Human Body, Motion and Behavior (Part I), edited by Vincent G. Duffy
17. LNCS 12778, Digital Human Modeling and Applications in Health, Safety, Ergonomics and Risk Management: AI, Product and Service (Part II), edited by Vincent G. Duffy

18. LNCS 12779, Design, User Experience, and Usability: UX Research and Design (Part I), edited by Marcelo Soares, Elizabeth Rosenzweig, and Aaron Marcus
19. LNCS 12780, Design, User Experience, and Usability: Design for Diversity, Well-being, and Social Development (Part II), edited by Marcelo M. Soares, Elizabeth Rosenzweig, and Aaron Marcus
20. LNCS 12781, Design, User Experience, and Usability: Design for Contemporary Technological Environments (Part III), edited by Marcelo M. Soares, Elizabeth Rosenzweig, and Aaron Marcus
21. LNCS 12782, Distributed, Ambient and Pervasive Interactions, edited by Norbert Streitz and Shin'ichi Konomi
22. LNCS 12783, HCI in Business, Government and Organizations, edited by Fiona Fui-Hoon Nah and Keng Siau
23. LNCS 12784, Learning and Collaboration Technologies: New Challenges and Learning Experiences (Part I), edited by Panayiotis Zaphiris and Andri Ioannou
24. LNCS 12785, Learning and Collaboration Technologies: Games and Virtual Environments for Learning (Part II), edited by Panayiotis Zaphiris and Andri Ioannou
25. LNCS 12786, Human Aspects of IT for the Aged Population: Technology Design and Acceptance (Part I), edited by Qin Gao and Jia Zhou
26. LNCS 12787, Human Aspects of IT for the Aged Population: Supporting Everyday Life Activities (Part II), edited by Qin Gao and Jia Zhou
27. LNCS 12788, HCI for Cybersecurity, Privacy and Trust, edited by Abbas Moallem
28. LNCS 12789, HCI in Games: Experience Design and Game Mechanics (Part I), edited by Xiaowen Fang
29. LNCS 12790, HCI in Games: Serious and Immersive Games (Part II), edited by Xiaowen Fang
30. LNCS 12791, HCI in Mobility, Transport and Automotive Systems, edited by Heidi Krömker
31. LNCS 12792, Adaptive Instructional Systems: Design and Evaluation (Part I), edited by Robert A. Sottilare and Jessica Schwarz
32. LNCS 12793, Adaptive Instructional Systems: Adaptation Strategies and Methods (Part II), edited by Robert A. Sottilare and Jessica Schwarz
33. LNCS 12794, Culture and Computing: Interactive Cultural Heritage and Arts (Part I), edited by Matthias Rauterberg
34. LNCS 12795, Culture and Computing: Design Thinking and Cultural Computing (Part II), edited by Matthias Rauterberg
35. LNCS 12796, Design, Operation and Evaluation of Mobile Communications, edited by Gavriel Salvendy and June Wei
36. LNAI 12797, Artificial Intelligence in HCI, edited by Helmut Degen and Stavroula Ntoa
37. CCIS 1419, HCI International 2021 Posters - Part I, edited by Constantine Stephanidis, Margherita Antona, and Stavroula Ntoa

38. CCIS 1420, HCI International 2021 Posters - Part II, edited by Constantine Stephanidis, Margherita Antona, and Stavroula Ntoa
39. CCIS 1421, HCI International 2021 Posters - Part III, edited by Constantine Stephanidis, Margherita Antona, and Stavroula Ntoa

http://2021.hci.international/proceedings

15th International Conference on Universal Access in Human-Computer Interaction (UAHCI 2021)

Program Board Chairs: **Margherita Antona,** *Foundation for Research and Technology – Hellas (FORTH), Greece,* **and Constantine Stephanidis,** *University of Crete and Foundation for Research and Technology – Hellas (FORTH), Greece*

- João Barroso, Portugal
- Rodrigo Bonacin, Brazil
- Laura Burzagli, Italy
- Pedro J. S. Cardoso, Portugal
- Silvia Ceccacci, Italy
- Carlos Duarte, Portugal
- Pier Luigi Emiliani, Italy
- Andrina Granic, Croatia
- Gian Maria Greco, Spain
- Simeon Keates, UK
- Georgios Kouroupetroglou, Greece
- Barbara Leporini, Italy
- I. Scott MacKenzie, Canada
- John Magee, USA
- Daniela Marghitu, USA
- Jorge Martín-Gutiérrez, Spain
- Troy McDaniel, USA
- Maura Mengoni, Italy
- Silvia Mirri, Italy
- Federica Pallavicini, Italy
- Ana Isabel Paraguay, Brazil
- Hugo Paredes, Portugal
- Enrico Pontelli, USA
- João M. F. Rodrigues, Portugal
- Frode Eika Sandnes, Norway
- J. Andrés Sandoval-Bringas, Mexico
- Volker Sorge, UK
- Hiroki Takada, Japan
- Kevin Tseng, Taiwan
- Gerhard Weber, Germany

The full list with the Program Board Chairs and the members of the Program Boards of all thematic areas and affiliated conferences is available online at:

http://www.hci.international/board-members-2021.php

HCI International 2022

The 24th International Conference on Human-Computer Interaction, HCI International 2022, will be held jointly with the affiliated conferences at the Gothia Towers Hotel and Swedish Exhibition & Congress Centre, Gothenburg, Sweden, June 26 – July 1, 2022. It will cover a broad spectrum of themes related to Human-Computer Interaction, including theoretical issues, methods, tools, processes, and case studies in HCI design, as well as novel interaction techniques, interfaces, and applications. The proceedings will be published by Springer. More information will be available on the conference website: http://2022.hci.international/:

General Chair
Prof. Constantine Stephanidis
University of Crete and ICS-FORTH
Heraklion, Crete, Greece
Email: general_chair@hcii2022.org

http://2022.hci.international/

Contents – Part II

Universal Access to Learning and Education

Diagnosis for School Inclusion in Teacher Training in One Higher Normal
School in Mexico 3
  *Francisco Alvarez Rodríguez, Romelia Chávez, Mónica Carreño,
  and Olivia Fragoso*

TabGO: Towards Accessible Computer Science in Secondary School 12
  *Ken H. Andriamahery-Ranjalahy, Léa Berquez, Nadine Jessel,
  and Philippe Truillet*

Endless Running Game to Support Sign Language Learning
by Deaf Children 25
  Diego Roberto Antunes and Janaine Daiane Rodrigues

Analysis of the Impact of Educational Technology on Social Inequity
in the United States. 41
  Nicole Darmawaskita and Troy McDaniel

Accessible Block-Based Programming for K-12 Students Who Are Blind or
Low Vision 52
  *Meenakshi Das, Daniela Marghitu, Mahender Mandala,
  and Ayanna Howard*

Geo-education as a Valuable Support to Children
with Learning Difficulties. 62
  Marianna Di Gregorio, Monica Sebillo, and Giuliana Vitiello

The SL-ReDu Environment for Self-monitoring and Objective Learner
Assessment in Greek Sign Language 72
  *Eleni Efthimiou, Stavroula-Evita Fotinea, Christina Flouda,
  Theodor Goulas, Gkioulan Ametoglou, Galini Sapountzaki,
  Katerina Papadimitriou, and Gerasimos Potamianos*

An Assessment of Moodle Environment Tools for the Literacy
Environment of Deaf Children in the Context of the 3rd Year
of Elementary Education 82
  *Marta Angélica Montiel Ferreira, Laura Sánchez García,
  Tanya Amara Felipe, Juliana Bueno, and Suellym Fernanda Opolz*

Developing an Online Music Teaching and Practicing Platform via Machine
Learning: A Review Paper   95
   Fatemeh Jamshidi, Daniela Marghitu, and Richard Chapman

A Multimodal Platform to Teach Mathematics to Students
with Vision-Impairment   109
   Abhishek Jariwala, Daniela Marghitu, and Richard Chapman

Analysis of Design Elements for the Treatment of Language Disorders
in Autistic Children   118
   Miao Liu and Yingjie Wang

Communication Robot as a Weekly Online Quiz Presenter   138
   Shu Matsuura, Satoe Kon, and Sakura Kuwano

Evaluation on Moodle LMS Data Usage During the First Wave
of Covid-19's Pandemic   154
   Luis Pereira and Joel Guerreiro

Deaf Inclusion Through Brazilian Sign Language: A Computational
Architecture Supporting Artifacts and Interactive Applications and Tools   167
   L. S. Garcia, T. A. Felipe, A. P. Guedes, D. R. Antunes, C. E. Iatskiu,
   E. Todt, J. Bueno, D. de F. G. Trindade, D. A. Gonçalves, R. Canteri,
   M. C. Canal, M. A. M. Ferreira, A. M. C. Silva, L. Galvão,
   and L. Rodrigues

Accessible Media

Preferences of Deaf or Hard of Hearing Users for Live-TV
Caption Appearance   189
   Akhter Al Amin, Abraham Glasser, Raja Kushalnagar, Christian Vogler,
   and Matt Huenerfauth

Effect of Occlusion on Deaf and Hard of Hearing Users' Perception
of Captioned Video Quality   202
   Akhter Al Amin, Saad Hassan, and Matt Huenerfauth

Reading Experiences and Reading Efficiency Among Adults with Dyslexia:
An Accessibility Study   221
   Gerd Berget and Siri Fagernes

Easy-to-Understand Access Services: Easy Subtitles   241
   Rocío Bernabé and Piero Cavallo

Live Captioning Accuracy in Spanish-Language Newscasts
in the United States   255
   Nazaret Fresno

Dynamical Properties of Three-Rules Set Realizing Compressive
and Errorless Description of Digital Sound.   267
    Shota Nakayama, Jousuke Kuroiwa, Tomohiro Odaka, and Izumi Suwa

Multimodal Fusion and Sequence Learning for Cued Speech Recognition
from Videos.   277
    Katerina Papadimitriou, Maria Parelli, Galini Sapountzaki,
    Georgios Pavlakos, Petros Maragos, and Gerasimos Potamianos

Creative Media Accessibility: Placing the Focus Back on the Individual   291
    Pablo Romero-Fresco

The Minority AD: Creativity in Audio Descriptions of Visual Art.   308
    Silvia Soler Gallego

Designing Accessible Videos for People with Disabilities.   328
    Leevke Wilkens, Vanessa N. Heitplatz, and Christian Bühler

Universal Access in Virtual and Intelligent Assistive Environments

Criteria for the Adoption of a Support Information System
for People's Mobility.   347
    Laura Burzagli and Pier Luigi Emiliani

Networks to Stop the Epidemic Spreading   358
    Vincenzo Fioriti, Marta Chinnici, Andrea Arbore, Nicola Sigismondi,
    and Ivan Roselli

Multimodal Interaction Framework Based on Firebase
Real-Time Database   367
    Youssef Guedira and José Rouillard

Lending an Artificial Eye: Beyond Evaluation of CV-Based Assistive
Systems for Visually Impaired People   385
    Fotis P. Kalaganis, Panagiotis Migkotzidis, Kostas Georgiadis,
    Elisavet Chatzilari, Spiros Nikolopoulos, and Ioannis Kompatsiaris

Human Body Parts Tracking from Pressure Data: Toward Effective
Pressure Injury Assessment   400
    Carlos Lastre-Dominguez, Nasim Hajari, Chester Ho,
    Oscar Ibarra-Manzano, and Irene Cheng

Personalized Navigation that Links Speaker's Ambiguous Descriptions
to Indoor Objects for Low Vision People.   412
    Jun-Li Lu, Hiroyuki Osone, Akihisa Shitara, Ryo Iijima,
    Bektur Ryskeldiev, Sayan Sarcar, and Yoichi Ochiai

Smart City Concept Based on Cyber-Physical Social Systems
with Hierarchical Ethical Agents Approach   424
    Omar Mata, Pedro Ponce, Troy McDaniel, Juana Isabel Méndez,
    Therese Peffer, and Arturo Molina

Real-World Distance Reduction in a Virtual Reality-Based Wheelchair
Simulation on Flat Surfaces   438
    Kousuke Motooka, Takumi Okawara, Yuki Yamato, and Akihiro Miyata

Ski for Squat: A Squat Exergame with Pneumatic Gel Muscle-Based
Dynamic Difficulty Adjustment   449
    Priyanka Ramasamy, Swagata Das, and Yuichi Kurita

Mobile Application for Determining the Concentration of Sulfonamides
in Water Using Digital Image Colorimetry   468
    Pedro Reis, Pedro H. Carvalho, Patrícia S. Peixoto,
    Marcela A. Segundo, and Hélder P. Oliveira

Making Parking Lot Accessible Through IoT . . . . ;   485
    José Rafael Rojano-Cáceres, Jesús Antonio Rosas-Percastre,
    Teresita Alvarez-Robles, and J. Andrés Sandoval-Bringas

Blind-Badminton: A Working Prototype to Recognize Position of Flying
Object for Visually Impaired Users   494
    Masaaki Sadasue, Daichi Tagami, Sayan Sarcar, and Yoichi Ochiai

Framework for Controlling KNX Devices Based on Gestures   507
    Jedid Santos, Ivo Martins, and João M. F. Rodrigues

Effect of Olfactory Stimulation with Vanilla Odor on Degree of Electrical
Activity to Control Gastrointestinal Motility   519
    Eiji Takai, Takahiro Aoyagi, Keita Ichikawa, Yasuyuki Matsuura,
    Fumiya Kinoshita, and Hiroki Takada

Continual Learning for Object Classification: A Modular Approach   531
    Daniel Turner, Pedro J. S. Cardoso, and João M. F. Rodrigues

Author Index   549

Contents – Part I

Universal Access Methods, Techniques and Practices

Implicit Measures as a Useful Tool for Evaluating User Experience   3
  Rossana Actis-Grosso, Roberta Capellini, Francesco Ghedin,
  and Francesca Tassistro

The Ecosystem's Involvement in the Appropriation Phase of Assistive
Technology: Choice and Adjustment of Interaction Techniques.   21
  Charline Calmels, Caroline Mercadier, Frédéric Vella, Antonio Serpa,
  Philippe Truillet, and Nadine Vigouroux

Setting Diversity at the Core of HCI   39
  Nana Kesewaa Dankwa and Claude Draude

A Systematic Mapping of Guidelines for the Development of Accessible
Digital Games to People with Disabilities.   53
  Taynara Cerigueli Dutra, Daniel Felipe, Isabela Gasparini,
  and Eleandro Maschio

Discount Evaluation of Preliminary Versions of Systems Dedicated
to Users with Cerebral Palsy: Simulation of Involuntary Movements
in Non-disabled Participants   71
  Yohan Guerrier, Janick Naveteur, Christophe Kolski,
  and Françoise Anceaux

Accessibility Practices for Prototype Creation and Testing   89
  Nandita Gupta and Carrie Bruce

Methods of Usability Testing for Users with Cognitive Impairments   99
  Cathleen Schöne, Ulrike Große, Alexander Wölfel, and Heidi Krömker

Remote Evaluation in Universal Design Using Video Conferencing
Systems During the COVID-19 Pandemic   116
  Joschua Thomas Simon-Liedtke, Way Kiat Bong, Trenton Schulz,
  and Kristin Skeide Fuglerud

A Multidisciplinary User-Centered Approach to Designing an Information
Platform for Accessible Tourism: Understanding User Needs
and Motivations   136
  Pedro Teixeira, Joana Alves, Tiago Correia, Leonor Teixeira,
  Celeste Eusébio, Samuel Silva, and António Teixeira

Accessibility, Usability, User Experience and Technology Acceptance

Users Perceptions of Headphones and Earbuds in Norway and Brazil:
An Empirical Study Based on a Kahoot Quiz.   153
   Amanda Coelho Figliolia, Frode Eika Sandnes, and Fausto Orsi Medola

Extended Analysis Procedure for Inclusive Game Elements: Accessibility
Features in the Last of Us Part 2.   166
   Patricia da Silva Leite and Leonelo Dell Anhol Almeida

Image Search Versus Text Search Revisited: A Simple Experiment Using
a Kahoot Quiz   186
   Signe Aanderaa Eide, Ana-Maria Poljac, and Frode Eika Sandnes

Disadvantaged by Disability: Examining the Accessibility
of Cyber Security   197
   Steven Furnell, Kirsi Helkala, and Naomi Woods

Web Accessibility and Web Developer Attitudes Towards Accessibility
in Mozambique.   213
   Suraj Gupta, Terje Gjøsæter, and G. Anthony Giannoumis

Screen Reader Accessibility Study of Interactive Maps   232
   Sayed Kamrul Hasan and Terje Gjøsæter

How Young People Living with Disability Experience the Use
of Assistive Technology.   250
   Josefin Kristensen and Jessica Lindblom

Game Accessibility: Taking Inclusion to the Next Level   269
   Carme Mangiron

E-commerce Usability Guidelines for Visually Impaired Users   280
   Elisa Prati, Simone Pozzi, Fabio Grandi, and Margherita Peruzzini

Usability Testing on Tractor's HMI: A Study Protocol   294
   Elisa Prati, Fabio Grandi, and Margherita Peruzzini

Social Network Behavior, from Information Search to Purchase:
The Case of Generation X and Millennials.   312
   Célia M. Q. Ramos and João M. F. Rodrigues

Citizen Science for All?.   326
   Elisabeth Unterfrauner, Claudia M. Fabian, Johanna Casado,
   Gonzalo de la Vega, Beatriz Garcia, and Wanda Díaz-Merced

Design for All Applications and Case Studies

Collaborative Virtual Environment to Encourage Teamwork in Autistic
Adults in Workplace Settings   339
    Ashwaq Zaini Amat, Michael Breen, Spencer Hunt, Devon Wilson,
    Yousaf Khaliq, Nathan Byrnes, Daniel J. Cox, Steven Czarnecki,
    Cameron L. Justice, Deven A. Kennedy, Tristan C. Lotivio,
    Hunter K. McGee, Derrick M. Reckers, Justin W. Wade, Medha Sarkar,
    and Nilanjan Sarkar

Image Adaptation Based on Color Saturation and Linear Matrices
for People with Deuteranopia-Type Color Blindness   349
    Daniel Delgado-Cedeño and Mario Chacón-Rivas

Design of Digital Therapeutic Workshops for People
with Alzheimer's Disease.   369
    Anne-Marie Dery-Pinna, Alain Giboin, and Philippe Renevier-Gonin

Tasteful: A Cooking App Designed for Visually Impaired Users   384
    Yunran Ju, Zhenyu Cheryl Qian, and Weilun Huang

Effect of the Peripheral Visual Field Elements of 3D Video Clips
on Body Sway   394
    Fumiya Kinoshita, Honoka Okuno, Hideaki Touyama,
    and Hiroki Takada

An Enhanced Open Source Refreshable Braille Display DISBRA 2.0   405
    Alvaro Boa Vista Maia Bisneto, Victor Hazin da Rocha, and Diogo Silva

ParkinsonCom Project: Towards a Software Communication Tool
for People with Parkinson's Disease   418
    Káthia Marçal de Oliveira, Elise Batselé, Sophie Lepreux, Elise Buchet,
    Christophe Kolski, Mathilde Boutiflat, Véronique Delcroix,
    Hélène Geurts, Kodzo Apedo, Loïc Dehon, Houcine Ezzedine,
    Yohan Guerrier, Marie-Claire Haelewyck, Nicolas Jura, Philippe Pudlo,
    and Yosra Rekik

Designing a Consumer Framework for Social Products Within a Gamified
Smart Home Context.   429
    Juana Isabel Méndez, Pedro Ponce, Othoniel Miranda, Citlaly Pérez,
    Ana Paula Cruz, Therese Peffer, Alan Meier, Troy McDaniel,
    and Arturo Molina

Viva: A Virtual Assistant for the Visually Impaired.   444
    Zeeshan Ahmed Pachodiwale, Yugeshwari Brahmankar, Neha Parakh,
    Dhruvil Patel, and Magdalini Eirinaki

Designing 3D Printed Audio-Tactile Graphics: Recommendations
from Prior Research   461
   Emilia Christie Picelli Sanches, Juliana Bueno,
   and Maria Lucia Leite Ribeiro Okimoto

Adaptive Augmentative and Alternative Communication Systems
for People with Neuromuscular Pathologies   473
   Jhon Fernando Sanchez Alvarez, Gloria Patricia Jaramillo Alvarez,
   and Claudio Camilo Gonzalez Clavijo

Multimodal Tactile Graphics Using T-TATIL, A Mobile Application
for Tactile Exploration by Visually Impaired People   482
   Leonardo Zani Zamprogno, Bruno Merlin, João Ferreira,
   Heleno Fülber, and Allan Veras

An Evaluation of Eye-Foot Input for Target Acquisitions   499
   Xinyong Zhang

Emotion and Behavior Recognition for Universal Access

Affective Guide for Museum: A System to Suggest Museum Paths Based
on Visitors' Emotions   521
   Alex Altieri, Silvia Ceccacci, Luca Giraldi, Alma Leopardi,
   Maura Mengoni, and Abudukaiyoumu Talipu

2D and 3D Visualization of Eye Gaze Patterns in a VR-Based Job Interview
Simulator: Application in Educating Employers on the Gaze Patterns
of Autistic Candidates   533
   Michael Breen, James McClarty, Caleb Langley, Jamshid Farzidayeri,
   Kyle Trevethan, Brandon Swenson, Medha Sarkar, Joshua Wade,
   and Nilanjan Sarkar

Development of an Index for Evaluating VIMS Using Gaze Data   545
   Kazuhiro Fujikake, Rentaro Ono, and Hiroki Takada

The Analysis of Brainwaves to Measuring Music Tone Impact on Behavior
of ADHD Children   555
   Chalakorn Juiter and Ko-Chiu Wu

Contextual Cues: The Role of Machine Learning in Supporting
Contextually Impaired Users.   567
   Martin Kinch and Simeon Keates

Design and Validation of a Stress Detection Model for Use with a VR
Based Interview Simulator for Autistic Young Adults   580
   Miroslava Migovich, Alex Korman, Joshua Wade, and Nilanjan Sarkar

A Study of Classification for Electrogastrograms Before/After Caloric
Intake Using Autoencoder   589
  Kohki Nakane, Keita Ichikawa, Rentaro Ono, Yasuyuki Matsuura,
  and Hiroki Takada

Building an Ecologically Valid Facial Expression Database – Behind
the Scenes   599
  Francesca Nonis, Luca Ulrich, Nicolò Dozio,
  Francesca Giada Antonaci, Enrico Vezzetti, Francesco Ferrise,
  and Federica Marcolin

Supervised Contrastive Learning for Game-Play Frustration Detection
from Speech   617
  Meishu Song, Emilia Parada-Cabaleiro, Shuo Liu, Manuel Milling,
  Alice Baird, Zijiang Yang, and Björn W. Schuller

Parkinson's Disease Detection and Diagnosis from fMRI:
A Literature Review   630
  Guillermina Vivar-Estudillo, Nasim Hajari,
  Mario-Alberta Ibarra-Manzano, and Irene Cheng

State of the Art and Future Challenges of the Portrayal of Facial Nonmanual
Signals by Signing Avatar   639
  Rosalee Wolfe, John McDonald, Ronan Johnson, Robyn Moncrief,
  Andrew Alexander, Ben Sturr, Sydney Klinghoffer, Fiona Conneely,
  Maria Saenz, and Shatabdi Choudhry

Author Index   657

Universal Access to Learning and Education

Diagnosis for School Inclusion in Teacher Training in One Higher Normal School in Mexico

Francisco Alvarez Rodríguez[1]([envelope]) [ORCID], Romelia Chávez[2], Mónica Carreño[3] [ORCID], and Olivia Fragoso[4] [ORCID]

[1] Universidad Autónoma de Aguascalientes, Aguascalientes, Mexico
[2] Escuela Normal Superior Federal de Aguascalientes, Aguascalientes, Mexico
romelia.chavez@ensfa.edu.mx
[3] Universidad Autónoma de Baja California Sur, Baja California Sur, Mexico
mcarreno@uabc.mx
[4] Centro Nacional de Investigación y Desarrollo Tecnológico, Morelos, Mexico
ofragoso@cenidet.edu.mx

Abstract. Educational inclusion not only refers to the integration of students with disabilities, it also refers to the fact of minimizing or eliminating barriers that may represent a limitation for student learning and participation, that is, considering social and cultural diversity that influence the acquisition of expected learning, therefore when talking about inclusion, reference is made to the process through which the school seeks and generates the supports that are required to ensure the educational achievement of all students who attend it, and thus be able to guarantee equality of social conditions through education. The objective of this diagnosis was to identify the guidelines that allow an educational intervention assuming the inclusive education approach, rescuing elements such as: diagnosis of the group with which the intervention will be carried out, selection of educational materials and resources, trans-disciplinary work, and definition of the individual's profile for educational intervention. The work presented is an initial stage of a model of educational inclusion. The results obtained, as can be seen in the previous section, are satisfactory and allow us to corroborate the usefulness of the diagnosis presented.

Keywords: Inclusion diagnosis · Educational inclusion · Teacher training · Superior normal school

1 Introduction

Educational inclusion not only refers to the integration of students with disabilities, it also refers to the fact of minimizing or eliminating barriers that may represent a limitation for student learning and participation, that is, considering social and cultural diversity that influence the acquisition of expected learning, therefore when talking about inclusion, reference is made to the process through which the school seeks and

M. Antona and C. Stephanidis (Eds.): HCII 2021, LNCS 12769, pp. 3–11, 2021.
https://doi.org/10.1007/978-3-030-78095-1_1

generates the supports that are required to ensure the educational achievement of all students who attend it [1], and thus be able to guarantee equality of social conditions through education.

Some authors will consider that the integration of individuals in collaborative work through trans-disciplinarily could be an effective integration mechanism. It can be observed various works that try to integrate the collaboration of teams through trans-disciplinarily as a means for the integration of individuals with different disabilities [15].

In this framework, some educational systems promote actions to encourage higher education schools to move towards inclusion through a strategy based on the dimensions of inclusive education such as culture, educational policies and practices, considering collaborative work as a means [16] because there is the belief that it will allow students to be promoted towards the achievement of goals and objectives in which the capacities of each individual are enhanced.

In Mexico there have been important advances in this regard, as an example various provisions of the general education law were reformed and added, in the matter of inclusive education: "Article 2.- Every individual has the right to receive quality education under conditions of equity, therefore, all the inhabitants of the country have the same opportunities of access and permanence in the national educational system, simply by satisfying the requirements established by the applicable general provisions [2]". The legal structure as a framework for a possible operation of inclusion in education in Mexico is adequate. On the other hand, various works can be observed that attempt to integrate team collaboration through trans-disciplinarity as a means for the integration of individuals with different disabilities [8]. In other words, there is a concern for not only educating individuals with a disability, it is also intended to include them socially in social activities such as work.

In this framework, the Educational System (SE) promotes a strategy to encourage basic education schools to move towards inclusion through a strategy based on the dimensions of inclusive education such as culture, educational policies and practices, considering as collaborative work [6]. There are several models that allow to develop these integrations and in them there is the belief that it will allow to push students towards the achievement of goals and objectives in which the capacities of each individual are enhanced [9], in this sense it is worthwhile present some of the elements considered in these models of collaborative and inclusive learning [8–10]:

- Structure the process in several phases and schedule in several milestones to review how the work is developing.
- Offer the necessary time to generate debate and contrast ideas as well as establish the goals and objectives of the activity [3].
- Use varied methodologies and activities.
- Organize students into teams considering the diversity of the members.
- Act as a guide and conductor of the activity at the beginning, and let the students assume their responsibility gradually
- Promote communication and respect among students.

Another aspect to consider in this complex problem are the barriers to Learning and Participation [11], since it is these that determine which are the factors that disadvantage student learning, considering the student's own and cognitive aspects as a predominant factor for the acquisition of learning, also considering other elements from their context such as: teacher methodology, classroom, classroom and school infrastructure, the school context, the family context, the social one, among others. This determines the specific evaluations because it is located in which situation the student's area of opportunity is, as well as knowing their learning style and their motivation to learn [12].

On the other hand, considering the type of project in relation to the epistemic rationality of transdisciplinary research as a transformer of knowledge, it distances itself from practices to rethink them and acts in front of the environment, the historical and social circumstances of the context, retaking the category of reality. As an articulation of the processes involved [13]. From this and considering the different aspects reviewed in this introduction and general review of the concepts related to this work, it is considered to apply an investigation based on the reflective process [7].

These elements are considered for this preliminary study as a guide to exploit in a first diagnosis on the inclusion in the teaching practices of the students in training of the Professor José Santos Valdés State Superior Normal, considering the trans-disciplinary work. It is important to mention that the work described below is an initial diagnosis considering in the first stages of the reflective process mentioned specifically in the identification of the problem, analysis and planning. Giving the necessary inputs for the subsequent stages.

2   Elements of the Initial Diagnosis

This initial diagnosis had the objective of identifying the guidelines that allow an educational intervention assuming the inclusive education approach, rescuing elements such as: diagnosis of the group with which the intervention will be carried out, selection of educational materials and resources, trans-disciplinary work, and definition of the individual's profile for educational intervention.

The application of the reflective methodology is for the following reasons [17–19]:

- Allows immediate intervention.
- Modifications can be made from the first observations of the intervention.
- It can be iterated between the analyzes of the results obtained and new interventions.

On the other hand, the type of phenomenon to be studied (individuals in a classroom) involves different aspects that are difficult to control and, as has been demonstrated with other similar studies, this methodology can support the diagnosis presented in this work [20].

The diagnosis is part of a proposed model of educational inclusion in which it is essential to consider the monitoring and evaluation of educational practices as well as the inputs recovered by the different actors (students, parents, directors, specialists in special education and teachers). These actors will feed the processes of analysis, reflection and improvement of new processes in which the focus of educational inclusion is constant.

In this way, each educational intervention will give way to the reflective process that is illustrated in Fig. 1. As indicated in the introduction as a method of research and educational intervention for this project.

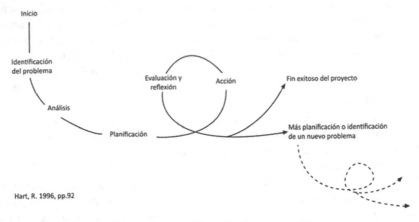

Hart, R. 1996, pp.92

Fig. 1. Phases of the reflective process [7]

As can be seen in Fig. 1, the diagnosis allows the identification of the problem for subsequent analysis and planning of the educational intervention. In other words, it generates the necessary related inputs for the following purposes:

• Detect the profile of the students who will participate in the intervention.
• Determine the tools that the facilitator has to carry out the intervention.
• Determine the predisposition of the school towards inclusion and the facilities it provides for this purpose.

Hence the importance of a preliminary diagnosis as the initial part of any intervention model. The method applied in this diagnosis consisted of two stages that are described below, in addition to the aspects involved.

2.1 Stages of Diagnosis Execution

It is important to mention that within the context of the initial diagnosis, different elements were considered as the actors that participate in a model of educational inclusion. In order to have the most complete information possible and therefore generate adequate planning, the main aspects for the elaboration of the diagnosis are listed below:

• Social and educational interaction that facilitates learning and participation of the entire educational community [4].
• Supports that help students overcome the difficulties they face in learning and participation [6].

- Participation of the entire educational community through actions that promote the inclusive education approach considering parents or guardians, students, teachers and educational authorities [5].

Two stages are defined for the execution of the diagnosis [14]:

(a) Planning and design of the diagnosis. It considers the organization of all elements of intervention including strategies, training, educational, social and special needs diagnoses, among others. Materials are prepared for the diagnosis of the inclusive intervention, considering the elements to create learning environments, adapted content, among others, to guarantee that all actors are trained and prepared for its implementation, considering this premise in the planning and design stage. of the diagnosis would guarantee an adequate inclusive intervention if the diagnosis shows the positive elements.
(b) Execution, monitoring and evaluation. The diagnosis of the intervention is carried out applying what was defined in the planning and design stage, also considering strategies that allow monitoring and evaluating the results obtained through different evidences.

The diagnostic design structure consists of the following elements:

(a) Analysis of the general context of the educational institution. Personnel and specialists involved, facilities, inclusive educational policies, students served, characteristics of the families served by the institution, etc.
(b) Analysis of the intervention space (room). Student characteristics, teacher teaching styles, learning environment, student learning styles, etc.
(c) Analysis of inclusive educational needs. Vulnerable group to which it belongs and / or type of disability to be treated, educational inclusion strategies, etc.

It can be seen how the diagnosis involves the elements mentioned at the beginning of the section, since it is considered essential that it encompasses all aspects related to the student (Fig. 2).

3 Results

A diagnosis was made as part of a first stage of an educational inclusion model and the diagnosis was made in its two phases: a. Planning and design, and b. Execution, monitoring and evaluation. The duration of this first application considering the two phases mentioned was 1 month corresponding to the semesters mentioned later, with 18 normal students and an intervention of groups of 30 students on average for each normalista (540 students participating in the diagnosis). The results obtained in the two phases are presented below:

(a) Planning and design of the diagnosis. At this stage the teachers of the Bachelor of Teaching and Learning of Spanish in Secondary Education (LEAEES), 3rd

Fig. 2. Intervention planning meeting.

semester, within the elaboration of the didactic sequences to develop Social Practices of Language (PSL), referred to: Exchange of reading experiences and Comprehension of texts to acquire new knowledge. They were in charge of planning and designing, according to the previous section, the diagnoses corresponding to the different groups (approximately 18) with 30 1st and 2nd year high school students in the state of Aguascalientes. The diagnosis in which they analyzed the contexts of the group in the family, social, school and of course the school characteristics. This made it possible to define conclusions to elaborate the didactic planning adapted to the needs of the group, as well as to make reasonable adjustments to attend to cases of students who faced barriers to learning and participation with the support of USAER (Service Units of Support to Regular Education) of the unit corresponding to the State of Aguascalientes.

(b)   Execution, monitoring and evaluation. The interactions between students and teachers, teaching and learning strategies, the use of resources and support materials were analyzed as part of the diagnosis, this helped to generate the evaluation as a means for the attention of all students considering their characteristics and the processes, use of time, participation, products, among others.

Each one of the normal students carried out a group evaluation following the structure of the previous section, below is a brief example of the result of a diagnosis made by some students in training as teachers (The texts captured in the different formats obtained from the diagnoses in the three examples below):

(a)   Analysis of the general context of the educational institution. *"The work carried out by the parents is very varied taking into account the level of studies, that is why 62 of them are employees and is followed by sales, commerce or tianguis and the third place is occupied by being a worker in a factory. Making the observation that many families their main income is street sales. Family income ranges between 3,000 and 5,000 pesos (60) per month at a higher rate, although there is a considerable number who earn from 5001 to more than 10,000 pesos. For their part, the mothers of families, their educational level is secondary (152) and they are followed by high school or high school, most of them being a housewife (201), followed by a federal employee. That is why the leading medical service is the IMSS (217), followed by the disappeared popular insurance".* Diagnostic evaluation 05–2019.

(b) Analysis of the intervention space (room). *"The group is made up of 38 students, which are 18 men and 20 women, of which there are none with special needs beyond the fact that there are problems, there is only the problem of low-income students, however, with special needs for part of secondary school there is inclusion by teachers, administrators and the students themselves because they manage to adapt to the learning pace of each of the students according to their needs".* Diagnostic evaluation 12–2019.

(c) Analysis of inclusive educational needs. *"It is worth mentioning that in the group that I have there is a student with autism and he attends USAER, to help him I did not want to ask him much because I was afraid that he was going to get sick because of what I asked him, in fact, on Thursday, October 4, the teacher put him to read and he started to get very nervous and he started to stutter and he started to get very nervous that he could not, but the teacher supported him so that he was not afraid, and that seems a bit worrying since I will be on the next day with him and I am afraid not to know or not be able to support him as it should since he needs special treatment so that he is controlled".* Diagnostic evaluation 15–2019.

The main findings of this diagnosis of educational inclusion are presented below:

- The experience and support of USAER specialists is necessary so that pre-service teachers can design strategies with reasonable accommodation for the learning and participation of students who face barriers to learning.
- The preliminary training and talks on awareness of promoting an education with an inclusive approach is a significant basis for defining the planning of didactic sequences with students who face barriers to learning and participation from the perspective of inclusive education.
- The coordination and support of the teacher trainers for the development of the diagnosis in its two stages was adequate as planned.

4 Conclusions

It can be seen in the work presented that this inclusion diagnosis allows us to analyze the different actors in the teaching and learning processes: teachers, specialists in educational inclusion, managers and of course students. The work presented is an initial stage of a model of educational inclusion. The results obtained, as can be seen in the previous section, are satisfactory and allow us to corroborate the usefulness of the diagnosis presented. As future work, it is intended to develop a new diagnosis in the following school term in order to improve the instruments and measurements to improve the results generated and thus systematize this practice as a regular activity in the training of future teachers of the aforementioned normal school. Another line of action is to extend the diagnoses to collaborative work extended to the family as a means of improving student learning.

References

1. Infante, M.: Challenges to teacher education: Educational. Estudios Pedagógicos. **35**, 287–297 (2010)
2. Ley General de Educación: Secretaría de Educación Pública (2018)
3. García-Valcárcel, A., Basilotta, V., Camino López: ICT in collaborative learning in the classrooms of primary and secondary education. Revista Científica de Educomunicación **42**, 65–74 (2014)
4. López-Gil, K.S., Natera, V.M.: Incidencia del trabajo colaborativo docente en la enseñanza y el aprendizaje de la escritura académica. Revista Electrónica de Investigación Educativa **20**(1), 1 (2018). https://doi.org/10.24320/redie.2018.20.1.1477
5. del Carmen, M., Palomino, P., De Jesús, M., Ruiz, C.: Actitudes y formación docente hacia la inclusión en Educación Secundaria Obligatoria. Revista Electrónica de Investigación Educativa **19**(1), 84 (2017). https://doi.org/10.24320/redie.2017.19.1.765
6. Barajas, A., Álvarez, F.J., Muñoz, J., Oviedo, A.C.: Process for modeling competencies for developing serious games. Revista Electrónica de Investigación Educativa. 18(3), 146–160 (2016). http://redie.uabc.mx/redie/article/view/1071
7. Hart, R.: La participación de los niños. De la participación simbólica a la participación auténtica. Editorial Gente nueva, Unicef, Colombia, junio de 1993 (1993)
8. Esparza-Maldonado, A.L., Margain-Fuentes, L.Y., Álvarez-Rodríguez, F.J., Benítez-Guerrero, E.I.: Desarrollo y evaluación de un Sistema Interactivo para personas con discapacidad visual. TecnoLógicas **21**(41), 149–157 (2018). https://doi.org/10.22430/225653 37.733
9. Alfageme, M.B.: Modelo colaborativo de enseñanza-aprendizaje en situaciones no presenciales. Universidad de Murcia, Tesis doctoral (2003)
10. Carrio, M.L.: Ventajas del uso de la tecnología en el aprendizaje colaborativo. Revista Iberoamericana de Educación **41**, 1–10 (2007)
11. Covarrubias Pizarro, P.: Barreras para el aprendizaje y la participación: una propuesta para su clasificación. In: Trujillo Holguín, J.A., Ríos Castillo, A.C., García Leos (coords.), J.L., Desarrollo Profesional Docente: reflexiones de maestros en servicio en el escenario de la Nueva Escuela Mexicana (pp. 135–157), Chihuahua, México: Escuela Normal Superior Profr. José E. Medrano R (2019)
12. Ainscow, M.: Desarrollo de escuelas inclusivas. Ideas, propuestas y experiencias para mejorar las instituciones escolares. Madrid. Narcea (2004)
13. Frodeman, R.: Interdisciplinarity. In: Sustainable Knowledge: A Theory of Interdisciplinarity, pp. 34–59. Palgrave Macmillan UK, London (2014). https://doi.org/10.1057/978113730 3028_3
14. Sobrado Fernández, L.: El diagnóstico educativo en contextos sociales y profesionales. Revista De Investigación Educativa. 23(1), 85–112 (2005). Recuperado a partir de https://revistas.um.es/rie/article/view/98351
15. Bourque, P., Robert, F.: Curriculum guidelines for undergraduate degree programs in software engineering. In: IEEE Computer Society & Association for Computing Machinery, Volume of the Computing Curricula Series (2015)

16. AMITI: Asociación. Asociación Mexicana de la Industria de Tecnologías de la Información (2018). Sitio web: https://amiti.org.mx (1) (PDF) Nuevos perfiles profesionales en TI caso ANIEI-New professional profiles in IT: case of ANIEI - Emergent Research Forum ERF paper.   https://www.researchgate.net/publication/335568502_Nuevos_perfiles_profesion ales_en_TI_caso_ANIEI-New_professional_profiles_in_IT_case_of_ANIEI_-_Emergent_ Research_Forum_ERF_paper. Accessed 05 May 2020

17. Esteve, O.: La observación en el aula como base para la mejora de la práctica docente. en Lagasabaster, D., Juan Manuel Sierra (eds.) (2004)

18. James, P.: Teachers in Action. Task for In-Service Language Teacher Education and Development. Cup, Cambridge (2001)

19. Lagasabaster, D., Juan Manuel Sierra, (eds.): La observación como instrumento para la mejora de la enseñanza-aprendizaje de lenguas, Cuadernos de educación, vol. 44. ICE-Horsori, Barcelona (2004)

20. Latorre, A.: La investigación-acción. Conocer y cambiar la práctica educativa. Graó, Barcelona (2003)

TabGO: Towards Accessible Computer Science in Secondary School

Ken H. Andriamahery-Ranjalahy[1]([✉]), Léa Berquez[2], Nadine Jessel[3], and Philippe Truillet[2]

[1] Musicology Department, Univ. Toulouse II Jean Jaurès (LLA-CREATIS), Toulouse, France
ken.andria@univ-tlse2.fr
[2] CS Department, Univ. Toulouse III Paul Sabatier (IRIT), Toulouse, France
lea.berquez@univ-tlse3.fr, Philippe.Truillet@irit.fr
[3] INSPE, Univ. Toulouse II Jean Jaurès (IRIT), Toulouse, France
Nadine.Baptiste@irit.fr

Abstract. While computing skills grow in importance in today's technology-centered society, the learning of these skills still isn't accessible easily for young visually-impaired students: in French schools for example, online platforms (like Scratch) are more and more used by teachers, but unfortunately these platforms rely heavily on visual elements. As an inclusive approach would suggest, modifications and adaptations of such platforms would favour collaboration between sighted and visually-impaired users: tangible stimuli are then favoured to compensate for visual elements, while visually-impaired and sighted communities are prompted to use the same tools. Even if tangible solutions are suggested through scientific studies in the accessibility field, a young visually-impaired student still can't use these solutions autonomously: many of these prototypes still require the intervention of a sighted third party. In this article, we describe our solution TaBGO (Tangible Blocks Go Online) which consists of enhanced tangible Scratch's blocks and an associated optical recognition software. We then present a planned user study to establish if this solution is usable and easily handled by young visually impaired and sighted students, considering users' feedback about usability, satisfaction and cognitive load.

CCS Concepts
• Human-centered computing • Accessibility • Accessibility systems and tools

Keywords: Algorithmic · Accessibility · Block programming · Tangible objects · Optical recognition

1 Introduction

With the technological improvements of the last decades, the field of computer science and associated computing skills grow to have an increased importance in today's world. Thus in France, the learning of these computing skills begins in primary school since

M. Antona and C. Stephanidis (Eds.): HCII 2021, LNCS 12769, pp. 12–24, 2021.
https://doi.org/10.1007/978-3-030-78095-1_2

the 2016 reform[1], and in secondary school using block-based Visual Programming Languages (VPL) like Scratch[2] or Blockly[3]. Thanks to these educational strategies, students can have a first introduction to computer science.

However, for visual impaired persons, these computing paradigms aren't accessible since they rely on visual elements [1]. Thus, this graphical user interface (GUI) prevents visually impaired students from this easy approach to computing skills, and subsequently doesn't encourage them to pursue a developer's career, nor towards socio-professional integration in today's technology-centered world [2]. The issue is clear: in secondary school, is it possible to give visually impaired student access to block-based VPL, and thus access to a simple acquisition method of these computing skills? This article presents the TabGO (Tangible Blocks Go Online) project, a tangible interface which allows Scratch programming in classrooms for people with visual impairments, using tangible blocks and an associated optical recognition software. First, previous existing technologies are presented and their influences on the TabGo project are highlighted. Then, the TabGo prototype is introduced, with an experiment to evaluate its usability. This article ends with future perspectives on the experimentation's results.

2   Related Works

Programming languages can be accessible for visually impaired users (especially when they are based on textual instructions), but such accessibility necessitates adaptations: some modifications concerning the IDE used or some other additional equipment like a screen reader (JAWS[4], for example). These accessibility-centered processes are *Assistive Technologies* [3, 4], and many of these solutions are based on audio and/or braille feedback to allow an intuitive navigation for visually-impaired users [5]. Moreover, the field of vocal synthesis (*Text-to-Speech*) has known many progresses during the last decades, representing an aural feedback: for example, *Javaspeak* [6, 7], *Emacspeak* [8] and *CAITLIN* [9] are all IDEs that include a vocal synthesis-based text editor; while the first two center around the accessibility of the Java language, CAITLIN targets the use of a design software. In additional equipment and in accessible IDEs, vocal synthesis is used as an efficient solution to make computer-based fields accessible for visually-impaired users.

In addition to vocal synthesis, it's important to highlight the focus on some languages, such as Java (in the previous examples) and Python. While these languages may present accessibility issues for visually impaired persons [10], they are nonetheless more and more used among scientific, engineering and computer-centered communities: as a consequence, blind programmers may learn to use it anyway, as some languages have "features that more than make up for any inconvenience that indentation may cause" [10]. While additional equipment and IDEs are useful tools for accessibility, the use of

---

[1] "Bulletin Officiel spécial n°11 du 26 novembre 2015", http://cache.media.education.gouv.fr/file/MEN_SPE_11/35/1/BO_SPE_11_26-11-2015_504351.pdf.

[2] https://scratch.mit.edu.

[3] https://blockly.games/?lang=fr.

[4] https://www.freedomscientific.com/products/software/jaws.

new languages, easier to learn, is also a point worth highlighting. Moreover, some languages are designed while consciously considering accessibility for visually impaired users, such as Quorum[5]: it is "evidence-based" (as they rely on scientific studies[6] [11]), and its syntax is specially designed to be easily read by a vocal synthesis engine. Quorum is therefore an accessibility solution which exemplifies the use of both vocal synthesis and modifications of IDE/existing programming languages.

If these studies contribute to making programming languages as accessible as possible, they aren't necessarily adapted for an integration in a classroom environment. However, this classroom integration can favour the possibility of collaboration between visually-impaired pupils and their visually-paired peers: this collaboration has a crucial role in the integration of visually impaired people [12], as seen in previous inclusive experiments in the classroom environment [13]. Moreover, it's important to highlight that for visually-impaired teenagers, the use of adapted interfaces give them an additional opportunity to develop their logical, cognitive and motor skills, and thus these interfaces may have a positive influence on their personal development, on both physical and psychological levels [14, 15].

For children, computing skills' learning is generally based on simpler IDEs, like Blockly, Scratch *StorytellingAlice* [16] and *LookingGlass*[7] [17]: it's worth mentioning these IDEs are often used by secondary school students. However, all these environments also rely heavily on visual elements, and thus need modifications to be accessible. For an easy and intuitive approach, one strategy is then to replace the visual stimuli by tactile stimuli: a tangible interface (TUI) is then preferred to a graphical one (GUI) [18].

Many studies have been conducted on usable TUIs in a scholar environment. In primary school, adapted TUIs are often derived from electronic audio-based toys: for example, Microsoft's CodeJumper/Torino project [19] rely on linkable blocks; Bee-Bot is a bee-shaped controller, linked to Lady Beetle and World of Sounds, two simplified music-centered programming softwares [20]. The modifications of toys into TUIs represent a simple but efficient way to introduce some computing basics to primary schools pupils, especially block-based toys: it's also possible to mention some block-based prototypes among scientific communities, such as the T-Maze [21], based on maze-construct maze-escaping tasks using tangible blocks; the P-Cube [22], based on RFID blocks and cards; and a grid-like LEGO-based TUI [23] that uses aural communication. To appeal to older students, other (more android-like) toys have been derived to act as feedback for simple algorithms, otherwise only accessible by sighted students since they rely on visual modifications of an avatar. For example, the Roamer is a turtle-like robotic toy, which would move entirely as the avatar would, translating visual stimuli into movements [24]. While a toy-based approach remains an effective one for accessibility, toys are not the only raw material for accessible TUIs helping visually-impaired pupils.

In secondary school, other tangible solutions have also been created: *Blocks4All* [25] presents a sensibly augmented IDE on Android tablet (which emulates different textures), while *AccessibleBlockly* [5] give access to every Blockly modules (*ArduBlockly*[8],

---

[5] https://quorumlanguage.com/.

[6] As advertised on https://quorumlanguage.com/evidence.html.

[7] http://www.alice.org/.

[8] github.com/carlosperate/ardublockly.

OzoBlockly[9], *BlockyTalky* [26]) through audio feedback. It's worth mentioning that this Blockly-based inclusive approach uses audio and tactile feedback, as did the solutions previously mentioned. Scratch has also been adapted for visually impaired users: the *Accessi-DV* Scratch briefcase [27] contains tangible programming blocks based on the Scratch blocks; the *CodeBox64* [28] is an Arduino-based Scratch controller. These two examples are crucial influences for the actual project TabGO [29]. All of these technologies consider the use of TUIs and hardware as possible accessible solutions that allow a first approach towards programming skills in secondary school.

While the prototypes mentioned above offer excellent guidelines, they still present issues for an implementation in the classroom environment. The *Codebox64*'s concept is issued from an Arduino-based approach and requires constructions and realizations from sighted competent teachers, for each student. These chain productions necessitate time and different components for each type of feedback required in each activity planned with it. Plus, this Arduino-based approach doesn't highlight Scratch's block-based logic and its benefits for young users [30]. However while the Accessi-DV briefcase does underline Scratch's block-based logic, the prototype doesn't allow the user to communicate directly with the Scratch online platform, and thus requires a sighted person to copy the algorithm completely on the Scratch online platform. While "activity-based unplugged coding and robotic coding training, integrated with the preschool education curriculum, enhanced the basic coding and robotic coding skills" [31], unplugged coding still have limitations: for example, the algorithm must be transposed to the Scratch platform for the user to experience feedback These solutions therefore require the help of a third party: to avoid involvement of this third party and to maximize autonomy, we have designed the TabGo solution.

3   The TabGO Project

In addition to related works, the TabGO project is also based on many others focused on the conception of block-based TUIs [32, 33], their use and efficiency [34, 35] or their reception by users [36–38]. Those works also include prior block-based TUIs prototypes [27, 39], improved to communicate with online Scratch. The actual TabGo prototype consists of two parts: a briefcase with tangible blocks, and an associated visual recognition device and software.

The blocks have been modeled corresponding to the virtual ones, both in aspect and in functions. They are wood-made or plastic-made (using a laser cutter through plastic sheets of 3 mm width), and are implemented with thin magnets (2 mm diameter $\times$ 3 mm width) that allow for connection between blocks, just like the Scratch system. These functions have been preserved since this system minimizes syntax errors, just like the online platform. While the blocks can be connected depending on their shape (like puzzle pieces) using incorporated magnets, the TabGo blocks also are enhanced with ropes in case of complex functions like conditional branches and Boolean loops, which are essential notions in the secondary school educational program.

In the Scratch platform, different colors indicate different function domains: for example, orange is associated with variables, while yellow is associated with events.

---

[9] ozoblockly.com.

For this useful characteristic, colors have been kept the same while designing the TabGo prototype, mostly for visually paired users. For visually impaired users, they have been carved with different patterns (such as straight lines, multiple dots, etc.) to mimic these colored functionalities: the logic applied here aims to compensate visual information by tangible stimuli.

Moreover, it's worth mentioning that even the briefcase has an indicative function here: the briefcase contains five compartments, one for each color/set of texture (see Fig. 1). The first blocks in the chain are in the top compartments: the event blocks in the top left compartment (such as the "when button pressed" event) and the micro:bit blocks in top right compartment. The center compartment holds the variable-based blocks (such as the "add 1 to my variable" function), as these notions are at the center, the heart of computing skills. The feedback blocks are placed at the bottom: the sound blocks are in the bottom left compartment (such as the "play alarm sound" function); while the Text-To-Speech blocks are in the bottom left compartment. This organization also places Scratch's basic functions at left and advanced extensions (Text-to-Speech and micro:bit) at right: Scratch's possibilities are organized left to right from simple to more complex. Thanks to this organization, a visually-impaired user can differentiate the blocks more easily, when trying to recreate an algorithm.

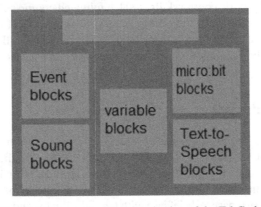

Fig. 1. Drawing representing the organisation of the TabGo briefcase.

While compensating for visual communication, it's important to note that the aural communication is also used: The TabGO project uses Scratch extensions to create non-visual feedback. Each of these extensions represents specific blocks that allow the integration of additional equipment or functions. Focusing on non-visual stimuli, we chose to adapt the "Text-to-Speech", "Music/Sound" (MIDI and musical language) and "Micro:bit"[10] extensions, which offer audio or tactile feedback. The TextToSpeech blocks use vocal synthesis (with functions like "pronounce hello world"); the music/sound blocks use and organize sample sounds in time (counted then as a fraction of time, 0.25 s for example) and the Micro:bit blocks allows the use of micro:bit cards, little

---

[10] https://microbit.org/.

electronic devices that integrates audio and vibrotactile feedback to Scratch algorithms (with functions like "when micro:bit shaked").

The blocks have been enlarged compared to the original interface (18 cm × 10 cm) to be enhanced by braille text and *cubarithms* to be identified by visually impaired users: the cubarithms here are little plastic cubes (1 cm × 1 cm × 1 cm) based on the Aubrey wheel[11]; they can be parameterized by users to hold a single braille cell. These cubarithms can then display numbers and variables' names. These enhancements aim to maximize the autonomy of visually-impaired users, since they can read and identify blocks, but also correctly set them to build customized algorithms.

As the first part of the TabGo prototype, the blocks presented here are derived from the Scratch's interface to retain the most useful features of this pupil-friendly approach to computer science, such as magnetic linking between blocks and color code. But they're also enhanced with many features favouring the blocks' correct identification and setup: these features are multiple, from the briefcase's organization to additional carved textures upon blocks.

While the precedent features were highlighted because they favour recognition by the user, the second part of the TabGo prototype centers around optical recognition of the algorithms (recreated with blocks) by the system. The solution presented here, in addition to blocks, centers around the use of a webcam to automatically recognize the *cubarithms* and the TopCodes[12] symbols placed upon the blocks.

Fig. 2. Full platform overview.

[11] https://www.utopiamechanicus.com/article/braille-display-2017/.
[12] http://users.eecs.northwestern.edu/~mhorn/topcodes/.

By adding TopCodes symbols and associated libraries, each block's type is optically recognized by the software part using a web-cam; while the values inside blocks are recognized by *cubarithms'* analysis: the TopCodes' analysis identify the types of blocks used in the algorithm; while the *cubarithms'* analysis identify the values held into such blocks. A JSON file and related resources are then generated as a SB3 file (common extension for Scratch language) to be read by Scratch (as shown in Fig. 3).

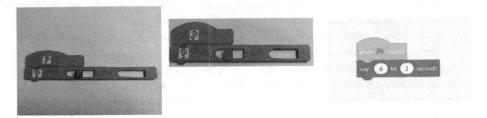

Fig. 3. From a simple algorithm to the algorithm in Scratch after the visual recognition.

The main objective is to give autonomy to visually-impaired students when using Scratch with the TabGO TUI (as shown in Fig. 4): thanks to this TUI, a visually-impaired user can use Scratch autonomously, from recreation of algorithms to optical recognition by the software, to a SB3 file exploitable by Scratch.

With the use of these enhanced blocks and this optical recognition software (as previously mentioned), it is then possible for users to design simple algorithms that help introducing important computing notions. So, these algorithms represent an easy way to enhance computing skills for students, whether they're visually paired or impaired. Finally, these algorithms also represent the first experimental phase for testing this solution's viability.

4   User Study

The tests planned to evaluate the efficiency of the TabGO solution are based on a multiple case study, centered around a sequence of four simple algorithms the subject has to build, four stages arranged by increasing difficulty. These algorithms were limited to a few blocks and were constructed accordingly to the French secondary school's program, thus remaining accessible for young students. Each stage of the experiment (except the first one) can be realized by one subject or by two subjects working together, mirroring the will previously mentioned to focus on (respectively) autonomy and inclusive collaboration. For instance, one of the first algorithms is based on a simple coin tossing machine (a six-block algorithm, see Fig. 4) inspired by an 8th grade assessment, introducing pupils to conditional branches and probabilities.

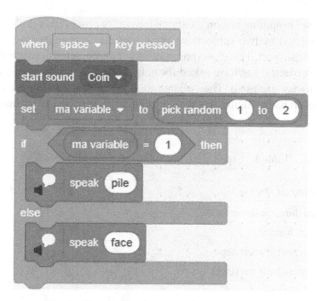

Fig. 4. Scratch interface – Coin Toss algorithm.

While the usability of this technology (as a first approach to computer science) is the main subject of these test series, parameters of age, technology affinity and braille knowledge are considered while evaluating efficiency of the TabGO prototype. Thus, four groups of sighted or visually impaired users of different ages will be confronted (P1 to P4).

- P1: Visually Impaired Teenagers
- P2: Sighted Teenagers
- P3: Visually Impaired Adults
- P4: Sighted Adults

The four groups are asked to construct specific algorithms following steps and instructions, under an informed instructor's watch. For each step, the instructor has to answer three questions, (1) how well does the subject identify blocks, (2) how well does the subject connect blocks and (3) how well does the subject experience feedback. Instructions are given to the test subject at the start of the task, and the instructor is told not to intervene, unless told to during crucial steps or if the subject encounters many difficulties. However, the instructor is also told to write any demand of intervention originated by the test subject: after he/she has been asked for help four times, the instructor is told to skip the actual task and begin the next one.

The parameters observed essentially focus on completion (or non-completion) of a given task, and the time necessary to complete each step/stage. Each parameter is appreciated by the observer with the use of a 5-point Likert scale (see Table 1). The experiment's duration is thus notated in relative (Likert scale) values, for each step and each stage. The experiment's completion includes progress between steps and between stages: these progresses indicate how well does the subject adapt to the prototype while apprehending new computing notions. Other parameters observed include collaboration if the stage is realized by two subjects working together and autonomy if the stage is realized by a single subject. These two parameters are appreciated according to the number of times the subject(s) has/have asked for help or verification, and also according to the number of tries for each step. The collaboration parameter also depends on the communication between users, higher if the communication is productive and/or enjoyable for each user.

Table 1. Experimental protocol – Observation grid

Parameter observed	1	2	3	4	5
Step duration (Likert scale)					
Block handling					
Progress between steps					
Progress between stages					
Collaboration					
Autonomy					
Total (/35)					
Stage duration (35 min at most):					
Number of times the subject asked for help:					
Number of times the subject asked for verification:					

At the end of each stage, the subject will also be asked to fill (indirectly by interview for visually impaired users) a satisfaction survey, a task load assessment (NASA-TLX) and a usability survey (SUS, or System Usability Scale). With these methods of data collection, many aspects and related questions will be answered to establish the actual efficiency of the TaBGo prototype.

Q1 - Were the blocks easily used and recognized by subjects? (Usability aspect, data collected by direct observations and by System Usability Scale).

Q2 - Was the task difficult for subjects? (Cognitive aspects, data collected by direct observations, NASA-TLX and by Satisfaction survey).

Q3 - Was the approach offered by using the TabGO prototype helpful for the subject to develop computing skills? (Progression aspect, data collected by direct observations and by NASA-TLX).

Q4 - Was the collaboration with other users pleasant and useful to subjects? (Collaborative aspect, data collected by direct observations and by satisfaction survey).

Q5 - Was the subject able to use the prototype autonomously? (Autonomy aspect, data collected by direct observations and by satisfaction survey).

All of the aspects of this sample experimental phase are summed up in Table 2 below.

Table 2. Experimental protocol – Aspects investigated and methods used to investigate them

Aspects investigated	Method of data collection
Usability	Direct observations, System Usability Scale
Cognitive load	Direct observations, NASA-TLX, Satisfaction survey
Progression	Direct observations, NASA-TLX
Collaboration	Direct observations, Satisfaction survey
Autonomy	Direct observations, Satisfaction survey

With these data collection methods combined, the experimental protocol presented here aims to be as complete as possible, considering both quantitative and finite aspects of task-resolving, as well as qualitative and human aspects in task-involvement. The subsequent stages imply different feedback and/or more complex algorithms, composed of multiple pairs of blocks connected together, or realized in collaboration with another user. Though knowledge progression and computing skills' acquisition (Q3) represent an important aspect of these tests, it is a secondary one as the main goal here is before and foremost to evaluate usability of the prototype in different conditions, with increasing difficulty.

The data collected are then analyzed to establish if there are differences in performance between each group of subjects, differences that can thus be linked to each subject's individual skills and experience. For each data collection method, the results' mean of each item is then calculated to establish if, overall, the TabGo TUI-based first approach towards programming skills' learning is actually intuitive enough to be used by secondary school students, whether they're visually impaired or sighted.

According to similar studies [28, 29], the results expected revolves around a clear apprehension and identification of the blocks used. The tasks composing the protocol are centered around the secondary school program, so the results shouldn't vary much from group to group, especially if the many enhancements reveal to be useful, as seen in similar studies [35, 39] and as announced by the first results of the pre-test phase. Though satisfaction may not be optimal for adults (as the tasks may not be particularly mentally challenging for them), we expect these tasks to be simple and enjoyable enough to encourage involvement and collaboration between all users, and especially between sighted and visually-impaired users. If the results are promising, the subsequent experimental protocols focus on the learning and acquisition of computing skills with the TabGo prototype. As previously mentioned, these results will help confirm hypotheses on the prototype's usability while also considering important factors playing a role in a learning (cognitive load, progression) and social (collaboration, autonomy) context: such data will help to establish if the prototype will be efficient and adapted in a classroom environment.

5   Conclusion

While pursuing the development of the TabGO prototype and while relating its progresses, this article has first presented possible guidelines for the conception of *Assistive*

Technologies for visually-impaired users to learn computing skills, in an educational context. Related works and major influences in the accessibility field were then presented, with an emphasis on classroom-integrated TUI solutions. Some characteristics have been highlighted: the use of block-based VPL (such as Scratch) may be adapted by the implementation of an adapted IDE centered on non-visual feedback (audio and tactile cues), and by the use of tangible blocks. By modifying and enhancing a learning tool, this inclusive approach has proven to improve collaboration between visually-impaired users and their sighted peers.

The TabGO project followed these guidelines and proposed a prototype composed of tangible enhanced Scratch blocks (with braille symbols, cubarithms, TopCodes and carved patterns) organized in a briefcase, and an associated optical recognition software (using a webcam), translating tangible block-based algorithms into exploitable files for the Scratch platform. With this prototype, the project is aiming to help visually-impaired users learn computing skills autonomously while still favoring inclusion and collaboration through a tangible activity in the classroom environment. With promising preliminary results, the experimental phase will soon be launched to evaluate the usability of this prototype.

Acknowledgments. This work is supported by the French UNADEV association (Grant 2019.49).

References

1. Carver, J. (ed.): Quality, nontechnical skills, blind programmers, and deep learning. IEEE Softw. **36**(2), 127–136 (2019). https://doi.org/10.1109/MS.2018.2883874
2. Kearney-Volpe Cl: Web Development Training for Students That Are Blind W4A 2019, 13–15 May 2019, San Francisco, California, USA (2019)
3. Senjam, S.: Assistive technology for students with visual disability: Classification matters. Kerala J. Ophthalmol. **31**(2), 86 (2019). https://doi.org/10.4103/kjo.kjo_36_19
4. Truillet, Ph.: L'informatique, pour un monde plus accessible. Bulletin de la Société informatique de France – numéro 15, avril 2020, France (2020)
5. Ludi, S., Merchant, W., Simpson, J.: Exploration of the use of auditory cues in code comprehension and navigation for individuals with visual impairments in a visual programming environment. In: ASSETS 2016, 23–26 October 2016, Reno Nevada, USA (2016)
6. Cheong, C., Burge, A. (eds.): Coding without sight: Teaching object-oriented java programming to a blind student. In: 8th Annual Hawaii International Conference on Education, Honolulu, Hawaii, 7–10 January 2010, pp. 1–12 (2010)
7. Francioni, J.M., Matzek, S.D., Smith, A.C.: A java programming tool for students, with visual disabilities. In: ASSETS 2000, November 2000, Arlington, Virginie, USA (2000)
8. Raman, T.V., Tauber, M.J. (eds.): Emacspeak—a speech interface. In: Proceedings of the SIGCHI Conference on Human Factors in Computing Systems (CHI 1996), pp. 66–71. ACM, New York, USA (199)
9. Vickers, P., Alty, J.L.: Musical program auralisation: a structured approach to motif design. Interact. Comput. **14**(5), 457–485 (2002). https://doi.org/10.1016/S0953-5438(02)00004-8
10. Teaching Modern Object-Oriented Programming to the Blind: An Instructor and Student Experience – Dr. Charles B. Owen, Michigan State University; Sarah Coburn, Michigan State University, Ms. Jordyn Castor

11. Kaijanaho, A.-J.: Evidence-Based Programming Language Design: A Philosophical and Methodological Exploration Information Technology Faculty. University of Jyväskylä, Ph.D. Dissertation (2015)
12. Archambault, D.: Interaction et usages des modalités non visuelles, accessibilité des contenus complexes, (Thèse) Université Pierre et Marie Curie - Paris VI, Paris (2010)
13. Metatla, O., et al.: Toward classroom experiences inclusive of students with disabilities. Interactions **26**(1), 40–45 (2018). https://doi.org/10.1145/3289485
14. Flammant, J.: De l'œil au regard. SIDVEM, Paris (2016)
15. Hatwell, Y.: Le développement perceptivo-moteur de l'enfant aveugle. Enfance **55**(1), 88 (2003). https://doi.org/10.3917/enf.551.0088
16. Kelleher, C., Kiesler, S., Pausch, R.: SAMMS girls to learn computer programming. In: CHI 2007 Proceedings, April–May 2007, California, USA San Jose (2007)
17. Chou, M.: Designing a community to support long-term interest in programming for middle school children, IDC 2012, 12–15 June 2012, Bremen, Germany (2012)
18. Brock, A.: Tangible interaction for visually impaired people: why and how. In: World Haptics Conference - Workshop on Haptic Interfaces for Accessibility, June 2017, Fuerstenfeldbruck, Allemagne. pp. 3. ffhal-01523745ff (2017)
19. Cecily, M., et al.: Physical programming for blind and low vision children at scale. Hum. Comput. Interact. (2019). https://doi.org/10.1080/07370024.2019.1621175
20. Jaskova, L., Kaliakova, M.: Programming Microworlds for Visually Impaired Pupils, Conférence de Constructionism 2014, Vienne, Autriche (2014)
21. Wang, D., Zhang, C., Wang, H.: T-Maze: a tangible programming tool for children, pp. 127–135 (2011). https://doi.org/10.1145/1999030.1999045.
22. Motoyoshi, T., Tetsumura, N., Masuta, H., Koyanagi, K., Oshima, T., Kawakami, H.: Tangible gimmick for programming education using RFID systems. IFAC-PapersOnLine. **49**, 514–518 (2016). https://doi.org/10.1016/j.ifacol.2016.10.608
23. Utreras, E., Pontelli, E.: Design of a tangible programming tool for students with visual impairments and low vision. In: Antona, M., Stephanidis, C. (eds.) HCII 2020. LNCS, vol. 12189, pp. 304–314. Springer, Cham (2020). https://doi.org/10.1007/978-3-030-49108-6_22
24. Virey, M., Renaud, P.: Le Roamer: un robot déjà ancien au service d'apprentissages bien actuels: Utilisation dans une Classe d'inclusion scolaire (Clis 1) de l'Yonne. La nouvelle revue de l'adaptation et de la scolarisation **52**(4), 231 (2010). https://doi.org/10.3917/nras.052.0231
25. Ladner, R.E., Milne, L.R.: Blocks4All: overcoming accessibility barriers to blocks programming for children with visual impairments. In: CHI 2018, Avril 2018, Montréal Canada (2018)
26. Deitrick, E., Sanford, J., Benjamin, R.: BlockyTalky: a low-cost, extensible, open source, programmable, networked toolkit for tangible creation. In: IDC 2014, 17–20 June 2014, Aarhus, Danemark (2014)
27. Boissel, S.: Mallette Accessi DV scratch « Scratch débranché en braille et gros caractères ». La nouvelle revue de l'adaptation et de la scolarisation **77**(1), 183 (2017). https://doi.org/10.3917/nras.077.0183
28. Marco, J.-B., Baptiste-Jessel, N., Truillet, P.: TabGO: Programmation par blocs tangibles. In: 30e Conférence francophone sur l'Interaction Homme-Machine (IHM 2018), 23 October 2018 - 26 October 2018, Brest, France (2018)
29. Amber, W., Zirui, W.: Evaluating a tactile approach to programming scratch. In: ACMSE 2019 Avril 2019 Kennesaw USA (2009)
30. Maloney, J., Resnick, M., Rusk, N., Silverman, B., Eastmond, E.: The scratch programming language and environment. ACM Trans. Comput. Educ. (TOCE). **10**, 16 (2010). https://doi.org/10.1145/1868358.1868363

31. Metin, S.: Activity-based unplugged coding during the preschool period.Int. J. Technol. Des. Educ. 1–17 (2020) https://doi.org/10.1007/s10798-020-09616-8
32. Sanchez, J., Aguayo, F.: Blind learners programming through audio. In: CHI 2005, pp. 1769–1772, 2–7 April 2005, Portland (2005). https://doi.org/10.1145/1056808.1057018
33. Shreekanth, T., Udayashankara, V.: A review on software algorithms for optical recognition of embossed braille characters. Int. J. Comput. Appl. **81**(3), 25–35 (2013)
34. Horn, M.S., Robert, J.K.: Tangible programming in the classroom: a practical approach. In CHI 2006 Extended Abstracts on Human Factors in Computing Systems (CHI EA 2006), pp. 869–874. ACM, New York, NY, USA. https://doi.org/10.1145/1125451.1125621
35. Observatoire des Ressources Numériques adaptées, Scratch 3D Magnet, janvier 2018, 13p. https://www.apmep.fr/IMG/pdf/Orna_Scratch3DMagnet.pdf
36. Capovilla, D., Krugel, J., Hubwieser, P.: Teaching algorithmic thinking using haptic models for visually impaired students. In: LaTiCE 2013, pp. 167–171, 21–24 March 2013. https://doi.org/10.1109/LaTiCE.2013.14
37. UN General Assembly: Convention on the Rights of Persons with Disabilities: resolution / adopted by the General Assembly, 24 January 2007, A/RES/61/106. http://www.refworld.org/docid/45f973632.html. Accessed 17 July 2018
38. Zuckerman, O., Grotzer, T., Leahy, K.: Flow blocks as a conceptual bridge between understanding the structure and behavior of a complex causal system. In: Proceedings of the 7th international conference on Learning sciences (ICLS 2006). International Society of the Learning Sciences, pp. 880–886 (2006). https://dl.acm.org/citation.cfm?id=1150162
39. Aymard, P.: Algorithmique Scratch et cécité. Exemple d'un support débranché et adapté (2018). http://revue.sesamath.net/spip.php?article1082

Endless Running Game to Support Sign Language Learning by Deaf Children

Diego Roberto Antunes$^{(\boxtimes)}$ ⓘ and Janaine Daiane Rodrigues ⓘ

Federal University of Technology – Parana (UTFPR), Ponta Grossa, PR, Brazil
drantunes@utfpr.edu.br, janainerodrigues@alunos.utfpr.edu.br

Abstract. The lack of access to information in Sign Language (SL) has been a problem faced by Deaf people, who are trying to use their natural language as the tool for communication and knowledge access. For Deaf children, this problem can be more aggravating, because 90% are children of hearing parents who generally do not know SL. Therefore, the design of educational resources that provide SL support such as animated movies, interactive stories and digital games, is essential for Deaf children. Digital Educational Games (DEG) are learning tools that has been showing benefits for children, providing a playful process and less rejection of the educational process in an environment that promotes greater motivation. This paper presents a methodology for DEG that combines the game style "Endless Running" and the concept of Iconicity to facilitate the learning of SL signs by Deaf children. The methodology was used to develop Ada Runner, a game about Traffic Education where the player can learn signs of Brazilian Sign Language. The game was validated by educators of Deaf children through the gameplay, the answer to 28 questions and a descriptive feedback. The validation presented positive results and considered that the game, based on the proposed methodology, is easy to use and can support the SL learning.

Keywords: Educational game · Sign language game · Accessibility · Game-based learning · Games for deaf

1 Introduction

According to World Health Organization, there are about 466 million people worldwide with hearing loss, total which includes 34 million children [17,24]. In the USA, for example, approximately 3.6% of the population (11 million) are deaf or have serious difficulty hearing [2]. In Brazil, approximately 9.3 million people have some deafness degree [4].

Deaf people around the world prefer to use a Sign Language (SL) as the tool for communication, knowledge access and culture [4]. The acquisition of a natural language has a fundamental role in a person's intellectual and social development [10]. Through language, the Deaf can enter education to learn the essential elements for daily life, enabling them to exercise their citizenship and contribute to society [19].

© Springer Nature Switzerland AG 2021
M. Antona and C. Stephanidis (Eds.): HCII 2021, LNCS 12769, pp. 25–40, 2021.
https://doi.org/10.1007/978-3-030-78095-1_3

However, a serious problem faced by Deaf people is the lack of access to information and digital tools in SL, an issue that creates many difficulties for the acquisition of SL and the educational process. Learning SL through books is not effective, since all the elements of a sign cannot be easily and accurately represented using static images [17].

For Deaf children, the lack of educational resources in SL can be more aggravating, because 90% are children of hearing parents who generally do not know SL and are not prepared to support their children in the learning process. The learning process becomes very slow and disappointing for Deaf children when they need to understand the spoken language [3].

In this context, these Deaf children do not have effective communication with their parents, creating a barrier to the development of SL and complicating their education [8]. Deaf children who have hearing parents need more linguistic resources and playful activities to assist in the acquisition of SL and enable their education [3].

Therefore, the design of educational resources that provide SL support is essential for this minority community. The SARS-CoV-2 pandemic has increased the demand for access of digital resources to support children's education at home, especially playful resources to increase the child's engagement.

Resources such as educational toys, animated movies, interactive stories and digital games can be used for playful learning [9]. Digital educational games are learning tools that provide a playful process and has been show positive results and benefits for children [11].

The use of digital games in education has increased over the years because it fascinates children and generates more engagement through entertainment [23]. Digital games can be used to minimize the lack of SL educational resources for Deaf children and contribute to improving the SL acquisition process [9].

In this sense, this paper presents a methodology to support the development of digital educational games that combines the game style "Endless Running" and the concept of Iconicity to facilitate the learning of SL signs by Deaf children. In the Endless Running or "Infinite Runner" genre, the player runs on a path dodging objects and earning points until all the attempts are over, in case of collision. The methodology was used for the development of Ada Runner, a game about the Traffic Education context where the player can learn signs of the Brazilian Sign Language and evaluate their learning during the game.

2 Background

2.1 Deaf People and Sign Language

The lack of access to information and knowledge has been a major problem faced by some minority communities. This is the case of the Deaf communities that have suffered over the years with isolation and social exclusion. The Deaf, in the context of this research, consist of individuals who are members of a minority community that has their own demands as citizens in social and political aspects of society [4].

The Deaf have their culture defined by the gestural-visual universe of Sign Language (SL), a linguistic tool used for their communicational relations and for the construction of knowledge [4]. Thus, a SL is considered the natural language of the Deaf and consists of an autonomous linguistic system that has rules of grammatical organization different from oral-auditory languages (e.g. English). SL have a structural complexity like any natural language, including all phonological, morphological, syntactic, semantic and discursive levels [4,6,12].

SLs are natural gestural-visual languages because communication is performed by the interlocutor through articulated movements (hands, arms and forearms) and non-manual expressions (facial expressions and body movements made by the head or torso) that are perceived through the visual channel [4].

A common problem is that the language most used in a country still dominates the resources of access to information and knowledge (e.g. in Brazil, Portuguese). Thus, most Deaf people are excluded from the communication process, where the social interactions are restricted. Additionally, it is observed that society (oral language) has poor knowledge of SL, which demands greater attention for the development of SL educational tools to support the Deaf [4].

Information and Communication Technologies (ICT) play an essential role in the construction of tools that provide the necessary support for access to information and an improvement in the social interactions of the Deaf. ICTs must have a clear understanding of the communication needs of Deaf people and make appropriate computational treatment of SL.

In this sense, it is important that tools built to support education or access to information use SL as the main resource for communication and interaction with users. The inclusion of SL in digital educational resources enables appropriate feedback during the interaction, assertiveness in understanding the information and, consequently, provides better usability and accessibility [4].

2.2 Digital Educational Games

Digital Educational Games (DEG) are resources built to teach while entertaining players, combining entertainment and education in an environment where the student is placed at the center of the learning experience [8].

DEG can assist the learning process by increasing student motivation and curiosity with a more interactive environment, enabling more effective learning results [25]. Educational resources presented in the form of DEG increase student engagement and improve their awareness of the educational process [18].

As immersive environments, DEG include interactive scenarios, challenges and rewards, interactions with objects and collaboration able to provide more contextual education considering real-world issues [13]. The use of digital games as a form of educational resources can provide less abandonment or rejection of the learning process, since the environment promotes greater motivation [25].

The use of games in the education of Deaf children is promising, because DEG enables visual and tactile feedback through vivid colors, interactive objects, videos with SL dialogues, challenges and tasks that refer to the real world, among other artifacts. Khenissi et al. (2015) [19] explains that the use of DEG provides more intellectual stimulation and increase creativity. It also enables collaboration and the development of social skills for the learner.

The use of games in education is supported by the Game Based Learning (GBL) methodology, considered an active learning methodology that has produced positive results with different levels of knowledge acquisition by learners in comparison to traditional approaches [8,9] and [22]. GBL provides an educational approach through an entertaining and relaxing game, an environment where students can acquire knowledge and use it to solve problems [23].

The GBL enables an innovative teaching method that reinforces learning through gameplay, which can engage learners with meaningful narratives and activities based on the game context [29].

GBL can be applied in different contexts such as use in the classroom, teacher support tool, resource for self-learning and as digital environments for interaction between parents and children (enabling collaborative learning and greater social interaction) between them [14]. In the learning process, the GBL can be used as: a) Self-Learning tool where the game has a built-in learning system that allows the player to create progress in an environment with challenges, but in an incremental way allowing progress with adequate feedback for the learning; b) DEG as a Pedagogical Tool where the game is used as a learning tool for teaching specific concepts and solving problems (e.g. mathematical operations); and c) DEG for Classroom Support where the teacher uses the game in conjunction with other approaches to provide a more interactive environment for learners to develop skills and knowledge (e.g. teaching home security situations) [28].

For Deaf children's education context, industry and academic research have used the games as more immersive and interactive artifacts to assist in the process of learning different concepts. The visual, spatial and dynamic nature of the games is well suited to assist in understanding the context and information, since the Deaf's use of SL consists of a visual-spatial language [4].

As an example of DEG for Deaf children, Canteri (2014) [7] presents a puzzle game style to teach basic signs of Brazilian Sign Language for the Animals, Personal Care, Transportation and Food themes (Fig. 1). The game goal is to find a correct group of three items: a sign, an image and the word that represents the concept. The game can be used to assist the teacher in the classroom to teach basic concepts, as well as be used to assess the child's previous learning.

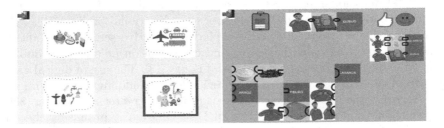

Fig. 1. Puzzle game for Deaf children with SL basic signs [7].

Another example is the SMILE [1] (Fig. 2A), which was developed to support the teaching of mathematics and science for Deaf children, using educational methods and motivational concepts in its design. CopyCat [5] (Fig. 2B) consists of an Adventure game to teach Deaf children to understand the signs of the American Sign Language (ASL), where the player performs signs requested by the game and increases progress if the sign is articulated correctly via camera. Sign My World [20] (Fig. 2C) was created for mobile devices focused on teaching Australian Sign Language (AUSLAN), where the player interacts with objects on screen, then a video appears with the sign. MemoSign [19] (Fig. 2D) consists of a memory game that teaches the concepts of SL combining the concepts of Avatar, Sign Writing[1] and the written language (English).

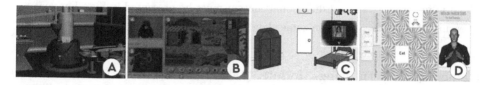

Fig. 2. A) SMILE [1]. B) CopyCat [5]. C) Sign My World [20]. D) MemoSign [19].

3 Methodology

3.1 Game Design for Deaf Children

Learning effectiveness using a DEG is a difficult task that depends on the proper relationship between the instructional process and game design. This is a complex activity, as game developers generally do not have the pedagogical and methodological knowledge of the educational area, while educational professionals do not have the technical knowledge for game development [16].

The development process for DEG involves the collaboration of multiple specialists, such as developers, designers and illustrators, pedagogical specialists, educators [16] and, in the case of Deaf people, the project may need an SL interpreter. In this sense, it is important that the DEG design process uses a methodology that considers all technical and pedagogical requirements, through the inclusion of several specialists or through guidelines.

In order to provide effective support in the DEG development for Deaf children, the proposed methodology uses the JEIS framework that includes concepts of Human-Computer Interaction, Educational Games, Education for the Deaf and Digital Games. The concepts of each area were used to define a set of criteria that each module must include to result in an effective DEG for Deaf children. JEIS was structured in four modules: *Teaching-Learning, Learner-Player, Gameplay and Tutoring, Graphics and Interface* [8] and [9].

---

[1] http://signwriting.org/.

Teaching-Learning Module. (Table 1) provides support in defining the educational content (objectives, structure, order, etc.) that will be covered in the game, based on the education and pedagogy literature for Deaf children.

Table 1. Teaching-Learning module criteria [7]

Fields of Experience	Inclusion of relevant concepts and content in Education of Children such as signs, letters, objects and words
Learning Rights	Includes themes considering instructional objectives: socialization, play, participation, exploration and expression
Game Goals Association	Each game goal must be related to teaching a concept
Sign Language	Educational content must be presented in Sign Language
Learning Support	The game should be a complementary learning tool

Gameplay and Tutoring Module. (Table 2) is responsible for defining the objectives and possibilities of interaction with the game in order to facilitate learning (i.e. the mechanics of the game related to the learning objectives).

Table 2. Gameplay and Tutoring module criteria [7]

Game Genre	Choose the most suitable game genre for children, such as: action, adventure and puzzle
Instructions	When starting the game it is necessary to show a video tutorial or using images to reinforce the mechanics
Goals	Goals must be clear and must be understood by Deaf children, according to their physical and cognitive abilities
Meaningful Choices	Choices must impact the environment and it must be clear to the player that their actions change the state of the game
Input and Controls	Limit the use of buttons and commands to reduce complexity. Prioritize native controls like touch, mouse and keyboard
Rewards	Set rewards when the player reaches the goals
Association with Experience Fields	Objectives and game mechanics must be directly related to educational content

Learner-Player Module. (Table 3) has the role of "monitoring" the progress and assisting in the learning assessment. If the learner doesn't reach the goal, the game must provide mechanisms to assist him (e.g. tips and new chances).

Graphics and Interface Module. aims to define all the graphic resources needed for DEG. As the target audience is formed by Deaf children, scenarios and illustrations play a fundamental role in communicating the context, educational content and narratives. The set of criteria is shown in Table 4.

Table 3. Learner-Player module criteria [7]

Performance Evaluation	Includes a mechanism to calculate the player's performance indicators, such as errors, accomplishments and time used
Scoring	Provides counters of results and performance indicators in real time during the game
Improvement Suggestions	Provides feedback when the player doesn't reach the expected performance (skills to improve and how to do)
Difficulty Adaptation	Mechanism for choosing the level of difficulty or automatic progressive adaptation
Hints	Provides assistance (e.g. suggestions of upcoming moves)

Table 4. Graphics and Interface module [7]

Colors and Shapes	Uses vivid colors, highlights important elements with strong colors and uses round shapes. This combination induces positive emotions and facilitates learning
Consistency	Keeps a positioning pattern of interface elements
Simple Menus	Presents simple menus using images and SL
Meaningful Icons	Uses icons with meanings related to the game and the theme, and should not distract the child
Cartoon Art Style	Uses child oriented illustrations in scenarios, elements and icons
Proper Feedback	Presents visual and quick feedback taking SL into account

3.2 Game Style

Lotfi et al. (2014) [21] presents a statistical study about the relationship between game genres and criteria such as age, area of application and game characteristics. The study showed that action, adventure and puzzle genres are more suitable for children in the context of education.

Many DEG for Deaf children, as previously mentioned, have used the Puzzle, Memory or Adventure approaches. Puzzle and Memory games provide simple interaction mechanisms, usually with a weaker narrative, and are generally used to learn isolated SL signs. The Adventure DEG type provides a broader context and presents an interactive environment related to the real world (e.g. park, house, shop, etc.) and enables simple gameplay through the interaction of objects on the screen, allowing the creation of more significant narratives.

In order to create DEG that can be applied in multiple contexts (such as self-learning, classroom support, resource for learning assessment or as a pedagogical resource for teaching specific knowledge), this methodology proposes the use of the Action genre, with the "Endless Running" sub-type. The Action type is interesting because it includes a broader coverage of gameplay features such as speed, interactive knowledge, entertainment, logic and intelligence [21].

Endless Running games usually consist of a linear run where the player must deflect objects by jumping or moving left or right. The difficulty of the game grows progressively by increasing the speed and the number of obstacles, and the goal is to go as far as possible without colliding with an obstacle. Popular games are Sonic Dash[2] and Super Mario Run[3]. Although it has simple gameplay, the Endless Running type is interesting because it instigates the player to always try to get better performance, reaching a greater distance or trying to make more points by deflecting objects or capturing rewards while running. This is an important factor because it enables greater engagement and motivation.

Additionally, it is important to note that when colliding with an obstacle or reaching a specific mark in the game (time, points obtained, number of attempts, etc.) it is possible to provide special feedback to the player. In the educational context, this interaction can be a hint, more knowledge or even a learning assessment, contributing to the mechanics of the game and the learning process.

3.3   Sign Language Approach

One of the educational contents indicated for Deaf children is the teaching of basic signs in a specific context. *"Learners in the initial stages of SL learning use iconicity as a mnemonic aid to remember new signs"* [17]. However, it is important to define a methodology for choosing and presenting the signs in order to maximize learning.

SL can express complex and abstract concepts through the combination of shapes and hand positions, location in space, movements and non-manual expressions. One of the sign formation processes is the Iconicity that uses the phonological parameters (hands, space, movement and expressions) to represent concepts, objects and actions of the real world with a certain similarity [27].

An iconicity process aims to provide mental images with iconic resemblance to the related concept, creating a linguistically valid sign [14] that can be described by the components of the linguistic system such as morphology and phonology.

The creation of iconic forms follows three steps: the first is the selection of the mental image that is associated with a real-world concept (e.g. a tree); the second is the extraction of essential characteristics (e.g. branches, trunk and plane); and the third is the encoding of the characteristics using the language resources (e.g. hands, movements, positioning, etc.) [27]. Since the concept of this paper is to support the SL initial learning based on a context, the use of iconicity can be a facilitator to introduce the SL for the Deaf child (i.e., the first signs). In this sense, the game must adopt iconic signs that belong to the context.

For example, consider the context of a park for the game. An object presented in this environment is a butterfly. A butterfly is an insect characterized in its mental image by the flapping of the wings, in this way, the SL can encode its sign using the iconic process with the hands to represent the wings, the hands overlapping (location) and the movement of the flapping wings (Fig. 3).

3.4   Educational and Game Mechanics

After defining the game context and the related signs, it is essential to define an instructional strategy in order to enable the Deaf child to explore the

---

[2] https://play.google.com/store/apps/details?id=com.sega.sonicdash.
[3] https://play.google.com/store/apps/details?id=com.nintendo.zara.

Fig. 3. Iconic sign for butterfly.

environment, and the game to present and explain the concepts and, eventually, evaluate this learning [15]. Therefore, the 4E educational approach was based on the concepts of the JEIS, relating the teaching-learning process directly with the game mechanics through the Explore, Expose, Explain and Evaluate phases.

In the **Explore** phase, the player will explore the game environment by running and dodging obstacles in the defined context. This context should simulate a real world environment, such as a park, a city street, a school, a home, etc. Thus, when running through the environment, the player will perceive the objects in the context and relate them to real-world situations. For example, in the traffic context the player will perceive objects such as cars and road signs.

During the Explore phase, the game will introduce the player to the educational content of the iconic signs that represent the objects and actions of the context. Thus, the **Expose** phase is responsible for showing the educational content in a floating window to the player. The triggers for the presentation of educational content can be activated in several ways, such as: specific score, time intervals or when the player collides with an obstacle (Fig. 4A). The mandatory requirement is that only the contents of objects already known to the player must be presented to him, that is, that the player has already seen the object during the game before the presentation triggers.

The content presented to the player will teach the sign of an object. This process is carried out by the **Explain** phase, which will present the object (illustration or image) on the left and the video of the sign made by an interpreter or by the educator on the right. An example is shown in Fig. 4B.

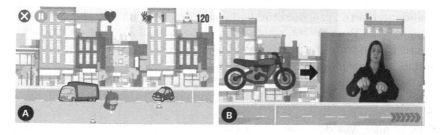

Fig. 4. Example of the Explore, Present and Explain phases in the developed game.

As the learner gains more experience in a phase of the game, it is necessary to evaluate the learning of the signs presented to him. The **Evaluate** phase is responsible for testing if the player has learned a sign already presented to him.

The evaluation can be performed in two ways: A) the game can present an object and the player must choose the correct sign that corresponds to this object in a group of videos (Fig. 5A); or B) the game shows the video of a sign and the player chooses which object correctly represents its meaning (Fig. 5B).

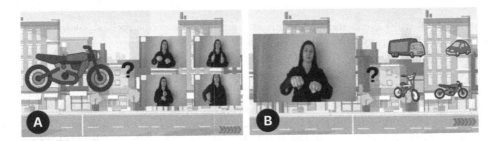

Fig. 5. Example of the Evaluate phase in the developed game [26].

This evaluation mechanism is also related to the mechanics of the game, that is, in addition to evaluating learning, the player must receive rewards when answering the test, for example, renewing the number of game attempts if he has already collided with an obstacle. In addition, in the "game over" event, it is possible to present a test to the players and reward them with an extra attempt if they answer correctly.

To avoid frustration if a player chooses an incorrect answer, the evaluation system should hide the incorrect alternative, giving more attempts for him. This is also a way for the player to recover the concept if he has not learned in the Explain phase. The reward system can also decrease the bonus after an error.

4   Development and Validation

The validation of the proposed methodology occurred through the development of the game Ada Runner [26], which uses the context of Traffic Education where the character Ada runs on the sidewalk to avoid obstacles (cones) (Fig. 6). The game development followed the methodology defining the contents of the game according to the criteria of the JEIS, it used the Endless Running style, adopted Iconic Signs as educational content and implemented the 4E educational approach and game mechanics.

Ada Runner was developed with the game engine Unity[4], a platform that provides 2D or 3D graphics engines, programming libraries, store for assets (3D models, illustrations, etc.) and several resources to assist the development of

---

[4] https://unity.com/solutions/game.

Fig. 6. Game tutorial and game scene for Ada Runner [26]

cross-platform games (mobile, computer, consoles, among others). The platform enables the entire configuration of the objects presented in the game as characters, camera views, scenes, actions, game physics and other settings.

In order to define the structure of the game, the GDD (Game Design Document) was defined following the criteria of the JEIS and the other steps of the proposed methodology. A summary of the GDD is shown in Table 5.

Table 5. Game document design abstract for Ada Runner [26]

Teaching-Learning	The objective is to teach basic signs of traffic elements. The defined signs are: "car", "motorcycle", "bicycle", "truck", "sidewalk", "crosswalk", "traffic light", "stop sign", "bus" and "seat belt"
Gameplay and Tutoring	An Action game where the player must dodge the cones. At the beginning, an animated tutorial is presented (Fig. 6A). The player gains 10 points by dodging the cones. Every 100 points a sign is presented. Eventually, after knowing a sign, a test will be presented to the player (randomly). If the player answers correctly, 1 point will be counted for the educational content
Learner-Player	Scoring is displayed at the top of the game screen in real time, counting the deflected cones and the correct signs. In addition, the number of attempts available is shown, initially 3. The difficulty increases progressively, increasing the number of cones and the game speed. As a hint, when choosing a sign, the game hides the incorrect alternative if chosen by the player (Fig. 7)
Graphics and Interface	The game's graphics are child oriented, with few menu options (home and close) and only the necessary information (attempts and score). Feedback is presented quickly, using SL and significant icons

In the Educational Approach, the teaching of signs related to traffic was defined as thematic. The signs were chosen by an education professional and Libras (Brazilian Sign Language) interpreter who researched and defined a set of 10 signs for the first phase of the game (Table 5). The interpreter then recorded the videos of the signs and made them available for inclusion in the game mechanics.

The game mechanics followed the proposed methodological process, using all stages of Explore (Fig. 4A), Present (Fig. 4B), Explain (Fig. 4B) and

Evaluate (Fig. 5). In the Evaluate stage (Fig. 7A), Ada Runner implemented the "help" mechanism that hides incorrect alternative chosen by the player, providing a "hint" to the player (Fig. 7B). If the player selects three incorrect alternatives, the evaluation mechanism still allows him to choose the correct alternative, enabling reinforcement in learning and maintaining the player's motivation. When the player hits or misses an alternative, the game provides visual feedback to the Deaf child using common and meaningful icons, for example, an emoji "smile" icon (Fig. 7 B-C). The process is shown in Fig. 7.

Fig. 7. Example of the Evaluation Process, with visual feedback and tips [26].

The game was evaluated using a questionnaire [9] formed by one discursive question for general feedback and 28 questions with a Likert scale ("I totally disagree", "disagree", "neutral", "I agree", "I totally agree") that considers the criteria of usability, suitability for Deaf children, gameplay, experience of use, support for learning and SL.

Ada Runner was released through a video on a social network in order to select education professionals (e.g. educators, teachers and researchers) to evaluate the game. At the end of the process, the game and the evaluation questionnaire were sent to 26 education professionals, who tested the game for a week and then answered the questions. The general results are shown in the Fig. 8.

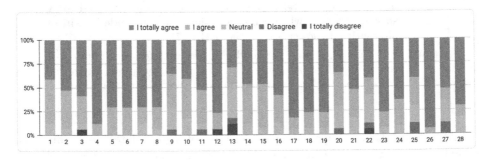

Fig. 8. Result of the evaluation questionnaire for the 28 questions.

5   Results and Discussion

The evaluators agreed that the game's design is suitable for the public, in accordance with the JEIS criteria. Question 1 ("the game design is attractive - interface, graphics, illustrations") obtained 88% of responses in agreement against 11% neutral. Question 2 ("the texts, colors and fonts match and are consistent") obtained 94.1% of answers in agreement against 5.9% neutral. Question 7 ("the fonts, size and style used in the game are legible") obtained 88.2% in agreement against 11.8% neutral. And, finally, question 8 ("the colors used in the game are understandable") obtained 94% of answers with agreement and 6% neutral.

Regarding usability, the evaluators also considered that the game is simple to learn and play, in addition to protecting the player from any errors and providing adequate feedback. Question 3 ("I needed to learn few things in order to start playing") obtained 88% agreement, 5.9% neutral responses and 5.9% of the evaluators disagreed. In question 4 ("learning to play this game was easy for me") the evaluators agreed 100%. And question 11 ("when I first looked at the game, I had the impression that it would be easy for me") 70.6% of the evaluators agreed, 5.9% were neutral and 5.9% disagreed.

The feedback with the player also obtained positive results, mainly in relation to the actions of the users and the recovery of errors. Question 9 ("the game prevents me from making mistakes") obtained 71% of responses in agreement, 23% neutral and only 6% disagreement. In question 10 ("when I make a mistake it is easy to recover quickly") approximately 82% of the evaluators agreed against 17% who were neutral. As for feedback, question 23 ("feedback for the user's actions is clear") resulted in 94% agreement.

The evaluation also pointed out that the game mechanics, implemented based on the methodology proposed, reached the objective of simplicity, adequacy to the public and to the potential uses of the game as a tool in the SL learning. In questions 5 ("I consider the mechanics of the game to be simple to understand") and 6 ("the rules of the game are clear and understandable") the evaluators agreed 100%. In addition, in question 14 ("the game offers obstacles, situations or variations at an appropriate pace") the evaluators agreed to 88%.

Educators also analyzed the game for issues related to learning and support in the teaching of SL. The results indicate that the game developed, using the proposed methodology, can be used in SL learning (as a supporting tool or self-learning tool). In the question ("I think I learned new things from this game"), 94% of the evaluators agreed while 6% disagreed. In question 17 ("I feel satisfied with the things I learned in the game") all the evaluators agreed. Regarding SL teaching, 100% of the evaluators agreed on question 26 that "the game supports SL teaching" and 82% agreed on question 28 that "a Deaf child could easily play this game".

In the discursive question, in order to collect general feedback, the evaluators mentioned that the game collaborates with social inclusion, that the methodology of presenting signs facilitates the learning of SL and that the game can be used during the literacy phase of Deaf children. As suggestions for improvement, the evaluators cited the inclusion of words in the oral language associated with objects in the context, assisting in the teaching of words.

Regarding the contexts of use, as shown by the validation questionnaire, the game developed based on the proposed methodology can be used as a support tool in the teaching of SL of Deaf children and used to learn basic SL signs (self-learning). In addition, the game can be used by hearing parents to assist in the initial learning of SL and to assist in the interaction with their Deaf children.

6   Conclusions

This paper presented a methodology for the development of digital educational games to support the learning of SL signs. The proposed methodology combined the game quality criteria of the JEIS, the game style "Endless Running" and the concept of Iconicity present in SL; producing a game approach directly related to the 4E educational strategy (Explore, Expose, Explain and Evaluate).

In the proposed 4E educational approach, the player can naturally explore objects presented in the game environment. Based on certain triggers, the game can highlight one of these objects and present the corresponding SL sign (teaching phase) to the Deaf child. Later, the game can evaluate the learning of this sign, showing a small test to the player who can earn rewards, as well as to evaluate and reinforce the learning.

The proposed methodology was validated through the development of the Ada Runner game, which used the Traffic Education context to support the learning of basic signs related to the theme, such as "car", "motorcycle", "crosswalk", among others. An evaluation was made by education professionals through the game test and a questionnaire, which showed great results directly related to the application of the proposed methodology: usability, gameplay, mechanics that allows teaching and learning evaluation, feedback and error control.

Although it is still necessary to test the use of it in the classroom, not performed due to the restrictions of the pandemic of COVID-19, the remote evaluation by educators showed that games developed based on the methodology can be used as a tool for teaching-learning SL or even for self-learning of basic signs.

The research intends to include in the methodology and in the games developed words of the oral language linked to the objects and signs used, in order to assist in the learning of the first words. In the Ada Runner game, this mechanic is already possible, but this concept needs to be better explored and integrated with the methodology and with the iconicity.

As a next step, the research intended to define an Infinite Runner style game template and incorporate it into an authoring tool [9] to enable educators, who don't have the technical knowledge for game development, to create games in an automated way. In this sense, the authoring tool would make it possible to use all the mechanics of Ada Runner, but with different characters, objects, scenarios and signs. This process can enable the generation of games for different teaching-learning contexts, in an easy way, contributing to the generation of educational materials in SL.

References

1. Adamo-Villani, N., Wright, K.: SMILE: an immersive learning game for deaf and hearing children. In: ACM SIGGRAPH 2007 Educators Program, SIGGRAPH 2007, p. 17-es. Association for Computing Machinery, New York (2007)
2. ADSC: Annual disability statistics compendium 2019 (2019). https://disability compendium.org/compendium/2019-annual-disability-statistics-compendium? page=6
3. AlShammari, A., Alsumait, A., Faisal, M.: Building an interactive e-learning tool for deaf children: interaction design process framework. In: 2018 IEEE Conference on e-Learning, e-Management and e-Services (IC3e), pp. 85–90 (2018)
4. Antunes, D.R.: Proposta de um Modelo Computacional para Representação de Sinais em uma Arquitetura de Serviços HCI-SL para Línguas de Sinais. Ph.D. thesis, UFPR - Federal University of Parana, Curitiba, September 2015
5. Brashear, H., Henderson, V., Park, K.H., Hamilton, H., Lee, S., Starner, T.: American sign language recognition in game development for deaf children. In: Proceedings of the 8th International ACM SIGACCESS Conference on Computers and Accessibility, pp. 79–86. Association for Computing Machinery (2006)
6. Brentari, D.: A Prosodic Model of Sign Language Phonology. A Bradford Book, 1st edn. MIT Press, Cambridge (1998)
7. Canteri, R.P.: Diretrizes para o Design de Aplicações de Jogos Eletrônicos para Educação Infantil de Surdos. Master thesis, UFPR - Federal University of Parana, Curitiba, PR (2014)
8. Canteri, R.P.: JEIS - Framework Conceitual e Ferramenta de Autoria para a Construção de Jogos Digitais para Educação Infantil de Surdos. Ph.D. thesis, UFPR - Federal University of Parana, Curitiba, Parana, Brazil (2019)
9. Canteri, R.P., García, L.S., Felipe, T.A., Galvão, L.F.O., Antunes, D.R.: Conceptual framework to support a web authoring tool of educational games for deaf children. In: Proceedings of 11th International Conference on Computer Supported Education - Volume 2: CSEDU 2019, pp. 226–235. INSTICC, SciTePress (2019)
10. Chomsky, N.: Knowledge of Language: Its Nature, Origin and Use. Praeger Publishers, New York (1986)
11. Echeverría, A., Barrios, E., Nussbaum, M., Améstica, M., Leclerc, S.: The atomic intrinsic integration approach: a structured methodology for the design of games for the conceptual understanding of physics. Comput. Educ. **59**(2), 806–816 (2012). https://doi.org/10.1016/j.compedu.2012.03.025
12. Fernandes, S.: Educação de Surdos, vol. 2. Editora IBPEX, Curitiba (2011)
13. Guigon, G., Humeau, J., Vermeulen, M.: A model to design learning escape games: SEGAM. In: Proceedings of 10th International Conference on Computer Supported Education - Volume 1: CSEDU, pp. 191–197. INSTICC, SciTePress (2018)
14. Guimarães, C., Antunes, D.R., García, L.S., Peres, L.M., Fernandes, S.: Pedagogical architecture - internet artifacts for bilingualism of the deaf (sign language/Portuguese). In: 2013 46th Hawaii International Conference on System Sciences, pp. 40–49 (2013). https://doi.org/10.1109/HICSS.2013.445
15. Hirumi, A., Stapleton, C.: Applying pedagogy during game development to enhance game-based learning. In: Miller, C. (ed.) Games: Purpose and Potential in Education, pp. 127–162. Springer, Boston (2009). https://doi.org/10.1007/978-0-387-09775-6_6

16. Hotte, R., Ferreira, S.M., Abdessettar, S., Gouin-Vallerand, C.: Digital learning game scenario - a pedagogical pattern applied to serious game design. In: Proceedings of the 9th International Conference on Computer Supported Education - Volume 2: CSEDU, pp. 87–94. INSTICC, SciTePress (2017)

17. Joy, J., Balakrishnan, K., Sreeraj, M.: SignQuiz: a quiz based tool for learning fingerspelled signs in Indian sign language using ASLR. IEEE Access 7, 28363–28371 (2019). https://doi.org/10.1109/ACCESS.2019.2901863

18. Kalogiannakis, M., Nirgianaki, G.M., Papadakis, S.: Teaching magnetism to preschool children: the effectiveness of picture story reading. Early Child. Educ. J. 46(5), 535–546 (2018). https://doi.org/10.1007/s10643-017-0884-4

19. Khenissi, M.A., Bouzid, Y., Essalmi, F., Jemni, M.: A learning game for deaf learners. In: 2015 IEEE 15th International Conference on Advanced Learning Technologies, pp. 418–422 (2015). https://doi.org/10.1109/ICALT.2015.98

20. Korte, J., Potter, L.E., Nielsen, S.: Designing a mobile video game to help young deaf children learn Auslan. In: Proceedings of the 26th Annual BCS Interaction Specialist Group Conference on People and Computers, BCS-HCI 2012, pp. 345–350. BCS Learning & Development Ltd., GBR, Swindon (2012)

21. Lotfi, E., Belahbib, A., Bouhorma, M.: Application of analytic hierarchical process method for video game genre selection. Int. J. Comput. Appl. 96 (2014). https://doi.org/10.5120/16881-6888

22. Mawas, N.E., Truchly, P., Podhradský, P., Muntean, C.H.: The effect of educational game on children learning experience in a Slovakian school. In: Proceedings of the 11th International Conference on Computer Supported Education - Volume 1: CSEDU, pp. 465–472. INSTICC, SciTePress (2019)

23. Mouaheb, H., Fahli, A., Moussetad, M., Eljamali, S.: The serious game: what educational benefits? Procedia. Soc. Behav. Sci. 46, 5502–5508 (2012). 4th World Conference on Educational Sciences (WCES-2012), Barcelona, Spain, 02–05 February 2012

24. Neto, N., Escudeiro, P., Galasso, B., Esdras, D.: Development of an inclusive multiplayer serious game for blind and deaf. In: 2020 15th Iberian Conference on Information Systems and Technologies (CISTI), pp. 1–6 (2020)

25. Papadakis, S., Trampas, A.M., Barianos, A., Kalogiannakis, M., Vidakis, N.: Evaluating the learning process: the "ThimelEdu" educational game case study. In: Proceedings of the 12th International Conference on Computer Supported Education - Volume 2: CSEDU, pp. 290–298. INSTICC, SciTePress (2020)

26. Rodrigues, J.D.: Aplicação do framework jeis no desenvolvimento de um jogo no estilo infinite runner para crianças surdas, 78f. Trabalho de Conclusão de Curso de Ciência da Computação - Universidade Tecnológica Federal do Paraná, December 2020

27. Taub, S.F.: Language from the Body: Iconicity and Metaphor in American Sign Language. Cambridge University Press, Cambridge (2001)

28. Thangagiri, B., Naganathan, R.: Online educational games-based learning in disaster management education: influence on educational effectiveness and student motivation. In: IEEE Eighth International Conference on Technology for Education (T4E), pp. 88–91. IEEE Computer Society, Los Alamitos, December 2016

29. Zahed, B.T., White, G., Quarles, J.: Play it safe: an educational cyber safety game for children in elementary school. In: 2019 11th International Conference on Virtual Worlds and Games for Serious Applications (VS-Games), pp. 1–4 (2019)

Analysis of the Impact of Educational Technology on Social Inequity in the United States

Nicole Darmawaskita and Troy McDaniel[✉]

The Polytechnic School, Arizona State University, Mesa, AZ 85212, USA
{ndarmawa,troy.mcdaniel}@asu.edu

Abstract. The desire to improve and modernize education through educational technology is met with a daunting wall, as educational technologies oftentimes reflect and exacerbate social inequities. This work explores the growth in United States' educational inequity stemming from the interdependent relationships between education, the digital divide, and social inequities. Diving into three case studies, this paper addresses the privatization consequences that result from the disproportionate funding barriers that schools in marginalized communities face in purchasing Smart Boards, as well as the dangerous impacts of SMART Technologies' techno-solutionist marketing in worsening educational inequities. In comparison, massive open online courses (MOOCs), which are designed with the goal of improving education equity, appear to circumvent the funding barriers that Smart Boards provide, but fail to address the more tailored educational needs of marginalized communities – ultimately landing at the same fate as that of Smart Boards in worsening educational inequities. Lastly, this paper investigates reading software related to improving education for students with reading issues and blind students. Massively popular and effective in helping these students be more engaged and independent in reading, reading software is overall successful in creating a positive push toward educational equity. However, individual reading software can easily fall to the same failures of Smart Boards and MOOCs in contributing to educational inequity.

Although improving educational equity requires a holistic approach, from a technology design standpoint, the following recommendations are made: (a) develop educational technology with the goals of improving education quality and equity, (b) circumvent as many barriers as possible to technology access through technology design, (c) work with marginalized communities to truly understand their needs and create a technology they will use, and (d) continue work toward equitable educational technology.

Keywords: Access to education and learning · Evaluation of accessibility · Usability, and user experience · Educational technology · Educational inequity · Digital divide · Educational technology integration

1 Introduction

Access to quality education is fundamental to bridging inequity gaps and raising socioeconomic mobility but is typically limited to students in privileged neighborhoods and/or

M. Antona and C. Stephanidis (Eds.): HCII 2021, LNCS 12769, pp. 41–51, 2021.
https://doi.org/10.1007/978-3-030-78095-1_4

those without disabilities [1]. In response, the era of smartphones and laptops has touted the rise of educational technology as a critical player in closing these gaps in education quality and access. However, the desire to improve and modernize education through technological solutions is met with challenges as new educational technologies often-times worsen the inequities they aim to resolve. Although educational technology has a role in improving education quality and improving socioeconomic mobility, it tends to fall flat in these goals and often exacerbates social inequities due to the following failures: (i) Failure to circumvent structural barriers to technology access through technology design, as demonstrated with the Smart Board; and (ii) Failure to consider why individuals may choose against utilizing technology, as demonstrated with MOOCs.

1.1 Education, Inequity, and the Digital Divide

The uneven distribution of quality education is built by design in the United States education system. Although school funding varies by state, in general, about half of school funding comes from property taxes, meaning that schools in lower income areas receive significantly less funds than those in higher income neighborhoods [2]. Furthermore, most states do not provide any additional funding to school districts that serve student populations of high poverty or color. When considering how equal funding doesn't result in equitable funding–as schools with many students in poverty or of color will require additional funds to provide specialized training for teachers and resources for students, such as free lunch, school supplies, ESL courses, etc.–the funding discrepancies in schools are especially extreme, as schools that are most in need receive severely inadequate funds [3]. (It should be noted that the root cause of these inequities historically stem from systemic racism, and although this paper does not go into the issue of racism, the divides in race, class, and education are heavily linked and complex [2–7]).

These funding discrepancies have huge ramifications, as underfunded schools struggle to receive extra funding and consider providing quality education as less of a priority. Since schools in the United States can receive additional funding off highly-ranked test scores on standardized exams and higher enrollment rates, these schools tend to emphasize test scores and "competitive" appearances against other schools, while cutting corners wherever possible due to lack of funding [8]. Additionally, highly qualified and experienced teachers appear to be one of the leading factors in improving academic achievement in students [2]. Unfortunately, unable to hire enough quality teachers, underfunded schools hire the highest number of unqualified teachers, who also contribute to the disproportionately high rate of attrition that these schools often face [1]. Furthermore, teacher professional development is distributed unevenly [1], worsening the inability of the education system to provide quality education for all. Students with disabilities, who already tend to experience a subpar education experience across the board, are even more so at a disservice in underfunded schools [4, 6, 7].

These inequities are then reflected into the population, as a student's socioeconomic status is strongly related to their educational achievement, school-dropout rate, mental health problems, drug usage, imprisonment rates, and teen birth rates [1]. Students of low income have disproportionately low representation in colleges/4-yr institutions, which results in labor market disparities [1]. Furthermore, the growing omnipresence of technology necessitates the development of digital skills for basic survival. This not only demands for the integration of technology in education, but also magnifies the widening gaps in education quality, achievement, and attainment [1], as the disparities in education become increasingly impacted by the disparities in technology access and usage.

The digital divide can be defined as the rankings and gaps in technology access and engagement [9]. This divide can stem from unequal opportunities to access and use various technology, as well as unequal engagement with technology [9]. Additionally, access to quality education, especially early education that incorporates educational technology, contributes to the digital divide [1], which again contributes to the cycle of inequity.

The digital divide is heavily expressed in education, as well-funded schools integrate technology into their curriculum to enhance learning, while underfunded schools, if they have the technology, tend to utilize it more as a form of babysitting [10]. Due to lack of funding, underfunded schools do not have the means to adequately train and provide sufficient technology support for their teachers, leading to situations like the one mentioned above [10]. Additionally, since teachers are one of the primary catalysts for adopting technology in their classrooms [11], the tendency for underfunded schools to hire teachers who lack experience and confidence with technology compounds the ineffectiveness of digital skills education in schools serving disadvantaged communities. Furthermore, high quality technology support is a major contributor of successful educational technology integration [11–13]. However, K12 technology support teams are typically grossly understaffed, overworked, and extremely lacking [14–16]–with only 34–48% of teachers deeming them adequate in 2018 [17]. Overall, teachers employed in underfunded schools, which tend to focus on exam score optimization and appearances, have higher dissatisfaction rates with educational technology than teachers in schools that emphasize students, inclusion, and quality instruction for all [8, 12].

A speculation for this is that the differences in school priority determines whether the school leadership will truly address the needs of their teachers and students, or whether they will cut corners on education quality, as it is not their focus. With the explosion in technology usage, schools that focus on quality instruction, which are typically well-funded, will be more prone to support, to the best of their ability, successful technology integration to enhance education, and vice versa–furthering discrepancies in education quality. Additionally, so many other factors–such as internet access and student support at home–disproportionately impact students of low income and of color [1]. Ultimately, these additional factors significantly impact the success of educational technology integration in classrooms, widening the digital divide and contributing to inequity [1].

Interestingly, technology access itself does not drive technology usage, as about 20% of those with internet access rarely, if ever, use it [10]. Race, income, and educational attainment are strongly correlated with internet usage–with white, high income, and high educational attainment each positively correlating with high internet use rates [10]. As a result, if, at the expense of other media outlets, the internet took on an even greater role in the distribution of information, the digital divide would significantly widen [10]. Although the incorporation of technology in education is critically important, the tendency for a significant portion of the population to avoid using technology highlights the need to holistically improve the United States' education system. The goals of improving education and reducing the digital divide can easily fall into the trap of techno-solutionism, as technology companies market their products as the simple solution to solving these complex issues. While technology can be part of the solution, its potential is often over-exaggerated, as in the case of the Smart Board.

2 Smart Boards and Educational Inequity

Developed by SMART Technologies, Smart Boards were regarded as the next transformative technology in the education environment, painting visions of students and teachers collaborating and connecting on multiple devices through a whiteboard of the future. Numerous research studies have been published indicating that Smart Boards do live up to their fanfare in helping students be more engaged and learn better [18–23]. However, their integration into the classroom has had mixed results, as some schools found great success with them, but others continue to phase them out [24–27].

Smart Board marketing, filled with techno-solutionist buzzwords such as "transformative, interactive, fun, efficient," [28] pressures schools into purchasing SMART's products, lest they be seen by parents as outdated [25]–adding to the compulsion underfunded schools have in placing a top priority on maintaining their competitive appearances. Parents want the best for their children, and when school funding cannot support the $300,000–$1,000,00 burden [25–27, 29] of Smart Boards–their updates, constant maintenance, continuous rotation of new and improved add-ons–parents step in with open wallets [25]. Consequently, when parent donations do not cover expenses, private businesses find opportunities to extend generous partnerships [25].

Consequently, parents with the means to donate find themselves more appreciated and heard, especially at school events involving fundraising, curriculum, and administration policies [25]. Inevitably, students with higher socioeconomic backgrounds begin to have more of their educational needs met by their school, while the needs of students in marginalized communities remain unheard. Moreover, these schools–in which parents of higher socioeconomic status comprises a significant portion of their parent population–are typically already well-funded and more able to utilize Smart Boards to enhance learning, due to the presence of experienced and qualified teachers, dedicated resources toward technology support and professional development, and utmost priority on quality instruction. The same, however, cannot be said for low-income underfunded schools.

Due to lack of funding, many schools simply cannot afford to purchase Smart Boards [1, 8, 12] or cannot afford to keep up with the continuous costs and are stuck with broken or outdated Smart Boards [26, 27, 29]. As a result, these schools may be deemed as less competitive and find their enrollment rates, and subsequently, their funding amounts dropping–in turn, potentially causing their teacher attrition rates to further increase. Ultimately, the students who remain in these schools are harmed, as their quality of education lowers. Due to their tendency to hire less qualified teachers and inability to provide beyond any basic, generic technology training and professional development [12, 25], low-income schools that are able to purchase Smart Boards are likely to be extra prone to using their Smart Boards as glorified projectors, a practice that is fairly common across all schools [25]. In this case, the purchase of Smart Boards becomes a waste of money as it provides no additional benefit to students, and instead, exhausts resources that could have been put toward beneficial items. Although, between the two situations mentioned above, perhaps the latter, in which schools ineffectively use their Smart Boards, is more attractive than the prior, in which schools lose funding. However, because most schools rely on business partnerships to purchase Smart Boards, underfunded schools that especially rely on these partnerships are likely to experience an exaggerated impact of these private businesses over school climate in comparison to well-funded schools.

Following these partnerships, private businesses may begin to gift students with logo-ridden stickers and pencils, while teachers find themselves in sponsorships with business partners and SMART Technologies, exchanging sale promotions for additional funds toward SMART product purchases [25]. These school-wide marketing tactics pit schools in a competition where they must continue purchasing technology and building relations with private business, as if it proves their dedication to quality instruction [25]. As mentioned earlier, well-funded schools may be better equipped to balance this competition with holistic dedication to quality education; but underfunded schools may find this pressure of privatization further compounds their tendency to maintain appearances at the expense of quality education.

Ultimately, the failure of the Smart Board in diminishing gaps in education quality stems from its inability to circumvent structural barriers to technology access, such as funding and the digital divide, through its design. It is likely that SMART Technologies did not have educational inequity in mind when developing the Smart Board. Nevertheless, the exorbitant costs of the Smart Board have contributed to the growing privatization of public schools and the widening gaps in education quality, the digital divide, and social inequity.

3   MOOCs and Educational Inequity

Massive open online courses (MOOCs) were, and still are, heralded as the new form of education that serves the public good and breaks down education barriers, providing the entire world with university-quality education [30, 31]. MOOCs are typically developed with university partnerships, and offer online education for free to anyone, regardless of previous academic achievement and university enrollment status [30, 31]. Since they are free, online, and are absent of typical university pre-selection requirements, MOOCs enable less privileged groups to potentially improve their career trajectory at a much lower cost in comparison to traditional higher education [32]. However, students in marginalized communities are vastly underrepresented in MOOCs, as most MOOC students are already educated and employed [32, 33]. In fact, minority students who participated in MOOCs often reported feelings of intimidation and reduced social presence [1]. Ironically, those who need the benefits of higher education–those who MOOCs were designed to specifically serve–are not benefitting from them. Instead, the benefits of MOOCs are provided toward those who are already educationally advantaged [32, 33]. While this situation may seem puzzling as there are much fewer barriers to MOOCs than traditional forms of higher education, the remaining barriers to MOOC access are significantly impactful.

Pollack Ichou noticed that the barriers marginalized students face in accessing MOOCs can be considered as a lack of access in four categories: material, mental, skills, and usage access, based on van Dijk's and Hacker's concept of four types of technology access [33, 34]. A lack of material access refers to an individual's lack of information and communications technology, such as computers and affordable and stable internet access–a lack that is commonly seen among low-income communities and globally in lesser developed countries [1, 8, 32–34]. Indisputably, compared to individuals of higher socioeconomic backgrounds, individuals of lower socioeconomic backgrounds are less likely to have material access. Although the choice for MOOCs to operate online seems to overlook the lack of material access that many people have, the majority of individuals in the United States have and use the internet, and the rate of internet usage and access continues to grow [35]. Accordingly, while the online aspect of MOOCs is imperfect in meeting the material access needs of everyone, it meets those needs for more people compared to traditional forms of higher education. Additionally, this highlights the limits of technology design in circumventing all structural barriers to technology and emphasizes the need for a holistic approach in tackling these complex issues. However, even with sufficient material access, individuals in marginalized communities may still refrain from participating in MOOCs for various reasons.

A lack of mental access refers to an individual's lack of elementary digital experience, which may be due to factors such as disinterest, technology anxiety, or hesitancy [34]. This lack of mental access can be seen among individuals in marginalized communities who avoid internet use, preferring to seek out alternative sources for information [10]. Consequently, these individuals are likely unaware of MOOCs, and even if they were aware, would be highly unlikely to participate. Unfortunately, even if an individual has sufficient material and mental access, they may still be unable to participate in MOOCs due to a lack of skills and usage access.

A lack of skills access refers to an individual's lack of digital skills [34], but can also be extended to include a lack of literary skills in the context of MOOCs [33]. Due to discrepancies in education quality, home technology access, and parent attitude, experience, and skills, digital literacy skills are developed unevenly, with individuals in marginalized communities typically lacking in digital skills when compared to their peers [33]. Furthermore, because nearly all MOOCs are taught in English and require college-level reading and writing, literary skills and English fluency are critical in the successful completion of MOOCs [33]. Similar to the case of digital skill development, literary skills and English fluency tend to be less developed for individuals in marginalized communities, further preventing them from participating in MOOCs. Perhaps most detrimental of all for individuals participating in MOOCs is a lack of usage access.

Many individuals in marginalized communities will have sufficient material, mental and skills access to participate in MOOCs, but they often lack usage access, or a lack of usage opportunities [33, 34]. In regard to MOOCs, this is demonstrated by the prevalence of abstract and high-level courses, such as artificial intelligence, which tend to be engaging for many already-educated students, but are simply not practical nor relevant to many students of marginalized groups [33]. Undoubtedly, if these courses are not applicable to marginalized students, they will be unlikely to participate in them.

Beyond these four access categories, MOOCs also fail to consider the varied education backgrounds of individuals in differing socioeconomic backgrounds. MOOCs tend to present the same material to all students in order to provide content equality. However, when considering how MOOCs will accept students regardless of prior academic achievement, the "equality" of MOOCs makes them arbitrarily too advanced or basic for any student. When reviewing the tendency of MOOCs to consist of mostly highly educated students [32, 33], MOOC instructors are then more likely to adjust their course materials to match the more advanced level of their students, rendering MOOCs to likely be too advanced for students with less educational attainment and possibly contributing to the feelings of intimidation and reduced social presence that minority MOOC students face [1].

Ultimately, the failure of MOOCs in diminishing gaps in education quality stem from their oversight in addressing the digital divide due to not fully understanding the tailored needs of marginalized communities. Although MOOCs were designed to circumvent as many barriers to higher education as possible, their failure to better uniquely tailor MOOCs toward marginalized communities has resulted in a lack of marginalized student representation–ultimately, furthering the digital divide, education gaps, and social inequity.

4 Reading Software and Educational Inequity

Unlike Smart Boards and MOOCs, reading software can arguably be seen as one of the few educational technologies that have truly made a positive push toward improving educational quality and equity. For purposes of this research, reading software can represent any software program that has reading aid functions, such as text-to-speech or optical character recognition (OCR, which is the capability to visually distinguish text in various formats, such as physical paper, images, or PDFs), regardless of whether the software's primary purpose is to aid in reading. For example, Apple and Microsoft products typically have built in text-to-speech screen reading technology [36, 37]; Google Drive has some OCR capabilities in transcribing files, such as PDFs or images that screen readers typically cannot read, into files that are compatible with screen readers [38]; and many reading software will contain text-to-speech and OCR capabilities that include highlighting individual words to match users' reading pace or as the words are read aloud [39–41]. For blind students, text-to-speech is vital for accessing information encountered in both school and daily life; for these individuals, text-to-speech enables reading, learning, and navigating digital media independently [42]. For students with reading issues, such as those stemming from dyslexia or ADHD, text-to-speech and/or OCR highlighting features can drastically improve their education, as these technologies help students be more engaged and independent in reading [39–41]. The massive popularity and commonplace adoption of reading software [39–41] indicates an overall ability in meeting both general access needs and the tailored needs of marginalized students.

As a category, reading software has demonstrated some positive impacts in educational equity, but individual reading software products can tend to replicate the failures of Smart Board and MOOCs in contributing toward educational inequity. Reading software can vary wildly in price with some being free or low cost to others costing in the range of thousands of dollars [42, 43]. Furthermore, not all reading software are built to the same standards, with the more affordable software often providing less or subpar features, such as poorer voice quality in text-to-speech or lacking strong OCR capabilities, in comparison to their more expensive counterparts [43]. The combination of pricing and quality differences between individual reading software products can prevent students with specialized needs and lower socioeconomic backgrounds from accessing the software they need due to cost, material access, and usage access barriers. While students who can afford these products may find their education quality improving, those unable to afford the expense may be left behind, widening the education quality gaps within marginalized communities and between marginalized and privileged communities. For individual technology businesses, striking a balance between improving equity and maintaining financial security can be challenging, but this balance tends to be a main factor in determining, from an organizational standpoint, whether an educational technology will positively or negatively impact educational equity.

5 Conclusion

Fundamentally, improving the education system with regards to social inequity requires a holistic approach that includes political and funding change; shifting views on school culture, administration, instructional practices, and privatization; and suitable educational technology [8]. Although educational technology is contributing to social inequity, for educational technology developers, there are several design factors to consider in creating positively impactful educational technology. The first of which is prioritizing education quality and equity. A developer that prioritizes positive impact first and profit second may be less likely to repeat some of the failures described in this work. By pushing back against techno-solutionism, perhaps future educational technology and their marketing can work to shift public mindset and school culture toward one where quality education is prioritized through meeting the needs of students, teachers, and staff, instead of through technology purchases.

Awareness of structural barriers to technology access is key for researchers and developers to circumvent these barriers as much as possible through technology design. As exemplified between Smart Boards and MOOCs, where MOOCs are much more accessible than Smart Boards, circumventing a significant portion of barriers is possible. To circumvent these barriers, we should develop technology that is free or low-cost, compatible with commonly used devices and the internet, and can be accessed by anyone regardless of educational standing. Since running a nonprofit educational technology business may not be financially feasible to most, potential options to maintain financial stability and low product cost may include setting up scholarship or donation systems, in which generous individuals can donate money toward school technology purchases, and well-funded schools can purchase educational technology at a suitable profit margin for business while underfunded schools are offered the technology for free or at a reduced cost.

Another potential option is to create partnerships with states, so that states can purchase educational technology to provide for everyone at no cost. For example, Arizona provides educational lab licenses of SketchUp Pro for free to schools that are involved with the state's licensing grant program [44]. Portland's Smart City PDX's Digital Divide project is another example, in which the state partners with community and nonprofit organization to reduce the digital divide–in an especially urgent manner due to the COVID-19 pandemic's impact in increasing technology dependence–by distributing technology devices, internet access, and digital skills training at no cost to those who are typically excluded from technology access [45]. By partnering with local government while keeping equity in mind, future educational technology may be able to shift public mindset and political policies toward focusing more on educational equity.

By working with marginalized communities, educational technology developers can better understand the tailored needs of these communities and why certain populations may choose against utilizing an educational technology. By providing a platform for marginalized communities to actively participate in developing technology for themselves, educational technology developers and community members can better create technology that will actually be used by these communities. As demonstrated by MOOCs, the oversight in understanding specific digital divide barriers for marginalized groups rendered MOOCs ineffective in their goal of equitably improving education.

Lastly, the continued work toward developing equitable educational technology is crucial. Although currently developed educational technology will likely cause some social harm because they cannot be truly equitable on their own–since technology alone is immensely limited in its ability to solve complex problems, as demonstrated by the limits in MOOCs of addressing material access–educational technology is incredibly important from a digital skill building standpoint, but also for those who cannot have a quality education without it, as demonstrated through reading software. These are significant positive impacts that, while overshadowed by the many significant negative impacts of educational technology, compel the continued development of educational technology.

Acknowledgements. This work is supported in part by the National Science Foundation (Grant No. 1828010).

References

1. Tawfik, A.A., Reeves, T.D., Stich, A.: Intended and unintended consequences of educational technology on social inequality. TechTrends **60**(6), 598–605 (2016). https://doi.org/10.1007/s11528-016-0109-5
2. Biddle, B., Berliner, D.: Unequal school funding in the United States. Educ. Leadersh. **59**(8), 48–59 (2002)
3. Morgan, I., Amerikaner, A.: Funding gaps 2018: an analysis of school funding equity across the U.S. and within each state. The Education Trust, Funding Gaps, pp. 1–13 (2018)
4. Cramer, L.: Inequities of intervention among culturally and linguistically diverse students. Penn GSE Perspect. Urban Educ. **12**(1) (2015). https://eric.ed.gov/?id=EJ1056724. Accessed 05 Dec 2020
5. Losen, D.J., Orfield, G.: Racial Inequity in Special Education. Harvard Education Publishing Group, Cambridge (2002)
6. Beratan, G.D.: Institutionalizing inequity: ableism, racism and IDEA 2004. Disabil. Stud. Q. **26**(2), (2006). https://doi.org/10.18061/dsq.v26i2.682

7. Sciuchetti, M.B.: Addressing inequity in special education: an integrated framework for culturally responsive social emotional practice. Psychol. Sch. **54**(10), 1245–1251 (2017). https://doi.org/10.1002/pits.22073
8. Warschauer, M., Knobel, M., Stone, L.: Technology and equity in schooling: deconstructing the digital divide. Educ. Policy **18**(4), 562–588 (2004). https://doi.org/10.1177/0895904804266469
9. Selwyn, N.: Degrees of digital division: reconsidering digital inequalities and contemporary higher education. RUSC. Univ. Knowl. Soc. J. **7**(1), (2010). https://doi.org/10.7238/rusc.v7i1.660
10. Dimaggio, P., Hargittai, E., Celeste, C., Shafer, S.: Digital inequality: from unequal access to differentiated use. In: Social Inequality, pp. 355–400 (2004)
11. Buckenmeyer, J.A.: Beyond computers in the classroom: factors related to technology adoption to enhance teaching and learning. Contemp. Issues Educ. Res. (CIER) **3**(4), 27 (2010). https://doi.org/10.19030/cier.v3i4.194
12. An, Y.-J., Reigeluth, C.: Creating technology-enhanced, learner-centered classrooms. J. Digit. Learn. Teach. Educ. **28**(2), 54–62 (2011). https://doi.org/10.1080/21532974.2011.10784681
13. Liu, F., Ritzhaupt, A.D., Dawson, K., Barron, A.E.: Explaining technology integration in K-12 classrooms: a multilevel path analysis model. Educ. Tech. Res. Dev. **65**(4), 795–813 (2016). https://doi.org/10.1007/s11423-016-9487-9
14. Berger, M.J., Harriger, A.R., Dooley, A., Heck, C.: Obstacles to Alice adoption in the high school classroom. In: Proceedings of the 2009 Alice Symposium, New York, NY, USA, June 2009, pp. 1–5 (2009). https://doi.org/10.1145/1878513.1878516
15. Federmeier, J.A., Clift, R.T.: Personal, professional, technical, and institutional factors involved in developing a computer-intensive english curriculum. In: Technology and Education: Issues in Administration, Policy, and Applications in K12 Schools, pp. 271–286. Emerald (MCB UP), Bingley (2006). https://doi.org/10.1016/S1479-3660(05)08018-2
16. Pierce, D.: School IT support: overworked...and understaffed. eCampus News (2009). https://www.ecampusnews.com/2009/03/02/school-it-support-overworked-and-understaffed/. Accessed 25 Nov 2020
17. Science and Engineering Indicators 2018, p. 1060 (2018)
18. Akça, Y., Özer, G., Işık, A.D., Çelik, E.: The user characteristics effects to smart board usage on technology acceptance model variables: the sample of Bartin highschool teachers. Int. J. Res. Bus. Soc. Sci. (2017). https://doaj.org. Accessed 06 Dec 2020
19. Cabus, S., Haelermans, C., Franken, S.: SMART in mathematics? Exploring the effects of in-class-level differentiation using SMARTboard on math proficiency. Br. J. Edu. Technol. **48**(1), 145–161 (2017). https://doi.org/10.1111/bjet.12350
20. Çoklar, A., Tercan, I.: Opinions of teachers toward the use of smart boards. Element. Educ. Online **13**, 48–61 (2014)
21. Gürbüztürk, O.: Investigation of elementary education students attitudes towards the use of smart boards. Int. Electron. J. Element. Educ. **11**(1), 55–61 (2018). https://doi.org/10.26822/iejee.2018143961
22. Kirbas, A.: Student views on using smart boards in Turkish education. Univ. J. Educ. Res. **6**(5), 1040–1049 (2018)
23. Mun, S.H., et al.: Active learning using digital smart board to enhance primary school students' learning. Int. J. Interact. Mob. Technol. **13**(7), 4–16 (2019). https://doi.org/10.3991/ijim.v13i07.10654
24. Korkmaz, O., Cakil, I.: Teachers' difficulties about using smart boards. Procedia. Soc. Behav. Sci. **83**, 595–599 (2013). https://doi.org/10.1016/j.sbspro.2013.06.113
25. Parks, A.N.: Smart boards, money and the pedagogy of watching. In: Clough, M.P., Olson, J.K., Niederhauser, D.S. (eds.) The Nature of Technology: Implications for Learning and Teaching, pp. 201–216. SensePublishers, Rotterdam (2013)

26. Replacement for broken SMART Board. The Spiceworks Community. https://community.spiceworks.com/topic/2243820-replacement-for-broken-smart-board. Accessed 06 Dec 2020

27. Smart Boards Fall Out of Favor—and Off the Budget—In Duluth, Minn., Schools. https://www.govtech.com/education/k-12/Smart-Boards-Fall-Out-of-Favor-and-Off-the-Budget-In-Duluth-Minn-Schools.html. Accessed 06 Dec 2020

28. Collaboration Software & Displays - SMART Technologies. https://www.smarttech.com/. Accessed 06 Dec 2020

29. What keeps causing the SMART Boards to lose their 'interactive' ability". https://community.smarttech.com/s/question/0D50P00002sa7xBSAQ/what-keeps-causing-the-smart-boards-to-lose-their-interactiveability?language=en_US. Accessed 06 Dec 2020

30. Mooc.org. Learn About MOOCs - Massive Open Online Courses|An edX Site." https://www.mooc.org/about-moocs. Accessed 06 Dec 2020

31. ASUx Free Online Courses from Arizona State University. edX. https://www.edx.org/school/asux. Accessed 06 Dec 2020

32. van de Oudeweetering, K., Agirdag, O.: MOOCS as accelerators of social mobility? A systematic review. Educ. Technol. Soc. **21**(1), 1–11 (2018)

33. Pollack Ichou, R.: Can MOOCs reduce global inequality in education? Australas. Mark. J. (AMJ) **26**(2), 116–120 (2018). https://doi.org/10.1016/j.ausmj.2018.05.007

34. van Dijk, J., Hacker, K.: The digital divide as a complex and dynamic phenomenon. Inf. Soc. **19**(4), 315–326 (2003). https://doi.org/10.1080/01972240309487

35. Demographics of Internet and Home Broadband Usage in the United States. Pew Res. Center Internet Sci. Tech. https://www.pewresearch.org/internet/fact-sheet/internet-broadband/. Accessed 07 Dec 2020

36. Accessibility – Vision. Apple. https://www.apple.com/accessibility/vision/. Accessed 07 Dec 2020

37. Microsoft Accessibility Features. Accessibility. https://www.microsoft.com/en-us/accessibility/features. Accessed 07 Dec 2020

38. Convert PDF and photo files to text - Computer - Google Drive Help. https://support.google.com/drive/answer/176692?co=GENIE.Platform%3DDesktop&hl=en. Accessed 07 Dec 2020

39. Lewandowski, L., Wood, W., Miller, L.A.: Chapter 3 - technological applications for individuals with learning disabilities and ADHD. In: Luiselli, J.K., Fischer, A.J. (eds.) Computer-Assisted and Web-Based Innovations in Psychology, Special Education, and Health, pp. 61–93. Academic Press, San Diego (2016)

40. Schiavo, G., Buson, V.: Interactive e-Books to Support Reading Skills in Dyslexia, p. 4

41. Zabala, J.: How does optical character recognition help kids with reading issues? https://www.understood.org/en/school-learning/assistive-technology/assistive-technologies-basics/how-does-optical-character-recognition-help-kids-with-reading-issues. Accessed 30 Nov 2020

42. Screen Readers|American Foundation for the Blind. https://www.afb.org/blindness-and-low-vision/using-technology/assistive-technology-products/screen-readers. Accessed 07 Dec 2020

43. Software Programs for Kids Who Struggle With Reading. https://www.understood.org/en/school-learning/assistive-technology/finding-an-assistive-technology/software-programs-for-kids-with-reading-issues. Accessed 07 Dec 2020

44. Resources: Educational Technology. Arizona Department of Education, 09 June 2016. https://www.azed.gov/standards-practices/k-12standards/educational-technology-resources. Accessed 07 Dec 2020

45. Digital Divide: Connecting Portland during the COVID-19 Crisis. Smart City PDX. https://www.smartcitypdx.com/covid-19-digital-divide-response. Accessed 29 Dec 2020

Accessible Block-Based Programming for K-12 Students Who Are Blind or Low Vision

Meenakshi Das[1]([✉]), Daniela Marghitu[1], Mahender Mandala[2], and Ayanna Howard[2]

[1] Auburn University, Auburn, AL 36830, USA
mzd0107@auburn.edu
[2] Georgia Institute of Technology, Atlanta, GA 30332, USA

Abstract. Block-based programming applications, such as MIT's Scratch and Blockly Games, are commonly used to teach K-12 students to code. Due to the COVID-19 pandemic, many K-12 students are attending online coding camps, which teach programming using these block-based applications. However, these applications are not accessible to the Blind/Low Vision (BLV) population since they neither produce audio output nor are screen reader accessible. In this paper, we describe a solution to make block-based programming accessible to BLV students using Google's latest Keyboard Navigation and present its evaluation with four individuals who are BLV. We distill our findings as recommendations to developers who may want to make their Block-based programming application accessible to individuals who are BLV.

Keywords: Accessibility · Block-based programming · Blind/Low Vision

1 Introduction

Block-based programming relies on visual cues and structures to convey information to users. In addition, they heavily utilize drag and drop gesture to create computer programs. This makes it inaccessible for people who are BLV to interact with them. We reviewed the current approaches to make Block-based programming accessible and used the following research questions in guiding us develop our solution:

1. What interaction techniques can BLV individuals use to understand the structure of a block-based program?
2. What interaction techniques can BLV individuals use to receive non-visual feedback from a block-based program?
3. What interaction techniques can BLV individuals use to debug a block-based program?
4. What are the benefits of a screen-reader vs a non-screen reader approach?

Our contributions ultimately built upon the Keyboard Navigation feature [1] which was released recently by Blockly (Google LLC, Mountain View, CA). Since many Block-based applications utilize the Google Blockly library as a base for their application, we concur building upon their already developed accessible keyboard navigation solution is the best standard approach.

© Springer Nature Switzerland AG 2021
M. Antona and C. Stephanidis (Eds.): HCII 2021, LNCS 12769, pp. 52–61, 2021.
https://doi.org/10.1007/978-3-030-78095-1_5

2 Related Work

There has been substantial effort in making Block-based programming accessible to individuals with vision needs. Google first released their accessible version of Blockly which replaced the drag and drop layout with a text layout for screen-reader compatibility [2]. Ludi and Spencer's work mainly focused on adding screen reader capability to Blockly, along with keyboard navigation, while maintaining its original block-based interface [2]. Google later released their own version of Blockly with Keyboard navigation for its blocks [1]. Although the blocks in this current version are navigable by keyboard, they neither produce audio output nor are accessible via screen readers. Milne and Ladner created Blocks4all, an iOS touch-based tablet application which is accessible via VoiceOver [3]. Kaushik and Lewis have proposed a non-visual blocks language called Psuedospatial blocks (PB), which distorts spatial layout, and is based on T.V.Raman's idea that instead of making spatial visual data accessible to screen-readers, the focus should be on making better non-visual representations of information. Their application uses synthetic speech instead of a screen-reader for providing output, although they state it will be possible to add screen reader support to it as well [4].

3 Our Solution

Custom Text-to-Speech. When Google conducted user studies with their initial Accessible Blockly approach, they found that many students were not comfortable using a screen-reader [5]. One of the most popular screen readers, Job Access with Speech (JAWS), is also quite expensive [6]. Some of the students come from low socioeconomic backgrounds and hence may not have had the financial means to purchase such screen-readers. Mac computers come with a free screen-reader called VoiceOver, but a Mac itself is quite expensive. Moreover, learning to use a screen-reader requires considerable practice and immersion making it challenging for users with recent vision loss to become adept at. Therefore, we developed a non-screen reader, self-voicing solution using synthetic speech and interactive text to speech approaches. The ability to use a screen-reader adeptly should not be a prerequisite or a barrier to learning to code, and hence we took this approach.

Retaining Spatiality. The Individuals with Disabilities Education Act (IDEA) requires that students with disabilities receive education in the least restrictive environment, i.e. alongside their non-disabled peers. We make this possible by using a spatial approach to convey information, instead of non-visual approaches which distort spatiality. Although non-visual approaches have been shown to have immense learning benefits for blind users [7], they are not very useful if blind and non-blind individuals want to collaborate and work together. In a study conducted on access overlays for blind users [8], it was shown that, "Access techniques that distort or remove spatial information may reduce users' spatial understanding and memory"; furthermore, this distortion makes it difficult for a blind person to collaborate with sighted peers. Peer programming is commonly used in professional settings and is often utilized by teachers in classrooms. Our approach maintains a spatial yet accessible organization of the block-based coding platform, making it easier for sighted and non-sighted peers to collaborate and learn programming together.

Auditory Cues. Auditory Cues such as earcons are distinctive sounds that convey certain information. In studies examining teaching robotics to BLV K-12 students, earcons were shown to improve learning of coding concepts [9]. In addition, using non-speech audio cues such as earcons can greatly reduce the cognitive burden that comes with sole speech output [10]. Blockly already features some auditory cues such as a *click sound* to denote the deletion of a block. Research has shown that sounds produced from different spatial locations are easier to distinguish [11]. For example, when you play video games, you can hear certain audio sounds from only the left/right ear of the headphones or certain sounds can feel "nearer" than others. Audio software enables this process by specifying audio coordinates in a 3D space. This type of binaural spatialization has been effective in math notation feedback and its use has also been investigated in Pencil Code (a block-based coding platform) with positive outcomes [12]. We used this technique to assist students to understand the opening and closing of nested code blocks. For example, a *click sound* is heard through the left and right side of the earphones respectively to denote the opening and closing of nested blocks.

4 Technical Details

Blockly fires an event for almost every change on its workspace [13]. All events contain properties that provide further information about that event. This was the key in developing the voice functionality as we could listen to specific event details on the workspace and convey them via speech to the user. Blockly currently has three cursors in their Keyboard Navigation functionality to navigate through the blocks. We chose the line cursor with few modifications since it closely mimicked a text editor - with the ability to move up and down and next and previous lines of code.

Adding Text to Speech. Text to speech was added for the following:

1. Toolbox: As the user navigates the toolbox through its various categories and blocks, multiple events are fired. The workspace listens to these events and uses the Web Speech API to communicate the details of that event to the user. In this case, it would be the name of a category or a block.
2. Block connections: Blocks have several connections such as an input connection, block connection, previous connection, next connection, and field connections. Figure 1 shows the different types of connections a block may have. Specific values from these connections were listened to and sent to Web Speech API, and then ultimately conveyed to the user.
3. Marking a connection: In order to connect a block to an existing block on the workspace, a connection has to be marked on the latter. This can be done through navigating to the desired connection and pressing the *Enter* key. This leads to the connection color flickering between red and blue. Since there is no audio feedback for this feature, we listened to this marking event and sent the spoken speech *Location marked* to the Web Speech API.
4. Connecting two blocks: After marking the desired connection on a block on a workspace, the user proceeds to add a block from the toolbox to connect to that block. We added spoken speech which conveyed the *moved* block that was connected to the *parent* block on the workspace. For example, if the *repeat block* was

Fig. 1. Image from Google Blockly's Keyboard Navigation Page which shows different connections of an *if-do* and *logic-compare* block.

already on the workspace, and the *print block* was to be inserted from the toolbox to the *repeat block's do connection*, the feedback would say, *Print block connected to the repeat block*. This way the user knows whether the block was inserted into the place it was intended to. If the two blocks are incompatible and cannot be connected, the feedback says, *This block can not be inserted at the marked location.*

Creating and Firing Custom Events. At some of the places which required a voice feedback, there was no event present. An example of the location is the dropdown options of a field on a block. In Fig. 2, a user was able to navigate up and down the dropdown list; however, no event was fired. Hence, there was no capability to add the voice feedback. After consulting with the Google Blockly team on their forum, we created our own custom events at the needed locations. In our case, for the Fig. 2 scenario, we added an UI event to go up and down the dropdown field in the core Blockly code, fired and listened to the event, which ultimately allowed us to add the voice feedback.

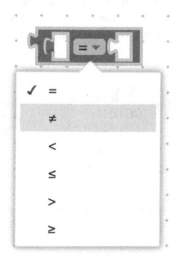

Fig. 2. Image from Google Blockly which shows the dropdown options of a *logic compare* block.

Adding Keyboard Shortcuts. Some features of Blockly such as accessing the Tooltip, deleting a block, are not accessible via the keyboard. A Tooltip in Blockly is a user interface element which provides more information on what a block does when you hover over it with a mouse. Hence, after consulting with the Blockly team on their forum, we added custom keyboard shortcuts for these features so a blind user could access them via the keyboard. After selecting a block, the user would have to press *CTRL + T* to access the tooltip and press the *DELETE* key to delete a block. In addition to this, we also added a shortcut to get the text representation of a block, including its nested children. For example, on pressing *CTRL + I* on the outer block in Fig. 3, the user would hear, *if (count = 3) do print " Hello"*.

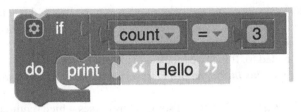

Fig. 3. A block of code with the following text representation: *if (count = 3) do print "Hello"*.

Adding Auditory Cues via Binaural Spatialization. To signify the opening and closing of a nested block, we made use of binaural spatialization, i.e., directing audio through the left or right audio channel. This was developed using the StereoPannerNode interface of the Web Audio API which provides the capability of panning an audio stream through the left or right. For example, in Fig. 4, when the cursor is on *print block's top connection* (as denoted with a red line), a beep is heard through the left audio channel to denote opening of the nested block. Similarly, when the cursor is on *print block's bottom connection* (as denoted with a blue line), a beep is heard through the right audio channel to denote closing of the nested block.

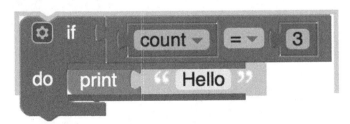

Fig. 4. A block of code with the following text representation: *if (count = 3) do print "Hello"*. *Print block's* top connection is marked with red, and bottom connection marked with blue.

Accessing Output. The focus of this work is on Accessible input, i.e. making block navigation, creating, inserting and moving blocks accessible to users who are BLV. For the purposes of testing, we added output in the form of print statements. Participants were asked to write code which printed some text depending upon the logic of the code. This is explained further in the evaluation section. We are currently examining the impact of adding voice feedback to outputs of code in the robot simulation as well. This involves the use of auditory cues and audio descriptions to let user know of the robot's movement and position in a simulation.

5 Evaluation

We evaluated our solution with four participants with varying vision needs-- low vision to total blindness. Two of these were experienced programmers, while the other two were low or inexperienced in programming. This was done to examine a variety of feedback. Table 1 below shows participant's demographic data. The participants were given some simple warm-up exercises such as entering the toolbox and navigating its categories and blocks, followed by a combination of some, all or related tasks below:

Table 1. Participant details

Participant	Age	Gender	Level of corrected vision	Screen reader proficiency
P1	18–22	Female	20/200 to 20/400 severe low vision	Moderate
P2	27–35	Male	Total Blindness with Light Perception	Expert
P3	14–17	Female	20/70 to 20/160: moderate low vision	Low
P4	14–17	Male	more than 20/1,000: near total blindness	Moderate

1. Write code using the *if-do block* which print's *Hello world* if the value of variable *test* is equal to *3*.
2. Write code using the *repeat while block* which prints *Hello world* until the value of a variable named *apple* reaches *10*.
3. Debugging: The following code in Fig. 5 is supposed to print *Hello world* until the value of *count* reaches *3*. Find the bug on one line.
4. Debugging: The following code in Fig. 6 is supposed to print *Hello world* until the value of *count* reaches *3*. Find the bug on one line.

Participant 1: Experienced Programmer working as a Software Engineer in Industry.

Observation: Participant at first was trying to connect two blocks without marking a connection on the workspace. Due to this, the blocks were simply inserted into the workspace and not connected to the desired block. She tried to move the block from the workspace and connect to the desired block, however current functionality only allows blocks to be connected via toolbox insertion. After this understanding, she was successfully able to complete all the tasks. However, she did not realize that binaural

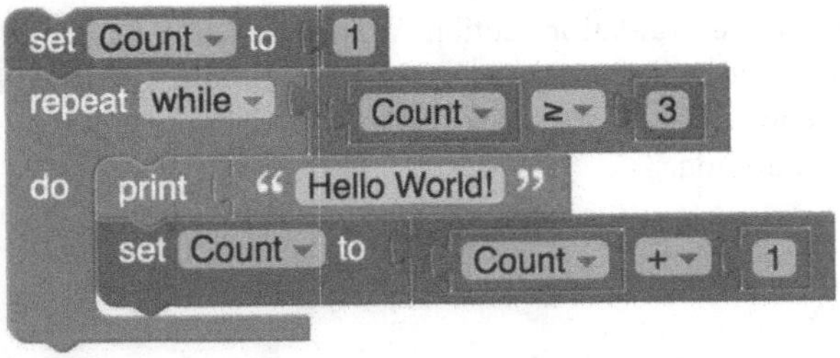

58 M. Das et al.

Fig. 5. A block of code with the following text representation: *set Count to 1, repeat while (Count greater than or equal to 3) do print "Hello World!", set Count to (Count + 1), end of do.*

spatialization was used for the nested blocks until specifically told about it. We concur she was still able to debug the statements successfully due to her having light perception and thus using it to understand the nested structure.

Fig. 6. A block of code with the following text representation: *set Count to 1, repeat while (Count lesser than or equal to 3) do print "Hello World!" end of do, set Count to (Count + 1).*

Feedback: Participant utilized the audio feedback most of the time with light perception guiding her to understand the structure of the code. As an experienced programmer who does not write code in linear fashion, the major frustration of the participant was not being able to move blocks across the workspace. As a person with moderate screen reader proficiency, she wanted a capability to increase speed of the audio feedback and more options to control the voice and verbosity. The participant liked the navigation and controls and found them easy to work with.

Participant 2: Experienced Programmer working towards a PhD in Computer Science.

Observation: When the participant tried to create a variable, there was no audio feedback provided as to whether the application was ready to take the variable name as input. This is due to the fact that when one clicks on the *create variable button* in Blockly, a JavaScript alert box pops up asking to type the variable name. In other words, this is not a part of the Blockly workspace, hence there were no audio feedback provided. We guided the participant to creating the variable in this case. This could have been mitigated if his screen-reader was on to read information outside of the workspace or if synthetic speech was added for this particular instance.

Another instance where we guided the participant was while changing the value of a math block. A value of math block can be changed by navigating to its field and pressing the *Enter Key* which leads to the current value being selected and thus can be changed. However, no audio feedback was provided after pressing the *Enter Key*. Hence, we guided the participant in this scenario as well.

In the current cursor, a user can navigate up and down lines/connections of code using keys W and S respectively and can navigate in and out a line of code by using keys A and D respectively. However, if the user reaches the start or end of a block using keys A and D, the cursor will automatically reach the first element of the block on new line, but *not* the new line's top or input connection. Hence, a connection could not be marked between the two blocks. This led to some confusion to the user as they remained unaware of the start of a new line. Figure 7 illustrates this issue. If a user keeps pressing the D key starting from the *if element* on line 1, they will eventually reach the *do element* as marked by orange square in the figure. However, access to the *do connection* is needed to insert a block between *if and do*, as illustrated by a black line in the figure. Using the D key does not reach this *do connection*. Constraining how a user navigates between lines can fix this issue. The participant completed all given tasks.

Feedback: The participant liked the workflow of marking and inserting blocks. He also liked the binaural spatialization to understand the structure of the code once we explained what they meant. The participant said they would have liked more feedback as to how the toolbox was arranged with a more hierarchical description.

Fig. 7. A block of code with the following text representation: *if (count = 3) do blank.*

Participant 3: High School Student with minimal programming experience.

Observation: The participant seemed to use a combination of mouse, zoom function and keyboard since she had moderate low vision. The participant experienced a bit of learning curve trying to understand the different connections and markings but once got used to it, was able to write code using blocks. She also had some understanding issues with the cursor as did participant 2. She did understand when a new line had started due to her moderate vision. However, same as participant 2, needed some help to navigate to the input connection of the next line as pressing the D key moved to the first element on the next line, and not its input connection.

Feedback: The participant said the software was easy to understand and the tasks helped her understand the basics of computer programming. She preferred having this synthetic voice than a screen reader because she felt that screen readers repeat words and read out unnecessary information. This can also be due to the fact she had low screen reader proficiency. She also mentioned she would have liked a custom zoom feature to zoom on individual blocks.

Participant 4: High School Student with no programming experience.

Observation: Due to technical difficulties arising from a Bluetooth Keyboard, we shifted our testing approach to a purely audio based one. Using our audio feedback solution, we went over a few programs and asked the participant to answer what the program printed. The programs contained *if-do, logic compare and repeat-while blocks.* After the participant got used to do the synthetic speech, he was able to answer most of the questions correctly. However, this was purely based on the researcher operating the keyboard and the participant only listening to the audio feedback. The participant had keyboarding skills and we concur with practice the participant should be able to use the keyboard commands successfully as well.

Feedback: We did not get any feedback on the Keyboard Navigation. However, the participant mentioned that they believed with practice they could get a strong understanding of the application.

6 Recommendations for Improvements

We propose working on the following to improve user experience informed by our usability studies:

1. Personalization: Add features to allow users to control the speed and verbosity of speech to match their audio comprehension needs.
2. Moving Blocks: Currently, there is no functionality to move blocks across the workspace. A block can be connected to another block only through toolbox insertion. We will modify the cursor to add this functionality.
3. Improved Audio Feedback: We will add audio feedback to the *creating variable* experience as explained in Observation data of Participant 2. Alternatively, we could:

   (a) move the create variable workflow to the Blockly workspace, as is in Open Roberta [14].
   (b) ask users to turn on screen-reader so content outside Blockly workspace is accessible to them.

   We will also make granular aspects of the workspace accessible. For example, adding audio feedback after pressing the *Enter Key* to change the math block value. We will also add audio feedback on some hierarchical information of the toolbox. An example of that could be: *Logic, category 1 of 9...*
4. Improved Cursor: We will constrain how the user can navigate through the blocks so that they are not able to go next or previous lines of code without using their respective keys specifically. This should fix most of the navigation issues such as not knowing if new line of code has begun as found in usability testing.

5. Other: We hope to add screen-reader support to blocks itself so experienced screen-reader users can benefit. This can be done by using the Aria Live region to communicate where the cursor is. Ludi and Spencer have already done work on this [2]. In addition to this, we will add a zoom feature to assist users with low vision.

After we make the following changes above, we will re-evaluate our solution with more users who are BLV.

Acknowledgments. We sincerely thank the Google's Blockly team for answering our technical questions on their public Blockly forum. This work is made possible due to an NSF Grant #1842092.

References

1. "KeyboardNavigation—Blockly." GoogleDevelopers. https://developers.google.com/blockly/guides/configure/web/keyboard-nav. Accessed 10 Feb 2021
2. Ludi, S., Spencer, M.: Design considerations to increase block-based language accessibility for blind programmers via blockly. J. Visual Lang. Sent. Syst. **3**(1), 119–124 (2017)
3. Milne, L.R., Ladner, R.E.: Blocks4All: overcoming accessibility barriers to blocks programming for children with visual impairments. In: Proceedings of the 2018 CHI Conference on Human Factors in Computing Systems, pp. 1–10, April 2018
4. Koushik, V., Lewis, C.: An accessible blocks language: work in progress. In: Proceedings of the 18th International ACM SIGACCESS Conference on Computers and Accessibility, Association for Computing Machinery, pp. 317–318. ACM Digital Library (2016). https://doi.org/10.1145/2982142.2982150
5. Google/Blockly-Experimental. 2019. Google, 2020. GitHub. https://github.com/google/blockly-experimental
6. Everything you need to know about screen readers. *Canadian Assistive Technologies Ltd.* https://canasstech.com/blogs/news/everything-you-need-to-know-about-screen-readers. Accessed 19 Feb 2021
7. Lewis, C.: Work in progress report: nonvisual visual programing. In: duBoulay, B., Good, J. (eds.) Proceedings of PPIG 2014 Psychology of Programming Annual Conference, 25th Anniversary Event. Brighton, England, 25th–27th June 2014 (2014)
8. Kane, S.K., Morris, M.R., Perkins, A.Z., Wigdor, D., Ladner, R.E., Wobbrock, J.O.: Access overlays: improving non-visual access to large touch screens for blind users. In: Proceedings of the 24th Annual ACM Symposium on User Interface Software and Technology, pp. 273–282, October 2011
9. Dorsey, R., Park, C.H., Howard, A.: Developing the capabilities of blind and visually impaired youth to build and program robots. J. Technol. Persons Disabil. **1**, 57–69 (2014)
10. Brewster, S.A.: Using non-speech sound to overcome information overload. Displays **17**, 179–189 (1997)
11. Murphy, E., Bates, E., Fitzpatrick, D.: Designing auditory cues to enhance spoken mathematics for visually impaired users. In: Proceedings of the 12th International ACM SIGACCESS Conference on Computers and Accessibility, ASSETS 2010, pp. 75–82. ACM, New York, NY, USA (2010)
12. Ludi, S., Wang, J., Chapati, K., et al.: Exploring the use of auditory cues to sonify block-based programs. J. Technol. Persons Disabil. **7**, 1–21 (2019)
13. Events—Blockly. Google Developers. https://developers.google.com/blockly/guides/configure/web/events. Accessed 10 Feb 2021
14. Open Roberta Lab. https://lab.open-roberta.org/. Accessed 10 Feb 2021

Geo-education as a Valuable Support to Children with Learning Difficulties

Marianna Di Gregorio[✉], Monica Sebillo, and Giuliana Vitiello

Department of Computer Science, University of Salerno, 84084 Fisciano, SA, Italy
{madigregorio,msebillo,gvitiello}@unisa.it

Abstract. In recent years, the way some subjects are now taught has changed to provide students with a thorough understanding of the dynamics and interconnections in the world, with an increasing emphasis on geography. However, so far, little has been done to provide adequate learning tools to support such an important transformation, and particularly for children with learning difficulties.

This paper proposes the integration of advanced geospatial technology into traditional interactive learning tools as a way to describe experiences that help students understand phenomena and improve their skills.

The system is the result of a usability engineering process aimed at providing users with learning difficulties an effective learning experience, by iteratively analyzing their expectations and needs with respect to georeferenced content. The results were encouraging and showed that improved learning can actually be achieved using the system.

Keywords: E-learning · Geographic information · User experience · Learning disorder · Visual environment

1 Introduction

One of the most common learning difficulties experienced by children and adults is dyslexia. Globally, an astounding 15% of the world's population is estimated to suffer from dyslexia [1].

Dyslexia is the most common learning disorder that affects the ability to read and write. Individuals with dyslexia typically read at significantly lower levels than expected, despite having normal or average intelligence scores.

A great deal of research is currently underway to explore the benefits of using information and communication technologies as a learning platform for individuals and especially children with such learning difficulties [2, 3].

Given the potential benefits, we focused on developing an interactive learning system achieved with the integration of advanced geospatial technology that could foster learning and help children improve some of their core skills, such as understanding phenomena and improving their skills.

However, no attempts have been made to support a multidisciplinary approach to education through e-learning. Additionally, little attention has been paid to hiding the

© Springer Nature Switzerland AG 2021
M. Antona and C. Stephanidis (Eds.): HCII 2021, LNCS 12769, pp. 62–71, 2021.
https://doi.org/10.1007/978-3-030-78095-1_6

increased complexity of learning components behind usable interfaces, which could help instructors create learner-tailored learning pathways while improving the engagement of learners with learning disabilities with a certain topic.

In this document, we address the challenges mentioned above and propose a usable and innovative geo-educational environment that supports instructors and learners in adopting the new model. The geoLO+ model allows users to manage teaching units in terms of the metadata used to describe different properties, including spatial and temporal properties.

We have built an ontology that organizes the concepts of disciplines, topics and levels (of education) in a three-dimensional space, enhanced by adding both a temporal and a spatial axis, together forming a new reference system for the allocation of resources. This ontology was conceived to allow learning content designers (e.g. school teachers) to organize resources based on semantic relationships, which can ultimately enable students to explore the interconnections between different educational topics.

We show that an emphasis on user experience (UX) when designing a geo-education environment can enable both instructors and students with learning disabilities to make the most of the high potential of geographic information and the semantic web. In fact, a usability engineering process was followed to develop the proposed Maps4Learning educational environment, aimed at providing users with an effective learning experience, iteratively analyzing their expectations and needs with respect to georeferenced content. The challenge we faced was the integration of advanced geospatial technology into traditional interactive learning tools.

In this paper, we present the methodology, design choices, implementation, and results of our preliminary assessment and evaluation of Map4Learnings, a geo education system which has turned out to be especially suitable for children with learning difficulties. The system was tested in the context of a middle school program. The preliminary results show the promising prospects that geo-learning has in such contexts.

To experiment with the approach, we have developed the new geoLO+ resource in the Moodle learning environment and implemented the Maps4Learning web application, where students can navigate the teaching units through their geographical references. The experimental usability study conducted in the context of a middle school, allowed us to analyze the impact of geoLO+ resources in terms of perceived quality, engagement and learning performance of students; The results were encouraging and showed that better learning can be achieved using Maps4Learning.

The paper is organized as follows. Section 2 recalls some relevant related work. Section 3 describes the contextual investigation process adopted to design the Maps4Learning educational environment. Section 4 describes the Maps4Learning visual environment and explains the relevant interaction design choices. Section 5 describes the experiment conducted in a middle school and analyzes the results obtained. Some final considerations are contained in Sect. 6.

2 Related Work

Dyslexia is a lifelong condition, and its symptoms can vary at different stages in a person's life, but timely and appropriate intervention can provide significant results.

Many methods of intervention are currently in use and more studies are needed to determine which interventions work best. Research is now focusing among others and on the potential benefits of using information and communication technologies (ICT) to develop interactive experiences and an optimistic learning environment, which can motivate and help children, thus helping them cope. their disability early on and possibly mitigate its various negative effects.

Digital technologies can be used to train, assist and even enable the learning process. Specifically, designed applications can stimulate student interest, but they can also help students with disabilities to fit and progress within traditional school environments [6]. Thomas considered ICT an enabling factor, as it can facilitate students' access by learning, increasing their motivation, fostering personal competition, improving their confidence and self-esteem [7]. Various implementations of ICT in education and learning have been researched, such as the use of websites as educational motivators for adults with learning disabilities [8], virtual environments [9, 10] and computer games [11, 12], implementations of portable writing aids and configurable word processing environments to support people with writing difficulties [13, 14]. A major group of people with special educational needs, such as dyslexia, could potentially benefit from ICT [6, 15]. Keates [16] explained the need for dyslexic pupils to access ICT for learning and to be introduced to appropriate ICT, including hardware and software (such as different word processors) for these pupils. It is also believed that the use of multimedia helps dyslexic students [17]. Multimedia applications not only allow, but also strengthen the bimodal presentation of information through visual and auditory channels; thus, information processing is accelerated, and mnemonic recall is facilitated [11].

The Maps4 Learning interactive learning environment has been designed taking into account the proven benefits of using technology and in this paper we show that it is especially useful for children with learning difficulties.

3   Requirement Analysis

In education, the adoption of user-centered approaches to design e-learning systems represents a promising innovative methodology compared to traditional approaches [5].

In this section, we summarize the contextual analysis process we followed for the Maps4Learning educational environment, aim to provide children with learning disabilities an effective learning experience and iteratively analyze their expectations and needs with respect to georeferenced content.

A first contextual survey was conducted among a group of 10 primary and middle school teachers, with a dual objective. Firstly, we wanted to understand the extent to which geographical references are used during teaching, to identify the subjects in which they are most commonly used, and to obtain information on the methods and tools currently adopted to enrich a given subject with geographical references. The second part of the survey was therefore dedicated to determining the extent to which the support of digital teaching at school and/or for homework is pursued, in particular, aimed at children with learning disabilities.

During the "Investigation Phase", therefore, we developed a survey aimed at parents with children with dyslexia, aged between 7 and 12 years. The process is based on carefully chosen questions; based on research and specialized methods, so that response data can be collected, and reliable results provided. We developed questions that involved the following areas: their children's demographics (age, gender, etc.), type of dyslexia the child struggled with, when and where symptoms were first noticed, with what tasks the children had difficulties, what were their treatment and their familiarity with ICT and cell phones.

The survey questions evaluate the views and opinions of parents, while offering a better understanding of the problems and difficulties their children face. The survey was conducted with 5 parents and the results gave us an overview of the main indicators of dyslexia and how parents come to observe and react to the first symptoms. Analyzing the responses, we noticed that most of the children did not have severe symptoms of dyslexia (the children were all diagnosed by specialists and speech therapists). The tasks that confused and upset most of the children were reading, writing and memorizing. All parents agreed that the design of a system based on a geo-educational component could improve the students' experience with didactic contents within a traditional e-learning system. The challenge was, on the one hand, to provide instructors with some usable interfaces capable of supporting geo-educational activities and, on the other, to improve the involvement of students with learning disabilities through innovative and personalized learning paths.

4   Map4Learning

The system, presented in [4], called Map4Learning is the result of a usability engineering process aimed at providing children with a stimulating and interactive experience able to facilitate the learning process of georeferenced contents.

Maps4Learning allows users to manage content in terms of learning objects called geoLO+, which are extended with spatial and temporal components and built according to standardized metadata.

Figure 1 shows the Maps4Learning visual environment used to query and explore the knowledge base that has been populated to date. In addition to using a legend that lists the POI categories stored in the knowledge base, it is possible to choose a temporal range and a geographic area through which POIs can be filtered. Additionally, criteria involving specific parameters related to didactic aspects, such as teaching level and disciplines, can be applied.

Once a query is executed, a historical map may be overlapped that contains POIs referring to the period selected through the temporal slider. On the bottom, a brief description of the period is recalled. By clicking on a POI, a link to DBpedia is shown with a preliminary description embedded, as shown in Fig. 2.

Finally, starting from a specific POI, semantically related topics can be accessed by simply invoking them from the preliminary description of the POI itself. Figure 3 shows POIs related to the Veiled Christ (Il Cristo Velato) sculpted by Giuseppe Sanmartino. Four POIs are displayed, each of them sharing a property with the statue, thus creating a multidisciplinary network of didactic units. Of particular note are the following:

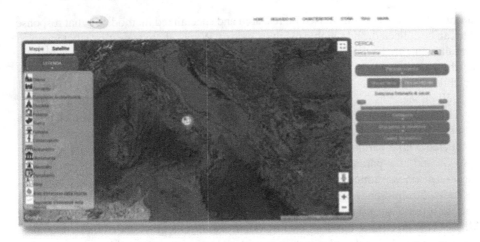

Fig. 1. The Maps4Learning environment.

Fig. 2. Exploring a geoLO+ in Maps4Learning.

- the Sansevero Chapel, where the masterpiece is currently located and where bio-chemical studies on human bodies are stored,
- the Historical Archive of the Bank of Naples (Archivio del Banco di Napoli), where one document refers to a down-payment of fifty ducats to Giuseppe Sanmartino signed by Raimondo di Sangro,
- the San Martino Museum (Museo di San Martino), where a terracotta scale model of the Christ by Corradini, the sculptor initially commissioned to complete the work, is preserved, and finally,
- Palazzo di Sangro, which belonged to the Sansevero princes.

When one of these POIs is selected, historically, geographically and semantically related POIs can be immediately displayed to emphasize their relationships and allow users to capture both different aspects of the same topic and the presence of a feature in different topics/disciplines.

Fig. 3. Exploring a topic through Maps4Learning

5 Evaluation of *Map4Learning*

The challenge was to improve the engagement of students with learning difficulties through innovative and personalized learning pathways. From the outset, it was obvious that for the design of such an application, we had to collect as much input as possible from students, teachers, and parents of students with learning disabilities.

Five students with dyslexia participated in this evaluation study. We classified them based on their level of dyslexia symptoms, gender, age, and treatment period in which they visited a therapist. Furthermore, the classification of dyslexia was based on the students' diagnosis by an expert, based on a psycho-educational assessment. The criteria used for the assessment of each individual were based on the age of the users and the level of learning difficulties. In an effort to develop conceptualizations and assessment methods for our learning application, a personal and contextual learning process was considered. It is important that the system is adapted to each student's learning level, recognizing their diversity and needs. It is also necessary to understand if a minimum initial level of knowledge is required, in order to acquire and learn from the application itself.

We also established a "control group" by recruiting 5 students of the same age group who were not assessed as having learning difficulties. The comparative use of the application and the subsequent data analysis also allowed us to determine whether the results of our assessment were actually related to learning difficulties or other factors (design choices, technology, IT experience, etc.). For example, knowledge of Italian has been isolated as an important prerequisite for users of this application.

We have chosen to develop the application in Italian in order not to create difficulties in completing certain levels due to their knowledge of the language. Finally, we interviewed the parents of the children to record their views and opinions, offering us useful information that helped us better understand the environment where children with dyslexia operate and the difficulty they encounter every day.

The main objectives for the evaluation of Map4Learning were:

- Observe students interacting with the system in a classroom and under the supervision of their teacher, obtaining qualitative and quantitative feedback. Also, identify design problems.
- Allow students to use the system unsupervised when assessors intentionally leave the classroom, in order to assess whether students find the application engaging or entertaining and whether they would continue to use it outside "classroom premises".

All students were asked to take a class test prepared by the teachers.

5.1 Procedure

To get the students involved in the experiment, we prepared a formal written consent form, which parents were asked to sign. Then, each class was divided into two groups of students of approximately equal size, forming the control group (CG) and the experimental group (EG). The first group received traditional lessons on the chosen topic; the latter took part in an interactive Maps4Learning lesson. Regarding the validity of the experiment, in order to avoid distortions resulting from the quality of the students in each group, the students were distributed by their teachers so that the average grades were comparable between the two groups. Considering the chosen topic, the first group of each class received two separate traditional lessons from the teachers of the associated team and the second group received a complete lesson from the main teacher using the geoLO + resource created. All students were asked to take a class test prepared by the teaching team. Grades below 6/10 were considered bankruptcies.

After evaluating the post-lesson test carried out by the students, the teachers were asked to answer a questionnaire intended to determine how much they perceived that the students had learned and the level of involvement of the students with the geoLO + used, also considering the environment visual of Maps4Learning.

The students who were in the second group of each class (which formed the experimental group), in turn, had to complete an anonymous online survey on their use of the geoLO + resource embedded in the given visual environment, answering questions about the degree of personal involvement and also with reference to the multidisciplinary nature of the resource explored and the degree of difficulty encountered during the execution of the tests [18, 19].

Overall, it took about three months to complete the experiment: March to May 2019.

5.2 Result

After the experimental evaluation had been conducted, we collected the results and analyzed students' progress. Our first significant observation was that all students showed their preference for learning through Map4Learning rather than traditional methods. The system helps children with dyslexia to focus and keep them focused, avoiding distractions. A result that indicates the importance of technology in today's learning methods. Students with different levels of dyslexia indicated differences in the duration of each test, while students with mild dyslexia symptoms completed the tests much faster than the others. Most of the students indicated a higher performance (based on the score obtained) than previous evaluations. Experimental results show that improved learning can be achieved using Maps4Learning.

Teachers' feedback on the perceived teaching efficacy of the proposed tool was considered paramount for deriving a qualitative measure for the tool's validity. Therefore, teachers were asked to respond to a brief questionnaire meant to evaluate students' ability to work in the hosting environment, the perceived learning progress and their engagement with the geoLO + they used during the experiment. Responses were based on a 5-point Likert scale to derive a qualitative measure of the three considered aspects.

To gain insights into how the students perceived the use of geoLO + within the given environment, we asked the students in the experiment group to respond to a questionnaire, again covering the aspects of usability, learning achievement, and engagement. As in the first questionnaire, responses were based on a 5-point Likert scale to derive a qualitative measure.

The bar chart in Fig. 4 summarizes the survey results of perceived usability, learning progress, and engagement of students.

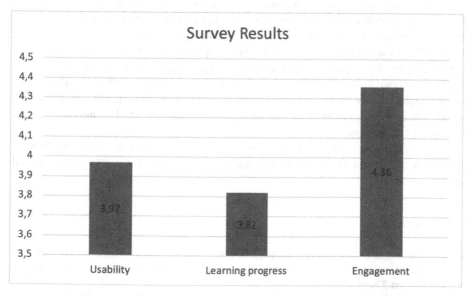

Fig. 4. Means of perceived usability, learning progress and engagement.

In all cases, the mean threshold value of 3 (the middle point in the Likert scale used) was exceeded, indicating that the platform was indeed recognized as a valuable tool by both groups of stakeholders.

In summary, the described experimental study allowed us to infer the following:

1. a statistically significant improvement was achieved, in terms of learning effect, using Maps4Learning with respect to traditional teaching methods
2. the learning progress was positively perceived by both groups of stakeholders, i.e., teachers and students, and
3. the proposed platform gained a satisfactory level of user acceptance.

While our current work may not be conclusive at this stage, preliminary results show promising prospects for geo learning in contexts where students have shown progress in their performance.

6 Conclusion

The term geo-education is a form of education which aims at enabling people to gain knowledge about the human and natural worlds and the interactions between them. To achieve that, geo-educators stimulate students to engage in geographical thinking, which is based on examining the Earth's past and evaluating the present, thus acquiring information from different points of view useful for the study of possible future scenarios.

Maps4Learning was also developed to pursue this goal. In this paper, we have shown that also students with learning disabilities can benefit from its adoption.

The usability test described in Sect. 5 has proven that the analysis of territorial elements, the search for information and the study of past events through geographic references can help students with learning disabilities gain a deeper understanding. This can help them memorize connections between topics more easily, thereby improving their geographic literacy and preparing them for a geographic thinking model.

The developed system based on geoinformation is quite universal and can be significantly adapted to any topic. The technology is implemented on specific examples but can be used to train students from various fields and different levels, thus ensuring the continuity of education.

In the future, we also plan to bring this new learning system to mobile devices, given the potential benefits of a mobile application, especially for children with special learning needs.

References

1. Dyslexia International: Better Training, Better Teaching (2017). Cited on https://www.dyslexia-international.org/wp-content/uploads/2016/04/DI-Duke-Report-final-4-29-14.pdf. Accessed on 3 Sept 2018
2. Cidrim, L., Madeiro, F.: Information and communication technology (ICT) applied to dyslexia: literature review. Rev. CEFAC 19(1), 99–108 (2017)
3. Adam, T., Tatnall, A.: The value of using ICT in the education of school students with learning difficulties. Educ. Inf. Technol. 22(6), 2711–2726 (2017). https://doi.org/10.1007/s10639-017-9605-2

4. Sebillo, M., Vitiello, G., Di Gregorio, M.: Maps4Learning: enacting geo-education to enhance student achievement. IEEE Access **8**, 87633–87646 (2020). https://doi.org/10.1109/ACCESS. 2020.2993507
5. Dix, A., Roselli, T., Sutinen, E.: E-learning and human-computer interaction: exploring design synergies for more effective learning experiences. Educ. Technol. Soc. **9**(4), 1–2 (2006)
6. Williams, P., Jamali, H.R., Nicholas, D.: Using ICT with people with special education needs: what the literature tells us. Aslib Proc. **58**(4), 330–345 (2006)
7. Thomas, M. (ed.): IT and students with emotional and behavioural difficulties. National Council for Educational Technology, Coventry (1992)
8. Johnson, R., Hegarty, J.R.: Websites as educational motivators for adults with learning disability. Br. J. Educ. Technol. **34**(4), 479–486 (2003)
9. Brooks, B.M., Rose, F.D., Attree, E.A., Elliot-Square, A.: An evaluation of the efficacy of training people with learning disabilities in a virtual environment. Disabil. Rehabil. **24**(11–12), 622–626 (2002). https://doi.org/10.1080/09638280110111397
10. Rose, F.D., Brooks, B.M., Attree, E.A.: An exploratory investigation into the usability and usefulness of training people with learning disabilities in a virtual environment. Disabil. Rehabil. **24**(11–12), 627–633 (2002). https://doi.org/10.1080/09638280110111405
11. Kazakou, T.A., Soulis, M., Morfidi, S., Mikropoulos, E.: Phonological awareness software for dyslexic children. Themes Sci. Technol. Educ. **1**(4), 35–54 (2011)
12. Larcher, J.: Information technology for children with language difficulties. In: Rinaldi, W. (ed.) Difficulties in an Educational Context. Whurr Publishers Ltd. (2000)
13. Nisbet P., Poon, P.: Special Access Technology (1998)
14. Nisbet, P., Spooner, R., Arthur, E., Whittaker, P., Supportive Writing Technology (1999)
15. Dickinson, A., Gregor, P., Newell, A.F.: Ongoing investigation of the ways in which some of the problems encountered by some dyslexics can be alleviated using computer techniques. In: Proceedings of the Fifth International ACM Conference on Assistive Technologies – Assets 2002, p. 97 (2002)
16. Keates, A.: Dyslexia and Information and Communications Technology: A Guide for Teachers and Parents (2002)
17. Abdul Rahman, F., Mokhtar, F., Alias, N.A.: Multimedia elements as instructions for dyslexic children. Int. J. Educ. Inf. Technol. **6**(2) (2012)
18. Bradley, C., Boyle, T.: The design, development, and use of multimedia learning objects. J. Educ. Multimedia Hypermedia **13**, 371–389 (2004)
19. Mangaroska, K., Giannakos, M.: Learning analytics for learning design: a systematic literature review of analytics-driven design to enhance learning. IEEE Trans. Learn. Technol. **12**(4), 516–534 (2019)

The SL-ReDu Environment for Self-monitoring and Objective Learner Assessment in Greek Sign Language

Eleni Efthimiou[1]([✉]), Stavroula-Evita Fotinea[1], Christina Flouda[1], Theodor Goulas[1],
Gkioulan Ametoglou[1], Galini Sapountzaki[2], Katerina Papadimitriou[3],
and Gerasimos Potamianos[3]

[1] Institute for Language and Speech Processing, Athena Research & Innovation Center,
Marousi, Athens, Greece
{eleni_e,evita,cflouda,tgoulas,ametoglou}@athenarc.gr
[2] Department of Special Education, University of Thessaly, Volos, Greece
gsapountz@sed.uth.gr
[3] ECE Department, University of Thessaly, Volos, Greece
{aipapadimitriou,gpotamianos}@uth.gr

Abstract. Here we discuss the design and implementation features of a platform aiming to provide two distinct modules for self-monitoring and objective assessment of learners of the Greek Sign Language (GSL) as L2. The platform is designed according to user needs of both learners and instructors. It incorporates the educational content of the A0 and A1 levels of CEFR. The platform provides a user-friendly environment that guarantees improvement of learner's skills, objectivity in learner assessment and enhanced SL knowledge grading. Active learner language production is assessed via an innovative SL recognition engine, while standard multimedia-based drills assess learners' comprehension skills.

Keywords: Sign language assessment · SL learner self-monitoring · Sign language as L2 · Computer vision · Human centred design · HCI

1 Introduction

European and national policies on inclusion and accessibility, as well as the official recognition of national sign languages, have led to a dramatic increase in the need for communication and education in sign language (SL), not only as mother language (L1) but also as second language (L2), well beyond the approximately 1‰ of the deaf population [1]. The legal, social, and educational demands of the current situation are such that non-native users of SLs compile an estimated 1% of the general population [2].

Regarding GSL, current educational practice does not provide tutors with any kind of automated assessment tool for the evaluation of student performance of either SL perception or production, avoiding altogether prompts in the audio modality.

© Springer Nature Switzerland AG 2021
M. Antona and C. Stephanidis (Eds.): HCII 2021, LNCS 12769, pp. 72–81, 2021.
https://doi.org/10.1007/978-3-030-78095-1_7

Failed efforts to evaluate SL performance based on humans have made it necessary to exclude student performance from the evaluated skills at the introductory learning levels, leaving perception evaluation as the only language skill that can be assessed, thus being detrimental to the academic value of SL introductory courses. The situation does not actually improve at higher learning levels, where it becomes mandatory to evaluate both perception and performance language skills. The currently used assessment procedures rely exclusively on human inspection of large amounts of video files or in-vivo inspection of small groups of students, thus being subject to the physical fatigue and even mood of the evaluator. Lack of both consistency and objectivity in marking are typical under these conditions, as is deviation in assessment among different evaluators in addition to extremely long evaluation time.

In this landscape, the demand for studying SL as L2 is rapidly increasing. The SL-ReDu project[1] addresses the current lag of natural human-computer interaction (HCI) in the domain of SL as L2 education. More specifically, the project works towards developing an assessment environment for both learner perception and performance skills [3]. The platform incorporates innovative algorithms of sign video recognition in order to allow integration of SL recognition technology, that supports the educational process in two distinct pillars:

i.   Self-monitoring of productive learning, and
ii. Objective learner assessment.

Here, we present the design of the platform that supports the self-monitoring and the objective evaluation modules to be exploited by learners and tutors of GSL as L2, focusing on those characteristics which on the one hand enable objective assessment of learners' knowledge, and on the other provide them with a self-monitoring tool, which currently lacks from GSL as L2 education.

To address these goals adequate functional specifications are combined with user-centred design principles [4, 5], which aim at robust performance which enables a satisfying user experience.

2   User Driven HCI Design in SL as L2 Learning

The SL-ReDu platform design aims to address the inherent obstacles of traditional practicing and testing methods in SL as L2 learning in providing two modules for learner's self-monitoring and objective learner assessment. In the design, educational considerations have played a crucial role, since interaction options had to take into account all aspects of SL linguistic systems from the semantic to the morpho-syntactic phenomena of SLs in both perception and production language activities.

Considering the situation in Greece, human presence in classroom alone has proved to be financially inefficient and very often geographically unachievable, in many cases requiring excessive traveling of both learners and instructors, also providing for very narrow time frames in which learners can practice in real life observation by instructors.

---

[1] https://sl-redu.e-ce.uth.gr.

These factors lead to significant costs, inefficient learning, and when considering the tutors' task of grading learners' performance, also in a workload and external conditions like human fatigue, that make objective assessment impossible. Similar obstacles are reported in respect to assessment methods for other European SLs as well [6–8].

In this landscape, SL-ReDu design allows for direct implementation of teaching methods and material in a web environment that entails different SL practice drills, which cover the phenomena of GSL from sign formation to complex syntactic and semantic utterance productions.

Exercise types include typical multiple-choice options which exploit image, video and text to trigger user response, as well as user input via video recording of their answers. SL-ReDu is unique in this respect, allowing the learner of GSL to actively sign, in order to enhance and solidify new knowledge, as well as to be assessed for her/his ability to produce grammatical utterances.

The system's video recognition engine provides signals to the user concerning the clarity and accuracy of her/his recording, based on the language model, provided by the platform (Fig. 1).

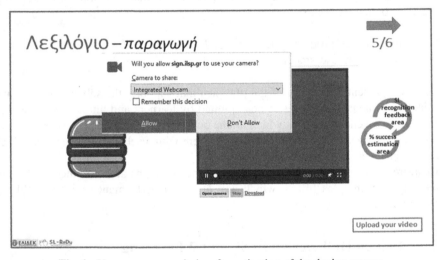

Fig. 1. User consensus window for activation of the device camera.

Thus, the platform design is targeted to successfully address a set of requirements which can be summarized as follows:

- Increase objectivity in learners' skills assessment
- Reduce the risk of errors by human evaluators
- Provide for a better grading process
- Develop a user-friendly environment

A basic design decision has been to focus on the task required each time, avoiding any unnecessary decorative features, so that the user concentrates on the linguistic content she/he must deal with.

A more detailed account of the SL-ReDu platform implementation is provided in the following Sect. 3.

3   The SL-ReDu Platform

The system is being developed as a web-based platform where only registered users can access the material provided. The web platform is available to both learners and instructors. The system modules for both self- and objective assessment incorporate different types of components, including the system database, frontend user interface, backend interface, images, and video files. The platform provides a user interface (frontent) for the learner and a content management system (backend) that is used by instructors to create learners' assessment tests and keep the record of learners' performance through time. The database provides the material hosted in both user interface and the content management system. The web-based platform is offered as a cross-device solution that can be accessed from everywhere as long as internet access is provided [9].

The two modules of the system address different user needs, although both are placed within the education context.

As far as the roles of the users are concerned, both learners and instructors must first login to the platform according to each group's credentials. The instructor can then create her/his own tests that will be addressed to the learners. To create a test, the instructor can retrieve exercises from a bank with all available exercise types and content. She/he can also keep a record of learners' performance, while the platform also supplies helpful tools for the tutor to adjust assessment parameters such as time limit and tolerance of acceptable answers.

If logged in as a learner, the user gains access to all educational material covering the different topics of the curriculum, as incorporated in the various exercise types of the system, in order to consolidate and improve her/his skills. When taking a test created by the instructor, a total score is saved after she/he submits the required answers (Fig. 2).

The platform's educational content derives from the language material defined as the target of L2 learning, and it is organized in three major axes, namely:

(i)   Lexical/semantic,
(ii) Morphological and
(iii) Syntactic

The educational material covers manual sign productions with emphasis on the single-sign manual productions, basic syntactic schemes and SL specific features with emphasis on formation, use and semantic interpretation of GSL classifiers.

The educational content further expands in lexical categories expected for communication at this level. The content in core grammar and lexicon enables the learner to experience the natural productivity of the language by comprehending the unlimited potentials for building of new utterances. This material allows for full development of the learner's skills in passive language tasks like comprehending signed language messages as well as productive language skills where the learner is required to produce his/her own linguistic message.

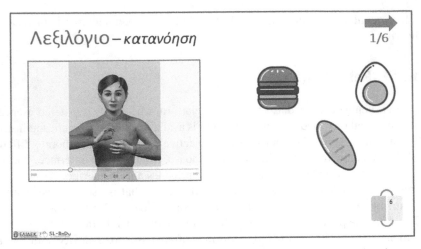

Fig. 2. GSL video driven multiple choice task testing lexicon comprehension

The system is planned to be evaluated in real class conditions, in two validation cycles, with the students at the Department of Special Education of the University of Thessaly in the context of learning and testing for the compulsory course *"Introduction to Greek Sign Language"* according to the department curriculum, aligned to the principles for A0 and A1 levels of the Common European Framework Reference for Languages (CEFR)[2]. The first validation study is expected to take place in June 2021.

3.1 The SL-ReDu Self-monitoring Module

The driving need for designing and development of the SL-ReDu self-monitoring module has been the limited time learners have in real classroom to practice with educational content and get corrected by a supervising tutor.

The environment allows the user to have full access to the whole of educational content of her/his level in the form of exercise drills, which she/he can repeat as many times as needed according to each user's individual learning needs.

The environment provides access to content via a tree structure that reflects the learning units. While performing the self-monitoring tasks, the user receives visual feedback as to her/his performance and the remaining number of available consolidation exercises (Fig. 3).

3.2 The SL-ReDu Objective Learner Assessment Module

The objective learner assessment module is the part of the end-user interaction environment [5], addressing the lack of assessment tools for evaluating the level of SL competence of non-native users (learners), and more importantly the need to ensure testing credibility and consistency.

---

[2] https://www.coe.int/en/web/common-european-framework-reference-languages/level-descri ptions.

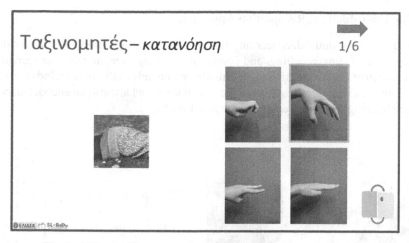

Fig. 3. GSL classifier comprehension test with active user selection

For the purposes of objective assessment, the instructor creates a test, by select-ing from the pool of available exercises. The learner is assigned the task to enter and complete the test in a specific time frame using her/his credentials. The learner in the objective assessment environment, is permitted to submit her/his answer only once for each exercise included in the test, unlike the multiple repetition options she/he is offered in self-monitoring environment (Fig. 4).

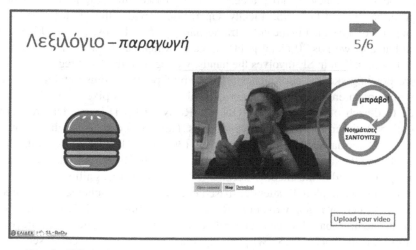

Fig. 4. GSL lexicon production task with feedback from recognition engine

3.3   The Embedded SL Recognition Approach

Here we present our initial deep learning-based system for GSL recognition from videos, targeting isolated, fingerspelling, and continuous signing. Specifically, our recognizer employs efficient visual detection of SL articulators, namely of the signer hands and body joints, visual feature representations of the articulators, and attentional encoder-decoder sequence learning for sign prediction (see also Fig. 5).

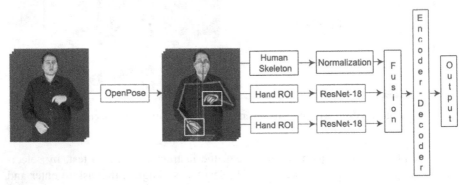

Fig. 5.   General architecture of the proposed deep learning-based system for sign recognition from video.

In more detail, our system commences with the detection of the signer's body skeleton via the OpenPose framework [10], a deep learning-based human joint detector of the body pose, hands, and face. Specifically, OpenPose provides the 2D location of 137 skeleton joints of the signer in the video frame, namely 25 body pose joints, 21 keypoints for each hand, as well as 70 facial joints, some of which can be seen in Fig. 6. Since dominant information in SL involves the hands, we segment the hand regions based on the corresponding skeletal coordinates returned by OpenPose, thus obtaining the two hand regions-of-interest (ROIs), each normalized to 224×224 pixels (see also Fig. 5). We then feed each of the two hand ROIs to a ResNet-18 [11] image feature learner, generating 512-dimensional appearance features. Next, we concatenate those together with the 15 2D normalized human skeletal joints (30-dim skeletal features) of the upper body (excluding the facial and hand points), thus getting 1054-dimensional features that we subsequently feed to the encoder-decoder module for the recognition task.

Specifically, we exploit an attention-based encoder-decoder scheme for the prediction task, motivated by recent work in ASR and machine translation [12, 13]. The model involves an attention-based recurrent neural network (RNN) that relies on bidirectional long short-term memory (BiLSTM) [14], equipped with an input feeding scheme. In its general form, the RNN encoder-decoder module comprises two processes: encoding and decoding (see also Fig. 6). In particular, our RNN encoder is fed with latent representations derived from the first GSL recognizer component generating hidden state representations, but instead of predicting the current state based on the past context as in the case of LSTMs [15], we apply BiLSTMs, where in addition to the previous observations there is also access to the future ones. Namely, one LSTM processes the

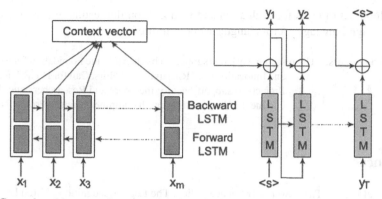

Fig. 6. General architecture of an attention-based RNN encoder-decoder based on BiLSTMs, with x denoting the latent representations derived from the first GSL recognizer component and y being the predicted elements of the output sequence.

input sequence in a forward fashion (left-to-right), while the second one processes it backwards (right-to-left), and both relate to the same output. These two calculations are concatenated generating hidden state representations. During decoding, the hidden state sequence is processed by the LSTM decoder [15] producing the elements of the output sequence, one by one. Further, encoder-decoder models equipped with attention are based on the alignment between input and output, driven by the "context" vector that expresses the likelihood of each chunk of the source sequence being related to the current output. More precisely, our model comprises a one-layer BiLSTM encoder and a one-layer LSTM decoder, both with hidden dimensionality fixed to 128. Training is carried out via the Adam optimizer [16] with initial learning rate of 0.001 decreased by a factor of 0.3. The alignment scores are computed through the function proposed in [12].

The developed SL recognition system is evaluated on two SL forms: (i) isolated signing via the Polytropon Greek SL (GSL) dataset [17], achieving word recognition accuracy of 90.39% and (ii) continuous fingerspelling in the American SL (ASL) employing the ChicagoFSWild dataset [18] with word recognition accuracy of 88.41%.

4 Conclusion

A platform encompassing the features discussed in Sects. 2 and 3 may have direct societal impacts for both learners and tutors of GSL. The platform's innovative technological features are expected to address the needs occurring from the large population of students and trainees, who are geographically scattered around the country, by enhancing their learning and/or self-correction experience. Similarly, the very small number of certified GSL instructors will benefit from an automated or even hybrid solution for the development of unified tests and grading mechanism.

The system will further lower costs of teaching and evaluation of GSL dramatically, while it is also able to adapt to the data of any SL with small adjustments, allowing for the development of tools for evaluation and feedback on the results of teaching SLs as second/foreign languages across language communities.

Acknowledgements. The research work was supported by the Hellenic Foundation for Research and Innovation (H.F.R.I.) under the "First Call for H.F.R.I. Research  Projects to support Faculty members and Researchers and the procurement of high-cost research equipment grant" (Project Number: 2456).

References

1. De Meulder, M.: The Power of Language Policy: The Legal Recognition of Sign Languages and the Aspirations of Deaf Communities, Ph.D. thesis, Faculty of Humanities, University of Jyväskylä (2016)
2. Cormier, K., Fenlon, J.F.: Possession in the visual-gestural modality: how possession is expressed in British sign language. In: McGregor, W.B. (ed.) The Expression of Possession, pp. 389–422, Mouton de Gruyter (2009)
3. Potamianos, G., Papadimitriou, K., Efthimiou, E., Fotinea, S.E., Sapountzaki, G., Maragos, P.: SL-ReDu: greek sign language recognition for educational applications. Project description and early results. In: Proceedings of PErvasive Technologies Related to Assistive Environments Conference (PETRA), Corfu, Greece (2020)
4. Efthimiou, E., Fotinea, S.-E., Kakoulidis, P., Goulas, T., Dimou, A.-L., Vacalopoulou, A.: Sign search and sign synthesis made easy to end user: the paradigm of building a SL oriented interface for accessing and managing educational content. In: Antona, M., Stephanidis, C. (eds.) UAHCI 2017. LNCS, vol. 10278, pp. 14–26. Springer, Cham (2017). https://doi.org/10.1007/978-3-319-58703-5_2
5. Efthimiou, Eleni., Fotinea, Stavroula-Evita., Goulas, Theodore, Kakoulidis, Panos: User Friendly Interfaces for Sign Retrieval and Sign Synthesis. In: Antona, Margherita, Stephanidis, Constantine (eds.) UAHCI 2015. LNCS, vol. 9176, pp. 351–361. Springer, Cham (2015). https://doi.org/10.1007/978-3-319-20681-3_33
6. Fischer, S.: Sign language and linguistic universals". Sign Language Linguistics **11**, 245–262 (2008)
7. Paludneviciene, R., Hauser, P.C., Daggett, D.J., Kurz, K.B.: Issues and trends in sign language assessment. In: Morere, D., Allen, T. (eds.) Assessing Literacy in Deaf Individuals. Springer, New York (2012). https://doi.org/10.1007/978-1-4614-5269-0_11
8. Haug, T.: Web-based sign language assessment: Challenges and innovations. In: Proceedings of ALTE International Conference on Learning and Assessment - Making the Connection (2017)
9. Mokhtar, S.A,. Anuar, S.S.S., Anuar, S.M.S.: , Web-based application for learning Malaysian sign language. In: Proceedings of the 11th International Conference on Ubiquitous Information Management and Communication (IMCOM 2017), pp. 1–6. Association for Computing Machinery, New York, NY, USA (2017)
10. Simon, T., Joo, H., Matthews, I., Sheikh, Y.: Hand keypoint detection in single images using multiview bootstrapping. In: Proceedings of the IEEE Conference on Computer Vision and Pattern Recognition, pp. 4645–4653 (2017)
11. He, K., Zhang, X., Ren, S., Sun, J.: Deep residual learning for image recognition. In: Proceedings of the IEEE Conference on Computer Vision and Pattern Recognition, pp. 770–778 (2016)

12. Bahdanau, D., Cho, K., Bengio, Y.: Neural machine translation by jointly learning to align and translate. CoRR, https://arxiv.org/abs/1409.0473 (2014)
13. Luong, M., Pham, H., Manning, C.D.: Effective approaches to attention-based neural machine translation. CoRR, https://arxiv.org/abs/1409.0473 (2015)
14. Schuster, M., Paliwal, K.K.: Bidirectional recurrent neural networks. IEEE Trans. Signal Process. **45**(11), 2673–2681 (1997)
15. Hochreiter, S., Schmidhuber, J.: Long short-term memory. Neural Comput. **9**(8), 1735–1780 (1997)
16. Kingma, D.P., Ba, J.: Adam: a method for stochastic optimization. CoRR https://arxiv.org/abs/1412.6980 (2014)
17. Efthimiou, E., Vasilaki, K., Fotinea, S.-E., Vacalopoulou, A., Goulas, T., Dimou, A.-L.: The POLYTROPON parallel corpus. In: Proceedings of the International Conference on Language Resources and Evaluation (2018)
18. Shi, B., Rio, A.M.D., Keane, J., Brentari, D., Shakhnarovich, G., Livescu, K.: Fingerspelling recognition in the wild with iterative visual attention. In: Proceedings of the IEEE International Conference on Computer Vision, pp. 5399–5408 (2019)

An Assessment of Moodle Environment Tools for the Literacy Environment of Deaf Children in the Context of the 3rd Year of Elementary Education

Marta Angélica Montiel Ferreira[1]([✉]), Laura Sánchez García[1], Tanya Amara Felipe[2], Juliana Bueno[3], and Suellym Fernanda Opolz[4]

[1] Informatics Department, Federal University of Paraná, Centro Politécnico, Jardim das Américas, Curitiba, PR, Brazil
[2] Departamento de Ensino Superior – DESU2, Instituto Nacional de Educação de Surdos, Rua das Laranjeiras, 232, Rio de Janeiro, RJ, Brazil
[3] Department of Design, Federal University of Paraná, Reitoria, Centro, Curitiba, PR, Brazil
[4] Prefeitura Municipal de São José dos Pinhais, São Jose dos Pinhais, PR, Brazil

Abstract. This research analyzed the existing tools in a Moodle VLE within an adaptation of a didactic sequence of bilingual literacy of deaf children. In this context, we proposed to use some of these tools and apply them to a virtual context for the bilingual literacy of deaf children in the 3rd grade of elementary school, who learn by the methodological principles of the direct way literacy. With this purpose, we carried out a literature review to verify the available resources in VLE by associating direct way literacy activities with a set of Moodle tools. Based on these usage scenarios, an expert teacher working with the research subjects evaluated the Moodle VLE tools and suggested the most appropriate ones for the audience in question.

Keywords: Virtual learning environment · Moodle · Deaf · Literacy

1 Introduction

The first conceptions of VLE (Virtual Learning Environments) occurred in the late 1990 s when these environments used WWW (World Wide Web) resources. The VLEs are systems with the integration of textual, graphic, and visual tools. They are developed for managing resources and pedagogical mediation in the distance learning modality and can also be adopted in the face-to-face modality [13].

Currently, these environments, such as Moodle (Modular Object- Oriented Dynamic Learning Environment), are extensively used as support resources in face-to-face courses. Moodle is widely appropriated by Brazilian universities [14]. Moodle provides tools for use in collaborative learning environments and in the teaching and learning processes [12]. In Moodle, there are administrative or managerial tools, which organize the participants in different profiles. For this research, only teacher and student profiles were

M. Antona and C. Stephanidis (Eds.): HCII 2021, LNCS 12769, pp. 82–94, 2021.
https://doi.org/10.1007/978-3-030-78095-1_8

selected since the studied environment would be the elementary school. Moodle also has informational tools, which make courses or subject's data available, and communication tools, which allow interaction between participants [13].

Advances in the application of information technology in education have led to an increase in the number of applications available. However, many are not yet accessible to the deaf. For example, Moodle environment itself does not provide a translation into the preferred and official language of deaf people [14]. In this case, studies on these VLEs are based on the adaptation/adequacy of resources and tools for the deaf.

This research adopts the term defined by [9], which considers Deaf with a capital "D" to denominate deafness as an intrinsic linguistic and cultural difference to those people who were born deaf. Therefore, there is a privilege regarding sign language as the preferred and mediating language [9].

The main objectives of this work was to evaluate the main tools and to identify the most appropriate ones for the target audience within the Moodle VLE. Thus, the research process presents the tools for a virtual learning environment for deaf children in the 3rd grade.

The methodological steps in this phase were a literature review and assessment of the most used resources (survey, glossary, tasks, grades, schedule, and news forum, among others). The literature review was carried out on the fundamental basis of computing events at the heart of human-computer interaction and computer science in education. After this analysis, a deaf professor specialized in the direct way literacy methodology (with a profile characterized in Sect. 4), who works with the target audience, assessed and suggested possible adaptations for the environment construction. This step investigated what tools of a VLE would be appropriate for deaf children and identified necessary improvements.

Thus, to present these reflections, this article is structured in the following sections: Sect. 2 presents the theoretical framework used and the related works, describes the direct way literacy and bilingual education of deaf children, and analyzes the Moodle VLE. Section 3, Materials and Methods, presents the study and describes the context and materials used. Section 4 presents the results and discussions, and Sect. 5 presents the Contributions, limitations, and future works.

2 Theoretical Background and Related Work

This section presents the theoretical context used in the research, highlighting its constitutive elements. The literacy method is the Direct Way Literacy, while the activity in the real world is the Bilingual Education of deaf children. Finally, the technology in consideration is the Moodle VLE. This section ends with the presentation of the related works.

2.1 Direct Way Literacy

Created by the French Association for Reading, the Direct Way methodology aims to develop critical readers capable of working/exploiting texts of various genres and in various ways [1]. Direct Way Literacy [10] has been used for more than 40 years in

French schools and had successful results in first language acquisition, as well as in second written language by foreign students. Our perspective adopts direct way literacy in action research, and we believe the literacy process needs to use themes/texts that arouse the interest of children. Thus, it can stimulate reading and developing the writing of a second language [7].

2.2 Bilingual Education for Deaf Children

The Brazilian urban deaf communities have their sign language, the Brazilian Sign Language - Libras, which is already official according to Law No. 10.436/2002 and Decree No. 5.626/2005. However, this linguistic minority still claims an official proposal of Bilingual Education that considers its language as the first language - L1, and Portuguese as a second language - L2, therefore respecting their linguistic, identity, and cultural rights. This proposal is necessary since only the majority language, i.e., Brazilian Portuguese, is imposed in most schools [9].

A Bilingual Education proposal features Libras as a language of instruction for the teaching and learning of other areas of knowledge, and Portuguese is usually adopted in its written modality [9]. The history of Deaf Education presents several political-pedagogical proposals since its beginnings, in 1863. Yet, in the National Curricular Common Bases of the Ministry of Education, Libras was not contemplated as part of the curricular proposal for Brazilian deaf children [8]. The research reported here proposes the teaching of the Portuguese language as L2.

The objective is to contribute to the teaching and learning of written Portuguese by proposing a support environment for bilingual literacy for deaf children (Libras and written Portuguese). Our study refers to the degrees of accessibility and utility in the process of the Moodle VLE tools.

2.3 Moodle-VLE

In virtual learning environments, there are virtual interactions between teacher and student [12]. Moodle is used in more than 241 countries, with 6,569.00 sites registered in Brazil [12]. It is an Open-source platform that can be installed, used, modified, and distributed [12]. VLEs have several resources and tools. In addition to standard features, each platform can provide different resources, such as access to social networks. The nomenclature of resources varies with each platform [11]. For our assessment, some of these resources were selected.

2.4 Related Work

The research aimed to verify how to include resources that adopted Libras as a mediating language in the written Portuguese Language literacy of deaf children. As for the specific issue of reading, the act of reading has changed with the new technologies, as [2] states. We partially agree with this statement because although the authors do not see the adoption of technology as a necessity, they defend its adoption as an instrument of social action capable of promoting new scenarios that facilitate the teaching-learning binomial.

When designing a VLE to support the literacy of deaf children, and, in learning the written Portuguese language (L2), it is necessary to adopt Libras, the preferred language (L1) and mediate language in the construction of knowledge [9]. In addition, the environment must also consider the usability requirements, among others of consensus in Human-Computer Interaction [3].

Throughout the process, we analyzed the main computing events in Brazil in the last five years and that relate to the research theme. The Events were the Brazilian Symposium on Human Factors in Computer Systems - IHC, and the Brazilian Symposium on Computers in Education- SBIE. The search found 181 articles for abstract and title readings. After the first reading, 40 articles were selected for the full reading stage and, after the subsequent reading, 6 (six articles) were selected for requirement extraction regarding the recommendations. Table 1 shows the list of authors and their main contributions to this research:

Table 1. Selected articles for data extraction

Authors	Main contribution
Ramos *et al.*	Adapted environment
Santos *et al.*	Lack of Libras in VLEs
Barrére *et al.*	Gamification by ranking in VLEs
Tavares *et al.*	Libras Learning from environmental resources
Cardoso *et al.*	Allow the control of video playback media for the deaf
Cavalcante *et al.*	Simple subtitles adapted to the deaf

The contributions ratified problems already known in the interaction in learning environments for the Deaf [14]. Among them, we highlight: 1) the lack of Libras as the mediating language of learning [17], and 2) the fact that the environments are not adapted to the cognitive level of the child [15]. Besides these, the following contributions will be considered in the environment development: insertion of simple and adapted subtitles [6]; use of text subtitles in the sound effects in videos (laughter, music, clapping) [6]; insertion of media control in the reproduction of videos [5]; provision of interpretation in Libras of pages [17, 18], adaptation of the environment according to the target audience [15]; use of simple texts with the use of images that contextualize the messages [6]; and use of gamification in the environment [4]. The reading showed that problems identified by the revised papers are recurrent. Despite the availability of these requirements in scientific articles, it is still necessary to draw attention to how these specific requirements must be included in the VLEs with a focus on deaf people.

3   The Study

This section describes how the study was conducted. Subsect. 3.1 presents details about the context, including the profile of the assessor and the researchers. Subsect. 3.2 presents the method used to conduct the study.

3.1 Context and Subjects

The present study was carried out by a team composed of 3 computer researchers on Human-Computer Interaction and Computers in Education, and 1 linguist researcher on Brazilian Sign Language and Deaf Education. A specialist teacher who has worked with the target audience for over nine years was responsible for the assessment stage. The teacher also uses the literacy method that was the reference of this research. In addition, the teacher knows the Portuguese Language because she was born, was literate, and grew up as a listener until mid-adolescence, then went deaf.

Therefore, this dual condition of being a former listener and deaf was considered since the teacher presents a bilingual conscience in the attentive observation of the literacy of deaf children. Such characteristics, added with her pedagogical practice in action-research in written Portuguese literacy since 2009, qualify her as an assessor.

3.2 Materials and Methods

Developing a VLE for deaf children requires an understanding of which media and resources will be most appropriate and of which languages (languages, modalities) should be used. From this premise, a computer researcher who works in Computers in Education proposed, for each resource, activities to enable its use and evaluation. Additionally, the researcher identified appropriate strategies and materials regarding each resource, according to the Direct Way methodology [16]. The didactic sequence chosen to be the activity/theme developed in this research had already been applied in a classroom learning context with the mentioned series/class and carried out by the assessor. That is the reason for the choice of the activity/theme. Thus, besides using a real context, the proposal also aimed to analyze all the tools provided by Moodle and thus adapt the didactic sequence in a context for a virtual learning environment with which the student can interact.

The activities employed strategies related to the preparation of content, and their respective interactions with the environment. Such strategies are derived from the action research reported in [7], which used the text "Alice in Wonderland" from the work of Lewis Carroll. Cherem and Opolz's (2018) research process was carried out with a 3rd-grade class from a bilingual school for the deaf. The work aimed to stimulate critical reading and develop socially situated writing practices within the direct way literacy methodology. It presented significant results in the construction of the referred knowledge [7].

The Moodle VLE used was the distance learning course version, in which the assessor teacher acted as mediator. For each tool, an activity was proposed, totaling 20 activities, following the methodology's steps (reading, interpretation, and linguistic analysis). All the tools were tested. However, due to space limitations, only two of them were described in this article.

At the same time, the intention was to identify strategies and materials that should be offered for each resource. Some resources would only serve as a query, and others would be for the execution of the activity. Table 2 shows the Moodle tools distributed according to the phases of activities in the direct way literacy methodology, each activity was produced and applied through the literacy method:

Table 2. Stages of activities in the direct way methodology. (Source: The authors).

1st-Activity-preparation	2nd-Activity-execution	3rd-Activity-extra resources	4th-Activity-finalization
Survey	Tasks	Glossary	Report
Links	Logbook	Forum	Groups
Quiz	Lesson	Database	Grades
Schedule	Assessment	Profile	
		Chat	

1. **Activity (Preparation of the content that will be used in the literacy stage):** The first activity consists of introducing the theme that will be worked on in the next class. At this stage, the teacher can ask open or closed questions to explore the content and measure/evaluate if the student knows the theme/subject. Activities include content preparation strategies to verify knowledge and the degree of student motivation.
2. **Activity (Application of the literacy activities):** The second section of activities consists of proposing the activities, in which the teacher can develop any type of material. This resource includes activities related to literacy. The teacher can provide a planned didactic sequence so that the student performs the activities, that can be done online or offline. An activity is a general name for a group of features in a Moodle course. An activity that the student will complete and interact with other students and/or the teacher.
3. **Activity (Extra Resources for literacy purposes):** The third option of activities consists of working with extra resources that exist in most VLE. Thus, they reinforce and debate what was learned in the previous stages. They highlight the option of the forum, which aims to enable a discussion on the subject seen and encourage students to exchange learning experiences.
4. **Activity (Working on the completion and results of activities):** These resources are intended for the teacher to answer questions from students, share the grades, divide students into workgroups, generate grade reports and activities carried out in the environment. The student can consult grades send questions to the teacher.

The teacher received the proposed activities and evaluated if each activity could be used in the preparation phase of the content. The tool link was chosen to share the text material with a video on YouTube[BR]. The objective was to verify if the student could easily access the link and understand its content. Figure 1 shows the proposed activity for the Link Tool. The teacher then assessed the suggested videos. The tools were assessed according to the Likert scale; Fig. 1 shows the evaluation screen for one of the tools - LINK - in the context of preparing material for the suggestion of various readings to the student:

Another example of an activity proposed for the evaluation was the Lesson tool, which can be used in the execution phase of the teaching. Its goal is to provide an activity for the student to develop. Figure 2 shows the lesson activity and the teacher's assessment:

- **Resource/Application- Link:** Continuing with the content preparation stage, a text and video was proposed for the student to access and get to know the subject with other types of reading, thus establishing the diversity of materials (a link to a website or a teacher post in the environment):

> ➤   Acess to YouTube[BR]: https://www.youtube.com/watch?v=Y-Ucu8ngu0c
> ➤   Acess to Web : https://www.bonslivrosparaler.com.br/livros/resenhas/alice-no-pais-das-

1.   On a difficulty scale of 1 to 5, how do you consider the ease of use of this resource?

Fig. 1. Evaluation screen of the Link tool, (Source: The authors)

- **Resource/Application- Lesson:** From the videos the student will visualize the narrated story and then make the story drawing using the drawing tool available in the environment, the activities are presented in page-by-page format, it is suggested to the student that he go through the sequence to complete the activity and draw your understanding of the narrated story:

> ➤   Watch the teacher's videos narrating the story, ask questions about it;
> ➤   View the written story next to the video;
> ➤   Draw the story using the environment and the drawing tool.

1. On a difficulty scale of 1 to 5, how do you consider the ease of use of this resource?

Fig. 2. Lesson assessment screen, (Source: The authors)

Since we have space restrictions, it was not possible to present all the proposed activities as a scenario for the evaluation of the tools in this article. The assessment of the tools consisted of investigating how a deaf child can use the VLE resources. The research questions defined were the following: 1) What applications/resources are appropriate for the target audience of the research? 2) What human factors should be considered in the interaction between the deaf child and the VLE tools? The tools selected for assessment are described in Table 3.

Table 3. Selected tools for assessment

Tool	Description
Survey	It allows checking the students' opinion on a question. It can be used to know the previous knowledge of the students; https://docs.moodle.org
Link	It allows access to another page, site, or document. It connects content to an activity but should be easy to navigate. https://docs.moodle.org
Questionnaire (quiz)	Presents questions to the student in a questionnaire format, with direct or indirect questions. https://docs.moodle.org
Schedule	Allows the export of appointment data to spreadsheets and other files. https://docs.moodle.org
Task	It is used so that the teacher can evaluate texts prepared and sent by the student. There is a space for comments and notes that are available individually to each student. https://docs.moodle.org
Logbook	This module corresponds to a reflection activity guided by a moderator. https://docs.moodle.org
Lesson	Presents content in a page-by-page format. Usually, at the end of each page, the student is required to answer a question. https://docs.moodle.org
Assessment	The teacher can assess the students based on the activities performed and the interaction with the environment. https://docs.moodle.org
Glossary	It is a resource that allows the visualization of terms and concepts related to the course content. https://docs.moodle.org
Forum	It is an asynchronous resource, allowing interaction without the need to occur at the same time. https://docs.moodle.org
Database	Allows the teacher or students to build, display and search a database of record entries on any topic, including images, files, among others. https://docs.moodle.org
Profile	It serves to modify the student's profile, displaying various information about the student. It is possible to check the messages that have been posted in the forum and access the activity report. https://docs.moodle.org
Chat	Students will be able to talk to the other participants in real-time (synchronous discussion). https://docs.moodle.org
Reports	This function allows the reports of all the students in the course to be viewed by the teacher. https://docs.moodle.org
Groups	It allows the personalized distribution of the students of the class in groups. https://docs.moodle.org
Grades	Contains all course grades grouped by class. https://docs.moodle.org

4 Results and Discussions

In the following section, we will discuss the assessor teacher's observations regarding the level of difficulty that the Deaf student may have in the use of each tool. In addition, there are suggestions on improvements to its use and its potential for supporting written Portuguese literacy in the context of bilingual education. The teacher's observations and evaluations were organized according to the Likert scale in Table 4.

Table 4. Result of the evaluations according to the Likert scale highlighting the level of difficulty of each assessed activity.

Application/Tool	1 Very difficult	2 Difficult	3 Neutral	4 Easy	5 Very easy
Survey				X	
Links				X	
Questionnaire	X				
Schedule				X	
Task			X		
Logbook		X			
Lesson				X	
Assessment				X	
Glossary					X
Forum			X	X	
Database			X		
Profile					X
Chat				X	
Reports				X	
Groups	X				
Grades	X				

- **Survey: (Level 4)** The teacher considered that, in the first moment, without considering the previous knowledge of the students, the information should be in Libras (L1). She suggested the inclusion of open or closed questions including icons and emojis used in social media (e.g., Like, I didn't understand, Love, among others).
- **Links: (Level 4)** The teacher considered the video with mimetic and iconic signs adequate because it illustrates, in a significant way, the narrative of the story. However, she considered it Level 3 for children who are not yet fluent in Libras. The text was adequate provided that it was used for the final stages; in the initial stage, an activity with infographics would be more appropriate.

- **Questionnaire: (Level 1)** The teacher mentioned that the Deaf child is still developing, starting the learning process in Portuguese under the perspective of a second language. Even a listener child does not yet write with complete fluency at this age. However, she believes it is necessary to stimulate the learner's autonomy by using a VLE without the need for mediation. The inclusion of a questionnaire with two non-mutually exclusive alternatives was suggested for the initial stage. This questionnaire in Libras would consist of drawings, icons, or infographics.
- **Schedule: (Level 4)** The assessor teacher mentioned that the child can experience the concepts of time. However, it is necessary to include an explanatory icon in Libras.
- **Task: (Level 4)** The teacher considered the proposal satisfactory. Yet, she highlighted the need to know the level of linguistic performance of the child in Libras, as well as the level of difficulty of the family in interacting with technologies. The assessor also pointed out that some students do not have access to adequate video recording tools. The text suggested in the proposed video link activity and the text in Libras were considered appropriate. She recommended the use of drawing tools and games, as they are well-accepted resources by children. Additionally, the teacher suggested the inclusion of text puzzle games, completion activities with keywords, associations of names to characters, and organization of text sentences.
- **Logbook: (Level 2)** The assessor teacher pointed out that it is necessary to identify the stage of linguistic development of the child in Libras, as well as the level of the approach of the children's family to the technologies. In addition, since many students have access to adequate tools and know how to interact with video recording in a meaningful way, she suggested the use of instructional videos.
- **Lesson: (Level 4)** The assessor suggested that children watch the video explaining the story narrated in Libras. This was proposed as an activity and also for other areas of knowledge in this schooling phase, according to the National Common Curricular Base (BNCC). After the video, students are encouraged to create mental images of the story and use the VLE to draw them. In this activity, without using written text, the video would be enough for the child to interpret the story and retell it through drawings or short sentences.
- **Assessment: (Level 4)** The teacher suggested the option to upload the child's video reading, added by the child or a family member. The video will show the child associating Libras with written Portuguese, performing interpretation with meaning.
- **Glossary: (Level 5)** The teacher considers the glossary an important resource for the students. She highlighted that the proposed activity for Libras and Portuguese glossary (bilingual) was interesting.
- **Forum: (Level 3 or 4)** The assessor noted that the forum can be used to develop argumentative skills. However, she pointed out that there is difficulty in interacting with this tool. The assessor suggested that, instead of a forum, there should be a space for virtual meetings in which the teacher and students could hold discussions in Libras.
- **Database: (Level 3)** The assessor teacher considered that it can be a useful tool, although she pointed out that the interaction should be simpler. There was also a reflection on the need to include a graphic editing space, such as a mural, to collectively create conceptual maps of the themes relating to the activities.
- **Profile: (Level 5)** The assessor believes that the child will be able to use this resource. Questionnaire: (Level 1) the teacher mentioned that the Deaf child is still developing,

starting the learning process in Portuguese under the perspective of a second language. Even a listener child does not yet write with complete fluency at this age. However, she believes it is necessary to stimulate the learner's autonomy by using a VLE without the need for mediation. The inclusion of a questionnaire was suggested, with two non-mutually exclusive alternatives for the initial stage. This questionnaire in Libras would consist of drawings, icons, or infographics.

- **Chat: (Level 4)** The assessor teacher highlighted that it is an important resource for both the chat and the discussion among the students.
- **Reports: (Level 4)** The assessor teacher suggested that the teacher and the child's family were assigned observation tables and graphical feedbacks instead of grades.
- **Groups: (Level 1)** the teacher stated that she has not used the strategy of asking children to form groups and, therefore, considered this tool unnecessary in the environment. However, the tool will be included in the final environment because we believe it can be useful in collaborative literacy scenarios.
- **Grades: (Level 1)** The teacher believes that this tool is unnecessary. But she suggested including, in the activities, a scoring option as in the "Gamification" with the use of emojis: Cool, Congratulations, Great, You can improve.

5 Contributions, Limitations and Future Works

This article described a research process that aimed to raise the levels of the suitability of the Moodle VLE main tools. The research was based on the assessment of a teacher who is active in the literacy of deaf children since 2009. To contextualize the evaluation, literacy activities based on the article "Alice in LIBRAS Country: an experience/pedagogical reflection of literacy for deaf students" [7] were proposed.

According to the assessor's perspective, a VLE for deaf children needs to address the specific needs of these students considering Direct Way Literacy practices. She stated that in the context of 3rd-grade deaf students, this platform is particularly useful. In addition, complementing her perspective, she reiterated that a VLE can be a complimentary resource for children regarding their learning, as it can be used outside the school environment. Due to the insufficiency of classroom workload, qualitative and meaningful literacy is lacking in regular classroom contexts. Thus, during breaks, the teacher needs to articulate the pedagogical time with the teaching of other areas of knowledge.

Therefore, the VLE serves as an additional pedagogical tool. Additionally, she pondered that families would have the opportunity to accompany and experience their children's learning to read and write. From the teacher's perspective, which we corroborate, in order to learn to read and write critically, it is necessary to constantly develop with the students the social function of reading and writing. Therefore, she mentioned that VLE can be a relevant opportunity for the child to develop these abilities with other resources.

From this research, it was possible to see that all multimedia resources and technological tools were considered useful to complement the teaching/learning process. The assessor teacher mentioned that it is necessary to reflect more deeply on the needs of the target audience. Among other considerations, we emphasize that the VLE interactions need to address the gestural-visual characteristic of Deaf communication with the world. It is also necessary to take constant care to approach compatible practices with the chronological age and level of cognitive-sensorial-motor development of the students, as well as their degree of access and their ability to interact with technological resources. The teacher's considerations were compatible with the contributions of the revised works.

Initially, we aimed at involving more teachers in the same assessment process – teachers who are active in the literacy of deaf children in the early grades of elementary school. We also intended to carry out an assessment process focusing on deaf students. However, the Coronavirus pandemic made it impossible to continue the research, which will be carried out in future works. The results presented here will, therefore, be expanded with the pending evaluations in order to contribute to the conceptual model.

The conceptual model of the VLE to support bilingual literacy of deaf children will be developed based on the results of the study described in this paper and on previous results. Previous results consist of two systematic reviews: one to collect the Avatar requirements and the other for the Literacy VLE requirements.

Acknowledgements. The authors are gratefull to Lúcia Cherem, who introduzed the Direct Way Literacy Methodology and facilitated the access to its creators. This study was financed in part by the Coordenação de Aperfeiçoamento de Pessoal de Nível Superior - Brasil (CAPES) - Finance Code 001. The Federal University of Paraná (UFPR) and the Postgraduate Program in Informatics (PPGINF) the development of this research.

References

1. ACTESDELECTURE: Les principes de la voie directe no 100. In: Paris: Association Française pour la Lecture (2007)
2. de Almeida, F.J., da Silva, M.da.G.M.: Reflexões sobre tecnologias, educação e currículo: conceitos e trajetórias. In: Valente, J.A., Freire, F.M.P., Arantes, F.L. (Orgs.), pp. 122–148. NIED/UNICAMP, Campinas, SP (2018)
3. Barbosa, S.D.J., Silva, B.S.: Interação Humano Computador. Elsevier Editora Ltda, Rio de Janeiro, Brasil (2010)
4. Barrére, E., Vitor, M.A., Almeida, M.A. de.: Ampliação das Possibilidades de Gamificação no Moodle. In: XXVIII Simpósio Brasileiro de Informática na Educação (SBIE), Recife-PE, pp. 605–614 (2017)
5. Cardoso, M.E. de A., Guilhermino, D. de F.T., Neitzel, R.A.L. da S.: A acessibilidade em Web sites na ótica da inclusão dos Surdos. In: Proceedings of the 14th Brazilian Symposium on Human Factors in Computing System, Salvador-BA, artigo N°: 46, pp. 1–4 (2015)
6. Cavalcante, N., Bacellar, S., Alves, A., Veiga, V., Tavares, E.: Compreensão de conteúdo multimídia na web por surdos pré-linguisticos: um estudo de caso com campanhas de saúde. In: Proceedings of the 14th Brazilian Symposium on Human Factors in Computing System, Salvador-BA, artigo N°: 2, pp. 1–9 (2015)
7. Cherem, L.P., Opolz, S.F.: Alice no País da LIBRAS: uma experiência/ reflexão pedagógica de letramento para educandos surdos. Leitura: Teoria & Prática, Campinas-SP, vol. 36, no. 74, pp. 91–108 (2018)
8. Felipe, T. A.: Diferentes Políticas e diferentes Contextos educacionais: educação bilíngue Para educandos surdos x educação Bilíngue inclusiva. INES. Revista Espaço, Rio de Janeiro, n° 49, Jan–Jun, pp. 189–220 (2018)

9. Felipe, T.A.: Aquisição da linguagem e escolas bilíngues para surdos. Amazônida: revista do programa de Pós-Graduação em Educação da Faculdade de educação da Universidade Federal do Amazonas, ano 17, n°1, Jan–Jun 2012 – Manaus: Editora da UFAM, pp. 37–62 (2012)
10. Foucambert, J.: A leitura em questão. Artes Médicas, Porto Alegre (1994)
11. de Lacerda, A.L., Da Silva, T.: Materiais e estratégias didáticas em ambiente virtual de aprendizagem. Rev. bras. Estud. pedagog. (online), vol. 96, no. 243, maio/ago, Brasília, pp. 321–342 (2015)
12. MOODLE. https://moodle.org/?lang=pt_brmoodle.org. Accessed on 02 Dec 2020
13. Pereira, V.C., De Albuquerque, D.C.S.H.: Construindo EAD: Primeiros Passos. In: Albuquerque, D.C.S.H., de e Pereira, V.C. (Orgs.) Cuiabá – MT (2013)
14. Pivetta, E.M., Saito, D.S., Ulbricht, V.R.: Surdos e Acessibilidade: Análise de um Ambiente Virtual de Ensino e Aprendizagem. Rev. Bras. Ed. Esp., vol. 20, no. 1, Jan–Mar, Marília-SP, pp. 147–216 (2014)
15. Ramos, D.B., de Oliveira, E.H.T., Ramos, I.M.M., Oliveira, K.M.T.: Trilhas de Aprendizagem em Ambientes Virtuais de Ensino-aprendizagem: Uma Revisão Sistemática da Literatura. In: XXVII Simpósio Brasileiro de Informática na Educação (SBIE), Macéio - AL, pp. 338–347 (2015)
16. Razet, C.: da leitura de uma história à leitura de uma escrita. In: Razet, C., Cherem, L.P., Rammé, V., N.S. e Olmo, P.F.C (Org.). Dossiê Especial: Didática sem Fronteiras. Revista X, Curitiba-PR, vol. 2, pp. 93–110 (2014). http://revistas.ufpr.br/revistax/issue/view/1899
17. Santos, F.T., Coutinho, F.J., Brito, P.H. da S.: Uma Revisão Sistemática sobre softwares educacionais para o ensino de LIBRAS. In: XXVII Simpósio Brasileiro de Informática na Educação (SBIE), pp. 896–905, Uberlândia-MG (2016)
18. Tavares, O. de L., Reinoso, L.F., Almeida, W.R. de.: CAP-APL: Plataforma para criação e uso de arquiteturas pedagógicas para aprendizagem de Português e Libras. In: XXVIII Simpósio Brasileiro de Informática na Educação (SBIE), Recife-PE, pp. 466–475 (2017)

Developing an Online Music Teaching and Practicing Platform via Machine Learning: A Review Paper

Fatemeh Jamshidi$^{(\boxtimes)}$, Daniela Marghitu, and Richard Chapman

Computer Science and Software Engineering, Auburn University,
Auburn, AL 36830, USA
{fzj0007,marghda,chapmro}@auburn.edu

Abstract. This article aims to lay a foundation for learning and practicing music online. Massive Open Online Courses (MOOCs) are growing as we are moving to online classes. Current music courses through MOOCs mostly focus on peer evaluation for assessing the students' performance. However, this technique may not be practical when it is applied to larger class sizes. Therefore, in this research, the main goal is to reduce the instructor's load and provide online real-time performance feedback. As a contribution to music education, we propose a new technological framework to automate music lessons for learning how to play any favorite songs via existing machine learning (ML) techniques for adaptability to various learning styles.

We discuss the main problems with existing online music lessons that ML techniques can resolve:

1. Finding or developing a music lesson based on the student's learning style, musical background, or preference.
2. Providing quantitative and qualitative assessments of the student's performance.

The paper discusses the tools for facilitating assessment where there is a semi-automatic assessment system that can train itself based on the instructors' real-life assessments on a small group and further assess larger sets of performances.

Keywords: Music technology · Machine learning · Computers in music education · Hidden Markov Model · Online music teaching · MOOCs

1 Introduction

Musical Human-Computer Interaction (HCI) techniques have empowered computer music systems to perform with humans via a broad spectrum of applications [14]. It is vital to have a consistent and focused approach when moving from traditional face-to-face (F2F) courses to Remote Learning (RL) courses using an online music teaching environment. Music students and teachers use

© Springer Nature Switzerland AG 2021
M. Antona and C. Stephanidis (Eds.): HCII 2021, LNCS 12769, pp. 95–108, 2021.
https://doi.org/10.1007/978-3-030-78095-1_9

different websites, online apps, and computer programs to learn, remix, and compose music. Existing music technologies allow digital or MIDI-enabled acoustic pianos to connect synchronously over the Internet, producing reliable instrumental audio, separate from the video-conferencing platform. Research is required to help teachers transition to the online format.

As RL music courses are becoming more common, graduate teaching assistants, or tutors, will become essential as instructor support mechanisms. We should train online teachers to have the necessary skills of online-music-teaching, communication, and assessment.

Based on [5], our analysis revealed four essential elements for online music courses:

1. Online music pedagogy (e.g., teaching philosophies, authentic music learning, openness to online music learning, institutional support, and learning approaches)
2. Course design (e.g., planning, organization, multimedia use, and curriculum)
3. Assessment (e.g., meaningful opportunities to demonstrate music learning)
4. Communication (e.g., methods for exploring subject content and technology tools)

This research identifies critical elements for developing a program for online music tutors. The goal is to train music teachers to master online skills and provide an online platform for people to practice music individually or as a group. Differences between F2F courses and online platforms include multimedia technology, social constructivist[1] learning activities, and developing practical online communication skills.

This research has two main questions:

1. What are the key components to teach online-music-skills to music tutors?
2. How can these components be adapted to implement an online automated tool that can train itself based on different students' skill and learning styles?

We are developing a teaching framework that helps music faculty members transition from traditional F2F classroom teaching to the online environment. This teaching framework is divided into three phases: 1) hybrid online courses; 2) a fully online study focused on social constructivist learning, and; 3) fully online classes with limited student interaction.

In this research, we also create a music technology curriculum and share the curriculum with expert music teachers to assess the chapters' and modules' possibilities. After analyzing the results provided by music teachers, we change the music modules accordingly. The second phase is to record different F2F classes in which music teachers teach our curriculum to students. In phase three,

---

[1] Social constructivism: Social constructivism teaches that all knowledge develops as a result of social interaction and language use, and is therefore a shared, rather than an individual, experience. Knowledge is additionally not a result of observing the world, it results from many social processes and interactions.

we implement an automatic online teaching model that can train itself based on the rehearsals and face-to-face recorded courses provided by music instructors. The system incorporates the techniques from different realms, including real-time music tracking (score following), beat estimation, chord detection, and body movement generation. In our system, the virtual music teachers' and students' behavior is captured based on the given music audio alone, and such an approach results in a low-cost, efficient and scalable way to produce human and virtual musicians' co-performance [6].

This paper presents various techniques, especially ML algorithms, to create Artificial Intelligence (AI) tutors and musicians that perform with humans. We focus on four aspects of expression in human-computer collaborative performance: 1) Chord and pitch detection, 2) timing and dynamics, 3) basic improvisation techniques, and 4) facial and body gestures.

Two of the most fundamental aspects of online-music-teaching are timing and dynamics. We create a model of different teachers performing as co-evolving time series. "Based on this representation, we develop a set of algorithms, to discover regularities of expressive musical interaction from rehearsals" [14]. Providing the learned model, an artificial performer generates its musical expression by interacting with a human performer, given a predefined curriculum. With a small number of rehearsals, the results show that we can employ ML to create more expressive and human-like collaborative performance than the baseline automatic accompaniment algorithm.

Body and facial movements are also essential aspects of online-music-teaching. We study body and facial expressions using the feature extraction models to create features based on teacher recordings. We contribute the first algorithm to enable our virtual teaching model to perform an accompaniment for a musician and react to human performance with gestural and facial expression. The current system uses rule-based performance-motion mapping and separates virtual tutor motions into three groups: finger motions, body movements, and eyebrow movements. Our result shows that the virtual tutor embodiment and expression enable more musical, interactive, and engaging human-computer collaborative performance [14].

In particular, we discuss the literature review in the next section. Then, we propose a music learning architecture for "How to play [song] on [instrument]" tutorial lessons when provided a favorite pre-recorded music piece as an input. In Sect. 4, we propose a method for automating the assessment of chord structure and beat detection via ML. In Sect. 5, we conclude the paper with a short discussion about the overall process of online music teaching and improvements to the prototype.

2   Literature Review

2.1   Machine Learning in Music

There are many useful music teaching applications using ML techniques. The main tasks in music that can be solved by ML are: music score following, chord recognition, musical instrument identification, beat tracking, rhythm tracking, source separation, genre classification, and emotion detection [8].

In music, most of the tasks need an initial feature extraction and classification. Some of the feature extractions that can be used for Music Information Retrieval (MIR) tasks include mel-frequency cepstral coefficients (MFCCs), chroma-based features, spectral flux, spectral centroid, spectral dissonance, and percussiveness [13]. Modeling the pattern of the extracted feature plays an important role in training the online automated model. Some of these models include Gaussian Mixture Models (GMMs), Hidden Markov Models (HMMs), and support vector machines (SVMs). With all of the current ML techniques available, we have the ability to automatically retrieve information about a piece of music [8]. This information may include the instrument type(s), key, tempo, musical notation, pitch(es), segments, and chords present in a song. By automatically obtaining this information from a piece of music, whether it be a novice student's recording or professionally recorded song, we may efficiently use this information for other automation tasks.

A number of metrics have been proposed to evaluate a real-time music tracking system. These metrics are mostly based on measuring the latency/error of every note event [12], or calculating the number of missing/misaligned notes during the process of score following [9]. There are, however two major issues in such evaluation methods. First, the performance of score following cannot fully represent the performance of an automatic accompaniment system operating in real-world environments, as it ignores the latency introduced in sound synthesis, data communication, and even reverberation of the environment. Second, note-level evaluation is suitable only for hard-onset instruments such as piano, while it is limited for soft-onset instruments such as violin, as the uncertainty of violin onset detection could propagate errors in the final evaluation results [6]. To solve these issues, we firstly propose an experimental setup which allows evaluation of the system in a real-world environment. Further, we provide a frame-level evaluation approach for general types of instruments, with intuitive visual diagrams that demonstrate how the system interacts with humans during the performance.

3 Proposed Framework of MOOCs for Music Learning and Performance

3.1 Module 1: Self-learning Tutorials

Online learning environments are divided into three categories: online video tutorials (e.g., YouTube), face-to-face video call with the teacher, and Massive Online Music (MOOCs) Courses. To learn music online, one needs to be self-motivated and self-disciplined. Online video tutorials may lack a real-time interaction with the learner, which is essential for music learning. The one-on-one video calls may present an interactive learning environment; however, they can not be practical in music learning when used for larger audiences. Therefore, to address the interactivity, scalability, and automating the development of music tutorials, machine learning models can be used. Figure 1 presents a framework for supporting MOOCs to increase their scalability to large audiences [1,11].

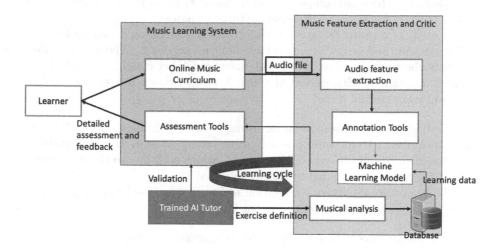

Fig. 1. Music education framework

The basics of the framework are: (1) Trained AI Tutor provides a music exercise using the Music Learning System (MLS); (2) learner uses interfaces for practice and learning. Then the learner uploads his/her The exercise's music performance to the MLS; (3) MLS sends the audio recording to Music Feature Extraction and Critic, where it is analyzed and further presented to the trained AI tutor for assessment.

To create automated lesson plans based on class recordings, some necessary information, including pitch, chord, beat, duration, rhythm, and dynamics, should be retrieved from the music file. This data can be used as valuable features for training a model to assess a students' performance while learning to play an instrument. One component of the model is the student practice and recording interface that can be easily tailored to specific exercises by the education content designer (music instructor). Our initial model provides better results with a simple instrument such as a flute in which the player can play one note at a time.

Our initial tests show that the face-to-face delivery of teacher performance followed by several student repetitions can be successfully imitated with such interfaces. The first session of this course will be offered during Summer 2021. The demonstrations of interfaces, results, and observations on user experience will be shared with the audience during the conference.

In this paper, we focus on the chord recognition task which is one of the most important tasks in Music Information Retrieval (MIR).

3.2   Module 2: Chord Recognition

In music, a combination of different notes that are played simultaneously is called harmony. The main components of harmony are chords, which are musical constructs that consist of multiple notes (three or more).

The result of a chord recognition task consists of dividing an audio file into smaller segments and assigning a chord label to each segment. "The segmentation represents the timeline of a chord, and the chord label classifies which chord is played during a specific period of time. A typical chord recognition system consists of two essential steps" [7].

– In the first step, the given audio recording is cut into frames, and each frame is transformed into an appropriate feature vector. Most recognition systems are based on chroma-based audio features, "which correlate to the underlying tonal information contained in the audio signal".
– In the second step, pattern recognition techniques are used to map each feature vector to a set of predefined chord labels.

Figure 2 represents a diagram of chord recognition process.

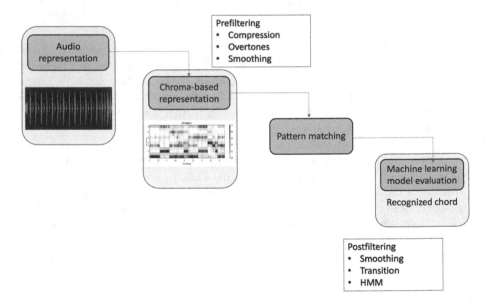

Fig. 2. Chord recognition diagram

Template-Based Pattern Matching. One of the techniques to detect a chord is through matching the chromagram of each segment with a predefined Template-based pattern matrix. For example we assume given a sequence

X = $\{x_1, x_2, ..., x_N\}$ and a set Λ of all chord labels. Template-based chord recognition aims to map each chromagram vector $x_n \in R^{12}$ to a chord label $\lambda_N \in \Lambda$, $n \in [1 : N]$.

Consider the following set:

$$\Lambda = \{C, C^\#, D, ..., B\} \qquad (1)$$

To simplify the problem, we convert all the possible intervals of chords to the main twelve major and twelve minor triads. Therefore, each frame $n \in [1 : N]$ is mapped to a major chord or a minor chord considered as λ_n.

We first pre-compute a set

$$\tau \subset F = R^{12} \qquad (2)$$

of templates denoted by $t_\lambda \in \tau$, $\lambda \in \Lambda$. Each template can be considered as a prototypical chromagram vector that represents a musical chord. Moreover, we fix a similarity measure by

$$s : F \times F \to R \qquad (3)$$

that allows comparing different chromagram vectors. Then, the Template-based procedure consists of classifying the chord label that maximizes the similarity between the corresponding template and the given feature vector x_n:

$$\lambda := argmax s(t_\lambda, x_n) \qquad (4)$$

In this procedure, there are three main concerns.

1. Which chords should be considered in τ?
2. How are the chord templates defined?
3. What is the best evaluation method to compare the feature vectors with the chord templates?

Based on [7], for the chord label set Λ, we select the twelve major and twelve minor triads. Considering chords up to enharmonic and up to octave shifts, each triad can be coded by a three-element subset of [0:11]. For example, the C major chord C corresponds to the subset 0, 4, 7. Each subset, in turn, can be classified with a binary twelve-dimensional chroma vector $x = (x(0), x(1), \ldots, x(11))$, where x(i) = 1 if and only if the chroma value $i \in [0 : 11]$ is in the chord.

For example, for the C -major chord, the resulting chroma vector is

$$t_C := x = (1, 0, 0, 0, 1, 0, 0, 1, 0, 0, 0, 0)^T \qquad (5)$$

The Template-based pattern mappings based on twelve major and twelve minor chords are shown in Fig. 3.

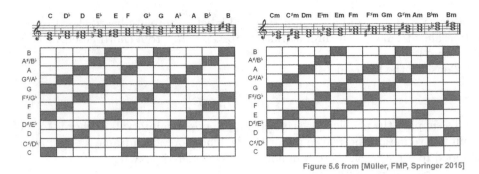

Figure 5.6 from [Müller, FMP, Springer 2015]

Fig. 3. Pattern matching [7]

3.3 Implementation

The following steps are performed and visualized in Template-based chord recognition:

1. First, the audio recording is converted into a chromagram representation. We use the STFT-variant.
2. Second, each chromagram vector is compared with each of the 24 binary chord templates, which yields 24 similarity values per segment. These similarity values are visualized in the form of a time–chord representation.
3. Third, for each frame, there is a chord label λ_n of the template that addresses the similarity value over all 24 chord templates. This yields our final chord recognition result, which is shown in the form of a binary time–chord representation.
4. Fourth, the manually generated chord annotations are visualized.

Figure 4 represents Template-based chord recognition results.

3.4 Hidden Markov Model (HMM)

"A Markov chain (MC) is useful when we need to compute a probability for a sequence of observable events. In many cases, however, the events we are interested in are hidden: we don't observe them directly. For example we don't normally observe the chord labels in a music audio signal" [2]. Rather, we see the audio sound and must infer the chords out of it. The sequence is called hidden because the elements has not yet been observed.

The HMM will provide an opportunity to add more features to our observation and keep with the same framework of that MC. In this paper, we will cover the main intuitions of HMM in chord detection.

The main answer that a HMM can give us is:

What is the most probable sequence of chords for a given sequence of observations?

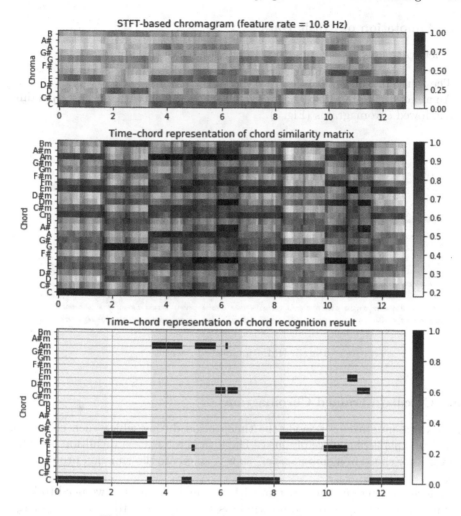

Fig. 4. Template-based chord recognition results

In order to answer this question we will need a few things from the MC and some new features:

- Chord Transition Probability Matrix: These are the notes probabilities explained in the MC section but having the chord transition probabilities instead.
- Emission probabilities: Probability of an observation to belong to each one of the chords $P(observation\|chord)$.
- Initial State Probability Matrix: Indicates what is the probability of a sequence to begin with a specific chord.

3.5   Annotation of Music Data

In order to be able to generate the probabilities above, we need:

1. The music files in order to extract the chromagrams
2. An annotated dataset, so we can join the chord labels with the corresponding windowed chromagrams (Fig. 5).

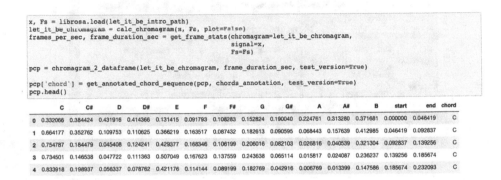

```
x, Fs = librosa.load(let_it_be_intro_path)
let_it_be_chromagram = calc_chromagram(x, Fs, plot=False)
frames_per_sec, frame_duration_sec = get_frame_stats(chromagram=let_it_be_chromagram,
                                                     signal=x,
                                                     Fs=Fs)

pcp = chromagram_2_dataframe(let_it_be_chromagram, frame_duration_sec, test_version=True)

pcp['chord'] = get_annotated_chord_sequence(pcp, chords_annotation, test_version=True)
pcp.head()
```

	C	C#	D	D#	E	F	F#	G	G#	A	A#	B	start	end	chord
0	0.332066	0.384424	0.431916	0.414366	0.131415	0.091793	0.108283	0.152824	0.190040	0.224761	0.313280	0.371681	0.000000	0.046419	C
1	0.664177	0.352762	0.109753	0.110625	0.366219	0.163517	0.087432	0.182613	0.090595	0.068443	0.157639	0.412985	0.046419	0.092837	C
2	0.754787	0.184479	0.045408	0.124241	0.429377	0.168346	0.106199	0.206016	0.082103	0.026816	0.040539	0.321304	0.092837	0.139256	C
3	0.734501	0.146538	0.047722	0.111363	0.507049	0.167623	0.137559	0.243638	0.065114	0.015817	0.024087	0.236237	0.139256	0.185674	C
4	0.833918	0.198937	0.056337	0.078762	0.421176	0.114144	0.089199	0.182769	0.042916	0.006769	0.013399	0.147586	0.185674	0.232093	C

Fig. 5. HMM annotated dataset

3.6   Calculate Framed Chromagram

Music data annotations provide the time period during which each chord was played in a particular piece of music. The idea is to create a definition of "what is a C Major chord in a chromagram" so we can create the emission probabilities matrix.

Before merging our chromagram with the annotation files, we need to know how much time each chromagram windows takes in order to be able to merge. To calculate the framed chromagram we send the windowed chromagram, the signal, and its sampling frequency to the model in order to know how many seconds each window is.

3.7   Calculate State Transition Probability Matrix

To calculate the state transition probability matrix, the model runs through all chords in the dataframe and will count all of the possible chord-to-chord transitions. Finally, in order to turn the count values into probability values, we will normalise all values so the probabilities of going from one chord to all others is always 1. The representation of state transition probability matrix is shown in Fig. 6.

```
transition_matrix = calc_transition_prob_matrix(pcp, test_version=True)
transition_matrix
```

sequence_chord	A:min	C	F	G
initial_chords				
A:min	0.972222	0.000000	0.027778	0.000000
C	0.000000	0.980198	0.000000	0.019802
F	0.000000	0.028169	0.971831	0.000000
G	0.014493	0.000000	0.014493	0.971014

Fig. 6. A representation of state transition probability matrix

3.8 Calculate Emission Probability Matrix

We calculated distribution assumptions of each chord according to the mean energy in the labeled chromagram. For HMM model with M states, mu-array will be shape [M, 12], where 12 are the 12 notes from the chromagram. It will show the average energy in each one of the 12 notes for each chord. For each chord of the HMM model, we will have a matrix of shape [12, 12] for each note. It will tell the HMM how, in each chord, the notes vary among themselves. For example, in a C major chord, we expect when the C note is high, the notes E and G are expected to be high as well. In this condition, state covariance matrix is of shape [M, 12, 12]. Then the model repeatedly runs on every chord and their respective chromagrams to calculates the mean energy and their covariance.

3.9 Calculate Initial State Probability Matrix (ISPM)

The reason initial state probability is needed is because at the beginning of the model training, the model doesn't know what have been the history of the chords played before. Therefore, an initial state probability matrix will start the estimation process by randomly estimating the beginning chord. For every step in the algorithm, we always calculate $P(chord_i \| chord_{i-1})$, i.e., the probability of observing a chord in a window given the previous chord at the previous window.

In this case, in order to calculate our ISPM, we ran through all our audio annotated files, counted all the initial chords, i.e., first chord of the music except for silence, and then normalized the number so the sum of the ISPM = 1.

3.10 Implementation

To implement HMM model we used the hmmlearn python package. This package abstract a few complicated mathematics, leaving an interface similar to sklearn machine learning packages, where we build and then predict over new observations.

- Because we are working with continuous emission probabilities, we build a hmm.GaussianHMM first and send the number of states. The covariance-type = "full" defines that the HMM understands that the notes can have a relationship, i.e., the amount of energy in one note is not independent of anyone else. For different HMM with different types of emission probabilities.

- We set the Initial State Probability Matrix
- Then Transition Probability Matrix
- Means and Covariance indicates the two parts of our emission probability as explained in section "Emission Probabilities".

Figure 7 illustrates the result of HMM model tested on the first 10 s of "Let-it-be" song.

```
COL_NAMES_NOTES = ["C", "C#", "D", "D#", "E", "F", "F#", "G", "G#", "A", "A#", "B"]

chord_ix_predictions = h_markov_model.predict(pcp[COL_NAMES_NOTES])
print('HMM output predictions:')
print(chord_ix_predictions[:50])

# create map between numerical state index and chord
chord_numbers = range(len(mu_array.index.values))
chords = mu_array.index.values
ix_2_chord = {ix_: chord_str for ix_,chord_str in zip(chord_numbers,chords)}

chord_str_predictions = get_hmm_predictions(chord_ix_predictions, ix_2_chord)
print('Translated chords HMM output predictions:')
print(chord_str_predictions[:50])

pcp['predicted'] = chord_str_predictions
```

```
HMM output predictions:
[1 1 1 1 1 1 1 1 1 1 1 1 1 1 1 1 1 1 1 1 1 1 1 1 1 1 1 1 1 1 1 1 1 1 1 1 1 1
 1 1 3 3 3 3 3 3 3 3 3 3 3]
Translated chords HMM output predictions:
['C' 'C' 'C' 'C' 'C' 'C' 'C' 'C' 'C' 'C' 'C' 'C' 'C' 'C' 'C' 'C' 'C' 'C'
 'C' 'C' 'C' 'C' 'C' 'C' 'C' 'C' 'C' 'C' 'C' 'C' 'C' 'C' 'C' 'C' 'C' 'C'
 'C' 'C' 'C' 'G' 'G' 'G' 'G' 'G' 'G' 'G' 'G' 'G' 'G' 'G']
```

Visual Evaluation

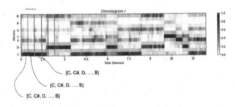

Fig. 7. The results of HMM model

4   Proposed Framework of MOOCs for Music Assessment

It is essential to have an automated performance assessment for large-scale class sizes to provide quantitative metrics for a faster assessment and real-time feedback to each music learner. The real-time assessment report is similar to the feedback provided by teachers in face-to-face classes. Feedback providing task involves extracting features from the student's audio and video performance to provide standard performance measures and quantitative metrics. Such methods would be more practical in music lessons since young generations learn faster and more efficiently when the provided report is instant and intuitive.

Since spectral modulation features via the modulation spectrum provide a simple visualization of rhythmic structures in music, these features can provide instant feedback for learning the rhythm of various simultaneous parts in a musical piece. In the next subsection, we focus on these features as an example to provide instant feedback for learning piano.

4.1   Modulation Spectral Features for Rhythmic Structures

Spectral Modulation features from the modulation spectrum can be practical in audio data mining tasks. In the music technology era, spectral modulation can address the classification and visualization of long-term and short-term rhythmic structures in music tempo and repeating patterns [10].

To demonstrate the potential of automatic assessment tools for this task, we plan on implementing a benchmark system that uses a well-known approach: assigning performance grades via mapping note level deviations computed from aligned transcriptions of the performance and the reference. Our benchmark system will be tested through a case study in Summer 2021 in a real-life scenario. The results of the study case will be presented at the conference.

5   Discussions and Future Work

Massive Online Courses (MOOCs) highlights a set of practical and thoughtful challenges that may not generally happen in smaller class sizes. This paper addressed two primary aspects of online music learning where machine learning techniques can be applied to enhance online music lessons for diverse learning styles and audiences' verity.

We demonstrated our proposal for the automated development of lesson plans that can train music lovers to play their favorite instruments and simultaneously have access to automated unique learning styles, varied musical backgrounds, and/or skills.

Furthermore, this paper proposed a quantitative assessment method of a student's progress in learning how to play a particular musical instrument. Proposed solutions in this paper can be useful for both individual learners or as an instructor who may need to assess the quality of a massive number of students' performance. "Previous research shows that interactive learning environments can also significantly contribute towards a student's interest, motivation, and discipline, and thereby enhance the commitment to learning" [1,3,4].

Future work would include the implementation of proposed methods and improving chord detection methods presented in the paper. In addition, accessibility methods of the online music teaching platform will be researched and implemented to support persons with disabilities such as visually impaired students.

References

1. Bozkurt, B., Gulati, S., Romani Picas, O., Serra, X.: MusicCritic: a technological framework to support online music teaching for large audiences. In: Forrest, D. (ed.) Proceedings of the International Society for Music Education. 33rd World Conference on Music Education (ISME), Baku, Azerbaijan, 15–20 July 2018. International Society for Music Education, Malvern (2018)
2. Jurafsky, D., Martin, J.H.: Sequence labeling for parts of speech and named entities. In: Speech and Language Processing (2020)
3. Jamshidi, F., Marghitu, D.: A web-based platform to teach music online (2020)
4. Jamshidi, F., Marghitu, D.: Using music to foster engagement in introductory computing courses. In: Proceedings of the 50th ACM Technical Symposium on Computer Science Education, SIGCSE 2019, p. 1278. Association for Computing Machinery, New York (2019). https://doi.org/10.1145/3287324.3293855
5. Johnson, C.: Developing a teaching framework for online music courses (2016)
6. Lin, Y.J., Kao, H.K., Tseng, Y.C., Tsai, M., Su, L.: A human-computer duet system for music performance. In: Proceedings of the 28th ACM International Conference on Multimedia, pp. 772–780 (2020)
7. Müller, M.: Fundamentals of Music Processing: Audio, Analysis, Algorithms, Applications. Springer, Cham (2015). https://doi.org/10.1007/978-3-319-21945-5
8. Muller, M., Ellis, D.P., Klapuri, A., Richard, G.: Signal processing for music analysis. IEEE J. Sel. Top. Sig. Process. 5(6), 1088–1110 (2011)
9. Orio, N., Lemouton, S., Schwarz, D.: Score following: state of the art and new developments. In: New Interfaces for Musical Expression (NIME) (2003)
10. Sephus, N.H., Lanterman, A.D., Anderson, D.V.: Exploring frequency modulation features and resolution in the modulation spectrum. In: 2013 IEEE Digital Signal Processing and Signal Processing Education Meeting (DSP/SPE), pp. 169–174. IEEE (2013)
11. Sephus, N.H., Olubanjo, T.O., Anderson, D.V.: Enhancing online music lessons with applications in automating self-learning tutorials and performance assessment. In: 2013 12th International Conference on Machine Learning and Applications, vol. 2, pp. 568–571. IEEE (2013)
12. Soulez, F., Rodet, X., Schwarz, D.: Improving polyphonic and poly-instrumental music to score alignment (2003)
13. Uhle, C., Dittmar, C., Sporer, T.: Extraction of drum tracks from polyphonic music using independent subspace analysis. In: Proceedings of the ICA, pp. 843–847 (2003)
14. Xia, G.: Expressive collaborative music performance via machine learning (2016)

A Multimodal Platform to Teach Mathematics to Students with Vision-Impairment

Abhishek Jariwala$^{(\boxtimes)}$, Daniela Marghitu$^{(\boxtimes)}$, and Richard Chapman

Department of Computer Science and Software Engineering, Auburn University, Auburn, USA
{avj0003,marghda,chapmro}@auburn.edu

Abstract. The advancements in Artificial Intelligence (AI) technologies in the last decade have led many developers, universities, and researchers to invest in the research and development of digital teaching platforms. This paper compares existing features implemented in the first prototype and provides visually impaired high-school students with a system to learn and practice mathematical problems. This project describes possibilities provided by open-source APIs such as Natural Language Toolkit (NLTK) and shows how to implement them to make education universal and accessible. We aim to achieve this by introducing an open-source platform, which will provide a set of modules for personalized speech recognition and accessible online tutoring. The system is divided into two modules: First, an intelligent conversational agent to help students learn new mathematical concepts, which opens up possibilities of providing students with a personalized response. Second, a mathematical expression parser and evaluator to help the student practice mathematical questions. The implementation and development of the system shall open doors towards self-directed learning for visually impaired students.

Keywords: Vision-impairment · Accessibility · High school.
mathematics · Natural Language Processing (NLP) with Python ·
Natural Language Toolkit (NLTK)

1 Introduction

Human-Computer Interaction (HCI) is a study of design, implementation, and evaluation of an interactive computing system for human use and studying the major phenomena surrounding them [14,17]. The abundant information available on the Internet and recent improvements in Human-Computer Interaction (HCI) technologies have improved the way we acquire, share and test our knowledge.

High-school mathematics is a foundation for students to learn and persevere in social and professional worlds. Recent advancements in technology have provided students with many virtual tools to improve their knowledge of mathematics. Students with visual impairments are at a disadvantage due to a lack

© Springer Nature Switzerland AG 2021
M. Antona and C. Stephanidis (Eds.): HCII 2021, LNCS 12769, pp. 109–117, 2021.
https://doi.org/10.1007/978-3-030-78095-1_10

of accessibility to the educational tools and the inability to process complex mathematical formulas and visual cues. This disadvantage leads to a significant knowledge gap between students with vision-impairment and students without disabilities. According to the U.S. Department of Education, as mentioned in [15], 15% of all visually impaired students are five or more grade levels behind their sighted peers. This knowledge gap leads to a staggering unemployment rate among disabled individuals.

The COVID-19 pandemic has affected everyone, but it has been challenging for visually impaired students [4]. While e-learning technologies have paved the way for self-learning during the COVID-19 pandemic, self-learning has not become a reality for vision-impairment people. According to the Royal National Institute of Blind People (RNIB) [1], two-thirds of visually impaired individuals have become less independent.

We reconsider the way high school students learn and practice mathematical questions. The prototype mentioned in [16] was developed with two goals: First, provide an easy-to-learn interaction mechanism to the students for clear communication with the application and integrate a highly interactive text-to-speech library that gives speech control to the student. The application uses a text-to-speech and a speech synthesizer JavaScript library that gives speech control to the user. This approach enables communication with the system but limits the responses to closed-ended questions. The developer must manually provide the questions and answers for the system to work as intended. The system intended to work for visually impaired students where clear communication is a key; this was a severe downside. To improve the human-computer interaction, we introduce an intelligent conversational bot. The paper proposes using NLTK to perform basic text operations on a given dataset to search for an answer to students' questions.

The prototype uses mXparser expression parser [18] to parse and evaluate mathematical equations. The major drawback of using the proposed library is that it lacks support for the Python programming language and provides step-by-step solutions to only limited mathematical concepts. This paper describes how an expression parser can be implemented and integrated with the system to help students practice mathematical questions.

The points mentioned above illustrate a need to improve the existing prototype of an interactive application for visually impaired students to learn high school mathematics concepts. The system is developed with the following goals:

- Improve the interaction by integrating NLTK to implement an intelligent bot for speech recognition.
- Integrate a JavaScript library to create an expression tree and implement an evaluator that solves the math problems and provides step-by-step solutions to students.

The rest of the paper is organized as follows: Sect. 2 introduces background and related research work to improve the online education experience for students with vision-impairment, Sect. 3 describes the proposed system along with the architecture. The paper is concluded in Sect. 4 with future research plans.

2   Background and Related Work

Over the years, with the technology advancements, there have been many improvements in how information is presented to students with vision-impairment, screen readers being the dominant mechanism. Many screen readers are also compatible with the websites developed under accessibility standards. However, that does not make the screen readers useful for visually impaired people because of several drawbacks. Visually impaired people often have to go through lots of irrelevant content before getting helpful information.

Although a digital copy of a text is useful for learning for visually impaired students, creating a digital copy of complex mathematical formulae is relatively difficult, as mentioned in [7,10]. When a complex mathematical formula, as shown in Eq. 1, is presented in digital format, many screen readers can interpret it in multiple ways. The digital copy of mathematical formulae often fails to convey the correct information. The authors in [21] introduced a non-ambiguous language MathSpeak, that can easily translate STEM materials into high-quality computer-synthesized voice.

$$3 + 2 + \frac{1}{x} \tag{1}$$

In paper [10], the authors evaluated the performance of the digital textbook vs. the traditional textbook while accessing algebra. The results demanded further research in the implementation of digital text in mathematics for visually impaired students. Regec [20] showed that the use of self-training tools was beneficial for teaching visually impaired students. The authors in separate studies [8,12] also showed the advantages of audio-tactile devices and speaking systems. Audio-tactile systems also increased motivation and curiosity for visually-impaired students.

Another useful approach, Process-Driven Math [13] was introduced to help blind students to be successful in college mathematics. Process-Driven Math is an auditory method that frees up students' working memory while solving equations by hiding complex numbers and symbols behind mathematical vocabulary layers. For example, the mathematical formula, "x2 + 2x + 1" will be presented to the student as "term + term + constant", freeing students' working memory and preparing the student to listen to the "elements" one by one. In this approach, the student is highly dependent on the trained reader-scribe for the information, which can be eliminated by developing an application that acts as a reader-scribe.

Davide and Volker [11] presented novel accessibility features of MathJax by generating tree representation of mathematical expressions. This extension mainly focuses on embedding complex mathematical expressions on the web and offering a similar user experience across all web browsers. This assistive technology extension also provides speech and tactile outputs of mathematical formulae.

In summary, the literature introducing new self-learning tools designed to teach visually impaired students illustrates the effectiveness of combining spoken systems with smart computing and the need for further research in this area.

3   System Architecture

The proposed system provides a platform for visually impaired students to learn and practice mathematical concepts. There are two objectives: First, creating an intelligent conversational agent that can teach new mathematical concepts and respond to students' questions. We use the NLTK library for data pre-processing and training the model. The decision to use NLTK was made because of its wide range of API features and precise documentation.

Second, providing step-by-step solutions to students to help them practice mathematical problems while providing hints whenever needed. This step is divided further into three steps: We use open-source JavaScript library math.js [2] to build an expression tree. It provides a flexible expression parser with support for symbolic computation and a large set of built-in functions and constants. Once we have an expression tree, we traverse the tree using inorder traversal and flatten the tree by simplifying math expressions to generate steps.

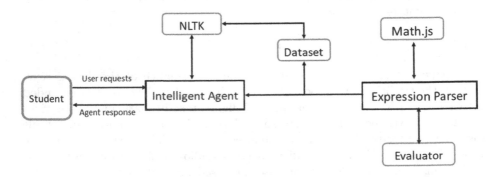

Fig. 1. System architecture.

Figure 1 shows the system architecture above. The system is divided into two steps:

3.1   An Intelligent Agent

The study of Natural language Processing (NLP) is studying the interaction between human language and computers. By utilizing NLP, researchers can organize and structure datasets to perform various automatic summarization, translation, and speech recognition tasks [19]. NLTK (Natural Language Toolkit) [9] is a leading platform for building Python programs to work with human language data.

For this research, we gathered over 1000 commonly asked questions that visually impaired students may ask while interacting with the system. The dataset includes questions and answers related to knowing more about the system, learning mathematical concepts, and asking for help. Figure 2 shows the structure of the data.

```
{"tag": "start_conversation",
 "patterns": ["Hi there", "Is anyone there?", "hey", "Hello", "Good day","Hi"],
 "responses": ["Hello", "Happy to have you here", "Good to see you."],
 "context": [""]
}
```

Fig. 2. Dataset structure.

The data is structured into tags, patterns, responses, and context.

- Tags: Categories that shows students' intention
- Patterns: Possible questions that students may ask
- Responses: Possible responses to the questions mentioned in patterns
- Context: Contextual words relating to a tag for better classification

Trying to build an intelligent agent is a complex task as the only knowledge the agent has access to is the information it has learned itself [6]. The dataset is stored in a JSON file. Since machine learning algorithms require data to be in a numerical feature vector rather than text, the dataset must be filtered carefully using statistical and numerical means. NLTK provides various text processing methods to clean the data:

- Conversion into lowercase or uppercase: In this step, the words are uniformly converted to lowercase or uppercase, so the algorithm does not treat the same words differently.
- Removing noise: This includes removing punctuation and special characters. This step also includes removing stopwords. Stopwords are the most common words in the text and removing those does not change the sentence's meaning. For example, "about", "me", "something", etc.
- Tokenization: In tokenization, sentences are broken into a list of words, i.e., tokens.
- Stemming or Lemmatizing: Stemming or Lemmatizing is the process of reducing tokens to their root. The slight difference between stemming and lemmatizing is that the stemming can often create non-existent words.

To train a model, we build a neural network with three layers. The first layer contains 128 neurons, the second layer 64 neurons, and the third output layer contains the number of neurons equal to the number of intents to predict the response. We trained the model with 200 epochs and a batch size of five. Figures 3 and 4 show the graphs of training accuracy vs. validation accuracy and loss, respectively.

After the initial processing phase, we need to transform the text into meaningful feature vectors. This process is called feature extraction. Bag-of-words is a simple and popular feature extraction method. In this method, the structure of words in a document is discarded and the model is only concerned with words in the document.

Once the model is trained and saved, the intelligent agent responds to students' questions with 99% accuracy. The example conversation with an intelligent agent is shown in Table 1.

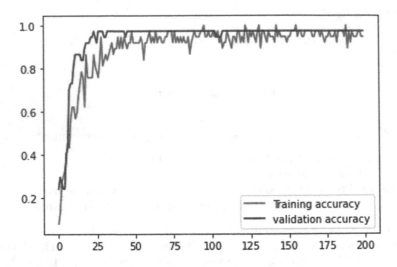

Fig. 3. Training accuracy vs. Validation accuracy.

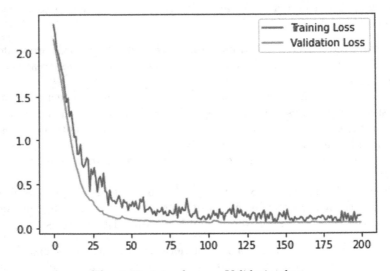

Fig. 4. Training loss vs. Validation loss

3.2 Math Expression Parser and Evaluator

We implemented an expression parser and evaluator that gives students options to practice mathematical concepts and ask for help along the way. The system shows the steps to solve a mathematical question as a tutor would. This idea is based on an open-source project, Socratic by Google [3,5].

There are three main parts in building expression parser and evaluator:

$$3 + 2 * x \tag{2}$$

Table 1. Example conversation with an intelligent agent

Entity	Communication
Student	Hi there
Agent	Hello there. Happy to have you
Student	Who are you?
Agent	I am Accessible Math. I can help you learn mathematical concepts
Student	What do you know about mathematics?
Agen	Ask me a question about linear equation and I will answer to the best of my knowledge

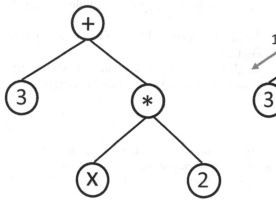

Fig. 5. Expression tree for Eq. 1   **Fig. 6.** Inorder tree traversal for Eq. 1

- Creating an expression Tree: Math.js is a powerful and open-source library that parses the mathematical equation string, generates an expression tree, and returns the tree's root node. An expression tree can be used to analyze, manipulate, and evaluate expressions. The example of a generated expression tree for the Eq. (1) is shown in Fig. 5.
- Flattening the tree: Once the expression tree is parsed, we use inorder traversal to traverse and simplify the expression to generate steps. The tree traversal is shown in Fig. 6.
- Simplifying expressions: Once we traverse through the tree, we find the best nodes to apply simplification rules and record it as a "step". This step provides necessary information such as operands, the operator, and the applied simplification rule. We store this information and wait for the student to practice the step. We only provide the information in speech format if students ask for hints.

4   Future Work and Conclusion

An accessible self-directed learning tool for visually impaired students is essential in the modern era with the increasing popularity of e-learning systems. It is necessary to integrate assistive technologies with e-learning platforms and designing educational content following accessibility guidelines. With our prototype's development and by introducing further improvements, our emphasis is to promote self-directed learning tools, especially for mathematics for visually impaired high school students.

The improvements presented in this paper are currently in beta testing but will be available as an open-source web application. The following improvements could be added in the future release of the work:

- We aim to assess the interaction with an intelligent agent for visually impaired students.
- Upon release, the application will be open-source and free to use to learn and understand the mathematical concepts.
- The current version only supports English as a primary language. In the future release, the application will be improved to support multiple languages.

References

1. The effect of lockdown and social distancing on blind and partially sighted people. https://www.rnib.org.uk/campaigning/priority-campaigns/inclusive-journeys/effect-lockdown-and-social-distancing-blind-and-partially-sighted-people. Accessed 05 Feb 2021
2. An extensive math library for JavaScript and Node.js. https://mathjs.org/. Accessed 05 Feb 2021
3. Get unstuck: learn better. https://socratic.org/. Accessed 05 Feb 2021
4. The pandemic is undermining visually impaired people's independence. https://theconversation.com/the-pandemic-is-undermining-visually-impaired-peoples-independence-heres-how-to-fix-this-142209. Accessed 05 Feb 2021
5. Stepping into math: open-sourcing our step-by-step solver. https://blog.socratic.org/stepping-into-math-open-sourcing-our-step-by-step-solver-9b5da066ae36. Accessed 05 Feb 2021
6. Abdul-Kader, S.A., Woods, J.: Question answer system for online feedable new born Chatbot. In: 2017 Intelligent Systems Conference (IntelliSys), pp. 863–869 (2017). https://doi.org/10.1109/IntelliSys.2017.8324231
7. Alajarmeh, N., Pontelli, E., Son, T.: From "reading" math to "doing" math: a new direction in non-visual math accessibility. In: Stephanidis, C. (ed.) UAHCI 2011. LNCS, vol. 6768, pp. 501–510. Springer, Heidelberg (2011). https://doi.org/10.1007/978-3-642-21657-2_54
8. Arlinwibowo, J., Retnawati, H.: Developing audio tactile for visually impaired students. Int. J. New Trends Educ. Implic. 6(4), 78–90 (2015)
9. Bird, S., Klein, E., Loper, E.: Natural Language Processing with Python. O'Reilly Media, Sebastopol (2009)
10. Bouck, E.C., Weng, P.L.: Reading math: a comparison of reading and listening to algebraic problems. J. Spec. Educ. Technol. 29(4), 1–13 (2014). https://doi.org/10.1177/016264341402900401

11. Cervone, D., Sorge, V.: Adaptable accessibility features for mathematics on the web. In: Proceedings of the 16th Web for All 2019 Personalization - Personalizing the Web, W4A 2019. Association for Computing Machinery, New York (2019). https://doi.org/10.1145/3315002.3317567

12. DePountis, V.M., Pogrund, R.L., Griffin-Shirley, N., Lan, W.Y.: Technologies used in the study of advanced mathematics by students who are visually impaired in classrooms: teachers' perspectives. J. Vis. Impair. Blind. **109**(4), 265–278 (2015). https://doi.org/10.1177/0145482X1510900403

13. Gulley, A.P., Smith, L.A.C., Price, J.A., Prickett, L.C., Ragland, M.F.: Process-driven math: an auditory method of mathematics instruction and assessment for students who are blind or have low vision (2017)

14. Hewett, T.T., et al.: ACM SIGCHI curricula for human-computer interaction. Technical report, New York, NY, USA (1992)

15. Blackorby, J., Chorost, M., Garza, N., Guzman, A.: The academic performance of secondary school students with disabilities (2003)

16. Jariwala, A., Marghitu, D., Chapman, R.: MyA+ Math: teaching math to students with vision impairment. In: Antona, M., Stephanidis, C. (eds.) HCII 2020. LNCS, vol. 12189, pp. 200–211. Springer, Cham (2020). https://doi.org/10.1007/978-3-030-49108-6_15

17. Lawrence, D.O., Ashleigh, M.: Impact of Human-Computer Interaction (HCI) on users in higher educational system: Southampton University as a case study. Int. J. Manag. Technol. **6**(3), 1–12 (2019)

18. mxparser - math expressions parser for java android c#.net/mono/xamarin - mathematical formula parser/evaluator library. http://mathparser.org/. Accessed 05 Feb 2021

19. Create your chatbot using Python NLTK. https://medium.com/@ritidass29/create-your-chatbot-using-python-nltk-88809fa621d1. Accessed 05 Feb 2021

20. Regec, V.: Mathematics in inclusive education of blind students in secondary schools in the Czech Republic. Procedia Soc. Behav. Sci. **174**, 3933–3939 (2015). https://doi.org/10.1016/j.sbspro.2015.01.1136. https://www.sciencedirect.com/science/article/pii/S1877042815011957. International Conference on New Horizons in Education, INTE 2014, Paris, France, 25–27 June 2014

21. Sheikh, W., Schleppenbach, D., Leas, D.: MathSpeak: a non-ambiguous language for audio rendering of MathML. Int. J. Learn. Technol. **13**(1), 3–25 (2018). https://doi.org/10.1504/IJLT.2018.091609

Analysis of Design Elements for the Treatment of Language Disorders in Autistic Children

Miao Liu and Yingjie Wang[⊠]

East China University of Science and Technology, Shanghai 200237,
People's Republic of China

Abstract. In order to improve the efficiency of toy intervention for the treatment of language disorder in autistic children, design elements related to toys are studied. Interviews were conducted with teachers and parents of children with autism, as well as professional rehabilitation teachers, and field observations were made at autism centers. Then related design elements stratified were selected from these researches. Hierarchical analysis (AHP) is used to quickly locate the main design factors from the inextricable influences in this study. The highly logical and scientific Hierarchical Analysis method, proposed by American scholar Saaty, can be applied to the scientific and efficient selecting of the related design factors in this topic. Through conducting single-case experiments on autistic children and comprehensive and quantitative evaluation on the results based on the theoretical framework of ICF-CY theory framework and MCELF language assessment forms to study the most effective Elements of toy design for treatment. In this paper, literature research, questionnaire research, interviews, and experimental analysis were used to identify the key design elements of special therapeutic toys for children with autism. The research can develop the further development and research of toy design for auxiliary therapy of autistic children with speech disorders, to fill the gap in the market, and to raise the attention to the needs of children with autism. The results of this study will provide a scientific basis for the selection of relevant toy design solutions, which is of theoretical significance and practical value.

Keywords: Product design · Children with Autism · AHP · Toy assisted therapy

1 Introduction

Autism Spectrum Disorders (ASD), also known as Autism or autistic disorder, is a broad spectrum of complex neurodevelopmental disorders in children [1]. The name Autism literally means "Within oneself" was first proposed by Leo Kanner in 1943. Patients close themselves in their own world, ignore and reject things in the outside world, and are unable to communicate with others normally. Nowadays, the scope of autism is extended to pervasive developmental disorders, covering more manifestations that do not satisfy Kanner's initial description of autism [2].

According to the latest edition of the "2019 China Autism Education and Rehabilitation Industry Development Report III", there are more than 10 million people with

© Springer Nature Switzerland AG 2021
M. Antona and C. Stephanidis (Eds.): HCII 2021, LNCS 12769, pp. 118–137, 2021.
https://doi.org/10.1007/978-3-030-78095-1_11

autism, with more than 2 million children aged 0 to 14 years old and growing at a rate of nearly 200,000 per year [3]. The most recent study, by 2020, found that one in 38 children has autism.

With the increasing number of autistic children, the research on autistic children has been gradually enriched. The literature research section is divided into three modules of research: 1. Study on the symptoms and causes of speech disorders in autistic children; 2. Research around intervention therapy for children with autism; 3. Research on intervention toys for autistic children and their market (Fig. 1).

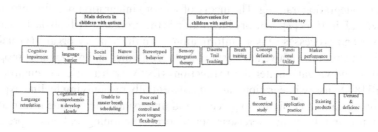

Fig. 1. Research framework

At present, the real cause of autism is still unknown in the world. It is a behavioral syndrome that begins in infancy and is accompanied by sensory and perceptual response disorders, behavioral disorders, language and expression disorders, and social relations and communication disorders [4]. Language serves as a medium for establishing interpersonal relationship, cognition of the world and calligraphy emotion. The existence of language barrier will seriously affect the healthy growth of autistic children, normal social interaction and connection with the world. There are five types of language disorders: abnormal pronunciation, confused language logic, misuse of personal pronouns, language fixation, lack of emotional expression [5]. The study found that the causes of language difficulties in autistic children are also multiple:

1. Delayed language development. Normal children with initiative language in about two years old, can independently communicate with others, compared with normal children, autistic children are widespread language retardation, cause autism children's vocabulary less, talk a lack of continuity, serious still can appear complete aphasia, these children only can make "ahhh" sounds to express themselves.
2. Delayed cognitive and comprehension development. Children with autism have unique and complex cognitive development that makes learning and comprehension more difficult and, to some extent, hindering the development of mature thinking.
3. Inability to master breath scheduling. Children with autism are less able to control their breath, so they often lose control of the loudness and pitch of their voice due to improper breath control, which affects their normal vocal production.
4. Weak oral muscle control ability and lack of tongue flexibility. Most children with autism have low frequency of exercise controlled by cavity muscles, which leads to reduced flexibility of the tongue and insufficient oral muscle control, and finally further aggravate children's language difficulties.

2 Autism Intervention Therapy and Its Related Research

The concept of early intervention is a remedial approach to compensatory education for children with environmental disadvantages, introduced in the United States in the 1960s [6]. Early intervention can effectively reduce language impairment and improve the cognitive and communication skills of children with autism, and targeted interventions can be adopted.Currently, there are several types of intervention strategies for language disorders:

1. Sensory integration training. The theory of sensory integration was first proposed by Dr. Ayres. J. in 1969 [7]. Sensory integration is the process by which the human brain analyses and processes sensory information from the sensory organs (visual, auditory, tactile, proprioceptive and vestibular) several times and responds appropriately so that the individual is better able to function effectively in a variety of environmental stimuli [8]. Sensory integration training is essentially by applying feeling experience to improve children's ability to perceive and understand the outside information.
2. Breath training. Blowing exercises improve oral functioning and oral expression by enhancing sensory awareness of the jaw, lips, and tongue, learning pronunciation positions, building specific muscle strength, and reducing or eliminating drooling.
3. Scenario-based teaching. Discrete Trail Teaching (DTT), based on the natural Teaching method, is also called "Discrete Operation Teaching Method" [4]. The complex task is divided into several specific small goals, and the learning of the whole task can be realized by guiding autistic children to complete one small goal after another. Naturalized teaching scenes can help children realize the generalization of behaviors immediately, as well as the acquisition training and transfer training of new behaviors [5].

In addition to these main types of intervention treatment, augmentative and Alternative Communication System (AAC) has also been developed to enhance children's social skills in situations where language cannot be developed in a conventional way, including Voice Output Communication AIDS (VOCA) and The Picture Exchange Communication System (PECS) [5]. The stage of 3–6 years old children in a critical period of brain development. Combined with the results of the survey, the target subjects of this study were selected as children with mild autism aged 3–6 who were more suitable for intervention treatment of language disorders.

3 Autism Intervention Toys

3.1 Autism Intervention Toys

Compared with the mature research on the direction of autism psychology, behavior and education, there are few research evidences on the intervention products for children with autism. At present, there is no unified definition of the standard concept of autism intervention toys, which is widely recognized as "the main function of autism toys is to reduce the impact of disorders, certain problem behaviors, emotional stress mitigation and cognitive correction" [9].

In Research on Toy Design for Autism Children, Long Chunxia clarified that the design of toys for autistic children should be based on the principle of intervention and treatment, and toys should be used as the carrier to stimulate and strengthen the therapeutic effect for autistic children in the use of toys [10].

Klein's theoretical research on play therapy has developed games into a systematic analysis method, which can study the condition of autistic children by analyzing the performance of children in games [11]. She emphasized that the use of toys is an essential part of game analysis, and children's toys in games should be small in size, neutral and safe, as well as suitable for specific symptoms of autistic patients [12].

Based on the results of the survey, this study defines autism intervention toys as devices that have certain therapeutic effects on the problem behaviors and disorders of autistic children. The special feature of intervention toys is that children with autism can indirectly complete the above therapeutic training in the process of using toys through the design of games, so as to achieve the effect of intervention therapy. Since the types of software toys are related to their specific contents, which are diverse and inconvenient to classify, and there are many related influencing factors, this paper mainly focuses on physical intervention toys and temporarily does not include software games in the scope of discussion.

3.2   Autism Intervention Autism Intervention Therapy Toy Market

Research on the current toy market finds that there are few toys to achieve marketization and the phenomenon of homogenization is relatively serious. Most of these toys are sensory system training toys and card teaching toys, which have a relatively single form of expression and lack of consideration for targeted intervention treatment of language disorders in autistic children. Now has some special autism toy shopping site, as www. discoverytoys.net, https://nationalautismresources.com, http://toysforautism.com and so on. These sites offer toy type is concentrated and mostly on retrieval method using age and efficacy as a condition of classification of sifting, rarely can assist users from the actual condition of children with autism, such as recommending according to the degree of language barrier.

Comprehensive market at present and relevant literature research results can be found that symptoms in children with autism and related rehabilitation education research is more, in the field of toys for children with autism intervention study is less, in the targeted language barrier intervention treatment related research in the field of toy more scarce, from the market point of view although there have been many has been put into use and autistic children language barrier intervention toys, but there is development of homogeneity tendency is serious and the lack of corresponding systematic design research support (Table 1).

Table 1. The main types of therapeutic toys available for autistic language disorder intervention

Picture	Instruction	Picture	Instruction
	Toy picture card. How to play: Through the letters and symbols in the card for spelling training, build sentences and paragraphs.		Intelligent Interaction. How to play: a large number of point-reading toys, a variety of interactive ways, able to carry out phonetic, cognitive assistant teaching.
	Feeling system training. How to play: Through external stimulation, children with autism can be trained in their perceptual ability and tactile sensitivity.		Combination toy puzzles. How to play: Combination puzzles to form words and sentences to achieve spelling training and assist communication.

4 Methods and Innovation of the Study

4.1 Methods of the Study

This study uses a combination of qualitative and quantitative research methods, including: literature collection and analysis, field research, user interviews and other related methods. First by reading the related literatures at home and abroad, combining with the existing theory of autistic children language barrier intervention toy requirements needed for systematic analysis and summary, based on the literature of autism group after reading cognition, rehabilitation center field visits, interviews with rehabilitation center faculty, obtain more detailed information for autistic children language barrier characteristics, behavior patterns and intervention treatment. At last, the conclusion about the language barrier intervention toy requires design factors is drawn.

4.2 Innovation and Significance of the Study

1. This study is an interdisciplinary study that summarises the design factors required for the design of therapeutic toys for autistic children language disorders through research in the fields of special child psychology, special child education, intervention therapy for autistic children and product design research, as well as practical observations and detailed information obtained through in-depth visits. This will enrich the research in the field of products for autistic children's language therapy, and increase the usefulness and support of design for autistic children's language therapy.
2. The AHP hierarchical analysis method is used to quantify the design factors and to determine the weighting framework of the design factors, so as to solve the problem of designers relying on subjective judgement in the design process. The weighting framework provides designers with a direction to think about, a design threshold and

a standard to evaluate the final product, allowing designers to more accurately grasp the distribution of the various elements of the product, to better exploit the design value of the product, and to improve the relevance and efficacy of the final product.

3. The weighting framework can also be applied to the selection of design solutions, helping designers, rehabilitation practitioners and parents of autistic children to select the most effective intervention toys to meet their actual needs.

4. Through the experimental study, the findings are applied to practice, providing experimental data to verify and improve the efficacy of the therapeutic intervention toys for autistic children, as well as providing some reference experience for the design and development of subsequent therapeutic intervention products for autistic children with language disorders.

5 Theoretical Basis

5.1 Analytic Hierarchy Process

In 1973, the American scholar Saaty introduced the famous hierarchical analysis method, which possesses a high degree of organization and scientific rigour in logical judgement [10]. Hierarchical analysis maximises the exclusion of subjective factors and allows complex issues to be analysed both qualitatively and quantitatively, leading to clear and accurate conclusions. There are many factors in the design of intervention toys for language disorders of autistic children. The application of AHP is more conducive to scientific comparison and analysis of various factors under various conditions.

Through literature research, combined with visits to rehabilitation centres for children with autism, interviews with instructors and observations of the real performance of children with autism, an evaluation model was constructed to stratify the influencing factors obtained, and the weight values of all influencing factors were calculated and ranked to produce scientific, quantitative results. The specific process is shown in the Fig. 2.

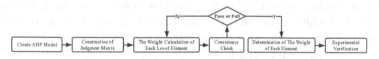

Fig. 2. The flow chart of AHP

5.2 Steps in Building AHP Model

Objective level: Optimal solution for the design of toys for autistic children with language disorders.

Criterion layer: Through literature research and field interviews, the design elements for the speech disorder intervention for children with autism were obtained, and the design elements of the criterion layer were identified as sensory experience, emotional comfort, security, interactivity, preference consideration, ease of use and adjustability.

Sub-criteria layer: According to the hierarchical construction method proposed by Saaty [13], the first level indicators of the criterion layer were divided into a total of eighteen second level indicators constitute the sub-criteria layer.

Through literature research and interviews, the design elements of the intervention therapy for autistic children with language impairment were finally summarised and the design elements of the hierarchical analysis criterion level and sub-criterion level were determined. The AHP model for toys for language disorder intervention for children with autism was constructed based on the principles of hierarchical analysis as shown in the Fig. 3.

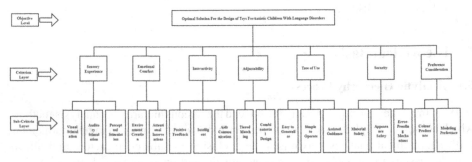

Fig. 3. AHP model

Criterion layer and its sub-index description:

Sensory experiences: A number of studies have shown that children's sensory enrichment experiences during the use of toys can be effective in strengthening children's perceptual skills.

1. Visual stimulation: A number of studies have shown that the use of images such as pictures, photographs and videos can be effective in teaching cognition to children with ASD. In addition, many children with ASD have an extreme fascination with rotating or brightly coloured objects, known as Sensory Seeking Behaviours [4]. Toys designed with images and rich colours can be stimulating and experiential for children with autism, enhancing their perceptual abilities.

2. Auditory stimulation: According to Anke Prothmann's research, children with autism are more sensitive to animal sounds, followed by nature, human sounds and finally the sounds of musical instruments [14]. Adding auditory stimulation to the design of toys can get more feedback from children.

3. Perceptual stimulation: Perceptual stimulation is achieved through pressure, vibration stimulation and enhanced tactile sensation, which can be achieved by changing the material of the toy and can effectively increase the autistic child's perception of the external environment and other objects.

Emotional comfort: Emotional comfort can ensure that children are in a more comfortable and stable state in the process of using toys, and ensure the smooth progress of intervention treatment.

1. Create a comfortable and familiar environment. Field survey found that many autistic children, once in a strange new environment, they need more time to adapt, toys through constructing game scenes. Toys should reduce children's sense of conflict and soothe anxious mood, build the scene, make children relax natural scene at the same time.

2. Attention intervention. On the one hand, to keep children's attention in the use of toys to reduce emotional anxiety, mobilize their emotions to maintain children's interest in toys, so that children can actively participate in the game. On the other hand, the overall coordination of toys should be considered in the design, so as to avoid distracting children's attention due to local protrusion.

Security: Children with autism have poor motor skills, poor coordination skills, and more rigid and repetitive behaviors than children in general. Therefore, the safety requirements of toys for autistic children will be higher.

1. Material Safety. In the selection of materials, in addition to non-toxic and odor-free safe and environment-friendly materials, we should also consider the possibility of inducing asthma attacks in children with autism. We should avoid plush materials that are easy to accumulate dust, so as to ensure that they are safe, reliable, durable and not prone to damage.

2. Appearance security. The survey found that children with autism often chew on toys during play, and there is a risk of them being eaten by children if they are too small, or hurt if they have sharp edges.

3. Error-proofing mechanisms. Children with autism have a tendency to seek vestibular pleasure. Children with autism have more extreme usage in the process of using toys. In addition, children with autism have unbalanced system, may use toys incorrectly, so in the design of toys to consider mistake proofing mechanism can ensure the safety of toys.

Interactivity: The interaction of toys strengthens children's sociability and expression desire through the interaction between children and toys. By constantly guiding children to make interactive connections in simple games, Social Adaptive Behavior can be enhanced to inspire the interaction between children through toys.

1. Toys provide feedback and reward mechanisms. Literature research has found that toys using sound and visual cues can effectively cultivate children's social communication skills, and also encourage and guide autistic children to interact with toys. The existence of reward mechanism can arouse children's interest.

2. Intelligent. The combination of software and hardware is realized by adding intelligent components, which changes the toy from static to dynamic, provides more functions such as accompanying and dialogue, and increases the interaction of children.

3. Aids communication. The initial relationship between autistic children and the rehabilitator can be quickly established through the toy as a bridge in the game, which helps the rehabilitator to carry out treatment quickly. On the one hand, rehabilitation

teachers can use toys to guide children; on the other hand, toys can assist children's expression.

Preference considerations: Numerous studies have shown that children with autism have preferences for many elements of toys that differ significantly from those of ordinary children, so the design of toys for children with autism cannot follow the design conventions of ordinary children's toys and needs to take into account the special preferences of the autistic child population.

1. Colour preferences. Children with autism have a more obvious and different colour preference than children in general, preferring green, blue, red, purple, orange and finally yellow, and preferring cooler colours to warmer ones [15].
2. Modeling preferences. Considering the cognitive impairment of autistic children, complex contour shapes should be avoided in the product design, and the overall shape needs to be simplified to facilitate the identification.
3. Attention preference. Song Luling's research found that children with ASD have a masculine cognitive preference, this cognitive style can lead to a preference for masculine style products, and children with ASD spend significantly less time looking at character and animal toys than normal children [16]. However, there are also studies show that attractive character toys for children with autism also exist. Therefore, there is some disagreement in the research on attentional preferences of children with autism, and there is not enough information to support this, so this design element will not be considered in this study.

Adjustability: Although children with autism are all part of the neurodevelopmental disorders category, they are very different from one another and the same toy or treatment programme may appear completely different to different children.

1. A hierarchy of levels of difficulty and matching criteria is used in the design of the toy, so that the user can determine which level of play to use in relation to the matching criteria, improving the relevance of the product.
2. Combination design, dividing the toy into individual components, which can be combined to obtain a variety of different functions to meet the different needs of children with autism at different stages of life.

Ease of use: If the use of toys is highly required, children will not be able to use them correctly and will not achieve the real effect of intervention therapy, and will be less interested in exploring them.

1. Easy to generalise. The ultimate goal of intervention training is that children with autism learn to naturally apply the skills taught by the rehabilitator in the designated environment to a real social setting, called generalisation.
2. Simple to operate. Children with autism have cognitive impairments that lead to learning difficulties, lower levels of hand-brain coordination and poorer dexterity than the average child. Toys for children with autism should not be too demanding in terms of operational and cognitive skills.

3. Assisted guidance. Adding visual cues and verbal guidance to the toy's function plays a supporting role. Visual cues can be used to help children with autism learn to play independently by showing the process and steps through some illustrations.

5.3 Construct a Judgement Matrix and Calculate the Weights of Each Indicator

An important step in the hierarchical analysis method is to reasonably construct a judgment matrix to compare the elements of the same level, and to score the relative importance of each indicator according to the value of the elements of the judgment matrix (as shown in Table 2) on a scale of 1–9 and its reciprocal, as proposed by the American operations researcher T.L. Saaty, based on a large amount of experimental data. The judgment matrix is shown in Table 3, Y_i represents the importance of each element in the criterion level to the target X, and y_{ij} represents the relative importance of each indicator in the sub-criteria level to the criterion.

Table 2. Judgement matrix

X	Y_1	Y_2	...	Y_n
Y_1	y_{11}	y_{12}	...	y_{1n}
Y_2	y_{21}	y_{22}	...	y_{2n}
...	...	...	...	...
Y_n	y_{n1}	y_{n2}	...	y_{nn}

Table 3. Judgement matrix scales and their meanings

Scales	Meanings
1	That two factors are equally important compared to each other
3	The former is slightly more important than the latter when compared to the latter
5	The former is more important than the latter when compared to the latter
7	The former is more strongly important than the latter when compared to the latter
9	The former is more extremely important than the latter when compared to the latter
2, 4, 6, 8	Median of the above adjacent judgements
Reciprocal	Two indicators representing the same hierarchy are of opposite importance

Considering the possible subjective bias in matrix assignment, in order to increase the rigor and credibility of the results, the rating samples in this study were selected in multiple dimensions to understand that the buyers, users and managers of toys for autistic children are often not the same person. In the intervention and treatment of children with autism, parents' participation in children's education have a great influence on the intervention and treatment effect. Teachers in special education institutions are indispensable in the whole intervention and treatment, so their evaluation is also very important. A total of 15 personnel including 5 professional rehabilitation teachers, 5 parents of autistic children and 5 design graduate students were selected to grade and assign values to each element, and the comprehensive multi-dimensional evaluation was evaluated, namely, Eq. (1).

$$y_{ij} = \left[\sum\nolimits_{x=1}^{k} (y_{ij}) \right]/k \tag{1}$$

5.4 Determination of Weights

According to Fig. 2, the seven criteria $Y_1, Y_2, Y_3, Y_4, Y_5, Y_6, Y_7$ in the criteria layer were used to refer to Ease of Use, Interactivity, Adjustability, Security, Sensory Experience, Emotional Comfort, Preference Consideration. Y_{11}, Y_{12}, Y_{13} are used to refer to Easy to Generalise, Simple to Operate, Assisted Guidance; Y_{21}, Y_{22}, Y_{23} are used to refer to Active Feedback, Intelligent, Aids communication; Y_{31}, Y_{32} are used to refer to Tiered Matching, Combination Design; Y_{41}, Y_{42}, Y_{43} are used to refer to Material Safety, Appearance Security, Error-proofing Mechanisms; Y_{51}, Y_{52}, Y_{53} are used to refer to Visual Stimulation, Auditory Stimulation, Perceptual Stimulation. Y_{61}, Y_{62} are used to refer to Environment creation, Attention intervention; Y_{71}, Y_{72} are used to refer to Colour Preferences, Modeling Preferences.

Square root method is used to calculate all indicators of the same level to obtain the corresponding weight value, namely Eq. (2).

$$W_i = \frac{W_i}{n} (i = 1, 2, 3....n) \tag{2}$$

5.5 Consistency Check

In practice, evaluators may think inconsistently before and after, so there is a need to test the consistency of the collected results to ensure that the inconsistency of the data is within an acceptable range and that the results are scientific. The consistency indicator of the judgement matrix is represented by CI.

$$CI = \frac{\lambda_{max}}{n-1} \tag{3}$$

λ_{max} represents the maximum eigenvalue and n is the order of the matrix. The consistency test of the hierarchical analysis is judged by the random consistency ratio of the matrix $C_R = \frac{CI}{RI}$. The average stochastic consistency index RI is only related to the order n of the matrix and can be determined directly from Table 4.

The judgment criterion is: when $CR < 0.1$ is judged to pass the consistency test, and vice versa, it does not pass the consistency test and need to recalculate the value. This thesis uses SPSS to conduct consistency tests on the judgment matrix constructed, and makes reasonable adjustments to the values that do not pass the consistency test. The final consistency test results are shown in Table 5.

Table 4. Average random consistency index table

n	1	2	3	4	5	6	7	8	9	10
RI	0.00	0.00	0.58	0.90	1.12	1.24	1.32	1.41	1.45	1.49

Table 5. Conformity test results

	0	Y_1	Y_2	Y_3	Y_4	Y_5	Y_6	Y_7
λ_{max}	7.038	3.004	4.115	2	3	3.004	2	2
CI	0.014	0.002	0.038	0	0	0.002	0	0
RI	1.36	0.52	0.89	0	0.52	0.52	0	0
CR	0.01	0.004	0.043	0	0	0.004	0	0

From Table 5 it can be seen that all judgment matrices met $CR < 0.1$ all passed the consistency test and the data was reasonably usable. The results of all indicators corresponding to the judgement matrix assessment were ranked as the final target weight ranking, as shown in Table 6.

Table 6. Comprehensive weight of hierarchical function index

Criterion layer	Weight W_i	Sub-criteria layer	Weight W_i	Combined weight	Sequence
Y_1 Ease of Use	33.262%	Y_{11} Easy to Generalise	64.833%	21.56%	1
		Y_{12} Simple to Operate	22.965%	7.64%	6
		Y_{13} Assisted Guidance	12.202%	4.06%	9
Y_2 Interactivity	10.325%	Y_{21} Active Feedback	51.125%	5.28%	8
		Y_{22} Intelligent	6.708%	0.69%	18
		Y_{23} Aids communication	22.428%	2.32%	14
Y_3 Adjustability	10.660%	Y_{31} Tiered Matching	83.333%	8.88%	2
		Y_{32} Combination Design	16.667%	1.78%	15
Y_4 Security	11.769%	Y_{41} Material Safety	22.222%	2.62%	12
		Y_{42} Appearance Security	11.111%	1.31%	17
		Y_{43} Error-proofing Mechanisms	66.667%	7.85%	5

(*continued*)

Table 6. (*continued*)

Criterion layer	Weight W_i	Sub-criteria layer	Weight W_i	Combined weight	Sequence
Y_5 Sensory Experience	11.107%	Y_{51} Visual Stimulation	64.833%	7.20%	7
		Y_{52} Auditory Stimulation	22.965%	2.55%	13
		Y_{53} Perceptual Stimulation	12.202%	1.36%	16
Y_6 Emotional Comfort	11.769%	Y_{61} Environment creation	25.000%	2.94%	10
		Y_{62} Attention intervention	75.000%	8.83%	3
Y_7 Preference Consideration	11.107%	Y_{71} Colour Preferences	75.000%	8.33%	4
		Y_{72} Modeling Preferences	25.000%	2.78%	11

6 Results Verification

6.1 TOPSIS

To verify the validity of the study findings, existing toy solutions were prioritised based on TOPSIS using the identified design elements and the corresponding target weights [17]. TOPSIS (Technique for Order Preference by Similarity to an Ideal Solution), also known as Approximation to an Ideal Value Ranking [18], is a method for decision analysis of multiple cases for one problem, in which the optimal and inferior sets of each index are obtained from the implemented design solutions, and other solutions are ranked by judging how close they are to the optimal set [19]. A more objective priority ranking of the three solutions was obtained through the TOPSIS method. Finally, the actual intervention treatment effects of the three toy programmes were experimentally examined to see if they were consistent with the results of previous studies.

6.2 Selection of Assessment Subjects

At the Huicheng Children's Rehabilitation Centre, which was selected in the preliminary research, the rehabilitation therapist of the rehabilitation centre was invited to select three of the most commonly used toy programmes for speech and language intervention for children with autism.

Option 1: Picture books with language training cards

Picture books and cards are the most frequently used language therapy toys in rehabilitation centres. They are usually used by teachers to guide children with autism in learning, but are less interesting and less potential for self-exploration.

Option 2: Animal Toy Piano

This toy piano uses the cartoon shape of animals, just press the keys, there will be lights emitted, different keys have different sound and light effects, clap the hand drum, each drum has different colours, the sound effects emitted from the clap are also different, can be through the light colour change, simulation of sound effects, when using can attract children's attention, guide children to imitate the sound, encourage children to vocalise, effectively assist children to practice the auditory system and articulation system.

Option 3: Mouth muscle toy

These toys are available in a variety of styles and guide the child through biting, chewing and blowing to achieve the effect of mouth muscle training, so that the child's oral muscles and tongue can be exercised and the child's ability to pronounce sounds can be improved to achieve the effect of speech impediment training.

6.3 Evaluation Process Based on the TOPSIS

Five teachers from the rehabilitation centre, five design students and five parents of autistic children from the rehabilitation centre were invited to score the three selected toy solutions against the design elements identified in the previous section, with a limited scoring range of $0 <$ very poor ≤ 3, $3 <$ poor ≤ 5, $5 <$ fair ≤ 6, $6 <$ good ≤ 8, $8 <$ good ≤ 10). The results are shown in Table 7.

Table 7. Initial evaluation matrix

Evaluation indicators		Option 1	Option 2	Option 3
Y_{11}	Easy to Generalise	6.36	7.56	6.43
Y_{12}	Simple to Operate	6.75	6.86	6.06
Y_{13}	Assisted Guidance	5.03	6.57	5.64
Y_{21}	Active Feedback	2.87	7.87	5.73
Y_{22}	Intelligent	1.25	7.93	1.44
Y_{23}	Aids communication	6.55	6.73	6.39
Y_{31}	Tiered Matching	7.54	5.67	5.08
Y_{32}	Combination Design	6.32	6.09	5.86
Y_{41}	Material Safety	6.89	6.74	7.94
Y_{42}	Appearance Security	7.73	7.67	7.56
Y_{43}	Error-proofing Mechanisms	5.25	5.84	5.07
Y_{51}	Visual-Stimulation	7.97	8.22	5.19
Y_{52}	Auditory Stimulation	1.12	8.35	5.22
Y_{53}	Perceptual Stimulation	1.07	7.73	6.79
Y_{61}	Environment creation	5.03	6.12	4.67
Y_{62}	Attention intervention	6.78	7.49	5.73
Y_{71}	Colour Preferences	6.73	6.85	6.44
Y_{72}	Modeling Preferences	6.03	7.69	6.57

Construct a weighting matrix based on the weights of each element. Firstly, the initial product evaluation matrix A is normalized to obtain the normalization matrix B (m is the number of programmes and n is the number of indicators)

$$B_{ij} = \frac{A_{ij}}{\sqrt{\sum_{i=1}^{m} A_{ij}^2}} \quad i = 1, 2, 3...m \ j = 1, 2, 3...n \tag{4}$$

The weighted normalised matrix Z is obtained by weighting the matrix B according to the weighting Table 8.

Table 8. Weighted standardized evaluation matrix

Evaluation indicators		Option 1	Option 2	Option 3
Y_{11}	Easy to Generalise	0.1163	0.1383	0.1176
Y_{12}	Simple to Operate	0.0453	0.0461	0.0407
Y_{13}	Assisted Guidance	0.0204	0.0266	0.0229
Y_{21}	Active Feedback	0.0149	0.0409	0.0298
Y_{22}	Intelligent	0.0011	0.0067	0.0012
Y_{23}	Aids communication	0.0134	0.0137	0.0131
Y_{31}	Tiered Matching	0.0625	0.0470	0.0421
Y_{32}	Combination Design	0.0107	0.0103	0.0099
Y_{41}	Material Safety	0.0145	0.0141	0.0167
Y_{42}	Appearance Security	0.0076	0.0076	0.0075
Y_{43}	Error-proofing Mechanisms	0.0441	0.0490	0.0426
Y_{51}	Visual Stimulation	0.0456	0.0471	0.0297
Y_{52}	Auditory Stimulation	0.0029	0.0215	0.0134
Y_{53}	Perceptual Stimulation	0.0014	0.0102	0.0089
Y_{61}	Environment creation	0.0161	0.0196	0.0149
Y_{62}	Attention intervention	0.0515	0.0569	0.0436
Y_{71}	Colour Preferences	0.0485	0.0494	0.0464
Y_{72}	Modeling Preferences	0.0142	0.0182	0.0155

Find positive and negative ideal solutions:

$$M_j^+ = max\{u_{1j}, u_{2j}, u_{3j}, ..., u_{nj}\}, (j = 1, 2, 3, ..., m) \tag{5}$$

$$M_j^- = min\{u_{1j}, u_{2j}, u_{3j}, ..., u_{nj}\}, (j = 1, 2, 3, ..., m) \tag{6}$$

$$X^+ = \left(M_1^+, M_2^+, M_3^+, ..., M_m^+\right) \tag{7}$$

$$X^- = \left(M_1^-, M_2^-, M_3^-, ..., M_m^- \right) \tag{8}$$

This equation gives the positive ideal solution for each option

$$X^+ = (0.1176, 0.0407, 0.0229, 0.0298, 0.0012, 0.0131, 0.0421, 0.0099, 0.0167,$$
$$0.0075, 0.0426, 0.0297, 0.0134, 0.0089, 0.0149, 0.0436, 0.0464, 0.0155)$$

This equation gives the negative ideal solution for each option

$$X^- = (0.1163, 0.0453, 0.0204, 0.0149, 0.0011, 0.0134, 0.0625, 0.0107, 0.0145,$$
$$0.0076, 0.0441, 0.0456, 0.0029, 0.0014, 0.0161, 0.0515, 0.0485, 0.0142)$$

Calculate the distance from each scheme to the ideal solution and the relative progress. The distance between each scheme and the positive ideal solution X^+ is

$$S_i^+ = \sqrt{\sum_{j=1}^{n} \left(u_{ij} - u_j^+ \right)^2}, (i = 1, 2, 3, ..., m) \tag{9}$$

The distance between each scheme and the positive ideal solution X^- is

$$S_i^- = \sqrt{\sum_{j=1}^{n} \left(u_{ij} - u_j^- \right)^2}, (i = 1, 2, 3, ..., m) \tag{10}$$

The relative progress of each scheme to the ideal solution is

$$C_i = \frac{S_i^-}{S_i^+ + S_i^-}, (i = 1, 2, 3, ..., m) \tag{11}$$

Finally, each scheme is sorted according to the value of relative schedule C_i. The higher the value of C_i is, the higher the priority of the scheme is, which is closest to the ideal solution. On the contrary, the smaller the value of C_i is, the lower the priority of the scheme is. The results are shown in Table 9.

Table 9. Euclidean distance and relative post progress

	S_i^+	S_i^-	C_i	Sequence
Option 1	1.3942	0.3441	0.1980	3
Option 2	0.2005	1.4274	0.8769	1
Option 3	0.9935	0.7563	0.4322	2

According to the results, the toy Option 2 is the closest to the ideal solution, which means that the final intervention effect of Option 2 is better than the other two toy schemes in theory.

6.4 Experimental Verification

With the help of the rehabilitation teacher, six mild autistic children with certain language ability in Huicheng children's rehabilitation center were selected as the experimental subjects. After the consent of the parents was obtained and the written informed consent was signed, the children were divided into three groups and the single subject experiment was used The intervention observation lasted for one month to verify the actual therapeutic effect of the three toys.

Before and after the beginning of the intervention experiment, the professional rehabilitation teachers used autistic child behavior checklist (ABC) and Child Autism Rating Scale (CARS) to evaluate the selected 6 autistic children. Language assessment includes basic communication skills, voice perception, voice production, word understanding and naming, sentence understanding and expression, and comprehensive application [20]. The final results were presented with a simplified scale, and the limited scoring interval was 0 < very poor ≤ 3, 3 < poor ≤ 5, 5 < General ≤ 6, 6 < good ≤ 8, 8 < very good ≤ 10). The average score of the two rehabilitation teachers was taken (Table 10).

Table 10. Evaluation form

Evaluation project		1			2			3		
		Before	After	Promotion rate	Before	After	Promotion rate	Before	After	Promotion rate
Language expression	Active communication	3.5	4.1	0.6	2.3	3.8	1.5	3.1	3.8	0.7
	Sentence expression	5.3	5.6	0.3	4.8	5.5	0.7	4.2	4.9	0.7
	Retelling ability	6.5	7.3	0.8	6.4	7.5	1.1	6.1	6.8	0.7
	Question answering	2.7	3.5	0.8	3.5	5.2	1.7	3.3	3.7	0.4
Language understanding	Name instruction	2.9	3.9	1	3.3	5.6	2.3	3.7	4.5	0.8
	Action command	5.6	6.3	0.7	5.2	6.1	0.9	4.9	6.1	1.2
	Identification behavior	3.7	4.2	0.5	3.5	4.7	1.2	3.8	4.7	0.9
	Vocabulary comprehension	4.3	5.8	1.5	3.8	4.3	0.5	4.5	5.3	0.8
Language imitation	Imitate pronunciation	6.3	6.6	0.3	5.9	6.8	0.9	6.1	7.3	1.2
	Imitative expression	5.2	5.7	0.5	5.7	6.8	1.1	5.5	6.8	1.3
Language perception	Language feedback	4.1	4.8	0.7	4.3	5.8	1.5	4.8	6.2	1.4
	Sound resolution	5.7	6.5	0.8	5.3	6.5	1.2	5.1	6.4	1.3
	Application of oral organs	6.2	6.8	0.6	5.7	6.9	1.2	6.3	7.5	1.2
Average promotion rate		0.7			1.2			0.97		

The data results show that the intervention effect of toy 2 is better than that of the other two toy schemes, and the intervention effect of toy 1 is the least obvious, which is consistent with the theoretical results calculated by TOPSIS combined with the target weight of design elements.

7 Summary

7.1 Shortcomings

This study also inevitably has many shortcomings. First of all, in the previous research, it is difficult to communicate with autistic children, and to obtain their ideas and needs. Autistic children have great differences, and it is difficult to meet every child, so the extraction and summary of design elements of intervention toys for autistic children with language disorders may not be able to perfectly meet the actual needs of every autistic child. In addition, at present, the definition of various design elements is still relatively broad, and further refinement is needed in the application. Some design elements are summarized vaguely, and some design elements cannot be summarized due to the lack of reference, so there is still room for further research on design elements.

Secondly, in the selection of experimental samples and research sites, only the mild autistic children in Huicheng rehabilitation center were selected as the subjects, so the same type of patients in a single place were selected as the samples, which made the experimental results and research results have certain limitations and narrowness. The lack of sample number and experimental time also affected the comprehensiveness of the experiment to a certain extent.

Finally, it is difficult to collect the data in the experiment, so we can only use the professional rehabilitation teacher to follow the observation to simplify the scale for evaluation. There are too many indicators that the rehabilitation teacher needs to observe, so it is difficult to collect the training results data comprehensively. In order to summarize, it is necessary to abandon some elements, so that the final results are not accurate enough.

7.2 Research and Prospect

This study attempts to locate the main design factors from the influencing factors of complex autism children's language disorder intervention toys by analytic hierarchy process (AHP) to form a systematic weight level. In the study, the influence of subjective factors is minimized by AHP and TOPSIS method. Through hierarchical and quantitative analysis, the design elements and weight levels of special toys with the most ideal therapeutic effect on language disorder of autistic children are summarized. The effectiveness is verified by experiments, which provides a reference for further development and research of adjuvant treatment of autistic children's language disorder. It provides a scientific and quantitative basis for the toy design of speech disorders, which makes the design output more scientific and reasonable, and helps to improve the actual treatment effect of special treatment toys.

Early intervention and treatment of language disorder is an effective means to help autistic children learn to communicate and express their language. As an indispensable and effective auxiliary tool, intervention and treatment toys need to be continuously optimized from a scientific and effective direction. Future research needs to constantly put forward and optimize scientific, systematic and quantitative theoretical basis, and finally form a complete and comprehensive framework for the intervention and treatment of language disorders in autistic children. Considering that autism, as a lifelong development disorder, is difficult to be completely cured, the care for autistic children also needs to consider the needs of autistic children's growth and life ability, so future research can continue to extend to the field of autistic life support products and even service design. In addition, it includes a series of more far-reaching issues such as whether the research can further help improve the future employment and social life of autistic children. In a word, there is a lot of research space in the field of autism, which is worth and needs us to invest more energy in.

References

1. Developmental Behavior Group of Chinese Medical Association Pediatrics Branch., Child Care Professional Committee of Chinese Medical Association Pediatric Branch., Expert Group on Children's Autism Diagnosis and Prevention Technology and Standards Research Project: Expert consensus on early identification and screening and early intervention for children with autism spectrum disorder. Chinese J. Pediatr. **55**(12), 890–897 (2017)
2. Su, S., Hu, H., Zhao, F.: A review of research on emotional intervention for children with autism spectrum disorder based on ICT. China Spec. Educ. (4), 47–53 (2019)
3. Multicolored deer Autism Research Institute: Report on The Development of Autism Education and Rehabilitation Industry in China. Tianjin Education Press, Tianjin (2019)
4. Baranek, G.T., David, F.J., Poe, M.D., et al.: Sensory experiences questionnaire: discriminating sensory features in young children with autism, developmental delays, and typical development. J. Child Psychol. Psychiatry **47**(6), 591–601 (2006)
5. Hou, T., Sun, T., Ma, C.: A review of language training in autistic children. J. Suihua Univ. (10), 68.0 (2019)
6. Wang, Y.: Analysis on the theoretical basis of early intervention. China Spec. Educ. (04), 1–3 (2000)
7. Chen, G.: Experimental Study on the Effect of Sensory Integration Training on Cognitive Ability and Motor Development in Children with Autism. Yunnan Normal University (2015)
8. Li, X., Huang, Y.: Research progress of sensory integration disorder . Chinese J. Pediatrics (9), 64–66 (2001)
9. William, F., Yuill, N.: An augmented toy and social interaction in children with autism. Int. J. Arts Technol. **5**(2/3/4) (2012)
10. Long, C.: Research on Toy Design for Children with Autism. China Academy of Art (2009)
11. Segal, H.: Klein. Karnac Books, London (1979)
12. Segal, J.: Melanie Klein. Sage publications, London (1992)
13. Long, Q.: Research on the application of AHP fuzzy comprehensive evaluation method in performance evaluation. Metall. Econ. Manage. (2), 45–48 (2007)
14. Prothmann, A., Ettrich, C., Prothmann, S.: Preference for, and responsiveness to, people, dogs and objects in children with autism. Anthrozoös **22**(2), 161–171 (2009)
15. Cao, S.Q., Wei, W., Sun, A.J.: Experimental study on color preference of 5-year-old children with autism. China Spec. Educ. **143**(5), 46–52 (2012)
16. Song, L.: Review and analysis on the research of toy preference of autistic children. J. Mod. Spec. Educ. **319**(16), 38–41 (2017)

17. Wang, M., Zhai, H.: Evaluation of mobile learning application design for autistic children based on TOPSIS method. Ind. Des. **000**(002), 60–61 (2020)

18. Wang, P.: Comprehensive evaluation of highspeed railway operation based on AHP and Topsis. Railway Econ. Res. (4), 26–30 (2018)

19. Huang, H., Li, Q., Tang, G.: Risk assessment of postoperative pulmonary thromboembolism based on AHP-TOPSIS comprehensive model. J. Chongqing Normal Univ. (Natural Science Edition) **36**(6), 79–86 (2019)

20. Guo, Q., Liu, Q.Y., Ma, N.J., et al.: A case study of ICF-CY in the assessment of language disorders in preschoolers with autism. Chinese J. Hear. Speech Rehab. Sci. (6) (2019)

Communication Robot as a Weekly Online Quiz Presenter

Shu Matsuura[1]([✉]), Satoe Kon[2], and Sakura Kuwano[2]

[1] Faculty of Education, Tokyo Gakugei University,
4-1-1 Nukuikita, Koganei, Tokyo 184-8501, Japan
shum00@u-gakugei.ac.jp
[2] Setagaya Elementary School Attached to Tokyo Gakugei University,
4-10-1 Fukasawa, Setagaya, Tokyo 158-0081, Japan

Abstract. To add a humorous interface to online quizzes for elementary school students, we demonstrate a video of a humanoid robot as a quiz presenter. The quiz was a fun way to learn various related knowledge starting with eating habits. The purpose of using a robot was to make the quiz interesting for students of all grades in elementary school and for them to enjoy the quiz with their parents. The video was a short quiz that lasted a few minutes wherein the robot interacts with a human voice, presenting the viewer with a multiple-choice quiz.

We distributed one robot-video quiz every week for six months, obtaining the following results. The number of students who responded to the quiz decreased sharply in the first month and stabilized at ~10% of the total number of students in the school. At first, most of the comments were about the quiz's difficulty, but gradually, most of the comments became about quiz's contents, suggesting the viewers established interest in the quiz topic. Many comments about the robot as a unique entity with its personality suggest that the viewers empathetically accepted the robot's existence.

Keywords: Online quiz · Humanoid robot · Robot's personality

1 Introduction

In Japan, a new school year for elementary schools starts in April. The Japanese government had closed elementary schools from March 2, 2020, to control the spread of COVID-19. Many schools delayed the new school year and took measures such as closing schools or dispersing school attendance.

Simultaneously, schools attempted online education to ensure learning was not interrupted. However, many parents became more anxious about raising their children during the school closure period [1]. According to a survey conducted by the Ministry of Education, Culture, Sports, Science and Technology for public schools that were temporarily closed, 100% of the schools imposed home study using textbooks and paper materials. However, only 29% of the schools could implement home learning using digital materials, and only 5% could implement home learning through simultaneous interactive online instruction [2].

M. Antona and C. Stephanidis (Eds.): HCII 2021, LNCS 12769, pp. 138–153, 2021.
https://doi.org/10.1007/978-3-030-78095-1_12

Two of the authors of this paper—a nutrition teacher and a nursing teacher—responded to these unexpected situations with on-demand and online instructional attempts. Before COVID-19, the nutrition teacher used to attach food-related quizzes to school lunch bookmarks to stimulate interest in school lunches and knowledge connected to daily life. Even after the reopening of the elementary school, the school took control measures through dispersed school attendance and simple school lunches.

Still, the children needed further reinforcement on education based on their lives. A good food-related education program for elementary school children and their parents creates health awareness [3]. However, our educational objective was to increase interest in the broader knowledge of life, culture, and science through food. With this goal, we began distributing weekly online quizzes on food and health to all students in the school in July 2020.

Reports show that weekly quizzes in higher education at moderate intervals effectively sustain learning [4, 5]. The quizzes' purpose in this study is not to determine the learning effect but to broaden the view of things and stimulate interest. It is to make thinking and learning more interesting. The idea of this quiz is to give students a sense of the richness of human life through a wide variety of knowledge.

Considering the level of knowledge, if we design the questions fit for younger students, they may be too easy for senior students, and senior students may not be interested. In consideration of younger students, hints to help them guess the correct answer will also be necessary. Thus, we must create the quiz content and its presentation carefully for all grades. It is also essential to create questions that will attract family members' interest and make the quiz engaging while giving it an atmosphere of humanity.

In this study, we focus on introducing the quiz and the quiz direction as well as attempting to use a video wherein a communication robot appears, talks to the quizzer, and presents the quiz to children as a humorous interface to enhance the enjoyment of the quiz. Humor appears in both verbal and visual forms [6, 7]. We examine the effects of this humor interface by analyzing the children's impressions.

2 Method

We used Microsoft Forms as the medium for the quiz. Children and their parents sent their answers and comments anonymously on the forms. Respondents were not asked to provide any personal information other than their grades.

The first quiz was a 10-question Yes–No quiz; subsequently, each set of quizzes consisted of about five questions, which we call a "quiz set." Two to four quiz sets were distributed for each session. Here we indicate "quiz set $n.m$" as the mth set of quiz sets sent out in the nth session.

Quiz sets 1 to 4 were a collection of various quizzes related to daily food. From quiz set 5 onward, each quiz set was created with a specific theme related to the season.

The quizzes were distributed by Setagaya Elementary School. The school is one of the elementary schools affiliated with Tokyo Gakugei University, a national university of education. The quiz URLs were distributed by e-mail to the parents of all 618 students every Monday evening. If the parents who received the URL did not inform their children, they could not take the quiz.

The communication robot used in this study was SoftBank Robotics NAO [8]. One of the authors worked as the principal of Setagaya Elementary School until March 2020 and had introduced NAO to the school; NAO is called "Little Principal" by the students and has been familiar to them as a mascot at the principal's address, etc. [9]. Therefore, in the 2020 school year, NAO is already a character for the second graders and above.

The video of the robot was saved on YouTube so that it could be played on Forms Quiz. As shown in Fig. 1, the quiz can be answered even if the children do not play video. They can read the questions and send their answers through the text forms. At the end of the quiz, a form asks for free comments on the quiz. The user is free to choose whether or not to write their impressions. In this study, we will classify and examine the contents of these free descriptions.

Fig. 1. Example of a form for the quiz set 22.1 including NAO's skit video, "A duck with green onion," where the upper text is the quiz text.

Excluding the first one, the NAO videos consisted of two parts: a prologue and a quiz. All of them are in the form of dialogs between an unseen human and NAO. The human uttered short words to avoid failing the speech recognition. The NAO prologue can be classified into three: explanation, comedy talk, and skit in dialog form about aspects related to the quiz topic, as shown below.

"Explanation":   The human speaks, and the NAO responds. This repetition is the main form wherein the person obtains knowledge from NAO. However, the following comic talk is also built in this type of dialog.

"Comedy talk":   It is based on the repetition of *"furi"* (bringing out the topic, beginning), *"boke"* (adding humor and development), and *"tsukkomi"* (ending) [10, 11]. In most cases, humans are in charge of *furi* and *tsukkomi* and bring out the fun of NAO. However, there are times when the human does *boke*, and NAO does *tsukkomi*.

"Skit":   It is a small play style by NAO and the human. For example, NAO played the role of the owner of a yakitori stall. During the play, NAO gave explanations and comedy talks.

NAO's speech is standard Japanese, but it has always had a specific characteristic in his tone of voice, which is characterized by a weak role language [12]. Its characters in its talking style are knowledgeable, a little cocky, and sometimes say things difficult to understand for children, but it has a nuanced way of speaking Japanese that is called "cute" by children.

The quiz set 4 and follow-ups were multiple-choice quizzes, in which, in most cases, NAO posed the questions, the human called out the choices, and NAO read out the choices. The reverse case was also exhibited for some cases. Table 1 shows the list of NAO videos added to the quiz sets analyzed in this paper.

Table 1. Lists of NAO videos.

Quiz index	Title	Time [min]	Type of prologue	Prologue	Quiz or questionnaire
5	*Somen* (thin noodles)	0:42	-	Say hello	What is the difference between *Udon* and *Somen* noodle?
6	Morning apples	1:07	Talk	Summer heat	Apples in the morning are gold
7.1	Sweat	1:03	Talk	Summer heat	Take salt on days when you sweat
8.1	*Yakitori* (grilled chicken)	1:09	Skit	Description of meat at NAO's *Yakitori* restaurant	What part of the meat is the liver?
9.1	*Ochazuke* (a bowl of rice in green tea)	1:26	Skit	Where is the Peach garden?	Add mackerel to your breakfast to boost your brain function
10.1	Good sleep	2:30	Explanation	Eating and harnessing the electrical energy of matters	Should one not play video games right before going to bed?

(continued)

Table 1. (*continued*)

Quiz index	Title	Time [min]	Type of prologue	Prologue	Quiz or questionnaire
11.1	Arranging lotus	1:33	Skit	The lotus flower opens and never closes after three days, symbolizing the enlightenment of the Buddha	What is the name of your favorite flower?
12.1	Picnics	2:47	Comedy talk	About the various "hunts" in Japan	About hunting, not taking anything, and just looking
13.1	Typhoon	1:50	Explanation	How typhoons develop	How to call a typhoon
16.1	Oyster	2:04	Comedy talk	A comic story about persimmons and oysters	How do you like your oysters cooked?
17.1	Halloween	1:01	Skit	Trick-or-treating on Halloween	What do you think of when you hear the word "Halloween"?
18.1	Sweet potato baker	1:51	Skit	The taste and nutrition of *Ishiyaki* potatoes	Will sweet potatoes replace rice as Japan's staple food?
21.1	*Oden* (soup)	2:36	Skit	The origin and the characteristics of *Oden*	What is *Oden* called in English?
22.1	Duck with green onion	2:30	Comedy talk	*Kobo-Daishi Kukai* and leeks	Meaning of the proverb, "A duck comes carrying a leek on its back."
23.1	Travel the world with food	3:03	Explanation	Christmas sweets	About the name of the German Christmas pastry, Stollen
24.1	Christmas	5:30	Explanation	About Christmas gifts and New Year's gifts	Why do we give gifts on special occasions?
25.1	*Toshigami* (great-year God)	4:43	Explanation	Each family prepares to welcome the New Year's god at New Year's	Why are *Kagami-mochi*, mirror-shaped rice cakes, displayed lying down?
26.1	*Zoni* (soup with *mochi* rice cakes)	4:02	Explanation	The Taste of Kyoto's White *Miso Zoni*	Why many new year festive dishes can be eaten without fire in Japan
27.1	*Mochi* (a rice cake)	4:35	Explanation	Things to keep in mind when eating rice cakes	A story about a chief who treated rice cakes poorly

(*continued*)

Table 1. (*continued*)

Quiz index	Title	Time [min]	Type of prologue	Prologue	Quiz or questionnaire
28.1	Cactus ice cream	2:55	Explanation	Taste preference of ice cream in summer and winter	About Cactus Ice Cream
29.1	Pancake	3:46	Explanation	Origin of pancakes	Origin of Pancake Day in Japan
30.1	*Setsubun* (the beginning of spring)	2:17	Explanation	Why do we roll beans on Setsubun the day before the beginning of spring?	On why, *Oni*, demons appear in the home

3 Results and Discussions

3.1 Change of Quiz Answer Submissions

Table 2 shows all the quiz sets we analyzed, including the quiz sets without NAO videos. These quiz sets were created by the same author. The fourth column of the table shows the number of quiz sets published simultaneously. The quiz sets shown in the table were created by one of the authors commonly. The numbers in the sixth column of the table indicate the numbers of NAO videos. Quiz sets 1 through 4 are generally quizzes on daily foods, but from set 5 onward, the quizzes were based on specific themes.

Table 2. Lists of quiz sets for analysis.

Session date	Index of session	Index of quiz set for analysis	Num. of quiz sets delivered at the same time	Title of the quiz set	NAO video
Jul-6-20	1	1	1	Daily foods	None
Jul-13-20	2	2.1	2	Daily foods	None
Jul-20-20	3	3.1	2	Daily foods	None
Jul-27-20	4	4.1	2	Daily foods	None
Aug-3-20	5	5	1	*Somen* (thin noodle)	1
Aug-11-20	6	6	1	Morning apples	1
Aug-18-20	7	7.1	2	Sweat	1

(continued)

Table 2. (*continued*)

Session date	Index of session	Index of quiz set for analysis	Num. of quiz sets delivered at the same time	Title of the quiz set	NAO video
Aug-24-20	8	8.1	2	*Yakitori* (grilled chicken)	1
Aug-31-20	9	9.1	2	*Ochazuke* (a bowl of rice in green tea)	1
Sep-7-20	10	10.1	2	Good sleep	1
Sep-14-20	11	11.1	2	Lotus flowers and rhizome	1
Sep-21-20	12	12.1	2	Picnics	1
Sep-28-20	13	13.1	2	Typhoon	1
Oct-5-20	14	14.2	2	Cluster amaryllises	None
Oct-12-20	15	15.1	2	Face masks	None
Oct-19-20	16	16.1	2	Oyster	1
Oct-26-20	17	17.1	2	Halloween	1
Nov-2-20	18	18.1	2	Sweet potato baker	1
Nov-9-20	19	19.1	2	Mushrooms	None
Nov-9-20	19	19.2	2	Ginkgo nuts	None
Nov-23-20	21	21.1	3	*Oden* (soup)	1
Nov-30-20	22	22.1	3	Duck with green onion	1
Dec-7-20	23	23.1	3	Travel the world with foods	1
Dec-14-20	24	24.1	3	Christmas	1
Dec-21-20	25	25.1	3	*Toshigami* (great-year God)	1
Dec-29-20	26	26.1	3	*Zoni* (soup with *mochi* rice cake)	1
Jan-4-21	27	27.1	2	*Mochi* (a rice cake)	1
Jan-12-21	28	28.1	4	Cactus ice cream	1
19-Jan-21	29	29.1	3	Pancake	1
Jan-27-21	30	30.1	4	*Setsubun* (the beginning of spring)	1

Figure 2 shows the chronological changes in the number of answers and comments sent from the respondents, and the number of views of NAO videos measured on YouTube Studio analysis for each time in Table 2. For quiz set 1, we received answers from nearly half of the all the children in the school; after the second quiz set, the number of answers decreased sharply.

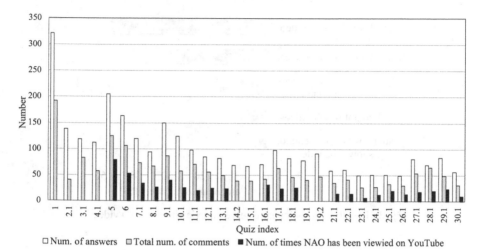

Fig. 2. Chronological changes in the number of answers, the number of comments from responders, and the number of video views of NAO measured on YouTube Studio.

Quiz set 5, which showed a sharp increase in the number of responses, was sent after the summer vacation. When sending out the quiz set to parents, an announcement was added: "This time, the robot teacher—NAO—is appearing for the first time in a long while." These factors may have contributed to the increase in the number of responses.

Quiz set 9.1 was the last week of the summer vacation, and an announcement was added to encourage students to prepare for the new term. Since quiz set 11.1, there has been a weak downward trend, but no significant increase or decrease, and the number of responses has remained $>\sim 50$.

The gray bars show the number of comments written after trying the quizzes. Except for quiz set 2.1, more than half of the people who sent in answers also wrote comments. Overall, 59.7% of the answer submitters wrote comments on their impressions.

The black bars in the figure indicate the number of times NAO videos were viewed. In the figure, the quiz indices without the black bars show the quiz sets do not include NAO video. Overall, 19.2% of the respondent-submitters watched the NAO videos. Even if they did not watch the video, they could still answer the corresponding quiz because the question texts are presented as seen in Fig. 1. Therefore, watching the video is not a necessary condition for answering. If a hint is needed for the answer, the hint is instead shown in the still image. We analyze the respondents' comments in Sect. 3.2. Figure 2 suggests that many comment senders have not watched NAO videos.

Figure 3 shows the aggregate results of the choice-based awareness survey on the extent of viewing NAO videos, which was included in the quiz set 29.1. Considering the measured value of the number of views counted on YouTube Studio shown in Fig. 2, the awareness of the degree of viewing is slightly higher than the actual number of viewing. This may reflect the student's intent to be more active in viewing.

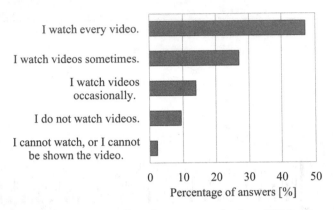

Fig. 3. Results of questionnaire survey on viewing of NAO video.

Figure 4 shows the results of questionnaires on the viewing devices for the quiz. This survey was conducted in the quiz set 28.1. Overwhelmingly, 76% of the users answered that they use smartphones as the viewing devices. Thus, the students mainly use their parents' smartphones, which they borrowed temporarily.

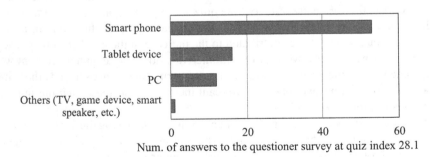

Num. of answers to the questioner survey at quiz index 28.1

Fig. 4. Results of questionnaire survey on the viewing devices.

Further, Fig. 5 shows the place students watch the quiz set. Most the quiz sets were viewed in the living room, a shared space; 43% of all the quiz sets were viewed with parents in the living room or at the dining table.

In a few cases, parents wrote comments on the quiz. It is assumed that these were cases where parents enjoy solving quizzes with their children. About 15% of the respondents watched the quizzes in their own rooms. Meanwhile, 8.6% of children solved the quiz sets outside the home, possibly during activities outside, after classrooms.

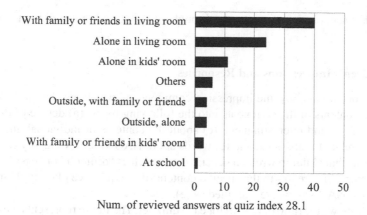

Fig. 5. Results of questionnaire survey on the places for viewing places.

Figure 6 shows the results of the grade level surveys after quiz set 11.1. The percentages for each grade level averaged over the entire period shown in the figure were 18%, 15%, 15%, 17%, 13%, and 7% for first, second, third, fourth, fifth, and sixth graders, respectively, and 15% for parents.

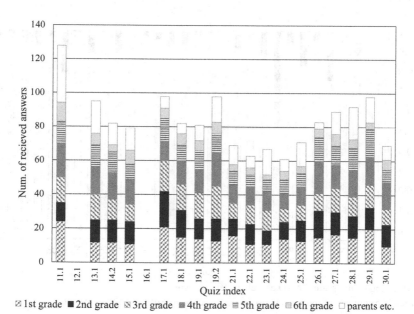

Fig. 6. Number of answers from each grade for each quiz set. Parents sent with their children.

Many quizzes are considered a little too difficult for the first graders, but parents and children possibly work on them together. Moreover, if parents are too busy, younger children may not solve the quizzes. However, Fig. 6 shows that each grade responded at the same rate throughout the period. There was no considerable decline in the younger grades; 6th graders had fewer answers throughout the period, but it did not decline to zero.

3.2 Children's Impressions and Responses

In this section, we analyze the impression comments after solving the quiz. We categorized the contents of the comments into the following types: (a) degree of difficulty, (b) degree of fun and interestingness, (c) about the contents of individual quizzes, (d) other words related to the quiz, and (e) words about NAO videos. Category (a) and (b) are comments that children wrote in general terms such as "difficult" or "easy," or "fun" or "interesting." If it refers to the specific content of the quiz, we classify them as (c). References to NAO videos are classified as (e).

Figure 7 shows the ratio of (a)–(e) for each quiz set. The figure represents the chronological change of the comment content. In the first quiz set, many of the comments indicated (a) "degree of difficulty" and (b) "degree of fun and interestingness." Then, (a) decreased over time, and the percentage of comments on (c) "individual quiz contents" increased. This tendency to mention the quiz's contents suggests a growing interest in the quiz's unique topics. Since there is no clear decreasing trend for (b), we can infer that people who feel enjoyment in the quiz contents stick to solving the quiz and sending comments.

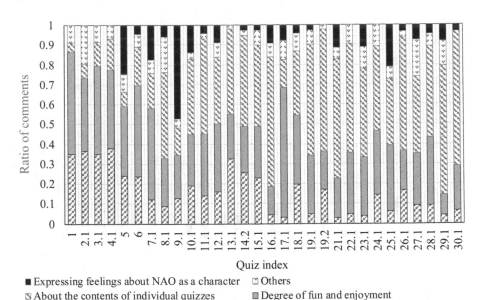

■ Expressing feelings about NAO as a character   ▨ Others
▨ About the contents of individual quizzes   ▤ Degree of fun and enjoyment
▨ Degree of difficulty

Fig. 7. Chronological changes in the ratios of five comment types.

As Figs. 2 and 6 indicate, there was a noticeable decrease in the number of responses during quiz sets 1–10, but in the later quizzes, the number of responses was indeed low but stable. During this period, the quiz contents shifted from general food knowledge to seasonal topics, changing to be associated with more familiar experiences. This association with daily life may also encourage respondents to be more aware of the quiz content.

We now turn our attention to the percentage of comments on NAO in Fig. 7. Since we introduced the first NAO video in quiz set 5, the response has reached 25%. In addition, in quiz set 9.1, we prompted comments on the NAO video in the feedback section, saying, "We are also happy to have messages from you to our robot teacher—NAO." As a result, 47% of the comments were on NAO. After the quiz set 11, comments about NAO were often less than 10%. Meanwhile, for quiz sets 14, 15, and 19 without NAO videos, we received the comments, "I miss NAO".

Next, we will try to classify the comments on NAO from two different perspectives. The first classification is as follows.

One-of-a-kind type: The robot appears as a unique entity with a mascot-like character. It has a lasting uniqueness.
Sight type: Perceived as a phenomenon or image of a machine that behaves and speaks. This type does not have a unique story with itself beyond the visible phenomena.

It is not easy to distinguish them clearly from the comments, but we made the following distinction on a trial basis.

One-of-a-kind type: The comment indicates with proper nouns. The sender calls the robot's name or greets it. The comment mainly expresses the feelings of the sender.

Sight type: The comment indicates with common nouns. It mainly expresses the sender's feelings about the observed phenomenon, such as a machine's movement.

The second and higher graders may remember a school time with NAO since NAO was the school mascot. As for the first graders, it is their first time seeing NAO, and they may get a unique story only through this quiz series.

We divided the comments on NAO images into the above two types and showed their percentages to the entire comments in Fig. 8 as a stacked bar graph.

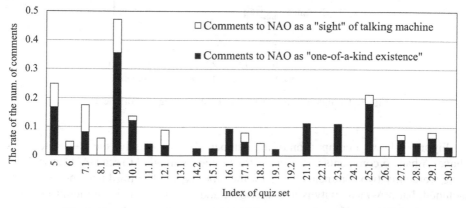

Fig. 8. Stacked bar graph of the rates of two comment types on NAO.

Overall, the one-of-a-kind type exceeded the sight type. In quiz set 5, many children sent comments such as "It was good to see NAO-sensei again" (classified as one-of-a-kind type). The percentage of one-of-a-kind type tended to increase after quiz set 10.1, although the number of comments on NAO was small. The viewers who answered the quiz will recognize NAO as a unique entity with a particular character through repeated quiz answering and viewing NAO dialogs related to each topic.

For the second classification of NAO comments, we introduced a method based on personal construction, as shown below.

A. "I_do and I_feel.": This is a first-person structure. The observer of the image is the central speaker. For example, "I met and was delighted."
B. "(I_see) it_is.": Potentially a first-person structure. "It's cute!" is similar to a narrative about an object in that it is (or appears to me to be) cute, but it is the subjective impression of the observer and is included in the first-person structure here.
C. Greetings: It is a typical second-person structure: "Hello, NAO-sensei, how are you?" The person to whom the comment is addressed is accepted as unique, or the observer constructs a unique second-person world.
D. "I_ask.": A question with a second-person structure. Questions like "What do you eat, NAO-sensei?" are utterances that usually follow from C. However, a common-sense routine question weakens the uniqueness.
E. "It_does and I_find.": Constructs with a third-person structure, such as "I am glad NAO-sensei came out," wherein the subject feels how an object such as NAO behaves. The combination of the third and first-person verbs can create a variety of comments.

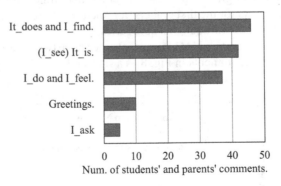

Fig. 9. Comparison of the number of A-E category comments.

Figure 9 shows a comparison of the number of comments for the A–E categories above. A had 35 comments of the same structure as "I am glad to see NAO-sensei" and there were only two comments found for the other types. The third person—NAO—is included, but NAO's activity is not described, and the emphasis is on the intrinsically first-person structure. Most of the early comments were on this A structure.

B: "(I_see) it_is." of the 35 comments in 42 were about impressions of NAO, similar to "NAO is good." The other seven comments were the topics targeting NAO videos, such as "NAO's video is good."

The utterances in the second-person structure of C and D, where the viewer virtually calls directly to NAO, can be said to be highly emotive; C was particularly frequent when it prompted a call to NAO. However, these types were a small number in the overall comments to NAO, stopping at 15.

E: "It_does and I_find."-type comments were numerous and were found throughout the period. A combination of the two types of comments (NAO activity, observer's awareness & impressions) enables expressing NAO's behavior and feelings about it. Table 3 shows the classification of the E-type comments. The content is diverse, and there is no significant bias. The children were happy that the NAO teacher showed up, disappointed that he was not there, and happy and interested that he would give them a quiz. They expressed various emotions about NAO's talk, including informative, interesting, fun, engaging, and clever.

Table 3. Combinations of "It_does" and "I_feel" type comments. Numbers in the parentheses indicate the number of cases.

It [robot]_does (verb)	I [human]_feel
Appear	delighted (4), enjoyed (2), feel it cute (1), other (1)
Not appear	sorry (4)
Talk	informative (3), amazed (3), funny (2), interested (2), delighted (1), relaxed (1), smart (1)
Make amusing talk	funny (2), enjoyed (1)
Question	interested (3), enjoyed (2), feel difficult (1), satisfied (1)
Act	funny (4), amazed (2), cute (1)
Play music	amazed (1), good (1)
Know	amazed (1)
Represent	failed (1)

As described above, in repeating the quiz with a specific topic each time, the respondents began sending more comments on individual contents. In addition, the respondents perceived NAO as a unique individual and tended to enjoy NAO's talks and quizzes.

In face-to-face classes at school, the teacher's essential role is to construct a mental foundation of the learning environment by stimulating children's interest and becoming an irreplaceable presence for them. In a face-to-face class at school, the teacher can be a source of empathy for the students. By contrast, in online quizzes, the communication robot may become a companion, instead of a real human teacher, as a unique presence for the students.

The origin of communication is between the questioner and the respondent in online quizzes. However, it may not be easy to feel the uniqueness of the questioner's personality when the questions are only submitted. Moreover, the students' encouragement to the robot is, in terms of sensitivity, indirectly encouraging to the questioner. Thus, this study suggests that the robot can emotionally mediate between the questioner and students by becoming an empathetic object for the students.

4 Conclusions

To add a humorous interface to an online quiz on daily life for elementary school students, we demonstrated a humanoid robot video presenting one of the quizzes in each quiz set. The quiz is a fun way to learn about various related fields of knowledge, starting with eating habits. The robot was an elementary school mascot before this project, appearing in front of the students frequently. Using this robot aims at making the quiz exciting and humorous for children of all grades and enjoyable with their parents. The videos were short—about a few minutes in length—and consisted of dialogs or skits, followed by a choice quiz for the viewer.

We distributed one robot-video quiz every week for six months and obtained the following results. The number of students who responded to the quiz plummeted in the first month. After that, the number of respondents stabilized at ~10% of the number of children in Setagaya Elementary School. An analysis of the comments that students voluntarily sent when answering the quiz revealed the following. At first, most of the comments were about the difficulty level of the quiz. However, gradually, most of the comments became about the quiz contents, suggesting the establishment of children's' interest in the quiz topic. Many comments on the robot as an individual and unique being suggest that the viewers sympathetically accepted the robot through the video.

We introduced the video of the robot as a humor interface. However, the results also suggested that the students' empathetic acceptance of the robot could lead to emotional mediation with the quiz contestant.

Acknowledgments. This work was partly funded by a Grant-in-Aid for Scientific Research (C) 19K02806 from the Ministry of Education, Culture, Sports, Science and Technology.

References

1. Takazu, R., Yokoyama, I.: What the COVID-19 school closure left in its wake: evidence from a regression discontinuity analysis in Japan. J. Public Econ. **195**, 104364 (2021)
2. MEXT: School closures to combat new coronavirus infections and learning guidance in public schools. https://www.mext.go.jp/content/20200421-mxt_kouhou01-000006590_1.pdf. Accessed 10 Feb 2021
3. Katz, D.L., et al.: Teaching healthful food choices to elementary school students and their parents: The Nutrition Detectives™ program. J. School Health **81**(1), 21–28 (2011)
4. Haigh, M.: Sustaining learning through assessment: an evaluation of the value of a weekly class quiz. Assess. Eval. High. Educ. **32**, 457–474 (2007)
5. Gholami, V., Moghaddam, M.M.: The effect of weekly quizzes on students' final achievement score. Int. J. Mod. Educ. Comput. Sci. **5**, 36–41 (2013)

6. Chandrasekaran, A., et al.: We are humor beings: understanding and predicting visual humor. In: Proceedings of the IEEE Conference on Computer Vision and Pattern Recognition, pp. 4603–4612 (2016)
7. Attardo, S.: Linguistic Theories of Humor. Mouton de Gruyter (1994).
8. Softbank robotics: https://www.softbankrobotics.com/emea/en/nao. Accessed 10 Feb 2021
9. Omokawa, R., Matsuura, S.: Development of thought using a humanoid robot in an elementary school classroom. In: Antona, M., Stephanidis, C. (eds.) Universal Access in Human-Computer Interaction. Virtual, Augmented, and Intelligent Environments. UAHCI 2018. Lecture Notes in Computer Science, vol 10908, pp. 541–552. Springer, Cham (2018). https://doi.org/10.1007/978-3-319-92052-8_43
10. Matsuura, S., Naito, M.: Shaping dialogues with a humanoid robot based on an e-learning system. In: 2016 11th International Conference on Computer Science & Education, IEEE Conference Publication, pp. 7–12 (2016)
11. Stocker, J.F.: Manzai, team comedy in Japan's entertainment industry. In: Davis, J.M. (ed.) Understanding Humor in Japan, pp. 51–74. Wayne State University Press (2006)
12. Kinsui, S.: Virtual Japanese—Enigmas of Role Language. Osaka University Press, Osaka (2017)

Evaluation on Moodle LMS Data Usage During the First Wave of Covid-19's Pandemic

Luis Pereira[✉] [iD] and Joel Guerreiro[✉] [iD]

FCT, ESGHT and SI, University of the Algarve, 8005-139 Faro, Portugal
{lpereira,jdguerreiro}@ualg.pt

Abstract. As the need for remote environments in education emerged during the first wave of COVID-19 pandemic crisis, Moodle learning management system (LMS) was widely used in higher education. Under these requirements, both students and teachers had to adapt and begin using different resources and activities within the platform. This research's aim is to compare Moodle LMS usage before, during and after the first wave of COVID-19 pandemic, what resources and activities were used and what future tendencies have come from this scenario in a Portuguese Higher Education University, Universidade do Algarve. Results show a huge growth of the LMS platform usage during the first wave and an increase afterwards, showing that teachers and students behaviors have changed and technologies can complement traditional on premises classes, improving teaching and learning methods.

Keywords: Moodle LMS · Knowledge Discovery in Database · COVID-19 pandemic · Learning Analytics

1 Introduction

Over the years, information technologies have revolutionized the educational industry with strategies to massify e-learning [1,2]. Many higher education institutions have adopted LMS as e-learning platforms for their pedagogical processes. With LMS platforms, synchronous or asynchronous virtual classes are included in teaching activities with the objective to promote meaningful learning [3]. With e-learning massification, a wider necessity emerged to analyze the registered data and contribute to the advance of Learning Analytics (LA) [4–6]. LA has the goal to collect, analyze and measure educational data, identifying behavior patterns to understand and improve learning processes, teachers and students performance and quality of courses [7,8].

In order to analyze data, Knowledge Discovery (KD), using data mining methods, is essential to extract useful information from large sets of data, optimizing and enhancing processes [9].

During the first phase of COVID-19 pandemic in Portugal, everybody was confined to their homes and asynchronous or synchronous classes had to be

© Springer Nature Switzerland AG 2021
M. Antona and C. Stephanidis (Eds.): HCII 2021, LNCS 12769, pp. 154–166, 2021.
https://doi.org/10.1007/978-3-030-78095-1_13

ensured. Teachers had to adapt their traditional teaching methods and apprehend, in a very short period of time, new technologies and systems to assure student's learning and evaluation. Thus, LMS were widely used to ensure learning continuity in higher education. Now, it is necessary to measure the impact on such systems, pedagogical processes and future tendencies that resulted from the massive use of those systems.

In this article, integrated on the education and learning topic, a research study was conducted using Moodle LMS data, learning analytics and knowledge discovery, for usage comparison, before, during and after the first wave of COVID-19 pandemic in Universidade do Algarve, Portugal. Universidade do Algarve is a traditional teaching institution and almost all courses are lectured on premises and only a few are synchronous, asynchronous classes. This paper contributes to the awareness of Moodle LMS data usage and resources, the perception of students knowledge acquisition and major differences in student evaluation during the COVID-19's pandemic first wave. Also contributes to the understanding of teacher's educational behavior after the confined period, analyzing and comparing if lectures continued using only traditional educational methods or began combining them with the technological methods apprehended, improving therefore educational procedures.

The remainder of this article is organized as follows: In Sect. 2 Related work is presented. Section 3 describes the knowledge discovery in database process used. Results are presented and analyzed in Sect. 4, while Sect. 5 concludes the article.

2 Related Work

The use of LMS was generalized over the last decade and many higher education institutions adopted these systems for e-learning [10]. Moodle is an open source software package that enables online learning and offers to teachers, administrators and students an integrated, robust and secure system for personalized environments [11]. In [12] a technological acceptance model (TAM) was developed with the objective to improve the use of Moodle LMS platform and learning processes using a questionnaire to discover students perception. The results presented by the authors reveal a moderate but positive attitude from students using virtual classrooms and reflect a good appreciation in Moodle's platform utility and usage facility.

T. Teo et al. [13] presented a study of the factors that influence student's intention to use Moodle in Macau. This study identified direct and indirect factors that influence student's intention to use Moodle like usefulness, attitudes, perceived behavioral control, output quality, trial-ability and technology complexity. Using a web survey to measure students perception towards Moodle usage, the authors in [14] presented their study. Results showed that student's mostly value the control over their educational progress and the communication facilitation between student and instructor and themselves.

In a Moodle case study, a correlation and performance study between different team members configurations was addressed by [15] using a tracking system. The authors goal was to access team configurations and determine which were quicker in resolving issues after they were reopened. The results confirm that combinations of different roles between team members correlated with reopened issues and changing team members resolved the referred issues.

In [16] Ubiquitous Learning, which has the purpose to provide adequate information anytime and anywhere based on student desires [17] and integrates learning spaces, digital resources, wireless networks, mobile devices enabling learning on demand [18], is addressed. With Moodle LMS, the authors developed a ubiquitous learning environment portal to find out the portal feasibility. The result showed that the principles of ubiquitous learning were applied and with the developed learning system, students indicated that the product has a good level of interactivity, easy to use and a friendly user interface.

From a digital transformation, resource optimization, improved data collection and analysis for decision-making point of view, a study was developed by [19] in order to present alternative options to enhance e-services using Information and Communications Technologies (ICT) resources on Universities. Using internal and external tools, plugins and advanced ICTs with Moodle, the authors conclude that deploying e-services through these technologies become an alternative for improving the management and administrative environment.

MILA, a LA tool was developed by [8] as a Moodle plug-in with the objective to support the LA processes, enhance courses quality and improve student's performance by analyzing student behaviors and learning processes used in University of Rome Unitelma Sapienza. A LA dashboard was developed by [20] to graphically visualize Moodle logs and obtain necessary data to improve teaching and learning processes.

Educational data mining was addressed in [21] where the authors designed and developed a custom software tool to collect, extract and present data over Moodle LMS. Their goal was to develop a flexible module user interface and present individual and statistical information in a user-friendly form.

Knowledge Discovery in Database (KDD) is the process to discover useful information in databases including extraction, preparation and interpretation of the observed data on which Data Mining techniques are widely used [22]. KDD is a iterative process with several steps to identify useful, valid and understandable patterns in data [23].

The authors in [24] explain that KDD is an iterative process of human-computer interaction with many steps, such as data pre-treatment, data conversion, data mining and evaluation.

Data mining consists in applying computational techniques in a KDD process to determine patterns over the data [25, 26]. refers to data mining "as one of the most prominent techniques to discover knowledge patterns, thus gaining richer insights into data".

F. Lei and C. Hexin in [27] described data mining as beforehand unknown connotative distilled process for potential useful information and knowledge from

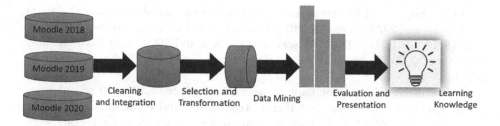

Fig. 1. KDD process.

fuzzy, noisy, incomplete plentiful and stochastic database, processing data and transferring information to useful knowledge (Fig. 1).

The six consecutive steps of data mining are described by Hou Z. in [28], business understanding, data understanding, data preparation, model establishment, model evaluation and result deployment, referring that the most important step is data preparation before the mining operation because it is the most critical part of the mining process. The author also refers that business and data understanding are essential to determine the mining target and data source. Throughout the process there must be performed a series of integration, cleaning, transformation and data reduction actions to improve data quality resulting in improved data mining.

Many different approaches have been researched and developed with KDD processes and with Moodle LMS data, but a learning analysis from usage the point of view determining if educational methods and behaviors altered, was not yet developed, as far as known.

In this article, a research study, using Moodle LMS in Universidade do Algarve, Portugal, is developed to compare resource and access usage, before, during and after the first wave of the COVID-19 pandemic, using knowledge discovery to collect, extract and analyze data to discover tendencies and behaviors from students and teachers.

3 Knowledge Discovery in Database Process

Universidade do Algarve has a particular implementation of Moodle LMS because it uses one database for each school year and integrates data from several systems like academic and human resources. To extract, identify tendencies and behaviors in order to understand teaching and learning usage differences within Moodle LMS data before, during and after first pandemic wave in Portugal, it is necessary to use a KDD process, data mining and leaning analytics.

The first wave of Corona Virus Pandemic in Portugal occurred during the second semester of 2020's school year, from February to July. Learning and teaching methods had to be adapted and technologies to be apprehended by both students and teachers.

This study uses Universidade do Algarve Moodle databases from the years 2018, 2019 and 2020, where the 2018 database has data of the entire school year of 2018/19, 2019 the 2019/2020 school year data and 2020, data from the first semester of 2020/21 school year, still not yet concluded (concluding in February 2021).

This study goal is to compare the second semester of 2018/19 school year, when all classroom lessons were mainly traditional and on premises, with the second semester of 2019/2020 school year, when most classroom lessons were synchronous with teachers and students confined to their homes, using only technologies and Moodle LMS to continue teaching and learning activities. In order to discover if behaviors and technologies usage changed when both teachers and students returned to the traditional on premises classroom lessons, after the referred confined period, the first semester of school year 2020/21 will be analyzed and compared with both other semesters.

In Fig. 1, KDD process used in this study is presented. The first step is cleaning and integration where all the inconsistent data has to be removed and the multiple data sources (three Moodle databases from 2018, 2019 and 2020 years) have to be combined into a new database. The second step is basically to select the relevant data to be analyzed and transform it into database tables appropriate for mining, also summarizing or aggregating data. The third step is Data Mining where mining methods are used to extract tendencies and patterns. In the last step, data patterns are evaluated and knowledge is presented.

The KDD process was implemented from the data registered in the tables and views from Universidade do Algarve's Moodle LMS presented in Table 1.

From the gathered learning knowledge, this study will provide important teaching and learning methods information changing both students and teacher's perception helping improve traditional teaching and learning methods with technological tools like Moodle LMS and the resources it uses.

4   Results and Analysis

For a better understanding of the results involved in the analysis, Table 2 is presented and shows the context of Universidade do Algarve in Moodle LMS. All of these values influence results, specially the number of teachers and students which directly effects resource usage, sessions, quizzes and work assignments registered in Moodle LMS. The number of courses and disciplines also influence the obtained results. As showed, in 2019 the number of teachers increased, the numbers of courses and disciplines are almost equivalent to 2018, but the number of students diminished. In 2020 all the parameters were reduced compared with 2018 and 2019, although the number or teachers was higher than 2018 but lower compared with 2019.

The following analysis focuses on the second school year semesters of 2018 and 2019 periods compared with the first semester of 2020, where 2018 is the previous semester of COVID-19's pandemic first wave, 2019's is the semester

Table 1. Moodle LMS tables and views used for KDD process.

Table or view	Description
mdl_user	Table where all Moodle users are registered
mdl_course	Courses in Universidade do Algarve registered
mdl_quiz	Quizzes that were registered
mdl_quiz_attempts	All quizz attempts that were registered
mdl_assign	Work assigns that were registered
mdl_chat	Chats registered
mdl_attendance	Student attendance to classroom
mdl_choice	Predefined inquiries registered
mdl_forum	All Forums created
mdl_glossary	Word glossary registered
mdl_lesson	Workbooks created
mdl_quizgame	Gaming quizzes registered
mdl_scorm	Activity files packages
mdl_survey	Surveys registered
mdl_wiki	Wikis created to explain subjects
mdl_workshop	Workshops registered
mdl_book	Books made available
mdl_file	Files made available
mdl_folder	Files folders created
mdl_page	Html pages created
mdl_url	Url registered
mdl_logstore_standard_log	Log table where user sessions are registered

Table 2. Universidade do Algarve context.

Parameter	2018	2019	2020
Number of teachers	1038	1223	1061
Number of courses	157	156	155
Number of disciplines	3650	3621	3344
Number of students	11196	10952	10315

of the pandemic confined period, where all classes were synchronous or asynchronous, and 2020 first semester, the data after the referred period. All results presented are filtered between this periods.

The first parameter analyzed was teachers and student's sessions registered, which are the number of times each user validated their credentials in Moodle LMS, demonstrating the interaction between users and the platform before, during and after COVID-19 first wave in Portugal.

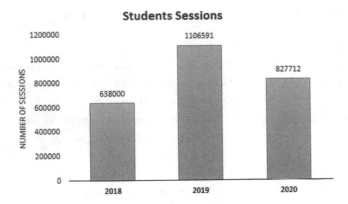

Fig. 2. Number of student's sessions

Figure 2 shows the number of students and Fig. 3, teachers sessions in Moodle LMS platform.

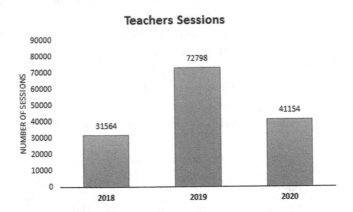

Fig. 3. Number of teacher's sessions

As presented, in the second semester of 2019, during COVID-19 first wave, the number of sessions was substantially higher compared with the same period of 2018 and with the first semester of 2020, meaning that more interaction and higher needs to access the platform data occurred. In 2020 the number of student and teacher sessions raised compared with 2018, showing a platform usage growth when traditional and non e-learning or remote teaching and learning methods are used.

This means that teachers and students realized the platform usage benefits, developed technological behaviors, applying them with traditional on premises classes, improving their teaching and studying methods.

Figure 4 shows all resources (quizzes, works assigns, chat, URL, wiki, files, etc.) used within the data periods analyzed. Resources in Moodle LMS are made available only by teachers. During COVID-19 first wave, a significant higher use of resources was registered compared with 2018 and 2020 periods where traditional education methods were applied, but in 2020 first semester, the number of resources increased compared with 2018.

The third and forth parameters are presented in Figs. 5 and 6, total number of quizzes registered and student evaluation results. In both figures, tendencies continue to be the same, a higher use of quizzes for evaluation during the COVID-19 first wave and in the first semester of 2020 the total number of quizzes is already higher than 2018 period, meaning that teachers began to believe and continue using the Moodle LMS for evaluation mixing it with the traditional educational methods. Figure 6 shows student success or failed evaluations.

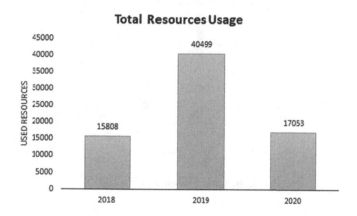

Fig. 4. Resources usage

The intention of analyzing this parameter is to verify if student's evaluation grades would change using these technologies. In 2018 and 2020, 77,1% and 78% of the student were successful in their quiz evaluation, but in 2019, when COVID-19 first wave occurred, only 68,3% were able to have positive grades in quizzes.

As showed, student's evaluation grades in 2019 were lower compared with the other semesters where the traditional education methods were applied, probably since the teachers were not physically present when students realized their quizzes, a tighter evaluation methodology was adopted. Nevertheless, results show that these technologies are able to evaluate students and the grades were not amplified and no benefiting occurred. Results also shows a higher Moodle LMS credibility because teachers increase quizzes usage in 2020, comparing the results with 2018.

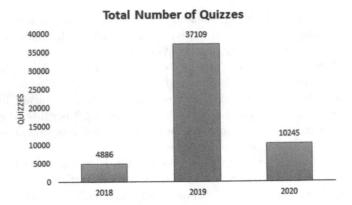

Fig. 5. Total number of quizzes

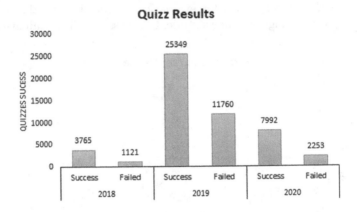

Fig. 6. Quiz evaluation results

Other parameters that can show the evaluation of Moodle LMS usage before, during and after the first wave of the COVID-19 pandemic are: work assignments and total number of files made available by teachers resources. Both parameters are presented in Figs. 7 and 8. Results show that the number of work assignments and files registered on the system, were much higher during the first wave and also the tendency of an increased use in 2020 compared to 2018.

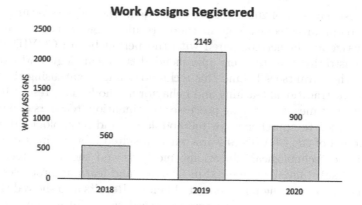

Fig. 7. Total number of work assignments

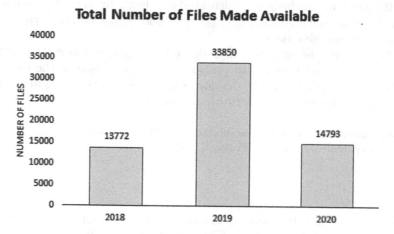

Fig. 8. Number of files made available

5   Conclusions and Future Work

Universidade do Algarve is a traditional institution where most classes are lectured on premises. During the first wave of COVID-19 pandemic all higher education institutions in Portugal were closed and both teachers and students had to adapt to new technologies and systems to continue the education activities.

In this article, a research study using knowledge discovery in database methods and learning analytics was conducted in order to evaluate usage and behaviors of both teachers and students before, during and after the first wave of COVID-19's pandemic period using Moodle LMS data in Universidade do Algarve.

Results show a huge increase of Moodle LMS usage and their resources during the COVID-19 first wave compared with the periods before and after. More accesses occurred e and more resources were used.

In the first semester of 2020, not yet concluded, when classes returned to the traditional on premises educational methods, results show that the accesses and resources usage are higher compared with the period before COVID-19's first wave, demonstrating that teachers apprehended the technologies, Moodle LMS system and the advantages behind this technology and began using them, complementing the traditional teaching and behavior methods. This research showed that, in difficult times, for learning processes continuation, teachers and students forced adaptation to apprehend new methodologies and technologies during the confined period of the COVID-19's first wave, resulted in a combine use of both traditional and technological educational methods and the use of technologies are nowadays substantially enhanced in teaching and learning processes, changing the educational paradigm implemented before. Results also showed that with Moodle LMS technologies and resources increased usage, future tendencies may end up in the implementation of active methodologies like project based learning (PBL) teaching methods in which students learn by actively engaging in real-world and personally meaningful projects and higher number synchronous classes and technologies usage.

For future work, the authors plan to develop a plug-in to integrate in Moodle LMS for teachers and students to evaluate usage and improve the education methods with this platform. The development of tools in this plug-in to create PBL teaching methods are also a future objective.

Acknowledgement. This work was supported by SI (Serviços de Informática) within UALG (Universidade do Algarve), Portugal.

References

1. Paechter, M., Maier, B.: Online or face-to-face? Students experiences and preferences in e-learning. Internet High. Educ. **13**, 292–297 (2010)
2. Mohammadyari, S., Simgh, H.: Understanding the effect of e-learning on individual performance: the role of digital literacy. Comput. Educ. **82**, 11–25 (2015)
3. Bedregal, N.,Tupacyupanqui, D.: Integración de metodologias activas y uso de aula virtual en los procesos enseñanza-aprendizaje de Matemática Discreta. In: Proceedings of the 16th LACCEI International Multi-Conference for Engineering, Education, and Technology: "Innovation in Education and Inclusion, Latin American and Caribbean Consortium of Engineering Institutions (2018)
4. Andrews, R., Haythornthwaite, C.: The Sage Handbook of E-Learning Research. SAGE, London (2007)
5. Anderson, T.: The Theory and Practice of Online Learning. Athabasca University Press, Edmonton (2008)
6. Haythornthwaite, C., Andrews, R.: E-Learning Theory and Practice. SAGE Publications Ltd., London (2011)
7. Harmelen, M.V.: Workman, Analytics for Learning and Teaching. JISC CETIS (2012)
8. Distante, D., Villa, M., Sansone, N., Faralli, S.: MILA: a SCORM-compliant interactive learning analytics tool for moodle. In: 2020 IEEE 20th International Conference on Advanced Learning Technologies (ICALT), IEEE, July (2020)

9. Fayyad, U., Piatetsky-Shapiro, G., Smyth, P.: From Data Mining to Knowledge Discovery in Databases. AI Magazine **17**, 37 (1996)

10. Escobar-Rodriguez, T., Monge-Lozano, P.: The acceptance of moodle technology by business administration students. Comput. Educ. **58**, 1085–1093 (2012)

11. About Moodle page obtained. http://docs.moodle.org/ Accessed 30 Oct 2020

12. Bedregal-Alpaca, N., Cornejo-Aparicio, V., Tupacyupanqui-Jaén, D., Flores-Silva, S.: Evaluación de la percepción estudiantil en relación al uso de la plataforma Moodle desde la perspectiva del TAM. Ingeniare. Revista chilena de ingeniería **27**, 707–718 (2019)

13. Teo, T., Zhou, M., Fan, A.C.W., Huang, F.: Factors that influence university students' intention to use moodle: a study in Macau. Educ. Technol. Res. Dev. **67**, 749–766 (2019)

14. Chung, C., Ackerman, D.: Student reactions to classroom management technology: learning styles and attitudes toward moodle. J. Educ. Bus. **90**, 217–223 (2015)

15. Assavakamhaenghan, N., et al.: Software team member configurations: a study of team effectiveness in moodle. In: 2019 10th International Workshop on Empirical Software Engineering in Practice (IWESEP), IEEE, December (2019)

16. Suartama, I.K., Setyosari, P., Sulthoni, S., Ulfa, S.: Development of ubiquitous learning environment based on moodle learning management system. Int. J. Inter. Mobile Technol. (iJIM), **14**, 182 (Aug 2020)

17. Yahya, S., Erny, A., Kamarularifin, A.: The definition and characteristics of ubiquitous learning: a discussion, . Int. J. Educ. Dev. Using Inf. Commun. Technol. **6**, 1–11 (2010)

18. Virtanen, M., Haavisto, E., Likanen, E., Kaarianem, M.: Student's perceptions on the use of a ubiquitous 360 learning environment in histotechnology: a pilot study. J. Histechnol. **41**, 49–57 (2018)

19. Chernogorova, Y., Dimova, R.: Digital transformation: a case study for providing e-services via moodle in universities. In: 2019 29th Annual Conference of the European Association for Education in Electrical and Information Engineering (EAEEIE), IEEE, September (2019)

20. Einhardt, L., Tavares, T.A., Cechinel, C.: Moodle analytics dashboard: a learning analytics tool to visualize users interactions in moodle. In: 2016 XI Latin American Conference on Learning Objects and Technology (LACLO). IEEE, October (2016)

21. Sykamiotis, G., Charitopoulos, A., Rangoussi, M., Koulouriotis, D.: Extraction and presentation of access and usage data from an e-learning platform (moodle): design and development of a software application. In: 2017 IEEE Global Engineering Education Conference (EDUCON), IEEE, April (2017)

22. Fayyad, U., Piatetsky-Shapiro, G., Smyth, P., Uthurusamy, R.: Advances in Knowledge Discovery and Data Mining. MIT Press, Menlo Park (1996)

23. Fayyad, U.: Data mining and knowledge discovery in databases: implications for scientific databases. In: Proceedings. Ninth International Conference on Scientific and Statistical Database Management (Cat. No. 97TB100150), IEEE Computer Society (1997)

24. Chen, Y., Wang, Y., Xiao, X., Shi, M.: Knowledge discovery technology based on access information mining on knowledge warehouse. In: 2011 Eighth International Conference on Fuzzy Systems and Knowledge Discovery (FSKD), IEEE, July (2011)

25. Fayyad, U., Piatetsky-Shapiro, G., Smyth, P.: From data mining to knowledge discovery: an overview. In: Advances in Knowledge Discovery and Data Mining. MIT Press, Menlo Park (1996)

26. Espinosa, R., Garriga, L., Zubcoff, J.J., Mazon, J.-N.: Linked open data mining for democratization of big data. In: 2014 IEEE International Conference on Big Data (Big Data), IEEE, October (2014)
27. Lei, F., Hexin, C.: Analysis methods of workflow execution data based on data mining. In: 2009 Second International Workshop on Knowledge Discovery and Data Mining, IEEE, January (2009)
28. Hou, Z.: Data mining method and empirical research for extension architecture design. In: 2018 International Conference on Intelligent Transportation, Big Data & Smart City (ICITBS), IEEE, January (2018)

Deaf Inclusion Through Brazilian Sign Language: A Computational Architecture Supporting Artifacts and Interactive Applications and Tools

L. S. Garcia[1(✉)], T. A. Felipe[2(✉)], A. P. Guedes[1(✉)], D. R. Antunes[3(✉)],
C. E. Iatskiu[4(✉)], E. Todt[1(✉)], J. Bueno[5(✉)], D. de F. G. Trindade[6(✉)],
D. A. Gonçalves[7(✉)], R. Canteri[8(✉)], M. C. Canal[1(✉)], M. A. M. Ferreira[1(✉)],
A. M. C. Silva[9(✉)], L. Galvão[1(✉)], and L. Rodrigues[1(✉)]

[1] Department of Informatics, Federal University of Paraná, Curitiba, PR, Brazil
[2] National Institute for Deaf Education, Rua das Laranjeiras, 232, Rio de Janeiro, RJ, Brazil
tfelipe@ines.gov.br
[3] Informatics Department, Federal University of Technology, Ponta Grossa, PR, Brazil
drantunes@utfpr.edu.br
[4] UniGuairacá Center, Guarapuava, PR, Brazil
[5] Department of Design, Federal University of Paraná, Reitoria, Centro, Curitiba, PR, Brazil
[6] Center of Technological Sciences, State University of Paraná, Bandeirantes, PR, Brazil
danielaf@uenp.edu.br
[7] Institute of Computing, University of Campinas, Campinas, SP, Brazil
[8] Federal University of Mato Grosso do Sul, Campus do Pantanal, Corumbá, MS, Brazil
[9] Engineering Department, State University of Pará, Belém, PA, Brazil

Abstract. In major hearing cultures, deaf people still face difficulties related to the teaching-learning processes, being computational tools one of them. This scenario triggered our research path in 2007 aiming to attend to the communicational needs of the Brazilian Deaf communities This effort has involved researchers from Computer Science and Linguistics in Participatory Design practices and developed an architecture for Brazilian Portuguese to Sign Language (Libras) machine translation together with interactive educational frameworks, applications and toolswhose bases were the Direct Way Literacy and the Bilingual Education for the Deaf. The architecture has as its principal component the CORE-SL, a computational formalism for the BSL phonology with indexing, storing, retrieving, and scalability properties, among others. We carried out a morphosyntactic evaluation of results available in related literature which allowed us to verify that those translators still generate signs and phrases considered ungrammatical by the deaf community.

Keywords: CORE-SL · Deaf · Brazilian Portuguese · Brazilian sign language ·
BSL · Libras · Literacy · Bilingual literacy

© Springer Nature Switzerland AG 2021
M. Antona and C. Stephanidis (Eds.): HCII 2021, LNCS 12769, pp. 167–185, 2021.
https://doi.org/10.1007/978-3-030-78095-1_14

1 Introduction

All around the world, deaf people have their identities and their cultures. Their sign languages are crucial for them. Sign languages are the preferential languages for deaf communities [1–3, 5], which are also used by indigenous populations with deaf members. Despite the legal support received in major hearing cultures that use oral-auditive languages, such as the Brazilian one, deaf people still face difficulties related to the teaching-learning processes. Computational tools that could potentially be instruments for social inclusion and plain citizenship is one aspect of these difficulties. This scenario triggered the beginning of our research path in 2007 through a research project which aimed to attend to the communicational needs of the Brazilian deaf communities and, in this way, contribute to their genuine social inclusion [33–37, 45–47].

This effort, continuously involving researchers from Computer Science and Linguistics through an interdisciplinary prism and Participatory Design practices together with deaf communities, developed an architecture with several modules for Brazilian Portuguese to Brazilian Sign Language - BSL (Libras) machine translation associated with referential products and interactive applications and tools [31].

In Brazil, several research groups focus on automatic and semi-automatic translation from oral to sign languages [2, 6, 16, 42–44, 48, 50] among others. Through the review of literature together with tests, it was observed that these translators still disregard morphosyntactic aspects of Libras, which, in turn, may cause the generation of ungrammatical sentences. According to [18–20], Libras is a flexing language, that is: there is a group of verbs that have morphosyntactic flexion. Therefore, for the generation of a sentence, or even a sign, a pertinent approach is the creation of a morphological model that formalizes the process of formation of signs employing rules. This model further generates the outputs using an avatar, that will also be generated from morpho-phonological rules.

Our architecture has as its principal component the CORE-SL [3–5], a computational formalism for the BSL phonology with indexing, storing, retrieving, and scalability properties, among others. By hypothesis, this formalism is universally valid within sign languages, since though they differ between them in phonological, morphological, syntactic, semantic, and discursive levels, the surface level, the phonological one, is determined by the set of possible physiological movements. The architecture was projected to include the computational representation of the other necessary linguistic knowledge: morphological, syntactical, semantic, and discursive. The main challenge of the project presented in this paper consists of the adequacy of the intelligent avatar BSL interpretation. The degree of adequacy can be measured by the intelligent avatar acceptance by the deaf communities.

The research work described in the present paper addresses all these linguistic levels within formal and computational languages. The architecture has, up to the present moment, its central formal module (CORE-SL), the sign register, the morphosyntactic rules, and the SignWriting generator. The other modules are currently in development.

A parallel track was defined to proceed to the development of deaf's educational supporting artifacts, tools, and applications. At this moment, the project has a few available artifacts, namely:

A structure was built to complete the requirements for collaborative environments. This structure adds deaf and interpreter actors and Libras intrinsic features which, together, allow for inclusion. A set of requirements for an environment to support critical bilingual literacy of deaf children in Libras and in written Brazilian Portuguese [7–9, 26, 27] and a set of requirements about testing questions for deaf [10, 11] were also constructed. A framework to inform game developers about the contents and the communicational needs of deaf children in early childhood [11–14, 29], as well as learning objects to support critical literacy [26, 27] were created. Additionally, educational games for deaf children emerged [12–14, 29].

As one of the Project's tools, we have the CORE-SL SignWriting generator, that converts sign representations to SignWriting [39–41]. The project also has a sign register (in the CORE-SL formalism) [38], the morphosyntactic structure of the lexicon [56], a tool for collaborative inclusive meetings [58–60], and an authoring tool for building educational games for deaf children [12–14]. A tool to support virtual concept map building for deaf education is under development.

All these artifacts, applications, and tools will be integrated as soon as the entire grammatical and discursive set of rules are developed and the intelligent avatar is working. These results and the ongoing work complete the project's innovative contributions that will support access to education, social inclusion, and full rights to Brazilian deaf communities.

This paper is organized as follows: Sect. 2 presents related work. Section 3 shows the architecture and its main components: the CORE-SL phonological base, the formal model, and a 3D avatar generation for syntactic-semantic-discursive and emotional expressions. Section 4 describes the main services developed and under developing. Section 5 rescues a few artifacts and applications, and, finally, Sect. 6 states the conclusions and current challenges.

2 Related Work

Results of some efforts towards the same goal as ours are available in the related literature and tools. TLibras Project [42, 43] aimed to develop a translator from PT-BR to Libras, as well as to create a set of phonological and morphosyntactic-discursive rules for the generation of signs and phrases from a corpus filmed in Libras. However, the team responsible for creating the avatar and the phonological level programming for the inclusion of signs was not able to finish this stage. Therefore, the team who worked with the production process created PUL0 – (Portuguese-UNL-LIST de Oralizer) [42, 44, 48]. PUL0 is a unidirectional automatic translation system, which translates an oral-auditory language, Brazilian Portuguese (Br-Portuguese), to the linear representation (Libras Script for Translation - LIST) of a gestural-visual language. Its goal would be to convert a sentence originally produced in Brazilian Portuguese into a specialized transcription of Libras, which would be signaled by an intelligent avatar from the phonological settings, i.e., the five parameters: hand configuration, articulation point, directionality, movement, and facial expressions. However, PUL0 creators were unable to test the program.

Another initiative was Prodeaf [52], a proposal of text and voice translation from Br-Portuguese to Libras. The translation is done by two tools: a mobile application and a plugin for websites. Prodeaf is currently owned by the HandTalk team - which evolved from a project called Falibras, a computer system that converts text and audio into Libras. HandTalk performs digital and automatic translation for Libras, through a website translator and an application. Another translator proposal is VLibras [6, 42], which consists of a set of tools aiming to translate digital content (text, audio, and video). According to the UFPB-LAVID Research Group that works with this application, the system had syntactic and semantic deficiencies and therefore there was a need to create an automatic translation component that brings a formal language of syntactic-semantic translation rules description and grammar [42]. The research on morphosyntactic and discursive issues of this translator through an avatar is still under development, being built, equally to our knowledge, in the form of academic products.

Research of [2, 16, 50] presented a rule-based machine translation system composed of a translator module that analyzes the inputs and then converts them into an intermediate representation. This system is called "Intermediate Language", which serves as the input for the animation module.

A morphosyntactic evaluation of these translators was presented by [56]. Considering an entry in PT-BR, it was observed if the output follows the grammar of Libras. It was possible to see that, although these translators have achieved their main goals, they still generate signs or phrases that are considered ungrammatical by the Deaf Community. Therefore, we hypothesize that such incongruity is due to the disregarding of phono-morpho-syntactic-discoursive rules for the equivalence between the unities in the two languages.

3 The Architecture and Its Main Components

Our will to design for the Deaf motivated our project. We drew on both the classical Natural Language Processing knowledge acquired during one of our project leader's doctoral thesis [30] and on Stokes' studies on Sign Languages structure based on American Sign Language [57], to launch our project in 2007. The proposal consisted of a Libras lexicon [45, 46], followed by the signs phonological decomposition built and populated through participatory workshops with a few deaf community students [3]. Even though phonology was a focus, the architecture already considered the development of additional linguistic modules and their integration into the phonological one. Additionally, there were three levels of software: i) the basic software, consisting of CORE-SL, the model that allowed the decomposition of signs by their minimal phonological elements; ii) the tools, which met the needs of different user profiles as well as the role of services for the applications; and iii) the artifacts and applications, which met the needs of distinct user profiles including that of the student, teacher, interpreter, and developer [31]. As the project went on, this architecture evolved. Figure 1 shows the revised version of the architecture.

During the initial structure of HCI-SL Architecture, it was realized that most of the fundamental computer services needed a structure for representation, storage, and recovery of signs. That is why, during the process, the modeling of gesture characteristics (hand configurations, location, orientation), spatial (movements), and non-manual

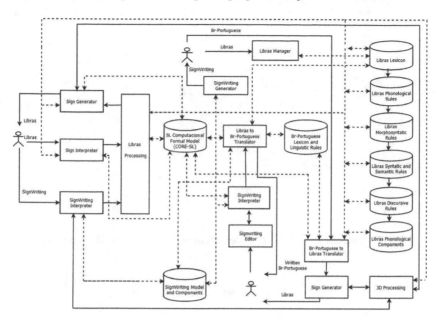

Fig. 1. The CORE-SL Arquitecture. Revised for this paper. (Source: The Authors)

expressions was necessary. Thus, it was sought to understand how the signs were structured linguistically and how to make an abstraction of this structure in a computational model.

Since then, the phonological model has evolved into a formal model with indexing, storage, scalability recovery properties.

Formalizaition of CORE-SL occurred through a Context-Free Grammar (CFG) whose structure was derived after an extensive study of several models of the phonology of sign languages. Thus, CORE-SL encompassed the necessary properties for the computational representation of the gestural and spatial characteristics (i.e., movements) of signs, enabling the description of any linguistically valid signs [4, 5].

Additionally, CORE-SL described a set of properties to enable the represented signs to be used in multiple architectural contexts: sequentiality and simultaneity (aspects of sign execution), recoverability (ability to recover the represented signs), correctness (guarantee of correct representation), universality (sign representation of any SL), reproducibility (sign generation for a 3D avatar or SignWriting), among others.

CORE-SL also explored the contexts of use of the formal model, such as the application in the linguistic contexts of translation as a meta-language, of input (automatic recognition via camera) and output through SignWriting and 3D Avatars, apart of tools for description and storage of signals. Figure 2 and Fig. 3 schematize the CORE-SL model.

To support the development of intelligent avatars from the point of view of 3D generation and considering the relevance of facial expressions in Libras, a system of synthesis of emotional expressions has been developed [32]. Most virtual interpreters represented by 3D avatars built using formal models that parametrize the specific characteristics of

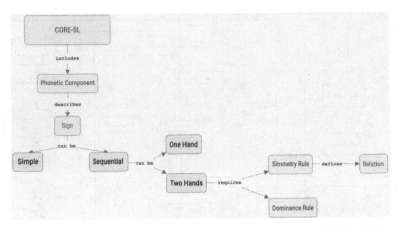

Fig. 2. Structure of CORE-SL model. (Source: Antunes et al. 2015, p. 102)

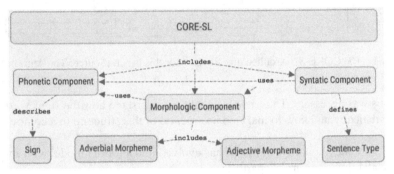

Fig. 3. The morphological component and how it relates to phonological and syntactic components. (Source: Antunes et al. 2015, p. 112)

sign languages still consider facial expressions as a minor resource in a sign language. Hence, these interpreters ignore the crucial role that facial expressions and emotions play in the context of the message conveyed, also for oral-auditory languages in the face-to-face spoken mode interaction.

In this research, in order to define a parameterized facial model for use in sign languages, a system of synthesis of facial expressions was proposed through a 3D avatar. Such avatar was built from a prototype that had a model of facial landmarks, separated by facial regions, and it encompassed a model of basic expressions, using the facial bases AKDEF and JAFEE as a reference. This system allows for representing complex expressions using interpolation of intensity values in geometric animation in a simplified way, with centroid control and independent region displacement in the 3D model. An application of the space-time model for facial landmarks was also proposed, with the aims of the behavior and relation of the centroids in the synthesis of the basic expressions, defining which geometric points are relevant in the process of interpolation and animation of the expressions. There was also the development of a system for exporting facial data according to the hierarchical format used in most 3D avatars sign language interpreters.

The purpose of this system is to encourage integration into formal computer models that already exist in the literature, also allowing the adaptation and alteration of values and intensities in the representation of emotions. Thus, the models and concepts presented intend the integration of a facial model for the representation of expressions in the synthesis of signals, offering a simplified and optimized proposal for the application of resources in 3D avatars. Figure 4 present the basic emotions and the animation process.

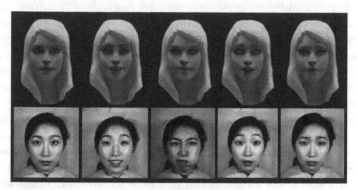

Fig. 4. Basic emotions represented in the virtual environment. The top row shows faces built with the 3D mesh, from left to right: Neutral, Joy, Anger, Surprise, and Sadness. The bottom row shows the samples of the JAFFE dataset used as a reference for deformations in the 3D mesh. (Source: Gonçalves D. A. 2017, p. 44).

Additionally, several other modules and bases of the Architecture have been developed, such as: the basis of primitives of the phonology of Libras; the CORE-SL-Sign-Register, a system that allows the registration and storage of signals from their description in the formal model CORE-SL and in the future will allow for the interpretation in Libras of the signs registered; the basis of primitives of SignWriting; CORE-SL-SignWriting-Generator, a system that, from the description of signs in the formal model, generates written representations in the SignWriting system; and Lex-Libras, which describes the morphosyntactic components of the inflected verbs in Libras and their corresponding complements from the phonological level, that is, parameters that compose the specific morphemes.

4 Services

After the development and formalization of the core of the architecture, the design and development of other linguistic-computer models stages began. A mini corpus of Libras was created in order to carry out concept tests of the services that were under development, as well as to allow their integration. Determined by a linguistic prism, this process consisted in the selection of a set of signs which were able to represent the main phenomena identified by the phonological and the morphosyntactic analysis, considering the specificities of the set of primitives of SignWriting. Another innovative feature of this process was its source: the signs were extracted from a real context use of

Libras, a didactic material for deaf children about Dengue fever [17, 22], and, therefore, the material did not consist on a simple collection of arbitrary signs. The "Pequeno Grande Vilão" ("The Little Big Villain", in free translation) deals with the problem of the Aedes Aegypti mosquito, a common vector in the tropics and during the summer in subtropical regions of Brazil [1]. This story was represented in the glosses system created by researcher Tanya Felipe for the Brazilian Sign Language from a system available for the American Sign Language [57]. Glosses had additions of diacritical signs and others that were not previously used by researchers from other countries, since the transcription considered the Brazilian Portuguese instead of English - which has no morpheme for gender mark, among other differences. It is also important to highlight that this mini corpus was created as a result of the change in strategy in order to solve the language issues in a bottom-up way, from the complexity of the Brazilian Portuguese to Libras translation process. The bottom-up approach sedimented the constructed linguistic-computational knowledge and previews the corpus extension for it to cover the phenomena being captured in the course of the process.

Considering the need for outputs in a graphic version of Sign Language, a basis of all the primitives of SignWriting was created and populated by our team. Subsequently, we developed the CORE-SL-SignWriting-Generator [39–41], a system that, from the description of a sign in the formal model, generates its written representation in the SignWriting system. SignWriting, in its turn, is a writing system that can graphically represent any sign language. In the related literature, several tools are found to provide support to the Deaf who wish to use SignWriting.

Felipe [17–19] created a gloss system of transcription that represented Libras signs in words of Brazilian Portuguese and graphic and typographic signs, aiming to present data about Libras sentence structure in context, through conversation and spontaneous narratives filmed and collected at the Deaf Association of Pernambuco, in the northeast of Brazil. Therefore, the scholar had to modify and add to meet the conventions used by linguists who used glosses in the English language. This gloss transcription system for Libras' linguistic description, also used for the database of data collected in Rio de Janeiro at the National Federation of Deaf Education, was used for the transcription of CORE-SL data when transcoding tests of the CORE-SL-SignWriting-Generator tool. The objective was to assess whether the tool had the potential to generate the SignWriting signals from the transcription of the Libras signs by CORE-SL. Figure 5 and Fig. 6 illustrate the generation process and its result. Figure 7 shows a hypothetical application.

After the development of CORE-SL, a further step was the creation of the CORE-SL-Sign-Register system, which allows the registration and storage of signals from its description in the formal CORE-SL and, in the future, will allow for the interpretation of the Libras signs registered [37].

The CORE-SL-Sign-Register is a computational tool to enable the proof of concept of the CORE-SL model, specifically at the phonological level of Brazilian Sign Language, that consists of hand configuration (HC), palm orientation, movement, and non-manual features, such as body and facial Expressions. The sign cataloging tool provides a standard textual representation for the signs and foresees the use of an intelligent avatar to interpret the inserted sign. The main expected result is an architecture with its

Signwriting Generator Operation

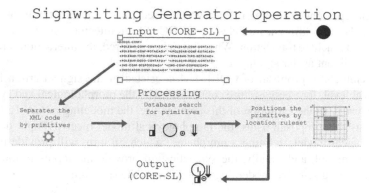

Fig. 5. Operation of the SignWriting generator from the CORE-SL. Figure 6 shows how the comic book could be printed in case the generator output was used. Operation of the SignWriting generator from the CORE-SL. (Source: Iatskiu C. E. 2018, p.1017)

Original do Gibi	O mosquito da dengue nasce e se desenvolve em água parada!
Glosa da Libras	ÁGUA LARGAD@. MOSQUITO D-E-N-G-U-E SURGIR DESENVOLVER
SignWriting	

Fig. 6. Original comic book text, translation to gloss, and SignWriting generator output. (Source: Iatskiu C. E. 2018 p.1020)

Fig. 7. Hypothetical version of the comic book with the SignWriting generator output. (Source: Iatskiu C. E. 2018 p.1020)

central sign representation model tested and revised for future integration of the registered signals with different modules of the HCI-SL architecture, such as the Libras dictionary and machine translation. When a sign is registered, the interaction screen will show the intelligent avatar signing it.

The architectural proposal of CORE-L 4 consisted of the sign insertion from its phonological level, foreseeing future connection with the morphological and syntactic-discursive levels. In the evolution of this architecture, the modeling of Lex-Libras [43] complements this proposal. Thus, the morphological model receives input data from the phonological model, defining a morpheme, which, in turn, will provide inputs to the syntactic model, and, finally, the syntactic will provide the inputs to the phono-morphosyntactic-discursive model. Figure 8 presents the structure.

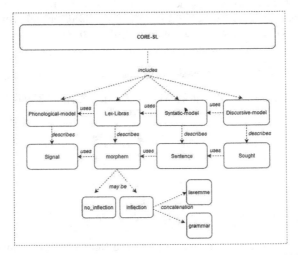

Fig. 8. CORE-SL operating structure. (Source: Silva A. M. C. 2020, p.19)

Lex-Libras presents two models, one in a Context-Free Grammar (GLC) formal structure, and the other in a tree-based model. It uses some phonological structures (the five parameters of Libras) as input, grouping them to represent a morpheme. The morpheme was described in two ways: inflection and no_inflection. The inflection node defines the signs that inflect. Meanwhile, the no_inflection node defines those that do not inflect [56] and that are described and specified by the phonological rules of CORE-SL.

5   Artifacts and Interactive Applications

Several conceptual frameworks were created with the potential to inform developers of services and applications for the Deaf the requirements of interaction Deaf culture via Computer and developed a series of applications in a fully participatory way with the various user profiles of our environments. These frameworks were created in parallel to the linguistic trail after the development of CORE-SL architecture, considering the high level of complexity of the translation between Brazilian Portuguese and Libras.

This set of products assumes Libras as the first language and mediating language in any interaction of the Deaf with other interlocutors, including computers and communication systems.

Aiming to support the bilingual education of deaf children, advocated both by the communities themselves and by their reference educators [17–25], and encompassing the Direct Way Literacy [8, 9, 53, 54], this process was initiated through the specification of requirements for applications to support literacy. In this journey, the requirements of a Virtual Learning Environment (VLE) to support literacy in written Brazilian Portuguese were identified. This led to the creation of a pedagogical architecture to support literacy and education with certain requirements of accessible tests, a transdisciplinary methodology for the creation of games and games to support bilingual education. All these tools were included in the update of the conceptual model of the Virtual Learning Environment. These works are reviewed below. The broad extension of the Project, our willingness to cover it as a whole, and the short relative space for its description determined a panoramic approach. Therefore, for additional information about each one of them, as well as to consult their respective related works and references, the readers should refer to the works mentioned here.

5.1 Bilingual Virtual Learning Environment

Bilingual literacy, our educational assumption for the Deaf, consists on using Sign Language (L1) for the learning of a written form of a second spoken language, the Brazilian Portuguese (L2) in the Brazilian context. However, the bilingual school does not yet have a bilingual teaching/learning approach that equally weights the teaching of the two proposed languages. Therefore, in most cases, the school context also does not use computer artifacts as resources to support the acquisition of knowledge by deaf students. The work of [8, 9], adopts the methodology of Action Research with the motivation to confront and change this reality. The mentioned research advances in proposing changes in the bilingual school environment. Foucambert [28] and Razet's unite theory and practice in a project of bilingual literacy, which was mainly structured and systematized in the principles Direct Way Literacy [8, 9, 28, 53, 54], a French socio-interactionist method. This method conceives literacy as the acquisition of reading and writing skills from the social reality to the reading and writing, thus appropriating several textual genres likely to be of interest to the target audience of the process, in our case, deaf children. This Action Research project occurred over more than three years within a bilingual context school located in the Metropolitan Region of Curitiba, and it brought pedagogical benefits to the target school, providing qualitative support for the construction of the conceptual solution of a computational environment to support bilingual literacy of deaf children. In addition to the requirements derived from each axis of knowledge treated throughout the work, the research also presented a use case diagram, a class diagram, and a description of situations of use predicted for the environment based on the activities of the literacy project designed by Action Research in the target school, as well as the preliminary architecture of the computational environment outlined [8, 9].

The newly described requirements served as the basis for the construction of a literacy environment prototype. In the evolution of the Project and drawing on transdisciplinary knowledge, our understanding of the need for a virtual learning environment to support written Brazilian Portuguese acquisition [26, 27], through the determined requirements and the conceptual model of the virtual environment for bilingual literacy and learning. The environment is based on one hand, on the Virtual Learning Environments already appropriated by Brazilian education, such as Moodle, and, on the other hand, on the concept of Direct Way Literacy [8, 9, 26, 27, 53, 54].

Around the Virtual Bilingual Learning Environment, though also stand-alone, and attending both to the end user's and the developer's needs, we created some additional frameworks, tools, and applications. They are roughly described in the following subsections.

5.2   Inclusive Virtual Meeting Framework and Tool

The right of the Deaf to be co-creators of knowledge [58–60] motivated the study of this process in a Community of Practice (CoP), which was formed by Deaf and hearing students with the participation of an interpreter. The observations allowed us to determine some aspects presented as a conceptual framework to support the design of CoP collaborative virtual environments inclusive of the Deaf. Inclusion, in this context, mainly involves ensuring the possibility of mediation of an interpreter in the absence of a bilingual teacher. To verify its applicability, the framework aided the development of a tool for video conferencing that considers the most significant and critical aspects to promote interaction between Deaf and hearing students. Such a tool aims to support both the inclusive construction of knowledge and the construction of identity knowledge by deaf learners themselves.

5.3   Accessible Testing Requirements for Deaf Learners

The types of questions used in Computer-Based Assessment (CBA) in Virtual Learning Environments have accessibility problems in the context of deaf students. Due to these problems, the interaction with the types of questions is compromised, so deaf students may be prevented from completing the tasks as hearing students do. The work of [10, 11] presents a set of recommendations that were found in the literature related to the subject of research and classified in three categories (i.e., "Accessibility in AVAs for the Deaf", "Accessibility for Information and Communication Technology (ICT) project for the literacy of Deaf" and "Accessibility in CBA"). Some of the recommendations were fully maintained, while others were adapted and rewritten in the context of the question types in VLE. The set of recommendations built into the work was composed of accessibility recommendations for six types of questions (i.e., Association, Dissertation, Gap, Multiple Choice, Short Answer, and True/False). The recommendations were classified according to each of the six types of questions and their corresponding application in questions and answers. In addition to the recommendations, we defined three teachers, student, and developer profiles, and, for each recommendation, there were suggested uses. The set of recommendations was evaluated by IT specialists and deaf teachers. The results of this evaluation were positive both on the usefulness of the use of the recommendations, and their accuracy, clarity, and completeness in the context of the hypothesis.

5.4 Frameworks for Building Games to Support Early Childhood Education for Deaf Children

Three pillars built a conceptual framework for the design of educational games for deaf children: Teaching Methodology for Early Childhood Education, Educational Electronic Games, and Human-Computer Interaction. Based on the conceptual model, the effort resulted in an authoring tool that allows the construction of educational games to assist in the education of deaf children in early childhood, a crucial phase in human linguistic development. The target audience of the authoring tool is bilingual literacy teachers. On the other hand, the games are aimed at deaf children in early childhood. The work presented the main components that form the conceptual framework, a guide for the design of educational games for deaf children. The tool was developed for web environments, and some prototypes of games were developed. The artifacts and prototypes were evaluated in specific experiments with the deaf community. The results of the experiments were positive and validated the authorial tool and games underlying frameworks [12–14].

The recently described framework was complemented by CAJEDUS game design methodology (which in Brazilian Portuguese stands for Criação de Jogos para a Educação de crianças Surdas or "Game Creation for Deaf Children Education"). The methodology arose from the problem that games for deaf children in the literature were not entirely accessible or disregarded the real linguistic context and its significance [29]. In addition, there is a need for computational tools that support the acquisition of Bilingual Education by deaf children [12–14, 29]. Thus, CAJEDUS emerged as a methodology for creating educational games for 4 or 5-year-old deaf children, designed for game developers who have little or no experience with deaf children. The methodology considers ethical aspects, accessibility, implementation of games, and education based on official educational guidelines on Early Childhood Education [29]. A case study with specialists in game development was designed to validate the methodology. The specialists designed a Game Design Document (GDD) and a game prototype based on the forest environment context. This choice reflected the valorization of Brazilian indigenous culture, also intending to reflect upon culture diversity. From the feedback obtained in the case study, it was possible to ascertain the usefulness and importance of CAJEDUS, in addition to refining it to a simpler and more practical version.

6 Conclusions and Future Work

This article presented research outcomes that have been developed by a Research Group over 13 years. Our group consists of members from various subfields of Computing, Linguistics, and Deaf Education, and our main objective is to support bilingual education in BSL (Brazilian SignWriting - Libras)-Brazilian Portuguese. Therefore, continuously since its inception, in a multi and transdisciplinary way, the group has been generating knowledge that falls within all areas of knowledge and disciplines involved and in no particular one alone. As a second innovative feature, the project has continuously adopted and practiced, since its beginning, Participatory Design with deaf communities of Deaf Culture in Brazil.

The defined architecture has 3 levels: the formal model of description of BSL or Libras (CORE-SL) at the base, the intermediate level of services, and that of artifacts and applications. Given the high degree of complexity and the need to involve so many different researcher profiles and types of resources in the linguistic axis - such as intelligent avatar translation and signaling - we carried out a vein of parallel research in order to build knowledge so that, when the avatar was available, it could be integrated into the series of applications for bilingual education. Currently, the architecture has some bases and modules and, likewise, there is a set of different artifacts, applications and tools developed and under development for future integration.

The available and ongoing products from the project are centered around Libras - Brazilian Portuguese bilingual literacy. They are also structured around the general education virtual environment, which uses all the knowledge artifacts, tools, and linguistic-computational bases and models. Referring to the Brazilian Sign Language - Libras Project outcomes' expected appropriation, the virtual learning environment's profiles are the (Deaf) student, the teacher, the interpreter, and the developer. The brackets refer to the possibility of the VLE be appropriate in inclusive regular education. Apart from the VLE, the last profile also benefits from the knowledge concerning artifacts, learning about frameworks, requirements, methodologies, among others.

There are three more applications under development: a mobile application to report violence against women accessible to the Deaf [49]; a virtual reality environment to support deaf children's education [15], and an application for sexual education designed to target deaf young women [51]. We also intend to advance regarding the set of participant's profiles, to include deaf students in all participatory design processes.

As far as the linguistic axis is concerned, the conclusion of Libras' syntactic rules is expected, as well as the specification of its semantic-discursive rules, the construction of a minimum-maximum signal corpus from the formal computational point of view, and the population of a sign corpus extracted from Libras in context - but in a controlled situation of capturing the signs by image processing.

Despite the legacy of innovative knowledge, the project's participants (spread around Brazilian territory: the Federal University of Paraná, National Institute for Deaf Education, Federal University of Technology – Paraná, State University of Paraná, Guairacá University Center, Government State of Amapá, State University of Pará and the Federal University of Mato Grosso do Sul) are aware of the need to establish additional partnerships with other research groups to expedite the achievement of objectives and, above all, to be able to develop products robust enough to be truly accepted and appropriated by our deaf communities.

We believe in the innovative and social potential of partnerships, just as we defend the greater relevance of social action over the search for individual groups' achievements. In this sense, the current needs of the project demand collaboration with groups that know about generating 3D avatars from formal models of linguistic-computational descriptions, with research laboratories holding 3D technology and, finally, institutional or corporate financial support, maybe in accordance with the Informatics Brazilian law, in the production of Brazilian Sign Language - Libras with output in a grammatically accurate intelligent avatar. Our main objective is to develop free software based on the knowledge and prototypes available, both regarding the translator issue and the virtual learning environment. Only by fulfilling these current demands that the project will achieve its goals and will be fully accepted and appropriated by deaf communities in Brazil.

Acknowledgements. The authors thank particularly Lúcia Cherem for having introduced them to the Direct Way Literacy and facilitated the access to the research group that developed this methodology. This study was financed in part by the Coordenação de Aperfeiçoamento de Pessoal de Nível Superior - Brasil (CAPES) - Finance Code 001. The Federal University of Paraná (UFPR) and the Postgraduate Program in Informatics (PPGINF) the development of this research.

References

1. Alves, J.M.: Histórias em quadrinhos e educação infantil. Psicologia: Ciências e Profissão, Psicol. cienc. prof. **21**(3), 2–9 (2001)
2. Amaral, W.: Sistema de transcrição da Língua Brasileira de Sinais voltado à produção de conteúdo sinalizado por avatares 3D, Tese de doutorado, Departamento de Engenharia de Computação e Automação Industrial, Faculdade de Engenharia Elétrica e de Computação, Universidade Estadual de Campinas (2012)
3. Antunes, D.R., Guimarães, C., García, L.S., Oliveira, L., Fernandes, S.: A framework to support development of sign language human-computer interaction: building tools for effective information access and inclusion of the deaf. In: 5th International Conference on Research Challenges in Information Science, RCIS, Gosier, pp. 126–137 (2011)
4. Antunes, D.R., Guedes, A.L.P., García, L.S.: A context-based collaborative framework to build sign language databases by real users. In: Antona, M., Stephanidis, C. (eds.) UAHCI 2015. LNCS, vol. 9176, pp. 327–338. Springer, Cham (2015). https://doi.org/10.1007/978-3-319-20681-3_31
5. Antunes, D.R.: Proposta de um modelo computacional para representação de sinais em uma arquitetura de serviços HCI-SL para Línguas de Sinais, Tese de Doutorado, Programa de Pós-Graduação em Informática, Setor de Ciências Exatas, Universidade Federal do Paraná, Curitiba (2015)
6. Araújo, T.: Uma solução para geração automática de trilhas em Língua Brasileira de Sinais em conteúdos multimídia, Ph.D. Dissertation, Programa de Pós-Graduação em Engenharia Elétrica e de Computação, Universidade Federal do Rio Grande do Norte (2012)
7. Bueno, J., García, L.S., Ulbricht, V.R.: Cor, Forma e Estilo de desenho: um estudo exploratório sobre as preferências de crianças surdas. In: 6° Congresso Nacional de Ambientes Hipermídia para Aprendizagem (CONAHPA), João Pessoa, pp. 1–11 (2013)
8. Bueno, J., García, L.S.: Action research to generate requirements for a computational environment supporting bilingual literacy of deaf children. In: Universal Access in Human-Computer Interaction, Universal Access to Information and Knowledge; 8th International Conference on Universal Access in Human-Computer Interaction, Heraklion, Crete, pp. 245–253 (2014)
9. Bueno, J., García, L.S.: Pesquisa-Ação na Construção de Insumos Conceituais de um Ambiente Computacional de Apoio ao Letramento Bilíngue de Crianças Surdas. In: 26° Brazilian Symposium on Computers in Education/26° Simpósio Brasileiro de Informática na Educação (SBIE 2015); 4° Congresso Brasileiro de Informática na Educação, Maceió, pp. 887–895 (2015)

10. Canal, M.C., García, L.S.: Recomendações de Acessibilidade para Surdos dos Tipos de Questões Usadas na Avaliação Baseada em Computador em Ambientes Virtuais de Aprendizagem. In: Simpósio Brasileiro de Informática na Educação. Anais do 26o Simpósio Brasileiro de Informática na Educação, Macéio, pp. 812–821 (2015)

11. Canal, M.C., Sánchez García, L.: Research on accessibility of question modalities used in computer-based assessment (CBA) for deaf education. In: Stephanidis, C., Antona, M. (eds.) UAHCI 2014. LNCS, vol. 8514, pp. 265–276. Springer, Cham (2014). https://doi.org/10.1007/978-3-319-07440-5_25

12. Canteri, R., García, L.S., Felipe, T.A., Antunes, D.R., Iatskiu, C.E.: An evaluation method of educational computer games for Deaf Children based on design guideline. In: Universal Access in Human-Computer Interaction, Access to Learning, Health and Well-Being, 9th International Conference On Universal Access In Human-Computer Interaction, Los Angeles, pp. 409–419 (2015)

13. Canteri, R., García, L.S., Felipe, T.A., Galvão, L., Antunes, D.R.: Conceptual framework to support a web authoring tool of educational games for Deaf Children. In: 11th International Conference on Computer Supported Education, Heraklion, Crete, vol. 2, pp. 226–235 (2019)

14. Canteri, R., García, L.S., Felipe, T.A., Iatskiu, C.E.: Vídeo games in education of Deaf Children. In: 17th International Conference on Enterprise Information Systems, Barcelona, pp. 122–129 (2015)

15. Conceição, V.A.J., García, L.S., Felipe, T.A.: Investigando a Gamificação no Ensino de Estudantes Surdos. In: II Fórum da Pós-Graduação em Ciência da Computação do Paraná/I Mostra de Trabalhos de Pós-graduandos em Ciência da Computação do Paraná, Cascavel-PR, p. 25 (2020)

16. De Martino, J.M., et al.: Signing avatars: making education more inclusive. Univers. Access Inf. Soc. Int. J. **16**, 793–808 (2017)

17. Felipe, T.A.: Bilinguismo e surdez. Trabalhos em Lingüística Aplicada **14**, 101–112 (1989)

18. Felipe, T.: A relação sintático-semântica dos verbos e seus argumentos na Língua Brasileira de Sinais (LIBRAS): vol. 1, Tese de doutoramento, Programa de Pós-Graduação da Faculdade de Letras, Universidade Federal do Rio de Janeiro (1998)

19. Felipe, T.: A relação sintático-semântica dos verbos e seus argumentos na Língua Brasileira de Sinais (LIBRAS): vol. 2. Tese de doutorado, Programa de Pós-Graduação da Faculdade de Letras, Universidade Federal do Rio de Janeiro (1998)

20. Felipe, T.A.: Sistema de flexão verbal na LIBRAS: os classificadores enquanto marcadores de flexão de gênero. In: 1th Congresso Surdez e Pós-Modernidade: Novos Rumos para a Educação Brasileira; 7th Congresso Internacional do INES; Seminário Nacional do INES, Rio de Janeiro, pp. 37–59 (2002)

21. Felipe, T.A.: Os processos de formação de palavra na LIBRAS. ETD: Educação Temática Digital **7**(2), 200–217 (2006). Accessed 21 Nov 2020

22. Felipe, T.A.: O discurso verbo-visual na Língua Brasileira de Sinais – Libras. In: Bakhtiniana: Revista de Estudos do Discurso, vol. 8, no. 2, pp. 67–89 (2013). Accessed 19 Nov 2020

23. Felipe, T.A.: Banco de dados para línguas de sinais e seus sistemas de transcrição. In: Anagela Baalbaki, Beatriz Caldas (Org.) Instrumentos Linguísticos usos e atualizações. 1ed. Editora Cartolina, Rio de Janeiro, pp. 155–188 (2014)

24. Felipe, T.A.: Diferentes políticas e diferentes contextos educacionais: educação bilíngue para educandos surdos x educação bilíngue inclusiva. In: Revista Espaço, Rio de Janeiro, vol. 1, pp. 189–220 (2018)

25. Felipe, T.A.: O Campo Lexical Meios de Transporte na Libras. LÍNGUAS & LETRAS **20**, 70–95 (2019)

26. Ferreira, M.A.M., García, L.S., Bueno, J., Felipe, T.A.: Requirements for a framework of a virtual learning environment for Deaf People mediated by avatar. In: HCI Internacional 2019 - Posters; International Conference on Human-Computer Interaction, Orlando, pp. 365–370 (2019)
27. Ferreira, M.A.M., García, L.S.: Requirements for avatar in virtual environment of support learning in the literacy of Deaf People in Portuguese mediated by LIBRAS. In:17th Brazilian Symposium on Human Factor in Computing Systems, Belém (2018)
28. Foucambert, J.: Modos de ser leitor: Aprendizagem e ensino da leitura no ensino fundamental. Editora UFPR (2008)
29. Galvão, L., García, L.S., Felipe, T.A.: RPGJEIS: uma ferramenta de autoria de jogos educativos do gênero role-play game para o auxílio do letramento de crianças Surdas. In: 8th Congresso Brasileiro de Informática na Educação; Workshops (WCIBIE 2019), Brasília, pp. 1482–1486 (2019)
30. García, L.S.: Linx: Um Ambiente Integrado de interface para Sistemas de Informação Baseados em Conhecimento. Pontifícia Universidade Católica do Rio de Janeiro, Tese de doutorado. Departamento de Informática (1995)
31. García, L.S., Guimarães, C., Antunes, D.R., Fernandes, S.: HCI architecture for Deaf communities cultural inclusion and citizenship. In: International Conference on Enterprise in Information Science, Angers Loire Valle, France, pp. 126–133 (2013)
32. Gonçalves, D.A., Todt, E., Claúdio, D.P.: Landmark-based facial expression parametrization for sign languages avatar animation. In: Brazilian Symposium on Human Factors in Computing Systems. Proceedings of the XVI Brazilian Symposium on Human Factors in Computing Systems – IHC, vol. 16. pp. 1–6. ACM Press, New York, Joinville (2017)
33. Guimarães, C., Antunes, D.R., García, L.S., Guedes, A., Fernandes, S.: Conceptual meta-environment for Deaf Children Literacy challenge: how to design effective artifacts for bilingualism construction. In: 6th International Conference on Research Challenges in Information Science, Valencia, Spain, pp. 1–12 (2012)
34. Guimarães, C., Antunes, D.R., García, L.S., Peres, L., Fernandes, S.: Deaf literacy: a computational process to design Sign Language/Portuguese artifacts for Internet. In: 11th International Conference WWW/Internet - ICWI, Madrid, pp. 250–259 (2012)
35. Guimarães, C., Antunes, D.R., Trindade, D.F., Silva, R., García, L.S.: Structure of the Brazilian Sign Language (Libras) for computational tools: citizenship and social inclusion. In: Organizational, Business, and Technological Aspects of the Knowledge Society; 3th World Summit on the Knowledge Society - WSKS, Corfu, Greece, pp. 365–370 (2010)
36. Guimarães, C., Antunes, D.R., Trindade, D.F., Silva, R., García, L.S., Fernandes, S.: Evaluation of a computational description model of Libras (Brazilian Sign Language): bridging the gap towards information access. In: 5th International Conference on Research Challenges in Information Science, Gosier, pp. 485–494 (2011)
37. Herbig, G.R.B.: Core-SL-Sign Register: ferramenta computacional para a especificação de sinais da libras. Dissertação de Mestrado, Programa de Pós-Graduação em Informática, Setor de Ciências Exatas, Universidade Federal do Paraná, Curitiba (2018)
38. Iatskiu, C.E., García, L.S., Canteri, R., Antunes, D.R.: The low use of sign writing computational tools from HCI perspective. In: Universal Access in Human-Computer Interaction. Access to Interaction; 9th International Conference on Universal Access in Human-Computer Interaction – UAHCI, Los Angeles, pp. 373–382 (2015)
39. Iatskiu, C.E., García, L.S., Canteri, R.: Automatic generation of Libras signals by graphic Simbols of SignWriting. In: 17th International Conference on Enterprise Information Systems, Barcelona, pp. 71–78 (2015)

40. Iatskiu, C.E., García, L.S., Felipe, T.A., Antunes, D.R.: Sistema para a geração automática da escrita de sinais em SignWriting visando o apoio ao ensino e à aprendizagem da Libras. In: 29° Brazilian Symposium on Computers in Education/29° Simpósio Brasileiro de Informática Na Educação (SBIE 2018), Fortaleza, pp. 1013–1022 (2018)

41. Lima, M.: Tradução automática com adequação sintático-semântica para LIBRAS. Dissertação de Mestrado, Programa de Pós-Graduação em Informática, Centro de Informática, Universidade Federal da Paraíba (2015)

42. Lira, G.A.: Pro Lira, G.A.: O impacto da tecnologia na educação e inclusão social da pessoa portadora de deficiência auditiva: Tradutor digital português x Língua brasileira de sinais, Tlibras (2009). http://www.senac.br/BTS/293

43. Lira, G.A.: Projeto tradutor Português x Libras. http: www.acessobrasil.org.br

44. Martins, R., Pelizzoni, J., Hasegawa, R.: PULØ- Para um sistema de tradução semi-automática português-libras. In: XXV Congresso da Sociedade Brasileira de Computação. Unisinos- São Leopoldo-RS (2005)

45. Miranda, A.J., Ribeiro, M., Almeida, A., García, L.S.: SIGNBANKMOBILE: a data Collection Environment for Deaf Culture Handwriting Recognition System. In: 13th IADIS International Conference on WWW/INTERNET 2014; International Conference on Cognition and Exploratory Learning in the Digital Age (CELDA), Porto, pp. 66–73 (2014)

46. Miranda, A.J.: WiKLaTS: um ambiente de interface e interação para manipulação e formalização de conhecimento para tradução entre pares de línguas baseada em regras, Dissertação de Mestrado, Programa de Pós-Graduação em Informática, Setor de Ciências Exatas, Universidade Federal do Paraná (2009)

47. Miranda, A.J., García, L.S.: WIKLANG: a definition environment for monolingual and bilingual dictionaries to shalow-transfer machine translation. In: Proceedings of IADIS International Conference WWW/Internet 2010, Timisoara Press, Lisboa, pp. 159–167 (2010)

48. Nunes, M.: Projeto PULOs: Núcleo Interinstitucional de Linguística Computacional – NILC, São Carlos, SP, pp. 80–118 (2003)

49. Paim, P., García, L.S.: NÃO à Violência Contra Qualquer Mulher!: Requisitos de Aplicativos Inclusivos para Denúncias de Violência Doméstica. In: II Fórum da Pós-Graduação em Ciência da Computação do Paraná/I Mostra de Trabalhos de Pós-graduandos em Ciência da Computação do Paraná, Cascavel, pp. 83–84 (2020)

50. Paiva, F.: Tradução automática de português brasileiro para Libras e análise de processos de intensificação, Ph.D. Dissertation, Faculdade de Engenharia Elétrica e de Computação, Universidade Estadual de CampinaS-Unicamp (2019)

51. Pereira, E.: Educação Sexual Acessível para Adolescentes Surdas: Diretrizes para Plataformas Digitais de Ensino. II Fórum da Pós-graduação em Ciência da Computação do Paraná (2020). https://doi.org/10.13140/RG.2.2.11208.14081

52. PRODEAF: https://handtalk.me/br

53. Razet, C.: De la lecture d'une histoire à la lecture d'une écriture. Synergies Brésil. N. 10, páginas 59–74 (2012)

54. Razet, C.: Da leitura de uma história à leitura de uma escrita. traduzido por liliane mendonça. revisado por lúcia peixoto cherem. Dossiê Especial: Didática sem fronteiras. Cherem, Rammé, Pedra & Olmo orgs. Revista X, 2 (2014)

55. Rodrigues, L., García, L.S, Silva, L.: Gesture vocabulary for natural interaction with Virtual Museums: Case Study: a process created and tested within a Bilingual Deaf Children School. In: 16th International Conference on Enterprise Information Systems (ICEIS), vol. 2, pp. 5–13, Lisboa. SCITEPRESS – Science and Technology Publications, Setúbal (2014)

56. Silva, A.M.C.: Lexlibras: descrição das unidades morfossintáticas da Libras a partir dos parâmetros fonológicos para o processo de tradução automática por um avatar. Dissertação de Mestrado. Programa de Pos-Graduação em Informática do Setor de Ciências Exatas da Universidade Federal do Paraná, PR, Curitiba (2020)

57. Stokoe, W.C.: Sign Language Structure. Linstok Press, Silver Spring, M.D. (1960)
58. Trindade, D.F., García, L.S.: Framework conceitual de apoio ao design de ambientes colaborativos inclusivos aos Surdos. In: Brazilian Symposium on Computers in Education (Simpósio Brasileiro de Informática na Educação, Macéio, AL, pp. 457–466 (2015)
59. Trindade, D.F., Guimarães, C., Antunes, D.R, Silva, R., García, L.S., Fernandes, S.: Communication and cooperation pragmatism: an analysis of a community of practice by Non-Deaf and Deaf to study sign language. In: Information Systems, e-Learning, and Knowledge Management Research; 4th World Summit on the Knowledge Society, Mykonos, Greece, pp. 191–205 (2011)
60. Trindade, D.F., Guimarães, C., García, L.S.: Conceptual framework for design of collaborative environments: cultivating communities of practices for deaf inclusion. In: 15th International Conference on Enterprise Information Systems - ICEIS, Angers Loire Valle, France, vol. 2, pp. 206–215 (2013)

Accessible Media

Preferences of Deaf or Hard of Hearing Users for Live-TV Caption Appearance

Akhter Al Amin[1], Abraham Glasser[1], Raja Kushalnagar[2], Christian Vogler[2], and Matt Huenerfauth[1(✉)]

[1] Rochester Institute of Technology, Rochester, NY, USA
{aa7510,atg2036,matt.huenerfauth}@rit.edu
[2] Gallaudet University, Washington, DC, USA
{raja.kushalnagar,christian.vogler}@gallaudet.edu

Abstract. There is a wide range of visual appearance of captions during television programming (e.g. text color, typeface, caption background, number of lines, caption placement), especially during live or near-live broadcasts in local markets. The effect of these visual properties of captions on Deaf and Hard of Hearing (DHH) users' TV-watching experience have been less explored in existing research-based guidelines nor in the design of state-of-the-art caption evaluation metrics. Therefore, we empirically investigated what visual attributes of captions are preferred by DHH viewers while watching captioned live TV programs. We convened two focus groups where participants watched videos consisting of captions with various display properties and provided subjective open-ended feedback. By analyzing the focus-group responses, we observed DHH users' preference for specific contrast between caption text and background color such as, black text on white background or vice-versa, and caption placement not occluding onscreen salient content. Our findings also revealed for preferences genre-adaptive caption typeface and movement during captioned live TV programming.

Keywords: Caption · Evaluation · Metric

1 Introduction

Around 360 million people world-wide [2] rely on captions while watching live television programming. A good quality caption provides access to what is being said, who said what, and some additional information about background sounds, e.g. laughter, clapping, and music to express the emotion of onscreen speaker.

The contents of this paper were developed under a grant from the National Institute on Disability, Independent Living, and Rehabilitation Research (NIDILRR grant number #90DPCP0002). NIDILRR is a Center within the Administration for Community Living (ACL), Department of Health and Human Services (HHS). The contents of this paper do not necessarily represent the policy of NIDILRR, ACL, HHS, and you should not assume endorsement by the Federal Government.

© Springer Nature Switzerland AG 2021
M. Antona and C. Stephanidis (Eds.): HCII 2021, LNCS 12769, pp. 189–201, 2021.
https://doi.org/10.1007/978-3-030-78095-1_15

To ensure DHH users' access to this speech and non-speech information, several regulatory organizations have mandated that broadcasters provide captions with specific properties, i.e. captions should be verbatim, synchronous, and not occlude any salient onscreen content [3–5]. While these regulations, e.g. [3–5,14,15] somewhat improve the quality of captions, current captioning quality provided by TV broadcasters is not always satisfactory to DHH viewers [6,14]. Additional research is needed on how to evaluate caption-quality in regard to appearance characteristics, e.g. the contrast between caption text and background color, font size, movement or placement style, and other issues [4,7,8].

Providing quality captioning for live or near-live TV programming is particularly challenging, given the time constraints broadcasters face in such settings [9]. To periodically evaluate the quality of broadcast television captioning, regulators employ existing automatic or semi-automatic caption evaluation metrics. Such metrics mostly focus on measuring the transcription accuracy, i.e. whether the caption text is similar to the words spoken by the onscreen speakers [10,11,13,24]. Few of these metrics consider how visual attributes of captions may affect DHH users' TV-watching experience. For example, Ofcom produced annual report identifying DHH users' dissatisfaction with the quality of captions, even when transcription was near perfect [14], which suggests that other attributes of caption may affect DHH users' judgements about of caption quality.

In this paper, we use the term "properties" of captions to refer visual attributes, such as caption text color, background, font size, font typeface, placement, and movement. Some prior researchers have conducted user-studies to determine DHH viewers' preferred caption properties, with a focus on the number of lines in the caption, the caption movement (e.g. scroll-up or pop-up), caption placement onscreen, line segmentation, or other issues [8,16,18,19]. However, those studies have focused on a variety of settings, e.g. impromptu meetings or classroom environments; additional research is needed with a specific focus on live television programming.

Therefore, this study was designed to elicit DHH users' subjective open-ended preferences regarding a wide range of display properties about captioning during live TV programming. A total 17 DHH adults participated in one of two focus groups conducted on different days. We asked participants to share their opinions about visual properties of short video clips of television programming with captions, and to discuss their prior experience with such captions, during a group discussion lasting for 90 min. Our findings provide insights on DHH users' perspectives about current captioning appearance properties during local TV broadcasts. Further, our findings inform the design of future caption evaluation metrics of caption quality.

2   Related Work

This section discusses the relevant literature on prior caption placement methods (Sect. 2.1), user studies focusing on DHH viewers' preferred caption appearance style (Sect. 2.2), and existing caption evaluation metrics (Sect. 2.3).

2.1 Prior Work on Caption Placement

Prior investigations of DHH users' preferred caption location on the TV screen have focused on two key issues: (1) identification of the current speaker and (2) avoiding occlusion with onscreen salient information. Some prior research has suggested positioning captions close to the current person speaking onscreen, especially when several people are present on the screen at a time [17,21]. While a user study revealed that such speaker-following caption-placement methods improve users' ability to identify the current speaker [18], viewers can become confused by the caption location when there are off-screen speakers [22]. Other research proposed content-sensitive caption placement methods so that captions do not block onscreen salient information regions, such as the face of a person onscreen or some onscreen text [16,20]. However, prior research has revealed that DHH users need to expend extra effort to seek the location of the caption when caption location varies due to changes in speakers' location or camera angle, which poses additional cognitive challenges for DHH viewers [15,22]. Most work in this area employs automatic methods to identify salient information on the screen, and this work could be enhanced if researchers were to collect additional empirical evidence about DHH viewers' preferences.

2.2 Prior User Studies on Caption Appearance Style

Several user studies have been conducted to solicit viewers' preferences for caption appearance. Most studies have investigated viewers' preferences for specific text font size or color [23,27,28], or the usability of captions in various contexts, e.g. classrooms or one-to-one meetings [8,29,30]. Other studies have examined whether additional color or text highlighting assists in conveying additional information, e.g. the accuracy or importance of words [31]. Prior work has also examined how a long text should be best segmented into multiple lines to improve its readability for DHH viewers [32], and how to best represent any non-speech or non-verbal information (e.g. background music, emotion, or environmental noises) in a caption [33]. Relevant to our current work, a recent experimental study with 105 DHH participants investigated DHH users' preferred caption appearance style for online videos [8]. While those studies offer some insights regarding DHH users' preferences, these works did not focus on captions produced for live TV programming, and some had included non-DHH participants. In contrast, in our current work, we focus on eliciting DHH users' open-ended feedback on a broad-range of caption appearance properties.

2.3 Existing Caption Evaluation Metrics

Caption evaluation metrics allow regulators or other organizations, e.g. [3,5,14], to regularly assess the quality of captioned television broadcasts. A widely used metric is Word Error Rate (WER) [10] which compares a **hypothesis text** (the text actually shown during broadcast) and a **reference text** (the verbatim text spoken by onscreen speakers), to generate a numerical score by counting the number of words that differ (due to word insertion, deletion, or substitution). Some other caption evaluation methods depend upon trained human annotators [11], probabilistic models [12], or word importance models [13] to determine a weighted penalty for each insertion, deletion, substitution - specific to the word or context. However, as mentioned in Sect. 1, these metrics do not consider caption appearance aspects.

While prior studies on caption display properties have led to some empirical insights, we are unaware of any prior research which investigated the subjective opinion of DHH users regarding a wide range of caption display properties of live TV captioning services. Furthermore, existing caption metrics do not consider the effect of these attributes, which poses a challenge to regulators who seek to measure the quality of a captioned video from DHH viewers' perspective. Therefore, in this study (Sects. 3 and 4), we conducted two focus groups, in a round table setting, in which participants were shown captioned videos and images, prior to discussion. Our goal was to elicit participants' subjective opinions and observe their reactions to other participants' comments.

3   Methodology

We selected a focus-group methodology for this study due to the early phase of our work, and our goal of obtaining participants' open-ended opinions pertaining to a wide range of caption display properties for captioned live TV programs. This method enabled us to identify several underlying concerns and allowed significant flexibility in pursuing themes that emerged during the session.

3.1   Participant Recruitment

The screening criteria for our study was that participants identify as Deaf or Hard of Hearing, as someone who reads captions when watching videos or television, and be age 18 or above. Participants were recruited through email and social-media announcements distributed by our university and organizations related to the DHH community. Those interested in participating reached out to investigators by email for scheduling. Our Institutional Review Board approved this study, and each participant provided written informed consent on the day of the focus-group session. Participants were compensated with $40 cash for their participation. Eleven participants attended the first focus group, and six participants attended the second. Across two focus groups, a total of 17 people participated including nine females, eight males, aged 18 to 45 (median = 25). Twelve of our participants described themselves as D/deaf, and five, as hard of hearing. All but 4 participants mentioned using American Sign Language (ASL) at home or work on a regular basis. Twelve participants said they started learning ASL at age 9 or younger. The remaining participants reported using ASL for at least two years and regularly using ASL at work or school. Prior research has suggested that individuals with similar characteristics are more likely to partici-pate in open discussion during sessions [25]. Following this recommendation, we scheduled participants who were more comfortable with ASL in our first focus group, and participants with less (or no) ASL experience in the second focus group.

3.2   Data Collection Procedure

Each focus group lasted around 90 min, following the same procedure. We conducted our sessions in ASL and English, employing professional ASL interpreters and Communication Access Realtime Translation (CART) service providers. To keep participants engaged in the discussion, we organized a round-table setup to facilitate an effective communicative environment [1]. After each person was seated, we handed out two documents: an informed consent and a demographic form. After collecting the signed informed consent and providing light refreshment, moderators started the session with a brief ice-breaker exercise by introducing participants to one another and providing instructions for actively participating in the focus group session. We divided the session into 5 times segments. In each segment, the discussion was conducted focusing on the topics as follows: **(1) caption background, (2) caption font size, (3) caption text color and typeface, (4) caption movement, and (5) caption placement**. Each of these topics was displayed on a presentation slide, including multiple captioned short videos or sample images. After displaying the videos or images, the moderator asked participants to raise their hands to share their opinions about the captioned videos or images. At the end of this session, we collected demographic information from participants. Each focus group session was video recorded and transcribed verbatim by a professional transcriptionist. The completed transcript was then verified by a member of the research team against the original recordings prior to analysis.

3.3   Analysis

To analyze the open-ended data, a mixed-method was used. Initially, we performed an open coding by familiarizing ourselves with the transcripts. Then we cross-checked our transcripts with the video recording of the session and annotated each participant in our transcripts anonymously (P1, P2,...P17) so that their identity remained undisclosed. Subsequently, we tried to understand the overall context of responses for each question we asked during the session, i.e. what the researcher asked (and did not ask), and whether the respondent included things beyond what had been asked (e.g. sharing their personal experiences, even if we did not ask). Then we investigated the intensity of the responses, i.e. the depth of feeling in which the comments and feelings are expressed. Finally, we analyzed the internal consistency of the responses, i.e. how emphatic an individual respondent was, whether others in the group indicated agreement, and the specificity of the responses. For instance, responses that are very relevant to the questions asked by moderators are evidence of the close attention of respondents. Our systematic method of analysis is adapted from [26] and, as a result of this analysis, several significant themes and patterns in the data have been identified.

4   Results

We asked participants a number of questions throughout the two focus groups to share their open-ended feedback on various aspects of caption appearance. We obtained insightful open-ended feedback which revealed some major concerns, expectations, and suggestions regarding different visual attributes of captions. After performing thematic analysis, we grouped our focus group findings five-fold:

– Preferred Caption Background
– Preferred Caption Font Size
– Preferred Caption Text Color and Typeface
– Preferred Caption Movement Style
– Preferred Caption Placement

4.1   Preferred Caption Background

What Is Your Preference for Caption Background? We displayed captioned images consisting of three commonly used caption background as shown in Fig. 1: black, grey or transparent, and no background. We got total of ten responses across two focus group sessions and the responses clearly indicated participants' inclination (70%) for grey or transparent background. The visibility of background content plays a key role in their prioritization of such caption background over others. One participants' responses speculates on this choice in a precise manner.

Fig. 1. Leftmost image contains caption with grey or transparent background, middle image contains caption with black background and caption contains no background in rightmost image

I agree, the grey or transparent one is the best. You can still see some visibility of what is behind it. You can still see some behind it. (P11)

4.2 Preferred Caption Font Size

What Is Your Preference for Caption Font Size? After watching captions of three different sizes ascending from small to large as shown in Fig. 2, nine participants indicated their preference for medium size font. At the same time, two respondents expressed their preference as it was more readable in size. One participant commented:

Like [the] middle one but bigger is easier to read. (P9)

Interestingly, one participant expressed a context-specific preference regarding caption font size:

In a movie theater, I would like number 3. But here in this room, I like number 2. Number 1 is too small. (P13)

A consensus was observed pertaining to DHH viewers' preference for larger font size over the smaller one, largely motivated by better text readability.

Fig. 2. Leftmost image contains caption with smallest font size, middle image contains caption with medium font size and caption has biggest font size in rightmost image

4.3 Preferred Caption Text Color and Typeface

What Is Your Preference for Caption Color and Typeface? We noticed that some of our participants preferred a white text color, as participants are accustomed to that color for captions, with others favoring a yellow and gray text on a black background. Participants shared several comments about caption color:

I think we are all used to white on black since we grew up with it. If you change it on us, then it will be harder for us, since we need exposure to it. I'm sure we can get used to it eventually. (P12)

I agree with what you said. I took a film class with captions for movies. During this class, my teacher said that for people with visual issues, that Yellow font on Black background is more accessible. (P16)

Regarding the typeface of captions, three participants indicated that caption typeface should vary depending upon the TV program genre. One of them said:

I have never changed the font for captions, but it would be cool for fonts to match the genre of the show, e.g. Harry Potter (wizard style), or scary movie (spooky font). (P17)

4.4   Preferred Caption Movement Style

What Is Your Preference for Movement (Pop Up or Roll Up) Style of Caption? Across two focus groups, we observed diverse preferences in regard to caption movement style among participants. Four out of seventeen participants expressed their preference for pop-up caption appearance, as compared to roll-up appearance style, explaining their reasons as follows:

If there is scrolling, then my eyes need to follow the moving words as I am reading words. I wish they would step up instead of roll up. (P1)

In scrolling there is too much mental work to find where am I. (P6)

I like... pop up and should be smooth. (P11)

On the contrary, six participants stated their preference for roll-up over pop-up, explaining that they felt that captions remain longer on the screen during roll-up than pop-up. They indicated that then multiple words appear simultaneously during pop-up style captions, there is a need to read quickly:

Scrolling you can look previous words but pop up only one line. (P4)

Maybe a little faster, but stays longer onscreen, too. If that makes sense. (P12)

Three participants indicated that their preference between these caption appearance styles was conditional. Two participants indicated TV genre-specific preference, e.g. roll-up for news programs or pop-up for movies. One participant mentioned that the number of lines in the caption is an important factor in their preference.

For News or live program scrolling is fine but movies should have pop up. (P2)

Depends on how many words on line. I prefer one full phrase at a tie. If short prefers pop up and if not then scrolling. (P10)

4.5   Preferred Caption Placement

What Is Your Peference for Placement of Caption?
Several participants indicated that they would prefer for captions to be displayed near the speaker who is speaking at that moment. Two participants discussed their specific preference for captions that vary in location in a speaker-following manner when there are multiple people on the screen:

In movie would like to see who is speaking, I don't want to miss out the story looking at below to to see the captions. (P2)

Fig. 3. In Left image, caption is placed in Lower Center position, in the Right image, caption is placed near Speaker who is speaking right now.

When 2 people are having a conversation, then it is nice. In news, it is usually just the anchorperson talking to the audience. For a conversation, the moving style number 2 is nice. (P13)

On the other hand, some participants preferred captions being placed in a static location, and they raised concerns about captions popping up close to the speakers' location (Right image in Fig. 3):

My preference would be for the caption to stay in one place on the screen. It should show a new line if it is a new person speaking. I prefer captions to remain in one place so my eyes don't move all over. (P5)

I prefer central location so I don't need to look for caption. But there should indication who is speaking. If the people who are talking are introduced themselves by name I would like to move caption out of the way. (P7)

5   Discussion

The key themes that have emerged during our analysis of the focus-group sessions are discussed below:

Preferred caption text and background color. The majority of participants indicated that color contrast between the caption text and its background should be high, e.g. black and white. Also it has been observed that low color contrast, e.g. yellow caption text on a white background, may reduce caption readability significantly. Our findings regarding color contrast between caption text and background are aligned with regulation described by [3,4].

Visibility of onscreen graphical contents determines preference for caption background. Study participants indicated a preference for watching captions with a transparent or semi-transparent background, as it may increase the visibility of surrounding onscreen content to some extent. This reflected DHH users' preference that onscreen salient graphical elements, e.g. speakers' face or onscreen textual information, not be blocked by caption text. These issues have also been examined in prior work and incorporated into guidelines, e.g. [3,4,20,22]. Our findings revealed that onscreen graphical content being blocked by caption was specifically a motivation for DHH users' preference for transparent caption backgrounds.

Distance between viewers and streaming device regulates preference for caption font size. Regarding caption font size, several participants indicated that larger font increases readability. However, several participants expressed their preference for medium sized font among three standard caption font size that were shown during this session. These findings provide evidence of font size on readability, as in [23]. Moreover, participants' responses indicated that caption-size preferences may vary with respect to the distance between viewers and their devices.

TV program Genre-specific caption typeface is preferred. With respect to caption text color, participants indicated a preference for light-colored caption text such as white, yellow, or grey, likely due to users' familiarity with these text colors in captioning, typically on a black background, in alignment with existing guidelines [3,4]. However, some participants suggested that TV-program genre-specific caption styles would be of interest in some settings, e.g. a **fantasy** type movie, 'wizard' style caption font, and for **scary** movie 'spooky' style caption font. These findings may lead future work on such modifications of caption appearance for these genres.

TV program Genre-specific caption movement is preferred. We observed no consensus among participants regarding caption movement style. Some preferred roll-up over pop-up, and some preferred otherwise. During the focus-group discussion, some participants explained that their preference may depend upon the genre of TV program, e.g. roll-up for news or pop-up for for movies. Our findings motivate future empirical research to investigate whether TV program genre-specific caption movement is preferred by DHH viewers.

Concerns regarding speaker-following or dynamic caption placement. We observed mixed responses from participants regarding speaker-following or dynamic caption placement (in which caption location onscreen varies due to other onscreen elements). The concerns raised by some participants aligned with some prior findings [15,22] that non-static caption placement may confuse viewers, since viewers need to seek the caption location as it varies over time. This finding motivates additional research on exploring the acceptability of current dynamic caption placement methods among DHH community.

6   Limitations and Future Work

There were several limitations of our current research, some of which could be addressed through future research studies. Firstly, our research is entirely focused on user preference. While this is our preliminary stage of research, future research involving participants' ability to understand and recall information from captions would be useful to measure as well.

The total number of participants in our study was relatively small, and recruitment was largely focused on DHH individuals from a university setting, which only represents a subset of the DHH community. Future research should obtain caption preferences from a greater number of DHH individuals from more diverse backgrounds.

In this study, we specifically asked participants to consider particular characteristics of captions, such as the background, font size, etc. Additional research will be needed to devise a study focusing on a wider range of visual properties of caption, i.e. how emotions are conveyed, how speakers are identified, whether punctuation in captions matter, etc.

7 Conclusion

We conducted this focus-group study as an initial step in our research on the preferences of DHH viewers about various display properties of captions, with an eye to how the findings from this study might inform future empirical work. Using this focus group methodology, we asked participants to express their preferences regarding caption styles, especially among some specific sample videos showed during the session. The themes that emerged from our findings suggest that DHH viewers do have some specific preferences for particular caption appearance styles, e.g., caption background, placements that avoid occlusion of other content onscreen, sufficiently large caption font size, etc. At the same time, many of our participants indicated that it would be beneficial to vary appearance characteristics, e.g. caption typeface or movement, based on the TV-program genre, e.g. movies or news. This approach is not yet mainstream among television broadcasters, existing captioning guidelines, and or existing caption-evaluation metrics. While the small number of participants in our study limited our analysis, we believe that this study contributes to addressing gaps in current research-based guidelines and caption evaluation metrics. As empirical basis for that work, our study provides an in-depth understanding of DHH viewers' preferences for various visual properties of captions, and it provides a foundation for designing future experimental studies to explore these aspects. The ultimate goal is that this line of work will provide guidance for television broadcasters to provide captions that better meet the needs and preferences of DHH viewers, and may also shed light on how regulators or other organizations may more holistically evaluate the quality of captioning in current television broadcasts.

References

1. Malyshev: Modern technologies of education at the University. - SPb.: Department of operational printing, HSE, p. 134 (2011)
2. Blanchfield, B.B., Feldman, J.J., Dunbar, J.L., Gardner. E.N.: The severely to profoundly hearing-impaired population in the united states: prevalence estimates and demographics. J. Am. Acad. Audiol. **12**(4), 183–189 (2001)
3. Federal Communications Commission: Closed Captioning Quality Report and Order, Declaratory Ruling, FNRMP (2014). https://www.fcc.gov/document/closed-captioning-quality-report-and-order-declaratory-ruling-fnprm. Accessed 30 Dec 2020

4. The Described and Captioned Media Program: Captioning Key for Educational Media (2010). Rhttp://access-ed.r2d2.uwm.edu/resources/captioning-key.pdf. Accessed 23 Dec 2020

5. BBC: BBC Subtitle Guidelines (2019). https://bbc.github.io/subtitle-guidelines. Accessed 26 Dec 2020

6. Nam, S., Fels, D.I., Chignell. M.H.: Modeling closed captioning subjective quality assessment by deaf and hard of hearing viewers. IEEE Trans. Comput. Soc. Syst. **7**(3), 621–631 (2020)

7. Berke, L.: Displaying confidence from imperfect automatic speech recognition for captioning. Assoc. Comput. Mach. SIGACCESS Access. Comput. **117**, 14–18 (2017)

8. Berke, L., Albusays, K., Scita, M., Huenerfauth, M.: Preferred appearance of captions generated by automatic speech recognition for deaf and hard-of-hearing viewers. In: Extended Abstracts of the 2019 CHI Conference on Human Factors in Computing Systems (CHI EA '19), pp. 1–6. Association for Computing Machinery, New York, NY, USA (2019)

9. Media Access Group (WGBH): Closed Captioning on TV in the United States 101 (2019). https://blog.snapstream.com/closed-captioning-on-tv-in-the-united-states-101. Accessed 10 Dec 2020

10. Ali, A., Renals, S.: Word error rate estimation for speech recognition: e-WER. In: Proceedings of the 56th Annual Meeting of the Association for Computational Linguistics (Vol. 2: Short Papers), pp. 0–24. Association for Computational Linguistics, Melbourne, Australia, July (2018)

11. Romero-Fresco, P., Martínez Pérez, J.: Accuracy Rate in Live Subtitling: The NER Model. Audiovisual Translation in a Global Context. Palgrave Studies in Translating and Interpreting, Palgrave Macmillan, London (2015)

12. Apone, M.B.T., Botkin, B., Goldberg. L.: Caption accuracy metrics project research into automated error ranking of real-time captions in live television news programs (2011)

13. Kafle, S., Huenerfauth, M.: Predicting the understandability of imperfect English captions for people who are deaf or hard of hearing. ACM Trans. Access. Comput. **12**(2), (June 2019)

14. Ofcom: Measuring live subtitling quality, UK (2019). https://www.ofcom.org.uk/__data/assets/pdf_file/0019/45136/sampling-report.pdf. Accessed 19 Dec 2020

15. English-language Working Group: Closed Captioning Standards and Protocol for Canadian English Language Television Programming Services (2008). https://www.cab-acr.ca/english/social/captioning/captioning.pdf. Accessed 19 Nov 2020

16. Hong, R., Wang, M., Xu, M., Yan, S., Chua, T-S.: Dynamic captioning: Video accessibility enhancement for hearing impairment. In: Proceedings of the 18th ACM International Conference on Multimedia (MM '10) (2010)

17. Hong, R., et al.: Video accessibility enhancement for hearing-impaired users. ACM Trans. Multimedia Comput. Commun. Appl. **7S**, 1, Article 24 (2011), 19 p. https://doi.org/10.1145/2037676.2037681

18. Brown, A., et al.: Dynamic subtitles: the user experience. In: Proceedings of the ACM International Conference on Interactive Experiences for TV and Online Video (TVX 2015), pp. 103–112. Association for Computing Machinery, New York, NY, USA (2015)

19. Kushalnagar, R., Kushalnagar, K.: Subtitle formatter: making subtitles easier to read for deaf and hard of hearing viewers on personal devices. In: Miesenberger, K., Kouroupetroglou, G. (eds.) ICCHP 2018. LNCS, vol. 10896, pp. 211–219. Springer, Cham (2018). https://doi.org/10.1007/978-3-319-94277-3_35

20. Jiang, B., Liu, S., He, L., Wu, W., Chen, H., Shen, Y.: Subtitle positioning for e-learning videos based on rough gaze estimation and saliency detection. InSIG-GRAPH Asia Posters 15–16 (2017)
21. Hu, Y., Kautz, J., Yu, Y., Wang, W.: Speaker-following video subtitles. ACM Trans. Multimedia Comput. Commun. Appl. **11**(2), (2015)
22. Kurzhals, K., Göbel, F., Angerbauer, K., Sedlmair, M., Raubal, M.: A view on the viewer: caze-adaptive captions for videos. In: Proceedings of the 2020 CHI Conference on Human Factors in Computing Systems (CHI 2020), pp. 1–12. Association for Computing Machinery, New York, NY, USA (2020)
23. Kim, M., et al.: The effect of font and display sizes on the readability for mobile devices. In: Proceedings of HCI Korea (HCIK 2016), pp. 468–475. Hanbit Media Inc., Seoul, KOR (2016)
24. Brooks, M., Apone, T., Botkin, B., Goldberg. L.: Research into Automated Error Ranking of Real-time Captions in Live Television News Programs, National Center for Accessible Media (NCAM)
25. Krueger, R.A., Casey, M.C.: Focus Groups A Practical Guide for Applied Research. Sage Publications, London (2009)
26. Rabiee, F.: Focus-group interview and data analysis. Proc. Nutr. Soc. **63**(4), 655–660 (2004)
27. Vigier, T., Baveye, Y., Rousseau, J., Le Callet, P.: Visual attention as a dimension of QoE: Subtitles in UHD videos. In: Proceedings of the Eighth International Conference on Quality of Multimedia Experience. pp. 1–6 (2016)
28. Morón, O.G., Szarkowska, A., Woll, B.: The impact of text segmentation on subtitle reading. J. Eye Move. Res. **65**, 2 (2018)
29. Kushalnagar, R.S, Lasecki, W.S., Bigham, J.P.: Accessibility evaluation of classroom captions. ACM Trans. Access. Comput. **5**(3), 7 (January 2014), 24 p. https://doi.org/10.1145/2543578
30. Rander, A., Looms, P.O.: The accessibility of television news with live subtitling on digital television. In: Proceedings of the 8th European Conference on Interactive TV and Video (Tampere, Finland) (EuroITV 2010). Association for Computing Machinery, pp. 155–160. New York, NY, USA (2010). https://doi.org/10.1145/1809777.1809809
31. Kafle, S., Yeung, P., Huenerfauth, M.: Evaluating the highlighting key benefit of words in captions for people who are deaf or hard of hearing. In: The 21st International ACM SIGACCESS Conference on Computers and Accessibility (Pittsburgh, PA, USA) (ASSETS 2019). pp . 43–55, Association for Computing Machinery, New York, NY, USA (2019). https://doi.org/10.1145/3308561.3353781
32. Waller, J.M., Kushalnagar, R.S.: Evaluation of automatic caption segmentation. In: Proceedings of the 18th International ACM SIGACCESS Conference on Computers and Accessibility (Reno, Nevada, USA) (ASSETS 2016). pp. 331–332. Association for Computing Machinery, New York, NY, USA (2016). https://doi.org/10.1145/2982142.2982205
33. Lee, D.G., Fels, D.I., Do. J.P.: Emotive captioning. Comput. Entertain. **5**(2), 11 (April 2007), 15p. https://doi.org/10.1145/1279540.1279551

Effect of Occlusion on Deaf and Hard of Hearing Users' Perception of Captioned Video Quality

Akhter Al Amin, Saad Hassan, and Matt Huenerfauth[✉]

Rochester Institute of Technology, Rochester, NY, USA
{aa7510,sh2513,matt.huenerfauth}@rit.edu

Abstract. While the availability of captioned television programming has increased, the quality of this captioning is not always acceptable to Deaf and Hard of Hearing (DHH) viewers, especially for live or unscripted content broadcast from local television stations. Although some current caption metrics focus on textual accuracy (comparing caption text with an accurate transcription of what was spoken), other properties may affect DHH viewers' judgments of caption quality. In fact, U.S. regulatory guidance on caption quality standards includes issues relating to how the placement of captions may occlude other video content. To this end, we conducted an empirical study with 29 DHH participants to investigate the effect on user's judgements of caption quality or their enjoyment of the video, when captions overlap with an onscreen speaker's eyes or mouth, or when captions overlap with onscreen text. We observed significantly more negative user-response scores in the case of such overlap. Understanding the relationship between these occlusion features and DHH viewers' judgments of the quality of captioned video will inform future work towards the creation caption evaluation metrics, to help ensure the accessibility of captioned television or video.

Keywords: Occlusion · Stimuli · Caption · Metric

1 Introduction and Background

In recent years, the transcription accuracy of captions appearing on television programming has improved, a phenomenon attributed to the use of caption-evaluation metrics which allow efficient assessment of accuracy of captioned television broadcasts [29]. However, beyond the issue of whether the captions

---

The contents of this paper were developed under a grant from the National Institute on Disability, Independent Living, and Rehabilitation Research (NIDILRR grant number #90DPCP0002). NIDILRR is a Center within the Administration for Community Living (ACL), Department of Health and Human Services (HHS). The contents of this paper do not necessarily represent the policy of NIDILRR, ACL, HHS, and you should not assume endorsement by the Federal Government.

© Springer Nature Switzerland AG 2021
M. Antona and C. Stephanidis (Eds.): HCII 2021, LNCS 12769, pp. 202–220, 2021.
https://doi.org/10.1007/978-3-030-78095-1_16

are accurate transcript of the words spoken by individuals in the video, other factors are known to negatively affect DHH viewers' experience with captioned video, including whether captions occlude other visual content [10, 41]. The placement of captions can pose unique challenges for DHH viewers, such as reducing the overall amount of information viewers can perceive from the visual content [20, 21] or making it difficult to use speechreading if the face of the person onscreen is blocked by a caption [37, 42]. Captions can also block other important visual information content, e.g. non-verbal behaviors that indicate a speaker's emotional state; in addition, captions can block other onscreen text, e.g. headlines or scrolling "news tickers" on television news broadcasts [5].

Providing captions for spoken content is essential for providing full access to information contained in television programming, e.g. from TV news, talk shows, classes, meetings, and other sources. For instance, real-time captioned news is vital for providing DHH viewers access to critical information about their local communities, nationwide events, or emergencies [3]. Many specialized software and commercial vendors provide real-time captioning services for live television programming spanning news, current affairs, and sports [28]. There are many users of captioned programming, including people who are Deaf or Hard of Hearing (DHH), who constitute a large proportion of society. Over 360 million people worldwide experience hearing loss [9], and 15% of the U.S. adults are Deaf or Hard of Hearing (DHH) [8]. However, relatively few prior research studies with DHH participants have provided empirical evidence of how various visual properties of captions, e.g. onscreen placement, influence viewers' judgment of video caption usability.

While there exist standards and regulations in many countries about providing captioning during television programming, e.g. Federal Communication Commission guidelines in the U.S. [15], there is evidence that DHH viewers are not fully satisfied with the quality of the captioning, e.g. for live or unscripted television programming in smaller U.S. television geographic markets [4, 27]. To enable regulatory agencies or others to monitor the quality of captioning in various settings, metrics[1] are needed that can efficiently and accurately evaluate television captioning quality. While evaluation studies with DHH participants can be seen as a gold standard for such assessment, more automatic metrics would enable more frequent and pervasive monitoring of quality, as long as these metrics are well-correlated with the judgements of people who are DHH.

---

[1] Throughout this paper, we use the term "metrics" to refer to some formula or algorithm that can produce a numerical score to represent the quality of a captioned video, whether it requires some human judgements or is calculated in a fully automatic manner. Thus, a metric may consider various features, and research on the relationship between features and the judgements of DHH viewers is foundational to deciding to incorporate particular features into a metric. Furthermore, we use the term "features" to refer to the aspects or properties of captioned video that may contribute to its quality. For instance, some prior research has investigated how DHH individuals' judgements of the quality of captions may be influenced by: incorrect transcription of speech into text [32], the latency of the caption relative to the timing of speech [33], font size or color in captions [5, 7], and other features.

Prior automatic metrics for evaluating captioned television programming have largely focused on features relating to transcription accuracy, e.g. Word Error Rate (WER), Named Entity Recognition (NER), Closed-Caption Evaluator, Automatic Caption Evaluation (ACE) [1,4,23,32]. Some metrics have considered latency issues, i.e. detecting when the timing of the appearance of caption text does not align temporally with the timing of spoken words [30–36]. However, there are emerging trends in the field of computer vision, which may enable such metrics to consider a new set of features, which we investigate in this paper. As the accuracy of automatically identifying people or text in videos increases, it will become possible to automatically calculate occlusion features, i.e. whether a caption blocks information that appears at a particular location and time in the video, e.g. a speaker's face or some onscreen text.

Prior research has suggested that such occlusions are a concern among DHH viewers of captions [10], and in this paper, we conduct a two-part experimental study to examine whether two such occlusion features (whether captions block portions of a speakers face, whether captions block onscreen text) influence DHH viewers' judgements about quality of captions in a video. Prior to incorporating such features into existing caption-evaluation metrics, basic research of this nature is necessary, to determine how they may affect DHH viewers' judgements of caption quality. Specifically, in our study, DHH participants indicated "how useful" captions were, how much they "enjoyed watching the video with the caption," and how "easy the captioned video was to follow" when viewing videos that varied according to these features. Thus, the contributions of this paper are empirical: We provide evidence that both factors have a significant effect on DHH viewer's judgements of caption quality. These findings provide motivation for future work into how to calculate such features automatically, for incorporation into caption-quality metrics.

2   Related Work

As discussed above, several researchers have proposed different techniques of measuring the quality of captions and identified some DHH users' preferred caption attributes while watching captioned TV programs. To contextualize our work within these prior efforts, Sect. 2.1 explains features used within existing caption metrics, and Sect. 2.2 summarizes prior empirical evidence of how appearance features of captions influence DHH users' TV-watching experience.

2.1   Existing Metrics of Caption Quality

A variety of metrics (both automatic and some requiring human judgements) have been proposed for the evaluation of television captioning quality, but these metrics have largely focused on the issue of text transcription accuracy and certain related features. For instance, Word Error Rate (WER) is the standard approach for evaluating automatic speech recognition systems [1], and this metric simply penalizes individual words that have been incorrectly inserted, deleted, or replaced – when comparing what was actually spoken (the "reference" text) and what the captions displayed (the "hypothesis" text). The Number, Edition error, Recognition error (NER) metric [32] is a semi-automated metric that requires human experts to label the severity of individual errors in the text, to calculate an overall error score for a text. National Center for Accessible Media (NCAM) introduced a semi-automatic caption evaluation metric called the Closed Caption Evaluator, which is another weighted version of WER [4]. A recently proposed version of this metric is fully automatic, and it uses automatic speech recognition to analyze the speech in video broadcasts and then to compute the caption error using a statistical model [4]. While not proposed for evaluating television captioning (but rather for real-time captioning of live meetings), Kafle and Huenerfauth introduced the Automatic Caption Evaluation (ACE) metric, which uses an automatically calculated word-importance model [23]. This model considered the predictability of individual words, as well as the semantic distance between the reference and hypothesis word [23]. Furthermore, ERRICSON and BBC research unveiled an approach to reduce latency in live captioning. Specifically, they focused on reducing encoding and compensating time during live broadcasts [31]. Finally, a recent machine-learning model has been introduced to detect latency between audio and captions [30].

Although various metrics like those above have been proposed for evaluating the quality of captioned television programming, regulations often include provisions that captions should not only have high transcription accuracy but also have other desirable properties. For instance, regulation from the U.S. Federal Communications Commission has included provisions that captions be not only textually verbatim but also visually sound: Specifically, the caption should be complete, should be synchronously displayed with the speech, and should not conflict with any salient visual information [16] – in other words, it should not block other important visual content. However, these issues have not previously been included in prior proposed automatic metrics of caption quality.

While teams of human judges could view samples of captioned television programming to determine when some of these issues may be occurring, recent advances in several fields have made it possible to create software that can automatically process videos to identify which person in a video is speaking, or when captions may be blocking the faces of people in the video. For instance, in computer-vision field, researchers have created technologies which can be used for detecting human faces and onscreen salient text in videos. Some of these technologies include multi-frame fusion-based face recognition [39], natural scene text detection [40], and onscreen caption detection and type recognition [38]. Since it seems possible to soon identify these features in videos, research is now needed on whether these properties do influence DHH viewer's judgements of the quality of videos – and to what degree.

2.2   Features Affecting DHH Viewer's Perception of Captioned Video Quality

In addition to the features of text transcription accuracy and latency (discussed in the context of automatic metrics above), there has been prior experimental research to investigate how various other aspects of captions may affect DHH viewer's judgements of their quality. For instance, previous work has investigated the effect of latency between caption appearance and speakers' speech, in real-time captioning circumstances [24,25] and identifying the current speaker in a panel discussion [17]. Prior work has also examined how inserting correct punctuation or pauses during the captioned video can benefit DHH viewers and increase readability [19,36]. Other researchers have investigated how DHH users' subjective impression of the readability and quality of captions is influenced by aspects of caption appearance, e.g. styles, font, and background [5,12]. Prior experimental studies have also revealed that proper segmentation (caption boundaries aligning with syntactic boundaries) can improve caption readability [28,36]. Finally, caption speed has also been found to affect DHH viewers' comprehension of captions [11]. In addition to research on these various features above, some prior work has been even more closely related to the focus of our study, i.e. on captions visually occluding salient video content, as discussed below:

Captions Occluding Portions of an Onscreen Speakers' Face: As discussed above, prior research has found that text-visibility in captions and video-content being blocked by captions are common concerns among DHH viewers [10]. While some recent televisions support users re-positioning captions to a different location upon request [12,41], this is a relatively new feature, and it is unclear how often DHH users would actively use their remote control to change caption locations while viewing television programming. Other recent work has examined dynamically varying the placement of captions onscreen [22], in accordance with the underlying video content; however, this technology does not yet avoid occlusions with important video content and is still being evaluated with DHH viewers [2,35]. While even captions that remain in one location on the screen have the potential to block important content onscreen, as new dynamic placement technologies emerge, there may be an even greater possibility for visual occlusions across a wide range of the video region.

The concern here is that prior research has found that while captions are essential for providing access to spoken content for DHH viewers, they have the potential to reduce the amount of information DHH viewers perceive from other visual content on the video, e.g. facial movements of the speaker or onscreen text [20,21]. Captions blocking the face of the current speaker is a concern, as some DHH viewers may use speech and oral-based communication, e.g. performing speechreading while looking at the mouth of the speaker [34,37,42]. In addition, a prior experiment showed that even when an onscreen interpreter is present, DHH users still focus their gaze on a speakers' mouth for 12% of total television program time [37]. Thus, captions that block the mouth of the speaker may hinder the understandability, enjoyability and perception of captioned videos for such viewers. In addition, the facial expressions of the speaker may enable the viewer to understand the speaker's emotional state, as prior work has established that emotions are expressed through verbal and non-verbal forms, including body posture, facial expressions (e.g. raising or lowering the eyebrows), eye gaze, and etc. [26]. Thus, if captions block any of these portions of the body, the emotional state of speakers may be less apparent to DHH viewers. Given this prior work, in our study described below, we investigate the impact of captions blocking the eyes or mouth of the speaker.

Captions Occluding Portions of Onscreen Text: In addition to the speed of speech, how dynamically scenes change, the number of onscreen speakers, and their visibility, research has also established the importance of caption placement onscreen. Specifically, the existence, number, and layout of onscreen text elements should also be considered before placing captions on the video [13]. Captions overlapping with other text onscreen can be particularly problematic for live news broadcasts, as captions can hinder the ability of DHH viewers to read textual information transmitted as part of the video itself. This text content may include the name of the person who is speaking during a news interview, the headline of the current story, or the news ticker at the bottom of the screen, which often features additional facts or headlines for other stories. A prior experimental study revealed that DHH users focused on non-caption onscreen text 7% of a TV program's total time [37]. However, we found no prior research that had investigated quantitatively the effect of captions occluding onscreen news text on DHH viewers' judgments of captioned video quality. Recently, researchers have proposed methods that can detect text that appears in a video, either when this text appears in the real world and is simply captured by the video camera (as in the case of a real-world sign that is within the video frame) as well as text that has been added to a video image digitally (whether static or horizontally scrolling) as in a live news transmission [38,40]. Given these advancements, future metrics that assess the quality of a captioned video could penalize captions that block onscreen text, but research is needed to understand how such occlusion affects the judgements of DHH viewers.

3   Research Questions

As discussed above, prior work on automatic metrics of caption quality has not yet integrated occlusion features, i.e. information about the degree to which captions block other onscreen visual content that appears, potentially ephemerally, at a specific place and time in a video. As technologies emerge for automatically identifying speakers' faces or onscreen text in videos, there is a need to understand how occlusion of these forms of visual information may affect DHH viewer's judgement of the quality of captioned video. Therefore, in this study, we experimentally evaluate how variations in two such features may affect viewers' judgments of video quality, in the following research questions:

RQ1: Are DHH viewers' subjective judgments about whether captioned videos are useful, enjoyable, and easy-to-follow affected by whether captions overlap with the onscreen (a) speaker's eyes and (b) mouth?

RQ2: Are DHH viewers' subjective judgments about whether captioned videos are useful, enjoyable and easy-to-follow affected by whether captions overlap with onscreen text containing the (a) current news headline and (b) other news headlines?

4   Methodology and Results

Our experiment consisted of one-hour appointments with a set of DHH participants, with each appointment partitioned into two time-segments: In the first segment, we conducted a study to investigate RQ1, and in the second, we conducted another study to investigate RQ2. This section provides an overview of both studies, beginning with details that were common across both studies. Later, individual sub-sections below focus on the details that are unique to each of these studies.

4.1   Study Design and Question Items

For both studies, a website was developed to display to participants several videos with different variations of occlusion features, and participants responded to questions, to provide their subjective impression of the quality of the videos displayed. For the first time-segment of this study, participants viewed three stimuli videos on a webpage in a side-by-side manner, in which captions: (1) overlapped with speaker's eyes, (2) overlapped with speaker's mouth, or (3) did not overlap with speaker's face at all. For the second time-segment of this study, three stimuli videos were shown, in which captions: (1) overlapped with onscreen text displaying the headline of the current news story, (2) overlapped with a scrolling news ticker displaying headlines for other news stories, and (3) did not overlap with onscreen text at all. After participants watched each stimuli on the web page individually, they responded to three subjective scalar questions, of which Question 1 was adapted from [23] and Question 3 from [5].

Q1: How useful did you find the captions? ("Usefulness" question)
Q2: Did you enjoy watching the video with the caption? ("Enjoyability")
Q3: It was easy to follow the video. ("Easy-to-follow")

4.2   Data Collection Procedure

This study was originally planned to be conducted as an in-person study, in which a researcher would sit with participants to introduce the study and answer questions, in American Sign Language or spoken English, depending upon the participant's communication preference. The participants viewed the stimuli videos on a web page on a computer, and they responded to questions by writing responses on a paper answer sheet. However, partway through collecting data from our 29 participants, the experiment had to move to an online remote format, due the need to maintain social distancing during the COVID-19 pandemic. Therefore, while for the first 3 participants, the responses to these questions were taken on paper, for following 26 participants, these questions were embedded together with video stimuli in a survey hosted on SurveyMonkey. Our study had been approved by the university Institutional Review Board (IRB), and the modification of the study for online remote participant was also approved by the IRB prior to the final 26 appointments. We conducted the in-person segment of the study in our lab. A researcher started the experiment with participants by obtaining signatures on the informed consent form, and then participants filled out a demographic questionnaire. Next, the researcher showed participants the website (containing stimuli videos) that we had created and provided brief instructions about the study procedure. Then, a questionnaire form was handed over to the participants, consisting of the scalar and open-ended questions (described above), and participants responded to each set of questions after watching each video stimulus.

For the remotely conducted segment of the study, a researcher sent an informed consent form to our participants through email, which participants read and reviewed, prior to a video conference meeting between the researcher and the participant. Participants responded to a demographic questionnaire, which was presented as a Google Form. The researcher then sent the participant a link to the experiment, hosted on SurveyMonkey, which contained both the stimuli videos and the corresponding questions for each. We added a sample page at the start of the survey to familiarize our participants with the format of the study, to facilitate the researcher explaining the study procedure, which had been easier in the in-person format, since the researcher could point to on-screen elements of the survey.

4.3 Recruitment and Participants

Participants were recruited by posting an advertisement on social media websites. The advertisement included two key criteria: (1) identifying as Deaf or Hard of Hearing and (2) regularly using captioning when viewing videos or television. Participants received $40 cash compensation for either the in-person or the remotely conducted hour-long study conducted using a video-conferencing. A total of 29 people participated in the study including 14 females, 14 men, and one non-binary, aged 18 to 55 (median = 25). 19 of our participants identified as deaf and 10 identified as hard of hearing. All our participants except 2 reported regularly using American Sign Language at home or work. 20 of our participants reported that they began learning ASL when they were 9 years old or younger. The remaining participants reported using ASL for at least 2 years and that they regularly used it at work or school.

4.4 Sub-study 1: Face Occlusion

For the first time-segment of the experiment appointment, we conducted our
"face occlusion" study, to investigate how captions overlapping with the onscreen
speakers' face during live captioned TV programming may affect DHH viewer's
judgment of caption quality. There were three different placements of the caption
shown during this study:

– captions overlapped with the speaker's mouth,
– captions overlapped with speaker's eyes, and
– captions not overlapped with the speaker's eyes or mouth.

Fig. 1. Video stimuli samples from Face Occlusion sub-study.

For this study, we created nine video stimuli, based on video sources collected
from the YouTube distribution channels from mainstream television news agencies. Each of these video stimuli was around 30 s long, and it consisted of a news
broadcast with a single individual speaking. We avoided videos related to any
sensitive, trending, or polarizing issues, in an effort to keep the content as neutral as possible. Our rationale for this selection was that videos containing these
issues might lead to divergent reactions among participants. We truncated each
video to the desired length using FFMPEG [14], an open-source video-editing
tool. We extracted the caption files for each video, which consisted of Advanced
Substation Alpha files. We manually inspected each caption file to ensure that
there were no word omissions or other errors in the text, to prevent errors in
text quality from influencing DHH viewers' judgements of the captioned video.
We manipulated the settings within the caption file, to adjust the placement of
the caption on the video. For the condition in which the captions overlapped
with the speaker's mouth, we ensured that the overlapping occurs for the entire
length of the video. Similarly, for "overlapped with eyes" condition, we ensured
that the caption overlaps with speaker's eyes throughout the duration of the
stimuli video. Finally, we embedded the caption file in the stimuli video, and we
created three sample videos, for each condition, using the same source video.

Participants viewed three videos, with captions placed on different parts of
the screen (speaker's eyes, speaker's mouth, and at the bottom), serially, and
they answered three scalar questions for each video. Figure 1 shows the placement

of captions on the screen in each of the three videos. A Greco-Latin schedule was used to determine the left-to-right placement of the videos and their assignment to conditions to video stimuli.

Figure 2 displays a divergent stacked bar graph (with the neutral response item plotted on the midline of the x-axis) for responses to the "usefulness question" (Q1), "enjoyability question" (Q2), and "easy-to-follow question" for the Face Occlusion study, across the three conditions. All significant pairwise differences are indicated with double asterisk (**) in the figure if the p-value is less than 0.01. The statistical analysis performed for the two questions is described below.

To evaluate the responses to the "usefulness question," a Wilcoxon Signed-Rank test was used. The results indicated that participants found captioned videos with no overlapping (Median = 4) more useful than the videos in which the caption overlapped with speaker's eye (Median = 2), ($Z = -3.3456, p < 0.001$). In addition, participants found videos with no overlapping to be more useful than videos in which the caption overlapped with the speaker's mouth (Median = 2), ($Z = 2.6784, p < 0.01$). For the "enjoyability question," a Wilcoxon Signed-Ranks test revealed that DHH participants found captioned videos with no overlapping (Median = 4) more enjoyable than videos in which the caption overlapped with speaker's eye (Median = 2), ($Z = -3.0001, p < .01$), or than videos in which captions overlapped with the speaker's mouth (Median = 2), ($Z = .00236, p < .01$). Similar results were observed for "easy-to-follow question": with users preferring no-overlap vs. overlap-with-eyes ($Z = -2.688, p < .01$), and preference for no-overlap vs. overlap-with-mouth ($Z = -2.6416, p < .01$). For each of the above mentioned question item, no significant pairwise difference between responses for the "overlap with eyes" condition and the "overlap with mouth" condition was observed.

4.5 Sub-study 2: Text Occlusion

For the second time-segment of the experiment appointment, we conducted our "text occlusion" sub-study, to investigate how captions overlapping with onscreen text during live captioned TV programming may affect DHH viewer's judgment of caption quality. There were three different placements of the caption shown during this study:

- captions overlapped with onscreen 'current news' text (headline of the current story)
- captions overlapped with onscreen 'scrolling news' text (about other news stories)
- captions not overlapped with any onscreen text

For this study, we created nine video stimuli which were collected from the same video source as previous "face occlusion" study. These videos consisted of TV news and panel discussions which are identified by prior work as the video genres of the highest captioning importance [6]. In all of these videos, a region of the screen included some text indicating the topic of the current news story, and

212   A. A. Amin et al.

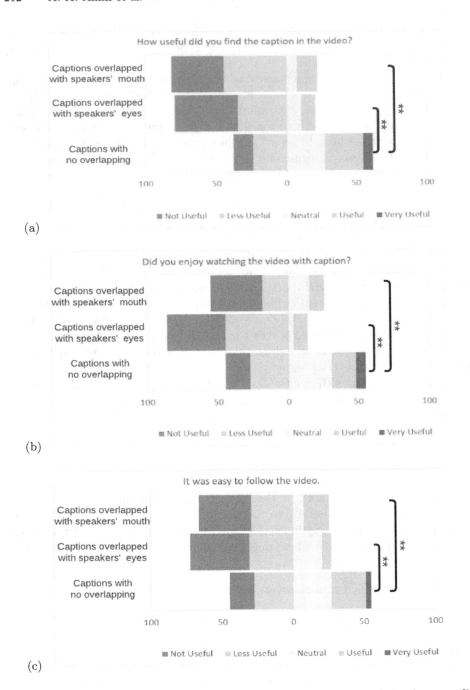

Fig. 2. Participants' subjective scalar responses for videos in each of the three conditions in the Face Occlusion sub-study, for (a) How useful did you find the caption? (b) Did you enjoy watching the video with the caption? (c) It was easy to follow the video. Double asterisks ** mark significant pairwise differences ($p < 0.01$).

another region contained a scrolling text area that presented headlines for other news stories. Both regions were near the bottom of the video image. As in the earlier "face occlusion" study, we cautiously selected videos in which speakers discussed a topic, which was not related to any political or trending issues, so that participants would not have strong emotional reactions to the content.

As before, to modify the caption transcript provided by the broadcaster, we extracted the caption file from the video source. Then we manually positioned the caption in such a way that a small fraction of 'current news' region (shown as black text on a white background in Fig. 3) was visible to participants. The rationale behind this decision to reveal a tiny amount of the 'current news' text was that if captions would completely overlap the text, then participants might not be aware that this text existed in the first place. We also ensured that there were no errors in the caption transcript, as we did in the first sub-study. Using FFMPEG, we created a total of nine videos, i.e. 3 sample videos produced under three different 3 caption-overlap conditions.

Fig. 3. Video stimuli samples from second segment of the study.

Participants viewed videos with captions placed on different positions such that it (1) overlapped current news text, (2) overlapped scrolling news text, or (3) did not overlap any text onscreen. On a screen that displayed three video stimuli side-by-side, participants viewed each video individually, and then answered the scalar questions after each. The left-to-right placement of the videos and the assignment of condition to each video was again determined using the Greco-Latin square method.

Figure 4 displays participants' responses to the "usefulness question" (Q1), "enjoyability question" (Q2), and "easy-to-follow question" (Q3) for the Text Occlusion sub-study across the three conditions. All significant pairwise differences are indicated with an asterisk (*), if the p-value is less than 0.05. The details of the statistical analysis performed for each question is described below.

For the "usefulness question," a Wilcoxon-Signed Rank test revealed that participants found captioned videos more useful when the caption does not overlap with any onscreen text (Median = 4) as compared to videos in which the caption overlaps with scrolling news text (Median = 3), ($Z = -2.0121, p < 0.05$). However, no significant difference was observed in the response to this question,

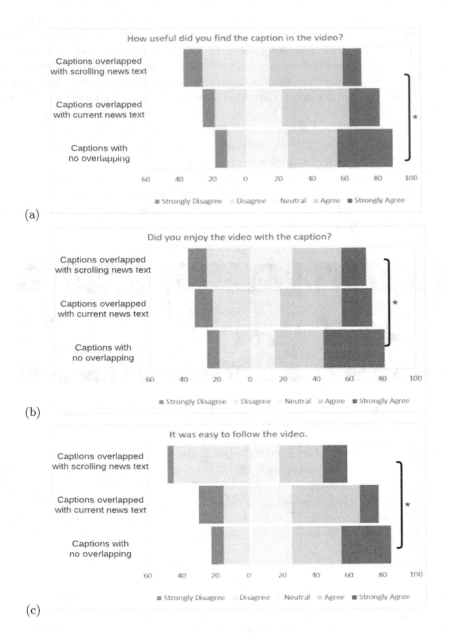

Fig. 4. Participants' subjective scalar responses for videos in each of the three conditions in the Text Occlusion study, for (a) How useful did you find the caption? (b) Did you enjoy watching the video with the caption? (c) It was easy to follow the video. Asterisks * mark significant pairwise differences ($p < 0.05$).

for any other pairs of conditions. For the "enjoyability question," a Wilcoxon-Signed Rank test revealed that participants preferred captioned videos in which the caption does not overlap with any text on screen (Median = 4) as compared to videos in which the caption overlapped with scrolling news text (Median = 3), ($Z = -2.128, p < 0.05$). Finally for "easy-to-follow" question, similar results were observed: preference for no-overlap vs. overlap-with-scrolling-news ($Z = -2.2012, p < 0.05$). However, no significant pairwise difference between responses for the "overlap with scrolling news" condition and the "overlap with current news" condition was observed for any of these three questions.

5 Discussion

Our experimental studies had examined each of our research questions, which concerned how variation in occlusion features in a captioned video may affect the judgements of DHH viewers about the video's quality, specifically in regard to whether users found the captioned video useful or enjoyable to watch.

RQ1: Are DHH viewers' subjective judgments about whether captioned videos are useful, enjoyable, and easy-to-follow affected by whether captions overlap with the onscreen (a) speaker's eyes and (b) mouth? In the Face Occlusion sub-study, we observed that participants found captioned videos in which the caption did not overlap with the "speakers' face", to be more useful, enjoyable and easy-to-follow, as compared to videos in which the caption overlapped with the speaker's eyes or mouth. These quantitative findings provide an answer to both part (a) and (b) of research question RQ1. This finding aligns with prior work, which had highlighted DHH viewers' opinion with the captions overlapping with critical onscreen content [5]. This finding also establishes that the onscreen speaker's face (their eyes and mouth, specifically) should be considered essential onscreen content, which should be visible to DHH viewers. Our findings also integrate with results of prior gaze-tracking studies with DHH viewers, which had revealed that users spend a significant amount of time focusing on a speakers' mouth [37] for speechreading. Above all, future design of caption evaluation metrics should be informed by this quantitative findings to reflect DHH viewers' judgment accurately.

RQ2: Are DHH viewers' subjective judgments about whether captioned videos are useful, enjoyable and easy-to-follow affected by whether captions overlap with onscreen text containing the (a) current news headline and (b) other news headlines? In the Text Occlusion sub-study, participants' responses revealed that captioned videos in which the caption did not overlap with any onscreen text were more useful, enjoyable and easy-to-follow, as compared to videos in which captions occluded scrolling text displaying headlines for other news stories. Our results did not show any significant difference between videos in which captions did not overlap any text and those in which captions occluded the current news story. Thus, our study only provided an answer to part (b) of research question RQ2 - indicating that our participants were bothered by captions blocking scrolling news headlines about other stories.

In addition to providing guidance for future caption-evaluation metrics, as discussed above for RQ1, both sections of our study have also illustrated methodologically how empirical responses can be collected from DHH participants in studies with captioned video. Such participation is essential in this research area, to ensure that DHH viewers' perspectives are considered in the design of caption-quality metrics.

6   Limitations and Future Work

There were several limitations in our study, some of which may suggest directions for future research, e.g. to generalize these findings to other groups of users or other video genres: Our study focused on DHH individuals that were recruited at a university, which reflects only a particular subset of the diverse DHH community. Future studies should examine the judgements of other potential users of captions, e.g. DHH individuals recruited from broader geographic settings or educational backgrounds, hearing individuals who may become DHH later in life, people with situationally induced hearing loss due to environmental noise, or specific sub-groups of the DHH community who prefer particular modes of communication (sign-language users vs. speech communication). In addition, a variety of educational factors or other demographic characteristics may affect how variations in these features may affect users' responses.

The motivation for our work has been to identify potential features for inclusion in new metrics for evaluating live television programs, where the near-real time context makes it more challenging for television broadcasters to provide high-quality captions. Given this focus, when preparing stimuli for our studies, we used videos of news broadcasts, including news anchors speaking to the camera, conducting interviews, panel discussions, or televised segments of speeches. Additional research would be needed to investigate a wider range of television genres, e.g. sports. A different set of critical onscreen content might be present in such videos, e.g. current scores during a sports competition, and such research may broaden the list of critical onscreen content that captions should not block.

Our study investigated DHH viewers' judgements of caption quality in regard to two specific questions, the usefulness of the caption (a question adapted from [23]) and how enjoyable the captioned video was. However, there are a variety of other measurement instruments that could be used to assess caption quality, either to gather further dimensions of subjective judgements, or to evaluate captions through some objective measure. For instance, our study did not explore the effect of occlusion on the understandability of onscreen text, which could be measured using objective comprehension questions.

While our study investigated two specific occlusion features, there may exist many other types of high-importance or high-information regions of videos which could be defined, which would further influence users' judgements of quality. More broadly, there are other features of caption quality that may have interaction effects with these occlusion features. For instance, in our "face occlusion" study, we observed the effect of one feature (captions overlapping with the speaker's face), for a set of videos that consisted of a single speaker in the video, and with perfect transcription accuracy. There is a potential for interaction effects between face-occlusion and other captioned-video qualities, e.g. the number of speakers in the video segment, the latency in the captioning, etc. In future work, a multi-factor study design would be needed to investigate whether such interactions may exist among caption properties.

7 Conclusion

Although transcription errors in live television captioning have reduced in recent years, with efforts driven in part by the availability of caption evaluation metrics [18], DHH users are still not fully satisfied with the quality of captions provided on live or near-live television broadcasters. Prior literature has suggested other important features of captioned video, such as whether captions occlude a speaker's face and other critical onscreen content. However, no prior empirical studies had examined the effect on DHH users' judgement of captioned videos from occlusion features, i.e. features relating to the overlap of captions with onscreen content that appears at particular times and locations in a video.

As discussed in our Introduction, to enable regulatory agencies responsible for monitoring the quality of captioned television programming to evaluate larger samples of captioned broadcasts, improved metrics are needed for automatically analyzing a captioned video to predict how it would correlate with DHH viewers' judgements. However, the currently available metrics do not account for whether captions occlude important video content, despite some regulations on caption quality that discuss this issue, e.g. [15,16].

Herein lies the key contribution of this study, namely: This research has identified properties of captioned video content – occlusion features – and has quantified the extent to which they affect DHH users' judgement of captioned videos. Basic empirical research, to examine how such features influence DHH viewer's quality-judgements, is foundational to the creation of high-quality, automatic metrics for efficiently evaluating captioned television programming. Having demonstrated this effect on DHH viewers' judgments, future research can investigate this relationship and examine how such features can be incorporated into existing metrics, which focus predominantly on text transcription accuracy. Since being able to measure something is often the first step toward improving it, by supporting the creation of metrics that consider a broader set of captioned video properties, this work may lead to more accessible television and video experiences for DHH viewers.

References

1. Ali, A., Renals, S.: Word error rate estimation for speech recognition: e-WER. In: Proceedings of the 56th Annual Meeting of the Association for Computational Linguistics, pp. 20–24 (2018)

2. Akahori, W., Hirai, T., Morishima, S.: Dynamic subtitle placement considering the region of interest and speaker location. In: Proceedings of 12th International Joint Conference on Computer Vision, Imaging and Computer Graphics Theory and Applications (2017)

3. Apone, T., Botkin, B., Brooks, M., Goldberg, L.: Research into automated error ranking of real-time captions in live television news programs. Caption accuracy metrics project. National Center for Accessible Media (2011). http://ncam.wgbh.org/file_download/136

4. Apone, T., Botkin, B., Brooks, M., Goldberg, L.: Caption accuracy metrics project. Research into automated error ranking of real-time captions in live television news programs. The Carl and Ruth Shapiro Family National Center for Accessible Media at WGBH (NCAM) (2011)

5. Berke, L., Albusays, K., Seita, M., Huenerfauth, M.: Preferred appearance of captions generated by automatic speech recognition for deaf and hard-of-hearing viewers. In: Extended Abstracts of the 2019 CHI Conference on Human Factors in Computing Systems (CHI EA 2019), p. 6. ACM, New York (2019). Paper LBW1713. https://doi.org/10.1145/3290607.3312921

6. Berke, L., Seita, M., Huenerfauth, M.: Deaf and hard-of-hearing users' prioritization of genres of online video content requiring accurate captions. In: Proceedings of the 17th International Web for All Conference (W4A 2020), pp. 1–12. ACM, New York (2020). Article 3. https://doi.org/10.1145/3371300.3383337

7. Berke, L.: Displaying confidence from imperfect automatic speech recognition for captioning. In: ACM Special Interest Group on Accessible Computing (SIGACCESS), no. 117, pp. 14–18 (2017). https://doi.org/10.1145/3051519.3051522

8. Blackwell, D.L., Lucas, J.W., Clarke, T.C.: Summary health statistics for U.S. adults: national health interview survey, 2012. National Center for Health Statistics. Vital Health Statistics. Series 10 (260) (2014)

9. Blanchfield, B.B., Feldman, J.J., Dunbar, J.J., Gardner, E.N.: The severely to profoundly hearing-impaired population in the United States: prevalence estimates and demographics. J. Am. Acad. Audiol. **12**(4), 183–189 (2001). http://www.ncbi.nlm.nih.gov/pubmed/11332518

10. Brown, A., et al.: Dynamic subtitles: the user experience. In: Proceedings of the ACM International Conference on Interactive Experiences for TV and Online Video (TVX 2015), pp. 103–112. ACM, New York (2015). https://doi.org/10.1145/2745197.2745204

11. Burnham, D., et al.: Parameters in television captioning for deaf and hard-of-hearing adults: effects of caption rate versus text reduction on comprehension. J. Deaf Stud. Deaf Educ. **13**(3), 391–404 (2008). https://doi.org/10.1093/deafed/enn003

12. Crabb, M., Jones, R., Armstrong, M., Hughes, C.J.: Online news videos: the UX of subtitle position. In: Proceedings of the 17th International ACM SIGACCESS Conference on Computers & Accessibility (ASSETS 2015), pp. 215–222. ACM, New York (2015). https://doi.org/10.1145/2700648.2809866

13. Dwyer, T., Perkins, C., Redmond, S., Sita, J.: Seeing into Screens: Eye Tracking and the Moving Image. Bloomsbury, New York (2018)

14. FFMPEG Developers: FFMPEG tool (version be1d324) [software] (2016). http://ffmpeg.org/

15. Federal Communications Commission: Closed Captioning Quality Report and Order, Declaratory Ruling, FNPRM (2014). https://www.fcc.gov/document/closed-captioning-quality-report-and-order-declaratory-ruling-fnprm

16. Federal Communications Commission: Closed captioning of internet protocol-delivered video programming: implementation of the twenty-first century communications and video accessibility act of 2010. Adopted rules governing the closed captioning requirements for the owners, providers, and distributors of video programming delivered using IP, and governing the closed captioning capabilities of certain apparatus on which consumers view video programming. MB Docket No. 11-154. FCC 12-9 (2012)

17. Glasser, A., Mason Riley, E., Weeks, K., Kushalnagar, R.: Mixed reality speaker identification as an accessibility tool for deaf and hard of hearing users. In: Proceedings of the 25th ACM Symposium on Virtual Reality Software and Technology (VRST 2019), pp. 1–3. ACM, New York (2019). Article 80. https://doi.org/10.1145/3359996.3364720

18. Government of Canada: Canadian Radio-Television and Telecommunications Commission, & Crtc. Broadcasting Regulatory Policy CRTC 2019-308 (2019). https://crtc.gc.ca/eng/archive/2019/2019-308.htm

19. Gower, M., Shiver, B., Pandhi, C., Trewin, S.: Leveraging pauses to improve video captions. In: Proceedings of the 20th International ACM SIGACCESS Conference on Computers and Accessibility (ASSETS 2018), pp. 414–416. ACM, New York (2018). https://doi.org/10.1145/3234695.3241023

20. Gulliver, S.R., Ghinea, G.: How level and type of deafness affect user perception of multimedia video clips. Univ. Access Inf. Soc. **2**(4), 374–386 (2003). https://doi.org/10.1007/s10209-003-0067-5

21. Gulliver, S.R., Ghinea, G.: Impact of captions on hearing impaired and hearing perception of multimedia video clips. In: Proceedings of the IEEE International Conference on Multimedia and Expo (2003)

22. Hong, R., Wang, M., Xu, M., Yan, S., Chua, T.-S.: Dynamic captioning: video accessibility enhancement for hearing impairment. In: Proceedings of the 18th ACM International Conference on Multimedia (MM 2010), pp. 421–430. ACM, New York (2010). https://doi.org/10.1145/1873951.1874013

23. Kafle, S., Huenerfauth, M.: Evaluating the usability of automatically generated captions for people who are deaf or hard of hearing. In: Proceedings of the 19th International ACM SIGACCESS Conference on Computers and Accessibility (ASSETS 2017), pp. 165–174. ACM, New York (2017). https://doi.org/10.1145/3132525.3132542

24. Kushalnagar, R.S., Lasecki, W.S., Bigham, J.P.: Accessibility evaluation of classroom captions. In: ACM Special Interest Group on Accessible Computing (SIGACCESS), p. 24, vol. 5, no. 3, January 2014. Article 7. https://doi.org/10.1145/2543578

25. Lasecki, W.S., Miller, C.D., Bigham, J.P.: Warping time for more effective real-time crowdsourcing. In: Proceedings of the SIGCHI Conference on Human Factors in Computing Systems (CHI 2013), pp. 2033–2036. ACM, New York (2013). https://doi.org/10.1145/2470654.2466269

26. Lee, D.G., Fels, D.I., Udo, J.P.: Emotive captioning. Comput. Entertain. **5**(2), 15 (2007). https://doi.org/10.1145/1279540.1279551. Article 11

27. Nam, S., Fels, D.I., Chignell, M.H.: Modeling closed captioning subjective quality assessment by deaf and hard of hearing viewers. Proc. IEEE Trans. Comput. Soc. Syst. **7**(3), 621–631 (2020). https://doi.org/10.1109/TCSS.2020.2972399

28. NIDCD: National Institute of Deafness and Other Communication Disorder: Captions for Deaf and Hard-of-Hearing Viewers (2017). https://www.nidcd.nih.gov/health/captions-deaf-and-hard-hearing-viewers

29. Ofcom: measuring live subtitling quality, UK (2015). https://www.nidcd.nih.gov/health/captions-deaf-and-hard-hearing-viewers
30. Oskar Olofsson: Detecting Unsynchronized Audio and Subtitles Using Machine Learning, Dissertation (2019). http://urn.kb.se/resolve?urn=urn:nbn:se:kth:diva-261414
31. Press Release: World-first approach to reduce latency in live captioning. Ericsson (2016). https://www.ericsson.com/en/press-releases/2016/6/world-first-approach-to-reduce-latency-in-live-captioning
32. Romero-Fresco, P., Pérez, J.M.: Accuracy rate in live subtitling: the NER model. In: Audiovisual Translation in a Global Context. Palgrave Macmillan, London (2015)
33. Sandford, J.: The impact of subtitle display rate on enjoyment under normal television viewing conditions. In: Proceedings of IET Conference Proceedings (2015). https://doi.org/10.1049/ibc.2015.0018
34. Strelcyk, O., Singh, G.: TV listening and hearing aids. PLoS ONE **13**(6), e0200083 (2018). https://doi.org/10.1371/journal.pone.0200083
35. Vy, Q.V., Fels, D.I.: Using placement and name for speaker identification in captioning. In: Miesenberger, K., Klaus, J., Zagler, W., Karshmer, A. (eds.) ICCHP 2010. LNCS, vol. 6179, pp. 247–254. Springer, Heidelberg (2010). https://doi.org/10.1007/978-3-642-14097-6_40
36. Waller, J.M., Kushalnagar, R.S.: Evaluation of automatic caption segmentation. In: Proceedings of the 18th International ACM SIGACCESS Conference on Computers and Accessibility (ASSETS 2016), pp. 331–332. ACM, New York (2016). https://doi.org/10.1145/2982142.2982205
37. Wehrmeyer, J.: Eye-tracking Deaf and hearing viewing of sign language interpreted news broadcasts. J. Eye Move. Res. (2014). https://core.ac.uk/download/pdf/158976673.pdf
38. Zedan, I.A., Elsayed, K.M., Emary, E.: Caption detection, localization and type recognition in Arabic news video. In: Proceedings of the 10th International Conference on Informatics and Systems (INFOS 2016), pp. 114–120. ACM, New York (2016). https://doi.org/10.1145/2908446.2908472
39. Zhang, Z., Wang, C., Wang, Y.: Video-based face recognition: state of the art. In: Sun, Z., Lai, J., Chen, X., Tan, T. (eds.) CCBR 2011. LNCS, vol. 7098, pp. 1–9. Springer, Heidelberg (2011). https://doi.org/10.1007/978-3-642-25449-9_1
40. Zhou, X., et al.: EAST: an efficient and accurate scene text detector. In: The Proceedings of 2017 IEEE Conference on Computer Vision and Pattern Recognition (CVPR) (2017)
41. Brown, A., et al.: Dynamic subtitles: the user experience. In: Proceedings of the ACM International Conference on Interactive Experiences for TV and Online Video (TVX 2015), pp. 103–112. Association for Computing Machinery, New York (2015). https://doi.org/10.1145/2745197.2745204
42. English-Language Working Group: Closed Captioning Standards and Protocol for Canadian English Language Television Programming Services (2008). https://www.cab-acr.ca/english/social/captioning/captioning.pdf. Accessed 19 Nov 2020

Reading Experiences and Reading Efficiency Among Adults with Dyslexia: An Accessibility Study

Gerd Berget[1]([✉]) [iD] and Siri Fagernes[2] [iD]

[1] Department of Archivistics, Library and Information Sciences, Oslo Metropolitan University, Postboks 4 St. Olavs plass, 0130 Oslo, Norway
gerd.berget@oslomet.no
[2] Mobile Technology Lab, Department of Technology, Kristiania University College, Pb 1190 Sentrum, 0170 Oslo, Norway

Abstract. Dyslexia is a common reading disorder that typically affects reading, concentration and short-term memory. Consequently, for people with dyslexia, reading fictional books might be challenging. Several studies have addressed layout and typography of digital texts. Less attention has been directed towards printed books. It has been suggested that e-readers might be beneficial for some people in this cohort. In this study, however, all the participants preferred reading fictional books on paper. This study investigates whether different line lengths affect reading experiences and reading efficiency of people with dyslexia. The overall purpose is to get a better understanding of how to produce accessible books. The experiments involve 20 adults reading excerpts from three fictional books in four different conditions where line length is the only independent variable. A screening-test for dyslexia was applied, in addition to eye-tracking and interviews. The findings indicate that the participants do not prefer narrow line lengths. However, the results show no significant impact of line lengths on reading speed or comprehension. The main conclusion is that line lengths seem to affect reading motivation, but not performance.

Keywords: Dyslexia · Line lengths · Reading

1 Introduction

Dyslexia affects spelling and fluent word level reading [1]. This cognitive impairment is prevalent in approximately 7% of any population [2], with some variations between languages. The Norwegian written language has a frequent use of double consonants, silent consonants, consonant clusters, silent vowels, and words with irregular orthography, all of which people with dyslexia typically find challenging [3–5]. Consequently, learning to read can be demanding for many Norwegian children [4].

In Norway, the organisation *Books for Everyone* produces accessible literature in six different categories targeting various user groups (Table 1). The *Easy to Read* category comprises books written specifically for users who find reading challenging, for instance

© Springer Nature Switzerland AG 2021
M. Antona and C. Stephanidis (Eds.): HCII 2021, LNCS 12769, pp. 221–240, 2021.
https://doi.org/10.1007/978-3-030-78095-1_17

people with dyslexia, users with ADHD, non-native English speakers, inexperienced readers, or people who are ill. Such books are typically referred to as high-content/low-skills or high-interest/low-level books [6], hereby referred to as *Hi-Lo books*. Hi-Lo books typically have a reading level below the actual age of the reader, but address topics appropriate for the reader's age. Consequently, these books should not be mistaken for easy-to-read books for children learning how to read. Books in the *Easy to Understand* category are also modified in content, and the intended user group is people with severe developmental impairments. The remaining categories have modifications based on font sizes (*Big Letters*) or the inclusion of alternatives to plain text.

Table 1. Book categories applied by *Books for Everyone.*

Category
Easy to Read
Easy to Understand
Big Letters
Braille and Tactile Pictures
Sign Language and Norwegian with Sign Support
Alternative Communication Signs

In the production of Hi-Lo books, *Books for Everyone* alters various aspects of the books to ensure they are easy-to-read, e.g., using short sentences, avoiding long or complicated words, ensuring concrete content and keeping consistency between text and illustrations. Paper quality, typography and layout are also considered. Although Hi-Lo books are intended for various user groups, this paper will focus on one target group, namely people with dyslexia.

Typography has been reported to significantly affect accessibility for readers with dyslexia [7]. Several researchers have investigated how to best present text visually for people with dyslexia, addressing font types [7], font sizes [8], letter spacing [9], line spacing [10] and line lengths [11, 12]. However, most of these studies focus on reading on screen, less attention is directed towards printed books. Hi-Lo Books produced by *Books for Everyone* have a layout with a high frequency of very short line lengths, from approximately 10 characters and up (Fig. 1). The purpose is to enhance the reading experience by providing small amounts of text at a time. According to representatives from *Books for Everyone*, the reason for this layout is the assumption that it makes the text more accessible for people with reading impairments. However, applying short line lengths implies that even relatively short sentences are split over several lines (Fig. 1, first and second sentence), requiring vertical eye movements in the middle of a sentence. Consequently, the reader must remember the text before the line shift until continuing reading the next line.

Dyslexia is often associated with reduced short-term memory capacity [13]. It is also claimed that the eye movements follow a different pattern compared to readers without dyslexia. However, Starr and Rayner [14] suggest that the reading impairment associated with dyslexia may cause irregular eye movements, not the other way around. The purpose of this study is to investigate whether short line lengths support the reading of people with dyslexia, or whether having sentences spread over several lines makes the text more difficult to read. This study is motivated by the assumption that frequent line shifts and numerous vertical eye movements within sentences may interfere with the reading fluency. Moreover, if the reader must re-read a sentence (e.g. due to forgetting content or decoding errors), longer vertical eye movements are required to navigate back to the beginning of the sentence. This study explores the following research questions:

RQ₁: Do line lengths affect the reading experience for people with dyslexia?
RQ₂: Do line lengths affect the reading efficiency for people with dyslexia?

Søndag
Jeg lager spinatpai og en gresk salat
ved siden av. Jeg har kjøpt fetaost
og oliven. Jeg har bakt brød også.
Urtebrød.
Klokka fem er alt klart.
Hun kommer sikkert litt over fem.

Fig. 1. Lindkvist [15], excerpt from page 17, reproduced with permission.

Reading experience comprises subjective measures acquired from qualitative interviews. Reading efficiency is commonly associated with reading speed, and has been applied as a measure either alone or combined with other units for decades [16]. High reading speed, however, does not necessarily entail successful reading, since comprehension is also important [16, 17]. According to Perfetti [18], reading efficiency may be regarded as a ratio of outcome to effort, where time is the proxy for effort. It is argued that the ability to retrieve words is more important than speeds. In this study reading efficiency is related to a combination of objective scores from reading experiments, namely reading speed (words per minute) and reading comprehension (number of correct answers about the previously read content).

2   Background

Dyslexia occurs in many forms and severities, and the definition is still under debate [19]. However, there seems to be consensus that dyslexia is related to challenges with fluent or accurate word recognition and spelling, and affects reading comprehension [20]. Other common cognitive markers are impaired short-term memory capacity [13] and reduced concentration [21]. One of the main challenges for people with dyslexia is reading long texts [22], such as books. Consequently, there is a need to consider how to produce accessible books, with the aim to facilitate the reading process.

2.1 Accessibility and Universal Design

Producing accessible books, such as the *Hi-Lo* books developed by *Books for Everyone,* represents an inclusive strategy, where the aim is to provide low proficient readers with suitable and accessible materials that hold a high literary quality. However, accessibility in general, and modified books in particular, are scarcely discussed in the research literature. Thiessen and Dyson [23] reported that children with dyslexia prefer books that resemble books read by their peers over books that are regarded as easier to read by typographic convention. This finding is in accordance with Berget and Fagernes [24], who found that adults with dyslexia in general were sceptical towards books that appeared to be modified because the books *"looked like elementary school books"* and *"they did not want to feel stupid"*. The same finding was reported by Brante [25]. Consequently, it seems like the universal design perspective might be more purposeful.

Universal design concerns designing and developing products, services and environments so that they can be used by everyone, regardless of their level of functioning. One of the goals of universal design is to avoid adapted solutions for people with specific impairments, but rather design user-friendly solutions for 'everyone'. Motivations for universal design are manifold, such as human rights, social inclusion, and the ability for everyone to participate in the society on equal premises [26–28].

2.2 Reading Skills

Leisure reading is considered important to develop social skills such as empathy [29] and improve reading skills, especially for users with reading impairments [30]. According to Gambrell [31], students will never reach their full literacy potential without a high reading engagement. Gambrell [31] defines motivation to read as *"likelihood of engaging in reading"* and emphasises the importance of promoting intrinsic motivation. Further, Gambrell [31] suggests seven rules of engagement, including *"students will be more motivated if they have opportunities to be successful with challenging texts"*. The reader is likely to give up reading if the text is too difficult, but also if it is too easy. Moreover, according to Schunk and Zimmerman [32], self-esteem might be an important factor related to reading experience and efficiency.

Low self-esteem is reported as a key issue for both children and adults with dyslexia in general [33–35], and females in particular [36]. In the context of reading, Gambrell [31] reported that all students would like to be perceived as reading challenging books, and people with reading impairments often choose books for pleasure reading that are too difficult to read. Consequently, Gambrell [31] recommends to not label books as *easy, average* or *difficult*, since the people who would benefit from reading the "easy books" would probably avoid them.

Becker and McElvany [37] found that children who enjoy reading as a leisure activity read frequently and develop good reading skills. In contrast, children who read primarily because of extrinsic motivation have less developed reading skills. Consequently, it seems important for children with dyslexia to have access to books they have an intrinsic motivation to read. Based on the assumption that this also applies to adults with dyslexia, the main purpose of this study is to gain an understanding of how to develop books that motivate adults with reading impairments to read. According to Becker and McElvany

[37] the reason why people with reading challenges do not succeed in their reading may not always be lack of motivation. The challenges might also be a result of previous experience of little or no progress in enhancing reading skills. It is therefore important to develop books that give a sense of coping, but at the same time increase in complexity and difficulty.

Leinonen and Müller [38] studied the reading habits of adults with dyslexia and found a relationship between reading speed and frequency of reading, where the faster readers read more in their everyday lives. Moreover, teaching people with dyslexia faster reading styles might be important to keep the person motivated to read. A relevant measure often applied in this context is reading fluency, a measure that has been defined differently over the years. However, Wolf and Katzir-Cohen [39] argue that reading fluency should be regarded as both component-based and developmental-based, where reading rate and speed are subskills of reading, while automaticity and accuracy result from reading and reading fluency.

Memory was early assumed to play a vital part in reading, and it has been suggested that differences in working memory may be reflected in reading comprehension [40, 41]. Short-term memory represents an important contributor to reading comprehension [42], from the basic level of reading letters and assembling them into words to remembering previously read words and putting them together in a sentence. Finally, previously read content must be recalled, so the new sentences can be put into a context. People with dyslexia typically have reduced short-term memory capacity [13], causing additional challenges with reading comprehension.

2.3 Layout and Typography

The impact of physical characteristics of a text, and how those affect reading has been discussed for decades. Samuels and Eisenberg [43] point out that these characteristics may influence reading speed, the nature of eye movements and overall reading strategy. According to Rello and Baeza-Yates [7], the layout and typography of a text is fundamental for people with dyslexia. Several researchers have investigated which layout and typography that best accommodate users with dyslexia primarily addressing reading on screen. Moreover, Jackson [44] reported that most of the research related to typology has been conducted on participants under 18 years, and often younger children. Consequently, there is a need to look further into these issues in the adult population with dyslexia.

It has been argued that there are benefits for people in general to read in a printed over digital format, especially in the context of learning [45], and for some users with dyslexia [46]. An advantage of screen reading is the possibilities for personalization, such as adjusting font sizes or zoom in on certain content. Nevertheless, previous research has reported overwhelming preferences for printed books over digital media [47, 48]. Moreover, students who read texts on paper have been reported to receive better reading comprehension scores than students who read digitally [49].

Typography has been discussed in the context of dyslexia. It has been suggested that fonts without serifs are most accessible, both on paper [50] and screen [7]. Rello and Baeza-Yates [51] found that sans serif, monospaces and roman font styles improved reading efficiency on screen, while serif, italic and proportional fonts were not optimal.

Special font types for people with dyslexia have also been developed, for instance *Sylexiad*, aimed at adult readers with dyslexia [52], *OpenDyslexic* and *font Dyslexie* [53]. Marinus and Mostard [54] tested the readability of *font Dyslexie* and concluded that it was not the shape of the letters, but the spacing between the letters, that benefited users with dyslexia. Zorzi and Barbiero [9] concluded that extra-large spacing between printed letters supported readers with dyslexia. In the context of screen reading, Rello and Pielot [10] concluded that line spacing had no effect on digital readability.

According to O'Brien and Mansfield [8], people with dyslexia rely on larger letters than readers without dyslexia to accomplish maximum reading speed. The British Dyslexia Association [50] recommends 12–14-point font size, and suggests that some users with dyslexia might prefer even bigger fonts. Rello and Pielot [10] reported that font size has a significant effect on the readability and comprehension of a text and suggest 18-point font size.

Few studies address line lengths. For books in general, line lengths should not surpass 70 characters [55]. However, according to Davidov [56], common line lengths in books are 80–100 characters. Bernard and Fernandez [57] looked at the differences between adults and children regarding line lengths (not including participants with reading impairments) while reading digital texts. They found no differences in reading times or efficiency for either groups. However, medium line lengths (55 characters per line) were considered optimal for reading.

Schneps and Thomson [12] studied people with dyslexia and their use of e-readers. In a POD condition, the text was on average displayed with line lengths of 12.7 characters per line, compared to 67.2 characters in a PAD condition. Schneps and Thomson [12] concluded that shorter lines could be beneficial. This finding contrasts with the guidelines from British Dyslexia Association [50], recommending 60–70 characters per line. Rello and Baeza-Yates [11] investigated reading on screen and concluded that line lengths had no significant effect on the readability for people with dyslexia. Moreover, some participants preferred wide columns, because the text seemed shorter [11]. Consequently, typography may not only affect readability, but also motivation.

3   Methods

This study applied a within-subjects design, using a triangulation of methods, namely screening tests, interviews, and reading experiments involving eye tracking equipment.

3.1   Participants

The study comprised 20 people based on the following inclusion criteria; age above 18 years and a formal diagnosis of dyslexia. Participants could not rely on reading spectacles, since glasses would interfere with the eye tracking equipment. A total of 22 participants were recruited. However, two people were excluded because of too high scores on the dyslexia screening test. No control group was included, since the purpose of the study was to investigate the accessibility of adapted books targeted specifically at readers with dyslexia.

Participants were mainly recruited through the organisations *Books for Everyone* and *Dyslexia Norway*. The participants (Table 2) were aged between 18 and 40, with an average age of 26.2 years. The gender distribution was 11 females (55%) and 9 males (45%). No participants had any relations to the experimenters.

Table 2. Participant characteristics.

Participant	Gender	Age	Educational level
P1	Male	25	Bachelor of Information Technology
P2	Female	29	Bachelor of Arts and Design
P3	Female	36	Bachelor of Information Technology
P4	Female	30	Bachelor of Preschool Education
P5	Male	40	Completed apprenticeship
P6	Female	25	Master of Education
P7	Female	22	Student (3rd year Bachelor of Business)
P8	Female	23	Bachelor of Economics
P9	Male	22	Upper secondary school
P10	Male	35	Completed apprenticeship (carpenter)
P11	Male	26	Student (3rd year, Bachelor Paramedics)
P12	Male	23	Student (1st year, Bachelor Information Technology)
P13	Male	28	Completed apprenticeship (helicopter technician)
P14	Female	23	Student (1st year Bachelor Information Technology)
P15	Male	22	Student (1st year Bachelor Information Technology)
P16	Female	18	Student (1st year Bachelor Nursing)
P17	Female	18	Upper secondary school pupil (3rd year)
P18	Male	19	In apprenticeship (2nd year electrician)
P19	Female	23	Student (1st Bachelor of Library- and information science)
P20	Female	37	Bachelor of Library- and Information Science

3.2 Procedure

Each session lasted for approximately one hour and followed the same procedure for all participants. First, participants got general information about the study and signed a consent form, followed by registration of background data such as gender, age and diagnoses.

Two screening tests were then conducted, one for visual acuity and one for dyslexia. A Landolt C visual acuity test was applied at a distance of 40 cm for short vision, according to the European Standard [58]. The purpose of the test was to ensure that the reading efficiency was not affected by reduced or blurred vision. The inclusion criterion was set at a visual acuity of 0.8 with both eyes open, within limits of what is regarded as normal vision [59]. A Norwegian Word Chain Test [60] was applied to screen for dyslexia. The purpose of this test was twofold; to confirm the diagnosis without accessing sensitive diagnostic papers, and to provide information about the decoding skills of each participant.

The participants were interviewed about their general reading habits and their preferences of the design and layout of printed books. After freely discussing characteristics affecting their motivation to read a book and which criteria they used when selecting a book, the participants were presented with six attributes (number of pages, number of illustrations, amount of text per page, line lengths, font type and font size) and asked to rate them from most to least important. Each interview was succeeded by a reading experiment. The participants wore SMI eye-tracking glasses 2 Wireless (SMI ETG 2W) through the entire reading session. Eye movements were recorded with a tracking ratio of 60 Hz. The sound recorder option was activated.

The participants read texts from all books in four different line lengths. Each text was read once, in one condition only. The participants read the texts silently in their own pace. After completing each text, the participants answered two questions about the content. All questions had been piloted and modified to ensure equal levels of difficulty. In the post-interview, participants were asked about overall preferences for each condition, with the purpose of getting subjective measures of the reading experience.

3.3 Stimulus

The stimulus comprised twelve texts and included four pages each from three different fictional novels in the *Books for Everyone* category *Easy to Read*. Every page had been selected so the story would make sense without reading the whole book. It was also important to ensure that the pages were equivalent in terms of length and reading level to enable comparisons between conditions. The excerpts were therefore analysed according to word count. In cases where the pages did not have an equal number of words, the text was slightly edited by removing the exceeding number of words, typically adjectives. This revision did not affect content or reading level.

The books were analysed according to the use of compound words, double consonants, silent consonants, consonant clusters, silent vowels and words with irregular orthography. The purpose was to ensure an even distribution of linguistical elements that people with dyslexia typically find challenging [3–5].

The texts were printed in black ink on pearl white 130-g paper in A4-size based on the recommendations by the British Dyslexia Association [50] to avoid large contrasts between text and background. The font type Arial was used, a font-type without serifs which is frequently suggested to be accessible for people with dyslexia [7, 50]. The font size was 14 points, corresponding with the font size originally applied in the books. This size is also recommended by the British Dyslexia Association [50] and applied in other studies e.g. Zorzi and Barbiero [9]. The layout comprised left-justified text with ragged right edge, which is commonly reported to be beneficial for people with dyslexia [50].

Each text was printed in four conditions, where line length was the only independent variable. The line lengths were either 40, 60 or 80 characters including white space, hereby referred to as L40, L60 and L80 (Fig. 2) In addition, the original, unmodified version by Books for Everyone was included, hereby referred to as BfE. The line length of 60 characters was based on guidelines by the British Dyslexia Association [50], recommending 60–70 characters, while 40 and 80 were based on studies such as Rello and Baeza-Yates [11].

BfE version:

> Jeg lager spinatpai og en gresk salat ved siden av. Jeg har kjøpt fetaost og oliven. Jeg har bakt brød også. Urtebrød. Klokka fem er alt klart. Hun kommer sikkert litt over fem. Kvart over fem er jeg utålmodig. Og sulten. Halv seks ringer jeg uten å få svar. Kvart på seks spiser jeg. Det smaker ikke så godt som jeg hadde trodd.

L40:

> Jeg lager spinatpai og en gresk salat ved siden av. Jeg har kjøpt fetaost og oliven. Jeg har bakt brød også. Urtebrød. Klokka fem er alt klart. Hun kommer sikkert litt over fem. Kvart over fem er jeg utålmodig. Og sulten. Halv seks ringer jeg uten å få svar. Kvart på seks spiser jeg. Det smaker ikke så godt som jeg hadde trodd.

L60:

> Jeg lager spinatpai og en gresk salat ved siden av. Jeg har kjøpt fetaost og oliven. Jeg har bakt brød også. Urtebrød. Klokka fem er alt klart. Hun kommer sikkert litt over fem. Kvart over fem er jeg utålmodig. Og sulten. Halv seks ringer jeg uten å få svar. Kvart på seks spiser jeg. Det smaker ikke så godt som jeg hadde trodd.

L80:

> Jeg lager spinatpai og en gresk salat ved siden av. Jeg har kjøpt fetaost og oliven. Jeg har bakt brød også. Urtebrød. Klokka fem er alt klart. Hun kommer sikkert litt over fem. Kvart over fem er jeg utålmodig. Og sulten. Halv seks ringer jeg uten å få svar. Kvart på seks spiser jeg. Det smaker ikke så godt som jeg hadde trodd.

Fig. 2. Excerpts from stimuli (Lindkvist, 2013: p. 17) in the four conditions, reprinted with permission.

Six experimental folders were assembled where books and conditions appeared in different orders. However, all pages from the same book were read in sequence and ascending order, to avoid frequent shifts in writing styles and content. The condition for each text varied, but all books were represented in every version in the document corpus. Each participant got one folder, and the folders were equally distributed among the participants.

3.4 Analysis

Data from the interviews addressing reading habits and preferences were categorised and analysed qualitatively. Preferences from the post-interview were used as subjective measures for reading experience. Reading efficiency measures were acquired from the reading experiments and analysed quantitatively. Reading speed and comprehension scores were used as objective measures of reading efficiency.

For each participant, reading speed (words read per minute) was computed for each read text based on the eye-tracking recordings. One of the goals was to investigate whether the text format with respect to line lengths affected the reading efficiency of the users. Consequently, the mean and median reading speeds were computed, as well as the total amount of correct answers given for each text format. The latter was used as a measure of reading comprehension. The use of measures for objective readability, objective comprehensibility and subjective preferences is in accordance with the study by Rello and Baeza-Yates [11].

Finally, it was tested for correlation between reading speed and line lengths for the different formats. The BfE format does not specify any standard line lengths, which implies that the line lengths vary. The estimated reading speeds of this format were hence not included in the correlation tests. For subsets of the data with very large variation in reading times, the eye-tracking data was visually inspected to investigate whether any particular behaviour stood out.

3.5 Ethical Considerations

The project was approved and ethically screened by the Norwegian Centre for Research Data (project number 50953). All data was anonymised. Participants could withdraw from the study at any time without justifying the decision.

4 Findings

4.1 Pre-interviews

In the context of reading habits, 11 participants rarely or never read fictional books, 2 of which had never read a whole book. While 3 people read on a monthly basis, only 6 participants read daily or weekly. Several participants expressed a wish to read more. Of the participants who read frequently, 2 people referred to this as an intentional strategy to improve reading skills.

When reading fictional books, all participants preferred reading in printed format. Their main justification was either concerned with e-books being tiresome to read or related to compensating strategies. Several participants mentioned using a white paper or their finger as navigational support while reading, a strategy they found difficult to apply when reading digital media.

The participants mentioned several characteristics of books that affected their motivation to read. Typography was the most frequently mentioned issue. 10 participants emphasised different perspectives on white space, between words, lines or paragraphs, the amount of text on each page and/or the total amount of white space on each page, while 6 mentioned either font type, font size or both. Easy language ("*but not too easy*") was mentioned by 9, while 8 focused on the actual content, such as "*a catchy topic*", the blurb, genre or title. Design was mentioned by 8 persons, with a focus on the cover and illustrations. Some relied on recommendations by others or the reputation of the book or author, a criterion mentioned by 7 of the participants. The structure of the book was mentioned by 4 people, such as a preference for short paragraphs or chapters, while only 1 person mentioned number of pages of the book.

When asked to rank 6 specific attributes (Fig. 3), text per page was ranked as the most important aspect by 7 participants, 3 emphasised either number of pages, font type or font size, while 2 ranked illustrations or line lengths at the top. There was more cohesion regarding the aspect considered least important. In total, 11 people considered illustrations as least important, 6 the total number of pages and 3 font type. None of the three remaining categories were ranked last.

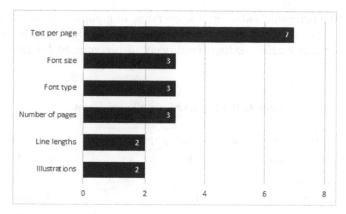

Fig. 3. Characteristics considered important when selecting a book

The rankings were averaged across all participants (Table 3), where the attributes considered most important received the lowest scores (1 being top ranking). The total amount of text per page and line lengths were considered most important, followed by font size and type. Number of pages and illustrations were rated as least important.

Table 3. Attributes scored according to importance (1 being top ranked).

Attribute	Score
Text per page	2.3
Line lengths	2.9
Font size	3.2
Font type	3.3
Number of pages	4.5
Illustrations	4.9

4.2 Reading Experiment

The measured reading speeds varied among the participants with respect to which format resulted in the shortest and longest reading time, but also regarding the computed reading speed across conditions. A comparison of average reading speeds for each condition for all participants showed little variation between the mean values (Table 4). L60 and L80 seem to generate slightly faster reading than the BfE and L40 format. The standard deviations are also comparable in size.

As the participants varied with respect to their score on the Word Chain Test, they were divided into 'subgroups' based on their individual scores. The groups were based on percentiles, so that participants in group 1 had test scores within the 25th percentile, group

2 within the 50th percentile and so on. The overview of groups, number of participants in each group and the range of test scores are presented in Table 5. The quantitative measures, mean and median reading speed, were also computed for each individual group.

Table 4. Reading speeds for all participants

Condition	Reading speed (mean)	Reading speed (median)	Range (min, max)
BfE	141 (SD: 40)	139	(60, 222)
L40	141 (SD: 44)	138	(46, 222)
L60	148 (SD: 53)	141	(52, 280)
L80	142 (SD: 48)	130	(48, 253)

Table 5. Grouping of participants based on test scores

Group #	Scores	Participants
1	12, 18, 21	P3, P4, P5, P10, P14, P20
2	26, 31, 32, 33	P13, P16, P17, P19
3	34, 37, 38, 39	P2, P7, P11, P12, P15, P18
4	40, 49, 51	P1, P6, P8, P9

Comparing the mean reading speed for each group did not provide any clear patterns with respect to which format resulted in the best reading efficiency. Comparisons of the values for the different groups (Table 6, 7, 8 and 9) show that the reading speed on average is higher in the groups with higher scores on the Word Chain Test. For the group with the lowest test scores (Table 6) and the group that scored within the 75th percentile (Table 8), L60 resulted in the highest mean value of reading speed, while the BfE format gave the best results with respect to mean reading speed in group 2 (Table 7) and 4 (Table 9).

Table 6. Reading speeds for group 1 (25th percentile)

Condition	Reading speed (mean)	Reading speed (median)	Range (min, max)
BfE	116 (SD: 36)	111	(63, 192)
L40	124 (SD: 50)	112	(46, 208)
L60	129 (SD: 67)	112	(52, 280)
L80	126 (SD: 56)	120	(48, 236)

Table 7. Reading speeds for group 2 (50th percentile)

Condition	Reading speed (mean)	Reading speed (median)	Range (min, max)
BfE	144 (SD: 27)	139	(122, 222)
L40	132 (SD: 28)	130	(92, 189)
L60	139 (SD: 28)	128	(102, 200)
L80	133 (SD: 29)	128	(92, 189)

Table 8. Reading speeds for group 3 (75th percentile)

Condition	Reading speed (mean)	Reading speed (median)	Range (min, max)
BfE	155 (SD: 38)	155	(82, 221)
L40	163 (SD: 40)	168	(97, 222)
L60	169 (SD: 45)	163	(92, 236)
L80	158 (SD: 49)	155	(88, 236)

Table 9. Reading speeds for group 4 (100th percentile)

Condition	Reading speed (mean)	Reading speed (median)	Range (min, max)
BfE	156 (SD: 42)	175	(95, 200)
L40	143 (SD: 44)	152	(82, 210)
L60	154 (SD: 52)	133	(104, 270)
L80	152 (SD: 47)	146	(96, 253)

Correlation was checked between mean reading speed and line lengths for each compared format, both overall, and for each participant group. The results indicated no or little correlation (approximately zero) for all participant groups. Summarizing the number of correct answers also did not differ much between the different layouts.

The reading efficiency for each format for each participant was also compared with the preferred reading format. Several of the participants (P1, P3, P8, P12, P13, P14, P16) preferred the wider formats L80 and L60, and disliked the BfE format, but actually read faster when the book pages were formatted in the BfE style. Another group of participants (P4, P6, P7, P9, P15, P20) both preferred and read fastest when the texts were in one of the wider formats (L60 and L80).

4.3 Post-interviews

L80 and L60 were ranked as the preferred format by 9 participants, while 2 preferred L40. No participants preferred the BfE format. Regarding the least preferred format, 12 people ranked the BfE version last, followed by L80 rated by 4 people, while L40 and L60 were voted last by 2 people each. The preference scores for line lengths were also averaged (Table 10). Top ranked formats got a value of 1, while least ranked format got 4. Again, the longest lengths (L80 and L60) were preferred over the shorter lines (L40 and BfE).

Table 10. Ranking of preferred line lengths (1 being top marked)

Format	Average rank
L80	1.8
L60	1.95
L40	2.7
BfE	3.55

The participants discussed several aspects of line lengths, with a main focus on four perspectives, namely navigation, reading fluency, reading experience and self-esteem.

Navigating the text was fundamental for many participants, and often related to punctuation and eye movements. A majority emphasised sentences as the most important unit, and the placement of the punctuation seemed more essential than the line lengths. Several participants mentioned that it was more important where in the sentence they had to navigate to a new line than how much content they had read before doing so. It seemed most vital not to split sentences over many lines.

The participants emphasised that it should not take too much effort to navigate between sentences or back to the beginning of a sentence. One participant said: "*I prefer when sentences end at one line and are not spread over several lines. In the original* [BfE] *it became difficult to navigate back to the beginning*" (P9). Another participant related a preference for L60 to eye movements: "*If I have to reread, I can just move my eyes back, not up and down*" (P18). A different participant stated that L40 and L60 "*had sufficient line lengths which makes it possible to keep pace with my eyes*" (P4). This participant often lost the overview during line shifts and always double-checked that she was navigating the text correctly when sentences were split over several lines.

Participants seemed to prefer longer line lengths than the BfE format provided. However, too long lines (L80) would make navigation difficult due to the horizontal distance they had to move their eyes. One participant elaborated on this issue: "*this version is too dense, then I will navigate to the wrong line, I will be utterly confused, and have to reread sentences*" (P19).

Regarding reading fluency, most participants did not favour the BfE version because the sentences were split over too many lines. This typography often led to many line shifts (and more vertical eye movements) per sentence, causing a halting reading: "*This one* [BfE] *is annoying, it doesn't flow as well because you have to move your eyes so often* [...] *it is easier to read when the lines are so long that I don't have to shift line that often*" (P18). Another participant stated: "*with lines with one or few words, the reading becomes very staccato*" (P9). Others got confused about the genre, believing that the

BfE version was poetry: *"I get a very poem-like feeling of the adapted* (BfE) *text. I do not like reading that [...] it affects my reading flow"* (P17).

Many participants discussed the overall reading experience. One participant said: *"the adapted* (BfE) *version kills fiction"* (P11), and thought the text seemed fragmented due to the short lines which negatively affected the reading fluency and reading experience: *"where is the love of reading then?"*. Another participant tied the short sentences to emotions: *"I cannot manage to get feelings from short sentences"* (P17).

Other participants mentioned a close relationship between the structure of the text and memory: *"I did not like it when the lines became very short,* (it was) *difficult to focus. It became so fragmented that it was hard to remember things from the start until the end. [...] When reading the short lines, it was difficult to grasp the content"* (P7).

Several participants mentioned that the BfE version reminded them of elementary school books, and that they preferred books resembling the books read by their peers: *"It should not be obvious that this book is made for someone with dyslexia. You shouldn't have to feel different"* (P7). Another participant stated that this format affected the motivation: *"If they try to stupefy the text too much, it doesn't encourage to reading"* (P11), while another said *"I associate this version* [BfE] *with elementary school, then I don't want to read it"* (P17) and *"one doesn't want the text to be so adapted that one feels stupid"* (P10).

5 Discussion

RQ1 addressed whether line lengths impact the reading experience of people with dyslexia. The participants were quite unanimous in their perceptions that short line lengths negatively affected reading flow and reading experience, and hence also the motivation to read. Most participants preferred longer line lengths (L60 and L80). Moreover, longer line lengths resulted in fewer lines overall, giving the visual impression that the text was shorter. This finding corresponds with Rello and Baeza-Yates [11]. These results support the guideline by the British Dyslexia Association [50] to avoid narrow columns and correspond with the IFLA (International Federation of Library Associations and Institutions) easy-to-read guideline stating that sentences should fit on a single line [61].

It also seems purposeful to direct attention towards navigation during reading, which is a topic for further research. Decoding errors occur frequently among people with dyslexia [20]. Consequently, it might be especially important to consider how to support navigation between sentences. Challenges relating to remembering content during frequent line shifts were also mentioned, suggesting that impaired short-term memory might affect the reading experience.

Another issue mentioned by most participants was the impact of frequent line shifts in the middle of sentences, causing a halting reading. This finding supports the assumption that line lengths can affect how a text is read [43]. Since intrinsic motivation [31] and progress [37] are reported to be important factors in developing reading skills, overall reading experience should be addressed in future research.

The finding that the Books for Everyone books were perceived as "stupefied" is in accordance with other studies on reading and motivation, suggesting that it is important that books targeted at people with reading impairments are not conceived as different from other books [23, 31, 32]. This is particularly important since people with dyslexia often seem to have reduced self-esteem [33]. This finding supports the universal design paradigm, where the products are usable for all types of users, and not particularly designed for one user group. This is also the overall purpose for Books for Everyone. For instance, Easy to Read books are developed for a diversity of users who might find reading challenging for various reasons. Consequently, by producing books that appeal to a wide spectrum of user groups, the need for "special books" would no longer exist. However, more research is needed on how to develop such books. It has been suggested that making products accessible for people with dyslexia typically benefit other users as well [62], which makes further studies on readers with dyslexia purposeful within the universal design context.

RQ2 addressed the relationship between line lengths and reading efficiency. To summarise the findings related to reading efficiency, which involves taking both reading speed and comprehension into consideration, this study has not been able to detect any clear patterns regarding which of the compared formats that result in the best performance, at least when each of the sub-groups of participants are studied individually (Table 6, 7, 8 and 9). For the entire group, however, L60 resulted in the highest reading speed among the participants, both with respect to mean, median and maximum number of words per minute. The large standard deviations associated with the calculated means may indicate that there are other aspects than the format with respect to line length that affect the reading speed.

The results of this study indicate no effect of line lengths on reading efficiency, neither in reading times nor in comprehension. This finding contradicts Schneps and Thomson [12]. The study comprised e-readers, and the studies are not directly comparable. The results, however, seem to be in accordance with Rello and Baeza-Yates [11], although that study was also conducted on a digital platform.

Regarding reading habits of adults with dyslexia, the participants rarely read fictional books or spent time on leisure reading, confirming the findings by Leinonen and Müller [38]. Several participants expressed a desire to read more but did not have the energy because other tasks were demanding, such as studying. Leisure reading is reported to be especially important for people who find reading challenging [30], but users need to develop fast enough reading speed and reading styles to keep motivated to read [38]. Moreover, people with reading challenges do not seem to read less because they lack motivation, but because they do not perceive progress [37]. Consequently, it is important to look further into how to provide such skills and among people with dyslexia. This is also a key issue for adults who have finished school and are not attended to by teachers and/or school librarians. Relevant topics to address in future research would be compensating strategies to make reading more efficient and how to produce accessible books targeted at adult readers.

Previous research on reading and dyslexia has mainly addressed digital formats [11, 12]. It has been suggested that e-readers might be beneficial for some people in this cohort [46]. However, in this study all the participants preferred reading fictional books on paper. This finding is in accordance with research on reading in general, that reading printed books is more beneficial than digital books [47–49]. Moreover, the results suggest that more research is needed on layout and typography on printed books for people with dyslexia.

The pre-interviews produced data on motivational criteria for selecting a book to read. Based on the findings in this study, it seems reasonable to assume that the amount of white space in general is important. This finding is in accordance with guidelines on both accessibility on digital [62, 63] and printed formats [50]. The number of pages, however, was not regarded as relevant. This was surprising, since people with dyslexia typically spend much time reading a text [20] and oftentimes have challenges with concentrating on a task for a long time [21].

Finally, from the pre-interviews it was apparent that the participants were very diverse with respect to the amount of reading experience. While some participants hardly read anything for leisure, others stated that they enjoyed reading, and would read up to several hours a day. Some participants had very little or no higher education, while others had completed bachelor or master's degrees. As the amount of reading experience is expected to have significant impact on reading efficiency, it seems likely that this factor may be one of the explanations to the large standard deviations in the computed means of reading speed in this study.

6 Conclusion

Based on this small-scale study, line lengths might impact the reading experience of users with dyslexia, affecting reading fluency and the motivation to read, and may be worth investigating further in a large-scale study including a control group. In contrast, line lengths might possibly not affect reading efficiency. In the context of line lengths and fiction, it might be most purposeful to consider user preferences over reading efficiency, to ensure the production of books that people with dyslexia are motivated to read.

Some key issues require particular attention in future research. First, intrinsic motivation is very important to support the reading of people with dyslexia. Second, there is a need to design books that better support navigation between sentences for people with impaired short-term memory. Moreover, there is a need for research on how punctuation and the layout of sentences may affect reading efficiency. Further, the preferences for printed books implies a need for more research on how to make printed text readable for people with dyslexia.

Due to a limited number of participants, it is not possible to generalise the findings from this study. Further, the participants read excerpts from books. The results might have been different if they for instance had read an entire book from start to finish. However, since reading is an especially demanding task for people with dyslexia, such an experiment would have had to be conducted in several sessions over a long period of time.

References

1. Nergård-Nilssen, T., Hulme, C.: Developmental dyslexia in adults: behavioural manifestations and cognitive correlates. Dyslexia **20**(3), 191–207 (2014)

2. Peterson, R.L., Pennington, B.F.: Developmental dyslexia. Lancet **379**(9830), 1997–2007 (2012)
3. Helland, T., Kaasa, R.: Dyslexia in English as a second language. Dyslexia **11**(1), 41–60 (2005)
4. Lyster, S.-A.H.: Reading development and reading disabilities: focus on Norway. In: Scruggs, T.E., Mastropieri, M.A. (eds.) International Perspectives, pp. 21–55. Emerald Group, Bingley (2007)
5. Høien, T., Lundberg, I.: Dysleksi: fra teori til praksis [Dyslexia: From Theory to Practise]. Gyldendal, Oslo (2012)
6. Spadorcia, S.A.: Examining the text demands of high-interest, low-level books. Read. Writ. Q. **21**(1), 33–59 (2005)
7. Rello, L., Baeza-Yates, R.: Good fonts for dyslexia. In: Proceedings of the 15th International ACM SIGACCESS Conference on Computers and Accessibility, pp. 1–8. ACM, Bellevue, Washington (2013)
8. O'Brien, B.A., Mansfield, J.S., Legge, G.E.: The effect of print size on reading speed in dyslexia. J. Res. Reading **28**(3), 332–349 (2005)
9. Zorzi, M., et al.: Extra-large letter spacing improves reading in dyslexia. Proc. Natl. Acad. Sci. **109**(28), 11455–11459 (2012)
10. Rello, L., et al.: Size matters (spacing not): 18 points for a dyslexic-friendly Wikipedia. In: Proceedings of the 10th International Cross-Disciplinary Conference on Web Accessibility, pp. 1–14. ACM, Rio de Janeiro (2013)
11. Rello, L., Baeza-Yates, R.: How to present more readable text for people with dyslexia. Univ. Access Inf. Soc. **16**(1), 29–49 (2015). https://doi.org/10.1007/s10209-015-0438-8
12. Schneps, M.H., et al.: Shorter lines facilitate reading in those who struggle. PLoS ONE **8**(8), e71161 (2013)
13. Perez, T.M., et al.: Functional alterations in order short-term memory networks in adults with dyslexia. Dev. Neuropsychol. **40**(7–8), 407–429 (2015)
14. Starr, M.S., Rayner, K.: Eye movements during reading: some current controversies. Trends Cogn. Sci. **5**(4), 156–163 (2001)
15. Lindkvist, E.: Ditt røde hår, Unn [Your red hair, Unn]. Solum, Oslo (2013)
16. Jackson, M.D., McClelland, J.L.: Processing determinants of reading speed. J. Exp. Psychol. Gen. **108**(2), 151–181 (1979)
17. Sabatini, J.P.: Efficiency in word reading of adults: ability group comparisons. Sci. Stud. Read. **6**(3), 267–298 (2002)
18. Perfetti, C.: Reading ability: lexical quality to comprehension. Sci. Stud. Read. **11**(4), 357–383 (2007)
19. Ryder, D., Norwich, B.: What's in a name? Perspectives of dyslexia assessors working with students in the UK higher education sector. Dyslexia **24**(2), 109–127 (2018)
20. Peterson, R.L., Pennington, B.F.: Developmental dyslexia. Annu. Rev. Clin. Psychol. **11**(1), 283–307 (2015)
21. Mortimore, T., Crozier, W.R.: Dyslexia and difficulties with study skills in higher education. Stud. High. Educ. **31**(2), 235–251 (2006)
22. Snowling, M.J.: Dyslexia. Blackwell, Oxford (2000)
23. Thiessen, M., Dyson, M.C.: Typography for children with reading difficulties: preferences for type in reading books. Int. J. Book **6**(2), 115–122 (2009)
24. Berget, G., Fagernes, S.: "I'm not stupid" - Attitudes towards adaptation among people with dyslexia. In: Masaaki, K. (ed.) Human-Computer Interaction: Theories, Methods, and Human Issues, pp. 237–247. Springer, Cham (2018)
25. Brante, E.W.: 'I don't know what it is to be able to read': how students with dyslexia experience their reading impairment. Support Learn. **28**(2), 79–86 (2013)

26. Iwarsson, S., Ståhl, A.: Accessibility, usability and universal design—positioning and defini-tion of concepts describing person-environment relationships. Disabil. Rehabil. **25**(2), 57–66 (2003)
27. Story, M.F., Mueller, J.L., Mace, R.L.: The Universal Design File: Designing for People of all Ages and Abilities. Center for Universal Design, Raleigh (1998)
28. UN: Convention on the rights of persons with disabilities (2006). https://www.un.org/disabi lities/documents/convention/convoptprot-e.pdf. Accessed 25 Jan 2021
29. Bal, P.M., Veltkamp, M.: How does fiction reading influence empathy? An experimental investigation on the role of emotional transportation. PLoS ONE **8**(1), 1–12 (2013)
30. Mol, S.E., Bus, A.G.: To read or not to read: a meta-analysis of print exposure from infancy to early adulthood. Psychol. Bull. **137**(2), 267–296 (2011)
31. Gambrell, L.B.: Seven rules of engagement: what's most important to know about motivation to read. Read. Teach. **65**(3), 172–178 (2011)
32. Schunk, D.H., Zimmerman, B.J.: Social origins of self-regulatory competence. Educ. Psychol. **32**(4), 195–208 (1997)
33. Carawan, L.W., Nalavany, B.A., Jenkins, C.: Emotional experience with dyslexia and self-esteem: the protective role of perceived family support in late adulthood. Aging Ment. Health **20**(3), 284–294 (2016)
34. Humphrey, N.: Teacher and pupil ratings of self-esteem in developmental dyslexia. British J. Spec. Educ. **29**(1), 29–36 (2002)
35. Riddick, B., et al.: Self-esteem and anxiety in the educational histories of adult dyslexic students. Dyslexia **5**(4), 227–248 (1999)
36. Alexander-Passe, N.: How dyslexic teenagers cope: an investigation of self-esteem, coping and depression. Dyslexia **12**(4), 256–275 (2006)
37. Becker, M., McElvany, N., Kortenbruck, M.: Intrinsic and extrinsic reading motivation as predictors of reading literacy: a longitudinal study. J. Educ. Psychol. **102**(4), 773–785 (2010)
38. Leinonen, S., et al.: Heterogeneity in adult dyslexic readers: relating processing skills to the speed and accuracy of oral text reading. Read. Writ. **14**(3), 265–296 (2001)
39. Wolf, M., Katzir-Cohen, T.: Reading fluency and its intervention. Sci. Stud. Read. **5**(3), 211–239 (2001)
40. Daneman, M., Carpenter, P.A.: Individual differences in working memory and reading. J. Verbal Learn. Verbal Behav. **19**(4), 450–466 (1980)
41. Rayner, K., et al.: Psychology of Reading. Psychology Press, New York (2012)
42. Burton, C., Daneman, M.: Compensating for a limited working memory capacity during reading: evidence from eye movements. Read. Psychol. **28**(2), 163–186 (2007)
43. Samuels, S.J., Eisenberg, P.: A framework for understanding the reading process. In Pirozzolo, F.J., Wittrock, M.C. (eds.) Neuropsychological and cognitive process in reading. Academic Press, New York (1981)
44. Jackson, J.E.: Towards universally accessible typography: a review of research on dyslexia. J. Technol. Persons Disabil. **2** (2014)
45. Myrberg, C., Wiberg, N.: Screen vs. paper: what is the difference for reading and learning? Insights **28**(2), 49–54 (2015)
46. Schneps, M.H., et al.: E-Readers are more effective than paper for some with dyslexia. PLoS ONE **8**(9), e75634 (2013)
47. Kretzschmar, F., et al.: Subjective impressions do not mirror online reading effort: concurrent EEG-Eyetracking evidence from the reading of books and digital media. PLoS ONE **8**(2), e56178 (2013)
48. Benedetto, S., et al.: E-Readers and visual fatigue. PLoS ONE **8**(12), e83676 (2013)
49. Mangen, A., Walgermo, B.R., Brønnick, K.: Reading linear texts on paper versus computer screen: effects on reading comprehension. Int. J. Educ. Res. **58**, 61–68 (2013)

50. British Dyslexia Association: Dyslexia style guide. http://www.bdadyslexia.org.uk/common/ckeditor/filemanager/userfiles/About_Us/policies/Dyslexia_Style_Guide.pdf. Accessed 13 Jan 2021

51. Rello, L., Baeza-Yates, R.: The effect of font type on screen readability by people with dyslexia. ACM Trans. Accessible Comput. **8**(4), 1–33 (2016)

52. Hillier, R.: Sylexiad. A typeface for the adult dyslexic reader. J. Writ. Creative Pract. **1**(3), 275–291 (2008)

53. Boer, C.T.: Font Dyslexie (2017). https://www.dyslexiefont.com/en/typeface/. Accessed 13 Dec 2020

54. Marinus, E., et al.: A special font for people with dyslexia: does it work and if so, why? Dyslexia **22**(3), 233–244 (2016)

55. Ling, J., van Schaik, P.: The influence of font type and line length on visual search and information retrieval in web pages. Int. J. Hum. Comput. Stud. **64**(5), 395–404 (2006)

56. Davidov, A.: Computer screens are not like paper: typography on the web. In: Sassoon, R. (ed.) Computers & Typography. Intellect, Bristol (2002)

57. Bernard, M.L., et al.: The effects of line length on children and adults' perceived and actual online reading performance. Proc. Hum. Factors Ergon. Soc. Ann. Meet. **47**(11), 1375–1379 (2003)

58. ISO: ISO 8596 Ophthalmic Optics: Visual Acuity Testing – Standard Optotype and its Presentation. ISO, Geneva (2009)

59. Zhang, P., et al.: Binocular balance in normal vision and its modulation by mean luminance. Optom. Vis. Sci. **88**(9), 1072–1079 (2011)

60. Høien, T., Tønnesen, G.: Ordkjedetesten [The Word Chain Test]. Logometrica, Bryne (2008)

61. Nomura, M., Nielsen, G.S., Tronbacke, B.: Guidelines for Easy-to-Read Materials. IFLA Professional Reports 120. International Federation of Library Association and Institutions, The Hague (2010)

62. McCarthy, J.E., Swierenga, S.J.: What we know about dyslexia and web accessibility: a research review. Univ. Access Inf. Soc. **9**(2), 147–152 (2010)

63. Santana, V.F., et al.: Web accessibility and people with dyslexia: a survey on techniques and guidelines. In: Proceedings of the International Cross-Disciplinary Conference on Web Accessibility, pp. 1–9. ACM, Lyon (2012)

Easy-to-Understand Access Services: Easy Subtitles

Rocío Bernabé$^{(\boxtimes)}$ and Piero Cavallo$^{(\boxtimes)}$

International University SDI München, Baierbrunner Str. 13, 81379 Munich, Germany
rocio.bernabe@sdi-muenchen.de

Abstract. Easy-to-understand access services use cognitive text simplification and methods, such as Easy-to-Read or Plain Language. These services aim to provide access for viewers who struggle to understand audiovisual content for reasons, such as reading, learning, or cognitive difficulties. Subtitles that have been created this way can, thus, be labelled as easy-to-understand subtitles, in short, easy subtitles.

Bernabé and Orero (2019) described the lack of easy-to-understand access services within the realm of audiovisual translation for the first time. Then, to tackle the need for parameters to create easy subtitles, Bernabé and García (2019) compared the Spanish standard UNE 153010:2021 for subtitling for the Deaf and Hard-of-Hearing, in short SDH, with the Easy-to-Read guidelines *Information for All* by Inclusion Europe. This short article discusses the results of applying the identified parameters to subtitle a short, informative video.

Keywords: Easy-to-read audiovisual content · Easy-to-understand subtitles · Reading and learning difficulties · Cognitive disabilities

1 Introduction

Accessibility, or the ability to access physical and digital environments, information, and technologies, is recognized as a principle in the Convention on the Rights of Persons with Disabilities (CRPD). Moreover, the CRPD considers accessibility to be an enabler of other rights (e.g., freedom of expression, education) and self-determination (UNGA 2006). Following this line of thought, a lack of accessibility can create a risk of exclusion for those who cannot participate equally (European Commission 2010; European Parliament 2016; Greco 2016; Inclusion International 2009; Johansson 2016; Tomljenović 2018; UNGA 2006).

A lack of accessibility in multimodal communication can be due to sensory and physical barriers, or difficulties in understanding. Persons who face difficulties making meaning out of content are a heterogeneous part of the population. These profiles include those with low levels of literacy, intellectual disabilities, dyslexia, aphasia, temporary impairments, or limited language skills (e.g., second-language learners, immigrants, or displaced populations), and the elderly, to name a few (Murman 2015; Ruer et al. 2015; World Wide Web Consortium [W3C] 2018).

© Springer Nature Switzerland AG 2021
M. Antona and C. Stephanidis (Eds.): HCII 2021, LNCS 12769, pp. 241–254, 2021.
https://doi.org/10.1007/978-3-030-78095-1_18

When understanding is at stake, cognitive text simplification can reduce textual complexity while avoiding loss of content (Carroll et al. 1998; Coster and Kauchak 2011; Chandrasekar et al. 1996). Research in this field started back in the 1990s with a focus on syntactic simplification. Later, scholars researching in the field of persons with special needs studied its effectiveness for persons with intellectual disabilities (Fajardo *et al.* 2014; Feng *et al.* 2009), readers with dyslexia, aphasia or deafness (Bachmann 2013; Saggion 2017), adults with low literacy levels (Aluísio *et al.* 2010), language learners (Urano 2000), and non-mother tongue speakers (Cornelius 2010).

Arfé et al. (2017, p. 2191) explain the concept of cognitive text simplification: "the aim [...] is not simply to reduce the linguistic complexity of the text, but to improve text coherence and the structure of information in the text." This view is based on the idea that less is not always more. In other words, removing linguistic complexity at lexical or grammatical levels alone does not necessarily support (literal or inferential) comprehension, as shown in young less-able readers (Di Mascio et al. 2011) and second-language learners (Urano 2000).

Researchers in this field have identified readability and understandability as the two elements that influence the degree to which a reader understands a text (Siddharthan 2014; Wissing et al. 2016; Wray and Janan 2013). Understandability is related to a person's skills and abilities to make meaning out of a text in a specific context (Siddharthan 2014; Saggion 2017; Wray and Janan 2013). Conversely, readability is external to a person's capabilities and can be measured based on text-dependent variables such as perceptual and linguistic factors (Burtt 1949; European Commission 2009; Ma and Rau 2011; Siddharthan 2014; Saggion 2017).

Perceptual factors influence the process of decoding written and oral information during the first interaction between a reader and a text, i.e., legibility. Perceptual factors in written texts range from typographical to paratextual (e.g., font-size, font-type, contrast, ratio text-to-white space) (European Commission 2009; Inclusion Europe 2009; Kouroupetroglou 2015; Marks 2009; Nietzio et al. 2014; Yuste Frías 2012; Tinker 1963). For its part, perceptual factors in oral texts are prosodic ones, such as pitch, intonation, stress, or sound quality (Fryer 2016; Rodríguez 2017; Starr and Braun 2020, Van der Heidjen 2007; Walczak and Fryer 2017).

Linguistic factors of readability include lexical/syntactical, stylistic and discursive factors that make texts more or less readable. Lexical and syntactical factors that are considered to play a role in making a text more or less readable include the number of syllables, sentence length, the semantic familiarity of words, type of grammatical constructions, or order (European Commission 2009, Hockett 1961; PLAIN 2011; Saggion 2017).

Style factors concern linguistic choices such as the use of active voice, a canonical subject-verb-object order, and mechanics (European Commission 2009; Hockett 1961; IFLA 2010; Inclusion Europe 2009; PLAIN 2011; Saggion 2017). Lastly, discursive factors, such as coherence, cohesion, and pragmatics, aim to avoid semantic gaps. The underlying idea is that lack of explicitation or intertextuality may lead to misunderstandings or misinterpretations, or hinder understanding (Neves 2009; Saggion 2017).

The leap from this theoretical framework to the practical application facilitates two writing methods that consider both perceptual and linguistic factors of readability: Easy-to-Read and Plain Language. The first is defined by the International Federation of Library Associations and Institutions, in short IFLA, as follows (IFLA 2010, p. 6):

> "easy-to-read" [...] means a linguistic adaptation of a text that makes both reading and comprehension easier. The aim of easy-to-read publications is to present clear and easily understood texts appropriate for different age groups. To achieve such a product, the writer/publisher must take into consideration content, language, illustrations, as well as graphic layout."

Similarly, the Plain Language Action and Information Network (PLAIN) states "Plain Language is communication your audience can understand the first time they read or hear it." (PLAIN n.d.). As a method, Plain Language builds on recommendations related to the design and linguistic simplification – syntax, grammar and lexis.

2 Merging Best Practices

The idea of text simplification as a way to render the core parts of a message, and of readability as a factor that influences understandability, is also found in audiovisual translation (Díaz-Cintas and Remael 2007; Di Giovanni and Gambier 2018; Georgakopoulou 2009). Indeed, De Linde and Kay (1999) identified that a higher lexical density in the subtitles (Halliday 1989) and a possible loss in lexical cohesion might affect understandability. Furthermore, Neves (2009) outlined that a lack of cohesive elements will force the audience to infer the meaning themselves and, thus, increase the cognitive load.

In subtitling, simplification has been used to overcome time and space constraints when conveying aural information visually. With it, researchers have focused either on language or sensory barriers or both (Díaz-Cintas and Remael 2007; Díaz-Cintas 2010, 2013; Szarkowska 2013). Conversely, research with a focus on cognitive disabilities is scarcer with a limited number of scholarly contributions. One example is the case study by Alba Rodríguez (2014), who explored how to identify cues and types of information to create subtitles that can support persons with intellectual disabilities. Other examples include the research by Silvia Hansen-Schirra and Christiane Maaß in Germany (2020) or the work by Carlo Eugeni (2017) about simplification strategies in real-time subtitling[1].

In 2019, Bernabé and García (2019) tackled the lack of parameters for creation by merging current guidelines from subtitling for the Deaf and Hard-of-Hearing (SDH), which also consider audiences with limited reading skills, and those from Inclusion Europe (2009). The result was a first set of 19 subtitling parameters that include Easy-to-Read recommendations regarding visual, temporal, and editorial aspects of subtitling, and background voices. The comparison also identified a lack of Easy-to-Read recommendations about how to subtitle music, sounds, contextual information or how to identify speakers or characters in case of ambiguity.

---

[1] This topic is also part of the Erasmus+ project LiveTextAccess on real-time intralingual subtitling (KA 2018-1-DE01-KA203-004218).

Identifying parameters from a experience-based method, such as the recommendations by Inclusion Europe, with parameters from evidence-based knowledge on SDH brings together information about a field that has (scarcely) been researched before, i.e., easy subtitles. Though the validity of such practice remains limited, Saldanha and O'Brien (2014) describe this type of research in a new field as a secondary-data based research.

3   Parameters for Easy Subtitles

This section presents the identified parameters and illustrates their application in an example. The tables below show the parameters organized according to the sections of the Spanish standard for SDH: visual aspects, temporal aspects, background voice, and editorial criteria (AENOR 2012) (Tables 1, 2, 3 and 4).

Visual aspects concern how subtitles should be presented visually on-screen. Visual aspects can be verbal and non-verbal and aim to support legibility as the ability to perceive and decode information. Temporal aspects refer to the time subtitles are displayed on a screen. This interval is closely related to a person's reading speed and their ability "to decode easily and continuously and to maintain their concentration" during reading (Shanahan 2019: 1). Background voice aims at resolving ambiguity as to who is speaking when a voice narrates what the viewer sees on a screen. Lastly, editorial parameters encompass four main linguistic categories: grammar, mechanics, usage, and style.

Table 1. Visual aspects

Parameter	Recommendation
1. On-screen placement: all subtitles except sound information	• Lower bottom of the screen • Subtitles should be in the same position on the screen throughout the whole video
2. Number of subtitling lines	• Try not to use too many layers of subtitles
3. Sentences per line	• Always start a new sentence on a new line
4. Minimum font size	• Legible according to the size of the screen • Check that you can also read them on a small screen • Always use large writing. You should use writing which is at least the size of Arial 14
5. Maximum font size	• Subtitles should be easy to read. For example, use larger than usual writing in movie subtitles
6. Font type	• Use a font-type with the greatest legibility • Try to use only 1 type of writing in your text • Never use a special writing design • Never use serif fonts • Never use writing that is too close together

(*continued*)

Table 1. (*continued*)

Parameter	Recommendation
7. Contrast: box and text	• There must be a strong contrast between subtitles and the background: one way is to have a dark line at the bottom on which the subtitles appear. But this line should be transparent so you can still see the film • If there is not enough contrast between the background and the subtitles, change the font colour, not the position
8. Text alignment	• Align your text to the left • Never justify your text
9. Customisation options: (personalisation)	• It should be possible for the viewer to hide the subtitles at any time

Table 2. Temporal aspects

Parameter	Recommendation
10. On-screen time	• Viewers should have enough time to read the subtitles
11. Synchrony	• Subtitles should be on the screen as long as possible

Table 3. Background voice

Parameter	Recommendation
12. Off-screen voice: speaker identification	• A background voice should only be speaking about things that people can see on the screen • If you use a background voice, it can be helpful to present the person first before he or she starts talking in the background

Table 4. Editorial criteria

Parameter	Recommendation
13. Line breaks	• If you have to write 1 sentence on 2 lines, cut the sentence where people would pause when reading out loud • Where possible, 1 sentence should fit on 1 line
14. Hyphenation	• Never split 1 word over 2 lines. This means never use a hyphen (-)
15. Suspension points	• Avoid all special characters where possible

(continued)

Table 4. (*continued*)

Parameter	Recommendation
16. Grammatical rules and punctuation	• Keep the punctuation simple
17. Speakers and speech	• Use correct grammar and spelling unless they are used to covey information which is necessary to understand the plot • Do not use dialects
18. Abbreviations and symbols	• Avoid abbreviations • Avoid all special characters where possible
19. Numbering	• Write numbers as digits, not as words • Never use Roman numerals • Where possible, write dates out in full

This first set of parameters and recommendations gives a hint about the difficulties and support that a subtitler will have upon creation. For instance, while editorial criteria are specific, temporal parameters are general and do not provide subtitlers with reference values. Additionally, some recommendations may not be possible to apply automatically with specific subtitling software, for instance, left-alignment of two-line subtitle events. Others, such as providing personalization options, might imply providing users with E2U instructions about how to turn on/off subtitles.

3.1 Simplification Example

The table below provides a list of subtitles that were simplified by applying the above-mentioned parameters. The original video is in Swedish with English closed captions. The video can be found here: https://vimeo.com/391929186. The video is called "Textmakthavare Mike möter Olle NY"[2].

A total of 28 subtitle events were created[3]. The table below shows the original English subtitles on the left column and the simplified ones on the right. The easy-to-understand (E2U) subtitles followed the SDH recommendations of a maximum of 37 characters per line, two-line subtitle events, and reading speeds of 15 cps as recommended by Romero-Fresco (2010) for adults with a hearing loss. The E2U subtitles follow the BBC guidelines for subtitling[4]. Nonetheless, an effort was made to follow subtitling best practices for the web, which advise to use 32-character lines (University of North Carolina 2021) and a maximum speed at around 12 cps, as recommended for children with hearing impairment (Tamayo 2016) (Table 5).

---

[2] The subtitles were created within the Erasmus+ project EASIT (2018-1-ES01-KA203-050275).
[3] The sample video is available here: https://youtu.be/w0KVk3UxnRE.
[4] https://bbc.github.io/subtitle-guidelines/.

Table 5. Easy subtitles

English subtitles from vimeo	E2U subtitles
1 00:00:00,400 --> 00:00:04,160 How can those who have power over text make language more accessible?	1 00:00:00,400 --> 00:00:04,160 How can we make simpler texts?
2 00:00:07,080 --> 00:00:13,080 I'm Olle Burman. I work as a marketing communicator at the Nordic Museum	2 00:00:07,080 --> 00:00:08,800 I am Olle Burman
	3 00:00:09,350 --> 00:00:13,080 I work at a museum in Stockholm, in Sweden
3 00:00:13,680 --> 00:00:17,800 I have a text from our exhibition "Homes and Interiors"	4 00:00:13,680 --> 00:00:17,800 There are many texts in the museum
4 00:00:17,960 --> 00:00:21,600 This paragraph is displayed at the exhibition	5 00:00:17,960 --> 00:00:21,600 This text is an example
5 00:00:21,760 --> 00:00:26,880 13% of all Swedish adults have some form of reading difficulty	6 00:00:21,760 --> 00:00:26,880 Many people in Sweden find reading difficult
6 00:00:27,720 --> 00:00:31,600 - Hello, I'm Mike - I'm Olle. What do you think of this text?	7 00:00:27,720 --> 00:00:31,600 Hi, I am Mike Olle. How do you find this text?
7 00:00:32,040 --> 00:00:36,320 It's really hard for me as there are a lot of difficult words	8 00:00:32,040 --> 00:00:36,320 I find it difficult Many words are difficult
8 00:00:36,480 --> 00:00:39,360 This is a bit hard, and this…	9 00:00:36,480 --> 00:00:39,750 This word is difficult And this one, too
9 00:00:40,200 --> 00:00:42,120 Could I change it a bit?	10 00:00:40,200 --> 00:00:42,120 Can I change it a bit?
10 00:00:42,280 --> 00:00:43,760 - Of course! - Okay	11 00:00:42,240 --> 00:00:43,760 Of course Okay

(*continued*)

Table 5. (*continued*)

English subtitles from vimeo	E2U subtitles
11 00:00:47,320 --> 00:00:52,280 Everyone takes it for granted that you can read. If you can't, you're stupid	12 00:00:47,320 --> 00:00:49,790 People think that you can read
	13 00:00:50,350 --> 00:00:52,380 If not, they call you stupid
12 00:00:53,040 --> 00:00:56,080 I have ADHD and severe dyslexia	14 00:00:53,040 --> 00:00:57,150 I find it hard to concentrate And I can confuse letters
13 00:00:57,520 --> 00:01:01,200 I used to fight, because I wasn't understood	15 00:00:57,420 --> 00:01:01,300 I used to get upset Because people did not understand me
14 00:01:01,760 --> 00:01:05,680 But now I use a pen, and they're even more afraid	16 00:01:01,760 --> 00:01:06,070 Now I prefer to write And people understand me better
15 00:01:06,640 --> 00:01:09,680 I've changed it a bit, exchanged a few words…	17 00:01:06,640 --> 00:01:09,680 I made some changes
16 00:01:10,040 --> 00:01:13,120 Bourgeois to middle-class	18 00:01:10,040 --> 00:01:13,120 "Bourgeois" is now "middle-class"
17 00:01:13,280 --> 00:01:17,080 I've also made shorter paragraphs	19 00:01:13,280 --> 00:01:17,080 The parts are shorter
18 00:01:17,240 --> 00:01:21,320 and added a space here so you have time to think	20 00:01:17,240 --> 00:01:21,320 And I separated the parts Then you have time to think
19 00:01:21,480 --> 00:01:23,480 Very clear…	21 00:01:21,480 --> 00:01:23,480 Very clear
20 00:01:24,640 --> 00:01:28,200 My message to those that write texts is:	22 00:01:24,640 --> 00:01:28,200 I want to say to people:
21 00:01:28,560 --> 00:01:30,960 Don't make such complicated texts	23 00:01:28,400 --> 00:01:31,040 Complicated texts are difficult

(*continued*)

Table 5. (*continued*)

English subtitles from vimeo	E2U subtitles
22 00:01:31,120 --> 00:01:35,160 Make them short, but filled with information	24 00:01:31,120 --> 00:01:35,160 Short texts with information are better
23 00:01:35,720 --> 00:01:37,480 - Many thanks! - Thank you!	25 00:01:35,560 --> 00:01:37,480 Many thanks! Thank you
24 00:01:38,040 --> 00:01:40,720 Mike's given me very valuable input	26 00:01:38,040 --> 00:01:40,720 Mike gave me useful tips
25 00:01:40,880 --> 00:01:44,480 which I will use when I develop text at work in the future	27 00:01:40,880 --> 00:01:44,480 I will use these tips at work
	28 00:01:49,200 --> 00:01:54,000 You can read more about how to make simpler texts here:

4 Discussion

The list of parameters facilitated guidance, especially with regards to visual and editorial aspects. At a visual level, legibility was supported by using static lines, a larger font than the original, i.e., Verdana size 18, a solid-black box to ensure a good contrast of over 4.5:1 throughout the video. Indeed, the contrast ratios[5] for cyan is 12.9:1, for yellow 16.3:1 and 19.7:1 for white, which meets the triple AAA requirements for regular and large texts set in the Web Content Accessibility Guidelines (WCAG 2.1[6]).

It was also possible to make simpler sentences. For instance, it was possible to transform nine subtitle events encompassing one sentence running over two lines into subtitle events with lines encompassing single simple sentences. Moreover, the original included a sentence that ran over two subtitle events and comprised three lines (see subtitles 17–18). After simplification, the number of subtitle events was kept the same, but three simple sentences were created instead. In a nutshell, visual recommendations were applied, with one exception, i.e., the left alignment of the text within the box.

As for the temporal aspects concerning on-screen time, SDH recommendations were followed due to the lack of specific ones for E2R. All lines have a maximum of 37 characters, including spaces and punctuation. The mean on-screen time is 10.28 cps,

---

[5] Measured with Color Contrast Analyzer.
[6] https://www.w3.org/WAI/standards-guidelines/wcag/.

or 123.32 words per minute (in short, wpm[7]). Thus, all subtitle events meet the 15 cps recommendation. To meet this requirement, it was necessary to choose between speed, explicitation, and speaker's style, within certain limits. For instance, in subtitle 13 ("If not, they call you stupid."), a more explicit version would have been: "If you cannot read, then people call you stupid.". However, this version was too long and had to be dismissed. An alternative simplification would have been to change both this and the previous subtitle by saying: "People call you stupid, if you cannot read." However, this option reflects the speaker's style to a lesser extent. Similarly, in subtitle 15, it could have been possible to eliminate the pronoun "me" at the end of the sentence and prioritize speed over explicitation. In this case, the decision was taken to prioritize explicitation. Eventually, this was possible by increasing the on-screen times a hundredth of a second.

Synchrony was kept as defined in SDH. To do so, we used the exact times as in the original in most cases. To meet the E2R recommendation to a minimum extent, some subtitles were left on the screen for a longer time period and, in some cases, subtitles appear slightly earlier than in the original. Nonetheless, we presume that the changes are not significant.

The subtitles will be validated in the near future by end-users of Easy-to-Read within the frame of the Eramus+ project Train2Validate[8]. We presume that some subtitle events would still be too fast for some readers. We assume that this could be the case for the events with on-screen times between 13–15 cps (e.g., 9, 13, 14, 15, and 20).

Regarding editorial simplification, we were able to apply all the recommendations in the table. To this end, we relied on English grammar, mechanics, and language usage. Nonetheless, the subtitles were revised by an English native speaker.

As for other linguistic aspects, explaining difficult words (e.g., ADHS and dyslexia), led to a higher number of characters. This also occurred when adding the name of the country, Sweden, to the third subtitle, resolving abbreviations (e.g., I'm, It's, Don't), making verbs and pronouns explicit (e.g. "Bourgeois" is now "middle-class", Because people did not understand me.). This higher number of characters shows that cognitive text simplification does not always mean linguistic reduction, which in the case of easy subtitling increases the challenge of making longer on-screen times possible.

Other editorial aspects were to avoid negative sentences and percentages, as recommended by Inclusion Europe (2009: 10, 11). To do so, we changed the original (i.e., Don't make such complicated texts) to a positive sentence (i.e., Complicated texts are difficult). Similarly, the percentage in the fifth subtitle event in the original (i.e., 13% of all Swedish adults have some form of reading difficulty.) was expressed by the word "many" to explain that it concerns a significant part of the population.

Lastly, the E2U subtitles use the colors white, yellow and cyan according to the BBC guidelines. The use of colors in E2R texts is not recommended by the guidelines published by Inclusion Europe. However, validation practice in E2R has shown that the colors in headings and sub-headings support E2R readers (Real Patronato sobre la discapacidad 2015). The Spanish standard on Easy to Read (UNE 153101 EX) also agrees with this view and lists the use of color as a technique to visually separate headings from the running text in printed documents (AENOR 2018). Another aspect to be considered

---

[7] A word was considered to be five characters, including spaces and special characters.
[8] https://plenainclusionmadrid.org/train2validate/ (Erasmus+ 2020-1-ES01-KA203-082068).

is that using colors to identify the speakers enabled eliminating special characters such as dashes in dialogues.

5 Conclusion

At first glance, creating easy subtitles seems relatively straightforward because several parameters and strategies are at hand. While the recommendations by Inclusion Europe already guide subtitlers closely at editorial and visual levels, there are still many questions to be answered and researched, especially concerning temporal aspects. Some of these questions are: Are simplified subtitles less faithful to the speaker's style and the register than verbatim or less simplified ones? Is it possible to explain or simplify complex or technical terms while keeping a maximum of 32 characters as recommended by some generally accepted best practices (UnivW3C 2021)? Which on-screen times are adequate for persons with reading and learning difficulties? What are other accompanying products to the subtitle events that can support readability and understandability? For instance, should an explanation in Easy-to-Read language always be provided along with the subtitles? Should an extended transcription should be provided? Should the concept of "extended audio description" be used for subtitles as well? If so, what genres, such as news items, more suitable than others such as films?

Because there are not enough empirical data to provide answers to these questions at this stage, this short article and the presentation at the conference is aimed at fostering research, triggering a discussion and raising awareness about the topic.

References

AENOR: Subtitulado para personas sordas y personas con discapacidad auditiva (Norma UNE 153010:2012) (2012)

AENOR: Lectura Fácil. Pautas y recomendaciones para la elaboración de documentos. (Norma UNE 153101 EX) (2018)

Alba Rodríguez, T.: Traducción audiovisual accesible a personas con discapacidad intelectual mediante el uso de subtítulos adaptados. Estudios De Traducción **4**, 199–209 (2014). https://doi.org/10.5209/rev_ESTR.2014.v4.45376

Aluisio, S., Specia, L., Gasperin, C., Scarton, C.: Readability assessment for text simplification. In: Tetreault, J., Burstein, J., Leacock, C. (eds.) NAACL HLT 2010 Fifth Workshop on Innovative Use of NLP for Building Educational Applications, pp. 1–9. The Association for Computational Linguistics, Los Angeles (2010). https://www.aclweb.org/anthology/W10-1001.pdf

Arfé, B., Mason, L., Fajardo, I.: Simplifying informational text structure for struggling readers. Read. Writ. **31**(9), 2191–2210 (2017). https://doi.org/10.1007/s11145-017-9785-6

Bachmann, C.: Può un font essere uno strumento compensativo per i lettori con dislessia? Gradimento e prestazione nella lettura in Times New Roman e in EasyReading[TM] di alunni dislessici e normolettori della classe quarta primaria. Dislessia. Giornale italiano di ricerca clinica e applicative **10**(2), 243–262 (2013). http://www.easyreading.it/wp-content/uploads/2017/01/ricerca_bachmann.pdf

Bernabé, R., Orero, P.: Easy to read as multimode accessibility service. Hermeneus **21** (2020). https://doi.org/10.24197/her.21.2019

Bernabé, R., García, Ó.: Identifying parameters for creating easy to read subtitles. CoMe **4**(1), 49–70 (2019)

Burtt, H.: Typography and Readability. Element. Eng. **26**(4), 212–221 (1949)

Carroll, J., Minnen, G., Canning, Y., Devlin, S., Tait, J.: Practical Simplification of English Newspaper Text to Assist Aphasic Readers (1998). https://www.researchgate.net/publication/274 0075_Practical_Simplification_of_English_Newspaper_Text_to_Assist_Aphasic_Readers

Chandrasekar, R., Doran, C., Srinivas, S.: Motivations and methods for text simplification. In: 16th International Conference on Computational Linguistics – (COLING 1996), vol. 2, pp. 1041–1044. Association for Computational Linguistics (1996). https://doi.org/10.3115/993268.993361

Cornelius, E.: Plain language as alternative textualisation. South. Afr. Linguist. Appl. Lang. Stud. **28**(2), 171–183 (2010). https://doi.org/10.2989/16073614.2010.519106

Coster, W., Kauchak, D.: Simple English Wikipedia: a new text simplification task. In: Lin, D. (Chair) 49th Annual Meeting of the Association for Computational Linguistics: Human Language Techonologies [Shortpaper], vol. 2, pp. 665–669. Association for Computational Linguistics, Portland (2011). https://www.aclweb.org/anthology/P11-2117.pdf

De Linde, Z., Kay, N.: The Semiotics of Subtitling. Routledge, New York (1999)

Di Giovanni, E., Gambier, Y.: Reception Studies and Audiovisual Translation. John Benjamins, Amsterdam (2018)

Di Mascio, T., Gennari, R., Vittorini, P.: The design of the TERENCE adaptive learning system. In: Bastiaens, T., Ebner, M. (eds.) ED-MEDIA 2011-World Conference on Educational Multimedia, Hypermedia and Telecommunications, pp. 1609–1617. Association for the Advancement of Computing in Education, Waynesville (2011). https://www.learntechlib.org/primary/p/38077/

Díaz-Cintas, J.: Subtitling. In: Gambier, Y., van Doorslaer, L. (eds.) Handbook of Translation Studies, vol. 1, pp. 344–349. John Benjamins, Amsterdam (2010)

Díaz-Cintas, J., Remael, A.: Audiovisual Translation: Subtitling. Routledge, London (2007)

Eugeni, C.: La sottotitolazione intralinguistica automatica: valutare la qualità con IRA. CoMe Studi di Comunicazione e mediazione linguistica e culturale (2017). https://www.academia.edu/7030302/La_traduzione_audiovisiva_sottotitolazione_e_fansubbing_a_confronto

European Commission: Guideline on the readability of the labelling and package leaflet of medicinal products for human use (2009). https://ec.europa.eu/health/sites/health/files/files/eudralex/vol-2/c/2009_01_12_readability_guideline_final_en.pdf

European Commission: European disability strategy 2010–2020: a renewed commitment to barrier-free Europe (2010). https://eur-lex.europa.eu/LexUriServ/LexUriServ.do?uri=COM%3A2010%3A0636%3AFIN%3AEN%3APDF

European Parliament: Directive EU. 2016/2102 of the European Parliament and of the Council of 26 October 2016 on the accessibility of the websites and mobile applications of public sector bodies. Off. J. Eur. Union (2016). https://eur-lex.europa.eu/legal-content/EN/TXT/?uri=uriserv:OJ.L_.2016.327.01.0001.01.ENG&toc=OJ:L:2016:327:TOC

Fajardo, I., Ávila, V., Ferrer, A., Tavares, G., Gómez, M., Hernández, A.: Easy-to-read texts for students with intellectual disability: linguistic factors affecting. J. Appl. Res. Intellect. Disabil. **27**(3), 212–225 (2014). https://doi.org/10.1111/jar.12065

Feng, L., Elhadad, N., Huenerfauth, M.: Cognitively motivated features for readability assessment. In: 12th Conference of the European Chapter of the Association for Computational Linguistics, EACL, pp. 229–237. Association for Computational Linguistics, Stroudsburg (2009). https://doi.org/10.3115/1609067.1609092

Fryer, L.: An Introduction to Audio Description. A Practical Guide. Routledge, London (2016)

Georgakopoulou, P.: Subtitling for the DVD industry. In: Díaz Cintas, J., Anderman, G. (eds.) Audiovisual Translation – Language Transfer on Screen, pp. 21–35. Palgrave MacMillan, New York (2009)

Greco, G.M.: On Accessibility as a human right, with an application to media accessibility. In: Matamala, A., Orero, P. (eds.) Researching Audio Description. New Approaches, pp. 11–33. Palgrave MacMillan, London (2016)

Halliday, M.A.K.: Spoken and Written Language, 2nd edn. Oxford University Press, Oxford (1989)

Hansen-Schirra, S., Maaß, C.: Easy language, plain language, easy language plus: perspectives on comprehensibility and stigmatisation. In: Hansen-Schirra, S., Maaß, C. (eds.) Easy Language Research: Text and User Perspectives (Easy – Plain – Accessible 2), pp. 17–38. Frank & Timme, Berlin (2020)

Hockett, C.: Linguistic elements and their relations. Language 37(1), 29–53 (1961). https://doi.org/10.2307/411248

IFLA (International Federation of Library Associations and Institutions): Guidelines for Easy-to-Read Materials (2010). www.ifla.org/files/assets/hq/publications/professional-report/120.pdf

Inclusion Europe: Information for All. European standards for making information easy to read and understand (2009). http://sid.usal.es/libros/discapacidad/23131/8-4-1/information-for-all-european-standards-for-making-information-easy-to-read-and-understand.aspx

Inclusion International: Better education for all: when we're included too; a global report; people with an intellectual disability and their families speak out on education for all, disability and inclusive education (2009). https://unesdoc.unesco.org/ark:/48223/pf0000186192

Johansson, S.: Towards a framework to understand mental and cognitive accessibility in a digital context. Ph.D. thesis, KTH Royal Institute of Technology – School of Computer Science and Communication, Stockholm, Sweden (2016). http://kth.diva-portal.org/smash/record.jsf?pid=diva2%3A908641&dswid=3185

Kouroupetroglou, G.: Text signals and accessibility of educational documents. In: 11th International Conference on Educational Technologies (EDUTE 2015), pp. 45–51. United Emirates, Dubai (2015). http://www.wseas.org/main/books/2015/Dubai/EDUTE.pdf

Ma, L., Rau, P.-L.: Reading Chinese in e-book readers: a review. In: Rau, P.L.P. (ed.) IDGD 2011. LNCS, vol. 6775, pp. 211–219. Springer, Heidelberg (2011). https://doi.org/10.1007/978-3-642-21660-2_24

Marks, E.: A prosody-enriched dynamic text presentation technique for enhanced reading of electronic text. Ph.D. thesis, Howard University, Washington DC (2009). https://www.academia.edu/435771/A_Prosody-Enriched_Dynamic_Text_Presentation_Technique_for_Enhanced_Reading_of_Electronic_Text

Murman, D.L.: The impact of age on cognition. Sem. Hear. 36(3), 111–121 (2015). https://www.thieme-connect.com/products/ejournals/html/10.1055/s-0035-1555115

Neves, J.: Interlingual subtitling for the deaf and hard-of-hearing. In: Díaz Cintas, J., Anderman, G. (eds.) Audiovisual Translation: Language Transfer on Screen, pp. 288–302. Palgrave Macmillan, New York (2009)

Nietzio, A., Naber, D., Bühler, C.: Towards techniques for easy-to-read web content. Procedia Comput. Sci. 27, 343–349 (2014). https://www.sciencedirect.com/science/article/pii/S1877050914000404

PLAIN: Federal Plain Language Guidelines (2011). https://plainlanguage.gov/media/FederalPLGuidelines.pdf

Rodríguez, A.: Audiodescripción y propuesta de estandarización de volumen de audio: hacia una producción sistematizada. Ph.D. thesis, Universitat Autònoma de Barcelona, Barcelona, Spain (2017). https://www.tdx.cat/bitstream/handle/10803/459247/alro1de1.pdf?sequence=1&isAllowed=y

Romero-Fresco, P.: Standing on quicksand: hearing viewers' comprehension and reading patterns of respoken subtitles for the news. In: Díaz Cintas, J., Matamala, A., Josélia, N. (eds.) New Insights into Audiovisual Translation and Media Accessibility: Media for All 2, pp. 175–194. Rodopi, Amsterdam (2010)

Ruer, P., Gouin-Vallerand, C., Zhang, L., Lemire, D., Vallières, E.F.: An analysis tool for the contextual information from field experiments on driving fatigue. In: Christiansen, H., Stojanovic, I., Papadopoulos, G.A. (eds.) CONTEXT 2015. LNCS (LNAI), vol. 9405, pp. 172–185. Springer, Cham (2015). https://doi.org/10.1007/978-3-319-25591-0_13

Saggion, H.: Automatic Text Simplification. Synthesis Lectures on Human Language Technologies. Morgan & Claypool, San Rafael (2017)

Saldanha, G., O'Brien, S.: Research Methodologies in Translation Studies. Routledge, London (2014)

Shanahan, T.: How important is reading rate? (2019). https://www.readingrockets.org/blogs/shanahan-literacy/how-important-reading-rate

Siddharthan, A.: A survey on text simplification. Int. J. Appl. Linguist. **165**(2), 259–298 (2014). https://pdfs.semanticscholar.org/8a30/f16ed3a83734c4ec087191401a8f241aa3a9.pdf

Starr, K., Braun, S.: Audio description 2.0: re-versioning audiovisual accessibility to assist emotion recognition. In: Braun, S., Starr, K. (eds.) Innovation in Audio Description Research. Routledge, London (2020, forthcoming)

Szarkowska, A.: Towards interlingual subtitling for the deaf and the hard of hearing. Perspect. Stud. Translatol. **21**(1), 68–81 (2013)

Tamayo, A.: Reading speed in subtitling for hearing impaired children: an analysis in Spanish television. J. Spec. Transl. **26** (2016). https://www.jostrans.org/issue26/art_tamayo.pdf

Tinker, M.A.: Legibility of Print. Iowa State University Press, Ames (1963)

Tomljenović, R.: Regulatory authorities for electronic media and media literacy: comparative analysis of the best European practices (2018). https://rm.coe.int/regulatory-authorities-for-electronic-media/1680903a2a

UNGA: Convention on the rights of persons with disabilities (CRPD) (2006). https://www.un.org/development/desa/disabilities/convention-on-the-rights-of-persons-with-disabilities.html

University of North Carolina: Subtitles, closed captions, transcriptions (2021). https://access.web.unc.edu/subtitles-or-closed-captions/

Urano, K.: Lexical simplification and elaboration: an experiment in sentence comprehension and incidental vocabulary acquisition. Master's thesis, University of Hawaii, Hawaii, USA (2000). https://www.urano-ken.com/research/thesis.pdf

Van der Heijden, M.: Making film and television accessible to the blind and visually impaired. Master's thesis, Utrecht School of the Arts, Faculty Art, Media & Technology, Utrecht, Netherlands (2007). https://static.aminer.org/pdf/PDF/000/288/838/spoken_subtitles_making_subtitled_tv_programmes_accessible.pdf

W3C: Overview of "Web Accessibility for Older Users: A Literature Review" (2018). https://www.w3.org/WAI/older-users/literature/#cognitive

Walczak, A., Fryer, L.: Vocal delivery of audio description by genre: measuring users presence. Perspect. Stud. Translatol. **26**(1), 69–83 (2017)

Wissing, G., Blignaut, A.S., van den Berg, K.: Using readability, comprehensibility and lexical coverage to evaluate the suitability of an introductory accountancy textbook to its readership. Stellenbosch Papers Linguist. **46**, 155–179 (2016). https://doi.org/10.5774/46-0-205

Wray, D., Janan, D.: Readability revisited? The implications of text complexity. Curriculum J. **24**(4) (2013). https://doi.org/10.1080/09585176.2013.828631

Yuste Frías, J.: Paratextual elements in translation: paratranslating titles in children's literature. In: Orero, P., Gil-Bajardí, A., Rovira-Esteva, S. (eds.) Translation Peripheries, pp. 117–134. Peter Lang, Frankfurt am Main, Berlin (2012)

Live Captioning Accuracy in Spanish-Language Newscasts in the United States

Nazaret Fresno[(✉)] [iD]

The University of Texas Rio Grande Valley, Brownsville, TX 78520, USA
nazaret.fresno@utrgv.edu

Abstract. In addition to English-speaking networks, the United States has a number of broadcasters that target the Hispanic community by offering their full programming in Spanish. According to the closed captioning regulations in place, they need to provide closed captions to their audiences, which have to be acceptable in terms of completeness, placement, synchronicity and accuracy. This paper provides the main findings of the first scholarly accuracy assessment conducted in the United States for Spanish-language live closed captions. Taking the national newscasts aired by two major Spanish-speaking networks as the focus of study, this article reports on their accuracy and reduction rates, and provides a detailed account of the number, type and severity of the errors encountered. Overall, our assessment revealed improvable accuracy levels, which were mainly caused by omissions of relevant information in combination with an increased presence of minor errors in the form of misspellings, punctuation errors and technology-related issues.

Keywords: Live captioning · Accuracy · Quality · Live subtitling · Media accessibility · Spanish

1 Introduction

In line with what Greco [1] calls the universalist account of Media Accessibility, we would argue that closed captions benefit viewers with hearing loss, as well as anyone who cannot access the soundtrack of a given program for whatever reason (for instance, being in a noisy environment). Therefore, closed captioning is understood in this paper as a service not for some, but for all, which should strive for the best possible quality.

According to the most recent data published in 2019 by the United States Census Bureau, over 41.5 million people in the US speak Spanish at home. From those, 38.6% state that they speak English "less than very well", with that percentage surpassing 59% in the group over 64 years old [2]. The broadcasting industry has not been oblivious to the fact that the Hispanic community is the largest minority in the country [3] and has been providing broadcasting services to this target population since the creation of the first full-time Spanish-language TV station in 1955 [4]. Today, a number of US-based networks broadcast their full programming in Spanish and, as mandated by the Federal Communications Commission (FCC), the primary authority for communications law and regulation, they need to provide closed captions [5].

© Springer Nature Switzerland AG 2021
M. Antona and C. Stephanidis (Eds.): HCII 2021, LNCS 12769, pp. 255–266, 2021.
https://doi.org/10.1007/978-3-030-78095-1_19

This article will deal with the accuracy of the live captions accompanying Spanish-language national newscasts. It will begin by briefly reviewing the existing research on this topic, as well as the instruments used to assess live captioning accuracy, before moving on to present the main findings of the first accuracy assessment undertaken in the US for Spanish-language live closed captions.

2 Live Captioning Accuracy: Metrics and Research

The US has been promoting closed captioning on television for several decades, after the FCC mandated in the late 90s the provision of closed captions for both English and Spanish programs [6]. After working to ensure that the new programming in both languages would be captioned, the FCC issued the first quality regulations in 2014, with which the Commission acknowledged not only the need to close caption pre-recorded and live broadcasts, but also the fact that captions should meet certain quality criteria in terms of completeness, placement, synchronicity and accuracy [5].

Accuracy, which is the focus of the current article, refers to the extent to which the closed captions in a given program faithfully convey the message that was uttered by the speakers. Accuracy has traditionally been regarded as an indicator of quality, as acknowledged by regulators in national closed captioning guidelines [5, 7–9], and by users who have taken part in research projects or surveys [10–15]. However, stakeholders and scholars have not agreed on a universal method to estimate it. Instead, several methodologies have been used by the closed captioning industry, as well as by researchers in this field.

One of the first studies on this topic was commissioned by the US National Captioning Institute and undertaken by Jordan et al. [16], who analyzed 69 h of televised content focusing, among other things, on accuracy. The researchers assessed "how closely the closed captions matched the audio track in both timing and veracity" [16]. A decision on the accuracy of each program was reached after taking into account if the closed captions were verbatim, if they included the complete message, and if they were understandable and meaningful, that is, if their errors did not prevent viewers from comprehending the program. Following this methodology, they found that only 25% of local news included "clear captions" that would allow users to follow most of the program, while the remaining 75% were either confusing or difficult to understand. When it came to national news, 82% of the segments assessed provided "clear captions" to their viewers, while 18% were classified as "somewhat unclear".

Focusing only on national newscasts, Fresno [17] analyzed the quality of over 11,000 closed captions contained in 500 min of news segments uploaded to the websites of four US broadcasters and offered to viewers as reshows. As far as accuracy is concerned, this study revealed misspellings and typos (present in 58% of the programs analyzed), together with omissions of relevant information (present in 52%), to be frequent causes of accuracy issues.

Other researchers have adopted metric systems to assess accuracy in live captioning. For instance, in the frame of the Caption Accuracy Metrics Project, Apone et al. [18] explored the application to the field of closed captioning of the Word Error Rate (WER), which was used to measure the accuracy of speech recognition. WER estimates the accuracy of a recognized text by comparing it to its transcript based on the number of words subtracted, deleted and inserted. These discrepancies are considered errors and all of them have the same weight in WER calculations. As a development to the WER model, Apone et al. [18] proposed the Weighted Word Error Rate model (WWER), which estimates accuracy based on the same items as WER (substitutions, deletions and insertions), but provides a specific weight to each error according to its severity. The errors that are more likely to cause comprehension issues to closed caption readers are considered more severe than those that do not prevent them from following the program and, thus, they have a heavier weight in the accuracy rate calculations. As part of the Caption Accuracy Metrics Project, Apone and his team used the WWER model to assess the accuracy rate of 20 news programs and found that 55% of them reached good accuracy levels, 35% showed accuracy issues that would pose challenges for viewers, and 10% of the programs included very inaccurate closed captions.

Both the WER and the WWER models follow a word-based approach since their unit of accuracy assessment are words. However, as pointed out by Romero-Fresco [19], this may be problematic when applied to human-produced live closed captions due to the fact that captioners may rephrase the message transmitted in a program but still provide the same meaning. For instance, a speaker saying "how are you doing?" could be captioned as "how are you?" and no information would be lost despite one word being dropped. Even though the viewer would receive the idea in full, word-based metrics would treat the deletion of "doing" as an accuracy mistake (unless a human revision was implemented to account for this kind of reformulation).

As an alternative to better account for closed captioning as performed by humans, Romero-Fresco and Martínez [20] devised the NER model. With this meaning-based instrument, originally designed to assess the accuracy of respoken subtitles[1], an accuracy rate is calculated for a given captioning sample according to the formula below, where N refers to the number of words and punctuation marks in the captions, E stands for the edition errors in the sample and R reflects recognition mistakes:

$$\frac{N - E - R}{N} \times 100$$

Edition errors are those caused by poor decisions made by the captioners. A typical example would be the omission of a full sentence that was available to the viewers who could access the soundtrack of the program, but was left out of the captions. Recognition errors are those that stem from an unsuccessful interaction between the captioners and their technical equipment. A typical example occurs when voice writers dictate to their speech recognition software, but the machine is unable to recognize their message and shows captions with different words that do not transmit the same ideas. Unlike word-based metrics, the NER model takes meaning, not words, as the main unit to assess accuracy. Consequently, if a caption renders the same idea that was shared by a speaker using a different wording, the reformulation would not be considered an error as long as meaning is kept. NER only labels as "errors" those instances in which captions do not convey the same meaning as the transcript, be it because they lack relevant information that was presented in the program or because they provide an altered message that does

---

[1] Respeaking is usually known as voice writing in the US.

not match the original. After identifying the mistakes and classifying them in edition or recognition errors, NER categorizes them according to their severity as minor, standard or serious. Minor errors (for instance, spelling mistakes or the omission of adjuncts) do not have a negative impact on the users' comprehension because, despite the mistake, it is still possible to understand the main idea expressed in the caption. Standard errors take place when viewers miss relevant information and, therefore, see their comprehension compromised. This is the case, for instance, when captioners omit a full sentence from the program, which is not included in the captions. Finally, serious errors (for instance, a wrong figure) are those in which the viewer is provided with incorrect or misleading information and cannot perceive the mistake. For live subtitles to be of acceptable quality according to the NER model, they need to reach 98% accuracy rate.

The NER model has been used in several countries to assess the accuracy of live subtitling. It was the instrument chosen by Ofcom, the UK-based regulator, in the largest live subtitling quality analysis undertaken to date [21]. It is also recommended in the Spanish standard on subtitling for the deaf and hard of hearing [9], as well as in the Canadian broadcasting regulatory policy for English-language closed captioning [22]. In addition to regulators, Media Accessibility researchers have also used the NER model. For instance, Romero-Fresco [23] reports on the results of the Ofcom project, which analyzed over 78,000 live subtitles with this instrument. The NER model has also been used in the US in several smaller-scale studies assessing the quality of the live captioning provided in widely watched televised events, such as the 2016 final presidential debate [24] and the Super Bowl LII [25]. Finally, when it comes to Spanish-language captioning, Spain is conducting its first live subtitling quality assessment at the national level, also using the NER model, in the frame of the on-going QualiSpain project, which released its first tentative results in 2019 [26].

3   Closed Captioning Accuracy in US National Newscasts in Spanish

Even though scholarly research on live captioning quality is by no means extensive, it has increased at a fast pace in the last years, with several recent studies dealing with this issue in the US [16, 24, 25]. Although the existing research has focused exclusively on English-language closed captions, over 12.5% of households in the US speak Spanish as their main language at home [2], a fact that has not been ignored by the broadcasting industry. In order to appeal to the Spanish-speaking community, a selection of US-based networks offer all their programming, both at the local and national level, in Spanish. Their broadcasts are also subject to the current FCC regulations and, as such, live programs need to be closed captioned [5]. The following sections present the main findings of what, to the best of our knowledge, is the first scholarly study dealing with closed captioning accuracy in Spanish programming in the US.

3.1   Materials

For the current research, we focused on the national newscasts aired by the two main Spanish-speaking broadcasters in the US: Telemundo and Univision. Twenty news programs aired by these networks between December 2019 and June 2020 were recorded from television together with their captions. After visualization, 10 min of each program were selected for the accuracy assessment, making sure that the final 200 min of programming included in this study accounted for news pieces equally distributed at the beginning, in the middle and at the end of the newscasts. The original captioning files were then extracted, and an accurate transcript of the selected segments was prepared to facilitate the accuracy analysis.

3.2 Methodology

The accuracy assessment was performed using the NER model [20], although the instrument had to be slightly adapted for the purposes of the present research. As explained in Sect. 2, in the original NER model mistakes are classified as edition and recognition errors. However, in the adaptation of the NER model that we used for the current analysis, we did not make such a distinction because the cause of some of the mistakes that we encountered was not clear and we could not always tell if they were due to human or technical issues. For instance, the sentence "Están *Ucrania*, Canadá, Alemania, Reino Unido (...)" was captioned as "Están *Italia*, Canadá, Reino Unido (...)". In this example we could not ascertain if the captioner said (or typed) "Italia" instead of "Ucrania" (edition error), or if s/he said (or intended to type) "Ucrania" but the caption read "Italia" due to a misrecognition (recognition error). Therefore and since we could not confirm the exact production method of our captions[2], we just estimated the accuracy rate according to the following formula, where 'N' stands for the number of words and punctuation marks in the captions, and 'Er' refers to the errors found in the sample, regardless of their cause:

$$\frac{N - Er}{N} \times 100$$

3.3 Results

Overall, the average accuracy rate (AR) found in our samples was 97.04% (or 3/10), which according to the NER model is substandard. From all the samples analyzed, one featured a very good AR, two showed acceptable accuracy levels, and the remaining seventeen samples had substandard ARs[3]. When disaggregated by broadcaster, the samples by Telemundo and Univision showed very similar ARs (97% and 97.10%, respectively). These results may be explained in terms of reduction rate and errors.

Reduction Rate
Even though closed captions in the US are expected to be as verbatim as possible [5], literality is not always feasible when captioning live programs, especially when overlapping or fast speakers need to be captioned. In these cases, captioners deliver edited

---

[2] Despite contacting both broadcasters several times, we obtained no satisfactory response and could not confirm how the closed captions that we analyzed had been produced.

[3] The NER model defines accuracy as follows [23]: "excellent" (AR above 99.5%), "very good" (AR 99%–99.49%), "good" (AR 98.5%–98.99%), "acceptable" (AR 98%–98.49%) and "substandard" (AR below 98%).

(non-verbatim) captions, which tend to be shorter than the original message, in order to keep pace. The reduction rate (RR) estimates how much shorter the text in the captions is as compared to the original message, and it is calculated by subtracting the number of words in the captions from the number of words in the transcript of the same segment. In the samples analyzed in the present research, the average RR was 26%, with five programs featuring RRs below 20%, twelve newscasts showing RRs between 20% and 40%, and three samples surpassing 40%. When looking at our samples by broadcaster, Telemundo featured an average 23% RR, while that for Univision reached 30%.

The RR illustrates the degree of editing performed by the captioners, including correct and incorrect edition. Correct edition describes instances in which captioners reformulate the speakers' message using a different wording. This may sometimes mean paraphrasing, condensing information, or even omitting ideas that were already known to the viewer. As a result, correctly edited captions tend to have fewer words than the transcript, but still provide all the necessary information for the viewers to comprehend the message. On the other hand, RR may also be an indication of incorrect edition, which takes place when the editing performed causes the users to miss ideas that were not known to them and that would be needed to fully understand the message delivered in the program. In this case, edited captions hamper the viewers' comprehension because they do not convey the full meaning of the oral text. When it comes to our samples, only 35% of all the closed captions analyzed were verbatim, 24% showed correct edition, and 41% included at least one error.

Error Analysis

A quantitative analysis revealed 13 errors per minute on average in our samples. From those, 82% of the mistakes were minor and would not have a negative impact on comprehension, 16% were standard and would prevent the viewers from understanding the message, and 2% were serious, which would provide inaccurate information to the user. When disaggregated by broadcaster, averages of 15 errors/minute and 11 errors/minute were found in the samples by Telemundo and Univision, respectively. Figure 1 shows the distribution of minor, standard and serious errors per broadcaster.

An in-depth study of the errors encountered revealed four problematic areas in the closed captions in our sample: omissions of information; orthotypographical and grammar mistakes; punctuation errors, and technical issues.

Omissions

Omissions of information accounted for 38% of all the mistakes identified in our samples. They were more frequent in Univision (48%) than in Telemundo (32%), and included the elision of both full sentences and adjuncts.

Punctuation Errors

These mistakes added up to 33% of all the errors encountered. They were particularly frequent in the closed captions by Telemundo (46%), and less common in Univision (12%). They involved missing punctuation (e.g. missing question marks, quotation marks, commas or full stops) and mistaken punctuation marks (for instance, the addition of a full stop in the middle of a sentence).

Technical Issues

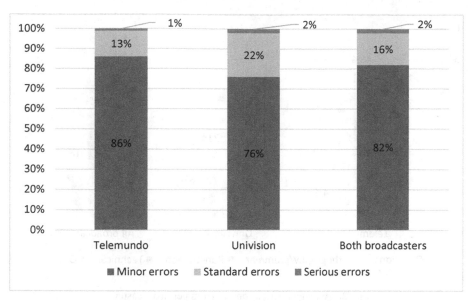

Fig. 1. Distribution of minor, standard and serious errors.

In addition to omissions of relevant information and punctuation mistakes, we identified another type of error that seemed to have a technical cause. The mistakes in this category were found in captions with incomprehensible text (e.g. "mi dprants"), and what looked like recognition issues (e.g. "te me por su vida" instead of "teme por su vida" or "incidentes de audio" instead of "incidentes de odio"). These problems, which seemed to have been originated by unsuccessful interactions between the captioners and their technical equipment, added up to 16% of the mistakes identified in our samples. They were more frequent in Univision (21%) than in Telemundo (12%).

Orthotypographical and Grammar Errors
The last group of inaccuracies identified in our samples were misspellings and improper grammar, which caused 8% of all the errors. Most of the mistakes included in this category were missing or incorrect accent marks (e.g. "sus *suplicas*", instead of "sus súplicas"), misspelled words (e.g. "*Dias* Balart" instead of "Díaz Balart"), incomplete words (e.g. "miré al *avió*", instead of "miré al avión"), and occasional grammar mistakes (e.g. "*habían* más", instead of "había más"). Univision showed more errors of this kind (11%) than Telemundo (6%). Figure 2 shows the average distribution of errors per broadcaster.

4   Discussion

To the best of our knowledge, no prior research that has tackled accuracy in live closed captions accompanying televised news programs in the US has reported on AR. Therefore, at the time of writing this paper it is only possible to compare the results summarized in Sect. 3 with similar studies undertaken for this genre in other countries. For instance,

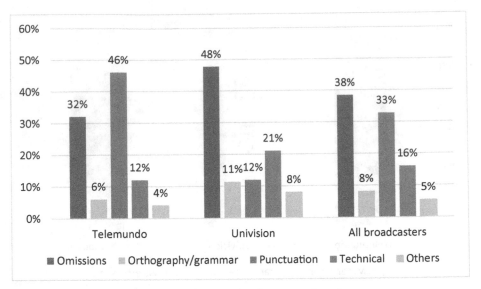

Fig. 2. Average distribution of errors per broadcaster.

in the UK, the Ofcom project assessed the accuracy of the live subtitles in four batches of news programs broadcast over a two-year period. The findings gathered for each batch allowed the implementation of specific measures aimed at improving the accuracy of subsequent batches, which led to increased ARs in news samples as the project progressed. To allow for fair comparisons with our current research, it may be more interesting to look at the results of the first UK batch, as opposed to focusing on the entire corpora of news programs, since this one contained the only samples that had not undergone quality interventions when assessing their accuracy. The first batch of live subtitles analyzed as part of the Ofcom project reached an average AR of 98.49% [23], higher than the average in our study (97.04%), and higher than the ARs reported for each of the two networks included in the present research (97% and 97.10%).

In addition, it may also be worth to review the existing studies dealing with live programs captioned in Spanish. The tentative results of the QualiSpain project [26] revealed that the live subtitles produced for news programs in Spain reached an average AR of 98.85%. According to these figures, the US captions analyzed in the current study (with an average AR of 3/10) can be considered less accurate than those in the news programs assessed so far in the UK and Spain (6/10). As mentioned before, these weaker results have to do with the RR and the errors found in the captions that composed our samples.

4.1 Reduction Rate

The RRs revealed in our study (23% for Telemundo, 30% for Univision, and 26% on average) showed the captioned text in our samples to be around one fourth shorter than the message originally delivered in those news segments. Usually, closed captions show reduced content when edition has been applied as a strategy to keep pace. Therefore, it is interesting to look at the RR together with the program speech rate. In the case of our newscasts, the speech rate averaged 167 wpm.

When comparing these figures to prior research, the Ofcom project reported an average RR of 13% and an average speech rate of 175 wpm [23], while QualiSpain found news programs to have a 20% RR on average, and a speech rate of 169 wpm, also on average [26]. These figures show that, when faced with news programs delivered at similar speech rates, the captioners who worked in our samples reduced the text in their captions more than respeakers in Spain and the UK. It should be noted, however, that the UK and Spain use a different methodology as compared to the US when it comes to live captioning of news programs, which probably influenced the RR obtained in each case.

In the UK and Spain, the so-called "hybrid mode", which combines pre-prepared and real-time subtitles, is used when dealing with news programs. The in-studio segments, in which anchors read from a teleprompter, tend to be prepared beforehand by the respeakers, who have access to the script of the news before the program is aired. That allows them to transform the scripted text into subtitles, which they launch during the live transmission of the newscast as the presenter reads those lines. By contrast, live connections with reporters are subtitled in real time as the reporting develops. Pre-prepared subtitles, which follow closely the text in the teleprompter, are more literal than subtitles produced in real time, which respeakers edit more often in order to keep pace with the spoken text. The use of this hybrid methodology often leads to the same program displaying pre-prepared and real-time subtitles featuring different characteristics. This was the case in the QualiSpain project, in which the subtitles for the scripted stories and live connections were analyzed separately and showed different trends in terms of RR. Namely, for scripted segments, which had an average speech rate of 170 wpm, relying on pre-prepared subtitles helped respeakers keep a low RR of 13%. However, when it came to live connections, which had to be subtitled in real time, the RR more than doubled, reaching almost 30% despite the fact that the average speech rate (167 wpm) was very similar to that in in-studio segments. In the US it is not customary to provide captioners with the script of the news and, thus, no pre-prepared captions can be created in advance. Interestingly, the RR found in our US newscasts (26%) is well above the RR for the scripted segments assessed in Spain (13%), but comparable to the RR reported for the QualiSpain unscripted stories (30%), which were delivered at the same average speech rate as the US news samples (167 wpm).

The RR revealed in the present study indicates that substantial editing was performed. RR reflects both correct edition, which we found in 24% of the captions in our study, as well as incorrect edition, which led to mistakes identified in 41% of the captions. This suggests that, while editing possibly allowed captioners to keep pace, it was also an important source of errors. In order to understand the impact that this editing may have had on viewers' comprehension, it is necessary to consider the aforementioned RR data together with an analysis of the errors encountered.

4.2   Errors

The closed captions in this study included 13 errors per minute on average. 82% of them were minor and would not have a negative impact on comprehension, 16% were standard and would hamper the viewers' understanding of the program, and 2% were serious, which would provide misleading information to the user. In the samples by Telemundo, an average of 15 errors/minute was found, with 86% of minor errors, 13% of standard errors and 1% of serious errors. The segments from Univision had 11 errors/minute on average, with 76% of the mistakes classified as minor, 22% of errors being standard, and 2% considered serious. According to these figures, the closed captions delivered by Univision included fewer mistakes than those broadcast by Telemundo. However, more of those errors were standard and serious and, therefore, more of them would prevent viewers from understanding the message that the captions intended to convey.

When compared to prior research dealing with live subtitling, 66% of the total errors identified in the Ofcom project for news programs were minor, while the remaining 33% were standard. As far as subtitles in Spanish are concerned, the tentative results of the QualiSpain project revealed an average of 6 errors per minute in non-scripted news segments with subtitles produced in real time. From those, 74% were minor, 22% were standard, and 4% were serious. The fact that the percentage of standard and serious errors was kept at a low 18% in the US (as compared to 33% in the UK and 26% in Spain) suggests that good efforts were made to deliver closed captions that conveyed the main ideas accurately. Even so, however, the AR of many of these samples was below par, which could be explained by looking at the total number of errors per minute (13 in the US and 6 in Spain). In other words, even though most of the inaccuracies identified in the present research involved petty mistakes or the omission of adjuncts not necessary to understand the main ideas, our American newscasts showed twice as many errors per minute as the live subtitles analyzed in Spain. This abundance of mistakes, rather than their severity, was the main factor leading to substandard ARs. Although these errors are believed to be noticed by the viewers without hampering their comprehension, live captioning research has yet to explore how an increased number of minor mistakes may affect the viewers' understanding. Isolated misspellings, omissions of information or punctuation errors may not prevent viewers from following a program. However, segments with a concentration of minor mistakes in their closed captions may pose more challenges, despite the apparently low severity of their errors.

In terms of error typology, omissions of information, which accounted for 38% of the total errors encountered, and punctuation mistakes, which added up to 33%, were the most frequent issues in our samples, followed by technical mistakes, which made up 16% of the total errors. Furthermore, the typology of errors varied across broadcasters. In the captions offered by Telemundo, punctuation (missing or misplaced punctuation marks) was especially problematic since it caused 46% of all the errors encountered. The second and third most frequent issues were omissions, which led to 32% of the identified mistakes, and technical issues, which reached 12%. In the case of Univision, omissions were the most common problem (48% of the total errors), followed by technical mistakes (21%) and a similar percentage of punctuation and orthotypographical errors (12% and 11%, respectively). These data suggest that the errors found in the samples by Telemundo were more related to formal aspects, while those in the captions by Univision were more content-based.

5 Conclusions

This article has presented the main findings of the first accuracy study conducted in the US for Spanish-language live captions. Our NER-based assessment of 200 min of samples from national newscast broadcast by Telemundo and Univision revealed improvable ARs below the 98% threshold for both networks. These results were due to a significant RR, caused by incorrect edition instances and by a substantial number of errors per minute, most of them minor. Omissions of relevant information, punctuation mistakes and technology issues were the most frequent types of mistakes encountered.

The analysis provided in this paper may be useful for Spanish-speaking live captioners and trainers working in the US, who may benefit from having identified the main weaknesses of current news captions in order to address them. In addition, the study presented here may be understood as a partial picture of the closed captioning accuracy found in news programs in the US, which could be completed in the future with an equivalent assessment for English-language segments. Furthermore, the research described in this paper may be seen as the first step toward a full quality assessment of the closed captioning delivered in news programs in the US, which should combine findings such as those reported here with additional data regarding closed captioning completeness, placement and synchronicity, both in terms of captioning speed and delay.

It is hoped that these findings will provide valuable data to those making good efforts to make Spanish programs in the US accessible to their intended audiences.

Acknowledgement. This research was conducted within the framework of the research group GALMA (Galician Observatory for Media Accessibility).

References

1. Greco, G.M.: The nature of accessibility studies. J. Audiov. Transl. 1, 205–232 (2018). https://doi.org/10.47476/jat.v1i1.51
2. US Census Bureau: Language Spoken at Home (2019)
3. US Census Bureau: Hispanic Heritage Month 2020 (2020)
4. Wilkinson, K.T.: Spanish-Language Television in the United States: Fifty Years of Development. Routledge, New York (2016)
5. Federal Communications Commission (FCC): Report and Order, Declaratory Ruling, and Further Notice of Proposed Rulemaking (2014)
6. Federal Communications Commission (FCC): Closed Captioning of Video Programming (1997)
7. Australian Communications and Media Authority: Broadcasting Services (Television Captioning) Standard 2013 (2013)
8. Canadian Radio-Television and Telecommunications Commission: Broadcasting Regulatory Policy CRTC 2016–435 (2016)
9. AENOR: Subtitulado para personas sordas y personas con discapacidad auditiva (UNE 153010) (2012)
10. Canadian Association of the Deaf: Understanding User Responses to Live Closed Captioning in Canada - Summary Report (2018)

11. Twenty-First Century Captioning Disability and Rehabilitation Research Project (Captioning DRRP): Comments on Telecommunications for the Deaf and Hard of Hearing, Inc. et al. Petition for Declaratory Ruling and/or Ruling Making on Live Closed Captioning Quality Metrics and the Use of Automatic Speech Recognition Technologies (2019)
12. Reid, B.E.: Survey Report by Telecommunications for the Deaf and Hard of Hearing, National Association of the Deaf, Hearing Loss Association of America, Technology Access Program at Gallaudet University (2015)
13. English Language Broadcasters Group: EBG Report on Efforts to Improve the Quality of Closed Captioning (2014)
14. Romero-Fresco, P.: Quality in live subtitling: the reception of respoken subtitles in the UK. In: Remael, A., Orero, P., Carroll, M. (eds.) Audiovisual Translation and Media Accessibility at the Crossroads, pp. 111–131. Rodopi, Amsterdam (2012). https://doi.org/10.1163/978940 1207812_008
15. Matthews, L.: Getting the full picture? Viewers' experiences of television subtitling (2015). https://doi.org/10.7748/en.15.10.12.s17
16. Jordan, A.B., Albright, A., Branner, A., Sullivan, J.: The State of Closed Captioning Services in the United States. An Assessment of Quality, Availability, and Use (2003)
17. Fresno, N.: Closed captioning quality in the information society: the case of the American newscasts reshown online. Univers. Access Inf. Soc. (2020)
18. Apone, T., Botkin, B., Brooks, M., Goldberg, L.: Caption Accuracy Metrics Project Research into Automated Error Ranking of Real-time Captions in Live Television News Programs, pp. 1–16 (2011)
19. Romero-Fresco, P.: Subtitling Through Speech Recognition Respeaking. St. Jerome Publishing, Manchester (2011)
20. Romero-Fresco, P., Martínez, J.: Accuracy rate in live subtitling. The NER model. In: Díaz-Cintas, J., Baños-Piñero, R. (eds.) Audiovisual Translation in a Global Context: Mapping an Ever-changing Landscape, pp. 28–50. Palgrave MacMillan, London (2015)
21. Ofcom: Measuring the quality of live subtitling (2013)
22. Canadian Radio-Television and Telecommunications Commission: Broadcasting Regulatory Policy CRTC 2019–308 (2019)
23. Romero-Fresco, P.: Accessing communication: the quality of live subtitles in the UK. Lang. Commun. **49**, 56–69 (2016). https://doi.org/10.1016/j.langcom.2016.06.001
24. Fresno, N.: Of bad hombres and nasty women; the quality of the live closed captioning in the 2016 US final presidential debate. Perspect. Stud. Transl. Theory Pract. **27**, 350–366 (2019). https://doi.org/10.1080/0907676X.2018.1526960
25. Fresno, N., Sepielak, K., Krawczyk, M.: Football for all: the quality of the live closed captioning in the Super Bowl LII. Univers. Access Inf. Soc. (2020). https://doi.org/10.1007/s10 209-020-00734-7
26. Fresno, N., Romero-Fresco, P., Rico-Vázquez, M.: The quality of live subtitling on Spanish television. In: Media for All 8 Conference. University of Stockholm, Stockholm (2019)

Dynamical Properties of Three-Rules Set Realizing Compressive and Errorless Description of Digital Sound

Shota Nakayama[1], Jousuke Kuroiwa[1(✉)], Tomohiro Odaka[1], and Izumi Suwa[1,2]

[1] University of Fukui, Fukui 910-8507, Japan
jou@u-fukui.ac.jp
[2] Jin-ai Women's College, Fukui 910-8507, Japan

Abstract. In the present paper, we investigate dynamical properties of a three-rules set of one dimensional cellular automata with two sets and three neighbors (hereafter referred as 1-2-3 CA), which realize compressive coding of digital sound without reproducing error. In the present paper, we apply our description method to two types of digital sound: The first is thirty six pronounced words which are taken from six different kinds of word pronounced by both three men and three women provided from ATR. The last is 150 music data which are taken from four classic and one JPOP music CD with the 1 s interval. All the data is quantized with 16 bits, which means that the data is described by 1-2-3 CA with 16 cells. For each data, we investigate dynamical properties of the top five resultant three-rules sets in less data amount. Dynamical properties are characterized with Wolfram's class and Chua's complexity. Almost three-rules sets consist of the rules of hua's complexity of 2. All the three-rules sets are composed with the rules of Wolfram's class 1 and 3 or 1, 2 and 3. However, all the these rules change to be class 3 for large number of cells. Thus, the rules of Wolfram's class 1 possess the diversity of the simplicity in small degree of freedom and the complexity in large degree of freedom. We guess that the rule with the diversity plays important roles in realizing compressive and errorless description of digital data.

Keywords: Cellular automata · Digital sound · Rule dynamics

1 Introduction

In the present paper, we investigate dynamical properties of a three-rules set of one dimensional cellular automata with two sets and three neighbors (hereafter referred as to 1-2-3 CA), which realize compressive coding of digital sound without reproducing error. For a few decades, chaotic and/or dynamics have attracted scientific interesting, and have been understood more an more [1,2]. In addition, there exist challenging investigations that chaotic dynamics can be applied to realizing complex information processing or complex control via certain simple rules [3–9].

© Springer Nature Switzerland AG 2021
M. Antona and C. Stephanidis (Eds.): HCII 2021, LNCS 12769, pp. 267–276, 2021.
https://doi.org/10.1007/978-3-030-78095-1_20

Therefore, we have investigated a description method with deterministic rules of 1-2-3 CA related with "rule dynamics" proposed by Aizawa and Nagai [10–14]. From the point of view of "rule dynamics", the rules should dynamically change to realize a complex dynamics, processing and control. In usual, 1-2-3 CA generates a complex dynamics including chaos [15,16]. On the other hand, in our investigation, we search for rule dynamics which describes time development of a digital sound as an example of complex dynamics.

Recently, we have succeeded a compressive and errorless coding of digital sound with three-rules set of 1-2-3 CA and Huffman coding for various digital sound [17]. Thus, we have succeeded to extract "rule dynamics" of digital sound with the three-rules set of 1-2-3 CA. The resultant rule sequences of the three-rules set for digital sound could reflect its dynamical features. Based on Kolgmorov complexity, the data amount of the description code should represent the complexity of the sound [18]. In discussing the complexity of the sound from the description code, therefore, it is important to eliminate redundancy of the code as possible and then we aim to achieve a compressive and errorless coding.

From the viewpoint of "rule dynamics", the rule sequences which realize the description of digital sound data could represent their dynamical characteristic features. Therefore, the purpose of the present paper is to investigate dynamical properties of three-rules sets of 1-2-3 CA.

2   Description Method with 1-2-3 CA

2.1   1-2-3 CA

In 1-2-3 CA, each cell is arranged on one-dimensional chain, and a cell state takes 0 or 1. In the present paper, the ith cell state at the t steps is denoted by a_i^t, and the updating rule is represented by,

$$a_i^{t+1} = f(a_{i-1}^t, a_i^t, a_{i+1}^t). \tag{1}$$

A function f corresponds to

$$f(0,0,0) = f_0, \ \ f(0,0,1) = f_1, \ \ f(0,1,0) = f_2$$
$$f(0,1,1) = f_3, \ \ f(1,0,0) = f_4, \ \ f(1,0,1) = f_5 \tag{2}$$
$$f(1,1,0) = f_6, \ \ f(1,1,1) = f_7,$$

where $f_i = 0$ or 1 $(i = 0, 1, \cdots, 7)$ and there exit 256 possible rules in 1-2-3 CA.

In order to specify a rule, we apply "rule number" of $\#r$ defined as

$$\#r = \sum_{k=0}^{7} 2^k f_k, \tag{3}$$

which was introduced by Wolfram [15].

2.2   Description Method with Three-Rules Set

Let us explain the description method with three-rules set in 1-2-3 CA briefly. In the description, at first, we determine a three-rules set of $\mathcal{R}^1 = \{\#r_1, \#r_2, \#r_3\}$ from 256 possible rules in 1-2-3 CA and a boundary condition for boundary cell states. The cell state of 1-2-3 CA at the t steps, $\mathbf{a}^t$, is regarded as "an amplitude of digital sound signal" at t steps. The time development of digital sound signals from $\mathbf{a}^t$ to $\mathbf{a}^{t+1}$ is reproduced by applying a certain rule of r, that is, $\mathbf{a}^{t+1} = r \circ \mathbf{a}^t$. As the appropriate rule of r, we employ the rule sequence with the shortest length of k by applying the elements of rule sets $\mathcal{R}^k$ ($k = 1, 2, \cdots$). It means that, starting from $k = 1$, we increase k until getting the target digital sound signal of $\mathbf{a}^{t+1} = r^k \circ \mathbf{a}^t$. Note that $r^k \in \mathcal{R}^k$ and $\mathcal{R}^k = \mathcal{R}^{k-1} \otimes \mathcal{R}^1$ where $\otimes$ means Cartesian product.

3   Computer Experiments

3.1   Method

In the present paper, we apply our description method to two types of digital sound: The first is thirty six pronounced words which are taken from six different kinds of words pronounced by both three men and three women provided from ATR. The last is 150 music data which are taken from four classic and one JPOP music CD with the 1 s interval. All the data is quantized with 16 bits, which means that the data is described by 1-2-3 CA with 16 cells. In prepossessing for reducing data amount, we apply gray coding to the subtraction between digital sound signals at the time steps t and $t + 2$. As the fixed boundary condition, we employ L1-R0 where L1 means that the boundary cell at the left of the 16th cell is fixed at unity. and R0 means that the boundary cell at the right of the 1st cell is fixed at zero.

   In the description, we search for appropriate rules among the limited number of three-rules sets according to the results of preliminary experiments since all the possible number of three-rules sets is extremely large. Now, we have completed in describing 18/36 pronounced words and 4/150 music data. For each data, we investigate dynamical properties of the top five resultant three-rules sets in less data amount. Dynamical properties are characterized with Wolfram's classification and Chua's complexity [15,16]. In the present paper, Wolfram's classification is performed by DP method.

3.2   Results

Several typical examples of dynamical features are given in Tables 1, 2 and 3, where three rules, their Chua's complexity, Wolfram's class and compressibilty are presented. In Chua's complexity, all the three-rules sets consist of ones of Chua's complexity of 2 or 3, and almost 2. In Wolfram's classification, all the three-rules sets are composed with ones of Wolfram's class 1 and 3 or 1, 2 and 3. Fromm the results, the candidates of the three-rules sets resemble each other

Table 1. Dynamical features and compressibility for pronounced data of "knife".

(a) woman 1

rank	#r_1	#r_2	#r_3	compressibility
1	90 $\kappa=2$ class 3	106 $\kappa=2$ class 3	180 $\kappa=2$ class 1	0.938
2	90 $\kappa=2$ class 3	166 $\kappa=2$ class 3	180 $\kappa=2$ class 1	0.940
3	90 $\kappa=2$ class 3	182 $\kappa=2$ class 3	180 $\kappa=2$ class 1	0.942
4	90 $\kappa=2$ class 3	118 $\kappa=2$ class 2	180 $\kappa=2$ class 1	0.943
5	90 $\kappa=2$ class 3	150 $\kappa=3$ class 3	180 $\kappa=2$ class 1	0.945

(b) woman 2

rank	#r_1	#r_2	#r_3	compressibility
1	90 $\kappa=2$ class 3	106 $\kappa=2$ class 3	180 $\kappa=2$ class 1	0.916
2	90 $\kappa=2$ class 3	210 $\kappa=2$ class 3	180 $\kappa=2$ class 1	0.918
3	90 $\kappa=2$ class 3	182 $\kappa=2$ class 3	180 $\kappa=2$ class 1	0.919
4	90 $\kappa=2$ class 3	166 $\kappa=2$ class 3	180 $\kappa=2$ class 1	0.920
5	62 $\kappa=2$ class 2	102 $\kappa=2$ class 3	180 $\kappa=2$ class 1	0.921

(c) man 1

rank	#r_1	#r_2	#r_3	compressibility
1	90 $\kappa=2$ class 3	106 $\kappa=2$ class 3	180 $\kappa=2$ class 1	0.912
2	90 $\kappa=2$ class 3	182 $\kappa=2$ class 3	180 $\kappa=2$ class 1	0.913
3	90 $\kappa=2$ class 3	118 $\kappa=2$ class 3	180 $\kappa=2$ class 1	0.914
4	90 $\kappa=2$ class 3	150 $\kappa=3$ class 2	180 $\kappa=2$ class 1	0.915
5	90 $\kappa=2$ class 3	166 $\kappa=2$ class 3	180 $\kappa=2$ class 1	0.915

(d) man 2

rank	#r_1	#r_2	#r_3	compressibility
1	90 $\kappa=2$ class 3	106 $\kappa=2$ class 3	180 $\kappa=2$ class 1	0.871
2	90 $\kappa=2$ class 3	182 $\kappa=2$ class 3	180 $\kappa=2$ class 1	0.872
3	90 $\kappa=2$ class 3	150 $\kappa=3$ class 3	180 $\kappa=2$ class 1	0.872
4	90 $\kappa=2$ class 3	166 $\kappa=2$ class 3	180 $\kappa=2$ class 1	0.872
5	90 $\kappa=2$ class 3	118 $\kappa=2$ class 2	180 $\kappa=2$ class 1	0.874

among data. In Table 4, the top four three-rules sets in appearance frequency are given. The top four three-rules sets are exactly the same irrespective of the kind of pronounced words or music data.

We compute Wolfram's classification with 17 cells, which corresponds to the quantization of the target signals. For rules with class 1 and class 2, we perform Wolfram's classification with 101 cells, again. In DP method, we compute a bit-pattern sequence by executing performing XOR operation between original bit-pattern and one for performing bit invert to the center cell corresponding the 9th for 17 cells and 51th cell for 101 cells, respectively. In class 1 and 2, the

Table 2. Dynamical features and compressibility for pronounced data of "pocket".

(a) woman 1

rank	$\#r_1$	$\#r_2$	$\#r_3$	compressibility
1	90 $\kappa=2$ class 3	182 $\kappa=2$ class 3	180 $\kappa=2$ class 1	0.712
2	90 $\kappa=2$ class 3	150 $\kappa=3$ class 3	180 $\kappa=2$ class 1	0.713
3	90 $\kappa=2$ class 3	166 $\kappa=2$ class 3	180 $\kappa=2$ class 1	0.714
4	62 $\kappa=2$ class 2	102 $\kappa=2$ class 3	180 $\kappa=2$ class 1	0.715
5	30 $\kappa=2$ class 2	166 $\kappa=2$ class 3	180 $\kappa=2$ class 1	0.715

(b) woman 2

rank	$\#r_1$	$\#r_2$	$\#r_3$	compressibility
1	90 $\kappa=2$ class 3	150 $\kappa=3$ class 3	180 $\kappa=2$ class 1	0.711
2	90 $\kappa=2$ class 3	182 $\kappa=2$ class 3	180 $\kappa=2$ class 1	0.712
3	90 $\kappa=2$ class 3	166 $\kappa=2$ class 3	180 $\kappa=2$ class 1	0.713
4	90 $\kappa=2$ class 3	118 $\kappa=2$ class 2	180 $\kappa=2$ class 1	0.715
5	62 $\kappa=2$ class 2	210 $\kappa=2$ class 3	180 $\kappa=2$ class 1	0.715

(c) man 1

rank	$\#r_1$	$\#r_2$	$\#r_3$	compressibility
1	62 $\kappa=2$ class 2	210 $\kappa=2$ class 3	180 $\kappa=2$ class 1	0.874
2	62 $\kappa=2$ class 2	102 $\kappa=2$ class 3	180 $\kappa=2$ class 1	0.875
3	54 $\kappa=2$ class 2	90 $\kappa=2$ class 3	180 $\kappa=2$ class 1	0.876
4	30 $\kappa=2$ class 2	166 $\kappa=2$ class 3	180 $\kappa=2$ class 1	0.877
5	62 $\kappa=2$ class 2	150 $\kappa=3$ class 3	180 $\kappa=2$ class 1	0.878

(d) man 2

rank	$\#r_1$	$\#r_2$	$\#r_3$	compressibility
1	90 $\kappa=2$ class 3	106 $\kappa=2$ class 3	180 $\kappa=2$ class 1	0.756
2	90 $\kappa=2$ class 3	182 $\kappa=2$ class 3	180 $\kappa=2$ class 1	0.756
3	90 $\kappa=2$ class 3	166 $\kappa=2$ class 3	180 $\kappa=2$ class 1	0.758
4	90 $\kappa=2$ class 3	118 $\kappa=2$ class 2	180 $\kappa=2$ class 1	0.759
5	62 $\kappa=2$ class 2	210 $\kappa=2$ class 3	180 $\kappa=2$ class 1	0.760

resultant bit-pattern sequence becomes zero for all the cell site. In class 3, on the other hand, some non-zero cells of the resultant bit-pattern sequence remains.

Typical resuts are given in Figs. 1 and 2. From the analysis, these rules are divided into two types. The first is that the transient duration becomes longer as the cell number increases, and transient state belongs to class 3 but steady state belongs to class 1 or 2 as shown in Fig. 1. The last is that transient and also steady state belong to class 3 for 100 cells even if steady state belongs to

Table 3. Dynamical features and compressibility for music data of "JPOP".

(a) interval 1

rank	#r_1	#r_2	#r_3	compressibility
1	26 $\kappa=2$ class 3	60 $\kappa=2$ class 3	120 $\kappa=2$ class 1	0.994
2	90 $\kappa=2$ class 3	106 $\kappa=2$ class 3	180 $\kappa=2$ class 1	0.995
3	60 $\kappa=2$ class 3	70 $\kappa=2$ class 2	120 $\kappa=2$ class 1	0.995
4	90 $\kappa=2$ class 3	166 $\kappa=2$ class 3	180 $\kappa=2$ class 1	1.000
5	90 $\kappa=2$ class 3	182 $\kappa=2$ class 3	180 $\kappa=2$ class 1	1.001

(b) interval 2

rank	#r_1	#r_2	#r_3	compressibility
1	30 $\kappa=2$ class 2	106 $\kappa=2$ class 3	180 $\kappa=2$ class 1	0.980
2	30 $\kappa=2$ class 2	90 $\kappa=2$ class 3	180 $\kappa=2$ class 1	0.980
3	30 $\kappa=2$ class 2	166 $\kappa=2$ class 3	180 $\kappa=2$ class 1	0.983
4	30 $\kappa=2$ class 2	150 $\kappa=3$ class 3	180 $\kappa=2$ class 1	0.983
5	30 $\kappa=2$ class 2	102 $\kappa=2$ class 3	180 $\kappa=2$ class 1	0.986

(c) interval 3

rank	#r_1	#r_2	#r_3	compressibility
1	60 $\kappa=2$ class 3	70 $\kappa=2$ class 2	180 $\kappa=2$ class 1	0.983
2	90 $\kappa=2$ class 3	106 $\kappa=2$ class 3	180 $\kappa=2$ class 1	0.986
3	90 $\kappa=2$ class 3	166 $\kappa=2$ class 3	180 $\kappa=2$ class 1	0.992
4	90 $\kappa=2$ class 3	182 $\kappa=3$ class 2	180 $\kappa=2$ class 1	0.992
5	90 $\kappa=2$ class 3	118 $\kappa=2$ class 2	180 $\kappa=2$ class 1	0.993

(d) interval 4

rank	#r_1	#r_2	#r_3	compressibility
1	90 $\kappa=2$ class 3	106 $\kappa=2$ class 3	180 $\kappa=2$ class 1	0.971
2	60 $\kappa=2$ class 3	70 $\kappa=2$ class 2	180 $\kappa=2$ class 1	0.973
3	90 $\kappa=2$ class 3	166 $\kappa=3$ class 3	180 $\kappa=2$ class 1	0.976
4	90 $\kappa=2$ class 3	182 $\kappa=2$ class 3	180 $\kappa=2$ class 1	0.977
5	90 $\kappa=2$ class 3	118 $\kappa=2$ class 2	180 $\kappa=2$ class 1	0.978

Table 4. Top four three-rules sets in appearance frequency.

(a) pronounced words

rank	#r_1	#r_2	#r_3	frequency
1	#90	#182	#180	17/18
2	#90	#166	#180	16/18
3	#90	#118	#180	14/18
4	#90	#106	#180	14/18

(b) music data

rank	#r_1	#r_2	#r_3	frequency
1	#90	#182	#180	3/4
2	#90	#166	#180	3/4
3	#90	#118	#80	3/4
4	#90	#106	#80	3/4

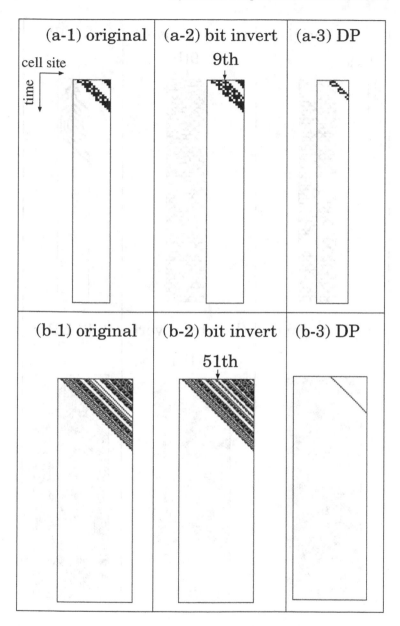

Fig. 1. Result of DP method for #180. (a-1) and (b-1) original bit-pattern sequence generated by the rule of #180 for 17 cells and 101 cells respectively with the L1-R0 fixed boundary. (a-2) and (b-2) bit-pattern sequence of bit invert of the center cell corresponding to the 9th and the 51th cell respectively. (a-3) and (b-3) bit-pattern sequence of DP method.

274   S. Nakayama et al.

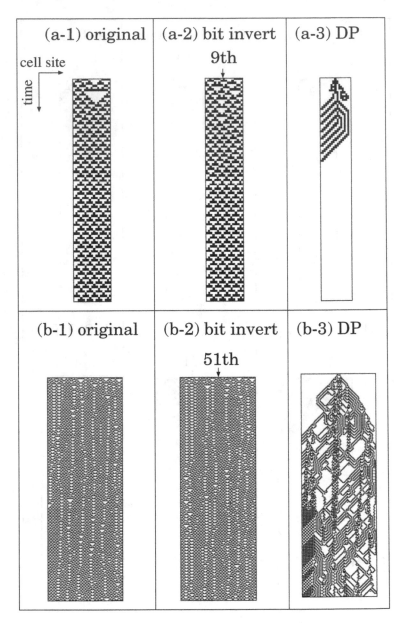

Fig. 2. Result of DP method for #54. (a-1) and (b-1) original bit-pattern sequence generated by the rule of #54 for 17 cells and 101 cells respectively with the L1-R0 fixed boundary. (a-2) and (b-2) bit-pattern sequence of bit invert of the center cell corresponding to the 9th and the 51th cell respectively. (a-3) and (b-3) bit-pattern sequence of DP method.

class 1 or 2 for 17 cells as shown in Fig. 2. We call these types of class 1 or 2 as pseudo-class 1 or 2.

4   Discussions

All the thee-rules sets are composed of ones with Chua's complexity of $\kappa = 2$ or 3, indicating that the rule in Boolean cubic representation is linearly inseparable and complicate. In addition, all the rules of class 1 or 2 are ones with pseudo-class 1 or 2, suggesting that transient state shows chaotic. Thees types of rules with pseudo-class 1 or 2 are special ones, indicating a feature of linearly inseparable, and stable feature that steady state belongs to class 1 or 2 but complex feature that transient state does to class 3 (chaotic). In the description, these types of rules could play an important role since the same rule are not applied repeatedly and then the transient state are employed. The reason why three-rules sets are exactly the same regardless of data type, pronounced words or music data, would be the limited number of these types of rules. In near future, we investigate characteristic features of each data by analyzing spatio-temporal pattern generated by rule sequence of the three-rules set at each step as "rule dynamics".

5   Conclusions

In the present paper, from viewpoint of Wolfram's classification and Chua's complexity, we investigate dynamical properties of the three-rules sets of 1-2-3 CA which realize realizing compressive and errorless description of digital sound. Results are as follows:

- In Chua's complexity, all the three-ruels sets belong to Chua's complexity of 2 or 3, and almost 2.
- In Wolfram's classification, all the three-rules sets are composed with Wolfram's class 1 and 3 or 1, 2 and 3.
- The rules with Wolfram's class 1 and 3 indicate a feature of linearly inseparable, and stable feature that steady state belongs to class 1 or 2 but complex feature that transient state does to class 3 (chaotic), called as pseudo-class 1 or 2 in the present paper.
- The top four three-rules sets in appearance frequency are exactly the same irrespective of the kind of pronounced words or music data.

The further problem is to investigate characteristic features of each data by analyzing spatio-temporal pattern generated by the rule sequence of the three-rules set at each step.

References

1. Aihara, K., Matsumoto, G.: Chaotic oscillations and bifurcations in squid giant axons. In: Holden, A.V. (ed.) pp. 257–269. Manchester University and Princeton University Press, Princeton (1987)
2. Freeman, W.J.: Tutorial on neurobiology: from single neurons to brain chaos. IJBC **2**, 451–482 (1992). https://doi.org/10.1007/978-3-642-79119-2_18
3. Tsuda, I., Koerner, E., Shimizu, H.: Memory dynamics in asynchronous neural networks. Prog. Theor. Phys. **78**, 51–71 (1987)
4. Tsuda, I.: Chaotic itinerancy as a dynamical basis of hermeneutics in brain and mind. World Futures **32**, 167–184 (1991)
5. Tsuda, I., Yamaguchi, A.: Singular-continuous nowhere-differentiable attractors in neural systems. Neural Net. **11**, 927–937 (1998)
6. Aihara, K., Takebe, T., Toyoda, M.: Chaotic neural networks. Phys. Lett. A **144**, 333–340 (1990)
7. Nara, S., Davis, P., Kawachi, M., Totsuji, H.: Chaotic memory dynamics in a recurrent neural network with cycle memories embedded by pseudo-inverse method. IJBC **5**, 1205–1212 (1997)
8. Nara, S.: Can potentially useful dynamics to solve complex problems emerge from constrained chaos and/or chaotic itinerancy? Chaos **12**, 1110–1121 (2003)
9. Kuroiwa, J., Nara, S., Aihara, K.: Response properties of a single chaotic neuron to stochastic inputs. IJBC **11**, 1447–1460 (2001)
10. Aizawa, Y., Nagai, Y.: Dynamics on pattern and rule - rule dynamics. Bussei Kenkyu **48**, 316–320 (1987). (in Japanese)
11. Nara, S., Abe, N., Wada, M., Kuroiwa, J.: A novel method of sound data description by means of cellular automata and its application to data compression. IJBC **9**, 1211–1217 (1999)
12. Wada, M., Kuroiwa, J., Nara, S.: Completely reproducible description of digital sound data with cellular automata. Phys. Lett. A **306**, 110–115 (2002)
13. Kuroiwa, J., Nara, S.: Errorless description with two rules of cellular automata for digital sound data. IJBC **23**, 135048-1–135048-8 (2013)
14. Terai, R., Kuroiwa, J., Odaka, T., Suwa, I., Shirai, H.: Three-rules set of one dimensional cellular automata with two states and three neighbors improves description ability. NOLTA. IEICE **6**(4), 534–541 (2015)
15. Wolfram, S.: A New Kind of Science, Wolfram Media Inc., Champaign (2002)
16. Chua, L., Sbtnev, V., Yoon, S.: A nonlinear dynamics perspective of Wolfram's new kind of science Part III: predicting the unpredictable. IJBC **14**, 3689–3820 (2004)
17. Tai, K., Kuroiwa, J., Odaka, T., Shirai, H., Suwa, I.: Compressive performance of digital sound data with two-rules and three-rules set in Cellular automata. In: 2019 International Symposium on NOLTA2019, pp. 237–240, Kuala Lumpur (2019)
18. Kolgomorov, A.N., Uspensky, V.A.: Algorithms and Randomness. In: Proceedings of the 1st World Congress of the Bernoulli Society, pp. 3–53 (1987)

Multimodal Fusion and Sequence Learning for Cued Speech Recognition from Videos

Katerina Papadimitriou[1]([✉]), Maria Parelli[2], Galini Sapountzaki[3], Georgios Pavlakos[4], Petros Maragos[2], and Gerasimos Potamianos[1]

[1] Department of Electrical and Computer Engineering,
University of Thessaly, Volos, Greece
`aipapadimitriou@uth.gr, gpotam@ieee.org`
[2] School of Electrical and Computer Engineering,
National Technical University of Athens, Athens, Greece
`maragos@cs.ntua.gr, el15155@central.ntua.gr`
[3] Department of Special Education, University of Thessaly, Volos, Greece
`gsapountz@sed.uth.gr`
[4] Electrical Engineering and Computer Sciences,
University of California, Berkeley, CA, USA
`pavlakos@berkeley.edu`

Abstract. Cued Speech (CS) constitutes a non-vocal mode of communication that relies on lip movements in conjunction with hand positional and gestural cues, in order to disambiguate phonetic information and make it accessible to the speech and hearing impaired. In this study, we address the automatic recognition of CS from videos, employing deep learning techniques and extending our earlier work on this topic as follows: First, for visual feature extraction, in addition to hand positioning embeddings and convolutional neural network-based appearance features of the mouth region and signing hand, we consider structural information of the hand and mouth articulators. Specifically, we utilize the OpenPose framework to extract 2D lip keypoints and hand skeletal coordinates of the signer, and we also infer 3D hand skeletal coordinates from the latter exploiting own earlier work on 2D-to-3D hand-pose regression. Second, we modify the sequence learning model, by considering a time-depth separable (TDS) convolution block structure that encodes the fused visual features, in conjunction with a decoder that is based on connectionist temporal classification for phonetic sequence prediction. We investigate the contribution of the above to CS recognition, evaluating our model on a French and a British English CS video dataset, and we report significant gains over the state-of-the-art on both sets.

Keywords: Cued speech recognition · Convolutional neural networks · Time-depth separable convolutional encoder · Connectionist temporal classification · OpenPose · Skeleton · 2D-to-3D hand-pose regression

© Springer Nature Switzerland AG 2021
M. Antona and C. Stephanidis (Eds.): HCII 2021, LNCS 12769, pp. 277–290, 2021.
https://doi.org/10.1007/978-3-030-78095-1_21

1 Introduction

Speechreading is essential to speech perception for the hearing impaired, albeit inaccurate due to the confusability of visual speech patterns, as multiple phonemes share identical mouthing (visemes). To address this problem, Cornett [6] introduced the cued speech (CS) communication system, complementing mouthing patterns with hand positional and gestural cues. In CS, the simultaneous articulation of mouthing patterns, hand-shapes, and hand positioning relative to the mouth provides a complete visual representation of the spoken language phonological system that is valuable to the speech and hearing impaired. Not surprisingly, CS has been adopted in many languages and dialects. For instance, as also shown in Fig. 1, French CS comprises 5 hand positions that encode vowels, as well as 8 hand-shapes that encode consonants in conjunction with 8 lip contour patterns, yielding 34 phonemes [15]. Similarly, CS for British English encapsulates 4 hand positions for monophthongs (12 monophthongs) and 4 hand slips for diphthongs (8 diphthongs) encoding, as well as 8 hand-shapes for the encoding of 24 consonants in conjunction with lip patterns (44 phonemes in total). Example video frames of CS articulation in French and British English are shown in Fig. 2, obtained from corresponding corpora [21, 22].

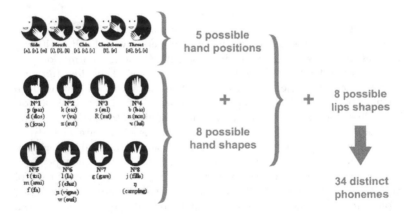

Fig. 1. French CS phonetic encoding system (figure adapted from [1])

Since CS information is primarily delivered by mouthing and gestural patterns, its automatic recognition from video data necessitates the integration of lipreading [28] and sign language recognition techniques [2, 29]. The topic has attracted recent interest in the literature, facilitated by the availability of CS data resources [19, 21, 22]. For example, on the visual front-end side of automatic CS recognition systems, early approaches rely on artificial markings for detecting the articulators of interest [15, 16], while more recent works utilize deep learning for lip tracking and hand region segmentation [21, 25], possibly assisted by a traditional image pre-processing pipeline [25]. This process is typically followed by appearance-based visual feature extraction, most often by means of convolutional neural networks (CNNs) [21,23,25]. On the back-end side, most phonetic sequence modeling approaches employ hidden Markov models [1,15,16,23] or more recently a deep learning-based attentional encoder-decoder [25]. In addition to the above, an important CS aspect is the inherent asynchrony between hand-shape and mouthing articulation. Indeed, as shown in [1], the former precedes the latter by roughly one syllable. The issue is also considered in [20,22,23].

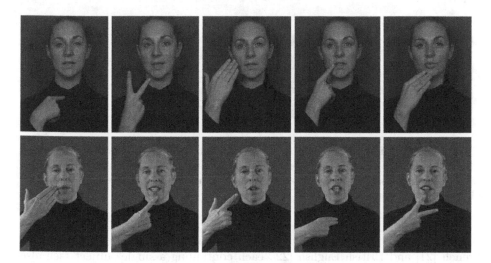

Fig. 2. Example video frames from the French CS dataset [21] (upper row) and the British English CS database [22] (lower row) that are used in this paper, showing various combinations of hand shapes, mouthing patterns, and hand positions.

In this paper, we address the problem of automatic CS recognition from upper-body videos with no artificial markings, by significantly extending our earlier work on this topic [25]. That CS recognition system commenced with a hybrid approach for mouth and hand region tracking (based on a traditional image preprocessing pipeline and 2D-CNNs), it then extracted appearance features of these regions by employing 3D-CNNs, as well as hand positional embeddings relative to the mouth based on 2D-CNNs, and finally concatenated these three visual feature streams and fed them to a deep attentional encoder-decoder [25].

Here, we modify the aforementioned system in multiple ways: We utilize the OpenPose framework [30] for skeletal data acquisition of the CS interpreter, and, by extension, for hand and mouth region segmentation. We then consider additional feature streams that capture structural information of the articulators of interest in order to investigate their benefit to CS recognition. Specifically, we first consider the 2D lip points and 2D hand skeletal coordinates of the signer, provided by OpenPose. Further, we infer 3D hand skeletal coordinates from the 2D ones, by exploiting a powerful architecture [24] that we recently used for 2D-to-3D hand-pose regression in sign language recognition [26], thus enriching knowledge about the trajectory of hand movement by enabling its observation in 3D. Finally, we modify the sequence learning model, by considering its time-depth separable (TDS) convolution block structure [11,25] used to encode the fused visual features, in conjunction with a decoder that is based on connectionist temporal classification (CTC) [10] for phonetic sequence prediction. Note that our approach does not rely on explicit synchronization of the hand and mouth feature streams prior to their fusion, instead expecting our model to learn such implicitly.

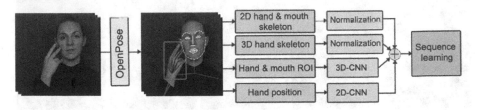

Fig. 3. Architecture of the introduced CS recognition system that generates phonemes from CS videos, following the detection of hand and mouth articulators (left), the extraction and fusion of various feature streams (middle), and sequence learning for phoneme prediction (right).

We evaluate our proposed system on two publicly available CS datasets in French [21] and British English [22], each containing a single subject (see also Fig. 2). We compare our approach against alternative sequence learning models and investigate the combination of various of the aforementioned visual feature streams for CS recognition. Our proposed system turns out superior, significantly exceeding the state-of-the-art on the two datasets that was reported in our earlier work [25]. In particular, we observe a significant absolute phoneme error rate (PER) reduction of 8.87% (from 29.12% to 20.25%) in the French CS corpus and 3.67% (from 36.25% to 32.58%) in the British English CS set.

2   The CS Recognition System

We next present our proposed system for CS recognition from videos. The system is schematically depicted in Fig. 3 and contains multiple components: Visual detection of the articulators, visual feature extraction of multiple streams relating to hand and mouth articulation, their fusion, and, finally, sequence learning for phoneme prediction. All system modules are detailed next.

2.1   Hand and Mouth Detection

Since CS relies on manual articulation together with mouthing patterns, it is clear that a successful CS recognition system should be able to accurately track both articulators in space and time. For this purpose, we utilize the OpenPose framework [30], which relies on deep convolutional pose models to provide a detailed representation of the human body in the form of multiple 2D keypoints. In particular, OpenPose can estimate up to 137 "human skeleton joints" in the 2D image pixel coordinate system, yielding 70 facial, 25 body-pose, and 42 hand-pose (21 for each hand) keypoints, as also shown in Fig. 4(a),(d).

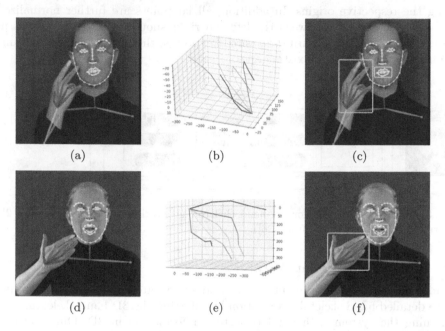

Fig. 4. Examples of articulator detection and keypoint feature extraction on the French CS dataset (upper row) and the British English CS corpus (lower row). Shown, column-wise, left-to-right: (a,d) 2D "skeletal" joints returned by OpenPose; (b,e): inferred 3D keypoints of the signing hand; (c,f): bounding boxes of the signing hand and mouth regions-of-interest derived based on the corresponding OpenPose 2D keypoints.

We further employ the hand and mouth keypoints to generate respective hand and mouth regions-of-interest (ROIs), as also depicted in Fig. 4(c),(f). We then feed these ROIs (after appropriate rescaling) to CNNs for appearance feature generation, as discussed in Sect. 2.4. Note that occasionally OpenPose fails, most likely due to the fact that only part of the signer's body is visible in the datasets considered here (see also Fig. 2). In such cases, we revert to the detection, tracking, and ROI extraction scheme of our earlier work [25].

2.2   2D Hand and Mouth Keypoint Features

Our CS system exploits 41 keypoints returned by OpenPose, namely 21 skeleton joints of the signing hand (this happens to be the right hand in the two datasets), and 20 facial keypoints associated with the lip region, all provided as 2D coordinates. This yields 42-dimensional (dim) features for the hand and 40-dim features for the mouth (82-dim in total). These features are normalized before being fed to the fusion module, to counter possible variations in the subject and camera relative positions. Specifically, the 2D points of interest are converted to a local coordinate system with the wrist keypoint and the upper-middle lip keypoint being the respective origins. In addition, all keypoints are further normalized based on the distance between the left and right shoulder joints. Note that in case OpenPose fails to return the desired keypoints, the missing feature streams are filled by the previous existing ones.

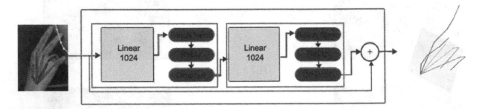

Fig. 5. Model architecture for 3D hand skeleton generation from corresponding 2D information (figure adapted from [26]).

2.3   3D Hand Keypoint Features

In addition to 2D hand keypoint features, we investigate the benefit of exploiting more detailed hand skeletal information by inferring the 3D hand skeleton, thus enriching the system with hand trajectory information in 3D. Our approach extracts the desired 3D hand joints by regressing the 2D hand joint locations to the 3D space [26]. Specifically, after extracting the 2D human skeleton of the hand via OpenPose, we feed its 2D hand coordinates to the hand-pose regression model, producing a series of hand keypoints in the 3D space. We zero-center both 2D and 3D poses around the wrist joint, so as to ensure translation invariance. The regression model, depicted in Fig. 5, is a deep neural network with two layers, each containing two basic blocks that share a residual connection. The network basic building block is a linear layer, followed by batch normalization, a rectified linear unit (ReLU) activation, and dropout. Incorporating batch normalization and dropout increases model robustness to noisy detections, whereas residual connections improve model generalization.

The model yields 21 3D joints for the signing hand, thus producing 63-dim feature vectors (see also Fig. 4(b),(e)). Note that prior to their fusion with other feature streams, these are normalized based on the distance between the hand shoulder and elbow joints, and regarding the wrist as the system origin.

2.4   Hand and Mouth Appearance Features

In addition to the aforementioned features, we extract spatio-temporal appearance features from the ROIs of the signing hand and mouth, as in our earlier work [25]. Specifically, we resize each ROI to 96 × 96 pixels and apply a 3D-CNN feature learner on three temporally adjacent ROIs of the signing hand or mouth. For this purpose, we utilize the 3D ResNet-34 network [12], which contains 3D convolutions (3 × 3 × 3) and 3D pooling and is pre-trained on the Kinetics dataset [3], obtaining feature maps from the output of its global average pooling layer. This process yields 512-dim feature vectors for each of the hand and mouth ROIs.

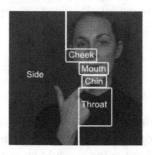 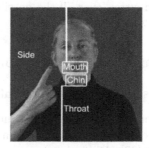

Fig. 6. Example frames of the French CS (left) and British English CS (right) datasets, showing the location-based area division of possible signing hand positions relative to the mouth, which we use to obtain hand positional embeddings in Sect. 2.5.

2.5 Hand Position Detection and Representation

As discussed in Sect. 1, hand positioning relative to the mouth plays a crucial role in CS. For this purpose, we use the 2D coordinates of the upper skeletal joint of the signing hand to detect the hand relative position, and then we pass this information through a five-layer 2D-CNN with three fully-connected layers to extract 64-dim hand positional embeddings. Specifically, the CNN is a multi-class model, with each class corresponding to the several possible location areas of the signing hand relative to the mouth. There are five such classes (location areas) for French CS and four for British English CS, as also depicted in Fig. 6.

2.6 Feature Fusion

The aforementioned feature streams are fused by simple vector concatenation, producing a 1233-dimensional feature vector for each video frame: 42 for 2D hand skeletal features, 40 for the mouth keypoints, 63 for the 3D hand skeletal stream, 512 for hand appearance, 512 for mouth appearance, and 64 for hand positional embeddings. These fused vectors are then passed to the sequence learning module for predicting the phonetic sequence of the CS video.

2.7 Sequence Learning

Viewing phoneme recognition in continuous CS videos as a sequence-to-sequence prediction task, we address it by employing a TDS convolutional encoder [11, 25], followed by CTC decoding [10]. Specifically, the resulting latent-representation vectors generated in Sect. 2.6 are modeled by a TDS convolutional encoder, which comprises two blocks: a 2D convolution over time, followed by a fully-connected block. In particular, the first sub-block involves a 2D convolutional layer complemented with a ReLU non-linearity and a normalization layer, while the fully-connected layer block consists of two convolutions with ReLU non-linearity in between and a normalization layer. The TDS convolutional encoder output is later subjected to linear projection followed by a log-softmax, yielding a probability distribution over all the possible phoneme labels prior to computing the CTC loss.

3   Experimental Evaluation

3.1   Datasets and Experimental Framework

As already mentioned, our experiments are conducted on two single-subject, continuous CS corpora, namely the French CS dataset [21] and the British English CS database [22]. All experiments are carried out using ten-fold cross-validation, with 80% of each fold used for training, 10% for validation, and 10% for testing.

In more detail, the French CS dataset contains 238 French sentences, each repeated twice, yielding a 476-sentence set with 11,770 phonemes in total belonging to 34 classes, and it is performed by a professional CS interpreter with no hearing disorders. The collected RGB video data include the upper body of the subject and are available at 50 frames per second (fps) and a 720×576-pixel resolution. On the other hand, the British English CS dataset is significantly smaller, containing only 97 sentences (with 44 phonetic classes) and is recorded by a professional CS speaker with no hearing impairment. The collected RGB video data include the upper body of the subject and are available at 25 fps and a 720×1280-pixel resolution.

3.2   Implementation Details

We implement our system in the PyTorch framework [27] and carry out its training using GPU acceleration.

For 3D hand skeleton network (Sect. 2.3) training, we use the Rendered Hand-Pose Dataset [33], a large-scale 3D hand pose dataset based on synthetic hand models [33]. This dataset utilizes 3D human models with corresponding animations from Mixamo 2 [9], while the software Blender 3 [5] is used for image rendering. It features 20 characters performing 39 actions, and different camera locations are selected randomly for each frame. The dataset provides 41,258 images for training and 2,728 images for evaluation with a resolution of 320×320 pixels. We train the network for 150 epochs using Adam optimizer [18], a batch size of 64, a starting learning rate of 0.001, and exponential decay. The weights of the linear layers are set by Kaiming He initialization [13].

For hand and mouth appearance feature extraction (Sect. 2.4), we apply a 3D ResNet-34 [12], trained by stochastic gradient descent with momentum at

0.9 with an initial learning rate of 0.1 decreased by a factor of 0.001. We perform 500 complete passes over the data with a mini-batch size of 256 images.

For the sequence learning model of Sect. 2.7, we employ a TDS convolutional encoder with two 3-channel, three 5-channel, and six 7-channel TDS blocks with kernel sizes 3×1. Additionally, we compare our approach to a number of alternative sequence models, differing in encoder type. Specifically, we evaluate our system using a one-layer long short-term memory (LSTM) [17] encoder and a one-layer gated recurrent unit (GRU) [4] encoder, both with 256 hidden units, as well as a Transformer [32] encoder with hidden dimensionality equal to 512.

We conduct the training of all sequence learning models by the Adam optimizer [18] with a learning rate of 0.003 decayed by a factor of 0.85 and use a batch size of 128. We employ 0.1 dropout and 0.1 label smoothing [31]. During decoding, we apply the beam search strategy of [8] with beam width equal to 3.

Table 1. Phoneme error rate (%) on the French and British English CS datasets, employing various feature stream combinations in conjunction with the sequence learning model of Sect. 2.7.

Feature streams						CS datasets	
Hand 3D-CNN (512-dim)	Mouth 3D-CNN (512-dim)	Positional 2D-CNN (64-dim)	2D Hand skeleton (42-dim)	2D Mouth keypoints (40-dim)	3D Hand skeleton (63-dim)	French	English
✓	✓					38.50	44.11
✓	✓	✓				25.64	35.13
		✓	✓	✓		38.87	47.10
		✓		✓	✓	37.54	45.89
✓	✓	✓	✓			25.58	33.68
✓	✓	✓		✓		24.93	33.29
✓	✓	✓			✓	25.06	33.50
✓	✓	✓	✓	✓		22.17	32.91
✓	✓	✓	✓	✓	✓	**20.25**	**32.58**

3.3   Results

The performance of our proposed approach for continuous CS recognition from videos is reported in Table 1. There, the phoneme error rate (PER) (%) obtained by the introduced sequence learning model relying on the TDS convolutional encoder and CTC decoding and operating on various feature stream combinations is shown on both CS corpora. It is apparent that the best results are achieved when all feature streams are concatenated, showcasing the benefit of incorporating multiple feature representations into the CS recognition system.

Comparing the best results of the table to our earlier work [25] that represents the state-of-the-art in the field, we obtain significant improvements on both datasets: An 8.87% absolute PER reduction (from 29.12% to 20.25%) for French

CS and a 3.67% one (from 36.25% to 32.58%) on British English CS. Such improvements can be attributed to the redesign of both visual feature extraction and sequence learning modules of our system. Indeed, from Table 1 it is obvious that the earlier used appearance and hand positional features alone lag behind the much richer feature representation proposed here. Further, the introduced sequence learning model improves over our earlier model that was based on the TDS convolutional encoder and attentional convolutional decoder, achieving a PER reduction of 3.48% (from 29.12% to 25.64%) for French CS and 1.12% (from 36.25% to 35.13%) for British English CS, revealing the power of CTC decoding in CS recognition (note that these results refer to the combination of appearance and hand positional features, since only these were considered in [25]).

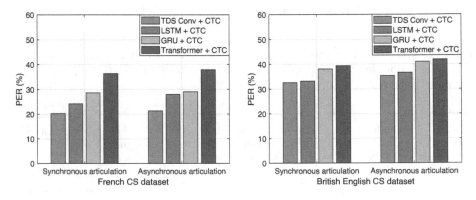

Fig. 7. Comparative evaluation of various sequence learning models on both datasets in terms of PER (%) using all feature streams fused synchronously or with a fixed delay (asynchronously).

Concerning the various feature combinations considered in Table 1, we observe that discarding hand positional embeddings results in the worst PERs on both datasets, demonstrating their importance to CS recognition. Notably, substituting hand and mouth appearance features with the respective skeletal data yields significantly higher PERs on both datasets than their combination. This demonstrates that skeletal data constitute descriptive representations conveying valuable information that can complement the corresponding appearance features, and thus their combined use is essential. Moreover, the 3D hand skeleton seems to be a robust representation, since it performs better than the corresponding 2D hand skeleton when added to the fusion module, and its incorporation on top of all other streams boosts system performance. It can also be seen that the 2D mouth keypoints representation performs well as additional mouth articulatory information, reducing PER on both datasets. This is primarily due to the fact that facial keypoints are more robustly detected by OpenPose than the hand joints that are often occluded. Finally, it can also be observed that there is a significant difference in PERs between the two datasets, most likely due to the limited size of the British English set.

Next, in Fig. 7, we investigate the performance of the various sequence learning models described in Sect. 3.2 on both CS datasets, when employing all feature streams (1233-dim vectors). Due to the asynchrony between hand and mouth articulation with the former preceding by approximately one syllable [1], we consider two feature fusion schemes: one that concatenates all features disregarding this asynchrony (as we do in our proposed system), referred to as "synchronous articulation" in Fig. 7, and another one, where the hand-related feature streams are artificially delayed by a fixed amount in time in the hope of better matching the mouth-related streams (referred to in the figure as "asynchronous articulation"). Specifically, we use a delay of 12 frames for French CS (as proposed in [1]) and 15 frames for the British English set. As it can be observed from Fig. 7, the proposed sequence learning model (TDS convolutional encoder and CTC decoding) yields the best results on both sets when features are directly concatenated with no enforced time shift. It can also be seen that the worst results for both datasets are obtained by the Transformer encoder-based model, while the LSTM encoder gives significantly better results compared to the respective GRU model, but still lagging our model. Further, enforcing a time delay of the hand features yields consistently worse results across all models compared to synchronous fusion.

Lastly, we investigated the performance of our model under a number of variations in the appearance feature learner and the number of TDS blocks in the TDS convolutional encoder. Specifically, we replaced the 3D-CNN with a 2D-CNN (ResNet-18 [14]) for appearance feature extraction of the hand and mouth ROIs. That model uses 3×3 convolutional kernels, downsampling with stride 2, and is pretrained on the ImageNet corpus [7]. This modification degraded PER significantly, by over 2% absolute (from 20.25% to 22.74% PER) for French CS and by about 3.5% (from 32.58% to 36.12% PER) for British English CS. Regarding the TDS convolutional encoder, we increased the number of channels keeping the same receptive field from (3, 5, 7) to (10, 12, 14), (10, 14, 18), and (10, 10, 14), but in all cases we ended up with worse PERs on both corpora.

4   Conclusions

In this paper, we investigated the incorporation of multiple representation streams into a state-of-the-art deep-learning based sequence learning model for CS recognition from upper-body videos. In particular, our CS recognition system relied on spatio-temporal feature extraction and fusion learned via a TDS convolutional encoder, followed by CTC decoding without the use of any explicit stream synchronization. We highlighted how the inclusion of skeletal data to the feature fusion module benefits system performance. Notably, inferred 3D hand skeletal data boosted CS recognition when added on top of all other spatio-temporal streams. The conducted evaluation on two CS datasets demonstrated that the proposed model outperformed other sequence learning architectures, surpassing the state-of-the-art in the field.

Acknowledgments. This research work was supported by the Hellenic Foundation for Research and Innovation (H.F.R.I.) under the "1st Call for H.F.R.I. Research Projects to support Faculty Members & Researchers and the procurement of high-cost research equipment grant" (Project "SL-ReDu", Project Number 2456).

References

1. Attina, V., Beautemps, D., Cathiard, M., Odisio, M.: A pilot study of temporal organization in cued speech production of French syllables: rules for a cued speech synthesizer. Speech Commun. **44**(1), 197–214 (2004)
2. Bheda, V., Radpour, D.: Using deep convolutional networks for gesture recognition in American Sign Language. CoRR abs/1710.06836 (2017)
3. Carreira, J., Zisserman, A.: Quo Vadis, action recognition? A new model and the Kinetics dataset. In: Proceedings of IEEE Conference on Computer Vision and Pattern Recognition (CVPR), pp. 4724–4733 (2017)
4. Cho, K., Merrienboer, B.V., Gülçehre, C., Bougares, F., Schwenk, H., Bengio, Y.: Learning phrase representations using RNN encoder-decoder for statistical machine translation. In: Proceedings of the Conference on Empirical Methods in Natural Language Processing (EMNLP), pp. 1724–1734 (2014)
5. Community, B.O.: Blender - a 3D modelling and rendering package. Blender Foundation, Stichting Blender Foundation, Amsterdam (2018). http://www.blender.org
6. Cornett, R.O.: Cued speech. Am. Ann. Deaf **112**(1), 3–13 (1967)
7. Deng, J., Dong, W., Socher, R., Li, L.J., Li, K., Fei-Fei, L.: ImageNet: a large-scale hierarchical image database. In: Proceedings of the IEEE Conference on Computer Vision and Pattern Recognition (CVPR), pp. 248–255 (2009)
8. Freitag, M., Al-Onaizan, Y.: Beam search strategies for neural machine translation. CoRR abs/1702.01806 (2017)
9. Fuse, M.: Mixamo: Quality 3D Character Animation in Minutes (2015). https://www.mixamo.com
10. Graves, A., Fernández, S., Gomez, F., Schmidhuber, J.: Connectionist temporal classification: labelling unsegmented sequence data with recurrent neural networks. In: Proceedings of the International Conference on Machine Learning (ICML) (2006)
11. Hannun, A., Lee, A., Xu, Q., Collobert, R.: Sequence-to-sequence speech recognition with time-depth separable convolutions. CoRR abs/1904.02619 (2019)
12. Hara, K., Kataoka, H., Satoh, Y.: Learning spatio-temporal features with 3D residual networks for action recognition. In: Proceedings of IEEE Conference on Computer Vision and Pattern Recognition (CVPR), pp. 3154–3160 (2017)
13. He, K., Zhang, X., Ren, S., Sun, J.: Delving deep into rectifiers: surpassing human-level performance on ImageNet classification. In: Proceedings of the IEEE International Conference on Computer Vision (ICCV), pp. 1026–1034 (2015)
14. He, K., Zhang, X., Ren, S., Sun, J.: Deep residual learning for image recognition. In: Proceedings of the IEEE Conference on Computer Vision and Pattern Recognition (CVPR), pp. 770–778 (2016)

15. Heracleous, P., Beautemps, D., Aboutabit, N.: Cued speech automatic recognition in normal-hearing and deaf subjects. Speech Commun. **52**(6), 504–512 (2010)
16. Heracleous, P., Beautemps, D., Hagita, N.: Continuous phoneme recognition in cued speech for French. In: Proceedings of the European Signal Processing Conference (EUSIPCO), pp. 2090–2093 (2012)
17. Hochreiter, S., Schmidhuber, J.: Long short-term memory. Neural Comput. **9**(8), 1735–1780 (1997)
18. Kingma, D.P., Ba, J.: Adam: a method for stochastic optimization. CoRR abs/1412.6980 (2014)
19. Liu, L., Feng, G.: A pilot study on Mandarin Chinese cued speech. Am. Ann. Deaf **164**(4), 496–518 (2019)
20. Liu, L., Feng, G., Beautemps, D.: Automatic temporal segmentation of hand movements for hand positions recognition in French cued speech. In: Proceedings of the IEEE International Conference on Acoustics, Speech and Signal Processing (ICASSP), pp. 3061–3065 (2018)
21. Liu, L., Hueber, T., Feng, G., Beautemps, D.: Visual recognition of continuous cued speech using a tandem CNN-HMM approach. In: Proceedings of Interspeech, pp. 2643–2647 (2018)
22. Liu, L., Li, J., Feng, G., Zhang, X.: Automatic detection of the temporal segmentation of hand movements in British English cued speech. In: Proceedings of Interspeech, pp. 2285–2289 (2019)
23. Liu, L., Feng, G., Beautemps, D., Zhang, X.P.: Re-synchronization using the hand preceding model for multi-modal fusion in automatic continuous cued speech recognition. IEEE Trans. Multimedia **23**, 292–305 (2021)
24. Martinez, J., Hossain, R., Romero, J., Little, J.J.: A simple yet effective baseline for 3D human pose estimation. In: Proceedings of the IEEE International Conference on Computer Vision (ICCV), pp. 2659–2668 (2017)
25. Papadimitriou, K., Potamianos, G.: A fully convolutional sequence learning approach for cued speech recognition from videos. In: Proceedings of the European Signal Processing Conference (EUSIPCO), pp. 326–330 (2021)
26. Parelli, M., Papadimitriou, K., Potamianos, G., Pavlakos, G., Maragos, P.: Exploiting 3D hand pose estimation in deep learning-based sign language recognition from RGB videos. In: Proceedings of the ECCV 2020 Workshops, pp. 249–263 (2020)
27. Paszke, A., et al.: Automatic differentiation in PyTorch. In: Proceedings of the NIPS-W (2017)
28. Potamianos, G., et al.: Audio and visual modality combination in speech processing applications. In: Oviatt, S., Schuller, B., Cohen, P., Sonntag, D., Potamianos, G., Krüger, A. (eds.) The Handbook of Multimodal-Multisensor Interfaces, Volume 1: Foundations, User Modeling, and Common Modality Combinations, pp. 489–543. Morgan-Claypool (2017)
29. Rao, G.A., Syamala, K., Kishore, P.V.V., Sastry, A.S.C.S.: Deep convolutional neural networks for sign language recognition. In: Proceedings of the Signal Processing and Communication Engineering Systems (SPACES), pp. 194–197 (2018)
30. Simon, T., Joo, H., Matthews, I., Sheikh, Y.: Hand keypoint detection in single images using multiview bootstrapping. In: Proceedings of the IEEE Conference on Computer Vision and Pattern Recognition (CVPR), pp. 4645–4653 (2017)
31. Szegedy, C., Vanhoucke, V., Ioffe, S., Shlens, J., Wojna, Z.: Rethinking the inception architecture for computer vision. In: Proceedings of the IEEE Conference on Computer Vision and Pattern Recognition (CVPR), pp. 2818–2826 (2016)

32. Vaswani, A., et al.: Attention is all you need. In: Proceedings of the Conference on Neural Information Processing Systems (NeurIPS), pp. 5998–6008 (2017)
33. Zimmermann, C., Brox, T.: Learning to estimate 3D hand pose from single RGB images. In: Proceedings of the IEEE International Conference on Computer Vision (ICCV), pp. 4913–4921 (2017)

Creative Media Accessibility: Placing the Focus Back on the Individual

Pablo Romero-Fresco^(✉) (iD)

Universidade de Vigo, GALMA, Vigo, Spain
promero@uvigo.es

Abstract. Although the emergence of integrated and collaborative approaches to media accessibility and audiovisual translation, such as accessible filmmaking, often require creative approaches, professionals trained in this area are hard to come by. The aim of this paper is, firstly, to explore why media accessibility does not seem to have pursued this creative route consistently until now. The focus is placed here on the currently prevailing experimental turn, which favours quantitative approaches and has been used to inform current media accessibility guidelines. Secondly, the paper defines creative media accessibility and seeks to identify and analyse the work of an emerging movement of artists, with especial attention to Liza Sylvestre, who uses media accessibility as a source of creativity. Her work constitutes a valuable contribution to research and training in media accessibility, placing the focus back on the individual as a necessary complement to the currently prevailing emphasis on quantitative studies in this field.

Keywords: Accessible filmmaking · Audiovisual translation · Creative media accessibility · Qualitative research

1 Introduction

Media accessibility (MA) has evolved considerably over the past decade and perhaps more especially so over the past few years. This state of flux may be at least partially accounted for by the three shifts that, according to Greco [1], are currently taking place in the general area of accessibility: a shift from a particularist account of access to a universalist account (which concerns users with and without disabilities who do not have access to original audiovisual productions), a transition from reactive to proactive models (access from inception rather than as an afterthought) and a shift from a maker-centered to a user-centered approach (the users as contributors to MA). An instantiation of these three shifts is the model known as accessible filmmaking, which requires "the consideration of translation and/or accessibility during the production of audiovisual media (normally through the collaboration between the creative team and the translator) in order to provide access to content for people who cannot access or who have difficulty accessing it in its original form" [2, pp. 5–6].

© Springer Nature Switzerland AG 2021
M. Antona and C. Stephanidis (Eds.): HCII 2021, LNCS 12769, pp. 291–307, 2021.
https://doi.org/10.1007/978-3-030-78095-1_22

The collaboration with filmmakers envisaged within the accessible filmmaking model is starting to reveal a new approach to MA that focuses not only on facilitating the viewers' comprehension of a film but also their engagement with it. This engagement-based approach to MA is explained in Romero-Fresco [3] and summarized in Fig. 1.

CURRENT APPROACH	NEW APPROACH
Centred on impairments	Centred on dis/abilities
Focused on compensation of missing content (providing information to make up for loss)	Focused on facilitating the user's experience
Takes the "able" expert as a reference	Takes the user as a reference
Concerned with comprehension	Concerned with engagement
Focused on one sense	Focused on more than one sense
Echoes of the medical model	Echoes of the social model
Results in "technicians" applying guidelines	Results in a more artistic and collaborative approach
Conducive to separation between production and translation/access	Conducive to collaboration with filmmakers (accessible filmmaking), although it can be applied without it

Fig. 1. Comparison between a comprehension-based approach to MA training and practice and an engagement-based approach [3]

This is resulting in the increasing use of MA practices that do not adhere to standard guidelines and that instead aim to enhance the users' experience in a creative and imaginative way. Partly related to the notion of transcreation and to the emergence of cybersubtitles [4, p. 141], which are produced "outside the commercial imperatives that regulate professional practice", creative media accessibility (CMA) encompasses "those practices that do not only attempt to provide access for the users of a film or a play, but also seek to become an artistic contribution in their own right, often enhancing user experience in a creative or imaginative way" [5]. This may also be referred to as alternative MA, in so far as it stands in opposition to most audiovisual translation (AVT) and MA guidelines, at least in their current state.

Unfortunately, although examples of these creative practices abound, they are somewhat disjointed and disconnected. They have been largely ignored in academic publications and, more importantly, they are normally not included in most MA courses. The emergence of accessible filmmaking means that companies are now looking for experts who can provide creative subtitles, captions, audio description or sign language, but professionals trained in this are hard to come by. The aim of this paper is, firstly, to explore why MA does not seem to have pursued this route consistently until now. The focus is placed here on the currently prevailing experimental turn in AVT [6], which favours quantitative approaches and has been used to inform current MA guidelines. Secondly, the paper seeks to identify and analyse the work of an emerging movement of artists, with especial attention to Liza Sylvestre, who use MA as a source of creativity. Their work constitutes an invaluable contribution to research and training in MA, placing the focus back on the individual as a necessary complement to the currently prevailing emphasis on quantitative studies set by experimental research in this field.

2 From Quantitative to Qualitative Research in MA

Of all the different methods and technologies used as part of the experimental turn undergone by AVT and MA, eye-tracking is perhaps the most common one [7]. The same goes for film studies, where eye-tracking research has gained significant traction over the past years, becoming a key area to inform and develop cognitive film theory [8]. Some of the current debates in film studies between cognitive film theorists and scholars adopting more introspective approaches based, for instance, on film-philosophy, can go a long way towards explaining the impact that eye-tracking studies have had on AVT and MA.

In his article "Politicizing Eye tracking Studies of Film" [9], published in the special issue of Refractory: a Journal of Entertainment Media, film-philosophy scholar and filmmaker William Brown reacts to a contribution in the same issue by Tim Smith [10], one of the leading researchers in eye-tracking-based cognitive film theory. What follows in the articles and in the comments section of the journal website is an insightful and very enlightening discussion on the benefits and drawbacks of adopting quantitative and qualitative methods for the study of film. While acknowledging the undeniable value of their findings, Brown identifies three aspects of eye-tracking studies (as conducted so far) that may be problematic: 1) with their emphasis on statistical significance, they tend to favour majority views and neglect marginal viewers or marginal ways of watching films; 2) they have so far been biased towards Hollywood and mainstream films and have not been so concerned with "marginal" films and 3) they have a political agenda or, at the very least, political impact, in that by focusing on attention, they validate and encourage a type of homogeneity that is more common in commercial films than in independent or more idiosyncratic cinema. For Brown [9], by exploring what is successful in terms of eliciting attention (and thus getting bums on seats and making money), eye-tracking studies reaffirm "the economic hegemony of one style over others" and validate "in some degree a homogeneity of product (and of audience?) – all within a 'cinematic' economic system that is itself predicated upon gaining attention". From his point of view, despite presenting itself as apolitical, eye-tracking research is anything but, given that it does not only tell us what viewers look at but it also may end up shaping what and how directors and producers decide to film.

Before looking at how much of this applies to AVT and MA, it is important to highlight the impact that eye tracking has had on this field. Going back to guidelines, which is particularly relevant for the case made in this paper, the first examples were predominantly based on the experience of well-seasoned professionals [11]. This has now changed radically. The cognitive turn experienced by (audiovisual) translation over the past decade [12, 13] has helped to provide guidelines with an empirical and scientific basis [14], and the proliferation of audience-reception studies has added a much needed user-informed dimension, as per Greco's above-mentioned shifts [1]. In a way, guidelines have been democratised in so far as many of them now include the input of a majority of viewers, or of a group that is statistically significant enough to be considered as a majority. This has undeniably strengthened our discipline, but it should not keep us from considering what has fallen by the wayside, for which addressing the above-mentioned points raised by Brown may be useful.

Eye-tracking studies in AVT and MA have inevitably placed strong emphasis on statistical significance. What matters is where most of the participants look at (Puss in Boots in Fig. 2 below).

Fig. 2. Gaze behavior of 15 viewers converging around the central figure during a clip from the teaser trailer for Puss in Boots [8].

While this helps to identify scientifically solid patterns that can reveal how different groups of viewers process audiovisual media, it also tends to flatten out differences. Researchers focus mainly on what is common to all, at the expense of what is not. More attention is thus paid to the average data of a group of viewers than to the full data provided by a single participant. This is even more pronounced with participants whose cognitive behaviour, or whose gaze patterns in the case of eye tracking, differs dramatically from the rest (see Fig. 3).

Fig. 3. Marginal viewer's gaze behavior during a clip from the trailer for Puss in Boots [8].

These marginal participants are often classified as outliers and their data are routinely discarded in empirical research as problematic, unrepresentative and useless [15]. The first issue identified by Brown above thus applies to AVT/MA, as the view of the majority is favoured over marginal ways of watching films or marginal viewers. This is perhaps particularly problematic in the case of MA research, whose raison d'être was from the beginning to account for those who are left behind and excluded from accessing audiovisual media [16]. It should be possible for researchers in this area to engage with these outliers meaningfully in a way that complements the quantitative and statistically significant data obtained with experimental reception studies.

The second criticism levelled by Brown to eye-tracking studies (bias towards Hollywood and mainstream films, at the expense of more marginal films) may also apply to AVT and MA, but it is the third one (validation and encouragement of a more or less homogenous approach to filmmaking) that is particularly relevant here. As mentioned above, many guidelines are now underpinned by empirical research, as they have been informed by the results of reception studies. Whereas this democratization of the guidelines is a very positive move away from the expert-based approach that prevailed in the past, it has also led to the validation of a homogeneous application of MA that may limit its potential creativity. As Brown [9] puts it, "Cinema is both business and art, but if art is one thing it is unique/different, and so a move towards homogeneity is a move towards the reduction of art in favor of business". Current guidelines normally encourage the same use of MA regardless of the particular nature of every film. Every other stage in the filmmaking process is adapted to the idiosyncrasy of the film in question, except for AVT/MA, which tends to build the same ramp for every building. This can result in situations where while the original viewers of a film can access the creative vision of the filmmaker, the audience of the accessible versions are provided with a much more standardised, comprehension-based access route.

In sum, there is no doubt that the current experimental turn in AVT/MA has been critical to provide a solid scientific basis for widely used guidelines that until now have been based on the personal views of experts. These studies are as necessary now as they have been over the past ten years. However, it is also worth looking at what has fallen by the wayside. The emphasis on statistical significance means that we have preferred to learn "a little bit about a lot of participants" than "a lot about a few participants". We have been more concerned with what is shared by all (or most) than with what sets us apart. This has been useful to consider participants as a group, but it has left behind the individuals, particularly those who do not conform to the general patterns and who are discarded as outliers. This has resulted in guidelines that, while valuable and democratic, encourage a homogeneous use of MA, regardless of the individual nature of every film.

It is therefore the idiosyncratic, the individual, or the "I", that is missing in both current research and practice. The next section presents the work carried out by Liza Sylvestre as an example of CMA that is suited to the particular piece in which it is being used, while serving as an unapologetically subjective and radically individual piece of qualitative research. It is through the creative use of MA that this artist and many others take us back to the individual.

3   The Radical Subjectivity of Creative Media Accessibility

In the 9th edition of the Media for All conference, I delivered a video presentation covering some of the content of this article: the reasons why a creative approach to MA does not seem to prevail in current research, training and practice as well as a definition and a brief analysis of some creative uses of MA and AVT [17]. This included the creative subtitles produced for a BBC Newsnight programme on Brexit and for the films Ons [18] and Film Socialisme [19], the creative audio description for the short film Tiempo de Blues [20] and the overall creative accessibility of the film La catarsis de Jude [21]. I situated those examples along a continuum ranging from inconspicuous to conspicuous, depending on whether they leaned towards blending in the style of the film (the film as protagonist) or towards standing out (translation or access claiming some degree of protagonism).

The conspicuous extreme was taking up by the so-called "Navajo subtitles" used by Godard for the English version of Film Socialisme. Instead of including full sentences, Godard's subtitles only feature a few key and often disjointed English words, which give us at best partial access to the original French dialogue: "German Jew Black" over the shot of a cook who is overhearing a conversation where those words are said (amongst many others) or "nochoice" to translate the narrated words "Constance, vous ne pouvait pas faire une chose" ("Constance, there is nothing you could do about it"). Godard puts the viewers of the English-subtitled version of the film at a disadvantage in comparison with the viewers of the original version, making it hard for them to access the dialogue and narration in the film. For some critics, this is Godard's revenge after years of classic Hollywood films where Native Americans were made to sound as though they spoke in choppy sentences, which here become the only way in the dialogue of the film for English-speaking viewers [22]. For others, Godard is making a larger point to question the (often overlooked) difference involved in producing different language versions for a film:

> It is quite obvious that Film Socialisme is not the same film if one understands French, English, or both languages. But isn't it the case, arguably to a lesser extent, when one watches any foreign film with subtitles? I think that if Godard took the principle of reduction inherent to subtitling to an extreme (and added other

peculiarities of his own), it is, among other things, to show how relative it is to try and assess a film without acknowledging the inevitable changes in perception caused by subtitling. [23]

Drawing on Godard's creative and disruptive of subtitles, I proposed in my video presentation for the Media for All conference the use of subtitles to question the very basics of translation and accessibility, namely the fact that subtitles must provide an account of the characters' dialogue. This was followed rather clumsily by a moment of silence where a few subtitles were displayed on screen showing an imaginary dialogue with the chair of the panel:

"CHAIR: You have 5 min left. Do start wrapping up, please."

"PABLO: God! I thought I was doing better! I'll do my best!"

Fortunately, subsequent research has shown that some artists (such as Liza Sylvestre, Christine Sun Kim or Caroline Lazard) have recently started to test this idea in a much more talented and artistic manner. They have a heterogeneous background, including filmmaking, visual arts, disability art and crip theory [24], a bold contemporary discourse that brings together disability and queer studies. An analysis of the common features of these artists and their work would merit a separate article, but suffice it to highlight here two of their driving forces: the refusal to treat access as an afterthought (one of the defining principles of accessible filmmaking) and the consideration of accessibility as the very material with which art is made, that is, "a generative site for poetic, humorous, and critical perspectives" [25] - the defining feature of CMA. A particularly apt example of this is Liza Sylvestre's Captioned Series [26].

3.1 Liza Sylvestre's *Captioned Series*

Liza Sylvestre is a US-based multimedia artist whose work, often addressing issues of communication, speech and hearing, has featured at renowned venues (such as the Weisman Art Museum) and obtained significant recognition by way of grants (fellowship from the National Endowment of Art) and awards (Citizens Advocate Award from the Minnesota Commission of Deaf, DeafBlind and Hard of Hearing). As a young girl with hearing loss, Sylvestre often had to watch TV films and programmes for which no captions where available, which had a critical impact on the way she related to audiovisual media and to society at large:

Out of boredom, but also out of my desire to fit in and hide the fact that I had no idea what was going on, I started documenting what I could understand. To anyone else in the class it probably looked like I was taking notes on the film, which I was. But not notes on any of the information shared audibly. I made up stories about people. I described their features. I declared assumptions. I had an entire and complete experience that was separate from any of my classmates' experiences. In my Captioned series, I transform these meandering reactions and thoughts into the captioning text that the film lacks. [27]

Drawing on this experience ("an activity I've been participating in my entire life" [27]), in her Captioned Series Sylvestre produces captions for the 1934 screwball comedy Twentieth Century and for a series of uncaptioned scenes from different TV programmes found while switching through channels. As explained above, these captions do not account for the dialogue on screen, which viewers without hearing loss can hear, but rather for her experience of exclusion from audiovisual media.

Some of the captions (see Fig. 4) include the artist's plot assumptions and interpretations, which show both how much is lost when there are no access tools available and what aspects excluded viewers need to cling on to in order to make sense of what is happening on screen:

Fig. 4. Captions with plot assumptions in Captioned Series

Other captions include a few descriptions of the little information Sylvestre obtains from the audio and especially detailed visual descriptions of the scenes. As highlighted in the above-mentioned engagement-based approach to MA [3], Sylvestre's audiovisual experience as a viewer with hearing loss is not only characterized here by the almost complete lack of access to the audio, but also by her reliance on the visuals and her ability to obtain information from them. This allows her to notice aspects that take place in the margins of the frame and that may go unnoticed by many hearing viewers. In Fig. 5, the main character is on the phone with a friend, writing down an address as he reads it out, while in the background a truck is getting ready to tow away his car. The framing of the shot, the acting and the dialogue point at this main character as the main focus, where the viewers' attention is expected to be. Yet, it is here the marginal viewer (the outlier that is excluded from eye-tracking data and that is more generally excluded from society when no captions are used) who uses creative captions to draw our attention to what is really happening on screen.

Fig. 5. Attention to the background in Captioned Series

In other cases (see Figs. 6 and 7), Sylvestre draws attention to visual aspects that may have gone unnoticed even for members of the creative team.

Fig. 6. Attention to visual detail in Captioned Series

I think IMDB should hire hard of hearing people to catch those trivia bloopers.

Fig. 7. Attention to visual detail in Captioned Series

In conveying her visual experience, many of the descriptions included Sylvestre's captions could work as an audio description –the accessibility modality that is normally used for blind and partially sighted users and any other people who may not be able to access the images (see Fig. 8).

She smiles knowingly.

Her face is so pale it glows.

Fig. 8. Captions with (audio) description in Captioned Series

This captioned description, while detailed and accurate, has no intention to be objective or comprehension-based, and is mainly concerned with the viewer engagement with the film (see Fig. 9). This is in line with the above-mentioned engagement-based approach to MA, with current practices of integrated audio description in the theatre [28] and with scholars who for some time now have been advocating for a more subjective approach to audio description [29]:

Fig. 9. Captions with detailed and subjective description in Captioned Series

Finally, the captions also include Sylvestre's personal commentary about her views on the plot, the sexism inherent to the cartoons she is watching, her experience trying to make sense of the visuals and, most importantly, her personal account of social exclusion (Figs. 10, 11, 12 and 13):

Fig. 10. Personal commentary in Captioned Series

Fig. 11. Further personal commentary in Captioned Series

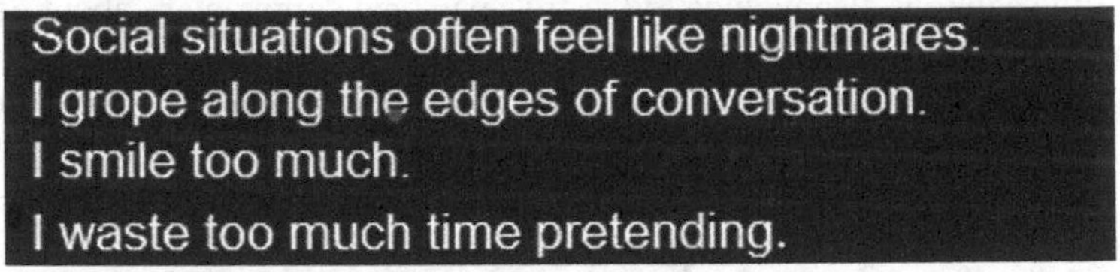

Social situations often feel like nightmares.
I grope along the edges of conversation.
I smile too much.
I waste too much time pretending.

Fig. 12. Captions with a personal account of exclusion in Captioned Series

3.2 Impact on Practice and Research

Film dialogue is often said to have a horizontal dimension (the characters talk to one another) and a vertical dimension (the filmmaker and the film "talk" to the viewers, conveying meaning, values, ideas, etc.) [30]. Captions or subtitles for viewers with hearing loss may be seen as also having two dimensions, as some captions account for the dialogue between the characters (horizontal dimension) whereas others represent the voice of the captioner describing sounds and music to the viewers (vertical dimension). Profoundly deaf viewers can only access film sounds second hand, through the descriptions of hearing captioners who do not share their world. In her *Captioned Series*, Sylvestre turns this vertical dialogue around and uses captions to convey the voice of a viewer with hearing loss. It is not the hearing captioner who is talking to the viewers with hearing loss through captions here, but rather a viewer with hearing loss who is using captions to let us all in her world.

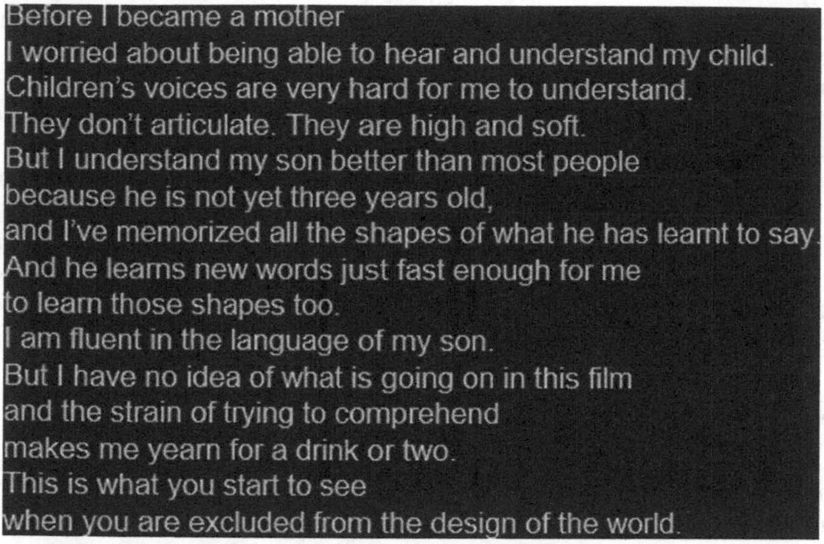

Before I became a mother
I worried about being able to hear and understand my child.
Children's voices are very hard for me to understand.
They don't articulate. They are high and soft.
But I understand my son better than most people
because he is not yet three years old,
and I've memorized all the shapes of what he has learnt to say.
And he learns new words just fast enough for me
to learn those shapes too.
I am fluent in the language of my son.
But I have no idea of what is going on in this film
and the strain of trying to comprehend
makes me yearn for a drink or two.
This is what you start to see
when you are excluded from the design of the world.

Fig. 13. Captions with a personal account of exclusion in Captioned Series

As an example of CMA, the captions are not conceived here as a ramp to access the film. Instead, they are a defining feature of its artistic nature, which asks us to consider, amongst other issues, the impact that access (be it through dubbing, subtitles, captions, audio description, etc.) has on the viewers' film experience. We tend to take for granted that we are all watching the same film, but are the differences inherent to the various translated and accessible versions of a film significant enough so that it effectively becomes a different film? Godard makes this point from an intellectual and political stance in Film Socialisme [19] by exaggerating some of the defining features of standard subtitles in order to partially exclude, or at least provide a very different experience to, the viewers of the English version of his film. Sylvestre does not need to exaggerate anything in order to tackle this difference in experience –she only needs to draw on her life as someone who has been excluded and does not share the same content (whether it is a film or life in general) as others.

Sylvestre's film embraces this notion by providing a very different experience to her viewers: whereas viewers with hearing loss can focus on the visuals and the captions (and probably relate to what is being explained), hearing viewers have a much more difficult job. They have to process dialogue and images that go together and captions that do not refer to the dialogue and that are mainly concerned with providing a window into the artist's life. And it is this emphasis on the "I", this radical and unapologetic subjectivity that makes this little film valuable not only as an artistic piece, but also as a research output. There is no attempt by Sylvestre here at being statistically significant or representative of anything else other than her personal account. Yet, her piece asks us to revisit some of the widely held assumptions at play in MA and poses questions that can lead to new avenues of research (including experimental studies): To what extent are we all watching the same film? Can access be provided by professionals who do not share the same world as the viewers? If not, how can these viewers be involved in the process? What does the well-known slogan "Nothing about us without us" really mean and how can it be implemented? And, more specifically, what can we learn from the way in which viewers with hearing loss engage with the visuals? Is captioning training accounting for this visual focus (and is audio description training accounting for the role played by sound for users)? Given the type of visual descriptions included by Sylvestre in her captions, is it possible to have audio descriptions written by viewers with hearing loss? And can captions about sound and music be written by blind and partially sighted users? Can some of the most subjective and poetic descriptions produced in this piece by Sylvestre, which address at the same time elements of image and sound, be used as both captions and audio description? Is thus subjectivity and poetry the meeting point between subtitles for viewers with hearing loss and audio description?

4   Final Thoughts

This article is an initial attempt to explore the notion of CMA and some of the potential reasons why it has not been developed further until now. Current debates between cognitive and philosophical approaches to film studies can be useful to throw light on the impact that the so-called experimental turn has had on AVT and MA research, training and practice. The proliferation of reception studies, not least those using eye-tracking technology, has been essential to provide a solid ground on which to move forward with (scientific) confidence and to involve users in research. The guidelines, no longer based on experts' views but more democratized and empirically solid, are one of the ways in which this research has been transferred to the professional world and to society at large. However, the notion of CMA points at areas that may have been neglected by this experimental turn, which seems to have prioritised, in practice and training, comprehension over engagement and technique over art; and, in research, the view of the majority over the input of individuals. None of this is particularly conducive to an artistic approach to MA.

Yet, there is a new wave of visual artists who are actively engaging with CMA, using access as an artistic contribution in its own right and, in some cases, as the very defining aspect of their art. Against a general tendency to ignore the differences brought about by translation and access, these artists embrace these differences, turn them into art and throw them back at us to question many of the widely held assumptions we are working with. This includes our role as sighted and hearing mediators for users who do not share our world. In some of these practices, artists are doing away with us and producing a new type of media that may be regarded as unmediated media. They do so from a radically subjective perspective that may be seen as a weakness in experimental research (where this marginal and anecdotic view can be ruled out as an outlier) but that here becomes a driving force to open a window into the world of the individuals for which access was created in the first place. Research in MA may benefit from using some of these examples of CMA to develop a qualitative avenue that can complement experimental findings. After more than a decade looking at groups of viewers and what they have in common, it is worth turning our attention to individuals, what they share with the group and also what sets them apart, for, as put by Brown [9],

It is in our differences that we show to the world what it is that humans can be. This idiosyncrasy, emphasis on difference, idiocy, it is the humanities as I understand them (idiosyncratically, differently, idiotically). It is humanity. To understand humans and indeed the cinema that they produce and watch, we need to account for this, for our differences are every bit as important as the humanity that we all otherwise share.

The emergence of CMA may be seen as a logical social development. Now that, mostly thanks to international and national legislation, the amount of MA provided in many countries is approaching 100% percent (although there is work to be done in other countries and generally in online content), it makes sense to shift the focus to the quality or the nature of this access. Over the past years, this has led many of us in this area to work on guidelines. But as this work was being done, two other important developments were taking place to increase quality in access: the integration of access into the production process (be it through the accessible filmmaking model, integrated access in the theatre, etc.) and the transition from access to inclusion and participation [31], which, as explained by artist Jodee Mundy in a tweet in 2017, means ensuring that users can not only walk through the door but also sit at the table, eat the meal and talk about it. These two developments may go a long way towards explaining why CMA is now gaining ground.

This article is nothing else than a gentle call for trainers, professionals and researchers in MA to embrace this new movement and what comes with it. From the point of view of training, this can be an interesting complement to guideline-based teaching. It can provide students with a safe shelter where the human input is not too likely to be replaced by automation in the near future and it can help them develop an artistic dimension that may be useful to diversify their portfolio.

As far as research is concerned, now that the foundations of AVT and MA are becoming more solid, it may be the right time to let this artistic approach engage critically with them, questioning them if needed. This will hopefully help to strengthen this area with a combination of quantitative and qualitative research methods and to consolidate its role as a driving force for social change.

Finally, professional translators and access experts looking to work with filmmakers and artists in general can take heart from the increasingly collaborative and integrated approach to access currently adopted in the theatre and the growing number of accessible filmmakers using this model too. It may be useful to move away from the question (often asked) of whether this approach will ever become mainstream: firstly, because some of the work presented here exists precisely as an opposition or even resistance to mainstream practices; and secondly, because the time and energy required to persuade large companies to change their approach to access may be best spent in the rewarding task of working with accessible artists who are looking for translators and access experts to collaborate with.

Creative MA and AVT promise exciting times for those of us working on this area, for this is not only a new way to approach accessibility and translation, but a new way to make art. One that we can all be part of.

Acknowledgment. This research has been conducted within the frameworks and with the support of the EU-funded project 'EASIT: Easy Access for Social Inclusion Training' (2018-1-ES01-KA203-050275), as well as the Spanish-government funded project 'The Quality of Live Subtitling (QuaLiSub): A regional, national and international study' (Convocatoria 2020 - «Proyectos de I+D+i», Spanish Ministry for Science and Innovation) and the Galician-government funded project Proxecto de Excelencia 2017 'Observatorio Galego de Accesibilidade aos Medios'.

References

1. Greco, G.M.: The nature of accessibility studies. J. Audiovis. Transl. **1**(1), 204–232 (2018)
2. Romero-Fresco, P.: Accessible Filmmaking: Integrating Translation and Accessibility into the Filmmaking Process. Routledge, London (2019)
3. Romero-Fresco, P.: Accessible filmmaking and media accessibility. In: Ji, M., Laviosa, S. (eds.) The Oxford Handbook of Translation and Social Practices, pp. 325–353. Oxford University Press, Oxford (2020)
4. Cintas, J.D.: 'Subtitling's a carnival': new practices in cyberspace. JoSTrans, J. Spec. Transl. **30**, 127–149 (2018)
5. Romero-Fresco, P.: Moving from accessible filmmaking towards creative media accessibility. Leonardo (Special issue edited by M. Ji)
6. Greco, G.M., Jankowska, A., Szarkowska, A.: Methodological issues in experimental research in audiovisual translation: experiences and recommendations. Transl. Spaces **11**(11), Call for papers (2020)
7. Kruger, J.-L.: Eye tracking in audiovisual translation research. In: Pérez-González, L. (ed.) The Routledge Handbook of Audiovisual Translation, pp. 350–366. Routledge, London (2019)
8. Smith, T.J.: Watching You Watch Movies: Using Eye Tracking to Inform Cognitive Film Theory, pp. 165–191. Oxford University Press, New York (2013)
9. Brown, W.: Politicizing eye-tracking studies of film. Refract. J. Entertain. Media **25** (2015)
10. Smith, T.J.: Read, watch, listen: a commentary on eye tracking and moving images (2015)
11. Carroll, M., Ivarsson, J.: Code of Good Subtitling Practice. European Association for Studies in Screen Translation, Berlin (1998)
12. O'Brien, S.: Cognitive Explorations of Translation. Bloomsbury, London (2011)
13. Chaume, F.: An overview of audiovisual translation: four methodological turns in a mature discipline. JoSTrans, J. Spec. Transl. **1**(1), 40–63 (2018). https://www.jatjournal.org/index.php/jat/article/view/43/3
14. Orero, P., et al.: Conducting experimental research in audiovisual translation (AVT): a position paper. JoSTrans, J. Spec. Transl. **30**, 105–126 (2018)
15. Zimmerman, D.: Increasing the power of nonparametric tests by detecting and downweighting outliers. J. Exp. Educ. **64**(1), 71–78 (2010)
16. Cintas, J.D., Remael, A., Orero, P.: Media for All: Subtitling for the Deaf, Audio Description, and Sign Language. Rodopi, Amsterdam (2007)
17. Romero-Fresco, P.: Creative Media Accessibility (2021)
18. Zarauza, A.: Ons. Maruxiña Films, Spain (2020)
19. Godard, J.-L.: Filme Socialisme. Vega Films, Switxerland (2010)
20. Font, M.Á.: Tiempo de Blues. When Lights are Low, Spain (2019)
21. Bas, J.: La catarsis de Jude, Spain (2018)
22. Akbar, A.: Cannes diary: stars lined up for BBC rom com. The Independent (2010)

23. Bréan, S.: godard english cannes: The Reception of Film Socialisme's 'Navajo English' Subtitles. Sens. Cinema **60** (2011). https://www.sensesofcinema.com/2011/feature-articles/godardenglishcannes-the-reception-of-film-socialismes-navajo-english-subtitles/#5

24. Ruer, R.M.: Crip Theory: Cultural Signs of Queerness and Disability. NYU Press, New York (2006)

25. Watlington, E.: Critical creative corrective cacophonous comical: Closed captions. Mousse Mag. **68** (2019). http://moussemagazine.it/critical-creative-corrective-cacophonous-comical-closed-captions-emily-watlington-2019/?fbclid=IwAR2Nf5MrCESIcKTjjjDEPXEVMcblQJCjrkEf4PdHuAk4oRoFIdR7y26oFQE

26. Sylvestre, L.: Captioned Series, US

27. Hamilton, A.: Captioned: An Interview with Liza Sylvestre. Sixty Inches From Center (2019)

28. Fryer, L.: Staging the audio describer: an exploration of integrated audio description. Disabil. Stud. Q. **38**(3) (2018). http://dsq-sds.org/article/view/6490/5093

29. Ramos-Caro, M.: Testing audio narration: the emotional impact of language in audio description. Perspect. Stud. Transl. **24**(4), 606–634 (2016)

30. Vanoye, F.: Conversations publiques. Iris **3**(1), 99–118 (1985)

31. Di Giovanni, E.: Audio description for live performances and audience participation. JoSTrans, J. Spec. Transl. **29**, 189–211 (2018)

The Minority AD: Creativity in Audio Descriptions of Visual Art

Silvia Soler Gallego$^{(\boxtimes)}$ (ID)

Colorado State University, Fort Collins, CO 80523, USA
ssoler@colostate.edu

Abstract. Several studies have described the most frequent features of visual art audio description (AD), but less frequent or minority features have received less attention. This article offers a description and discussion of minority features in visual art AD as instances of more creative practices that can foster a variety of experiences for the diversity of users of this type of intersemiotic translation. For this purpose, a qualitative analysis of a multilingual corpus of visual art ADs and their context of creation and implementation was carried out, drawing on Langacker's *Cognitive Grammar* (1987/2008) and its further development by Croft and Cruse (2004). The results show that some ADs conceptualize the artwork as a process and utilize an internal viewpoint. The focus of attention is sometimes shifted to the technique or the subjective impressions elicited by the work, with a few ADs showing especially high levels of subjectivity. In a group of ADs, universal accessibility translates into low specificity, understood as the amount of information and detail. The prevalent constitution of the work is altered so the identification is postponed, and the interconnections between the visual components are profiled. The typical general-to-specific progression is not followed and, instead, the AD imitates the artwork's composition. In a small number of ADs, the location of the visual components is not conveyed through lexis but implied in the discourse sequence, while the paralinguistic features of voice tempo, tone, and intensity are utilized to translate the composition and sensory impressions elicited by the artwork.

Keywords: Audio description · Visual arts · Creativity · Cognitive linguistics

1 Introduction

According to Eisner (2002), the goal of art education programs should be to help learners develop their capacity to have aesthetic experiences in their daily lives and this aesthetic seeing "requires one to search for qualitative relationships and to note the quality of experience they engender" (26). Individual interpretation and experience are essential components of the gallery teaching method advanced by Burnham and Kai-Kee (2011), who state that "When the interpretation is shaped into 'an experience', we make it possible that our viewers will leave the museum changed, perhaps transformed" (65). These voices coincide in the importance of subjective and creative interpretations and

© Springer Nature Switzerland AG 2021
M. Antona and C. Stephanidis (Eds.): HCII 2021, LNCS 12769, pp. 308–327, 2021.
https://doi.org/10.1007/978-3-030-78095-1_23

experiences in art education. However, creativity in the creation of audio description (AD) of visual art has received very little attention so far within AD studies.

In previous corpus-based descriptive studies of visual art AD (Soler 2016, 2018), I have described the linguistic and contextual features of this translation phenomenon. However, these studies have focused on the most frequent features, while less frequent or minority features have received less attention. One of these minority features is subjectivity, which has recently been addressed in corpus-based studies that have shown considerable levels of this feature in visual art AD (Lima and Magalhães 2013; Luque 2016; Soler 2019; Luque and Soler 2020). The goal of this article is to offer a description and discussion of this and other minority features in visual art AD as instances of more creative practices that can foster a variety of experiences for the diversity of needs and expectations of the users of this type of intersmiotic translation. For this purpose, I carried out a qualitative analysis of a multilingual corpus of visual art ADs, both recorded and live, and contextual information related to their creation and implementation. In this analysis, as in previous studies of this translation modality, I draw on Langacker's *Cognitive Grammar* (1987/2008) and its further development by Croft and Cruse (2004) to analyze the conceptualization of the visual artwork in the AD. Similarly, within Translation Studies, Krüger (2013) and Halverson (2013) have proposed that cognitive linguistic theories be used to study translation shifts. The following section expands on this theoretical approach and its application in the current study.

2   A Cognitive Approach to Visual Art Audio Description

I consider theories that attempt to describe and explain linguistic communication based on theories of human cognition to be especially relevant to the study of intersemiotic translation phenomena. The reason for this view is that these theories help us to understand the cognitive operations behind the linguistic differences observed in ADs. Besides, they also help us to describe AD not only as a linguistic product, but also as a cognitive process that occurs in different languages and cultures. The goal of cognitive linguistics since it emerged has been to give an account of language in connection with general features of human cognition (Dirven 2002: 76). This discipline is guided by the cognitive commitment. According to it, language is determined by humans' experience of the world, and therefore, the principles described in cognitive linguistics should reflect theories of human cognition postulated in other disciplines (Evans and Green 2006: 27–28).

In *Cognitive Grammar*, Langacker proposes that language is a symbolic system consisting of structures with a semantic and a phonological pole (2008: 15). Lexicon, morphology, and syntax are all symbolic structures within this system, and they are combined to form symbolic assemblies. The phonological pole invokes or provides access to a conventionalized semantic value that consists of conceptual content and a particular construal imposed on that content. The conceptual content consists of a matrix of cognitive domains, which are defined as any kind of conception or mental experience (44). The construal is related to humans' cognitive capability to describe the same situation in different ways. Langacker uses a visual metaphor to explain this phenomenon: "[conceptual] content is likened to a scene and construal to a particular way of viewing it," and in viewing that scene, "what we actually see depends on how closely we examine it, what we choose to look at, which elements we pay most attention to, and where we view it from" (55). Accordingly, Langacker identifies four dimensions of the construal: Focus, Prominence, Specificity, and Perspective. Focus refers to the conceptual content selected to be conveyed through language, while Prominence is the focus of attention on specific elements of that conceptual content. Specificity is the level of precision and detail used to describe a situation, and Perspective is the viewing arrangement, the overall relationship between the viewers and the situation being viewed. In a language usage event, conventional linguistic symbols are combined with humans' encyclopedic knowledge, mental capabilities, and apprehension of the context to create a conceptualization, i.e., a meaning. For this reason, a usage event is never the same for the sender and the addressee. However, successful communication is possible, provided that there is a considerable similarity between the two (458).

Croft and Cruse (2004) compiled and reviewed previous research on cognitive linguistics, psychology and phenomenology, including that of Langacker, and proposed four dimensions of the construal. These construal dimensions are based on the type of cognitive operations involved in each case: Attention/salience, Judgement/comparison, Perspective/situatedness, and Constitution/Gestalt (46 ff.). Within the attention dimension, they distinguish four subcategories: selection or focus, scope, scalar adjustment, and dynamic attention. The first three are static, while the last one is dynamic. Selection is a cognitive operation by which we attend to parts of our experience, while we ignore others that are irrelevant. The scope of attention is what surrounds this focus or selection. The scale used in that conceptualization can have different levels of granularity, from a coarse-grained view to a fine-grained view. This is illustrated with the phrases "along the road" (in a line), "across the road" (in a two-dimensional space), and "through the road" (in a three-dimensional space), and "triangle" (shape with 3 sides) versus "polygon" (shape with several sides). This category seems to be related to the Specificity dimension in Langacker's proposal, and therefore, it is here used to discuss the quantity of information and detail used in the ADs. Finally, the attention can be static or move across the scene. The former is a summary scanning, as in "the collapse of Boston Bridge", while the latter is a sequential scanning, as in "Boston Bridge collapsed."

The Judgment/comparison operations comprise categorization, metaphor, and figure-ground alignment. Categorization consists of applying a word, morpheme or construction to an experience by comparing it to prior experiences and judging whether it belongs to the same class. Metaphor involves the relationship or comparison between a source domain (the literal meaning of the metaphorical expression) and a target domain (the experience being described by the metaphor). Figure-ground alignment is the expression of spatial relations through language by indicating the position of one entity (figure) relative to another (ground).

Perspective/situatedness operations are related to spatiotemporal location, as well as to knowledge, believes and attitudes, to our "situatedness" in the world. It includes the subcategories of viewpoint, deixis, and subjectivity/objectivity. Viewpoint refers to the position in a three-dimensional space ("in front" versus "behind") and in the vertical dimension ("above" versus "below") used to describe a scene. Deixis consists on using the speaker's position to designate something in a scene, as in "I", "you", "this," and "that". Subjectivity/objectivity refers to ways of including oneself in the conceptualization of a scene, from more subjective ways ("Don't lie to me") to more objective ways ("Don't lie to your mother").

The Constitution/Gestalt operations deal with "the very structure of the entities in a scene" and are the "most basic level of constituting experience and giving it structure or a Gestalt…" They are related to Gestalt psychology principles, which deal with "how human minds construe a single complex object from seemingly fragmented perceptual sensations" (63). Under this category, Croft and Cruse list three operations: structural schematization, force dynamics, and relationality (entity/interconnection). Within the structural schematization category, we find the individuation subcategory. Individuation is related to "whether or not entities are individuated (boundedness), and if so, their unity and relation to their parts, and their multiplicity if more than one individual is construed" (64). For instance, the same entity is construed differently in "foliage" and in "leaves." The former construes the entity as unbounded, as a relatively homogeneous substance without clear boundaries, while "leaf" construes the entity as a bounded individual and its plural "leaves" multiplies the individual. Force dynamics refers to the conceptualization of causation or the "forces" that act upon the participants in an event. For instance, in "I kicked the ball", "I" is the causer who forces the causee to move, while in "I held the ball", the causer resists the causee's tendency to move. Finally, within the relationality category, we find relational and non-relational entities. A relational entity is one that implies the existence of another entity, such as the adjective ROUND, which cannot be conceived of without something that is round, or the verb RUN, which cannot be conceived of without someone who runs. On the contrary, a non-relational entity, such as TABLE, can be conceived of by itself, without reference to another entity. According to Langacker, a relational concept profiles the interconnections between entities, while a non-relational concept profiles the entities that are interconnected. Thus, CIRCLE is non-relational because it profiles the points (or entities) that make it up, while ROUND is relational because it profiles the interconnections between those points, which define the curvature of the circle.

Based on this theory, one might hypothesize that different translators would create different construals of the artistic source text and that therefore, no significant regularities would be found in the analysis of a corpus of ADs of visual art. However, previous studies have showed the existence of frequent features in this type of intersemiotic translation. The goal of this article is to offer a description of less frequent or minority features in the AD of visual art as instances of creativity in this type of intersemiotic translation for the four dimensions of the construal proposed by Croft and Cruse (2004), and to illustrate them along with more frequent or majority features observed in the corpus. The following section is dedicated to describing the data compiled and analyzed in this study, as well as the data collection and analysis methods.

3 Materials and Methods

To carry out this study, I collected and analyzed two types of data: a corpus of visual art AD, and contextual information on the creation and implementation of the ADs. To collect this information, I used the following tools and procedures: bibliographical review, autonomous visit, visit in guided tour organized by the museum, semi-structured interview, and survey. The following data collection procedure has been followed in a cyclical way from the beginning of my research of visual art AD, in 2010. Firstly, I identify museums that offer verbal description resources by searching their respective websites and other relevant publications. The audio descriptive guide is then accessed if it is available online. Additionally, I collect contextual data on their accessibility resources from the museums' websites and other reliable publications. Secondly, the museum is visited whenever possible in order to study the available audio description guides and tactile materials in situ. Then, I send a survey to the museum and the organization and/or freelance audio describer responsible for creating the audio descriptive guide and the tactile materials, or interviews are conducted if possible. Finally, I request access to the script and audio files of the audio descriptive guide and/or permission to attend and audio record an audio descriptive guided tour, if it can be conducted, during the interview or else via email. If permission to audio record an interview or audio descriptive guided tour is not granted, notes are taken to record the main information provided and observed during the interview or the tour. The guide in charge of conducting the tour is also interviewed before or after the activity whenever possible.

In my study of visual art AD, I have been able to identify the following visual art AD resources from art museums and exhibitions: 43 audio descriptive guides and 42 audio descriptive guided tours. Of these resources, I have been able to compile the audio and/ or script of 29 audio descriptive guides (or part of them) and 8 audio descriptive guided tours, which together make up the corpus used for this study. This is a multilingual and multimodal parallel corpus consisting of the artistic source texts and their intersemiotic translations into either Spanish, French or English. In some cases, the audio descriptive guide can be accessed via a website or a mobile app. In other cases, I requested access to the guide files of the museum or company holding the copyright and my petition was, in some cases, denied or ignored. The audio descriptive guided tours compiled for the study are video recordings that are available online, as well as audio recordings of tours that I attended. Regarding the context of the creation of these resources, I have compiled information through semi-structured interviews and surveys from eighteen museum accessibility coordinators, and the describers for twenty-five permanent collections and exhibitions (fourteen of audio descriptive guides and eleven of audio descriptive guided tours). In some cases, the creator of the audio descriptive guide is also the person that gives the audio descriptive guided tour, while in other cases they are different professionals. In addition to these data, I observed eight audio descriptive guided tours and did twelve autonomous visits with audio descriptive guide to permanent collections and exhibitions. Finally, I was able to collect additional information through a bibliographical review of different types of publications for thirty-three art museum permanent collections and exhibitions.

For this study, I carried out a qualitative analysis of the visual art AD corpus just described in order to identify the less frequent or minority features in connection with the four dimensions of the construal as proposed by Croft and Cruse (2004), and of the contextual data related to their creation and implementation. The following section offers a description and discussion of the most salient minority features of the corpus.

4 Minority Features in Visual Art Audio Description

In previous studies of AD in art museums (Soler 2016, 2018, 2019), I concluded that the artwork is mainly described as a static product, using static verbs and focusing on the states of the visual components. Within these visual components, iconic signs, composition, and color are more frequently described (Attention/salience). Although subjective descriptions, which include the sensations, feelings and ideas elicited or triggered by the work in question, may be used, often by means of a metaphor, on the whole, objective language and content are preferred (Judgement/comparison). The work is described from an external viewpoint, from the viewpoint of a visitor who contemplates the artwork (Perspective/situatedness), and progresses from a general description to a more specific one (Constitution/Gestalt). Most ADs begin with the information provided on the label: the title, author, year, and media or materials. This is followed by an overall description of the subject matter (i.e. the iconic signs) when the work is not wholly abstract, followed by the style (medium and technique), composition and color. Next, the AD offers a detailed description of the different visual components. This detailed description is organized sequentially (top to bottom, background to foreground, left to right, etc.), using language to clearly indicate the location of the different elements within the space of the artwork. This sequential progress thus has three levels of specificity, by which we mean the amount of information and detail used to communicate the artwork through language (Attention/salience). When included, the more subjective, interpretive descriptions are often offered after the detailed and more objective description of the visual components. This is also the case with contextual information. To illustrate, here is the AD transcript of *Jack-in-the-Pulpit, Number Four* by Georgia O'Keeffe, composed by the education department of the National Gallery of Art in Washington DC (the painting and recorded AD may be accessed at: www.nga.gov/visit/tours-and-gui des/verbal-description-tour-east-building.html).

Georgia O'Keeffe, *Jack-in-the-Pulpit, Number Four*, oil on canvas, painted in 1930. This description is about three minutes long.

This painting measures three and a half feet tall by two and a half feet across. An oval form with wavy edges dominates the composition. The form extends beyond the edge of the canvas at the bottom in both sidúes. It is deep purple that blends into shades of slate gray and white at the center. This shape is surrounded by three bands of vibrant green against a cerulean blue background. The title suggests that O'Keeffe shows a stylized version of the Jack-in-the-Pulpit flower.

To explore the work in more detail we'll start at the lower center and work our way up and out to describe the flower and the background.

An elongated, knob-like form stretches upwards from the bottom center to about a quarter of the way up the canvas. This stalk-like form is called the spadex. The spadex swirls slightly at its rounded top. The center of the spadex is a vivid, deep indigo blue that graduates to black. This dark spadex is silhouetted against an eggshell white area that flares out and up to a point, almost like a candle flame. A narrow blade of white reaches upwards from the top center of the spadex and comes to a point that ends about three quarters of the way up the canvas.

Thin bands of indigo blue border the white form where it swells outwards. The main oval shaped petal nearly fills the composition. The petal is painted with deep plum purple and black, except where two lighter gray areas shade the oval near the upper left. The petal edges curve and dip irregularly, and the tip of the petal narrows to a twisted point. Green bands, perhaps leaves, seem to be layered behind and above the central petal. The innermost band is a vivid spring green where it touches the central petal, and the outer band is a sage color. In both bands the color fades from its brightest along the inner edge into deep black shadow, along the jagged and irregular outer edges.

The outer sage band is broken at the center and the blue background color shows through the gap. The corners of the canvas beyond fades from saturated indigo blue, where it touches the outline of a flower, to pale baby blue and white at the corners of the canvas.

I concluded that the focus of attention on the artwork as a product and on the domains of icon, composition and color, as well as the limited subjectivity, use of an external viewpoint, and the progressive discourse structure with the three levels of specificity observed in the corpus contribute to create the objective and detailed descriptions promoted by current guidelines. This may indicate that despite the cognitive ability of human beings to describe a given situation in different ways, contextual factors such as guidelines dictate AD creation for art museums. In the following sections, I compare the majority features and minority features for each dimension of the construal.

4.1 Attention/Salience

The results of the qualitative analysis performed for this study show that a small group of ADs describe the artwork as a process, thus shifting the attention from the artwork as a static product of the artistic process to the artist's actions and decisions that make it possible. The AD of Jackson Pollock's *Number 27*, created by Lou Giansante for Art Beyond Sight and the Whitney Museum of American Art in New York, focuses on the creative process and more specifically, on the painter's technique (the painting and recorded AD may be accessed at: http://www.artbeyondsight.org/amart/jackson-pol lock.shtml). Pollock's technique is especially relevant and therefore it is described in detail. But this description takes the form of a narrative; in other words, the describer moves from AD to "audio narration." Additionally, this audio narration is offered prior to the detailed description of the other visual components of the artwork, thus shifting the focus of attention to the artistic process and the artist's technique.

Jackson Pollock was an American painter and a major force in the Abstract Expressionist movement of the 1940s and 1950s. Works by the Abstract Expressionists were sometimes called action paintings, because they put a big emphasis on the physical act of painting itself as an essential part of a finished work. Pollock did his most famous action paintings during his so-called "drip period" between 1947 and 1950. Here's the story of one of those paintings, titled *Number 27*, simply because it was the 27th painting he did that year.

[**Click on, jazz music playing over small hi-fi speaker. Room ambience, some-one is moving around**] The year is 1950. In Jackson Pollock's studio, jazz, his favorite music, plays from a small phonograph. Pollock moves quickly around a large unstretched canvas lying on the floor. As he moves he dips a paintbrush into a can of paint. But instead of touching the brush to the canvas, he begins to drip the paint on the canvas, creating long threads, splatters, and pools of color. He does this again and again, staring intensely at the canvas as he works. Occasionally, instead of a brush he dips a stick into the paint, again using it to splatter and drip paint across the canvas. Sometimes he just picks up the can of paint and pours it on the canvas. Later Pollock switches to other cans of paint, each a different color, and eventually there are six colors in the painting *Number 27*. He continues to move energetically around all four sides of the canvas, almost as if in a dance, and he doesn't stop until he sees what he wants to see and he feels that the painting is finished. [**Music ends. Radio clicks off. Ambience out**] This description of Jackson's painting style makes clear that his paintings are abstract, not images that people could identify.

With that thought in mind, here's a verbal description of *Number 27*. It's a large oil painting on canvas, nine feet long horizontally and four and a half feet tall. The first impression of *Number 27* is that it looks like someone dripped and splattered different colored paints all over a canvas. At first glance, the painting looks accidental, even sloppy. But if you try to isolate a single color and follow its path through the painting, you'll see that actually Pollock carefully and deliberately constructed the painting, painstakingly building up the surface. The first color he put down was black. We can tell because all the colors are layered over it. In *Number 27*, Pollock used 6 colors: black, white, yellow, olive green, gray, and pale pink.

The tangled lines and layers of paint on the canvas are a record of Pollock's movements, fast or slow, arching or abrupt. And they are a record of the raw emotion he felt while in the creative process. Eventually he covered almost the entire surface of the painting, though there are many places where you can see the off white natural color of the canvas in the background. In putting paint on canvas the way he did, Pollock was expressing his deeply personal ideas and feelings.

We find a similar approach in Julie Treuman's AD of Pollock's *One Open Parentheses Number 31 Close Parentheses* for Acoustiguide and the Museum of Modern Art of New York (the painting and recorded AD may be accessed at: www.moma.org/audio/playlist/3/182). However, here the audio narration of the technique is offered after the work has been described as the static product of the creative process. Additionally, Treuman's use of the past tense still suggests the external viewpoint of a museum visitor who contemplates the work. In contrast, the present tense used in the previous AD implies the internal viewpoint of one who is present during the process of creation. This use of the present tense is a common way of narrating past events in English, but in this particular communicative situation it can have a significant impact on the experience of the AD user. I will discuss this further in the following section.

One Open Parentheses Number 31 Close Parentheses. Painted in 1950 by American painter Jackson Pollock, 1912–1956. Oil and enamel on canvas, eight feet ten inches high by seventeen feet six inches wide. 270 × 531 cm.

This picture hanging on this wall is painted on a very large, wide canvas. If you stand in the middle, it seems to expand indefinitely on either side of you. It's an abstract work, without any hint of representation. Its colors are sombre: black, blue, grey, brown and white on an off-white background.

It's painted in Jackson Pollock's famous 'drip' technique. And there's no better way of describing the way it looks than to explain the way it was painted. Pollock laid the canvas flat on the floor. Then he walked around with a can of paint, using first one colour and then another, pouring and dripping paint all over the canvas. He would not pour the paint directly from the can. Rather, he dripped it from brushes, or from sticks used for mixing house paint. As he walked, he would fling his arms in sweeping gestures, so the paint trails in long, blobby ropes across the canvas – some are straight, some curve and they vary in length. He was able to control where the paint would be thick and where it would form fine, thin lines. He carried on until he had covered the canvas with a deep, dense web of trailing ropes of paint.

The bare, off-white surface of the canvas is visible in many places, particularly around the edges and corners of this unframed painting. One can imagine the experience of running one's hands over its knobby surface, and following the trails of paint with one's fingertips.

With regard to specificity or granularity in visual art AD, there are two groups of describers, both from the fields of linguistics and translation, who promote a universal accessibility approach to art museum AD; namely GVAM (Accessible virtual guides for museums) in Spain, and The Art Project in Poland. This low level of specificity is also found in some ADs created by the educators of the Museum of Fine Arts in Boston, and represents a dramatic contrast with the ADs generally created by the art museums in this corpus. An example of this approach is the following AD of a painting entitled *Naranjas y limones* (Oranges and Lemons) by Julio Romero de Torres, developed by GVAM for the Museo Julio Romero de Torres in Córdoba, Spain (the painting and recorded AD may be accessed at: gvam.cordoba.es/webtest1/index?id=444&ad=true). A transcription of the original segment from the guide on this work is included here, and the only two audio descriptive sentences are underlined. These are as follows (my translation): "The central figure is a woman naked from the waist up. The young woman holds oranges in her arms close to her chest [...] In the background of the composition, there are a series of archaeological pieces that the painter often uses as a decoration motif." The rest of the text offers contextual information related to the artist, as well as interpretive information based on the contextual and formal analysis of the work typical in Art History.

Esta obra corresponde a 1927. Es la representación peculiar y muy personal del tradicional tema del bodegón. A las naturalezas muertas, al bodegón frío de frutas y flores inexpresivas opone Romero de Torres esta representación de manera que mezcla el bodegón y la figura humana.

La figura central es una mujer desnuda de medio cuerpo. La joven sostiene entre sus brazos unas naranjas sobre su pecho. La singularidad de Romero de Torres está en darle a la fruta el valor de integrante protagonista del cuadro. La composición posee toda la sensualidad de los bodegones flamencos, pero además Romero de Torres aporta su original interpretación del tema con la participación del desnudo. En el fondo de la composición aparecen una serie de piezas arqueológicas que el pintor suele utilizar como motivo de decoración.

La pieza rebosa sensualidad y erotismo y supuso una verdadera provocación para los círculos más reaccionarios de la sociedad del momento.

4.2 Judgement/Comparison

In line with most existing recommendations and guidelines, objective language is preferred in ADs of visual art, but opinion lexis and more specifically, metaphors, are widely used in this type of AD (Luque 2016; Soler 2019). One AD from the analyzed corpus is especially subjective and metaphorical. It was created by Claire Bartoli for an audio descriptive guided tour she conducted at the Musée d'Art Contemporain du Val-de-Marne (MAC/VAL), in Paris, for an installation by Éric Hattan entitled *Lèche-Vitry-nes* (Window-shopping). I have included here my translation of an excerpt from the video recording of the audio descriptive guided tour (available at: vimeo.com/38136237; the installation may be seen at: www.macval.fr/Eric-Hattan-4410).

A fantasy of architects!
A very long horizontal window
cuts out a cinemascope landscape
over the trees in the garden
and the buildings in the background.

Making it angle, from window to window,
a second window, it, all vertical.
It rises from the same level as the first.

Help! Do not open the window!
The city is just behind.
The city, people's lives,
people's lives thrown away!
They stick, they clump there!
Behind the glass, they accumulate.
They begin to eat the garden!

Bartoli's AD includes both objective and subjective descriptions of the artwork. The subjective descriptions are related to the visual components of the installation and the subjective impressions it elicits. These impressions are created through numerous metaphorical operations: the painting's composition is a fantasy of architects, the landscape in the background is seen as a cinemascope, and the objects piled up in the installation are the lives of the city's inhabitants; thrown away, clumping, accumulating, eating the garden. Bartoli has a background in creative writing and acting and she is blind. In an interview conducted for this study, the coordinator of the education department of the Musée d'Art Moderne in Paris, another museum where she works as describer, said that to prepare the ADs for her museum, Bartoli interviewed different experts at the museum and used the information collected to create the artwork descriptions. The same coordinator thought that this type of descriptions could be useful for all types of visitors and stated that for Bartoli, it is important to include the subjective impressions of the describer because they help people build their own interpretation.

The subjective content and the formal features of this AD, with short sentences, omissions, and non-standard syntax, resemble those of ekphrastic poetry. In a narrow sense, literary ekphrasis has been defined as the description of a visual artwork, be it real (referential ekphrasis) or imaginary (notional ekphrasis) in literature (Pimentel 2003). According to Krieger (2000), the goal of literary ekphrasis is to create *energeia*, i.e. a highly vivid description that allows the reader or listener to see the represented object with their internal eye. Over the course of Bartoli's tour, this poetic description is combined with a more objective description, along with contextual commentary provided by a museum educator. Together, they constitute a great example of how to offer diverse ADs for a variety of AD users within a tour, and how this structure and effect may be recreated in an audio descriptive guide that contains multiple audio descriptive tracks for the same artwork.

In the AD of three canvases from the *Les Nymphéas* (Water Lilies) series by Claude Monet, composed by Julie Treuman for Acoustiguide and the Museum of Modern Art in New York, the information on the label is followed by a description of the viewer's sensory impression of the scale of the work (the painting and recorded AD may be accessed at: https://www.moma.org/audio/playlist/3/173). This subjective description reads "The scale of these three huge paintings allows one not just to look at them but rather to immerse oneself in them." By placing it at the beginning of the AD, immediately after the introduction containing the label information, the focus of attention shifts to the subjective impression created by the work in the viewer. Besides, this subjective impression is generated by a metaphorical mapping of the painting's scale onto the viewer's physical sensation of being surrounded by the canvases. The describer also offers contextual information regarding the visual abilities of the artist and suggests a connection between these abilities and the growing abstraction in his art. Here we note the difference between interpretive information based on contextual data, and interpretive information based on visual perception, aesthetic experience, and formal analysis of the work.

6–9. Water Lilies, painted 1914–26 by the French artist Claude Monet, 1840–1926. Oil on canvas. Three panels, each panel 6 ½ ft high by fourteen feet wide, 200 cm by 425 cm.

The scale of these three huge paintings allows one not just to look at them but rather to immerse oneself in them.

Water Lilies was painted late in Monet's career, at a time when his work had become increasingly abstract. This may have been a result of his failing eyesight. He had a cataract operation just a couple of years after these paintings were completed.

Each of the canvasses is completely devoted to water—the edge of the pond is never shown. It's a mysterious, shifting world. Nothing is clearly defined. The paintings are made up of blurry, merging brushstrokes, forming an abstract mist of colour. In the darker areas of the canvas, where the water seems to be in shadow, it has the cool green depth of a pine forest. Lighter areas reflect back the sky in the gleaming blues and greens of a peacock's tail. There are also vast, dancing surfaces of reflected sunlight, daubed onto the canvas in chaotic patches of creamy paint. Clusters of green floating lily-pads fill large portions of the pond. And flecks of pink, lilac and yellow on the pads convey the water-lilies themselves.

These paintings are a celebration of Monet's lifelong devotion to the effects of light. The result is as much a meditation in paint as it is a visual record of Monet's own garden and pond.

4.3 Perspective/Situatedness

In an earlier section, I suggested that Lou Giansante's use of the present tense, when narrating the creative process for one of Pollock's abstract expressionist paintings, endows it with an internal viewpoint, that of someone who is present during the process and shares the artist's time and space. While the viewpoint is still external to the work, it is internal to the creative process. A similar construal is found in his AD of *Early Sunday Morning* by Edward Hopper, created for Art Beyond Sight and the Whitney Museum of American Art (the painting and recorded AD may be accessed at: www.artbeyondsight.org/amart/edward-hopper.shtml; the annotations between square brackets are included in the online transcript). This AD also utilizes an internal viewpoint in the initial discourse section. However, here the internal viewpoint introduces the place depicted in this figurative painting. Therefore, it is an audio narration that refers to a different stage in the creative process, namely the selection of the scene. In both ADs, the describer reproduces the creative process based on contextual information, yet provides a more immersive experience of the artistic process. Additionally, it is not only an internal viewpoint of the creative process, but of the painting as well. The listener is first transported to the scene depicted in the painting, thus establishing an internal viewpoint for its subsequent detailed description. Even though this detailed description uses the external viewpoint commonly adopted in visual art AD, it is linked to the earlier internal narration through the following sentence that helps reinforce the immersive experience: "You see them as if you're standing across the street from them."

> **[Fade up empty street ambience. Low hum of distant traffic]** The year is 1930. The artist Edward Hopper is up very early on a Sunday morning, walking the streets of his neighborhood in Greenwich Village, New York City. **[A few birds. A man's footsteps on concrete. Slow, steady]** He walks alone… at this early hour the streets are empty of people… and that's just the way he likes it. Hopper's often drawn to painting scenes of American life like this empty street… or half-empty theaters, or railroad tracks, gas stations, or the windswept lighthouses of Cape Cod where he spends his summers. **[Ambience and footsteps continue. Distant barking dog]** Hopper is an intensely private man, and that shows in his paintings. They're realistic, but spare, often empty of people and nature. To some

people they're filled with loneliness. To others, they reflect Hopper's deep interest in being alone with his thoughts and feelings. **[Single '30s era car goes by]** On this particular Sunday morning, Hopper's walk takes him along Seventh Avenue South in Greenwich Village. He looks across the Avenue and his attention is drawn by a row of two-story buildings. They become the subject of his painting Early Sunday Morning. The buildings are in New York City, but Hopper leaves out details like street signs. So it could be any Main Street, in any small town in the United States, during the middle decades of the twentieth century. **[All sounds out]**

And now here's a detailed verbal description of Early Sunday Morning. It's a horizontal oil painting on canvas. It's 3 ft tall and 6 ft wide, so it's twice as wide as it is tall. It shows a block of three attached buildings, all two stories tall, with shops on the street level and apartments above them. The buildings extend horizontally across the painting from the left edge to the right edge. You see them as if you're standing across the street from them. (The description continues)

Giansante again uses this internal viewpoint in the AD of Lily Martin Spencer's *Kiss me and you'll kiss the 'lasses*, created for Art Beyond Sight and the Brooklyn Museum (the painting and recorded AD may be accessed at: www.artbeyondsight.org/amart/lily-martin-spencer.shtml; the annotations between square brackets are included in the online transcript). In this case, the describer reinforces the internal viewpoint by explicitly placing himself and the listener within the scene depicted in the painting. In the earlier ADs of Pollock and Hopper, the common technique of present tense narration of past events is used. In contrast, in this AD of Spencer's painting, the describer transforms himself and the listener into active participants when he says "and as we peek into the home of a young woman, she's busy at work putting up fruit, preserving it for the winter months" and later, "but her head is turned, looking straight at us with a playful smile on her face." In addition, the three ADs include ambient sounds related to the artwork and together, all these linguistic and sound techniques help the listener to mentally travel to the space-time coordinates of the narration. These choices may be related to the fact that Giansante has a background in radio communication.

Lily Martin Spencer was an enormously popular artist in the mid-nineteenth century because of her genre paintings, paintings that show realistic scenes from everyday life. Especially domestic scenes of women, like this scene. **[Quiet indoor ambience, birds outside, woman hums to herself while at work, wooden spoon taps bowl]** Summertime, 1856. Fruits are at their ripest... and as we peek into the home of a young woman, she's busy at work putting up fruit, preserving it for the winter months. The floor of the room has a carpet of white and red flowers. She wears an ankle-length dress, dark green, with short sleeves. The neckline of the dress shows a white ruffle. A pink apron tied at the waist covers the front of her dress. She has brown hair, pulled back into a bun at the back of her head. She's standing, at a table whose white tablecloth has been pulled to the right edge, so that she can work on the wooden tabletop without dirtying the tablecloth. She's standing in the center of the room with her body facing right, but her head is turned, looking straight at us with a playful smile on her face. Her look is teasing, even suggestive, probably because she's talking to a man. And what has she just said? **[Woman]** Kiss me and you'll kiss the 'lasses! The word 'Lasses is short for molasses. It's a moment of playful flirtation, for if the man she's addressing tries to kiss her, she'll give him a dousing of molasses from a wooden spoon she holds. **[All sounds fade out]** And that is the title of Lily Martin Spencer's painting... *Kiss me and you'll kiss the 'lasses.*

Now here's the rest of the verbal description of the painting. It's a small oil painting, only 29 in. high and 21 in. wide. On the right of the painting, the table she stands at is piled with various fruits. There's a bowl filled to the brim with dark red raspberries. Behind the bowl a basket overflows with pale yellow cherries tinged with light red. Next to the basket is a glass dish filled with round green fruit, possibly grapes. In the foreground in front of the table, a chair holds more fruit; a metal basin filled with green apples or pears, and the brown outer skin of two pineapples. (The description continues)

Interestingly, this enhanced internal viewpoint is used in the children's audio guide at the Museum of Modern Art of New York (the annotations between brackets are my own). Here, the expositive-interpretive discourse used in the general audio guide for adult visitors has been replaced with an evocative description designed to catch the attention of younger visitors and encourage their contemplation and analysis of the work. Rather than a static entity, the painting is described as a dynamic event where the visual elements come to life and the child-visitor becomes an actor. The viewpoint is again internal to the scene in the painting, as the describer places himself and the child inside it from the beginning by saying "Child! Pay attention. Do not step on the irises. Do not fall into the water. Does Mr. Monet know you are in his garden? Here you are, right on the edge of his famous pond of water lilies." It is combined with an external viewpoint, when the describer instructs the child where to stand in order to contemplate the work in "Now, walk to the middle of this enormous painting, step back, waaaay back" and later, "Walk to your right now, down toward the end of the painting."

[Voice 1] [Music: mysterious] Oh, my! Where am I?

[Voice 2: playful] You, there! Child! Pay attention. Do not step on the irises. Do not fall into the water. Does Mr. Monet know you are in his garden? Here you are, right on the edge of his famous pond of water lilies. Flowers, you know, that grow in the water. Now, walk to the middle of this enormous painting, step back, **[Music: magical, process] [Voice stress]** waaaay back. Can you see the round green leaves floating on the surface? **[Music: guitar and accordion, soft, melodic]** The flowers are pink and purple. **[Sound: birds and rowing]** Every morning, very early, I row out on this pond to get rid of old leaves, dead blossoms, the surface must be *parfait,* perfect for Mr. Monet. He paints the pond again and again and again. To paint water, it is very difficult. Water is clear, there is nothing to paint! But you **[Voice stress]** can paint the reflections in it, like the sky. Can you see bits of fluffy, pinkish white clouds in Mr. Monet's painting? The pond, it changes colors on cloudy or sunny days, in the morning and the evening, the reflections change as the clouds drift, or a breeze ripples the surface, or a frog jumps in **[Sound: frog croaking]**, or a bird lands in the water **[Sound: splash] [End of music]**. The pond looks different in shady places. Walk to your right now, down toward the end of the painting. **[Music: faster rhythm]**. *Fais attention!*

Don't crush the flowers! At this end, the pond looks green and brown, it seems darker and cooler here, maybe from the shadow of a willow tree on the bank, maybe there are fish in this part, maybe a turtle. But Mr. Monet paints only the water and the flowers. He loves to paint. Come close to the picture for a moment. **[Sound effect: xylophone notes simulating steps]**. Can you see the many, many marks of his brush? Perhaps you've noticed that this painting comes out from the wall as if it might wrap around you. Mr. Monet made it **[Voice stress]** big, so you would feel right in the middle of the water. He wanted to share what he saw. **[Sound: rowing]** So I am happy to row out to keep the pond beautiful in Mr. Monet's garden. **[Sound: rowing]**

In all of these ADs, a variety of sounds are used to translate the painting into a verbal discourse, thus adding another layer of intersemiotic translation. This practice has been advocated and put into practice by Neves (2012). She collaborates with sound producers to create "soundpaintings," where ADs include non-verbal sounds to facilitate the interpretation of the verbal elements and therefore, the visual artwork. The artwork AD is complemented with the translation into non-verbal sounds to create a multimodal target text that combines two intersemiotic translation types. Moving further in this direction, the National Gallery in London commissioned purely musical intersemiotic translations of a number of paintings to be included along with the verbal contents in the audio guide (available at: https://www.youtube.com/watch?v=jXUqCkqNKmo).

4.4 Constitution/Gestalt

Most ADs conceive of the artwork as the product of the artistic process. This type of AD typically begins with the label information, where the first visual components described are the size and the materials or medium, along with the work's title, author and date of production. The latter are not audio descriptive elements as such, but they help to identify the artwork as a singular entity. Then, a general description of the subject matter (iconic signs), color and composition is offered, followed by a more detailed, organized and sequential description of these and other visual components. When the artwork thus identified as a singular entity and museum item, and described as a group of visual components that are then individually described, it is understood as a non-relational entity.

However, a few ADs start with a single long sentence that highlights the connections between the different visual components of the work and relates them to the viewer's experience. This type of description highlights the connections between the constituent entities, as well as between the work and the person who experiences it, thus understanding it as a relational entity. Wendy Moor's AD of an Impressionist painting from the series *Les Nymphéas* by Claude Monet for Antenna International and the Tate Modern (the recorded AD is not published, but the painting may be seen at: www.tate-images.com/results.asp?txtkeys1=monet#) is an example of this. This AD details the materials and size of the work at the beginning, but leaves the title and artist's name for later. The typical discourse structure is altered, thus offering a different experience that actually resembles one experienced by one type of museum-goer: visitors who prioritize the sensory experience and view the work before reading its associated label and text panels. Additionally, the language of the AD imitates the artwork by describing the visual components in one unbroken sentence that connects the main visual components and translates the visual experience of first viewing the painting: "The misty pale greens, warm yellows, mauves and rosy pinks of this almost-abstract oil painting 13 ft wide and 6 and a half tall glow invitingly."

The misty pale greens, warm yellows, mauves and rosy pinks of this almost-abstract oil painting 13 ft wide and 6 and a half tall glow invitingly. It's hung low, in a simple burnished gold-red frame like bamboo pole. Viewed from close to, the encrusted canvas is an amorphous mass of splodged, swirling layers of multi-coloured paint. But with distance, separate shapes begin to emerge. Paradoxically, the further away from the painting we are the more it draws us in—and it's best appreciated from about 12 ft away, at the bench in the centre of this room.

It's called *Water Lilies*, and it was painted after 1916 by Claude Monet.

Eye-shaped areas of dark blue and mauve contain horizontal groupings of greeny-yellow and aquamarine ovals with blobs of red and pink water-lily leaves and flowers. These contrast with patches of vertical squiggles and smudges in greens, tans and pinks - like indistinct veils.

The work divides into three vertical sections slanting gently towards the right. Up each of the left and right sections are three lily groups - one above the other—with blurred areas between. Where on the left side there's a group, in the corresponding position on the right side is a blurred area—and vice versa, providing a kind of equilibrium. Towards the top the oval leaves are more squashed—hinting at the tilt of the water surface as it recedes from us.

The middle vertical section is predominantly pale pink and bounded by bulging mauve forms—suggesting the reflections of trees with a sunrise or sunset sky between. In the centre of this is a particularly smudged area, perhaps where the breeze has ruffled the water. And towards the top right of the work is another—maybe the fleeting movement of a weeping willow.

She also uses this technique in the AD of an abstract expressionist painting by Jackson Pollock entitled *Summertime Number 9A*, created for the same museum (the recorded AD is not published, but the painting may be seen at: www.tate.org.uk/art/artworks/pol lock-summertime-number-9a-t03977). In this AD, the description of line, color, shape, direction, and composition in a single, long sentence may be considered as a creative means of translating the perceptual, emotional and cognitive experience of first standing in front of the painting and contemplating it.

Within the tangled mass of swirling, looping black and grey lines taking up the cream canvas of this long dynamic abstract painting nearly 19 ft wide and only 2 and a half feet high, almost-vertical thicker black lines at more or less regular intervals, with blobs at top and bottom, suggest a frieze of frenzied dancers. This sense of rhythm is heightened by evenly spaced patches of yellow and blue—and smaller blotches of red, purple and other colours.

The work is called *Summertime Number 9A*, and the American artist Jackson Pollock created it in 1948 by literally dancing—or at least moving rhythmically around the canvas laid flat on the floor—dripping and flinging house paint from a stick or brush-handle, or pouring it direct from the can. Here he is talking about his method:

... I paint on the floor, which isn't unusual, because the Orientals did that. Most of the paint I use is a liquid, flowing kind of paint. The brushes I use are used more as sticks than as a brush. The brush doesn't touch the surface of the canvas—it's just above..."

The flowing lines here certainly have a calligraphic quality about them—and the sweeping arcs give a real sense of Pollock's arm swinging just above the canvas.

He tended to work in trance-like bursts, only stopping when he felt the painting looked as it should. He said that the floor allowed him to be completely in a painting, almost unaware of what he was doing—so the painting took on a life of its own. Pollock often listened to jazz while he worked.

Summertime Number 9A is probably the closest anyone could get to a visual representation of jazz without actually writing notes on a stave.

In the detailed and progressive description that is usually the norm in visual art AD, the location of the visual components is clearly indicated through language. In this way, the artwork is conceptualized as a bounded entity. However, one AD from the corpus conveys the composition and more specifically, the location of the visual components, without using any lexis related to space and location. Instead, they are implicitly indicated by means of the sequence in which these formal components are enunciated through language. The describer modulates the vocal tempo (speed) to "imitate" the repetition of vertical lines of alternate colors present in each of the multiple rectangular canvases that constitute this installation of paintings. By doing so, the describer also translates the visual impression caused by this composition into a verbal and aural semiotic mode. Besides, the dimensions and overall shape of the work are not mentioned, which also makes the boundaries of the work blurry, undefined, like foliage as opposed to leaves. The artwork is thus described as an unbounded entity. This is the AD of *Mures de peintures* (Wall of Paintings) by Daniel Buren, created by Claire Bartoli for the audio descriptive guide of the Musée d'Art Moderne in Paris. I have included here my translation of the AD (the recorded AD may be accessed at: soundcloud.com/mamvp-le-profil/mam-elu cubration-bartolienne; the work may be seen at: www.mam.paris.fr/fr/oeuvre/murs-de-peintures).

Black, white, black, white, black square. Small red, white, red, white, red square. Black square. Large orange, white, orange, white orange, white, orange square. Small blue, white, blue, white, blue rectangle. Gray square. Red rectangle. Horizontal red rectangle. Vertical orange, white, orange, white, orange. Large horizontal red, white, red, white, red rectangle. Vertical black, white, black, white, black. Large red square. Small gray rectangle. Horizontal long gray, white, gray, white, gray, white, gray. Small orange rectangle. Small blue, white, blue, white, blue rectangle. Vertical gray. Red. Large green, white, green, white, green, white, green square. Large red, white, red, white, red, white, red vertical.

This may be deemed what Wolf (1999) called "imitation" in his work on intermediality. Wolf distinguished between two types of verbal description of a painting: one limited to referencing the artwork or enumerating the objects represented, called "thematization", and another that follows the structure of the image and is called "imitation." Bartoli's AD falls within the second category, as the AD attempts to convey the formal features of the artwork by imitating its structure. Thematization is the most frequently used type of visual art AD. In thematization, the intersemiotic translation does not imitate the formal features of the source text but categorizes and qualifies its components. The art composition is explained with shorter sentences, following a clear sequence from the general to the specific, and using clear indications of space and location. This was illustrated at the beginning of this section with the description of Georgia O'Keefe's *Jack-in-the-Pulpit, Number Four.*

The same technique is used by Bartoli for an installation work entitled *L'ivrogne* (The Drunkard), by artist Gilles Barbier, during an audio descriptive tour that she conducted at the Musée d'Art Contemporain du Val-de-Marne (MAC/VAL) in Paris. I have included here my translation of an excerpt from the video recording of the audio descriptive guided tour (available at: vimeo.com/38136237; the installation may be seen at: www.macval.fr/Gilles-Barbier). Once again, the sequence used in the description is not the only tool used to translate the composition of the artwork. The describer uses variations of the vocal tempo, tone (pitch) and intensity (volume), to imitate the composition.

Up in the air, stars in the... Hey!
Sssss.... Snake
Earthworm, worm, worm, worm... Earthworm!
Spir... Spir... Respiration, spiral!
Oh, ooh, up there!

5 Conclusions

This article has described and discussed minority features in a corpus of recorded and live audio descriptions of visual art for the four dimensions of the construal as proposed by Croft and Cruse (2004). The results of the study show that some ADs conceive of the artwork as a process and use an internal viewpoint. Attention sometimes shifts to the technique or to the subjective impressions elicited by the work, with a few ADs displaying especially high levels of subjectivity and formal similarities with ekphrastic poetry. Within a group of ADs, universal accessibility translates into low levels of specificity or granularity, understood here as the amount of information and detail, which contrasts dramatically with the long and highly specific ADs that are predominant in the corpus. The prevalent structure of the work in the AD is altered so its identification is postponed, and the connections between the visual components are profiled, thus conceiving of the artwork as a relational entity. The general-to-specific progression that is typical of this intersemiotic modality is not followed. Rather, the describer's linguistic choices create a text that imitates the art composition and translates the visual experience of some museum-goers when first viewing it. In a small number of ADs, the location of the visual components is not conveyed through precise lexis but implied in the discourse sequence, while the paralinguistic features of voice tempo, tone, and intensity are used to translate the composition and the sensory impressions evoked by the work of art. In doing this, the work is conceptualized as an unbounded entity, with undefined boundaries, thus enabling a different experience of visual art.

In addition, this study has shown that describers of visual art have various professional and educational backgrounds. We hope that this study will increase awareness of these different profiles, which could lead to the emergence of even more creative and enriching practices in this field. If accessibility is to be improved at art museums and exhibitions, these institutions should benefit from working with individuals with different approaches to visual art AD. With regard to the minority AD features discussed in this study, guidelines and standards are helpful for promoting and improving accessibility, and this is also relevant for the creation of visual art AD. Based on research from different disciplines, they set high-quality standards that inform existing resources and facilitate the creation of new ones. However, the experience of AD users may be enhanced even further by working in close cooperation with them and acknowledging the diversity of their needs and preferences. This collaboration and acknowledgement can open productive paths to investigating and inventing more diverse forms of audio describing visual art.

References

Burnham, R., Kai-Kee, E.: Gallery teaching as guided interpretation. In: Burnham, R., Kai-Kee, E. (eds.) Teaching in the Art Museum. Interpretation as Experience, pp. 59–66. J. Paul Getty Museum, Los Angeles (2011)

Croft, W., Cruse, D.A.: Cognitive Linguistics. Cambridge University Press, Cambridge (2004)

Dirven, R.: Cognitive linguistics. In: Malmkjaer; K. (ed.) The Linguistics Encyclopedia, 2nd edn. pp. 76–82. Routledge, London (2002)

Eisner, E.W.: The Arts and the Creation of Mind. Yale University Press, New Haven (2002)

Evans, V., Green, M.: Cognitive Linguistics. An Introduction. Edinburgh University Press, Edinburgh (2006)

Halverson, S.: Implications of cognitive linguistics for translation studies. In: Rojo, A., Ibarretxe, I. (eds.) Cognitive Linguistics and Translation: Advances in Some Theoretical Models and Applications, pp. 33–73. Walter de Gruyter, Berlin (2013)

Krieger, M.: El problema de la écfrasis: Imágenes y palabras, espacio y tiempo (y la obra literaria) [The ekphrasis problem: Images and words, space and time (and the literary work)]. In: Monegal, A. (ed.) Literatura y Pintura [Literature and Painting], pp. 140–160. Arco Libros, Madrid (2000)

Krüger, R.: A cognitive linguistic perspective on explicitation and implicitation in scientific and technical translation. trans-kom (J. Transl. Tech. Commun. Res.) 6(2), 285–314 (2013)

Langacker, R.W.: Cognitive Grammar: A Basic Introduction. Oxford University Press, Oxford (1987/2008)

Lima, P.H., Magalhães, C.M.: A neutralidade em audiodescrições de pinturas: Resultados preliminares de um descrição via teoria da avaliatividade [Neutrality in audio descriptions of paintings: Preliminary results from a description based on Appraisal Theory]. In: Santiago Araújo, V.L., Ferreira Aderaldo, M. (eds.) Os Novos Rumos da Pesquisa em Audiodescrição no Brasil [New Directions in Research on Audio Description in Brazil], pp. 73–87. Editora CRV, Curitiba (2013)

Luque, M.O.: The embodiment of the metaphor: an analysis of the metaphors used to convey the human body in audio descriptive guides of museums for people with visual functional diversity. E-AESLA **2**, 326–334 (2016)

Luque, M.O., Soler, S.: Metaphor as creativity in audio descriptive tours for art museums: from description to practice. J. Audiovis. Transl. **3**(1), 64–78 (2020)

Neves, J.: Multi-sensory approaches to (audio) describing the visual arts. MonTi **4**, 277–293 (2012)

Pimentel, L.A.: Écfrasis y lecturas iconotextuales [Ekphrasis and iconotextual readings]. Poligrafías: Revista de literatura comparada **4**, 205–215 (2003)

Soler, S.: A corpus-based genre analysis of art museum audio descriptive guides. In: Alonso Almeida, F., Cruz García, L., González Ruiz, V. (eds.) Corpus-Based Studies on Language Varieties, pp 145–166. Peter Lang, Bern (2016)

Soler, S.: Audio descriptive guides in art museums: a corpus-based semantic analysis. Transl. Interpret. Stud. **13**(2), 230–249 (2018)

Soler, S.: Defining subjectivity in audio description for art museums. Meta: Transl. J. **64**(3), 708–733 (2019)

Wolf, W.: The Musicalization of Fiction: A Study in the Theory and History of Intermediality. Rodopi, Amsterdam (1999)

Designing Accessible Videos for People with Disabilities

Leevke Wilkens[✉] , Vanessa N. Heitplatz , and Christian Bühler

Department of Rehabilitation Technology, TU Dortmund University, Dortmund, Germany
{Leevke.wilkens,vanessa.heitplatz,
christian.buehler}@tu-dortmund.de

1 Introduction

The usage of videos is popular across a variety of disciplines and learning contexts (e.g. leisure time, school, higher education, and work). Educational videos meet the reception habits of children, adolescents as well as adults in their leisure time [4]. The usage of videos in educational contexts is associated with many benefits, such as the increased flexibility of learning, regarding time, place, and speed or repetition, and revisions [16]. For others, the usage of videos may pose new challenges (e.g. lack of accessibility or usability). The usage of videos in teacher education has gained more and more attention in recent years. For example, they offer the possibility, that classroom observations can be done from a distance, one situation can be analyzed from different perspectives, and new opportunities for theory-practice transfer arise [38]. Additionally, recent studies have shown that video-prompting via digital devices (e.g. tablets, smartphones) offers an added value for people with disabilities on the self-directed vocational task completion [11, 14, 20]. Increasing self-esteem, enhancing (digital) skills, and independence from caregivers are such benefits. However, videos have to be accessible for everyone to benefit from these potentials.

This paper aims to analyze videos from different education projects (higher education and vocational training) to answer the following questions: 'Where are differences and similarities of educational videos from different contexts?' and 'How is accessibility realized in these videos?'. This analysis can then be used to develop a guideline for producing accessible educational videos for people with disabilities.

2 State of the Art

Lifelong learning becomes increasingly important for all individuals in our ongoing digitalized society [31]. The usage of the Internet and digital technologies is changing the ways people interact, communicate, and learn [21, 36]. A good fit between the individual and his or her (learning) environment can improve cognitive skills, cooperative, and self-decided learning [30].

© Springer Nature Switzerland AG 2021
M. Antona and C. Stephanidis (Eds.): HCII 2021, LNCS 12769, pp. 328–344, 2021.
https://doi.org/10.1007/978-3-030-78095-1_24

2.1 Learning with Videos

Videos have provided various opportunities for learning and education. Mobile phones and other digital devices "have pushed forward new paradigms for using video in education" [45]. Today, people can create and broadcast their own digital videos for others and create new patterns of video-based information structures. This paradigm shift is used for advanced learning about complex topics in different education settings. Thus, it is no surprise that current studies examine the usage of videos in different learning contexts.

An analysis of the current state of research shows that many studies examine the effect of self-directed video prompting to enhance life-skills of people with disabilities, adolescents, and in higher education [11, 14, 44]. All these authors showed that participants were able to complete their tasks independently and correctly after an amount of time and training without the help of caregivers or other people from the social environment. Goo et al. showed that the usage of computer-based video instructions is an effective method for facilitating the acquisition and generalization of enhancing life skills for young students [20]. In a similar context, Payne et al. indicated that the usage of instructional videos can help students to teach life skills when living in their rooms or apartments [35]. Besides, videos can be valuable not only for learning and completing tasks but also for other areas of life. Zahn et al. proved that creating videos can contribute to gain deeper knowledge about a specific topic (in this case obesity) and to reduce stigmatizing attitudes by the social environment [45].

People with intellectual disabilities often struggle to find employment and show difficulties with vocational task acquisition and completion [14]. Ayres et al. found that people with moderate to severe intellectual disability are not employed within two years after finishing high-school [6]. Furthermore, only half of the people with intellectual (on any level) (51.8%) and 66.4% of individuals with Autism-Spectrum-Disorder were gainfully employed outside the home. Employment and living situations are the most important "post-school variables" to foster quality-of-life outcomes for these people. The usage of technologies cannot overcome all barriers but "skilled application of technology can increase many areas of independence" [6]. So far, only a few projects have focused on the improvement of employment situations for people with intellectual disabilities using digital technologies in general. Andreassen et al. developed an "Interactive Calendar with Mobile Phone Reminders (RemindMe)" to enable the users to take initiative and to plan, structure, and organize everyday life [5]. Other studies focused on the usage of digital technologies to improve social and personal skills [3, 8] or to promote activities in specific areas of the life of elderly people or people with disabilities (e.g. safety skills or functional activities) [7, 25]. Chiner et al. and Alfredsson et al. found that watching videos on YouTube is one of the most performed internet activities of people with disabilities [2, 12]. Bayor constitutes that "YouTube holds potential as a teaching and learning tool with a wealth of instructional videos available […]" [8]. In short, using digital technologies "as an instructional support for teaching chained tasks in the areas of life skills and vocational/employment skills" has been proven as valuable for people with intellectual disabilities [6].

Also, in higher education, for instance in teacher education, videos are seen as having various potentials:

- Authentic representation of the complexity and simultaneity of teaching
- Connection between theory and practice
- As a basis for reflection on teaching
- As a basis for focusing on quality characteristics of teaching [19, 29]

Even beyond teacher education, videos have been associated with various benefits for informal and formal knowledge transfer:

- Increased flexibility in time, place, speed
- Personalization and social presence for learners
- Unlimited repetition and revision
- Higher levels of student engagement
- Promotion of active learning pedagogy
- Language learning [16]

In this context, videos are used both - passively (watching videos) and actively (editing videos) - to transfer knowledge and initiate re-reflection in higher education teaching [24].

2.2 Accessible Video

Videos can contribute to the promotion of inclusive teaching through the multimodal presentation of information. However, it is important to note that the usage of videos can also exclude students if they are not designed to be accessible.

Non-accessible documents and other media are barriers to participation in digital education [17]. Even when implementing UDL or UDI principles using digital media, consistent attention must be paid to their accessibility. If students are offered a video as an alternative to text to implement the UDL principle of "presentations of information", students with hearing impairments, for example, will be excluded if the video has no captions. The same applies if the content is offered text-based as an alternative to an audio file, but the text document is not accessible [40]. Thus, even in the case of multiple presentations of information, consistent care must be taken to ensure that every form of presentation is accessible [10].

While educational videos differ depending on the audience, context, and objective, educational videos have similarities, such as the need for accessibility; this includes, captions as well as audio description [1]. While the creation of captions is seemingly easy - it can even be done automatically via Youtube - the design of audio description is more complex [43]. One reason is, that the amount of information, which is covered by the audio description is determined by the length of the gaps in the audio track [33, 34].

Depending on the audience, not only audio descriptions but also other requirements (e.g. easy language, using symbols for a better understanding), are necessary for accessible educational videos [9, 22, 27].

The decision about necessity lies with the person given the task, who needs to answer the question 'What is important?' or 'what competencies are focused on, and what are the learning objectives?' Therefore, providing videos for education involves didactical considerations, which have an impact on the accessibility of videos [43]. Consequently, not only the technical dimension for creating accessible videos but rather didactical dimensions should be considered to enable individual learning progress.

Therefore, the working group 'BIK für Alle' has formulated three requirements for the accessible usage of videos in university teaching:

- "an accessible video player
- captions
- translation of purely visual information (e.g. audio description)" [37]

The complexity of the accessible implementation of these requirements varies according to the intended usage of the video (see Fig. 1):

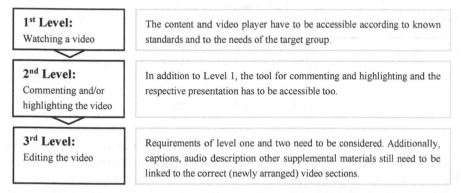

| 1st Level: | The content and video player have to be accessible according to known |
| Watching a video | standards and to the needs of the target group. |

2nd Level:	In addition to Level 1, the tool for commenting and highlighting and the
Commenting and/or	respective presentation has to be accessible too.
highlighting the video	

3rd Level:	Requirements of level one and two need to be considered. Additionally,
Editing the video	captions, audio description other supplemental materials still need to be
	linked to the correct (newly arranged) video sections.

Fig. 1. Levels of video usage (own figure)

Thus, accessible videos include an accessible video player, captions, audio descriptions but also content-related considerations such as visual support, easy language, etc. – always according to the intended target group. Also, considerations about the design and required resources (costs, time, personal) must be taken into account because they might pose new challenges, also for universities or research projects [37]. It is also important that accessibility features for one group may pose difficulties for another group, e.g. captions for people with Autism Spectrum Disorders [32].

3 Method

Five videos were examined, using the presented code system, additional material such as information on the webpage or the framework for lecturers was used to supplement the analysis.

To analyze the videos we developed a code system consisting of general information about the video and the four principles of accessibility: perceivable, operable, understandable and robust [41]. These dimensions were then categorized using accessibility features for videos, based on guidelines for accessible videos (see Fig. 2).

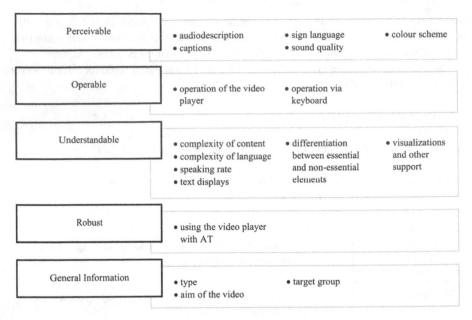

Fig. 2. Code system (own figure)

This approach makes it possible to consider both, aspects which are established in guidelines for accessible videos, such as audio description and captions but also aspects which are not covered by these guidelines, such as visual support or easy language.

Because of the explorative nature of this analysis and the respective research question, the analysis is not aiming for an evaluation of the quality of the provided accessibility aspects. Instead we focus on the differences and similarities of the analyzed videos.

3.1   Subject of Analysis

The videos used for the analysis are from two different projects at TU Dortmund University. Firstly, instructional videos designed for the miTAS - project [22]. The videos from the second context are from the research project "Degree 4.0 – Digital teacher education 4.0: video-based – accessible - personalized", where videos are used to initiate reflexive teacher education in different subjects.

Introducing the miTAS Project. The miTAS (multimedia individual training and working assistance system) project is funded by the Federal Ministry of Education and Research (duration October 2019 to September 2021). The project aims to "improve the employment situation of people with disabilities" on the first labor market by using digital technologies for vocational training and work processes [28]. miTAS is an application that can be operated on smartphones as well as tablets (iOS and Android) and can be used as a webpage to support everyday tasks of people with disabilities and their caregivers in different professional contexts [28]. By creating individually tailored profiles, working or everyday tasks (e.g. cleaning, sorting laundry, or assembling a desk chair) can be divided into step-by-step instructions which are provided with self-developed videos, descriptions, or voice memos to address different sensory channels. The miTAS application offers opportunities to enlarge the Interface and to use a read-aloud function. People with disabilities and caregivers can create and co-design working or everyday tasks in a collaborative process [22].

In addition to the miTAS application, a 'miTAS-Media-Box' offers learning materials (e.g. checklists, videos, descriptions) to familiarize the users with the miTAS application. The media box is designed as a website on which different materials are offered, based on the pedagogical concept of station learning [42]. "The combination of the miTAS application and the media boy enables a blended learning concept, which makes it easier to get to know the application a virtually supplements on-site use" [22]. A main focus of the media box is providing videos. There are different kinds of videos with different aims and for different target groups (e.g. image videos, instructional videos, screencasts), which are intended to explain certain aspects or familiarize users with the application.

In this analysis, the image video of miTAS, where the app is introduced and a video tutorial about the creation of a task in the app are analyzed.

Introducing the Degree 4.0 Project. The research project Degree 4.0 takes place at TU Dortmund University and is funded by the Federal Ministry of Education and Research (from October 2018 till July 2022). The aim of the project is the development of an accessible digital learning platform on which videos are provided to foster reflexive teacher education. The subjects Computer Sciences, German Studies, Mathematics and Music take part in the project and hence develop on the one video material. The subproject Rehabilitation Sciences is aiming at the accessibility of both the LMS and the videos itself [43].

For the analysis for this paper three videos from the subjects Computer Sciences, Mathematics and German Studies are used. Audio description and subtitles are done by TU Dortmund University's Department of Disability and Studies (DoBuS).

These videos differ not only in regard to content but also in the way accessibility aspects were implemented. Additionally, to the videos itself, a developed framework for the lecturer [43] is used as an additional source of information, because the audio description was not done by the lectures themselves.

4   Results

The analyzed videos are different with respect to the intended target group of these videos and the general design.

On the one hand, the miTAS videos are designed for people with intellectual disabilities and their caregivers. The aim of the videos is the presentation and advertisement for the miTAS app, respective presenting video tutorials for specific tasks to work with the App. The videos are designed partly as comics using icons and written text as well as users of the app, using the app to do a specific task (see Fig. 3).

Fig. 3. Screenshot MiTAS video

On the other hand, the Degree videos are in use in teacher education. In all videos, some sort of real-live situation is presented (in a classroom setting, a video of a teacher with a student, or screencast with additional clips showing the hands, keyboard (see Fig. 4)).

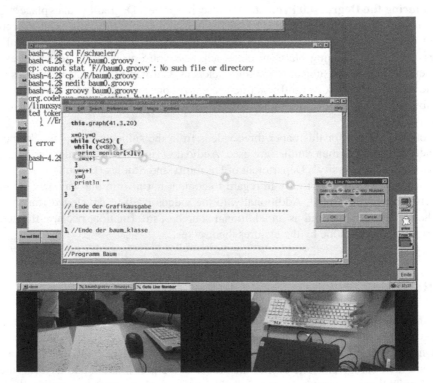

Fig. 4. Degree video-computer sciences [18]

In contrast to the miTAS videos, these videos are not intended to demonstrate something to the viewer. Instead, these videos are used to initiate reflection according to specific didactical questions.

The results of the analysis are presented corresponding to the dimensions of accessibility.

Perceivable

"Information and user interface components must be presentable to users in ways they can perceive" [41].

In both videos from miTAS the color scheme is not always optimal for people with visual impairments. Using a contrast analyzer by leserlich.info [26] it was found that at some points the contrasts in the speech bubble are not high enough (1,5:1), while others are compliant with WCAG Level AA to Level AAA (6,0:1 to 21,0:1) [41]. "The contrast ratio can range between 1 and 21 and is usually expressed in relation to 1 (21:1)" [26]. Also, writing text on a picture often results in low contrasts, especially, when the font color is black and the picture itself has dark colors in it.

In the second video the decision - making process, which step needs to be done next is presented with a green and red differentiation, these colors may pose problems for people who have a Red-green deficiency, even though "yes" and "no" are indicated as words.

In the Degree videos little to no influence can be exerted on the color scheme, because real life situations are filmed. Only the captions are presented on a black box to maximize the contrasts. But in one video, the teachers, who are in focus of the video, wear clothes in different colors (yellow, pink and grey). In the audio description these colors are used to differentiate the persons.

Due to the nature of the videos, the sound quality of the Degree videos is not as good as the miTAS videos. In the miTAS videos, the audio track is recorded by a narrator in a quiet environment. Thus, there is nearly no background noise. Two of the three analyzed Degree videos record "real life" situations, in the Computer Sciences video the audio track is deleted. The video from the German studies records a classroom situation, therefor one can hear students talk and move around. Not all students face the camera, thus what is said is not always easy to understand. The video from Mathematics does not have background noise, nevertheless the student speaks quieter than the teacher, making it harder to understand him.

One major difference between the miTAS and Degree videos are the provision of accessibility services. In both cases captions are provided, in the Degree videos these are verbatim captions, when possible, the editing is done at a minimum, including para- and extralinguistic elements in brackets. The proximity of the subtitles to the original sound differs between the different videos. We cannot say anything about the video from the Computer Sciences, because the original sound was removed, due to privacy reasons, in the captions of the video from the mathematics para- and extralinguistic elements are not as focused as in the video from German studies. The change of speaker is indicated with a color change (white and yellow).

The miTAS videos do not provide 'classic' captions. Instead, some of the spoken text is integrated in the image, as key points in the image or as text at the bottom of the image. These "captions" are edited and at some point, used as additional source of information, for example:

- Spoken text: "Put in another fuse"
- 'Captions': "Work steps are read out"

While the miTAS do not have an audio description, the audio descriptions of the Degree videos differ greatly (Table 1):

Table 1. Comparison audio description

Mathematics	Computer Sciences	German Studies
'Classic' audio description: description text is inserted in the gaps in the original sound • If possible, everything is described as a process, rather than end-product-oriented: "The student draws a circle and draws, three lines across – creating six squares. Then he crosses the circle out…	Written transcript • The written transcript includes the "spoken" words and the audio description • The program code shown in the video is provided as an extra text document, separately • Focus lies on changes the students make in the program code	Extended audio description: • If possible, the audio description is inserted in the gaps in the original sound • Before the video starts, the to be shown situation (classroom with teachers, blackboard) is described • Gaps are inserted or lengthened (black screen) to provide a longer audio description • Teachers are differentiated using the different colors of their clothes • Students are not differentiated

The audio description of the video from Mathematics and German Studies are spoken by a synthetic voice.

To be conform on the level AAA with the WCAG the provision of sign language for prerecorded audio content is necessary [41]. Also, the German Association of the Deaf points out, that captions are not always sufficient, because sign language differs from spoken language [15]. This should also be considered for educational videos. Nevertheless, none of the analyzed videos are translated into the sign language.

Operable
"User interface components and navigation must be operable" [41].

In light of accessibility, the operability of the video player is essential, which includes the size of the buttons as well as the operation via keyboard.

Because the learning platform for the Degree project is still under development, this category cannot be analyzed yet. But, in the development process the accessibility of the learning platform, including keyboard operations are specifically focused [43].

The miTAS videos are integrated into the 'miTAS media-Box'. The control system of the video player includes play and pause, volume, settings (resolution) and full screen, all control buttons can be operated via the keyboard. Thus, the video player meets the accessible criteria to be operable via the keyboard and it is possible to access the video without a mouse and most likely with alternative input devices.

Understandable
"Information and the operation of user interface must be understandable" [41].

Both miTAS videos are relatively easy to understand, icons and examples help the viewers to understand the content. Additionally, the used language resembles easy language and the content is often presented in bullet points. A visual focus tool (a with color supplemented mouse or a color frame around the picture, which is currently talked about), helps to focus and understand the content of the video. Another tool to support comprehension are demonstrations of given tasks or decisions which need to be made. Especially in the tutorial on how to create a task, it might have been even easier to understand the content, if the same example were used, instead of using different situations (baking, cleaning hands, setting a table).

To support understanding for the target group people with intellectual disabilities, elements such as pictures, symbols or short real live video sequences are used in the miTAS videos.

Additionally, the language is rather easy, there is not too much-written text (mostly bullet points), the primary channel to provide information is auditory with illustrations (Symbols, Personas), when setting a focus on a particular button this is done via speech as well as highlights in color.

However, while in the miTAS videos different approaches were used to reduce the complexity of the video and support understanding, the Degree videos show complex real-life situations, and no approaches were used to support understanding. Because no editing was done, these videos can be used with different focuses for an analysis. Only the given task for the students may support them to set a focus. Overall, in all three videos rather complex situations are shown, allowing student teachers to gain an insight into real-live classroom situations. Except for the video from the Computer Sciences, here two screens are combined in one video: a screencast of students in school and hands and keyboard of the students. A certain kind of prior knowledge is crucial to understand this video.

Also, the audio track is not as easy to understand as in the miTAS videos, once again due to the classroom situation (German Studies and Mathematics) and deleted audio track (Computer Sciences). There is no support integrated in the videos to help student teachers to focus on the "essential" elements of the task.

Robust
"Content must be robust enough that it can be interpreted by a wide variety of user agents, including assistive technologies" [41].

Regarding the usage of the videos with assistive technology (AT) the same as in the section 'Operable' must be said about the Degree videos. It is planned, that the video player can be used with AT, but a final evaluation is still pending.

The miTAS video player can be accessed via screen-reader and because of its usability via keyboard, it can be assumed, that it is possible to use the video player with different kind of control systems.

Although it seems in this analysis as if the video player is only important for accessibility in the principles 'Robust' and 'Operable', it is to be emphasized that the WCAG [41] with its four principles 'Perceivable', 'Operable', 'Understandable' and 'Robust' and the respective criteria and conformation levels should be the basis for the video player itself as well as the technical environment. This is especially important when developing new tools and/or learning platforms [43].

5   Discussion

This analysis clearly shows, that it is not sufficient to talk about the accessible video, as if the design criteria for such videos are clearly defined. Even though, there are standards and guidelines for accessible videos, the analysis of five different videos in our study implicates, that the design can look completely different. In order to design accessible videos, it is necessary to know the aim of the video. If videos have an intended target group, the needs of this group are mostly more focused than other needs.

An analysis tool to classify the videos regarding their target group, learning contents, and -the goal is the Training Compass [39]. The Training Compass is an instrument that considers the differences in learning contents, target groups, and learner's impact. It is structured based on the 'chain of effects' cascade [39]. Overall, the Training Compass includes six dimensions of learning effects on the learner (Fig. 5).

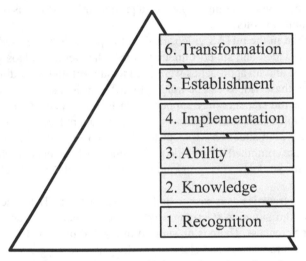

Fig. 5. Cascades of the training compass (own figure)

The (learning) impact of didactic materials and methods on the learner can be rated from very low (first cascade: recognition) to highest (last cascade: transformation). Most of the didactic materials serve for the recognition of a specific topic, for the acquisition of knowledge, or deepening knowledge (e.g. lectures, school lessons, learning videos). With this respect, lots of materials and didactic methods exist to ensure learning success. PowerPoint presentations, webinars, or providing materials on e-learning platforms are such didactic methods on the first three cascades. Thus, the learning goal of the first three cascades is to acquire knowledge and to enable learning repetitions that stabilize the acquired knowledge. In the last three cascades, the goal is to transfuse acquired knowledge into an individual context (e.g. learning context, business context) and to initiate changes (e.g. adapting procedures, strategies, routines or to strengthen team spirit). Videos can be used as methods or material to reach the specific goals at all cascades [39].

The analysis shows that the accessibility of the videos is realized in accordance with the respective target group of the videos and corresponding tasks. It is worthwhile to use different designs of videos following the intended aim: "What is the video for?". The main purpose of the studied miTAS image video is to provide information about the app and the media box. The video addresses a broad audience. The miTAS image video can be located on the first cascade of the Training Compass (recognition) and intended to make the viewer aware of the miTAS app. The instructional videos can be located on the cascades between knowledge (cascade two) and ability (cascade three). They aim to encourage the viewer to follow the instructions and to learn about the different functions, settings, and opportunities of the app and to gain first positive experiences.

The Degree videos aim to foster reflection as part of the professionalization of teachers. Even though "there is broad agreement that reflection is crucial for teacher education and teaching improvement and change, there is also, at the same time, similarly broad agreement that there is no clarity on what reflection is" [13]. In the Degree project, the student teachers of Computer Sciences have to describe and analyze the pupil's programming process, with the overarching goal that the student teachers reflect on the pupils' learning process [18].

Due to the complexity of reflection, and the different tasks which are used to initiate it, the Degree videos cannot be assigned to one cascade. Instead, all cascades are important and must be addressed by the Degree videos to target the reflection of student teachers.

The analysis of the videos in this study shows that although they are an important instrument as individual methods to gain knowledge and contribute learning success (see Sects. 2.1 and 2.2), they should also be embedded into an overreaching didactic concept that considers the various degrees of effectiveness and learning success for the learner. Whether this concept is a media box (in case of the miTAS project), an e-learning platform or any other concept is to be considered individually according to the needs of the target group or audience.

However, this study shows that the design of accessible videos can vary widely and that at some point decisions must be made, which needs have to be targeted primarily and which ones are not as important at the moment. This is concurrent with the "paradox of accessibility": different target groups have different accessibility needs. One thing, such as curbs can be a barrier for a person with a wheelchair, at the same time they serve as orientation for people with visual impairments [23].

This is also true for videos, while captions are necessary for people with hearing impairment, they may pose a barrier for people with autism [32] or providing two videos, one with audio description and one without may pose new challenges for people with intellectual disabilities.

6   Conclusion

Videos represent a good method to convey knowledge, to deepen or to give practical insights into different contexts. In this paper, we analyzed videos from different educational contexts in regard to their accessibility and it became clear, that the design of videos, which are supposed to be accessible, can look completely different. Aspects such as the respective target group, aim of the video and technical elements influence the implementation of accessibility in videos.

To ensure accessibility, we propose four steps before creating videos and implement accessibility (see Fig. 6).

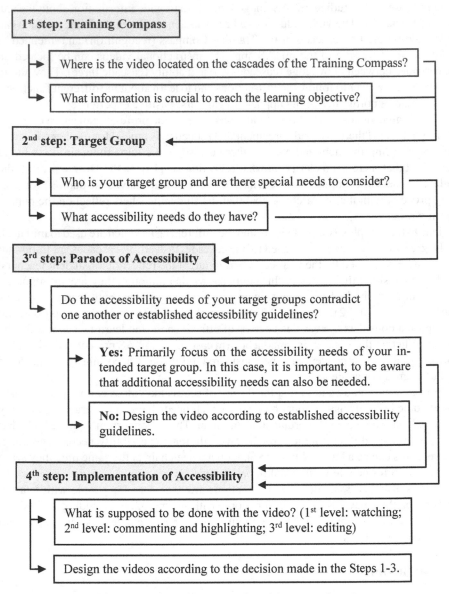

Fig. 6. Four steps before creating videos (own figure)

While there are guidelines on how to design videos accessible, videos in educational contexts may pose different challenges. Instead of primarily entertainment, educational videos are used with a specific objective. The analysis showed that videos for nearly the same target group, but with different content (Degree videos) can also differ in their accessibility. And videos from other educational contexts and with a different target group look completely different and consider different accessibility aspects.

However, considering didactical instruments such as the Training Compass [39], the guidelines and respective conformation levels of the WCAG [41] for every tool and player in use and the accessibility needs of target groups are essential to design videos for their intended use.

Technological development may also support the implementation of accessible videos in the future. By now, captions can be created automatically, translation software, such as DeepL using artificial intelligence are getting more and more advanced and also technology recognizing pictures already exists (Seeing AI by Microsoft). It seems possible, that these technologies can be used for creating accessible videos soon. Nevertheless, one cannot solemnly focus on the content, the technical environment (video player, website, etc.) plays an important role in the accessible usage of videos. To design such an environment the WCAG [41] should always be kept in mind.

Acknowledgements. The project on which this report is based was funded by the BMBF Bundesministerium für Bildung und Forschung [Federal Ministry of Education and Research] under the funding code 16DHB2130. The responsibility for the content of this publication lies with the authors.

The project on which this report is based was funded by the BMBF Bundesministerium für Bildung und Forschung [Federal Ministry of Education and Research] under the funding code FKZ 01PE18014B. The responsibility for the content of this publication lies with the authors.

References

1. AEM (n.d.): What Makes for High Quality Accessibile Videos? http://aem.cast.org/naviga ting/using-high-quality-accessible-video-for-teaching-and-learning.html
2. Alfredsson Ågren, K., Kjellberg, A., Hemmingson, H.: Digital participation? Internet use among adolescents with and without intellectual disabilities: a comparative study. New Media Soc. 1–18 (2019). https://doi.org/10.1177/1461444819888398
3. Alzrayer, N., Banda, D.R., Koul, R.K.: Use of iPad/iPods with individuals with autism and other developmental disabilities: a meta-analysis of communication interventions. Rev. J. Autism Dev. Disord. 1(3), 179–191 (2014). https://doi.org/10.1007/s40489-014-0018-5
4. Anders, P., Staiger, M., Albrecht, C., et al.: Einführung in die Filmdidaktik. J.B. Metzler, Stuttgart (2019)
5. Andreassen, M., Hemmingsson, H., Boman, I.-L., et al.: Feasibility of an intervention for patients with cognitive impairment using an interactive digital calendar with mobile phone reminders (RemindMe) to improve the performance of activities in everyday life. Int. J. Environ. Res. Publ. Health 17, 1–14 (2020). https://doi.org/10.3390/ijerph17072222
6. Ayres, K.M., Mechling, L., Sansosti, F.J.: The use of mobile technologies to assist with life skills/independece of students with moderate/severe intellectual disability and/or autism spectrum disorders: considerations for the future of school psychology. Psychol. Sch. 50, 259–271 (2013). https://doi.org/10.1002/pits.21673
7. Bassette, L.A., Taber-Doughty, T., Gama, R.I., et al.: The use of cell phones to address safety skills for students with a moderate ID in community-based settings. Focus Autism Other Dev. Disabil. 33, 100–110 (2018)

8. Bayor, A.A.: HowToApp: supporting life skills development of young adults with intellectual disability. In: Association for Computing Machinery (ed.) ASSETS 2019: The 21st International ACM SIGACCESS Conference on Computers and Accessibility, Pittsburgh, PA, USA, October 2019, pp. 697–699. Association for Computing Machinery, New York (2019)

9. Bosse, I.K., Pola, A.: Applying movie and multimedia to the inclusive learning and teaching in Germany: problems and solutions. In: Antona, M., Stephanidis, C. (eds.) UAHCI 2017. LNCS, vol. 10279, pp. 129–142. Springer, Cham (2017). https://doi.org/10.1007/978-3-319-58700-4_12

10. Burgstahler, S., Havel, A., Seale, J., Olenik-Shemesh, D.: Accessibility frameworks and models: exploring the potential for a paradigm shift. In: Seale, J. (ed.) Improving Accessible Digital Practices in Higher Education, pp. 45–72. Springer, Cham (2020). https://doi.org/10.1007/978-3-030-37125-8_3

11. Cannella-Malone, H.I., Brooks, D.G., Tullis, C.A.: Using self-directed video prompting to teach students with intellectual disabilities. J. Behav. Educ. **22**, 169–189 (2013). https://doi.org/10.1007/s10864-013-9175-3

12. Chiner, E., Gómez-Puerta, M., Cardona-Moltó, M.C.: Internet use, risks and online behaviour: the view of internet users with intellectual disabilities and their caregivers. Br. J. Learn. Disabil. **45**, 190–197 (2017). https://doi.org/10.1111/bld.12192

13. Clarà, M.: What is reflection? Looking for clarity in an ambiguous notion. J. Teach. Educ. **66**, 261–271 (2015). https://doi.org/10.1177/0022487114552028

14. Cullen, J.M., Alber-Morgan, S.R., Simmons-Reed, E.A., et al.: Effects of self-directed video prompting using iPads on the vocational task completion of young adults with intellectual and developmental disabilities. J. Vocat. Rehabil. **46**, 361–375 (2020). https://doi.org/10.3233/JVR-170873

15. Deutscher Gehörlosen-Bund e.V.: Stellungnahme zum überarbeiteten Entwurf für einen Medienstastsvertrag (2019). http://www.gehoerlosen-bund.de/sachthemen/barrierefreie%20medien

16. Dinmore, S.: Beyond lecture capture: creating digital video content for online learning – a case study. J. Univ. Teach. Learn. Pract. **16** (2019)

17. Emmerdinger, K., Gegenfurtner, A., Stern, W.: Barreirearmut an der Uni. Inklusion sehbeeinträchtigter Studierender durch die Implementierung assistiver Technologien und Universal Design in Lern-Managment-Systemen. spuren - Sonderpädagogik in Bayern **61**, 40–43 (2018)

18. Fischer, J., Romahn, N., Weinert, M.: Fostering reflexion in CS teacher education. A video-based approach to unveiling, analysing and teaching novices' programming processes. In: Kori, K., Laanpere, M. (eds.) ISSEP 2020, International Conference on Informatics in School: Situation, Evaluation and Perspectives 2020, pp. 128–139. CEUR Workshop Proceedings (2020)

19. Frommelt, M., Auf, F., der Maur, G., Biaggi, S., et al.: Videos in der Ausbildung von Lehrkräften: Förderung der professionellen Unterrichtswahrnehmung durch die Analyse von eigenen bzw. fremden Videos. Unterrichtswissenschaften **44**, 357–372 (2016)

20. Goo, M., Therroen, W., Hua, Y.: Effects of computer-based video instruction on the acquisition and generalization of grocery purchasing skills for students with intellectual disability. Educ. Train. Autism Dev. Disabil. **51**, 150–161 (2016)

21. Hastall, M.R., Heitplatz, V.N.: Soziotechnische Systemgestaltung für Therapie und Pflege. In: Posenau, A., Deiters, W., Sommer, S. (eds.) Nutzerorientierte Gesundheitstechnologien. Im Kontext von Therapie und Pflege, pp. 101–112. Hogrefe, Göttingen (2019)

22. Heitplatz, V.N., Nellen, C., Sube, L.C., et al.: Implementing new technological devices in social services: introducing the miTAS project. In: Miesenberger, K., Petz, A. (eds.) Future Perspectives of AT, eAccessibility and eInclusion, pp. 109–118. Open Access Compendium (2020)

23. Kastl, J.M.: Die Soziologie und das soziale Modell der Behinderung. In: Kastl, J.M. (ed.) Einführung in die Soziologie der Behinderung, pp. 35–55. Springer, Wiesbaden (2017). https:// doi.org/10.1007/978-3-658-04053-6_2

24. Krüger, M., Steffen, R., Vohle, F.: Videos in der Lehre durch Annotationen reflektieren und aktiv diskutieren. In: Csanyi, G.S., Reichl, F., Steiner, A. (eds.) Digitale Medien - Werkzeuge für exzellente Forschung und Lehre. Tagungsband; GMW 2012, pp. 198–210. Waxmann, Münster (2012)

25. Lancioni, G.E., et al.: Non-ambulatory people with intellectual disabilities practice functional arm, leg or head responses via a smartphone-based program. J. Dev. Phys. Disabil. **31**(2), 251–265 (2018). https://doi.org/10.1007/s10882-018-9636-7

26. leserlich.info (o.J.): Contrast calculator. Calculating and testing easily accessible colour combinations. https://www.leserlich.info/werkzeuge/kontrastrechner/index-en.php

27. Materna, D., Söffgen, Y., Wuttke, L.: Einsatz digitaler Medein für Menschen mit Lernschwierigkeiten in hauswirtschaftlichen Ausbildungsberufen. Ansätze und Ziele im Projekt LernBAR. Berufsbildung in Wissenschaft und Praxis (BWP) **48**, 53–54 (2019)

28. miTAS: miTAS – ein "multimediales individuelles Trainings- und Arbeitsassistenz-System" (2020). https://mitas-app.de/. Accessed 23 Apr 2020

29. Möller, K., Sunder, C., Todorova, M.: Förderung der professionellen Wahrnehmung bei Bachelorstudierenden durch Fallanalysen. Lohnt sich der Einsatz von Videos bei der Repräsentation der Fälle? Unterrichtswissenschaften **44**, 339–356 (2016)

30. Netzwerk Digitale Bildung: Wegweiser Digitale Bildung. Für zeitgemäßen Unterricht mit digitalen Werkzeugen (2020). https://www.netzwerk-digitale-bildung.de/wegweiser-digitale-bildung-3-0/

31. Neugebauer, R. (ed.): Digitalisierung. Springer, Heidelberg (2018). https://doi.org/10.1007/978-3-662-55890-4

32. Neumann, M.: Neumodische Videos und Barrierefreiheit bei Autismus (2017). https://dasfotobus.wordpress.com/2017/07/13/neumodische-videos-und-barrierefreiheit-bei-autismus/

33. Norddeutscher Rundfunk: Vorgaben für AUdiodeskription (2019). https://www.ndr.de/fernsehen/service/audiodeskription/Vorgaben-fuer-Audiodeskriptionen%2caudiodeskription140.html

34. Ofcom: Ofcom's Code on Television Access Services (2019). https://www.ofcom.org.uk/__data/assets/pdf_file/0035/179954/tv-access-services-code.pdf

35. Payne, D., Cannella-Malone, H.I., Tullis, C.A., et al.: The effects of self-directed video prompting with two students with intellectual and developmental disabilities. J. Dev. Phys. Disabil. **24**, 617–634 (2012). https://doi.org/10.1007/s10882-012-9293-1

36. Pelka, B.: Digitalisierung als soziale Innovation verstehen und umsetzen. In: Ückert, S., Sürgit, H., Diesel, G. (eds.) Digitalisierung als Erfolgsfaktor für das Sozial- und Wohlfahrtswesen, pp. 263–278. Nomos Verlagsgesellschaft mbH & Co, KG (2020)

37. Puhl, S., Lerche, S.: Barrierefreie Videos in der Hochschullehre. Eine Initiative von BIK für Alle und der Justus-Liebig-Universität Gießen. In: Tolle, P., Plümmer, A., Horbach, A. (eds.) Hochschule als interdisziplinäres barrierefreies System, p. 84. Kassel University Press c/o Universität Kassel - Universitätsbibliothek, Kassel (2019)

38. Scheidig, F.: Unterrichtsvideos. Neue Szenarien digitaler Praxisbezüge. journal für lehrerInnenbildung **20**, 28–41 (2020). https://doi.org/10.35468/jlb-01-2020_02

39. Steinmayr, S., Immecke, J., Rosomm, D.: Der Didaktik-Architekt. Wirksame Lernformate bauen, ohne Didaktik-Profi zu sein. wirmachendruck.de, Backnang (2020)

40. Thompson, T.: Video for all: accessibility of video content and universal design of a media player. In: Burgstahler, S.E. (ed.) Universal Design in Higher Education: From Principles to Practice, 2nd edn., pp. 259–273. Harvard Education Press, Cambridge (2015)

41. W3C: Web Content Accessibility Guidelines (WCAG) 2.1. W3C Recommendation 05 June 2018 (2018). https://www.w3.org/TR/WCAG21/#background-on-wcag-2. Accessed 21 Jan 2021
42. Wehrfritz (o.J.): Stationenarbeit—Methoden—Inklusion. http://www.inklusion-schule.info/methoden/stationenarbeit.html. Accessed 22 Jun 2020
43. Wilkens, L., Bühler, C., Bosse, I.: Accessible learning management systems in higher education. In: Antona, M., Stephanidis, C. (eds.) HCII 2020. LNCS, vol. 12189, pp. 315–328. Springer, Cham (2020). https://doi.org/10.1007/978-3-030-49108-6_23
44. Yucesoy-Ozkan, S., Gulboy, E., Kaya, F.: Teaching children with intellectual disabilities through video prompting: smartphone vs. tablet. Int. J. Early Childh. Spec. Educ. **10**, 33–49 (2018). https://doi.org/10.20489/intjecse.454433
45. Zahn, C., et al.: Video clips for YouTube: collaborative video creation as an educational concept for knowledge acquisition and attitude change related to obesity stigmatization. Educ. Inf. Technol. **19**(3), 603–621 (2013). https://doi.org/10.1007/s10639-013-9277-5

Universal Access in Virtual and Intelligent Assistive Environments

Criteria for the Adoption of a Support Information System for People's Mobility

Laura Burzagli[✉] and Pier Luigi Emiliani

CNR IFAC, Via Madonna del Piano 10, Sesto F.no (Firenze), Italy
l.burzagli@ifac.cnr.it

Abstract. In order to promote people's well-being, the configuration of intelligent environments (AmI environments) is possible due to the current development of communication and information technologies. In AmI environments it is possible to implement information systems able to support each person in performing activities necessary for living comfortably. In the paper information systems for supporting people in planning where to move and how to reach the chosen place are considered. First the meaning of the concepts as access to services in the environment (accessibility) and planning the movement to the place of interest (mobility) are considered, taking also into account the problem of possible barriers (physical accessibility). Then, existing applications for navigation are considered, pointing out the limitations from the perspective of the lack of adaptability to single users. Finally, the need of new support information systems is briefly discussed, from the perspectives of why they are needed, how they may be used, and how they can be implemented.

Keywords: Accessibility · Mobility · Support services

1 Introduction

In AmI environments intelligent objects may be interconnected among themselves and with the network exchanging data for the implementation of information systems able to support each person in performing activities necessary for living comfortably.

The availability of information systems able to support people in their daily activities, based on a careful study of the characteristics of the person and of the activities that she carries out in the everyday life, is particularly important. For example, with reference to nutrition [1], they may offer the remote control of household appliances, the management of the pantry in relation to quantities and expiration dates of contained items, the support in choosing recipes and help in cooking, and, if necessary, the remote control for the health care perspective.

Among the supports to the human activities necessary for living independently and comfortably, people need to know where they can have access to required services (accessibility) and how they can move from their present position to the place where the service providers are located (mobility).

© Springer Nature Switzerland AG 2021
M. Antona and C. Stephanidis (Eds.): HCII 2021, LNCS 12769, pp. 347–357, 2021.
https://doi.org/10.1007/978-3-030-78095-1_25

In the paper, after the summary of available definitions of accessibility and mobility in an urban environment in connection with the WHO standards, a short summary is made of available navigation applications, pointing out limitations in offering personalized information about important aspects of accessibility and mobility. Finally, why new support information systems are necessary and how they can be implemented and used is discussed.

2 Accessibility Versus Mobility

In planning living spaces (urban planning) a distinction is made between accessibility and mobility [2]. Accessibility is defined as "the potential for interaction" i.e. the potential of the environment to provide services[1] to people, while mobility is defined as "the potential for movement", i.e. the potential of people to move to the places where the services are available. Then, from the mobility perspective is also necessary that the physical accessibility is guaranteed, i.e. that physical obstacles (e.g. stairs) are not present.

2.1 Accessibility

In the implementation of AmI systems to support the activities of people based on ICT technologies, it is particularly important to consider the above definition of accessibility as a motivation to mobility, leading to the need of movement (e.g. walking or using transportation). This implies the need of identifying the knowledge necessary to evaluate the individual possibility of reaching the service of interest and using it. Then, it is necessary to develop methodologies for the identification of parameters which can quantify the level of accessibility of a place and the possibility of moving to it. In this sense and with respect to walking, there are already applications, such as Walk Scores [3], that assign a pedestrian accessibility value to an area. On this basis, some other commercial applications are also built, which demonstrate the value of the produced value.

Specific definitions of single aspects of accessibility in the context of urban planning are many, and also measured with different metrics [4], but the concept that emerges clearly is the potential offered by information about services in the environment to promote people's quality of life, a concept that goes beyond the absence of architectural barriers. In this sense, for example, a path richer of shops or other services (e.g. a post office or a bank) offers higher accessibility for people. This concept is not only important for the population as a whole, but it can have a fundamental impact in the specific situation of particular groups of people, such as elderly people. The increase in age generally corresponds to an increase in the difficulty of identification of useful services and of movement, for example the ability to access both public and private transport. With reference to transportation, they may have greater difficulty in driving cars, but also in the use of public transport (e.g. due to possible crowding, or to the management of timetables, or to the ability to find information on available routes).

---

[1] In the discussion about accessibility, service is any location as a bank, a post-office, a shop and so on useful for carrying out activities of interest.

Therefore, this concept of accessibility as a basis for the design of ICT systems to support people in moving around to access services is fundamental. It is also clear that the level of accessibility information necessary for a person goes beyond a precise representation of the obstacles present on the path, such as the presence of holes in the pavement or the absence of sidewalks. There are other aspects that can be considered, if one wants to address the need of improving the quality of life of people. For example, it may be convenient not to follow the shortest route, if the information system knows that the user does not like to walk in a specific street.

In the accessibility of information in electronic format, e.g. using Internet, guidelines have been identified and standardized, which in principle allow the accessibility to information to all people [5]. This should also be the case in accessibility and mobility, because the level of accessibility of the outdoor environment can give a measure of the possibility of a comfortable life of people in the built environment.

2.2 Mobility

Providing information and/or advice to move in the environment for access to necessary services is obviously very important for all people and particularly for groups as elderly people. However, the mobility needs of people to be considered for the identification of the features of information systems to support them require a deeper analysis.

Let us start from the general concept of mobility, which is undoubtedly identified as one of the fundamental activities of a person's life. To this purpose, reference is made to an international classification of the structures, functions and activities of the person, i.e. to the International Classification of Functioning and Disabilities (WHO-ICF) [6].

The ICF classification refers to the term mobility at two levels:

- the level of neuro-musculoskeletal functions, defined as *"functions of body movement, which include functions of joints, bones, reflexes and muscles"* (Chapter 7 of the Section relating to Body Functions)
- the level of the change in the basic positions of the body, in the position of objects, and in the real activity of walking and movement (Chapter 4 of the Section on Activities and Participations). This also involves walking on different surfaces and walking in the presence of obstacles.

Therefore, the structuring defined by the ICF shows the need for the support of people in limitations of abilities in body functions, as well as in mobility in the environments. Moving around requires information systems to support the person with data about her specific accessibility needs, routes to reach the corresponding services, and suggestions, when necessary, of specific assistive technology that identifies tools to overcome difficulties in the movement functions of the body (see Fig. 1).

Then, the ICF classification also devotes a chapter to mobility (see Figs. 2 and 3). The two levels (movement and mobility) are not disjointed, but the models of used support information systems are different. Movement can be characterized as a type of activity rather than as a function. There are also listed different types of mobility, such as crawling, running, climbing, and jumping. The function can then be considered with reference to the places to reach and, eventually, to the means of transport.

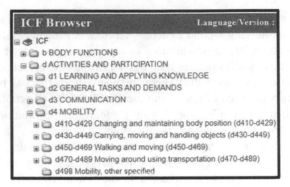

Fig. 1. ICF body functions [7]

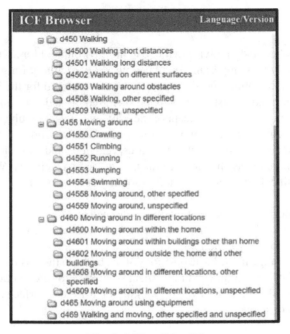

Fig. 2. ICF walking [7]

In order to build an information system for support to mobility, all the above reported activities and corresponding necessary abilities must be clearly considered in the definition of the requirements for its development. The used media are also of particular importance for the definition of the features of the information system.

Therefore, the design of an information system to support mobility is a complex task, due to extreme dispersion of the levels of activity to be considered. It is on the same level of complexity of all support information systems involving social interaction, as for example those against loneliness. This parallel is extremely useful to move toward a new way of designing support information systems, which must not be start from the

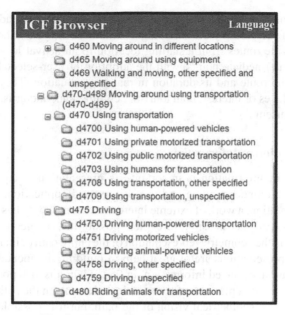

Fig. 3. ICF moving around and driving [7]

person's limitations of activities, but from the activity to be carried out. The main task is to develop support information systems and technologies necessary to make a person able to carry out activity with the available abilities.

3   Existing Navigation Applications

In order to define the state of the art in the accessibility and mobility field, it is extremely useful to look at the available applications (navigation applications), which are undoubtedly so many that one could believe that the field does not need any further contribution. An extensive analysis of existing applications would be beyond the scope of this contribution, but also a partial analysis of them is enough to point out a set of observations useful to discuss the points made above.

3.1   The Purpose of the Navigation Applications

Just to give a few examples, without pretending to be exhaustive, applications such as Wave, Google, OSM and Michelin can be considered [8–11]. These applications (along with many others), seen from the perspective of personal support, provide a considerable amount of information that is useful for moving around and are used daily by a large number of people.

They provide useful information for people's orientation in space. They are based on an extensive and continuously updated information base, with a complex structure. Selection criteria of various types allow the user to access information according to different methodologies, from the simple search for a street starting from its name, to the search for a point of interest, without the exact indication of the address. Through the introduction of increasingly advanced algorithms over the years, these applications can currently provide routes from a starting location to an arrival location, even with the definition of intermediate points, with the adoption of user-selectable filters, such as, the length of the route and its duration in real-time situation. They also allow the identification of places of interest, both touristic, commercial, and artistic (for example shops, hotels or museums).

3.2   The Presentation of Information

If the availability of information is important, its presentation is equally important, because it allows the understanding and use of the used application. At the level of information presentation, a work of extreme interest and complexity has been also made over the years: it is in fact possible to exploit possibilities of geometric or graphic interaction, showing the geometric representation of the entire path or images of the same. These different representations are of great help in building the mental representation necessary to exploit the received information. In fact, when it is also possible to receive an image of the destination place, or of some critical elements in the path, the user is not required to construct a geometrical vision of the path, but it is possible to see directly the real situation.

If we consider road junctions or areas of particular complexity (e.g. residential or industrial or exclusively dedicated to mobility, such as connections of communication arteries), these diversified levels of presentation represent a specific help for the user and simplify his mental process in supporting the personal mobility objective. For example, he can be a tourist in the historic center, or a courier who delivers the goods to an industrial area, who needs different forms of information and presentation. In addition, the difficulty of presentation on different devices can also be overcome by the adoption of rescaling criteria, resulting from the solution of multimodality problems.

To the information listed above, a real time component can be added, with the transition from static to dynamic information, where routes can also be selected on the basis of the occurrence of events, such as traffic jams or temporarily closed roads. Information collection has recently involved the access to social networks, resulting in collective data collection processes, which can be assimilated to a collective intelligence process. This places the user himself in the role of prosumer rather than of simple consumer of the mobility application.

In addition to these general mobility-related applications, there are also systems addressing specific elements, such as the possibility of renting locomotion equipment anywhere in the world. A non-exhaustive search for existing mobility-related applications available in various stores, showed that about 20% of applications are aimed at route management, while the remaining 80% are aimed at rental and car sharing.

3.3   Use of Available Navigation Applications

An observation of considerable interest that can be inferred from the above overview is that these applications are aimed to support mobility in unknown environments. They are based on universal criteria and therefore are usable by a person anywhere in the world or in a wide range of locations. The starting point of the application itself is the ability to provide unknown information about unknown places, according to numerous and extremely varied criteria.

A first conclusion with regard to all these applications is that they offer a useful contribution to the mobility of people in unknown environments in their daily lives and are widely used.

4 Why and How to Implement and Use Additional Information Systems?

Even if the available navigation applications are useful for many purposes, there is space for additional ICT systems aimed to support people in living more comfortably and increasing their wellness, as will be shown in the following. Maybe that some components of these systems are already available, but for many users it is necessary that they are integrated, easily accessible and adapted to the need of any specific user.

The main point to be made is that new support information systems must be designed in order to make available to people personalized information about the availability of services in their surroundings (accessibility - potential for interaction) and how they can move from their present position to the service (mobility - potential for movement), including possible obstacles in the way (physical accessibility).

4.1 Why Is It Necessary?

The main purpose of most available applications for navigation is the collection and management of information for moving around and the knowledge of geographical information, in real time too. The starting point for the implementation is not the person herself, but the amount of information available and collectible and the capability of managing it and filtering it as efficiently and completely as possible. They use techniques very advanced from a technological perspective, which transform them in a kind of a magic wand, whose use allows more and more people to feel no longer like strangers in an unknown environment. People can easily orient themselves through the use of a computer-based system as a smart phone, a tablet or a laptop.

The discussion of the need of additional support information systems for navigation must start not from available data but from people and the definition, collection and suitable presentation of the information really necessary to support them.

For accessibility, as previously defined, people need information about available services in the environments. On the basis of an initial profile of the person (for example she takes care of the house and needs information about shops for buying food or she is mainly involved in social activities and needs communication services), the information system must construct an initial database of sites of possible interest and be able to give information about the availability of them at walking distance, or in places that can be reached with public transportation or using a cycle or a car, if she is able and willing to do it.

The information system must also be able to learn from the use of the person updating the data base, for example adding services not mentioned in the initial profile, or increasing the weight, to be used in the reasoning, of the shop where she likes to buy bread, or adding sites where she has gone and has found them interesting enough to be willing to go there again. In the case of services which are not continuously available (e.g. mobile selling places that are present periodically), it is necessary that the system has information about their schedule.

For mobility, as previously defined, people need information about itineraries to reach services of interest. The itineraries must be adapted to the needs and preferences of the person. For example, the information system must have learned that going to buy vegetables the person normally does not want to use the shortest route but a route where many shop windows to be looked at are available. Therefore, it will offer this route as a first choice, changing to the shorted one if required. The information system should also be available for requests as the following: "*I want to walk for some times, but I need to be back before the bread shop closes*". The information system has learnt where normally the person likes to walk, is able to compute the available time, and knows the closing time of the shop. On this basis it plans an itinerary. However, it is also able to modify it if she asks to pass in front of a specific shop or service provider or if she stops to have a conversation with a friend. It also is able to give an alarm when the time to reach the bread shop risk not to be enough.

Obviously, if the service is not at walking distance, the support information systems must be able to give information about difficulties in going there with the car (if the user is able to use it) or using public transportation (including timetables, information about connections and possible physical barriers).

Finally, for some groups of people, as elderly people or people with ability limitations, information about possible physical obstacles (physical accessibility) is necessary. Moreover, this should be based on a network of people who is willing to update the information also in real time.

4.2 How to Use the Support Information System

A significant example, dealing with elderly people, is offered in order to exemplify the use of a support information system implemented to according to the criteria described above. There is no doubt that, as age increases, the ability to move is gradually decreasing [12], with regard to pedestrian mobility, to the ability of using private transport systems, i.e. driving a car, and to the ability of using public transport, many of which may not be equipped to accommodate degraded health conditions (in relation to the abilities necessary for mobility). Old people may move slower or have difficulty in climbing steps, which reduces movement abilities, or degraded vision and hearing, which reduce the ability to acquire information from the environment and, for example, may lead to a reduction in orientation.

For them, as far as accessibility is concerned, a support system can be characterized by the ability, once the user's profile and therefore part of her habits and needs are known, of optimizing the criteria on which suggestions of availability and localization of the necessary services are produced. For example, for the purchase of medicines, an activity common to many elderly people given the frequent presence of chronic diseases, the support information system is supposed to optimize the choice of pharmacy, depending on the time, the coincidence with the need of accessing other services, such as the purchase of groceries, or the possible meeting with other people, who frequent the area around a specific pharmacy. Accessibility should be measured and possibly optimized in order to increase the user's quality of life, and not only the use of the service.

Considering again elderly people, the optimization of mobility through a support information system may start suggesting the shortest itinerary, advising if it can be covered on foot, or using a public or private transport, according to the characteristics of the person. For example, if the user's profile describes a person dedicated to physical fitness, a choice will be proposed by giving greater priority to the pedestrian path, rather than to one with public transport.

The level of physical accessibility, on the other hand, requires first of all to know movement abilities of the individual and to compare them with barriers in the path, for example holes in the pavement or other obstacles possibly present in a pedestrian path. If the route is supposed to be taken with public transport, the support information system should point out the features of the vehicles that can create difficulties for the user, e.g. the height of the door steps, the height of the available seats, insufficient information for the identification of the position along the route.

4.3   How to Implement the Support Information System

For favoring accessibility and mobility of people with the goal of improving the person's quality of life, it is necessary not only to take care of a careful environmental planning (objective level), but also to offer support information systems able to produce recommendations for the individual user (subjective level), as outlined in Fig. 4. First, this involves, together with static and dynamic environment information, the implementation of a component able to manage the set of user profiles, which contains the initial information necessary to customize the support system for each user, mediating the levels of the person's abilities with her preferences, habits and commitments in daily life. This provides the information base on which the support system can prepare the most appropriate recommendations.

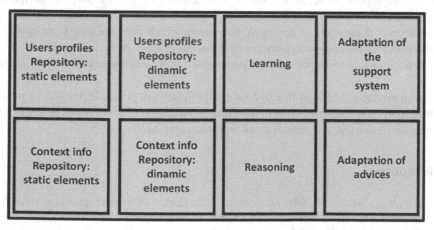

Fig. 4. Basic blocks of the support information system

However, this information, even if detailed, is not sufficient to guarantee a support system capable of supporting a person in her daily activities, because the management of her profile must also be based on a dynamic component, which takes care both the progressive modifications in the general state of the person and in her behavior, also in real-time. Therefore, a second component is necessary in the support system able to modify and/or increase the initial profile information through the acquisition of data extracted from the user's own activities, revealed, for example, through sensors present in the environment or wearable devices. Moreover, the user can also voluntarily provide information, such as the schedule of commitments or comments about recommendations provided in the past. This component requires the use of Artificial Intelligence technologies, capable of learning from the data themselves and inserting the results into the modeling of the suggestions to be provided. Machine learning techniques must therefore be evaluated and integrated for this purpose.

Since the information that generates the suggestion arises from the evaluation of the condition of the person and the environment, a further component is necessary in the information system to reason, for example through optimization algorithms, in order to provide the most appropriate recommendations on the basis of available information.

The last component of the support information system to be introduced and optimized, is the interface with the user. The presentation of the results of reasoning, i.e. the recommendation, will have to consider the device, or more generally the technological support available to the user, so that the information is presented in the most appropriate form. For example, the representation as a map of a path may be unsuitable in the presence of a small monitor and the information may be conveyed in a text version, which can be further supported with an audio component.

5   Conclusions

Accessibility and mobility as previously defined are of fundamental importance to support the well-being of people and for some people, for example elderly people, a personalized support is necessary, which is not offered by general purpose navigation applications.

To support these users an approach is required, which does not start from available information about the environments, but by the needs of the user, taking also into account that the needs are different for different persons and they can change in time, in real time too.

Using available Artificial Intelligence components is in principle possible to implement support information systems that are able to manage profiles of users, to learn from the way they are used, and reason about their changing needs.

References

1. Burzagli, L., Baronti, P., Billi, M., Emiliani, P.L., Gori, F.: Complete specifications of ICT services in an AAL environment. In: Cavallo, F., Marletta, V., Monteriù, A., Siciliano, P. (eds.) ForItAAL 2016. LNEE, vol. 426, pp. 51–60. Springer, Cham (2017). https://doi.org/10.1007/978-3-319-54283-6_4

2. Hansen, W.G.: How accessibility shapes land use. J. Am. Inst. Planners **25**(2), 73–76 (1959)
3. Walk Score Home page. https://www.walkscore.com/. Accessed 31 Jan 2021
4. Vale, D., Saraiva, M., Pereira, M.: Active accessibility: a review of operational measures of walking and cycling accessibility. J. Transp. Land Use **9**(1), 209–235 (2016)
5. W3C Web Accessibility Initiative Home Page. https://www.w3.org/WAI/. Accessed 31 Jan 2021
6. WHO: ICF International Classification of Functioning, Disability and Health. World Health Organization, Geneva (2001)
7. ICF Browse Home Page. https://apps.who.int/classifications/icfbrowser/. Accessed 31 Jan 2021
8. WAVE Home Page. https://www.waze.com/. Accessed 31 Jan 2021
9. GOOGLE MAPS Home Page. https://www.google.com/maps/. Accessed 31 Jan 2021
10. OPEN STREET MAP Home Page. https://www.openstreetmap.org/. Accessed 31 Jan 2021
11. MICHELIN Home Page. https://www.viamichelin.it/. Accessed 31 Jan 2021
12. Fatima, K., Moridpour, S., De Gruyter, C., Saghapour, T.: Elderly sustainable mobility: scientific paper review. Sustainability **12**, 7319 (2020)

Networks to Stop the Epidemic Spreading

Vincenzo Fioriti[1], Marta Chinnici[1(✉)], Andrea Arbore[2], Nicola Sigismondi[2], and Ivan Roselli[1]

[1] ENEA-C.R Casaccia, Via Anguillarese 301, 00123 Rome, Italy
{vincenzo.fioriti,marta.chinnici,ivan.rosselli}@enea.it
[2] ICT-Technical Consultant, Rome, Italy

Abstract. Today, only two methods are viable to immunize people against an epidemic spreading: vaccine and quarantine, but a prolonged quarantine extended to the whole population implies unsustainable costs, while vaccinations take a lot of time. Nevertheless, it would be possible to stop the propagation of viruses and alleviate the economic activities lockdown greatly, vaccinating or quarantining only a small percentage of the population using well-known methodologies to select people to immunize. From a practical point of view, it is necessary to provide the social or relational national network, which will constitute the spectral graph analysis, our primary methodological tool. This requires to generate a graph of many nodes (people) and links (relations, of any kind) mapping the whole population. The connections are extracted from the national register, media, web resources, cellular phones and any other source, possibly after an anonymizing step. The procedure is inherently dynamic since relations and people geo-localization change continuously; therefore, a real-time update must be implemented. Fortunately, internet data collection mechanisms can provide vast information to support the update step. Once the National Relation Network is available, individuals that could propagate more dangerously the infection (which is subtly different from propagating to more people the infection) will be identified quickly and immunized with high priority. A careful selection of these individuals may stop or slow down the spreading, safeguarding at the same time, the economic system. Likewise, the National Relational Network can directly indicate the subjects hit financially by the epidemic without additional computational costs. Moreover, the Graph theory usage will allow applying its numerous, impressive achievements to the epidemic containment. We warn that no real experiment has been conducted on a large scale, so no evidence is available; however theoretical demonstrations and computer simulations are encouraging. Finally, we do not intend to present a formal treatment of the issue or foster academic discussions; instead, we propose a practical approach to the epidemic spreading problem.

Keywords: Complex network · Graph theory · Big data · Epidemic spreading · Infective diseases

1 Introduction

During an outbreak, a significant issue to stop or mitigate the virus diffusion is identifying people to be immunised utilising vaccine with priority, since providing vaccines to

M. Antona and C. Stephanidis (Eds.): HCII 2021, LNCS 12769, pp. 358–366, 2021.
https://doi.org/10.1007/978-3-030-78095-1_26

millions within a short time-lapse may result difficult. It is also desirable to minimise the number of people to be quarantined to safeguard the economic system at the same time. Therefore, it is mandatory to resort to optimisation, meaning we should select the persons properly to vaccinate or quarantine, according to a mathematical procedure. The task is not trivial, because to identify them, a variety of counter-intuitive approaches are needed. Hence, several methodologies have been developed in the past years to solve the problem. Graph Theory (GT) is emerging as one of the most promising because of its unique synthesis and description [1, 2]. It is quite natural to represent an epidemic spreading using a graph: the node-link-node structure mirrors the interaction between two or more people simply and clearly, and nevertheless, allowing powerful elaborations. When the graph is derived from technological processes or natural phenomena it is called a network. For a long time, GT has been considered a theoretical field of mathematics. Still, today supercomputing makes it possible to elaborate massive quantity of data. GT has become the key to investigating vast complex networks, such as the entire nation's social network.

Here we want to answer the following questions: is it conceivable to stop the propagation across a vast social network neutralising only a small percentage of the population? How do we select people to immunise?

However, to answer these issues, no real experiment has been conducted on a large scale, so no decisive evidence is available, but theoretical demonstrations and computer simulations are encouraging.

This paper emphasises that the primary mathematical framework we utilise is the graph spectral eigenvalue analysis because of the remarkable results it can provide, but other techniques may give similar advantages. Moreover, we clarify our aim was not to provide complete or formal discussions, as the time for academic discussions lacks. The paper is organised as follows: Sect. 1 – Introduction; Sect. 2 – Background: National Relational Network (NRN); Sect. 3 – Methodology; Sect. 4 – Analysis and Results; Sect. 5 – Conclusions and Future Works.

2 Background: National Relational Network (NRN)

This section presents our proposal's essential points; we discuss the necessary tool, the network formed by citizens relations: the National Relational Network (NRN). Links (also called edges) are due to relation of different nature: physical and familiar mainly, but also the proximity, or even an email correspondence: the more, the better. Edges may last a few minutes or maybe created at any moment. For Italy, about 65 million nodes-inhabitants and their links must be considered, updated and elaborated in real-time to develop such a National Relational Network. Thus, an ad hoc structure should be planned, with supercomputing facilities full access to any web resources, social nets, media, and cellular phones.

When the network's resolution is too large it is possible to consider clusters of single nodes. Clusters may be represented by assisted living facilities, convents, barracks, ports, airports, stations, and scalable resolution (districts, towns, cities, regions, nations etc.). At this point, one could ask if it is feasible to detect automatically a specific, possibly small, cluster of individuals sharing common attributes. It is still an open issue, although efforts in this direction have been made [3–5], paving the way to a solution. A possible application of this kind of searching algorithms would be to recognise clusters with poor a priori knowledge, for example, a cluster of symptomless infected persons whose topology is somehow known, at least to a certain extent [6–9].

We are dealing obviously with a complex and many-sided issue, requiring a relatively high financial effort, not to mention the technological and legislative difficulties. An anonymisation step would be necessary, though it is compromising privacy in any case. On the other hand, essential advantages in crisis management may be gained, as illustrated in the following Paragraphs.

2.1 The Epidemic Threshold

Many scientists believe that the diffusion of a virus on a graph has a threshold. The threshold depends on two parameters, the infection rate β (average value) and the cure rate δ (average value). Above the threshold, the virus will propagate through the network; otherwise, it will expire more or less rapidly. Some threshold results are from scale-free graphs [10–12], while the most general is from Wang [13] for generic graphs. Generic means no assumption is made on the graph (scale-free, random, small-word, degree distribution). The main result of Wang is as follows:

$$\delta/\beta > \lambda_{max}(A_{NRN}) \tag{1}$$

where λ_{max} is the maximum eigenvalue of the graph adjacency matrix, in our case, ANRN. Now, according to Wang, if the (1) holds, the spread reduces.

Note that λ_{max} depends on the structure of the graph, therefore adding or deleting some links we can change easily the value of λ_{max}. We assume the ratio on the left side of (1) is fixed, since usually is not feasible to modify δ or β. Clearly, in this case, to promote the slowing down of the spreading, we must reduce λ_{max} which depends only on the graph topology.

However, we find here a trade-off between safety, represented by a small λ_{max}, and a good network connectivity expressed by a large λ_{max}. A network with large maximum eigenvalue means that every part of the network is well connected with the rest of the net throughout many connections (i.e. the economic system is safe, see [14]); on the other end, many connections mean the virus has many ways to propagate.

For example, the graph in Fig. 1 is badly connected, since the node 17 is the only link between the two clusters; on the other hand, each cluster is very well connected per se, as each node is linked to everyone else. For example, if the node 2 is infected, removing node 17 implies the infection cannot propagate from the cluster containing node 2 to the other cluster, but it can only spread inside the same cluster. Simultaneously, the two clusters without node 17 could be isolated; therefore, they can no longer work together, possibly causing an economic damage.

2.2 Critical Nodes

Some node-individuals are particularly important to facilitate or prevent the diffusion. Sometimes the reason is evident, but often no apparent motivation is clear. For example, a man with a very active social life that meets many other people is prone to infect a large number of people; on the network, such an individual is called a "hub", a node with many links (the node "degree") to other persons. This seems direct and intuitive, as Fig. 1: node 17 has only two links, all others nodes seven links, but node 17 is a bridge between two clusters, therefore if we could immunize or remove only one node (or one link), a right choice would be to immunize node 17 (or one of its links) [12]. Since we have just a few nodes, there is no need for calculations. Unfortunately, the real world is more complicated.

When a graph contains millions of nodes, visualizing them is almost impossible (see Fig. 2). Thus automatic elaborations are mandatory, provided powerful calculation resources are made available. Even so, classifying nodes is not easy. Many algorithms have been devised to this end, always trying to reduce their mathematical complexity that limits the computational capabilities. Finding the most "influential" or critical nodes (individuals) is still today one of the central issues of research studies in this field. Anyway, significant results have been achieved and are ready for the implementation.

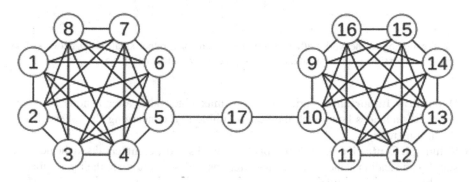

Fig. 1. A bridge (node 17) links two completely connected clusters ("cliques" in the jargon).

3 Methodology: Identifying the Most Critical Nodes

Various algorithms called centrality measures are available to classify the importance of nodes. We list just a few of them. Some of these methods are very simple; nevertheless, it may be cost-effective. We believe the spectral algorithms are by far the best ones, see [15]. Using one or more of the above methods, all nodes are ranked from the most dangerous to be immunized as soon as possible, to the less influential:

- **Degree:** merely the number of links from/to a node. Intuitively a high degree node, e.g. a "hub", maybe more influential.
- **Closeness:** the sum of the shortest geodesic path lengths between a given node and all other nodes in the graph. If a node is located at the periphery of the network, the closeness is small.
- **Betweenness:** total number of shortest paths between every possible pair of nodes that pass through the given node.

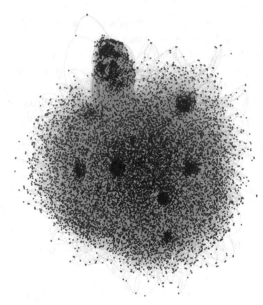

Fig. 2. Technological network with 16000 nodes. Even for a rather small-sized network, it is practically impossible to understand the graph's structure with the naked eye.

- **Dynamical Importance:** variation of the max eigenvalue after a node has been removed. Indicates how much the node is influential concerning the others. It is a spectral method.
- **Subgraph Centrality:** is the "sum" of closed walks of different lengths in the network starting and ending at the vertex. It characterizes nodes according to their participation in subgraphs of the network.
- **K-core:** is a recursive pruning of the least connected nodes to disentangle the structure of networks focusing on their central cores. Nodes are ranked accordingly.
- **AV11:** selects a subset of k nodes all at once, according to spectral combinatorial methods. The selected subset may be optimal or suboptimal concerning the brute-force method and is not unique. It is a spectral method [15]. In the simulations, the AV11 stopped the spreading in some small real technological networks immunizing less than 17% of the nodes [24].

Finally, an attractive economic interpretation of the influential node ranking is mandatory. The first-of-the-list are the most "important" nodes in a topological sense, and the last the less critical nodes. However, following Leontief [14], we can associate them with economic status, meaning the last nodes might be supported financially during the crisis. An experiment conducted in 2016 showed how to find the most affluent individuals among 108 phone users [26]. Authors constructed a social phone call network, correlating individual financial information with their social locations in the network.

They state [26]: ≪The inequality in communication patterns between the top economic class and the lowest is striking and mimics the economic inequality at the country level. It is visually apparent that the top 1% (accounting for 45.2% of the total credit in the country) displays an entirely different communication pattern than the bottom 10%≫. Thus, people to be supported may be identified directly from the NRN, without additional computational costs.

3.1 Minimum Number of Immunized People

Now we know the most critical nodes but still have to decide how many of them need to be vaccinated to stop or slow down sufficiently the spreading. Equivalently, we have to determine the minimum number of persons to be quarantined during the lockdown phase to minimize the economic damages and, at the same time, stop or slow down sufficiently the spreading. It appears that the term "sufficiently" implies a precise amount of arbitrariness, submitted to the decision-making [27].

The minimum number of individuals is obtained using λ_{max}, the maximum eigenvalue of the adjacency matrix of the National Relational Network Graph, A_{NRN}. From our perspective to vaccine or quarantine, a person means to remove a node from the NRN Graph, which means to reduce λ_{max}. We do so until:

$$\lambda_{max}(A_{NRN}) \leq \delta/\beta$$

In other words, one removes a group of the first-of-the-list nodes, then calculates (1). If (1) is right, the procedure stops; otherwise, a larger group of the first-of-the-list nodes is chosen sequentially, and λ_{max} is recalculated.

Moreover, since a complete theoretical treatment of the epidemic threshold for dynamic networks is sorely lacking, best we can do is to repeat this procedure every time interval, defined by the computing capabilities.

Of course, here the working hypothesis is that we have estimated δ and β previously, by field measurements. Actually, it is complicated to know the numeric value of the infection rate β (average value) and the cure rate δ (average value), even worst, probably there is no average value. Therefore, we must resort to a different estimation for the maximum eigenvalue of the adjacency matrix A^{NRN}, remembering we need to reduce as much as possible λ_{max}, to leave as much as possible intact the connectivity of the NRN because it would mean the economic system will save most of its capabilities [14, 16–21].

One alternative solution is the use of the Laplacian matrix L, defined: $L = D - A^{NRN}$, where D denotes the diagonal matrix of vertex degrees, whose second eigenvalue λ_2^L is positive *iff* the graph is connected. Therefore, as far as $\lambda_2^L > 0$, we can reduce λ_{max} immunizing the top "influencers" of the list previously described, while maintaining efficient the economy.

Here we do not provide demonstrations or numerical simulations, but formal details and simulations may be traced in [24, 25, 28, 29].

3.2 Minimum Number of Immunized Relations

Another strategy to minimize "sufficiently" the economic damages during the lockdown phase, is to immunize the links (also called edges) - i.e. relations among individuals, rather than quarantine the nodes. Moreover, the term sufficiently implies a precise amount of arbitrariness, submitted to the decision-makers. Removing or quarantining a relation means to prevent physical contacts and communications of any kind between two people, even if is the reason not directly understandable or intuitive. Pruning an edge affects similar [21–24] to remove a node [28, 29]. Thought one has to prune many edges for quarantine a node, it may be less traumatic both to people and the economy. Limited social activity is preferable to no social activity; on the other hand, quarantine people are undoubtedly simpler than controlling personal life aspects.

4   Results and Discussion: NRN as a Dynamical Graph

As previously discussed, we have extracted information on the critical nodes. The NRN is inherently dynamic since new edges are created/eliminated continuously. The most apparent reason is people mobility that determines interactions of any type. These must be traced and real-time recorded on the NRN database, integrated with other information, which means to create (destroy) a large number of links at any moment. Useful hints may derive from web media; for example, Twitter traffic can track concerns related to the disease and estimate the spreading in real-time, a couple of weeks in advance concerning standard methods [25].

The technology to do so is available for a long time; therefore, the only (apart from the privacy and legislative) problems are due to the absolutely mandatory supercomputing facilities.

5   Conclusions and Future Works

In this paper, we do not intend to discuss our proposal's mathematical tools; instead, we want to expose a practical approach to the epidemic spreading problem directly. Algorithms may well be changed, provided the goal remains the proper selection of people to immunize primarily to optimize the vaccine distribution and reduce the lockdown costs while stopping or slowing down the epidemic spreading. A word of caution: it is well-known that the internet big data analysis has been used for a long time by nation-states and private enterprises to study and forecast people behaviours. Graph theory algorithms may enhance its capabilities consistently, requiring even more careful supervision by the public opinion. Summarizing:

- It seems possible to minimize the number of individuals to immunize by vaccine or quarantine during an outbreak selecting these persons properly. The spreading could be stopped, and the lockdown may be alleviated this way.
- The algorithms can identify the most influential or critical individuals, meaning those who propagate more dangerously the disease.
- The NRN can directly indicate the subjects that hit financially by the epidemic, without additional computational costs.
- Particular clusters of individuals can be identified by topological information with acceptable precision.

- The minimization procedure requires a continuously updated graph, formed by the relations among citizens due to linkages of different nature: physical, proximity, information from the internet, cellular phones.
- Some sub-graphs, corresponding to small areas of the region affected by the spreading, could show the small-world property. Depending on people mobility, the small-world property increases the propagation speed dangerously, especially at the outbreak's initial stage.

References

1. D'Agostino, G., Scala, A.: Networks of Networks: The Last Frontier of Complexity. Springer, Heidelberg (2014). https://doi.org/10.1007/978-3-319-03518-5
2. Otte, E., Rousseau, R.: Social network analysis: a powerful strategy, also for the information sciences. J. Inf. Sci. **28**(6), 441–453 (2002)
3. Fioriti, V., Chinnici, M.: Identifying sparse and dense sub-graphs in large graphs with a fast algorithm. EPL **108**, 50006 (2014)
4. Benzi, M., Klymko, C.: J. Complex Netw. **1**, 124 (2013)
5. Estrada, E., Rodrıguez-Velazquez, J.A.: Phys. Rev. E **71**, 056103 (2005)
6. Miller, B., et al.: Lincoln Lab. J. **20**, 10 (2013)
7. Miller, B., Bliss, N., Wolfe, P.J.: A spectral framework for anomalous subgraph detection. ArXiv:1401.7702v1 [cs.SI] (2014). Accessed 29 Jan 2014
8. Miller, B., Beard, M.S., Bliss, N.T.: Matched filtering for subgraph detection in dynamic networks. In: IEEE Statistical Signal Processing Workshop (2011)
9. Yan, S.J., Chughtai, A.A., Macintyre, C.R.: Utility and potential of rapid epidemic intelligence from internet-based sources. Int. J. Infect. Dis. **63**, 77–87 (2017)
10. Vespignani, A.: Modelling dynamical processes in complex socio-technical systems. Nat. Phys. **8**, 32–39 (2012)
11. Pastor-Satorras, R., Vespignani, A.: Epidemic spreading in scale-free networks. Phys. Rev. Lett. **86**(14), 320–3203 (2001)
12. Chakrabarti, D., Wang, Y., Wang, C., Leskovec, J., Faloutsos, C.: Epidemic thresholds in real networks. ACM Trans. Inf. Syst. Secur. **10**(4), 1–26 (2008)
13. Wang, Y., Chakrabarti, D., Wang, C., Faloutsos, C.: Epidemic spreading in real networks: an eigenvalue viewpoint. In: SRDS Conference (2003)
14. Leontief, W.: The Structure of American Economy 1919–1929. Oxford University Press, Oxford (1951)
15. Arbore, A., Fioriti, V.: Topological protection from the next generation malware: a survey. Int. J. Crit. Infrastruct. Inderscience Enterprises Ltd, **9**(1/2), 52–73 (2013)
16. Fioriti, V.A., D'Agostino, G., Bologna, S.: On modeling and measuring inter-dependencies among Critical Infrastructures. In: IEEE COMPENG Conference 2010, Rome (2010)
17. Atay, F.A., Bıyıkoglu, T., Jost, J.: Network synchronization: spectral versus statistical properties. ArXiv:0706.3069v1 [cond-mat.dis-nn] (2007). Accessed 20 June 2007
18. D'Agostino, G., et al.: Methodologies for inter-dependency assessment. In: CRIS 2010 (2010)
19. Chen, Z., Ji, C.: Measuring network-aware worm spreading ability. In: IEEE INFOCOM Conference 2007 (2007). http://web.eng.fiu.edu/zchen/paper/metric.pdf
20. Kuramoto, Y.: Chemical Oscillators. Springer, Berlin (1994)
21. Matamalas, A., et al.: Effective approach to epidemic containment using link equations in complex networks. Sci. Adv. **4**, 4212 5 (2018)

22. Le, L.T., Eliassi-Rad, T., Tong, H.: MET: a fast algorithm for minimizing propagation in large graphs with small eigen-gaps. In: SDM, Computer Science (2015)
23. Tong, H., Prakash, B.A., Eliassi-Rad, T., Faloutsos, M., Faloutsos, C.: Gelling, and melting, large graphs by edge manipulation. In: CIKM, pp. 245–254 (2012)
24. Fioriti, V., Chinnici, M., Arbore, A.: Suboptimal topological protection from advanced malware. In: Congresso Nazionale SIMAI, Politecnico di Torino (2012)
25. Arbore, A., Fioriti, V., Chinnici, M.: The topological defense in SIS epidemic models. Chaos Solitons Fractals **86**, 16–22 (2016)
26. Signorini, A., Segre, A.M., Polgreen, P.M.: The use of Twitter to track levels of disease activity and public concern in the U.S. during the influenza A H1N1 pandemic. PLoS ONE **6**(5), (2011)
27. Luo, S., Morone, F., Sarraute, C., Travizano, M., Makse, M.A.: Inferring personal economic status from social network location. Nat. Commun. **8**, 1–7 (2017)
28. Chinnici, M., Fioriti, V., Arbore, A.: The network topology of connecting things: defence of IoT graph in the smart city. In: Rodrigues, J.M.F., et al. (eds.) ICCS 2019. LNCS, vol. 11540, pp. 84–96. Springer, Cham (2019). https://doi.org/10.1007/978-3-030-22750-0_7
29. Chinnici, M., Fioriti, V.: Node seniority ranking in networks. Stud. Inf. Control **26**(4), 397–402 (2017)

Multimodal Interaction Framework Based on Firebase Real-Time Database

Youssef Guedira[✉] and José Rouillard

Univ. Lille, CNRS, Centrale Lille, UMR 9189 – CRIStAL, Centre de Recherche en Informatique Signal et Automatique de Lille, 59000 Lille, France
`{youssef.guedira,jose.rouillard}@univ-lille.fr`

Abstract. Relying on one technology with a single interaction modality may benefit some users but would certainly exclude a lot more if they have impedances to use that modality. The solution then becomes the inclusion of multiple modalities in the initial design of the interactive system making it more adaptable to the needs of many more users. Including many modalities can rapidly increase the number of interaction objects that need to receive the stream of user commands. This is especially true if the user needs to interact with multiple artifacts in a home automation environment. In this paper, we present the general architecture of an ongoing project for multimodal home automation system. This system relies on a web based database called Firebase for the exchange of user input and the issuing of commands to the multiple artifacts. The user input is acquired using a smartphone and a webcam equipped computer. They capture the user's tactile input, vocal phrases, eye gaze as well as head pose features like tilt and face direction. We were able to achieve a reliable data transfer between the database and the different input acquisition interface. As a first step in the prototyping of the system, we were able to control two separate game interfaces developed using Unity3D software.

Keywords: Quality of life technologies · Multimodal · Interaction design · Disability · Special needs

1 Introduction

With the advancements in the development of smart homes and connected environments, people nowadays are able to control their home environment through intelligent and adaptive interfaces. In fact, these technologies greatly benefit users with special needs especially. This is especially the case when moving around the house, reaching for artifacts and manipulating them becomes a heavy and painful task, sometimes impossible without external assistance. However, with the varying profiles of this category of users, inclusion matters come into play. A system relying solely on voice command would exclude any user with speech impediments. The solution is to adopt a multimodal interaction approach from the beginning stages of the system design.

In this paper, we present our ongoing work on the notion of multimodal interaction in the context of Human-Computer Interaction to improve quality of life. Since Richard

© Springer Nature Switzerland AG 2021
M. Antona and C. Stephanidis (Eds.): HCII 2021, LNCS 12769, pp. 367–384, 2021.
https://doi.org/10.1007/978-3-030-78095-1_27

Bolt and his famous "Put that there" [1], it is well known that multimodal interaction can provide more natural and easy to use interfaces. In our research, we focus more on the use of multimodal interfaces to interact with a connected environment especially for user with special needs. In fact, our discussions with patients and healthcare professionals in care-centers revealed the need for such environment control. On one hand, the connected environment allows the user to interact with multiple objects without needing to move around the space and with minimal to no need for physically reaching for the objects. This is especially beneficial when the person suffers from reduced mobility. On the other hand, the use of multiple modalities for interaction would allow users having various levels of ability with regards to sensory-motor functions to still benefit from the use of such technologies.

Elouali et al. [14] suggested benefiting from this mobile technology for multimodal interaction. More specifically, smartphones are nowadays equipped with multiple sensors (gyroscope, compass, microphone, camera…) which can be used to acquire a large spectrum of user input and utilizing a various interaction modalities. In fact, the work of Guedira et al. [12] introduces power wheelchair steering on a smartphone application. Combining these ideas can give rise to a holistic interactive system that utilizes the smartphone technology to both interact with the environment and drive the wheelchair.

In our work, we particularly focus on users suffering from neuromuscular diseases. For instance, in our team, we are working on Hybrid BCI (Brain-Computer Interfaces) for Duchenne Muscular Dystrophy (DMD). DMD is a severe pathology of skeletal musculature. This genetic disorder causes an absence of dystrophin, a protein that supports muscle strength and muscle fibers cohesion, which leads to progressive muscle degeneration and weakness [2]. Hybrid BCI means that various other ways to communicate are used beside EEG (Electroencephalogram). As we consider multiple user profiles and various interaction possibilities, one of the challenges to the system design is that users can change the way they interact when they become tired, for example, switching from a direct muscular interaction to another one (voice, gaze, EEG…). Interfaces that handle these changes may not be very easy to conceive, implement and manage. One of the challenging aspects is the exchange of data bits between the multiple input acquisition interfaces, the central interaction engine and the output devices. Jacket el al. [13] proposed an architecture for an ambient assisted living framework relying on a Zigbee protocol to relay information between multiple components of the interactive system. Nowadays, various tools allow us to store and retrieve data in the cloud instantly. In this paper, we explore the use of a lighter weight communication through a Firebase web database.

The rest of the article is organized as follow: in Sect. 2 we give the architecture of the proposed multimodal system. We detail the different modalities that are used to get user input. After that, we detail how the input is centralized using the web based database Firebase. We then give an overview from the literature on how the input coming from different modalities can be leveraged to then send it as a user command to the object of interaction. In Sect. 3, we illustrate via two computer simulations how this data exchange was achieved between two or more separate devices. Then, in Sect. 4, we give a brief overview of the upcoming step in our design which is about an experiment using a Wizard of Oz technique. We conclude in Sect. 5 with a summary of the work and a brief outline of this next experiment.

2   Architecture

For better efficiency, we have chosen a modular architecture. Multiple interfaces acquire user input, each interface capturing one or more interaction modality. This would allow each user to select the input interface(s) that best suit their needs without affecting the rest of the interaction chain. The different input signals are then centralized on a web based database and treated to synthesize one user command. The system then reacts accordingly. Throughout the execution of the intended task, the system can prompt messages to the user either asking for more clarification or informing him/her on the progression of the task. The prompted messages themselves can be conveyed through different channels in order to accommodate for the user's needs/preferences without being scarce or cumbersome. The schematic in Fig. 1 gives a large scale overview of the architecture. To the latter is added a Wizard of Oz [9] (see Sect. 4) which interacts, through the same database, with the user's home automation environment.

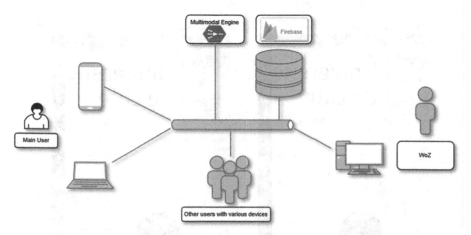

Fig. 1. Architecture of our multimodal interaction framework based on Firebase Realtime Database

In this section we give a detailed description of the system's architecture. For each module/sub-module, we will give a technological solution that can be used in the system. The specific solutions given in this section can be thought of as lightweight especially for prototyping but can also be used in real life deployment of the system. Other solutions can be used as long as they provide similar functionalities.

2.1   User Input Acquisition

When designing a system to improve the quality of life of users with special needs, one should keep in mind that different users may have varying levels of ability on each basic function. If we take neuromuscular diseases [3] as an example, the spectrum of manifestations can be very large: some patients may only have mobility problems while others may not be able to speak or even breathe naturally. In [4], authors discuss multiple manifestations of these diseases and how they can impact the design of a wheelchair steering system. The wide spectrum of deficiencies caused by such disease makes it hard to encompass a large spectrum of users with a single modality. In order to level up the plane field in terms of interactive system design, we need to think about including diverse input interfaces that can make use of each person's residual abilities to allow them to accomplish the needed tasks. For this reason, the input interface presented in this paper consists of several input acquisition modules, each one captures user actions through a particular channel and makes use of a specific modality.

Tactile Interaction. The user can issue commands by touching a tactile interface. This is performed via two different paradigms: continuous-input tactile pad and discrete tactile buttons.

These two paradigms themselves can either be physical (physical buttons) or virtual (tactile graphical interface). In our implementation, we have chosen to use a mobile application that contains both a virtual tactile pad and discreet buttons (Fig. 2 top).

Fig. 2. A screenshot of the tactile control interface (top) and how it interacts with the Firebase web database. The tactile pad is represented by the orange rectangle. The user's touch is represented by the black circle. TTS stands for Text To Speech (Color figure online)

The virtual pad (orange rectangle in Fig. 2) registers the users' touch (represented using the large black circle in Fig. 2) which allows them to perform free gestures. The discreet buttons allow for the selection between different choices (for example between tasks).

The two paradigms can be used either as alternatives or as complements to each other. When used as complements to each other, the user can make a gesture on the pad and either confirm or undo the gesture by tapping on one of two buttons. When used as alternatives to one another (in a two-choice selection for example) the user can make a gesture to the right on the pad (equivalent to tapping the right button) and make a gesture to the left (equivalent to tapping the left button) and vice versa.

Speech Recognition. The user can utter a sentence or a phrase to issue a command to the system. In our implementation of the multimodal system, we have chosen to make use of the Google API for speech recognition[1].

The utterance can initiate an interaction, specify it or halt it. The significance of the utterance can be absolute or contextual. For example: if the user needs to close the windows for the bedroom and the guest room. The user can say "close the windows of the bedroom". In this case, the utterance can be interpreted at face value and the system will close the windows of the bedroom. To close the windows of the guestroom, the user can either substitute "bedroom" by "guestroom" in the previous utterance or utter "and do the same thing for the guestroom". The system should understand from the context that the overall interaction is not done yet and that "the same thing" is a contextual substitute for "close windows".

Last but not least, the utterance can specify the interaction. We can take the previous example. The user can utter "close the windows". The system recognizing multiple rooms, can ask for specification of the command. The user can then specify "bedroom" or "guestroom".

Head Movement Command. By the means of a normal web camera, the system captures the head movement of the user. The system detects head orientation and tilt using the face detection feature of the Dlib and OpenCV libraries. For the first iteration, we decided to limit the user's actions to a left/center/right face orientation (Fig. 3) and a left/straight/right head tilt.

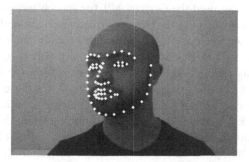

Fig. 3. Illustration of head movement (face looking to the left) detection using OpenCV and Dlib libraries

---

[1] More information on the API available on the official page: https://cloud.google.com/speech-to-text.

Eye Gaze. The user can make eye movements in order to interact with the system. For prototyping purposes in our implementation of the multimodal system, the eye gaze is captured via video camera relying on OpenCV library for face feature detection (Fig. 4). The reason behind it is that we did not opt for a precise target acquisition using this modality. It comes as a picking mechanism for a limited number of discrete choices presented on a screen in front of the user.

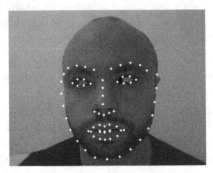

Fig. 4. Illustration of eye gaze detection (eyes looking to the right) using OpenCV and Dlib libraries.

The risk while using eye gaze to interaction is that this channel can be the main tool for exploring the environment. Thus, the user might be simply looking at an object in the environment while the system may register this action as an instruction bit. For this reason, the eye gaze detection interface requires a confirmation via a blink in order to register the gaze action. The user's gaze is detected as either left, or right as a mechanism of choosing between two different options each presented on the left or the right side of the screen. In order to send a gaze instruction the user needs to gaze in the intended direction then blink so that the gaze action is registered.

In our current implementation, we have included all the mentioned modalities. As stated above, we mainly relied on existing libraries for input acquisition as our goal is not to re-implement them but rather give a proof of concept of their integration in a holistic system. Namely, we have used the Google API for speech recognition, and OpenCV was used to process camera input from the user. We are well aware that trying to explore each modality on its own and trying to optimize it thoroughly can improve the quality of input acquisition and may have a positive impact on the quality of interaction as a whole. However, following the main goal of this first implementation, the focus is more on the integration rather than the study of each modality. Now that these building blocks are fully integrated in the system, the modularity of the latter makes it feasible to isolate each modality and optimize it as much as possible without hindering the functioning of the system as a whole. Further developments should introduce the use of Electromyography (EMG) signals [15] that gives data about muscular activation that reflects muscular activity as well as a brain-computer interface through the use of Electroencephalography (EEG) signals [16]. The multimodal fusion engine should be well calibrated to adapt to a given user depending on the acquired signals and the input acquisition time window.

2.2 Centralizing User Input

In order to benefit from the multiple modalities in the interaction, it is necessary to centralize all the actions coming from the user on a single platform. This platform needs to have constant updates of the input signals coming from all the acquisition devices then transmit them to the central decision making component that should make sense of all the input signals and interpret them according to the situation. For our implementation, we have decided to use a web-based database called "Firebase Database" to centralize the user input.

Communication with Firebase. Firebase[2] is a web NoSQL database provided by Google that supports storage as well as real-time data access. It is a lightweight solution for exchanging information between multiple clients that are subscribed to the database. It provides support for multiple development platforms such as Android, IOS. Support is also provided to connect the database to a C++, C# or a Python script.

In our implementation, each client is a component in the multimodal system architecture. Each component is connected to the internet and sends data to Firebase. In the real-time database, the state of each input acquisition interface is registered and changes upon user action. The data are updated in real time so the central decision making component can periodically and frequently check for new arriving commands. Figure 5 gives a brief screenshot of the database we use in our architecture.

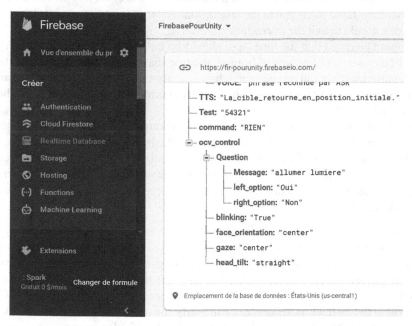

Fig. 5. Example of content available in a Firebase Realtime Database

---

[2] Details about the Unity Firebase integration available on: https://firebase.google.com/support/release-notes/unity.

2.3 Synchronization of User Input

As we have established, the system makes use of multiple modalities to interact with the user. Each input acquisition interface captures a certain modality and sends the registered input to the central decision making system. The system needs to make sense of the continuously changing state of the input interfaces in order to form a complete instruction. In addition, the instruction may be composed of multiple bits from different input interfaces. The question then becomes: when does the system detect the start/end of an instruction acquisition?

A Time Based Acquisition of User Input. The first paradigm in the acquisition of an instruction can be based on a time window. Within this time lapse, the user can issue multiple bits of the instruction through various channels. The system needs to wait for the duration of this time window after which it can start analyzing the user input. The time window can start from the moment the system asks a certain question like "What do you want to do?" If the user wants to dim the lights of the room, he/she can utter "dim" and click on the "lights" icon on the screen. The user is provided a time lapse of 10 s for example to complete all the needed bits for the full understanding of the command. After the 10 s time frame is over, the system can proceed to the processing of the instruction. In the case of an incomplete instruction, e.g. the user utters "dim" and does no further action before the 10 s time lapse is over, the system can use that bit of the instruction to ask for clarification: "What do you want to dim?" The user then is provided with an additional time lapse to complete the instruction. After several unsuccessful trials, the system can decide to halt the interaction.

It should be noted that the time lapse should be customized according to the capabilities of the user. If he/she suffers from a condition that renders his/her movements too slow, the time lapse should be large enough to accommodate for that. On the contrary, if the user is able to issue the command bits in a short period of time, the time lapse should be shortened.

On the plus side, this paradigm sets a relatively known duration of the input acquisition and can avoid getting stuck. On the minus side, it can be inconvenient to the user when he/she needs more time to think or just gets delayed by an external distraction. Hence, the user may not be able to complete the command bit in time which then lengthens the duration of the interaction and increases the needed exchanges between the user and the system.

An Action Based Acquisition of User Input. In this interaction paradigm, the system can issue an instruction request to the user. In order for the instruction sequence to start, a certain action is needed as a sort of "start recording" action. The changes to the state of each input interface is then registered. The user can then, through another key action signal the end of an instruction sequence. If the system was not able to make sense of a certain bit in the instruction sequence, it can notify the user asking for clarification. The same procedure is then required to issue the missing bit of information.

On the plus side, this paradigm offers the possibility for the user to take their time while issuing the different command bits. This can be beneficial especially for people suffering from a physical or mental condition that reduces considerably their action speed. On the minus side, it requires two additional actions (start and finish) which can add more physical and mental load to the interaction.

Choosing between these two input fusion paradigms may not be always clear. There can be situations where one is more adapted compared to the other. For this reason, we intend utilize both depending on the use case and the specific context of the interaction.

For the first implementation of our multimodal input fusion engine, we have utilized a time based approach. A lapse of time is given to the user to provide all the needed input bits for the task at hand. At the end of this time lapse, the system treats the multiple bits which are then converted into a complete instruction understandable by the system. This is better illustrated in a simple drawing application (Fig. 6). The drawing application runs on the user's smartphone (smartphone 1). It provides a basic interface with "yes/no" buttons, a display for system message prompts, a large drawing area and a "clear" button. On a separate smartphone (smartphone 2) runs the multimodal fusion engine. This is a separate application that regulates the acquisition of user input and cycles every 10 s. As we established earlier, the information bit exchange between these two devices is mitigated through Firebase real-time web database to which both devices are subscribed. Within this 10 s time lapse, the user can touch on a location in the drawing area (on smartphone 1) and utters "draw house". At the end of this time lapse, the system gets the information that a house needs to be drawn at the same location indicated by the user's touch, then the application shows a small house icon.

Fig. 6. Left: Illustration of the functioning of the multimodal fusion engine running on smartphone 2. Right: Multimodal drawing application running on smartphone 1.

2.4 Handling Multiple Input Signals

Within the context of a multimodal interaction, the system listens to the user input coming from multiple channels. The question then becomes: how does the system handle the various inputs coming roughly at the same time? More specifically which signal to consider? And what role is it supposed to play in the interaction?

In the literature, this question can be answered in multiple ways depending on the design of the system and the requirements of the specific interaction. Multiple papers have laid out the different concepts and paradigms for multimodality [5] and [6]. These concepts and definitions have been revised since like in [10] but have retained the overall paradigms. In this section, we give a reminder of the main paradigms from these articles of literature and reposition them in the context of interaction for people with special needs.

Complementarity. In this paradigm, the interactive system relies on the combination of multiple signals coming from different modalities to get the full input message. Each modality brings one or more bits to the input message and without the contribution "synergistically" of the other bits from the different modalities, the input message is incomplete. An example in our case is the scenario where the user taps the "light bulb" icon on a screen and utters "switch ON". Each bit of information is incomplete by its own until associated to the other bit to give the instruction "switch ON the light bulb".

In the context of people suffering from neuromuscular diseases for example, this paradigm can be useful if for a person who has just enough motor ability to move over a couple of buttons while still being able to talk. When the same operations can be performed on two different artifacts (ON/OFF can be applied to a light bulb and to a TV set), then the tactile interface can be made more compact and more reachable by the user without diminishing the usability of the whole system.

Fig. 7. Illustration of the combination of M1 (modality 1) and M2 (modality 2) brings the system from a state S to a state S' (taken from [7]).

Equivalence. In this paradigm, the multiple modalities allow for the same message being issued (Fig. 7). In the case of switching on a light bulb, the user can tap a "light bulb switch" or utter "switch on the light bulb". Both modalities (touch and voice) allow the user to issue the same command. In the context of interaction for people suffering from neuromuscular diseases for example, the patient can have his/her motor abilities decline with various external factors like cold. When that happens and the user can hardly move his/her hand to the "light bulb switch", he/she can issue the command by voice.

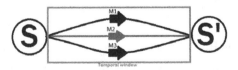

Fig. 8. Illustration of how M1 (modality 1), M2 (modality 2) and M3 (modality 3) can all bring the system from a state S to a state S'. The user chooses M2. Taken from [7]

When the user decides to issue the same command using more than one modality, then the paradigm is called a redundancy (Fig. 8). This however puts the constraint on the system when fusing the data from the different modalities to handle any apparent conflict. If the user taps the "lights OFF" button and utters "dim the light", the system either needs to ask for clarification or ignore one of the channels.

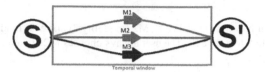

Fig. 9. Illustration of how M1 (modality 1), M2 (modality 2) and M3 (modality 3) can all bring the system from a state S to a state S'. The user chooses M1 and M2 redundantly. Taken from [7]

Assignment. In this paradigm, the user can issue the instruction only using one modality (Fig. 9). When the combination modality-task is system imposed, we talk about a system assignment paradigm. Depending on the use case this paradigm may be obsolete when the user suffers from a disability that inhibits the utilization of that modality for any length of time. This would require a different design for each category of users (suffering from a given disease) or worse different designs for the same user when his/her condition fluctuates. If the switching on of the light bulb in the previous example were only possible by tapping the tactile switch, then the user would not have been able to perform the task in colder weather conditions.

Fig. 10. Illustration of how only M1 (modality 1) can bring the system from a state S to a state S'. Taken from [7]

A more adapted paradigm is the Agent Assignment (Fig. 10). Here, the system design resembles that of the Equivalence case. However, the choice belongs to the user to always use one single modality. Taking the same light bulb switching example, if the user is completely paralyzed and can only interact with eye gaze, even if the interaction is achievable via multiple modalities, the user will always choose eye gaze interaction for that matter. The only caveat in this paradigm is that the system still listens for the other channels although they will not be used by the person. In this case, the system can dynamically prune one or more channels if, over time, they are not used.

3 Simulation Prototypes

As part of our prototyping process, we developed two applications on Unity3D game development software. The goal is to see how we can use multiple machines (clients) that are subscribe to Firebase. The user can provide input on one or more machines, the Firebase database collects this input and sends it to the machine that is required to perform the task. This section gives a brief description of the two applications.

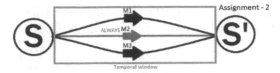

Fig. 11. Illustration of how M1 (modality 1), M2 (modality 2) and M3 (modality 3) can all bring the system from a state S to a state S'. The user always chooses M2. Taken from [7].

3.1 A Unity3D Game on Two Distinct Machines

The first application is a simple game developed on Unity3D software running on a computer (Fig. 11). At the start of each round, a green or red ball drops on the top level. On a smartphone, the user has a tactile interface with a number of button among which a "left" and "right". Using these two button, the user needs to move the ball down the different levels to the corresponding bucket.

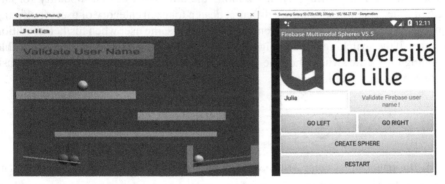

Fig. 12. Example of Unity standalone application (left) controlled by a smartphone Android application (right) across Firebase Realtime Database

The goal of this simple game is to show how, using Firebase real-time database, the user could provide input on one machine while the central system processes the input signal and executes it on another machine. Both are subscribed to the Firebase database. So, when the user presses a button, the smartphone application sends the data to the web database, the computer running the 3D game receives the update and then moves the ball.

3.2 Controlling a Robotic Arm

The example presented in Fig. 12 shows how a standalone application generated with Unity3D can be connected to an Android smartphone across Firebase. The user moves the target placement object (purple rectangle) thanks to the direction arrows of the mobile application. By clicking the button on the PC application, a trajectory plan is requested for the Nyrio robot arm, via a ROS (Robots Operating System)[3] instance, running in a Docker container[4] (Fig. 13).

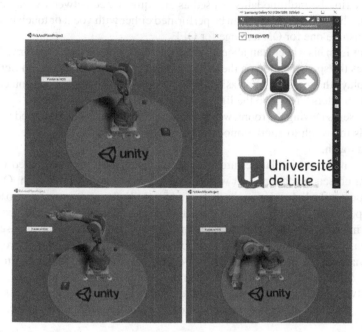

Fig. 13. Example of Unity standalone application controlled by a smartphone Android application across Firebase Realtime Database, using ROS on a Docker Container.

4 Examples of Interaction Scenarios: Acting on the Surrounding Environment

In this section, we take three different scenarios of interactions that the user may be able to accomplish with the multimodal input of the system. In each scenario, we illustrate some of the paradigms in Sect. 2.4 and detail how the system makes sense of different input signals in order to act on the user's environment. These scenarios constitute the basis for the first interactions developed for the user testing of our system. We are currently testing in laboratory the whole system usability, according to various parameters (user's disability level, kind of multimodality allowed, help from Wizard of OZ or not…).

In all these scenarios, the user is confined to the use of a power wheelchair. The latter is equipped with a computer (screen in front of the user for display), a tablet is attached to the armrest showing the interface Fig. 12 capturing user taps as well as utterances to the voice command. A webcam is attached to the computer screen facing the user in order to capture eye gaze and head movement.

---

[3] More information on the Robots Operating System available on: https://www.ros.org/.

[4] The implementation of the robotic control is inspired from the "pick and place" project provided by Unity3D: https://blogs.unity3d.com/2020/11/19/robotics-simulation-in-unity-is-as-easy-as-1-2-3/.

4.1 Switching On/Off the Lights

In this scenario, the goal for the user is to switch on/off the lights of the bedroom. In this scenario, the multimodality is used as an equivalence between vocal and touch interaction. The on/off switching can be performed either with vocal or touch interaction. We will illustrate one for ON and one for OFF.

The user is on his wheelchair about to enter the room and the lights are turned off. The user touches the speech button on the tablet and utters "switch on bedroom lights". The computer plays the message "You asked to switch on bedroom lights, do you confirm?" The user then utters "Yes" and the lights are switched on.

As the user is leaving the room, we suppose that the user gets too fatigued by talking, so he needs to switch to another modality to perform the same task. Here, the chosen modality is touch.

The user makes a circular gesture on the tablet pad and is then presented with a list of potential objects he can interact with displayed on the computer screen. One of the objects indicates the lights. Using the "left" and "right" buttons, he navigates to the lights icon then performs a check gesture on the tablet pad. The screen then shows the two options to interact with the lights "switch on" and "switch off". As the user selects the right button corresponding to the right choice a message is shown on the screen to ask for confirmation. The user then performs a check gesture on the tablet pad to confirm the choice, and the lights are switched off in the bedroom.

These two interactions illustrate how the user can interact with an object from the surrounding (bedroom lights) using two different modalities interchangeably.

4.2 Switching an Air Conditioning Fan and Controlling the Fan Speed

In this scenario, we make the supposition that the user is on a wheelchair and suffers from a severe case of Duchenne Muscular Dystrophy. His ability to talk is reduced to single, simple words as talking tires him. He also has very reduced hand mobility but can still move a couple of fingers over his phone screen that is attached to the armrest of his wheelchair.

We make the assumption that the environment control system is context aware. In other words, as the user gets into a room, the list of objects that the user can interact with are displayed on the screen in front of him/her. A rectangle is drawn over the selected object. The user can still access objects that are in other rooms through a separate menu.

In this scenario the user is in the living room, on a hot day, and needs to switch on the air conditioning fan. The speed of the fan can be set to various levels of speed. A fan, a TV set, a light bulb and window stores are presented on the screen as the user enters the room.

The user's fingers are on the tactile pad drawn on the phone screen. With any movement on the pad, the selection rectangle is moved from one object to another. To select the intended object, the user blinks for 500 ms and the object is illuminated. To cancel the selection the user can blink again for 500 ms and the illumination disappears. When an object is illuminated (the air conditioning fan for example), a dialog window is displayed on the screen with two different options ON and OFF. The user tilts his head to the right to switch the fan on. The system keeps the dialog window for 5 s after the switching ON of the fan. If the user wants to cancel the action, he can switch the fan OFF by tilting the head to the left. After this 5 s time lapse, the interaction object menu reappears again to allow the user to interact with more objects in the room if needed.

As soon as the fan is switched on, the system registers that the fan is on and puts itself in the context. This is useful for the user in case he wants to change the fan speed. By simply uttering "faster" and confirming by a 500 ms blink the user can increment the fan speed. The user can–but is not required to–specify the intended interaction object since the fan is the only switched ON object in the context that has a "speed property".

As the user wants to leave the room, he would like to switch the air conditioning fan back OFF. He proceeds with the same steps as for switching on the fan.

4.3 Simulating the Control of a Waste Separation Robotic Arm

In this scenario, the user is also on a wheelchair and is suffering from a mild case Duchenne Muscular Dystrophy [8]. She cannot walk but she can talk freely without getting tired and can even move her hands, and handle very light objects. To assist with heavier objects, she uses a robotic arm that can be positioned on her wheelchair or put independently somewhere else inside the house. Both her input acquisition interface (smartphone application shown in Fig. 12) and the robotic arm's control interface are connected wirelessly to Firebase so she can, if needed, control the arm from while she is in another room. Her wheelchair is equipped with a screen where she can visualize a third person shot of the robotic arm so she can control it from a distance. It is worthy to note that she tries to be ecologically responsible so she makes sure to separate her waste bags into recyclable and non-recyclable. The bags however can be heavier than she can handle so she uses the robotic arm.

At the start of the interaction, she is in the living room on her wheelchair. The robotic arm is positioned on the kitchen counter, with the recycling bin on the right and the non-recyclable bin on the left and the trash bags to separate are in the middle. The trash bags and the bins are reachable by the robotic arm.

Using a tactile application similar to Fig. 12, she is able to steer the robotic arm over the bag she wants to pick. Then she utters "pick". The robotic arm picks up the trash bag. We suppose that this bag needs to go to the recycling bin. When the robotic arm picks up the bag, the user then utters "to recycle" and the robotic arm, knowing the position of the recycle bin through various sensors, moves the bag over the bin. We note that the robotic arm relies on movement planning through the Robotics Operating System (ROS) that runs via Transmission Control Protocol (TCP) connection on a server inside the house similar to the application shown in Sect. 3.2.

However, we stipulate that due to occasional technical lags, the arm may position the bag slightly besides the intended bin. For this reason, a fail-safe was installed: if the arm is slightly off target, the user can correct its position using the tactile pad on her phone just like she did to pick up the bag, but this time, only a slight correction is needed. It is then that the user can utter "release" and the bag is released in the recycle bin.

5   Wizard of Oz

Wizard-of-Oz (WoZ) is a common technique enabling HCI researchers to explore aspects of interaction not yet implemented in a real interactive system [9]. In this architecture, the WoZ module can be seen as a client who subscribes to all messages passing through the network. Instead of automatically reacting as the other modules of the architecture, this one lets the evaluator interpret the user's intentions and give an appropriate response.

The WoZ module is an important part of the system because it allows seeing, at a glance, all the necessary information needed for an evaluator to make a quick decision, letting the user think that this decision is taken by the "intelligent system".

An evaluator (the WoZ) observes interactions between a user and the system (computers, robots, etc.) and decides to interpret or not various interaction elements (speech, gaze, gesture, EEG, etc.) performed by the user [11]. Hence, a supposed intelligent system could interpret the sentence "It's too hot in this room", by proposing to switch on a fan. If this part of the system (ASR, semantic interpretation…) if not yet really available, the WoZ can switch on a fan "manually" remotely, in order to let the user think that this reaction was made by the intelligent system.

6   Conclusion

Multimodal interaction is widely used and studied as a subpart of Human-Computer Interaction, and researchers of this domain are often trying to improve the users' quality of life.

We have presented a general architecture of a multimodal interaction framework based on Firebase Realtime Database. Obviously, when designing and developing multimodal user interfaces, it is useful to have a powerful and fast way to send and receive information through various communication devices.

Thanks to Unity Firebase SDK, it is now possible to create 2D and 3D standalone applications for Windows, Mac and Linux, connected to Firebase Realtime Database. Mobile applications can be also connected to Firebase to push and pull such kind of data. We used App Inventor[5] and an experimental component named "Firebase DB" in order to create quickly and easily some mobile applications to deploy and test our prototypes.

Within this framework, our preliminary tests have shown that it is possible to handle multimodal interactions from the user, thanks to a Firebase Realtime Database, used as a quick and robust bus communication. We successfully tested various kinds of interaction (touch on a smartphone screen, speech recognition, eye gaze, tilt head…) in order to allow equivalent multimodality.

As our proposition is based on a shared real-time database, we will also be able to carry out evaluations of tasks for which the protagonists could interact remotely with the multimodal systems (voice, teleoperation gesture, visual and haptic remote perception, etc.).

Future work will consist of evaluating the system for free (painting) or imposed (home automation) tasks. We also plan to test multiple fusion paradigms (such as complementarity) to perform these same tasks. We will determine if the system is usable

---

[5] Web page available on: http://ai2.appinventor.mit.edu/.

according to the handicap declared by the user or detected by the system during interactions. We will be able to use the WoZ technique in our framework, in order to allow experimenters to simulate the behavior of machines. Finally, we will increase the number of sensors by adding endogenous (EEG, EMG…) and exogenous (camera, temperature sensor, etc.) data.

References

1. Bolt, R.: "Put-that-there": voice and gesture at the graphics interface. ACM SIGGRAPH Comput. Graph (1980). https://doi.org/10.1145/965105.807503
2. Rouillard, J., Duprès, A., Cabestaing, F., Bekaert, M.-H., Lecocq, C., et al.: Relevant HCI for Hybrid BCI and Severely Impaired Patients. HCII 2015, pp. 313–323. Los Angeles, USA (2015). https://doi.org/10.1007/978-3-319-20816-9_30. (hal-01361922)
3. Jasvinder, C.: Stepwise approach to myopathy in systemic disease. In: Frontiers in Neurology, vol. 2. Article 49 (2011)
4. Guedira, Y., Brohm, P.-E., Dervin, D., Farcy, R., Bellik, Y.: Conception et Evaluation d'une Interface Tactile pour le Pilotage de Fauteuils Roulants Electriques pour des Personnes Atteintes de Maladie Neuromusculaires. Journal d'Interaction Personne-Système (8), 1 (2019)
5. Caelen, J., Coutaz, J.: Interaction homme-machine multimodale: problèmes généraux. IHM'91. Dourdan (1991)
6. Bellik, Y., Teil, D.: Les types de multimodalités, dans les actes des 4ièmes Journées sur l'ingénierie des interfaces Homme-Machine, IHM'92, pp. 22–28. Telecom Paris Publ., Paris (1992)
7. Pirau, J.: Modeling and resolving conflicts and apprehensions in multimodal models. Student Thesis: Master Thesis in Computer Science (2016)
8. Duprès A., Cabestaing, F., Rouillard, J., Tiffreau, V., Pradeau, C.: Toward a hybrid brain-machine interface for palliating motor handicap with Duchenne muscular dystrophy: a case report. Annals of Physical and Rehabilitation Medicine. Elsevier Masson (2019). https://doi.org/10.1016/j.rehab.2019.07.005
9. Hoffman, G.: OpenWoZ: a runtime-configurable Wizard-of-Oz framework for human-robot interaction. In: Conference: AAAI Spring Symposium on Enabling Computing Research in Socially Intelligent Human-Robot Interaction At: Palo Alto, CA (2016)
10. Martin, J.C.: Six primitive types of cooperation for observing, evaluating and specifying cooperations. In: Proceedings of AAAI (1999)
11. Salber, D., Coutaz, J.: Applying the Wizard of Oz technique to the study of multimodal systems. In: Third International Conference, EWHCI 1993. Moscow, Russia (1993). https://doi.org/10.1007/3-540-57433-6_51
12. Guedira, Y., Brohm, P.-E., Dervin, D., Farcy, R., Bellik, Y.: A Tactile interface to steer power wheelchairs for people suffering from neuromuscular diseases. In: HCI in Mobility, Transport, and Automotive Systems. Driving Behavior, Urban and Smart Mobility, Second International Conference, MobiTAS 2020, Held as Part of the 22nd HCI International Conference, HCII 2020, Copenhagen, Denmark, July 19–24, 2020, Proceedings, Part II (2020)
13. Jacquet, C., et al.: An ambient assisted living framework with automatic self-diagnosis. Int. J. Adv. Life Sci. 5(1–2), 10p (2013)

14. Elouali, N., Pallec, X.L., Rouillard, J., Tarby, J.-C.: MIMIC: leveraging sensor-based interactions in multimodal mobile applications. In: International Conference on Human Factors in Computing Systems, CHI 2014. Toronto, Canada (2014)
15. Sun, Y., et al.: Intelligent human computer interaction based on non redundant EMG signal. Alexandria Eng. J. **59**(3), 1149–1157 (2020)
16. Botte-Lecocq, C., Cabestaing, F.: Les interfaces cerveau-machine pour la palliation du handicap moteur sévère. In: Handicap'2008, pp. 180–189. Paris, France (2008)

Lending an Artificial Eye: Beyond Evaluation of CV-Based Assistive Systems for Visually Impaired People

Fotis P. Kalaganis$^{(\boxtimes)}$, Panagiotis Migkotzidis, Kostas Georgiadis, Elisavet Chatzilari, Spiros Nikolopoulos, and Ioannis Kompatsiaris

Centre for Research and Technology Hellas, Information Technologies Institute, MKlab, 57001 Thermi-Thessaloniki, Greece
kalaganis@csd.auth.gr

Abstract. The autonomy of the visually impaired, expressed by their ability to accomplish everyday tasks on their own even when help by others is not available, is of paramount importance. Hence, the rapid growth of computer vision in the last decade has given rise to a large number of assistive applications aiming to help the visually impaired in perceiving the world in a similar way to the seeing ones. In this study we investigate the usability of a hybrid system, named e-Vision, that couples the natural and seamless adoption provided by an external camera embedded on a pair of glasses with the processing power and the penetration rate of modern smartphone devices. The ultimate benefit which e-Vision hopes to bring to the visually impaired is greater autonomy, and the increased wellbeing. To assess e-Vision's performance, a month-long pilot study took place and people with actual visual impairment used the system in their daily lives. This procedure enable the system's evaluation under real conditions. Although the e-Vision's evaluation provided indications for a promising system, the obtained results were below our expectations with respect to practical usage. Since the employed computer vision modules were based on state-of-the-art deep learning models capable to achieve top-level performance, we identified the shortcomings and the limitations that typical computer vision-based practices set to the creation of assistive technologies for the visually impaired. Therefore, we propose potential remedies capable of overcoming the identified obstacles in existing practices.

Keywords: Assistive system · Blind · Visually impaired · Computer vision · Guidelines · Practical limitations · Egocentric

This work is part of project e-Vision that has been co-financed by the European Regional Development Fund of the European Union and Greek national funds through the Operational Program Competitiveness, Entrepreneurship and Innovation, under the call RESEARCH – CREATE – INNOVATE (project code: T1EDK-02454).

M. Antona and C. Stephanidis (Eds.): HCII 2021, LNCS 12769, pp. 385–399, 2021.
https://doi.org/10.1007/978-3-030-78095-1_28

1 Introduction

Computer Vision (CV) is an inextricably connected component, and one of most prominent subfields of Artificial Intelligence (AI), that describes the ability of machines to process and understand visual data. The key concept of CV is to automate the type of tasks the brain's visual processing system, supported by the visual organs (i.e. eyes), typically does. The rapid growth of CV in the last decade has given rise to a large number of assistive technologies aiming to help the visually impaired in perceiving the world in a similar way to the seeing ones. Although CV-based assistive devices for visually impaired people have made great progress, they are confined to recognizing obstacles and generic objects without taking into account the context of the activities performed by the person. This context differentiates significantly the functional requirements of an assistive device.

One of the most notable efforts towards the creation of assistive technologies for the totally blind is the vOICe system [1] which offers the experience of live camera views through image-to-sound renderings and is based on the concept of sensory substitution. With a left to right scanning procedure, images are converted into sound where elevation is associated with pitch while brightness with loudness. From a theoretical neuroscience perspective, this could lead to synthetic vision with actual visual sensations, by taking advantage of the neural plasticity that governs the human brain, through training. A similar system, that transmits semantic information to the user through a mixed reality sonification interface was recently introduced [5]. This system leverages popular computer vision methods to localize 18 static and dynamic object classes in real-time. Another notable effort concerns the Tyflos system [3]. The Tyflos system consists of camera and Global Positioning System (GPS) sensors, microphones, an audio recording device and a 2D vibrating vest. A portable computer is used for the purposes of text-to-speech and language processing as well as image analysis. The Tyflos system incorporates a stereoscopic vision module, which is attached to a conventional pair of eyeglasses and is capable of creating a depth map from the surrounding environment. The acquired depth map is converted to a tactile vocabulary that allows the user to perceive his surroundings through a vibratory vest.

Recently, several commercial solutions have been introduced for assisting the visually impaired by exploiting recent computer-vision advances. These solutions can be divided into two different categories. The first category concerns the smartphone-based systems with the most indicative being seeingAI[1], Envision[2] and eye-D[3]. These applications employ the smartphone's built-in sensors (e.g. camera, accelerometer, etc.) and offer recognizing capabilities. More specifically, they allow the user to select from generic categories for recognition, such as reading text, barcodes scanning, detecting people, etc. Then, the recognized instances

---

[1] https://www.microsoft.com/en-us/ai/seeing-ai.
[2] https://www.letsenvision.com/.
[3] https://eye-d.in/.

are communicated to the user though earphones. Besides the mobile-based category, the second approach concerns systems that employ external camera-glasses. Notable examples of this category are OrCam MyEye2[4], eSight[5], NuEyes[6] and Eyesynth[7]. OrCam MyEye 2 is a portable device with an integrated camera that can be attached to the users' glasses and is capable of recognizing up to 100 custom objects according to user's input (e.g. selected products, people), read text and recognize barcodes. On the other hand, eSight and NuEyes are glass-based devices that work as digital magnifiers, and therefore are only suitable for people with partial visual loss. Finally, Eyesynth is a pair of glasses accompanied by a portable microcomputer that converts the user's 3D surroundings into intuitive sounds that are propagated through cochlear audio and their usability is focused on avoiding obstacles.

Here, we investigate the usability of a hybrid system, named "e-Vision", that couples the natural and seamless adoption provided by an external camera embedded on a pair of glasses with the processing power and the penetration rate of modern smartphone devices [7]. The system allows the user to capture the environment through the embedded camera while the smartphone returns via the auditory channel the extracted information as perceived by the CV algorithms. In addition to the system design, e-Vision's main novelty lies in the context-aware design of the application. "e-Vision" is structured towards supporting three distinct daily activities for the visually impaired. For each of the supported activities (i.e. supermarket visit, public administration visit and outdoor walk), several CV modules are exploited in a complementary manner. The exploited modules (i.e. object recognition, facial landmarks and emotion recognition, image classification, and optical character recognition) were selected so that each one can complement another towards a common goal, a context-aware assistive system for the visually impaired people.

The autonomy of the visually impaired, expressed by their ability to accomplish everyday tasks on their own even when help by others is not available, is of paramount importance [8]. To this end and in an effort to examine the actual benefits that "e-Vision" brings to the visually impaired community, a month-long pilot study was performed where twelve visually impaired participants used the "e-Vision" system in the three mentioned scenarios (i.e. shopping at a grocery store, outdoor walking and visiting a public administration building).

During this pilot study an advanced log system was developed that monitored and stored both the output of the system (the auditory information that was communicated to the user) and the captured images. This allowed us to annotate the captured images in a semantic level and compare them with the system's output. Consequently, this led to a quantitative evaluation of the system's reliability (separately for each supported activity) and offered an indication about the potential benefits it could bring to the visually impaired community.

---

[4] https://www.orcam.com/en/myeye2/.
[5] https://esighteyewear.com/.
[6] https://nueyes.com/.
[7] https://eyesynth.com/.

Although the obtained results of the evaluation appeared to be promising they were below our expectations (based on our in vitro preliminary experiments). Since the employed CV modules [10,13–15] were based on state-of-the-art deep learning models capable to achieve top-level performance, the system faced challenges that were not anticipated. Therefore it was within our scope to identify the limitations that typical CV-based practices set to the development of assistive technologies for the visually impaired.

In order to uncover such limitations and in an effort to identify the key factors that led to the sub-optimal performance of "e-Vision", a post-evaluation investigation took place. A great part of "e-Vision's" outcomes -and the present study's contribution- concerns the identification of the practical limitations that should be considered when creating a CV-based assistive system for the visually impaired. The main problem that was identified and was omnipresent in each of the supported activities, concerned the poor quality of the captured photos. This is attributed to the users' inability to accurately capture with the photographic lens the points of interest existing within their surrounding environment. While typical CV practices are based on the fact that the provided images clearly depict the points of interest [6,11], this is not a valid assumption when considering an application addressed to the visually impaired. To this end and beyond the presentation of the system accompanied by its quantitative evaluation, we aim to uncover all the crucial factors that should be considered in such applications. Moreover, we provide insights for the CV community and how its focus should be shifted to a new direction that will enable its actual employment in assistive technologies for the blind people.

2   Overview of e-Vision System

The principal objective of "e-Vision" is to promote the autonomy and independence of people with visual impairment. The e-Vision system consists of two hardware components. The first component is a pair of Wi-Fi enabled camera-glasses. More specifically, a wireless camera is integrated in a typical pair of glasses that can wirelessly transmit captured images or video in real-time through Wi-Fi protocol. The second component is a smartphone device, running either iOS or Android operating system, which hosts the e-Vision application and consequently realizes the CV components (modules). The system's feedback is provided to the user by means of narration though the auditory pathway using conventional earphones, a crucial component capable of ensuring the essential seclusion of the feedback. The combination of the aforementioned hardware components ensures both freedom in movement and sufficient computational power in order to realize the essential computer-vision functionalities.

As it is already stated, "e-Vision" is structured towards supporting three distinct daily activities for the visually impaired. The first provides the visually impaired with the ability to visit a supermarket and complete a session of grocery shopping. The system provides context-aware information to the users in two levels of abstraction. The first level will facilitate navigation in the supermarket, an issue of paramount importance for the visually impaired, providing only essential information to the user while ensuring low levels of frustration. In this direction, the proposed system will classify any given image into one of the three basic concepts/categories: a) product, b) shelf and c) trail. The second level will exploit the information provided by the first and will in turn identify the specific product, shelf or trail. Initially, an image classifier is employed for detecting the corresponding category and then OCR is used to extract the text that appears in the image. By exploiting a supermarket's product database an exact description with the respect to the aforementioned category is obtained. In case where the image is classified as a "product" the obtained description corresponds to the identified text included in the object with the largest bounding box (salient object). As a result, users will have access to detailed descriptions about the product they are holding or the trail/shelf they are aiming at [7].

The second concerns carrying out a task in a public administration building (e.g. getting a birth certificate), an extremely demanding task for the visually impaired people. Towards this direction, e-Vision supports several features specially tailored for the public administration case. The core feature of this scenario concerns the document narration by exploiting advances in OCR technology. Additionally, By taking advantage of recent object detection algorithms, the e-Vision system is capable of notifying the user about the existence of a ticket dispenser (e.g. take-a-number system) as well as other useful objects including chairs, desks and people. To increase the social aspect of this activity, by exploiting the advances in face and emotion recognition, the e-Vision system provides social context during a conversation or a transaction (e.g. "You are facing a happy man"). By employing a deep learning model, the system initially examines whether the image contains a document, a person, and/or an object. The results are then provided in a hierarchical order as follows: a) If both a text/document and a person are detected in the image, the information concerning both is communicated to the user, b) in case that only one of the above is detected (e.g. the photo depicts either a document or a person but not both at the same time) the information concerning only the detected entity is communicated to the user (e.g. only document reading or just a description of a person's gender, emotional state, etc.) and c) in case where no face or document/text is detected, then the identified objects shown in the image are transmitted to the user. We note that all the results are returned to the user via the auditory pathway.

The third of the targeted activities of e-Vision is an outdoor walk. Here the system serves a variety of purposes ranging from an immersive cultural experience through specifically designed soundscapes, all the way to users' friends identification and auditory portraiture of the user's surrounding. By exploiting the face recognition advances in CV, the system will is to identify detected faces and whether they belong to the user's social environment. To enable this feature, users must provide portraits of their friends, though a specifically designed interface, that will serve as the baseline for the face recognition module. The identified faces are communicated to the user through the auditory pathway (i.e. "Your friend John is approaching."). Moreover, in an effort to provide an auditory depiction of the surroundings, we take advantage of the object detection module. The user's surroundings are processed in order to extract the depicted set of identified objects and their corresponding location. Then the identified objects are converted into a comprehensive narration (e.g. "A bench on your right, a dog in front of you.") that is provided to the user using text-to-speech technologies. In an effort to avoid auditory -and consequently cognitive- overload, only the essential feedback is provided according to the user's individual preferences, by means of narration verbosity and feedback frequency, through the settings menu of the e-Vision application. We note that a detailed description of the e-Vision system and its capabilities can be found in [12].

3   Evaluation

This section provides the evaluation of the e-Vision application with objective criteria, based on data collected automatically during the pilot studies where users with actual visual impairment tested the developed system in natural settings. We note that an initial training took place, before the actual pilot study, on how to setup .and use the system. During the pilot trials the system was provided to the users for one month in order to use it at their own pace and convenience. The evaluation is presented per usage scenario of the application.

3.1   Supermarket

A total of 335 images from 12 users were evaluated for the Supermarket case. Before evaluating the reliability of the system, the images collected during the pilot testing had to be annotated. During the annotation process, each image was manually assigned with all the values that should be returned to the user by an ideal system that would work perfectly. These annotations are the basis for evaluating the reliability of the system as they enable a direct comparison of the results communicated to the user and the actual description that corresponds to each image. During the annotation process the following descriptions were assigned to each image:

- **Classification (Integer):** An image-level annotation that denotes if the image depicts a trail, a shelf, a product or something else (beyond the scope of this usage scenario).
- **Description (String):** A detailed annotation which describes exactly the concept depicted in the image with respect to the classification annotation. For example, if the image depicted a specific product this annotation could say "Barilla pasta No10, 1+1 offer" while in the case of a shelf it would say "spaghetti, pasta".

The first part of the evaluation concerns the classification of the image into one of the following three categories: a) trail, b) shelf and c) product [7]. Figure 1 shows the confusion matrix of the employed classifier (a combination of a Deep

Neural Network for feature extraction and a Support Vector Machine for classification) that classifies the images into one of the aforementioned categories. As
it can be seen from the first column (which is empty), the classifier was forced
to classify the images into one of the previously mentioned categories without
being able to identify the images that were not related - in some way - to the
supermarket use case.

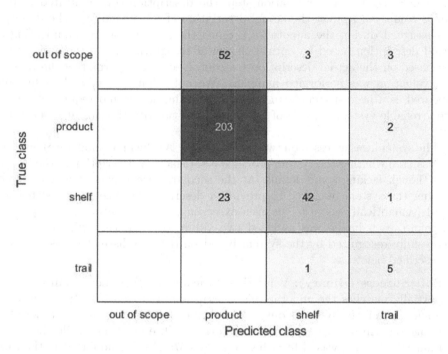

Fig. 1. The confusion matrix that describes the classification of images into one of the
following categories: a) trail, b) shelf, c) product.

It becomes apparent that, about 20% of the images are not related, in some
way, to the supermarket usage scenario. Most of these (out of scope) images
depicted an item which could not be purchased from a supermarket (e.g. a phar-
maceutical product) and this justifies why they have been classified as "product" since they exhibit the same visual characteristics as a supermarket product
image. Those images stemmed from actual users experimenting with the system
at their home using objects of any different kind. It should be noted that photos depicting actual supermarket products but taken outside a supermarket's
environment were still considered relevant in the annotation process. In a broad
sense of evaluation, a fairly high percentage of accuracy is observed reaching the
order of 75%. This percentage quantifies the system's inability to recognize "out
of scope" images. If these images are not taken into account and the system's

reliability is quantified by considering only the related, to the super market scenario, images (see the 3 × 3 bottom-right subtable of the confusion matrix), then the classification accuracy exceeds 90%. It is worth mentioning that the image classifier seems to confuse some shelf photos and classifies them as product photos. This shortcoming is attributed to very close-up photos where the camera focused on a particular product of the shelf.

The next essential step concerns a more detailed evaluation of the system as a whole. During this evaluation step, the description communicated to the user is compared against the actual description of the image (e.g. the description assigned during the annotation). Since the system was communicating a verbal description based on optical character recognition while the annotation was based on the actual description (as contained in a supermarket database), the evaluation was performed manually. We note that the manual evaluation appeared as a necessity since an automated evaluation would require an absolutely reliable system capable of comparing the two descriptions at a semantic level.

The system was assessed on two levels of rigor. At the first (moderate) level, it was assessed whether the system provided a satisfactory description of the image even though lacking some details. At the second (strict) level, it was assessed whether the system managed to provide a description of the image with high detail (semantically equal to, or even exceeding, the annotation's description). Therefore, each image was assigned two values that indicate whether it was successfully recognized by the system based on the two distinct levels of rigor, as described below:

- **Soft Success (Binary):** Value that indicates whether the system's output partially matches the annotation's description (1) or not (0). In the case of a success (1), the system's output should be an adequate but not a detailed image description (e.g. the system returned "Elite crackers" while the exact image description was "Elite wheat crackers 375 g"). We note that in the case of a success, although incomplete, the description produced by the system should not be misleading or partially incorrect.
- **Hard Success (Binary):** Receives a value of 1 if the system managed to produce an accurate description of the image and a value of 0 in case of incorrect or incomplete description. At this level, the system should produce a description semantically equal to or higher than (e.g. exact product and correct expiration date) the description provided to the image during the annotation.

As mentioned above, the inherent nature of the evaluation procedure, combined with concurrent technological barriers served as an obstacle to the automated assessment of system's the reliability. Since our evaluation approach called for a soft and hard success annotation, which involves human judgement, it becomes apparent, that the tactic of using human resources to evaluate the system appeared as a necessity. The above procedure showed that the success rate of the system under the strict evaluation criterion was 35% while with the moderate at 53%. Before considering any external factors that may have led to the aforementioned result, we should admit that the system does meet the expectations for an assistive system aiming to promote the daily tasks of visually impaired people.

3.2   Administration Building

A total of 264 images from the same, 12, users were evaluated for the administration building scenario. An essential step for the evaluation process concerns the manual annotation of the collected images. During the annotation process, each image was manually assigned all the attributes that should be returned to the user by an ideal system that would work perfectly. These annotations serve as the basis for evaluating the reliability of the e-Vision as they enable a direct comparison of the results communicated to the user and the actual description that corresponds to each image. During the annotation process, the following attributes were assigned to each image:

- **Meaningful Photo (Binary):** A binary value indicating whether the image was depicting something that could be semantically interpreted or not.
- **Category (Integer):** An integer indicating if the image was depicting a) a document, b) one or more faces, c) both of the aforementioned or c) an object (e.g. a ticket dispenser, a chair, etc.).
- **Description (String):** Includes all the semantic elements (text, facial attributes, objects etc.) that are capable of describing accurately the corresponding image.

Then, the system was evaluated by comparing the annotation attributes with the system's output. The first part of the evaluation concerns the categorization of the image into one of the following categories: a) document, b) person c) document alongside with a person and d) object. Figure 2 presents the confusion matrix of the image classification into one of the aforementioned categories. It becomes apparent from the confusion matrix that the image classification accuracy is approximately 75%. This percentage results only from the images that depicted something meaningful. It is observed that the system's inaccuracy stems from its inability to distinguish between images containing persons and documents at the same time as the ones containing only documents. This is attributed to the face recognition module that fails to detect faces with 100% accuracy (e.g. some objects are incorrectly identified as faces when they are not).

In a similar way to the previous case, after the evaluation of the image classifier, the system's performance as a whole was assessed. During this, second, evaluation step the system's output that was communicated to the users was compared to the annotation attributes at a semantic level. This evaluation step included two distinct levels of rigor. The first level (moderate) was indicating if the system managed to provide a satisfactory description even missing some details. The second level (strict) assessed if the system's output was governed by the same semantic complexity as the one provided in the annotation. Therefore, each image was assigned two values that indicate whether it was successfully

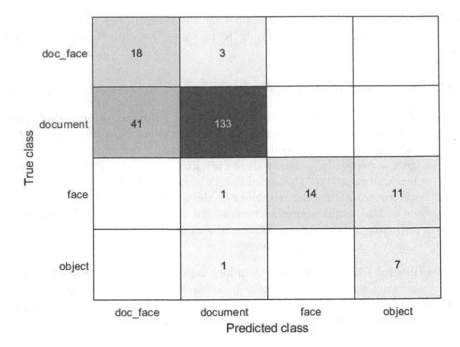

Fig. 2. The confusion matrix that describes the classification of images into one of the following categories: a) document, b) person, c) both document and person and d) object.

recognized by the system based on the two distinct levels of rigor, as described below:

- **Soft Success (Binary):** Value that indicates if the system's output partially matches the annotation's description (1) or not (0). In the case of a success, the system's output should be an adequate but not a detailed image description. We note that in the case of a success, although incomplete, the description produced by the system should not be misleading or partially incorrect.
- **Hard Success (Binary):** Receives a value of 1 if the system managed to produce an accurate description of the image and a value of 0 in case of incorrect or incomplete description. At this level, the system should produce a description semantically equal or even higher than the description provided to the image during the annotation.

Again, we note that it was the nature of the evaluation process that has lead to a human-centered assessment of the system (e.g. manual comparison of annotation and system's output on a semantic level). The evaluation procedure uncovered an overall 49% and 66% accuracy under the strict and moderate evaluation criteria respectively. A more detailed quantification of the system's reliability, per classification category, can be found at Table 1. Although the soft success accuracies appear to be sufficient, the system's reliability under the strict evaluation criteria fails to meet desired performance.

Table 1. Hard and Soft success values per classification category.

Category	Soft success	Hard success
Document	54%	35%
Face	100%	80%
Document and Face	71%	52%
Object	100%	62.5%

3.3 Outdoor Walk

For this supported activity, we initially considered 689 images that were taken by 12 users during the pilot testing of the e-Vision system. Among the three supported activities, the outdoor walk is the most generic of the three and the one that offers the user the greatest freedom of use. The main functionality that supports this activity is the object identification and description. Because it is practically impossible to locate and identify all the objects depicted in a picture of general interest, the images during the annotation process simply took on the following attribute indicating whether the image actually contains objects or is a poor quality photo with no meaningful elements.

– **Meaningful Photo (Binary):** Value that indicates if the image is depicting a detectable object or not (e.g. image depicting solely ground with no objects included).

Out of the full set of 689 images only 485 were annotated as meaningful photos while the rest 204 were images that did not depict a detectable object. Following the paradigm of the previous two use-cases, the assessment of system's reliability is performed in a comprehensive and thorough way since it assessed the information returned to the user at a semantic level. The process took place in exactly the same way as in the other usage scenarios. Therefore, each image was assigned by a human annotator two values indicating whether it was successfully described by the system based on the two following described distinct levels of rigor.

– **Soft Success (Binary):** Value that indicates if the system's output partially matches the annotation's expectation (1) or not (0) under moderate evaluation criteria. In the case of a success, the system's output should be an adequate but not a detailed image description. We note that in the case of a success, although incomplete, the description produced by the system should not be misleading or even partially incorrect.

- **Hard Success (Binary):** Receives a value of 1 if the system manages to produce an accurate description of the image and a value of 0 in case of incorrect or incomplete description. At this level, the system should produce a description semantically equal or even higher than the evaluator's expectations.

The evaluation process uncovered that the outdoor walk usage scenario is the most reliable in terms of the accuracy of the information provided to users. The system's assessment under the moderate level of rigor uncovers a reliability of 80% (considering only the meaningful images according to the annotation procedure). The assessment under the strict level of rigor leads to a reliability value of 45% approximately. We should note that at the strict level of rigor, all images were included (assigned either as meaningful or not during the annotation process) and the object detection module should detect no object on images annotated as not meaningful. The significant reduction observed in the reliability between the two distinct levels of rigor is due to the system's inability to locate all objects of interest depicted in images.

4   Beyond the System's Evaluation

Whereas CV models and algorithms have shown remarkable progress over the past few years, they usually perform well under artificially curated datasets with high-quality and clear images. Even images curated from the web intrinsically pass a human quality assessment of "worthy to upload to the internet". On the other hand, CV-based assistive systems for the visually impaired operate on real-life data originating from blind people. Images stemming from blind photographers typically are of poor quality, since blind people cannot validate the quality of the pictures they take. These images pose new challenges for modern vision algorithms. Furthermore, the prevailing assumption when collecting images to train a CV model is that meaningful information is actually contained in the given images. However, in practice, visually impaired people cannot ensure that a taken image fulfills this criterion since it may suffer from poor focus and lighting or is missing the content of interest.

A post-evaluation investigation that took place uncovered that the aforementioned limitations were the prevailing factors that led to the sub-optimal performance of e-Vision. During this process we examined both the quality and the content of photos that were recorded by the visually impaired. Figure 3 depicts indicative examples of photos taken by blind people during the pilot trials of e-Vision. It becomes apparent that even a human being, without knowing the image context, would not be able to provide the essential information that a visually impaired would be interested of (e.g. detailed document's text and exact product identification).

In an effort to examine the extend of the aforementioned phenomenon, we identified the photos that could not be interpreted by humans and we uncovered that approximately constitute 1/3 of the total photos collected during the

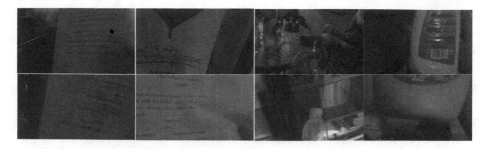

Fig. 3. Indicative examples of photos taken by visually impaired people during the pilot trials of e-Vision. The four left columns depict document images and the four right depict photos of products.

pilot trials. This measurement quantifies the users' inability to accurately capture with the photographic lens the points of their interest. Below, we aim to provide generic guidelines for the CV community that may serve as the basis for overcoming existing obstacles and will hopefully promote its employment in assistive technologies for the visually impaired people.

The great takeoff in CV technology is widely attributed to the collection of a large dataset of images properly annotated. Existing CV models and algorithms are trained on generic datasets governed by particular standards in terms of quality. Therefore, it should not be expected that these same models will able to operate decently on images of low quality as captured by visually impaired people. Towards this direction, several datasets containing actual images taken by visually impaired people have become lately publicly available. The most notable efforts concern visual question answering [2] and automatic image captioning [9]. From our point of view the CV community should exploit recent advances of the field and base its future efforts on such datasets in order to promote assistive technologies for the visually impaired.

A second crucial factor concerns the image quality assessment. A lot of researchers have been focusing on the investigation of what quality issues are observed in a given image and their progress typically stems from artificially constructed settings. Common practices concern the training and evaluation of algorithms on high-quality publicly-available datasets under distortion effects that simulate quality issues. However, these artificially generated environments typically lack the required sophistication to capture the wide variety of factors that modulate the quality issues in natural settings (e.g. insufficient camera hardware, poor lighting conditions, excessive camera shaking, scene obstructions, etc.). Moreover, the quality issues are typical detangled from whether they relate to the ability to complete specific vision tasks [4]. From our point of view we believe it is important to develop appropriate algorithms capable of a) deciding whether an image is of insufficient quality to recognize the content, b) uncovering which quality flaws are present in an image, and c) investigating whether a vision task is impossible due to unrecognizable content versus the content of interest being missing from the field of view. The development of such algorithms may drive both advanced assistive technological achievements and training procedures for the visually impaired in order to help them operate photographic means with high convenience.

5 Conclusion

The main goal of e-Vision is to support people with visual impairments. As described previously, this goal is achieved through the creation of a mobile application, accompanied by a set of camera-glasses, capable of improving the daily lives of visually impaired people. This application takes advantage of modern technological advances in the fields of computer vision and computational intelligence. However, taking into account the limitations of the existing technological reality, it becomes apparent that the development of a universal application capable of covering a wide variety of daily tasks is not feasible. Therefore, the development of the application revolved around the assumption that the design of the application should take into account the purpose of its use. To this end, e-Vision is structures towards supporting the following daily tasks: a) shopping at a grocery store, b) visiting an administration building and c) going an outdoor walk.

In order to support the aforementioned three tasks, the employment of suitable computer vision tools appears as a necessity. The basic computer vision modules that constitute the core of e-Vision are: a) optical character recognition, b) object recognition, c) classification and d) facial landmark recognition. For each of the supported activities, a combination of different computer vision modules is employed. More specifically, in the case of the supermarket, image classification algorithms (product, shelf and trail separation) and optical character recognition (for specifying the exact product, shelf or trail) are used. In the case of the administration building, e-Vision makes use of optical character recognition methods (reading text from signs and documents), facial landmark identification (gender and emotion recognition) and object recognition (uncovering objects of interest in the surrounding environment). Finally, in the scenario of an outdoor walk, object recognition algorithms are used for describing users' surrounding environment.

One of the key concepts of our study concerns the system's reliability assessment so as to quantify to what extend it may promote the autonomy of visually impaired people. Therefore, all the gathered images, during a pilot study involving the use of the e-Vision system by 12 visually impaired users for one month, were annotated so as to drive this assessment. The evaluation procedure indicated that the system, although useful, it did not meet the expectations that were formed during in vitro experiments. To this end, we propose guidelines in an effort to foster future efforts towards developing assistive systems for the visually impaired community.

References

1. Auvray, M., Hanneton, S., O'Regan, J.K.: Learning to perceive with a visuo—auditory substitution system: localisation and object recognition with 'the voice'. Perception **36**(3), 416–430 (2007)
2. Bigham, J.P., et al.: VizWiz: nearly real-time answers to visual questions. In: Proceedings of the 23nd Annual ACM Symposium on User Interface Software and Technology, pp. 333–342 (2010)
3. Bourbakis, N., Keefer, R., Dakopoulos, D., Esposito, A.: A multimodal interaction scheme between a blind user and the tyflos assistive prototype. In: 2008 20th IEEE International Conference on Tools with Artificial Intelligence, vol. 2, pp. 487–494. IEEE (2008)
4. Chiu, T.Y., Zhao, Y., Gurari, D.: Assessing image quality issues for real-world problems. In: Proceedings of the IEEE/CVF Conference on Computer Vision and Pattern Recognition, pp. 3646–3656 (2020)
5. Constantinescu, A., Müller, K., Haurilet, M., Petrausch, V., Stiefelhagen, R.: Bring the environment to life: a sonification module for people with visual impairments to improve situation awareness. In: Proceedings of the 2020 International Conference on Multimodal Interaction, pp. 50–59 (2020)
6. Deng, J., Dong, W., Socher, R., Li, L.J., Li, K., Fei-Fei, L.: Imagenet: a large-scale hierarchical image database. In: 2009 IEEE Conference on Computer Vision and Pattern Recognition, pp. 248–255. IEEE (2009)
7. Georgiadis, K., Kalaganis, F., Migkotzidis, P., Chatzilari, E., Nikolopoulos, S., Kompatsiaris, I.: A computer vision system supporting blind people - the supermarket case. In: Tzovaras, D., Giakoumis, D., Vincze, M., Argyros, A. (eds.) ICVS 2019. LNCS, vol. 11754, pp. 305–315. Springer, Cham (2019). https://doi.org/10.1007/978-3-030-34995-0_28
8. Gold, D., Simson, H.: Identifying the needs of people in Canada who are blind or visually impaired: preliminary results of a nation-wide study. In: International Congress Series, vol. 1282, pp. 139–142. Elsevier (2005)
9. Gurari, D., Zhao, Y., Zhang, M., Bhattacharya, N.: Captioning images taken by people who are blind. arXiv preprint arXiv:2002.08565 (2020)
10. Jourabloo, A., Liu, X.: Pose-invariant face alignment via CNN-based dense 3D model fitting. Int. J. Comput. Vis. **124**(2), 187–203 (2017)
11. Kuznetsova, A., et al.: The open images dataset V4: unified image classification, object detection, and visual relationship detection at scale. arXiv preprint arXiv:1811.00982 (2018)
12. Migkotzidis, P., et al.: e-vision: an AI-powered system for promoting the autonomy of visually impaired. Eur. J. Creative Pract. Cities Landscapes **3**(2), 33–53 (2021)
13. Qin, Z., Zhang, Z., Chen, X., Wang, C., Peng, Y.: FD-MobileNet: improved mobilenet with a fast downsampling strategy. In: 2018 25th IEEE International Conference on Image Processing (ICIP), pp. 1363–1367. IEEE (2018)
14. Redmon, J., Divvala, S., Girshick, R., Farhadi, A.: You only look once: unified, real-time object detection. In: Proceedings of the IEEE Conference on Computer Vision and Pattern Recognition, pp. 779–788 (2016)
15. Sun, Y., Wang, X., Tang, X.: Deep convolutional network cascade for facial point detection. In: Proceedings of the IEEE Conference on Computer Vision and Pattern Recognition, pp. 3476–3483 (2013)

Human Body Parts Tracking from Pressure Data: Toward Effective Pressure Injury Assessment

Carlos Lastre-Dominguez[1], Nasim Hajari[2(✉)], Chester Ho[3],
Oscar Ibarra-Manzano[1], and Irene Cheng[2]

[1] Universidad de Guanajuato, Guanajuato, Mexico
cm.lastredominguez@ugto.mx, ibarrao@ugto.mx
[2] MRC, Department of Computing Science, University of Alberta,
Edmonton, AB, Canada
{hajari,locheng}@ualberta.ca
[3] Department of Medicine, University of Alberta, Edmonton, AB, Canada
chho@ualberta.ca

Abstract. Pressure injuries (PI) cause significant co-morbidities to patients and are costly to the healthcare system, yet mostly preventable. The development of PI is multi-factorial and a major factor is the prolonged interface pressure between the body and the support surface. Monitoring interface pressure over time can reduce the risk of PI development, especially for high risk groups such as those with mobility issues, including seniors and patients with spinal cord injuries. PI can be monitored using pressure sensors. However, the current procedure relies on nurses checking the visualization screens periodically for snapshot pressure assessments, without longitudinal measurements and predictive analysis. We proposed a novel method to track target body parts from pressure data over time. The goal is to develop an automatic PI monitoring system, which will provide just-in-time alerts to care-givers and release nursing resources to higher priority tasks.

Keywords: Pressure injury · In-bed pose estimation · Body part tracking · Longitudinal monitoring · Sensor mattress

1 Introduction

Monitoring in-bed pressure can reduce the chance of developing pressure injuries (PI), especially for high risk groups including seniors and patients with spinal cord injuries. PI development is multi-factorial and the most important known factor is the prolonged interface pressure between the skin and supporting surface such as a bed. Prolong pressure will block the blood flow and hence develop PI. According to [13], there are over 2.5 million patients convalescent with PI in the US. This is just a sample of the problem dimension that captivates the interest of the World Health Organization (WHO). Although PI can be prevented and treated in the early stages, it can be life threatening in its later stages. 29,000 cases of death from PI have been reported in 2013, which is more than 100% increase from 1990 [2]. The prevalence of this condition is even higher in the Canadian healthcare setting (26%) compared to European healthcare setting (2%) [15]. Data from the Agency for Healthcare Research and Quality shows that the rate of pressure injuries in the United States rose by 6% from 2014 to 2017 [1]. Despite all the efforts to effectively monitor in-bed pressure and predict the chance of developing PI, it still remains a challenging task to-date.

The use of pressure mattresses has been considered as a possible intervention to bedsores. In this scenario the healthcare providers check the snapshot of a patient's pressure map at fixed time intervals and change the patient's posture accordingly. However, this method lacks the effective tracking of body parts that have been under pressure over time. The capability to automatically track the pressures exerted on target regions alerts nurses to adjust a patient's posture effectively. Applying computer vision techniques on pressure data for human pose estimation is a possible solution. However, the low resolution and noisy pressure data does not allow a clear visualization of the body silhouette, which makes it difficult to accurately locate the target regions such as head, shoulders, sacrum, and feet.

Pressure data analysis for in-bed pose estimation has been studied in the literature for patient monitoring, PI prevention and sleep pattern analysis. Some researchers used descriptors such as Histogram of Oriented Gradients (HOG) and Scale-Invariant Feature Transform (SIFT), with Support Vector Machine (SVM) and other classifiers to classify in-bed postures [3,6]. Ostadbabas et al. [17] used Gaussian Mixture Models (GMM)-based clustering approaches for posture classification and limb identification. Skeletonization-based pose estimation is the technique used by [9,19]. Independent Component Analysis (ICA) and Principal Component Analysis (PCA) are other techniques used for in-bed posture classification based on pressure data [21]. Artificial Neural Networks (ANN) are recently proposed in the literature [4,7,8,14] to estimate the in-bed postures from pressure data. Some of these techniques require a heavy pre-processing step to make the pressure data as close as possible to the optical data and then use a pre-trained pose estimation network to estimate the in-bed posture from the pressure data [8]. Note that the performance of these techniques depends on the quality of the pressure data. The pressure data are generally noisy and have lower resolution compared to optical data. This can reduce the accuracy of pre-trained ANN methods significantly. Other ANN approaches build their networks from scratch or through retraining existing networks with pressure data [4,14]. These approaches require a representative labelled training set, which can be difficult to get, especially if the training set needs a second data modality such as optical videos [12] or MoCap data to supplement the pressure data [5,11].

In this paper, we propose a novel body part detection and tracking approach based on the low resolution and noisy pressure data. We use signal processing techniques to enhance the pressure signal and find the local maxima in the signal sequence. The local maxima represent the high risk regions, which have higher probabilities to develop PI. These regions include head, shoulders, sacrum and feet. We use the publicly available pressure dataset, (PmatData) proposed by [18], to test our approach. The remaining of this paper is organized as follow: Sect. 2 describes the dataset. Pressure data enhancement is explained in Sect. 3. The algorithms for body part detection and tracking are explained in Sect. 4 and 5. Finally, Sect. 6 concludes our findings.

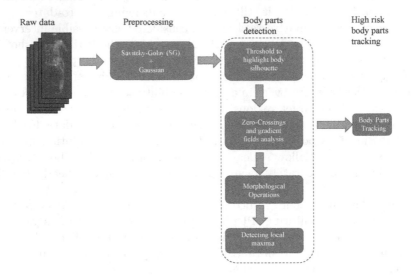

Fig. 1. Overview of the proposed approach

2 Dataset

The Pressure Map Dataset (PmatData) [18] is the first publicly available dataset which collected pressure data for different in-bed postures using two types of pressure measurement mats. The data can be used to visualize the in-bed body pose. There are 13 subjects in the dataset with various postures on supine, left lateral and right lateral, as well as different combinations of external objects and inclinations of the bed (see Table 1). The data is acquired using Vista Medical FSA SoftFlex 2048 and the distribution of pressure sensor in the mattress is 32×64. The sampling rate 1 Hz and each posture is captured around a 2 min period, generating 120 frames.

Based on this dataset, we describe below the proposed method. An overview of our approach is depicted in Fig. 1.

3 Pre-processing: Data Enhancement

One of the challenges of using the PmatData pressure dataset to localize body parts is the low resolution, and noisy pressure data as can be seen in Fig. 2(a).

To enhance the pressure data and remove the system noise, we applied smoothing techniques in our experiments. Smoothing techniques have been applied in the spatial domain for denoising and enhancing of body shape [8]. They can be categorized into two groups: linear and non-linear. The linear smoothing techniques estimate $p_i(x, y)$ considering a weight (normalization factor) w in the region determined by N. A general discrete convolution form is represented in Eq. 1.

$$p_i(x, y) = \sum_{m \in N} \sum_{n \in N} w(i - m, j - n) I(x, y) \tag{1}$$

Table 1. Data properties for experiment I

Index	Posture	Bed Incl. (degree)	Ext. Obj.
1	Supine	0	0
2	Right	0	0
3	Left	0	0
4	Right	0	1 Wedge
5	Right	0	2 Wedge
6	Left	0	1 Wedge
7	Left	0	2 Wedge
8	Supine	0	0
9	Supine	0	0
10	Supine	0	0
11	Supine	0	0
12	Supine	0	0
13	Right Fetus	0	0
14	Left Fetus	0	0
15	Supine	30	0
16	Supine	45	0
17	Supine	60	0

where $p_i(x, y)$ is the pixel estimation of point (x, y) in the image I, and w represents the weight which depends on the kernel (convolution matrix). The effect provided by this kernel is to diminish the different intensities between neighbourhood pixels. Analytically, this filter is equivalent to a low pass filter (LPF) applied in the spatial domain. We have tried different smoothing kernels such as uniform, circular, pyramidal, conical, binomial, Gaussian and Savitsky-Golay. The analysis results of these kernels show that Gaussian and Savitsky-Golay filters enhance the pressure signals more effectively. Therefore, we applied both filters on the raw data to smooth the pressure signal but at the same time preserve the local characteristics of it. These approaches are described below.

3.1 2D Gaussian Kernel

A 2D Gaussian kernel is given in Eq. 2.

$$K_g(x,y) = \frac{1}{2\pi\sigma^2} e^{-\frac{x^2+y^2}{2\sigma^2}} \tag{2}$$

where the variables x and y are interpreted as the distances from the origin in the horizontal and vertical axes, respectively, and σ is the standard deviation of the Gaussian distribution. Specifically, a cubic Gaussian kernel is employed in our experiments.

3.2 Savitzky-Golay Filter

Let $f(x,y)$ be a two-dimensional (2D) signal, where x and y are the discrete spatial coordinates. Considering a 2D polynomial that approximates the signal in a least-square error (LSE) manner. Over a horizon of length $H = 2M + 1$, where M are data points symmetric on both sides of the signal point (around the origin $(0,0)$), the data on the horizon are approximated by a polynomial of order N that minimizes the error between the selected data belonging to the horizon and its approximate polynomial signal.

Initially, we consider the cost function which is minimized by Eq. 3:

$$J = \sum_{x=-M}^{M} \sum_{y=-M}^{M} ((g(x,y) - f(x,y)))^2 \tag{3}$$

where:

$$g(x,y) = \sum_{i=0}^{N} \sum_{j=0}^{N} a_{i,j} x^i y^j \tag{4}$$

Substituting $g(x,y)$ from Eq. 4 in Eq. 3, we will have the following equation:

$$J = \sum_{x=-M}^{M} \sum_{y=-M}^{M} ((\sum_{i=0}^{N} \sum_{j=0}^{N} a_{i,j} x^i y^j - f(x,y)))^2 \tag{5}$$

Minimising this expression to zero and considering $0 \le p, q \le N$, we obtain:

$$\frac{\partial J}{\partial a_{pq}} = \sum_{x=-M}^{M} \sum_{y=-M}^{M} 2((\sum_{i=0}^{N} \sum_{j=0}^{N} a_{i,j} x^i y^j - f(x,y))) x^p y^q = 0 \tag{6}$$

Hence,

$$\sum_{x=-M}^{M} \sum_{y=-M}^{M} ((\sum_{i=0}^{N} \sum_{j=0}^{N} x^{i+p} y^{j+q} a_{i,j})) = \sum_{x=-M}^{M} \sum_{y=-M}^{M} x^p y^q f(x,y) \tag{7}$$

the following expression can be represented in matrix form:

$$\mathbf{A}^T \mathbf{A} \mathbf{a} = \mathbf{A}^T \mathbf{F} \tag{8}$$

where $\mathbf{F} = f(x, y)$, the matrix $\mathbf{A}$ is a $(2M+1)^2 \times (N+1)^2$ matrix depending of x and y. Considering $M = 1$ and $N = 2$, A is a form-polynomial matrix given as follows:

$$\mathbf{A} = \begin{bmatrix} 1 & x_0 & x_0^2 & y_0 & y_0^2 & x_0 y_0 & x_0 y_0^2 & x_0^2 y_0 & x_0^2 y_0^2 \\ 1 & x_1 & x_1^2 & y_1 & y_1^2 & x_1 y_1 & x_1 y_1^2 & x_1^2 y_1 & x_1^2 y_1^2 \\ \vdots & \vdots & \vdots & \vdots & \vdots & \vdots & \vdots & \vdots & \vdots \\ 1 & x_8 & x_8^2 & y_8 & y_8^2 & x_8 y_8 & x_8 y_8^2 & x_8^2 y_8 & x_8^2 y_8^2 \end{bmatrix} \tag{9}$$

Considering that $\mathbf{W} = (\mathbf{A^T A})^{-1} \mathbf{A^T}$, the coefficients of $\mathbf{a}$ can be computed as:

$$\mathbf{a} = (\mathbf{A^T A})^{-1} \mathbf{A^T F} \triangleq \mathbf{WF} \tag{10}$$

where the matrix $\mathbf{W}$ is a $(N+1)^2 \times (2M+1)^2$ matrix whose terms are independent of input data. According to [16] with an odd size kernel $H \times H$ and considering that $\mathbf{H} = \mathbf{AW}$, the estimation of $\hat{g}(x, y)$ as $\hat{\mathbf{G}}$ is given by Eq. 11.

$$\hat{\mathbf{G}} = \mathbf{Aa} = (\mathbf{AW})\mathbf{F} = \mathbf{HF} \tag{11}$$

where $\mathbf{H}$ represents the kernel matrix of the Savitsky-Golay filter. We used Savitzky-Golay (SG) based techniques developed by [10, 20] for data smoothing. Figure 2 shows some examples of applying two of the fastest filters (conical and pyramid) as well as binomial, Gaussian and Savitsky Golay filters for a subject in a right lateral position.

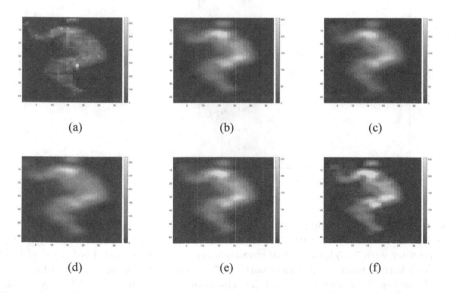

(a)   (b)   (c)

(d)   (e)   (f)

Fig. 2. Smoothing results on frame 20 for a subject in a right lateral position with different filters: (a) Raw data, (b) 7×7 conical filter, (c) 7×7 pyramid filter, (d) Gaussian filter with $\sigma = 1.4$, (e) 7×7 binomial kernel and (f) 7×7 Savitsky-Golayis.

3.3   Processing Time

We applied seven smoothing filters with different configuration parameters such as kernel size or σ. Figure 3 shows the average processing time for each filter. As Fig. 3 depicts, the computational cost depends on the kernel size. For example a Savitsky Golay filter with a 3×3 kernel size is 50% faster than the same filter with a 5×5 kernel size and 67% faster than 7×7 kernel.

4   Body Part Detection

After enhancing the pressure data, a threshold is applied to eliminate insignificant data to better highlight the body silhouette. Figure 4(a) illustrates the highlighted body silhouette. As mentioned earlier, the high risk regions to develop PI are head, shoulders, sacrum and feet. Also, Fig. 4(a) shows that (with warmer colors, e.g. yellow and orange) these areas have a higher pressure interface compared to their neighbourhood. Therefore, detecting local maxima in the 2D pressure signals provides cues for the location of these parts. The local maxima are computed as the zero crossings in the gradient fields. Given the unit vectors $\hat{\mathbf{i}}$

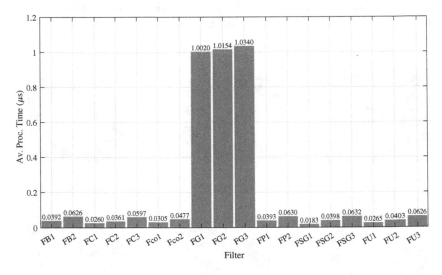

Fig. 3. Averaged processing time in microseconds (μs). FB1: binomial filter with 5×5 kernel, FB2: binomial filter with 7×7 kernel, FC1: circular filter with 3×3 kernel, FC2: circular filter with 5×5 kernel, FC3: circular filter with 7×7 kernel, Fco1: conical filter with 5×5 kernel, Fco2: conical filter with 7×7 kernel, FG1: Gaussian filter with $\sigma = 1$, FG2: Gaussian filter with $\sigma = 1.4$, FG3: Gaussian filter with $\sigma = 2$, FP1: pyramidal filter with 5×5 kernel, FP2: pyramidal filter with 7×7 kernel, FSG1: Savitsky-Golay filter with 3×3 kernel, FSG2: Savitsky-Golay filter with 5×5 kernel, FSG3: Savitsky-Golay filter with 7×7 kernel, FU1: uniform filter with 3×3 kernel, FU2: uniform filter with 5×5 kernel, FU3: uniform filter with 7×7 kernel.

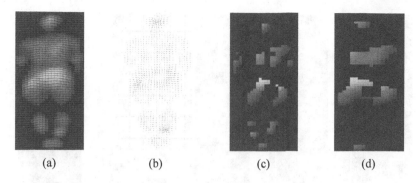

(a)   (b)   (c)   (d)

Fig. 4. (a) After applying a threshold to data smoothed by Savitsky Golay and Gaussian filter. (b) Gradient vector obtained from the pressure data. (c) Potential regions of interest detected based on local maxima. (d) More noticeable regions of interest after removing unrelated data and applying morphological operations.

and $\hat{\mathbf{j}}$ in the direction of the x and y coordinates respectively, the gradient is expressed by Eq. 12 and the gradient field is depicted in Fig. 4(b).

$$\nabla(f) = \frac{\partial f}{\partial x}\hat{\mathbf{i}} + \frac{\partial f}{\partial y}\hat{\mathbf{j}} \tag{12}$$

The local maxima regions can be estimated by Eq. 13 and the output is shown in Fig. 4(c).

$$\delta(x,y) = \begin{cases} 1, & \frac{\partial f}{\partial x} < 0 \text{ and } \frac{\partial f}{\partial y} < 0 \\ 0, & \text{otherwise} \end{cases} \tag{13}$$

Note that in Fig. 4(c) there are irrelevant regions, especially around arms and hands. We remove these regions using relative location information. We then use morphological operations, such as dilation and erosion, to remove small regions, which are not the high risk body parts.

The result of this post-processing step and the final detected regions are shown in Fig. 4(d).

After detecting the high risk regions, the next step is to label them automatically and accurately. Here we use a simple relational approach to label the regions. The intuition is that we are monitoring patients, who cannot move on the mattress by themselves and therefore the body orientation is relatively fixed. In other words, considering the result in Fig. 4(d), the body is divided into four regions. The top (first) and bottom (last) regions correspond to head and feet respectively. The second and third region corresponds to shoulders and sacrum. Figure 5 shows the detected body regions for different postures.

5   High Risk Body Parts Tracking

To track body parts over time, we need to find local maxima of enhanced signals in each frame. Figure 6 (Head) and Fig. 7 (Hips) show the pressure tracking

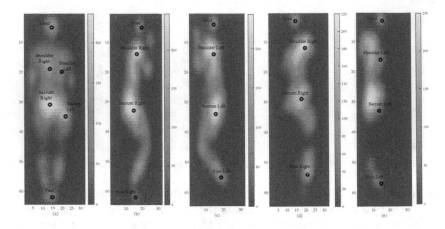

Fig. 5. An illustration of automatically detected local maxima, which correspond to the high risk body regions, e.g., head, shoulders, sacrum and feet.

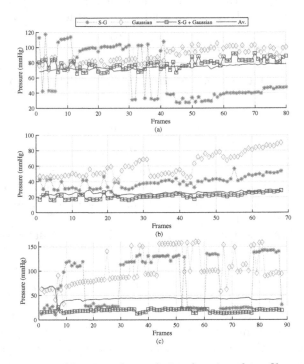

Fig. 6. Head pressure tracking on enhanced signals using three filters: Savitsky-Golay (S-G), Gaussian and S-G+Gaussian. The reference value is the average of the raw signals in the extracted region (Av.). (a) Head supine pose, (b) Head right lateral pose and (c) Head left lateral pose.

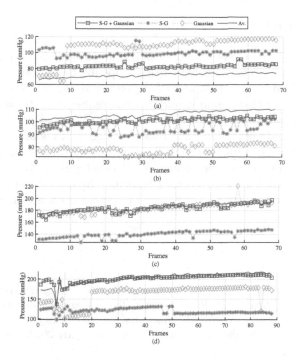

Fig. 7. Sacrum pressure tracking using enhanced signal by Savitsky-Golay (S-G), Gaussian and S-G+Gaussian filters. The reference value is the average of the raw signal in extracted region (Av.). (a) Hip supine pose-right section of sacrum, (b) Hip supine pose-left section of sacrum, (c) Hip right lateral pose and (d) Hip left lateral pose.

Table 2. Body tracking evaluation based on RMSE: K = 1 and K = 2 denote kernel size 3 × 3 and 5 × 5, respectively.

Head	SG + Gaussian (K = 1, σ = 1.4)	SG (K = 1)	Gaussian (σ = 1.4)
Head-supine RMSE	7.35	35.68	16.86
Head-right RMSE	5.02	15.55	38.20
Head-left RMSE	26.9	63.90	69.1
Hips	SG + Gaussian (K = 2, σ = 1.4)	SG (K = 2)	Gaussian (σ = 1.4)
Supine hip-right RMSE	11.4	27.78	37.97
Supine hip-left RMSE	5.58	11.55	27.86
Lateral hip-right RMSE	6.82	83.4	43.2
Lateral hip-left RMSE	3.85	44.5	4.65

over time using three different enhancement approaches for head and sacrum area respectively. We use the average of raw data in each extracted region as a ground truth for comparing the efficiencies of the enhancement approaches. Table 2 shows the root-mean-square error (RMSE) corresponding to Fig. 6 and Fig. 7, with respect to the average of the raw signals.

6   Conclusions

Monitoring in-bed pressure of patients can reduce the chance of developing pressure injuries (PI), especially for high risk groups including seniors and patients with spinal cord injuries. Developing PI depends not only on interface pressure, but also on the time that region is under pressure. Some body parts, including: head, shoulders, sacrum and feet, are more prone to PI development. We propose a novel method to detect, label and track the high risk regions from noisy and low resolution pressure data. Tracking body parts over time is a crucial first step in analysing and predicting the chance of PI development. In future work, we will address the problem of eliminating external objects, e.g. pillows put under the patients to reduce interface pressure, as external objects can affect body parts detection.

References

1. https://www.advisory.com/daily-briefing/2019/11/14/pressure-injury
2. Abubakar, I., Tillmann, T., Banerjee, A.: Global, regional, and national age-sex specific all-cause and cause-specific mortality for 240 causes of death, 1990–2013: a systematic analysis for the global burden of disease study 2013. Lancet **385**(9963), 117–171 (2015)
3. Beltrán-Herrera, A., Vázquez-Santacruz, E., Gamboa-Zuñiga, M.: Real-time classification of lying bodies by HOG descriptors. In: Martínez-Trinidad, J.F., Carrasco-Ochoa, J.A., Olvera-Lopez, J.A., Salas-Rodríguez, J., Suen, C.Y. (eds.) MCPR 2014. LNCS, vol. 8495, pp. 211–220. Springer, Cham (2014). https://doi.org/10.1007/978-3-319-07491-7_22
4. Casas, L., Navab, N., Demirci, S.: Patient 3D body pose estimation from pressure imaging. Int. J. Comput. Assist. Radiol. Surg. **14**(3), 517–524 (2018). https://doi.org/10.1007/s11548-018-1895-3
5. Clever, H.M., Kapusta, A., Park, D., Erickson, Z., Chitalia, Y., Kemp, C.C.: 3D human pose estimation on a configurable bed from a pressure image. In: 2018 IEEE/RSJ International Conference on Intelligent Robots and Systems (IROS), pp. 54–61. IEEE (2018)
6. Cruz-Santos, W., Beltrán-Herrera, A., Vázquez-Santacruz, E., Gamboa-Zúñiga, M.: Posture classification of lying down human bodies based on pressure sensors array. In: 2014 International Joint Conference on Neural Networks (IJCNN), pp. 533–537. IEEE (2014)
7. Davoodnia, V., Etemad, A.: Identity and posture recognition in smart beds with deep multitask learning. In: 2019 IEEE International Conference on Systems, Man and Cybernetics (SMC), pp. 3054–3059. IEEE (2019)
8. Davoodnia, V., Ghorbani, S., Etemad, A.: In-bed pressure-based pose estimation using image space representation learning. arXiv preprint arXiv:1908.08919 (2019)
9. Farshbaf, M., Yousefi, R., Pouyan, M.B., Ostadabbas, S., Nourani, M., Pompeo, M.: Detecting high-risk regions for pressure ulcer risk assessment. In: 2013 IEEE International Conference on Bioinformatics and Biomedicine, pp. 255–260. IEEE (2013)

10. Gowri, B.G., Hariharan, V., Thara, S., Sowmya, V., Kumar, S.S., Soman, K.P.: 2D Image data approximation using Savitzky Golay filter smoothing and differencing. In: 2013 International Mutli-Conference on Automation, Computing, Communication, Control and Compressed Sensing (iMac4s), pp. 365–371. IEEE (2013)
11. Harada, T., Sato, T., Mori, T.: Pressure distribution image based human motion tracking system using skeleton and surface integration model. In: Proceedings 2001 ICRA. IEEE International Conference on Robotics and Automation (Cat. No. 01CH37164), vol. 4, pp. 3201–3207. IEEE (2001)
12. Huang, W., Wai, A.A.P., Foo, S.F., Biswas, J., Hsia, C.C., Liou, K.: Multimodal sleeping posture classification. In: 2010 20th International Conference on Pattern Recognition, pp. 4336–4339. IEEE (2010)
13. Mansfield, S., Obraczka, K., Roy, S.: Pressure injury prevention: a survey. IEEE Rev. Biomed. Eng. **13**, 352–368 (2020)
14. Matar, G., Lina, J.M., Kaddoum, G.: Artificial neural network for in-bed posture classification using bed-sheet pressure sensors. IEEE J. Biomed. Health Inform. **24**, 101–110 (2019)
15. McInnes, E., Jammali-Blasi, A., Bell-Syer, S.E., Dumville, J.C., Middleton, V., Cullum, N.: Support surfaces for pressure ulcer prevention. Cochrane Database Syst. Rev. **21** (2015)
16. Menon, S.V., Seelamantula, C.S.: Sure-optimal two-dimensional savitzky-golay filters for image denoising. In: 2013 IEEE International Conference on Image Processing, pp. 459–463. IEEE (2013)
17. Ostadabbas, S., Pouyan, M.B., Nourani, M., Kehtarnavaz, N.: In-bed posture classification and limb identification. In: 2014 IEEE Biomedical Circuits and Systems Conference (BioCAS) Proceedings, pp. 133–136. IEEE (2014)
18. Pouyan, M.B., Birjandtalab, J., Heydarzadeh, M., Nourani, M., Ostadabbas., S.: In: 2017 IEEE EMBS International Conference on Biomedical Health Informatics (BHI) (2017)
19. Pouyan, M.B., Birjandtalab, J., Nourani, M., Pompeo, M.M.: Automatic limb identification and sleeping parameters assessment for pressure ulcer prevention. Comput. Biol. Med. **75**, 98–108 (2016)
20. Rajagopalan, S., Robb, R.A.: Image smoothing with Savtizky-Golai filters. In: Medical Imaging 2003: Visualization, Image-Guided Procedures, and Display. p. 773 (2003)
21. Yousefi, R., et al.: Bed posture classification for pressure ulcer prevention. In: 2011 Annual International Conference of the IEEE Engineering in Medicine and Biology Society, pp. 7175–7178. IEEE (2011)

Personalized Navigation that Links Speaker's Ambiguous Descriptions to Indoor Objects for Low Vision People

Jun-Li Lu[1,2]([✉]), Hiroyuki Osone[1], Akihisa Shitara[1], Ryo Iijima[1],
Bektur Ryskeldiev[1,2], Sayan Sarcar[1,2], and Yoichi Ochiai[1,2]

[1] Research and Development Center for Digital Nature, University of Tsukuba,
Tsukuba, Japan
jllu@slis.tsukuba.ac.jp
[2] Faculty of Library, Information and Media Science, University of Tsukuba,
Tsukuba, Japan

Abstract. Indoor navigation systems guide a user to his/her specified destination. However, current navigation systems face the challenges
when a user provides ambiguous descriptions about the destinations.
This can commonly happen to visually impaired people or those who
are unfamiliar with new environments. For example, in an office, a low-
vision person asks the navigator by saying "Take me to where I can take a
rest?". The navigator may recognize each object (e.g., desk) in the office
but may not recognize which location the user can take a rest. To overcome the gap of surrounding understanding between low-vision people
and a navigator, we propose a personalized interactive navigation system that links user's ambiguous descriptions to indoor objects. We build
a navigation system that automatically detect and describe objects in
the environment by neural-network models. Further, we personalize the
navigation by re-training the recognition models based on previous interactive dialogues, which may contain the corresponding between user's
understanding and the visual images or shapes of objects. In addition,
we utilize a GPU cloud for supporting computational cost and smooth
the navigation by locating user's position using Visual SLAM. We discussed further research on customizable navigation with multi-aspect
perceptions of disabilities and the limitation of AI-assisted recognition.

Keywords: Personalized navigation · Linking ambiguous descriptions
to objects · AI cloud

1 Introduction

Indoor navigation systems guide a user to his/her specified destination [2,3,5,
7,9–12,16,17]. However, current navigation systems face the challenges when a
user provides ambiguous descriptions about the destinations. This can commonly
happen to visually impaired people or those who are unfamiliar with new environments. For example, in an office, a low-vision person asks the navigator by

M. Antona and C. Stephanidis (Eds.): HCII 2021, LNCS 12769, pp. 412–423, 2021.
https://doi.org/10.1007/978-3-030-78095-1_30

saying "Take me to where I can take a rest?". A typical navigator may recognize each object (e.g., desk, chair, and printer) in the office but may not recognize which location can be satisfied the user's target destination, especially when the user describes the target destination ambiguously.

In advanced development of artificial intelligence (AI), the navigation devices and technology focused on utilizing recognition abilities of AI. For example, a work [11] detected the target of a object from visual images [4,21] and generate the map of a space by using LiDAR devices in assisting the navigation of visual impairments. In addition, the computational devices, such as movable robots, smartphones, and locating devices (e.g., GPS), were utilized in navigation systems. For example, a smartphone-based navigation with GPS-based locating [17] focused on assisting visual impairments in navigating across a relatively wide outdoor area. Furthermore, the design of interface or agile functions on a navigation system for blind users are important factors in quality of navigation. For example, a work [7] designed a suitcase-shaped navigation robot in assisting navigation of blind users with avoiding the collision of obstacles in the path. In addition, a work [2] focused on providing a smooth rotating experience when visually impaired people make a turn on corner, by using the tip of customizable rotating degrees.

However, few literature on navigation systems have dealt with or investigated on the gap or corresponding between the perception of visual impairments and the conditions of their existing space. Specifically, the spoken words from blind user's understanding to the surroundings could be quite different to the spoken words from normal people.

Therefore, to overcome the gap of surrounding understanding between low vision people and a navigator, we propose a personalized interactive navigation system that is able to link user's ambiguous descriptions to indoor objects. Specifically, we build a system that automatically detects objects and describes the detected objects in an indoor environment by using neural-network models. Further, for personalizing the navigation, we propose to re-train the recognition models based on the data of interactive dialogues, which contains the corresponding among the user's descriptions on target, the model's descriptions, and visual images or shapes of objects. Last but not least, we locate user's indoor positions by using Visual SLAM, and build a GPU cloud that runs recognition and machine learning for supporting computational cost of neural-network recognition.

In the demonstration, we showed a built prototype of our system and an application case that consisted of an initial navigation, collecting interactive dialogues, retraining recognition models, and personalizing the navigation. In addition, we observed that our personalized navigation was able to reduce the time of finding target destination, in the next time of similar navigation tasks. We list the key points of this work as follows.

- We advocate that there exists a gap of surrounding understanding between low vision people and a navigator.
- Therefore, we propose a personalized navigation system that detects and describes objects in environments, by re-training the recognition models using interactive dialogues during navigation.

– We demonstrated the usage of the system in a space of laboratory and discussed for facilitating further research.

2 Related Work

We discuss AI-assisted navigation, customized recognition that can be used in navigation, and the survey on navigation for low vision people as follows.

2.1 AI-Assisted Navigation Devices and Technology

Kayukawa et al. [11] detected object's position by camera's image and built the 2D map by using LiDAR. Guerreiro et al. [7] presented the design of a carry-on robot, which is an autonomous suitcase-shaped navigation robot that is able to guide users (especially for visual impairments) to a destination and avoids the collision of obstacles. Further, their designed function of a vibro-tactile handle for conveying directional feedback was found to be useful to blind people. Sato et al. [17] developed a smartphone-based navigation system that utilized localization capabilities of GPS-based measurement and focused on the evaluation on navigation tasks across a wide outdoor area, which was across multiple buildings. Ahmetovic et al. [2] advocated that the rotating error of making a turn could often happen for blind users, and thus proposed a neural-network approach that learned to revise the rotating degrees in making a smooth rotation for a user. Furthermore, in customized or personalized recognition, Ahmetovic et al. [3] developed a smartphone-based application that enabled blind users to automatically recognize their-own objects, especially for objects which could not be recognizable via tactile feature, and thus proposed a camera-aiming guidance to assist a user in locating objects.

2.2 Survey on Navigation for Low Vision People

Furthermore, we discussed about survey on navigation for blind or low vision people. Ohn-Bar et al. [15] found that, in smartphone-based navigation, there might exist a significant variability during the crucial elements of the navigation (e.g., turning and encountering obstacles). Therefore, Ohn-Bar et al. advocated the need to not only adjust interface timing and content to each user's personal walking pace, but also their individual navigation skill and style. Ahmetovic et al. [1] investigated the impact of expertise on interaction preferences and revealed that visually impaired had diversified needs for navigation instructions based on their abilities and preferences. Guerreiro et al. [6] investigated the assistance of navigation in airport accessibility for visual impairments and found that, even the route of navigation was challenging, blind users were able to complete the navigation independently.

These above works focused on navigation technology and blind users. However, these work might not focus on the gap or corresponding between the perceptions of visually impaired and real conditions of their existing space.

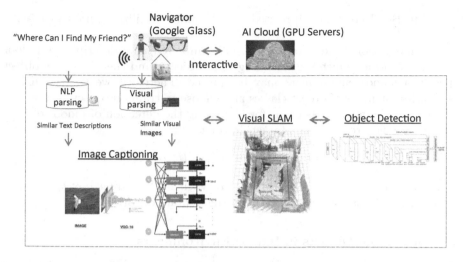

Fig. 1. We propose a navigation system that detects and describes objects in the environment by neural-network models of object detection and image captioning. Further, we personalize the navigation by re-training the recognition models based on interactive dialogues.

For example, the spoken words from blind user's understanding to the surrounding space could be quite different to the spoken words from normal people. To deal with the above issues, in this work, we aim to investigate the gap between user's understanding and conditions of the existing space. Further, we propose the approach of building personalized navigation for a user, how to re-train recognition models by using interactive dialogues during navigation, and which recognition models could be utilized.

3   Personalized Navigation Cloud: Detecting Objects, Describing Objects, and Locating Users in Indoor Environments

In Fig. 1, we propose a personalized navigation system for linking user's ambiguous descriptions to objects. Specifically, the system consists of detecting and describing objects in environments, personalizing navigation by interactive dialogues and re-training approach, locating users by Visual SLAM, and the construction of a GPU cloud.

3.1   Detecting Indoor Objects

We show the model that detects objects from a given image. For real-time usage and computational complexity, we consider to utilize speedy models, such as YOLOv4: Optimal Speed and Accuracy of Object Detection [4] and SSD (Single

Shot MultiBox Detector) [14] related models, and we utilize an implementation of YOLOv4[1].

In a navigation task, people or visually impaired may describe the indoor target destination, which are often large-size objects, and the number of object types in a indoor environment may be limited. Therefore, we train YOLOv4 with limited number of object classes and choose to train on objects whose size are relatively large, such as chair, for increasing the detection of indoor objects which may relate to the user's target destination.

$$F(m; \mathbf{W}) = \{(b_1, o_1), ..., (b_i, o_i)\}, \tag{1}$$

is the function that detects each object o_i with its bounding box b_i in input image m, and $\mathbf{W}$ is the set of weights of the neural-network model.

3.2 Describing Objects in Indoor Environments

After detecting objects, we show the model that describes the detected objects in the context of indoor environments. We utilize a classical model of image captioning[2] [20], which is a attention-based encoder-decoder model with LSTM [18] and ResNet [8].

The user's target destination may relate to a single object (e.g., desk). Therefore, if there are multiple objects detected in a single image, we choose to run image captioning $C(.)$ on each sub-image m_{b_i} of a detected object o_i.

$$C(m_{b_i}; \mathbf{W}) = T,$$

where output T is a sequence of words. Further, for describing the context of a object more completely, the textual description of each object contains both the textual description of the object's sub-image and that of the whole image, which is

$$C(m_{b_i}; \mathbf{W}) \cup C(m; \mathbf{W}). \tag{2}$$

3.3 Personalizing Navigation for Linking User's Ambiguous Descriptions to Objects

In a navigation task, the spoken description about the target from a user (especially visually impaired) may not match the correct description of target. Therefore, we personalize the navigation for a user by the following process.

1. In a navigation task, the user speaks the target description.
2. At a moment, the navigator (e.g., smart glasses), which is attached on the user, receives visual image and detect objects with their descriptions.
3. For each detected object, the navigator asks the user if the description of the object matches user's target destination?

---

[1] YOLOv4, https://github.com/Tianxiaomo/pytorch-YOLOv4.
[2] Image Captioning, https://github.com/sgrvinod/a-PyTorch-Tutorial-to-Image-Captioning.

4. If the user replies "yes", the related label data will be saved as: "the target description by user", "the description of the object by model", "is matched/close", and "the object with its sub-image". Otherwise, the process continues.
5. The step (2) to step (4) can be iteratively triggered when the user is asked to call for querying the target destination.

After collecting the label dataset from one or multiple navigation tasks, in our AI cloud, we can re-train the model of object detection $F(\mathbf{W})$ and the model of image captioning $C(\mathbf{W})$ by using the dataset. Therefore, with re-trained models, in the next navigation task of a similar environment or similar target, we may be able to provide the descriptions of objects that are relatively similar to the user's descriptions of target. For example, the target description, "Where I can take rest", from a user, may not be matched with the descriptions of detected objects by the model, at the first time of navigation. Therefore, after re-training models, we are possible to match the user's description to the target, i.e., the desk, in the lab.

3.4   Indoor Locating by Visual SLAM

In a navigation task, the navigator requires to know the location of a user in the indoor environment. However, we cannot sensor the location of the user in a indoor environment accurately by using GPS-based measurement. Therefore, we utilize Visual SLAM[3] [19] for detecting the indoor location of a user. Visual SLAM generates the map of a space based on multiple views of visual images of the space. Further, for increasing the accuracy of locating, in an indoor environment, we pre-build the generated map before running a navigation task. Note that the camera is required to run calibration for computing related matrices[4], which are used to get the corresponding between points of camera and points of the space, before running Visual SLAM.

Navigator. A navigator is an interface device that is used for visually sensing the surrounding as user and communicating between the user and our navigation system. In indoor navigation for low vision people, we advocate that the navigator should be wearable on a user for easy communication and sensing the surrounding. Further, we advocate to utilize smart glasses since the smart glasses can be wearable on the head in front of eyes and thus are able to sense as field-of-view of people. Especially, we recommend the latest Google Glass[5] that has both of high computation ability, which can support computer-vision preprocessing such as image compressed or filtering routines, and quality power savings, which can make long-time usage of navigation. In the demonstration of this work, a laptop PC is used as navigator for preliminary development.

---

[3] OpenVSLAM, https://github.com/xdspacelab/openvslam.
[4] https://docs.opencv.org/2.4/modules/calib3d/doc/camera_calibration_and_3d_reconstruction.html.
[5] Google Glass Enterprise Edition 2, https://www.google.com/glass/tech-spec.

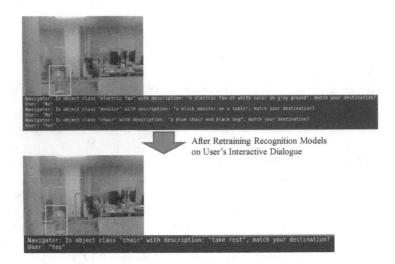

Fig. 2. A navigation task with the user's spoken destination, "Where can I take rest". In the initial time of navigation, the user's destination was known after three times of dialogues (the above case). After personalizing by re-training recognition using interactive dialogues, in the next time of navigation, the user's destination could be quickly known (the below case).

4   Demonstration

In the demonstration, we discuss the following questions. **Question 1**: Can our navigation system perform personalized navigation? How did our personalized navigation improve user's navigation tasks? **Question 2**: Did our method link the user's descriptions with indoor objects?

Navigation by Interactive Dialogues. We set a simple navigation task, which was located in a laboratory of an indoor environment. A participant took a laptop PC (as navigator) in front of himself or herself and performed a navigation task by interactive dialogues with the navigator. In the task, at first, the participant speaks out the target destination to the navigator, and thus the navigator will try to detect objects with the textual captions of the detected objects and ask the user that if the object relates to the target or not?

At the first time of navigation, the user spoke out the destination as "Where can I take rest". At a moment, as shown in Fig. 2, the navigator asked the user if each of detected object was matched the target or not, and until the third time of conversation, the user replied to "yes". Note that the user took three times of conversation for finding the target, and the dialogues during this navigation was recorded as data.

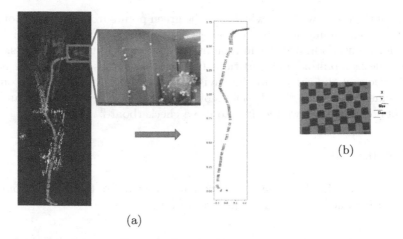

(b)

(a)

Fig. 3. Indoor locating results by Visual SLAM: (a) The movement tracing (green dots) of a user in a laboratory space, and note that 3D feature points (red dots) could be corresponding to 2D features points (yellow dots) of a camera's image in front of the user. (b) The camera was required to run calibration to compute related matrices before running Visual SLAM. (Color figure online)

Re-training Navigation Models. Therefore, to customize the navigation model, we re-trained our model of image captioning by using the dataset of interactive dialogues from the first navigation. A sample data was composed of the attributes of detected object, generated caption, matched user's target or not, and sub-image of the object (e.g., "electric fan", "a electric fan of white color on gray ground", "is matched"). In the training of image captioning model, we observed that the model could learned quality performance about after thirty epochs (i.e., loss was relatively low and accuracy was relatively high). Note that the number of samples was about the level of tens, and we set the ratio of training data and that of validation data as eighty percent and twenty percent.

Personalized Navigation by Interactive Dialogue and Retraining Models. After retraining the model, the user is asked to perform the same navigation task, with the same setting of the first time. In the second time of navigation, as shown in the below of Fig. 2, with the same user's target description, we observed that the user could find the target object by using less time of conversation with the navigator (i.e., one-time conversation). A preliminary results found that our navigation system might reduce the time of finding target, which was unclear from user's description, after our system learned the personalized navigation from interactive dialogues.

Indoor Locating Results by Visual SLAM. In the demonstration, we also showed the locating results of user's movement and the space of the laboratory in this navigation task by using Visual SLAM. In Fig. 3(a), we showed that the locating of the user's walking, which was the green points from the start point at below to the end point at above. By observing the locating results, we might be able to locate user's movement in a laboratory space with typical objects, such as chair, desk, monitor, and partition. In Fig. 3(b), we also showed the result of calibration on the camera of the navigator. For calibrating a camera on the correspondence between the 2D points of a image taken by the camera and the 3D points of the space, we required to use a checkerboard[6].

5   Discussion

We discussed on further research direction and showed the issues from the demonstration and AI recognition and re-training.

Facilitating Research on Customizable Navigation with Multi-aspect Perceptions of Disabilities and AI-Assisted Recognition. Through our demonstration, we showed the difficulty that visually impaired users may occur, such as multiple times of dialogues for getting the target destination. We also showed the opportunity to solve the issues by personalizing navigation using re-training recognition models with interactive dialogues. Since there exists some weak or disable sensing of disabilities, either visually or hearing impaired, an interesting research direction may be that complementing multiple-aspect sensing of disabilities with customizable and learnable AI-assisted navigation. Especially, how to complement sensing ability and how to customize AI recognition may relate to design of interaction during a navigation process.

Limitation on Unstable Trainable Recognition and Requiring Multi-aspect Modeling for Disabilities. How to approach the re-training of recognition models may still be challenging issues, since the machine-learning recognition results could be unstable and the complexity of environments (e.g., multiple and diverse types of objects) and the perception level of disabilities could make a machine hard to learn the same or close level of recognition to the environments. Further, how to control the learning of a customized navigation between user's own perceptions and the common recognition ability, could be issues. The reasons may be that if the navigation is customized for personal understanding and it may lose typical knowledge of recognition.

6   Conclusion

Current navigation systems face the challenges when a user provides ambiguous descriptions about the destinations. This can commonly happen to visually impaired people. In this work, to overcome the gap of surrounding understanding

---

[6] Checkerboard, https://markhedleyjones.com/projects/calibration-checkerboard-coll ection.

between low-vision people and a navigator, we propose a personalized interactive navigation system that links user's ambiguous descriptions to indoor objects. We build a navigation system that detects and describes objects in the environment by neural-network models. Further, we personalize the navigation by re-training the recognition models based on interactive dialogues, which may contain the corresponding between user's understanding and visual images or shapes of objects. In addition, we utilize a GPU cloud for supporting computational cost and locate the navigation by locating user's position using Visual SLAM. We discussed on customizable navigation with multi-aspect perceptions of disabilities and pointed limitation of AI-assisted recognition and issues of re-training models.

Acknowledgement. This work was supported by Japan Science and Technology Agency (JST CREST: JPMJCR19F2). Research Representative: Prof. Yoichi Ochiai, University of Tsukuba, Japan.

A   Neural Networks used in Recognition Models

We showed how to train our recognition models, as shown in Fig. 4, as follows. For detecting objects, we utilized the model of YOLOv4 [4], and there were eight object classes, which are "electric fan", "monitor", "chair", "locker", "door", "microwave", "blackboard", and "desk", trained in the demonstration. For describing objects in an environment, we utilized a typical model of image captioning [20]. In the demonstration, there were some sentences of user descriptions attached with the images of some objects. The spoken sentences from the user were translated by Google API[7]. Note that we ran transfer learning on the model of image captioning, since the basic recognition ability for textual descriptions on common visual images might be needed. We continued the training of image captioning on a model of weights, which were pre-trained on Microsoft COCO [13].

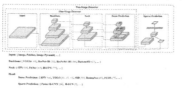

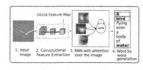

(a) Model of YOLOv4 from [4]

(b) Model of Image Captioning from [20]

Fig. 4. Neural networks used in recognition models.

---

[7] https://cloud.google.com/speech-to-text.

References

1. Ahmetovic, D., Guerreiro, J., Ohn-Bar, E., Kitani, K.M., Asakawa, C.: Impact of expertise on interaction preferences for navigation assistance of visually impaired individuals. In: Proceedings of the 16th Web For All 2019 Conference - Personalizing the Web, W4A 2019, San Francisco, May 13–15, pp. 31:1–31:9. ACM (2019)
2. Ahmetovic, D., Mascetti, S., Bernareggi, C., Guerreiro, J., Oh, U., Asakawa, C.: Deep learning compensation of rotation errors during navigation assistance for people with visual impairments or blindness. ACM Trans. Access. Comput. **12**(4), 19:1–19:19 (2020)
3. Ahmetovic, D., Sato, D., Oh, U., Ishihara, T., Kitani, K., Asakawa, C.: Recog: supporting blind people in recognizing personal objects. In: Bernhaupt, R., et al. (eds.) CHI 2020: CHI Conference on Human Factors in Computing Systems, Honolulu, April 25–30, pp. 1–12. ACM (2020)
4. Bochkovskiy, A., Wang, C., Liao, H.M.: YOLOV4: optimal speed and accuracy of object detection. CoRR abs/2004.10934 (2020)
5. Giudice, N.A., Guenther, B.A., Kaplan, T.M., Anderson, S.M., Knuesel, R.J., Cioffi, J.F.: Use of an indoor navigation system by sighted and blind travelers: performance similarities across visual status and age. ACM Trans. Access. Comput. **13**(3), 11:1–11:27 (2020)
6. Guerreiro, J., Ahmetovic, D., Sato, D., Kitani, K., Asakawa, C.: Airport accessibility and navigation assistance for people with visual impairments. In: Brewster, S.A., Fitzpatrick, G., Cox, A.L., Kostakos, V. (eds.) Proceedings of the 2019 CHI Conference on Human Factors in Computing Systems, CHI 2019, Glasgow, 04–09, May, p. 16. ACM (2019)
7. Guerreiro, J., Sato, D., Asakawa, S., Dong, H., Kitani, K.M., Asakawa, C.: Cabot: designing and evaluating an autonomous navigation robot for blind people. In: Bigham, J.P., Azenkot, S., Kane, S.K. (eds.) The 21st International ACM SIGACCESS Conference on Computers and Accessibility, ASSETS 2019, Pittsburgh, 28–30, October, pp. 68–82. ACM (2019)
8. He, K., Zhang, X., Ren, S., Sun, J.: Deep residual learning for image recognition. In: IEEE Conference on Computer Vision and Pattern Recognition, CVPR, Las Vegas, NV, USA, 27–30 June, pp. 770–778. IEEE Computer Society (2016)
9. Idrees, A., Iqbal, Z., Ishfaq, M.: An efficient indoor navigation technique to find optimal route for blinds using QR codes. CoRR abs/2005.14517 (2020)
10. Jabnoun, H., Hashish, M.A., Benzarti, F.: Mobile assistive application for blind people in indoor navigation. In: Jmaiel, M., Mokhtari, M., Abdulrazak, B., Aloulou, H., Kallel, S. (eds.) ICOST 2020. LNCS, vol. 12157, pp. 395–403. Springer, Cham (2020). https://doi.org/10.1007/978-3-030-51517-1_36
11. Kayukawa, S., Ishihara, T., Takagi, H., Morishima, S., Asakawa, C.: Blindpilot: a robotic local navigation system that leads blind people to a landmark object. In: Bernhaupt, R., et al. (eds.) Extended Abstracts of the 2020 CHI Conference on Human Factors in Computing Systems, CHI 2020, Honolulu, 25–30 April, pp. 1–9. ACM (2020)
12. Kuriakose, B., Shrestha, R., Sandnes, F.E.: Smartphone navigation support for blind and visually impaired people - a comprehensive analysis of potentials and opportunities. In: Antona, M., Stephanidis, C. (eds.) HCII 2020. LNCS, vol. 12189, pp. 568–583. Springer, Cham (2020). https://doi.org/10.1007/978-3-030-49108-6_41
13. Lin, T.Y., et al.: Microsoft COCO: common objects in context. In: Fleet, D., Pajdla, T., Schiele, B., Tuytelaars, T. (eds.) ECCV 2014. LNCS, vol. 8693, pp. 740–755. Springer, Cham (2014). https://doi.org/10.1007/978-3-319-10602-1_48

14. Liu, W., et al.: SSD: single shot multiBox detector. In: Leibe, B., Matas, J., Sebe, N., Welling, M. (eds.) ECCV 2016. LNCS, vol. 9905, pp. 21–37. Springer, Cham (2016). https://doi.org/10.1007/978-3-319-46448-0_2

15. Ohn-Bar, E., Guerreiro, J., Kitani, K., Asakawa, C.: Variability in reactions to instructional guidance during smartphone-based assisted navigation of blind users. Proc. ACM Interact. Mob. Wearable Ubiquitous Technol. 2(3), 131:1–131:25 (2018)

16. Plikynas, D., Zvironas, A., Gudauskis, M., Budrionis, A., Daniusis, P., Sliesoraityte, I.: Research advances of indoor navigation for blind people: a brief review of technological instrumentation. IEEE Instrum. Meas. Mag. 23(4), 22–32 (2020)

17. Sato, D., et al.: NavCog3 in the wild: large-scale blind indoor navigation assistant with semantic features. ACM Trans. Access. Comput. 12(3), 14:1–14:30 (2019)

18. Sherstinsky, A.: Fundamentals of recurrent neural network (RNN) and long short-term memory (LSTM) network. CoRR abs/1808.03314 (2018)

19. Sumikura, S., Shibuya, M., Sakurada, K.: OpenVSLAM: a versatile visual SLAM framework. In: Proceedings of the 27th ACM International Conference on Multimedia MM 2019, pp. 2292–2295 (2019)

20. Xu, K., et al.: Show, attend and tell: Neural image caption generation with visual attention. In: Bach, F.R., Blei, D.M. (eds.) Proceedings of the 32nd International Conference on Machine Learning, ICML 2015, Lille, France, 6–11 July, JMLR Workshop and Conference Proceedings, vol. 37, pp. 2048–2057. JMLR.org (2015)

21. Younis, A., Li, S., Jn, S., Hai, Z.: Real-time object detection using pre-trained deep learning models mobilenet-SSD. In: ICCDE 2020: The 6th International Conference on Computing and Data Engineering, Sanya, China, 4–6 January, pp. 44–48. ACM (2020)

Smart City Concept Based on Cyber-Physical Social Systems with Hierarchical Ethical Agents Approach

Omar Mata[1]([✉]), Pedro Ponce[1], Troy McDaniel[2], Juana Isabel Méndez[1],
Therese Peffer[3], and Arturo Molina[1]

[1] Tecnologico de Monterrey, Mexico City 14380, Mexico
{omar.mata,pedro.ponce,armolina}@tec.mx, A01165549@itesm.mx
[2] Arizona State University, Mesa, AZ 85212, USA
troy.mcdaniel@asu.edu
[3] University of California, Berkeley, CA 94720, USA
tpeffer@berkeley.edu

Abstract. A smart city is considered a sustainable city that manages needed resources and makes autonomous decisions to improve the quality of life of its citizens. On the other hand, Cyber-Physical Systems (CPS) have been implemented as isolated systems inside the city. For instance, the traffic lights, autonomous navigation for cars, and so on. Instead, consider a smart city with an integrated CPS for independent blocks that can be interconnected in a central unit. However, when a CPS makes decisions about the integration of ethical concepts based on human perception, social space must be added, and so a CPS must be transformed into a Cyber-Physical Social System (CPSS). Furthermore, a new type of social interaction between all the elements in a CPSS within a smart city presents human behavioral challenges such as virtual-morality. This paper first proposes an Artificial Moral Agent with machine learning algorithms to regulate the interaction within the CPSS, adding itself to all the subsystems' communication. Additionally, a moral agent structure is proposed with a morality filter as its fundamental component.

Keywords: Cyber-physical systems · CPSS · Social feature · Smart City · Moral agent · AI

1 Introduction

The idea of a "smarter" city to face different problems of urban areas by using technologies to create better life conditions has been around for many years [1]. As [2] shows in an extensive review, the chronological definitions of cities that link technological informational transformations with economic, political, and socio-cultural changes were often referred to as: digital city, wired city, green city, among others. The digital cities concept stands out at the beginning, as the internet started to develop, and it is based on the Information and Communication Technologies (ICT) where people and services are joined and shared to make a smarter community. However, the role of citizens was not prioritized.

© Springer Nature Switzerland AG 2021
M. Antona and C. Stephanidis (Eds.): HCII 2021, LNCS 12769, pp. 424–437, 2021.
https://doi.org/10.1007/978-3-030-78095-1_31

The smart city concept later appeared with the objective to improve the quality of urban life, but it does give the citizens the key role they deserve. Moreover, as ICT is also a prominent part, the digital city is becoming a subset of the smart city. But given the purpose of a smart city is often too large, many frameworks have been proposed to gather all the elements and the relationships between them. Unfortunately, as this concept may include many fields, it has been difficult to develop a straightforward definition.

Therefore, for the purpose of this work, a smart city refers to the management of the relationship between humans (citizens), natural resources, energy, mobility, and buildings to upgrade the quality of life by using the information and communication technologies for optimization.

As it is almost impossible to create a smart city from the ground up, it is easier to propose digital elements applied over the existing infrastructure for citizens to interact and promote social factors. Hence, artificial intelligence (AI) has been applied to many different areas within a smart city, using special agents that can perceive the environment through sensors and act upon that environment through actuators [3]. Some areas of implementation have been:

- Education
- Public spaces
- Smart economy
- Mobility, transport, and logistics
- Energy and smart buildings
- Public safety
- Environment and natural resources
- Health and assistance

In the smart city scenario, some agent-based solutions have been proposed, from evacuation models [4] and emergency responses [5] to driver's decisions on traffic situations [6] and coordination of traffic lights [7].

But the incorporation of AI systems may bring some risks, either because the AI is used to directly cause harm or because somehow the AI becomes unintentionally negative. Eitel-Porter [8] proposes three categories in which the AI risks in a corporation could be organized and tackled:

1. Compliance and governance. Refers to the risk of breaching regulations. The AI could be biased unintentionally during development.
2. Brand damage. Refers to the risk of breaching social norms. The AI could learn bad behavior that could damage the reputation of what it represents.
3. Third-party transparency. Refers to the risk that anybody could generate an AI as a "black box" tool in which the management would not know how it works.

Although these risks are mentioned within a corporation, it is easy to extrapolate the same to a smart city scenario.

On the other hand, AI integration in automation of complex systems has recently made much progress in CPS. These systems integrate computing, communication, and storage capabilities to monitor and control physical processes as is shown in Fig. 1. The CPS focuses on the intersection of the physical and cyber world. This type of system has been demonstrated to provide advantages in sensing, communicating, and processing information locally and globally. However, the interaction with humans is not one of the main strong points of this type of system.

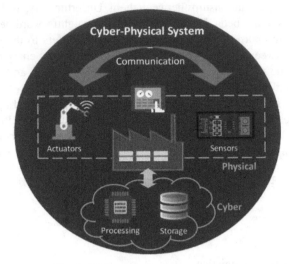

Fig. 1. Cyber-physical system diagram

These kinds of systems manage a large amount of information that is often found in the cloud, as the objective is to represent processes of the physical world by collecting, processing, and managing information [9].

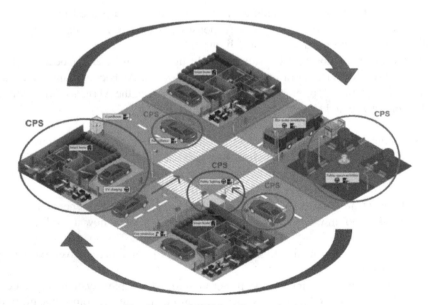

Fig. 2. Set of CPS inside a smart city

Many CPS can be combined in the same environment. If a set of CPS are used under a city environment, this set can resemble some definitions of a smart city. Figure 2 shows an implementation of a smart city with many CPS: an autonomous vehicle driving around the city, the automated traffic lights system, resources control in public spaces, energy consumption in smart buildings, among others.

But as mentioned before, the interaction with humans is not one of the main features of CPS. Although, for example, in autonomous vehicles [10] humans are involved, the true social behavior is not modeled as part of the solution. Therefore, a social component has been added to CPS to enable smart interaction between cyber, physical, and social spaces generating the Cyber-Physical Social Systems concept (CPSS) [11, 12] to meet people's social interaction demands and react to the physical world.

Hence, the human's role in CPSS now becomes fundamental as the social activities impact the smart city environment. Moreover, some social features help to better know the citizens, communities, and cities based on social terms [13–15].

Thus, new challenges regarding the added social space are identified [16]:

- *Device management.* Internet of Things (IoT) technologies and smart devices available today offer a wide range of applications that provide solutions to different CPSS problems. But as these devices lack a unified communication protocol or even a common framework, they require a lot of work to manage. Therefore, an interoperability model in which all the devices can communicate and share information should be developed for enabling CPSS. Besides, the information that is transmitted between devices and users has to be regulated according to ethical considerations.
- *Context-awareness.* Any information used to infer a specific situation of an agent is called a context. Therefore, context-awareness uses that information to provide tailored experiences. In the CPSS environment, the challenge becomes using different types of sensors to obtain data for inferring a context. Due to the high-volume of data, often machine learning algorithms are applied with knowledge-based approaches or even probabilistic approaches. For example, in [17–19], different user types are analyzed using artificial neural networks (ANNs) and fuzzy systems to understand user preferences for tailoring a service.
- *Social computing.* Social computing refers to the use of ICT that considers social context, where CPSS is the infrastructure that enables it. In this way, traditional context awareness moves toward socially aware computing in which the social interaction can be sensed by collecting information from large groups of people [16]. Applications include traffic congestion detection, pollution monitoring, and prediction of diseases. For this new social computing paradigm to improve the design of CPSS, alternative technologies must be considered.
- *Human-Machine Interfaces (HMIs).* Human-machine interfaces are interfaces in which a user can interact between the social, cyber, and physical spaces; a basic need of a CPSS. The interaction, therefore, should be user friendly and be able to adapt or change depending on user behavioral analysis. An example of a tailored HMI is proposed in [20] within a gamification structure that provides feedback and adjusts itself based on the user's profile and behavior to teach, motivate, and engage the end-user to perform specific goals.

- *User behavior-based proactive service.* The goal of this service is to predict human action's intention by understanding human behavior and its characteristics. This is challenging given the sheer variety of users [17].

As human involvement increases in the automation of a smart city under the definition of a CPSS, the systems must consider a new communication channel created between the added social space with moral principles. These moral principles have not been given enough attention as they are often viewed as a negligible side effect of new technologies. Therefore, not only must the moral misconducts of humans interacting with a system be regulated, but the system itself, as decisions involving humans can now be made.

One important concern is in regard to the use of data. As CPSS increases the availability of data, the possibilities of misuse also grow. For example, utility providers may use data to monitor and control appliances in private buildings to redistribute the resources as they better see fit [21]. Further, every technology such as cameras, sensors, devices for human interaction, etc., that collect data, can be subject to biased use that can compromise citizens' privacy.

Another common example of moral dilemma in autonomous machines is in emergency situations like whether a transportation vehicle choose who or what to crash into when it was unavoidable, or, in the case of victims of disasters, who to assist first and based on what criteria [22]. Table 1 shows other examples in relation to smart cities and their moral challenge.

Table 1. Examples of moral challenges

Application	Challenge
Autonomous transportation [23]	Who can get access to the service and how? Data sharing
Occupancy counting and tracking [24]	Using cameras for collecting private data may lead to discriminatory actions or misuse of information
Utilities monitoring systems [25]	Favoring certain people over others: economic status, age, behavior, etc.
Crime prediction [26]	Biased AI; algorithms may tend toward specific demographics
Elderly care [27]	How obtrusive should a system be? Some moral challenges are autonomy, privacy, and physical health

Moreover, the implementation of moral principles in any system is not a trivial task because there is not a global definition of rules or guidelines. Whether it is a philosophical approach, Kantianism and utilitarianism [28]; or an approach of moral theories like moral generalism and moral particularism [29]; or basic rules as Asimov's laws [30]; or even basic principles as fairness, accountability, transparency, explainability, and privacy [8], a common ground must be found where the artificial morality can be implemented.

Hence, this paper proposes an artificial moral agent structure with hierarchical control that can implement some moral guidelines based on a hybrid approach of bottom-up and top-down for artificial intelligence.

2 Proposal

A new type of social device is mentioned in [15] that uses actual technologies to develop a sensing, smart, and sustainable product to communicate between consumer-products and product-products. This proposal goes beyond that model and designs the environment necessary to understand citizens according to their social needs and moral guidelines inside a smart city. Suppose a CPS only dealt with technical data using sensors to monitor, validate, and manage a city. In that case, the city could not achieve the expected result for the citizens because the smartness, in smart city, has become an end in itself, but the needs of the citizens were not realistically tackled. What is needed is a people-centric approach where the CPS must be re-designed into a CPSS system to integrate social capability [31]. Therefore, the CPS should use special sensors to detect social activities and behavior in humans.

Wearables have been gaining popularity as their designs have improved, but also, the increase in functionality for users has made them more appealing. These devices are an example of social sensors used in projects ranging from health [32], to energy [33], to activities [34], and so on.

Developing artificial morality becomes urgent as computers are being designed to perform with greater autonomy [35]. As [36] presented, there have been implementations of AI used in societal environments that show partial and discriminatory responses. Therefore, a computer system should evaluate if its action is morally appropriate in a smart city environment. Such a system should be designed and built by a diverse and inclusive group of people. This is key for avoiding biases and discriminatory behavior against a particular part of the population.

Some approaches were proposed by [35, 37] for designing artificial moral agents (AMA). However, those approaches are not complete since they do not consider the following.

2.1 Top-Down Strategy

This task consists of transforming moral principles and theories into guidelines for morally appropriate actions. With current machine learning algorithms, this approach could be implemented on a computer system. Although, as Tolan [38] shows, biased training data makes predictive performance unreliable. Therefore, an exhaustive search for complete databases must be made to achieve better results. The fundamental example of this kind of strategy is Asimov's laws of robotics [30].

2.2 Bottom-Up Strategy

This task is meant to provide environments in which appropriate behavior is rewarded, i.e., learning through experience. Some machine learning algorithms can handle these kinds of tasks. Still, the risk is that the system does not necessarily learn a morally appropriate action, but an action that may be common in a determined society.

A hybrid strategy implementation of AMA is proposed in Fig. 3. The top-down strategy refers to explicit moral principles, guidelines and rules that are implemented on an agent and the bottom-up strategy looks for implicit values found in the behavior.

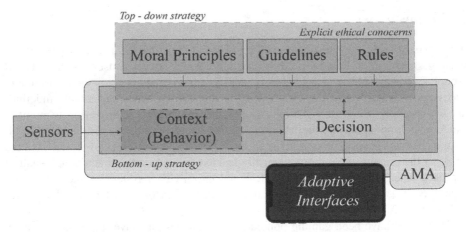

Fig. 3. Top-down strategy and bottom-up strategy involved for designing Artificial Moral Agents (AMA).

Therefore, both strategies merge within the AMA to present the best set of decisions to an adaptive interface. The AMA makes its decision based on the context of the environment and the explicit ethical concerns programmed. The context is deduced by the information gathered from the sensors in the CPSS.

Figure 4 depicts the first part of the proposal where the physical worlds' inputs rely on adaptive, dynamic interfaces that receive and send stimuli to citizens. The citizens actively interact with the interface to obtain information from the physical environment as part of the larger social cyber-physical system. In turn, knowledge from citizens is utilized in the form of social information.

Fig. 4. Moral agent supervising the communication within CPS architecture and the social features.

The CPS becomes a CPSS that can socially interact between them and with citizens using social interfaces. As a result, the CPSS can be defined as a set of social systems that integrate the virtual and physical world in social environments with conventional

CPS information. Still, the priority of CPSS is to improve the communication with humans drastically, and to understand the needs and expectations of citizens for providing social and technical solutions that are accepted by all agents within the smart city. Figure 5 shows how all communication channels between each CPSS space should go through the agent. The term social interface refers to sensing, modeling, managing, and interoperating social factors.

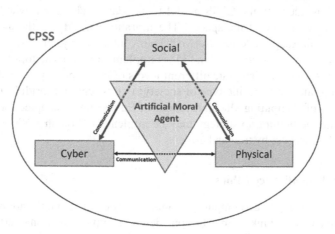

Fig. 5. Moral agent proposed for regulating communication.

Figure 6 shows the second part of the proposal: the moral agent internal structure in which:

$$AMA = \{C_{DS}, P_{DS}, S_{DS}, P_I, M_F, C_{DA}, P_{DA}, S_{DA}\} \qquad (1)$$

The inputs C_{DS}, P_{DS}, and S_{DS}, refer to Cyber, Physical, and Social sensorial devices that read environmental data. This part of the structure provides the context information to the agent by merging all the data to better understand its environment.

Then the information is passed to the processing P_I where social computing takes place. This is possible by using inference algorithms making the core of the AI. The algorithm then gives a set of actions as a result.

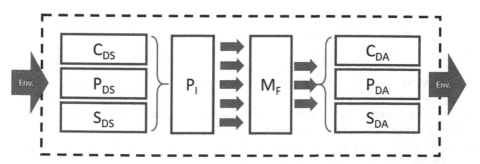

Fig. 6. Moral agent structure

All those possible actions are then passed to the morality filter $\mathbf{M_F}$ in which moral guidelines are applied to filter the most suitable action. This process ensures that the action will include some level of moral principles.

Finally, the $\mathbf{C_{DA}}$, $\mathbf{P_{DA}}$, and $\mathbf{S_{DA}}$ refer to the Cyber, Physical, and Social actuating devices that execute the action upon the environment. The execution of the action may be autonomous, or it may depend on the interaction of a human. In the case when the interaction of a human is needed, an HMI is implemented.

The AMA is added to the CPSS model to evaluate each action, whether morally appropriate, between any of the spaces. The morality part $\mathbf{M_F}$ of the agent may be implemented as an Adaptive Neural Network Fuzzy Inference System (ANFIS) in which a hybrid of both strategies proposed in [35] is implemented. For the top-down strategy part, the fuzzy system can integrate different levels of moral principles or theories that may be appropriate for a specific type of society; in this regard, Floridi [39] states that the Association of Computing Machinery Code of Ethics may be adapted for AMAs. On the other hand, the bottom-up strategy may be implemented on an ANN to let it learn somehow as humans do, by trial and error.

2.3 Artificial Intelligence Ethics

Giving a digital system, like a computer, a robot, or any other agent, the ability to engage in a human-like way of thinking may be considered an implementation of artificial intelligence. However, a precise definition is still a work in progress because even the word intelligence is up for discussion. Artificial intelligence has recently focused on imitating intelligent human behavior; and hence, there is a need to apply ethical guidelines [40].

To make responsible AI is primarily about human responsibility for developing intelligent systems and fundamental human principles and values. Therefore, some considerations have been proposed [41]:

- Ethics by design: integrating algorithms of ethical reasoning that can rule the behavior of AI.
- Ethics in design: analyzing and evaluating ethical implications of AI with engineering methods.
- Ethics for design: ensuring ethical behavior of the developers of AI systems and their users through standards, codes of conduct, among others.

AI ethics considers technological transformation to impact individuals. Europe proposed three ethical principles for a human-centric approach to AI [42]:

- No harm principle: AI algorithms promote inclusion and avoid manipulation and negative profiling to protect more vulnerable groups, like the elderly, children, and immigrants.
- Justice principle: AI developers and implementers must maintain unbiased freedom for all individuals and minority groups.
- Explicability principle: AI systems must be auditable and comprehensible by all types of individuals, either experts or non-experts.

Finally, AI experts should consider inclusion, diversity, and equity topics to augment humanities and social sciences as part of curricular training [43, 44].

Table 2. Moral agent improvement on CPS and CPSS: a comparison.

Smart city subsystem	CPS	CPSS	AMA
Energy	Implementation of smart grid technologies, control energy consumption, optimize power generation with renewable sources	User preferences and behavioral analysis for better optimization. Based on the user needs	The agent should prioritize equitable electric power supply for all users
Mobility	Coordination of public transport using geolocation. Private transport infrastructure automation. Customization of transport	Routing of trajectories based on user preferences: time, cost, comfort, etc.	The agent should use situational preference on routes and infrastructure, e.g., for emergency services. Prevention of high-risk situations like driving under the influence
Natural resources	Public monitoring and display of environmental data to reduce individual waste of resources	Tailored individual programs for resource savings. Public awareness	The agent should distribute natural resources equitably and penalize waste

Table 2 shows a comparison of a CPS and CPSS for a specific field but also how an AMA could improve the implementation. The first column is the subsystem within a smart city. The second column describes an example implementation of a Cyber-Physical System. The third column describes the added functionality when the social space is added in the Cyber-Physical-Social System. The last column describes how the Artificial Moral Agent may interact in the CPSS.

3 Discussion

The "inevitability" of automation in most activities' humans do makes us believe the necessity to develop AMAs. Not that every technological system may need a moral agent, but as the complexity level of AI increases, it will no longer be possible to know what they will do (or how they will react) in every situation. Thus, adding moral guidelines may prevent unwanted reactions and may also serve as guidelines for other humans. Moreover, it may prevent immoral use of the resources available or of the technology itself.

An implementation of an Artificial Moral Agent is still under development using machine learning algorithms. It is proposed to be added to the communication part between a Human Machine Interface that interacts between the user and all sensors and actuators found in a smart community. A smart city scenario could then be scaled by the integration of multiple communities each varying in size.

However, there are still some disadvantages of AMAs. To this day, it may not be possible to build a perfect moral agent as the technology tools are restricted on how to define ethics digitally. But this same restriction has not stopped the development of AIs from gaining expertise in diverse areas, so, perhaps, it will be the same case for morality. Another problem to face is that there is no universal agreement in ethics so it will not be possible to program it. Nonetheless, humans also face moral decisions where there is ethical vagueness, but it does not stop us to make moral judgments. Therefore, AMAs can also choose the best moral response with the information within reach.

4   Conclusion

CPS is mainly used as a technical solution in factories to increase productivity with less centered interaction between humans. However, adding a Social space for becoming a CPSS increases the human centralized interaction. A smart city environment is proposed as a CPSS where the citizens' needs become the center of the interaction. Moreover, the CPSS, instead of being modeled just as the integration of the social part in the system, is proposed to integrate an AI that acts as a moral agent to monitor and regulate the communication between all the spaces of the CPSS.

The moral agent implements a moral filter within the process of deciding the actions to implement; in this way, it can ensure not just a flawless technical operation of the proposed smart city environment but also an ethical operation as well.

Thus, this research paper does not try to substitute humans' moral responsibility in a smart city environment nor in its actions, but instead, proposes a path that could integrate the autonomous decisions making part, for the CPSS, based on moral aspects.

Acknowledgments. This research project is supported by Tecnologico de Monterrey and CITRIS under the collaboration ITESM-CITRIS Smart thermostat, deep learning, and gamification project (https://citris-uc.org/2019-itesm-seed-funding/), and the National Science Foundation under Grant No. 1828010.

References

1. Cocchia, A.: Smart and digital city: a systematic literature review. In: Dameri, R.P., Rosenthal-Sabroux, C. (eds.) Smart City. PI, pp. 13–43. Springer, Cham (2014). https://doi.org/10.1007/978-3-319-06160-3_2
2. Dameri, R.P., Rosenthal-Sabroux, C.: Smart city and value creation. In: Dameri, R.P., Rosenthal-Sabroux, C. (eds.) Smart City. PI, pp. 1–12. Springer, Cham (2014). https://doi.org/10.1007/978-3-319-06160-3_1
3. Russell, S., Norvig, P.: Artificial Intelligence: A Modern Approach (2020)
4. Satoh, K., Takahashi, T., Yamada, T., Yoshikawa, A., Terano, T.: Evacuation Behaviors in an Emergency Station by Agent-Based Approach, pp. 236–241 (2009). http://www.iadisportal.org/digital-library/evacuation-behaviors-in-an-emergency-station-by-agent-based-approach

5. Taboada, M., Cabrera, E., Iglesias, M.L., Epelde, F., Luque, E.: An Agent-based decision support system for hospitals emergency departments. Procedia Comput. Sci. **4**, 1870–1879 (2011). https://doi.org/10.1016/j.procs.2011.04.203

6. Vigueras, G., Orduña, J.M., Lozano, M., Jégou, Y.: A scalable multiagent system architecture for interactive applications. Sci. Comput. Program. **78**(6), 715–724 (2013). https://doi.org/10.1016/j.scico.2011.09.002

7. Klügl, F., Bazzan, A.L.C.: Route decision behaviour in a commuting scenario: simple heuristics adaptation and effect of traffic forecast. J. Artif. Soc. Soc. Simul. **7**(1), 1 (2004)

8. Eitel-Porter, R.: Beyond the promise: implementing ethical AI. AI Ethics **1**(1), 73–80 (2021). https://doi.org/10.1007/s43681-020-00011-6

9. Ahmed, S.H., Kim, G., Kim, D.: Cyber physical system: architecture, applications and research challenges. In: 2013 IFIP Wireless Days (WD), pp. 1–5. Valencia, Spain (2013). https://doi.org/10.1109/wd.2013.6686528

10. Awoyera, O.O., Sacko, O., Darboe, O., Cynthia, O.C.: Anfis-based intelligent traffic control system (ITCS) for developing cities. J. Traffic Logistics Eng. **7**(1) (2019)

11. Wang, F.Y.: The emergence of intelligent enterprises: from CPS to CPSS. IEEE Intell. Syst. **25**(4), 85–88 (2010)

12. Chourabi, H., et al.: Understanding smart cities: an integrative framework. In: 2012 45th Hawaii International Conference on System Sciences, pp. 2289–2297 (2012). https://doi.org/10.1109/HICSS.2012.615

13. Ponce, P., Meier, A., Miranda, J., Molina, A., Peffer, T.: The next generation of social products based on sensing, smart and sustainable (S3) features: a smart thermostat as case study. In: 9th IFAC Conference on Manufacturing Modelling, Management and Control, p. 6 (2019)

14. Ponce, P., Meier, A., Mendez, J., Peffer, T., Molina, A., Mata, O.: Tailored gamification and serious game framework based on fuzzy logic for saving energy in smart thermostats. J. Clean. Prod. 21167 (2020). https://doi.org/10.1016/j.jclepro.2020.121167

15. Mendez, J.I., et al.: Empower saving energy into smart homes using a gamification structure by social products. In: 2020 IEEE International Conference on Consumer Electronics (ICCE), pp. 1–7. Las Vegas, NV, USA (2020). https://doi.org/10.1109/icce46568.2020.9043174

16. Zeng, J., Yang, L.T., Lin, M., Ning, H., Ma, J.: A survey: cyber-physical-social systems and their system-level design methodology. Future Gener. Comput. Syst. **105**, 1028–1042 (2020). https://doi.org/10.1016/j.future.2016.06.034

17. Mata, O., Ponce, P., Méndez, I., Molina, A., Meier, A., Peffer, T.: A model using artificial neural networks and fuzzy logic for knowing the consumer on smart thermostats as a S^3 product. In: Martínez-Villaseñor, L., Batyrshin, I., Marín-Hernández, A. (eds.) MICAI 2019. LNCS (LNAI), vol. 11835, pp. 430–439. Springer, Cham (2019). https://doi.org/10.1007/978-3-030-33749-0_34

18. Méndez, J.I., Mata, O., Ponce, P., Meier, A., Peffer, T., Molina, A.: Multi-sensor system, gamification, and artificial intelligence for benefit elderly people. In: Ponce, H., Martínez-Villaseñor, L., Brieva, J., Moya-Albor, E. (eds.) Challenges and Trends in Multimodal Fall Detection for Healthcare. SSDC, vol. 273, pp. 207–235. Springer, Cham (2020). https://doi.org/10.1007/978-3-030-38748-8_9

19. Méndez, J.I., Ponce, P., Meier, A., Peffer, T., Mata, O., Molina, A.: Framework for promoting social interaction and physical activity in elderly people using gamification and fuzzy logic strategy. In: 2019 IEEE Global Conference on Signal and Information Processing (GlobalSIP), pp. 1–5. Ottawa, ON, Canada (2019). https://doi.org/10.1109/globalsip45357.2019.8969110

20. Ponce, P., Peffer, T., Molina, A., Barcena, S.: Social creation networks for designing low income interfaces in programmable thermostats. Technol. Soc. **62**, (2020). https://doi.org/10.1016/j.techsoc.2020.101299

21. Mohamed, N., Al-Jaroodi, J., Jawhar, I.: Service-oriented big data analytics for improving buildings energy management in smart cities. In: 2018 14th International Wireless Communications Mobile Computing Conference (IWCMC), pp. 1243–1248 (2018). https://doi.org/10.1109/IWCMC.2018.8450469
22. Bonnemains, V., Saurel, C., Tessier, C.: Embedded ethics: some technical and ethical challenges. Ethics Inf. Technol. **20**(1), 41–58 (2018). https://doi.org/10.1007/s10676-018-9444-x
23. Krisher, T.: Can Self-Driving Cars Withstand First Fatality? U.S. News & World Report. 20 March 2018https://www.usnews.com/news/business/articles/2018-03-20/arizona-death-brings-calls-for-more-autonomous-vehicle-rules. Accessed on 20 Feb 2021
24. Akkaya, K., Guvenc, I., Aygun, R., Pala, N., Kadri, A.: IoT-based occupancy monitoring techniques for energy-efficient smart buildings. In: 2015 IEEE Wireless Communications and Networking Conference Workshops (WCNCW), pp. 58–63 (2015). https://doi.org/10.1109/WCNCW.2015.7122529
25. Kim, J.S.: Making smart cities work in the face of conflicts: lessons from practitioners of South Korea's U-City projects. Town Plan. Rev. **86**(5), 561–585 (2015)
26. Bogomolov, A., Lepri, B., Staiano, J., Oliver, N., Pianesi, F., Pentland, A.: Once upon a crime: towards crime prediction from demographics and mobile data. In: Proceedings of the 16th International Conference on Multimodal Interaction, pp. 427–434 (2014). https://doi.org/10.1145/2663204.2663254
27. Misselhorn, C.: Artificial morality. Concepts, issues and challenges. Society **55**(2), 161–169 (2018). https://doi.org/10.1007/s12115-018-0229-y
28. Brożek, B., Janik, B.: Can artificial intelligences be moral agents? New Ideas Psychol. **54**, 101–106 (2019). https://doi.org/10.1016/j.newideapsych.2018.12.002
29. Bauer, W.A.: Virtuous vs. utilitarian artificial moral agents. AI Soc. **35**(1), 263–271 (2020). https://doi.org/10.1007/s00146-018-0871-3
30. Clarke, R.: Asimov's laws of robotics: implications for information technology-part I. Computer **26**(12), 53–61 (1993). https://doi.org/10.1109/2.247652
31. Trencher, G.: Towards the smart city 2.0: empirical evidence of using smartness as a tool for tackling social challenges. Technol. Forecast. Soc. Change **142**, 117–128 (2019). https://doi.org/10.1016/j.techfore.2018.07.033
32. Jiang, L., et al.: Wearable long-term social sensing for mental wellbeing. IEEE Sens. J. **19**(19), 8532–8542 (2019). https://doi.org/10.1109/JSEN.2018.2877427
33. Umetsu, Y., Nakamura, Y., Arakawa, Y., Fujimoto, M., Suwa, H.: EHAAS: energy harvesters as a sensor for place recognition on wearables. In: 2019 IEEE International Conference on Pervasive Computing and Communications (PerCom), pp. 1–10 (2019). https://doi.org/10.1109/PERCOM.2019.8767385
34. Jeyakumar, J.V., Lai, L., Suda, N., Srivastava, M.: SenseHAR: a robust virtual activity sensor for smartphones and wearables. In: Proceedings of the 17th Conference on Embedded Networked Sensor Systems, pp. 15–28 (2019). https://doi.org/10.1145/3356250.3360032
35. Allen, C., Smit, I., Wallach, W.: Artificial morality: top-down, bottom-up, and hybrid approaches. Ethics Inf. Technol. **7**(3), 149–155 (2005). https://doi.org/10.1007/s10676-006-0004-4
36. Coeckelbergh, M.: AI Ethics. The MIT Press, Cambridge, Massachusetts, USA (2020)
37. Wallach, W., Allen, C., Smit, I.: Machine morality: Bottom-up and top-down approaches for modelling human moral faculties. AI Soc. **22**(4), 565–582 (2008). https://doi.org/10.1007/s00146-007-0099-0
38. Tolan, S., Miron, M., Gómez, E., Castillo, C.: Why machine learning may lead to unfairness: evidence from risk assessment for juvenile justice in catalonia. In: Proceedings of the Seventeenth International Conference on Artificial Intelligence and Law, pp. 83–92 (2019). https://doi.org/10.1145/3322640.3326705

39. Floridi, L., Sanders, J.W.: On the morality of artificial agents. Minds Mach. **14**(3), 349–379 (2004). https://doi.org/10.1023/B:MIND.0000035461.63578.9d
40. Kok, J.N., Boers, E.J., Kosters, W.A., Van der Putten, P., Poel, M.: Artificial intelligence: definition, trends, techniques, and cases. Artif. Intell. **1**, 270–299 (2009)
41. Dignum, V.: Ethics in artificial intelligence: introduction to the special issue. Ethics Inf. Technol. **20**(1), 1–3 (2018). https://doi.org/10.1007/s10676-018-9450-z
42. Glasco, J.: Smart Education for Smart Cities: Visual, Collaborative & Interactive (2019). https://hub.beesmart.city/en/solutions/smart-people/smart-education/viewsonic-smart-education-for-smart-cities. Accessed on 28 Nov 2020
43. The Oxford Handbook of Ethics of AI. Oxford University Press (2020)
44. Mata, O., Mendez, I., Aguilar, M., Ponce, P., Molina, A.: A Methodology to motivate students to develop transversal competencies in academic courses based on the theory of planned behavior by using gamification and ANNs. In: 2019 IEEE Tenth International Conference on Technology for Education (T4E), pp. 174–177. Goa, India (2019). https://doi.org/10.1109/t4e.2019.00041

Real-World Distance Reduction in a Virtual Reality-Based Wheelchair Simulation on Flat Surfaces

Kousuke Motooka[1](✉), Takumi Okawara[1](✉), Yuki Yamato[1](✉), and Akihiro Miyata[2](✉)

[1] Graduate School of Integrated Basic Sciences, Nihon University, 3-25-40 Sakurajousui, Setagaya-Ku, Tokyo, Japan
[2] College of Humanities and Sciences, Nihon University, 3-25-40 Sakurajousui, Setagaya-Ku, Tokyo, Japan
miyata.akihiro@acm.org

Abstract. A virtual reality (VR)-based wheelchair simulator based on a combination of motions attainable by an electric-powered wheelchair and vection-inducing videos displayed on a head-mounted display has been proposed for patient rehabilitation and training. This simulator requires the actual physical distance traveled by the wheelchair and the distance traveled by the wheelchair in the virtual environment to be the same. This requirement limits the locations where users can use this simulator. We clarify the relationship between these distances and aim to reduce the physical distance required to perform VR-based wheelchair simulations. To this end, we conducted an experiment whereby participants drove a wheelchair on a flat ground at a constant speed and at a decreasing speed for 8 m. The experimental results showed that the required physical distance can be reduced by 30% and 20% using the constant speed and deceleration approaches, respectively. The results of this study are expected to contribute to the development of wheelchair simulators that require less space.

Keywords: Wheelchair simulator · Virtual reality · Vection

1 Introduction

Many virtual reality (VR)-based wheelchair simulators have been developed to reduce the anxiety experienced by people driving wheelchairs outdoors by providing them the opportunity to practice driving safely. These simulators have been used for patient rehabilitation and training owing to their higher feasibility compared to physical courses for wheelchair users. However, existing approaches have a cost/quality trade-off problem. Simulators that provide only visual feedback can be constructed at low costs but cannot provide users with a sense of motion. By contrast, simulators that provide both visual and motion feedback can yield rich experience but require expensive devices, including a motion platform.

© Springer Nature Switzerland AG 2021
M. Antona and C. Stephanidis (Eds.): HCII 2021, LNCS 12769, pp. 438–448, 2021.
https://doi.org/10.1007/978-3-030-78095-1_32

To address this issue, a VR-based wheelchair simulator using a combination of motion patterns attainable by an electric-powered wheelchair and vection-inducing videos displayed on a head-mounted display (HMD) was proposed [1]. Because this simulator is composed only of commercial products, it is relatively inexpensive and can give users the feeling of passing through barriers, such as slopes. This approach also requires real and virtual distances traveled by the wheelchair to be the same. Such a requirement limits the environment in which users can employ this type of simulator. Many studies in the field of VR have succeeded in making the moving distance in the real world shorter than that in the virtual space. However, for wheelchair simulations, the reduction of the real-world distance is difficult because its relationship with the virtual distance is unclear. In this study, we clarify this relationship, with an underlying aim of reducing the distance required for VR-based wheelchair simulations.

2   Related Works

2.1   Wheelchair Simulators

Wheelchair simulators can be broadly divided into those that provide only visual feedback and those that provide both visual and motion feedback [2,3].

First, simulators that provide only visual feedback mainly consist of a chair, display, and joystick. In this kind of simulators, a user aims to drive and avoid collisions between the wheelchair and objects in the virtual space. Examples of these simulators include a wheelchair simulator that allows children with severe disabilities to properly operate an electric-powered wheelchair [4] and a wheelchair simulator that allows children with multiple disabilities to become familiar with wheelchair driving [5]. Furthermore, there are quite a few simulators that use an HMD, whose prices are decreasing in recent years. The user sits on a chair and operates the joystick to move in the virtual space displayed on the HMD. For example, there is a wheelchair simulator that allows people who are new to wheelchair driving to improve their wheelchair driving skills [6]. In this system, the movements of the joystick and wheelchair in the real world are linked. The wheelchair in the real world is equipped with a camera, and the movie taken by the camera is displayed on the HMD.

Second, simulators that provide visual and motion feedback are highly realistic, which is the advantage of these simulators. In the real world, wheelchair users accelerate/decelerate and drive up/down slopes. Hence, from this point of view, a simulator that provides not only visual feedback but also motion feedback can provide users with a rich experience. For providing motion feedback, a motion platform called the Stewart platform [7] is commonly used. This platform consists of a parallel connection robot manipulator that provides motion with six degrees of freedom. In previous studies, this platform was equipped with an HMD [8] and a large hemispherical display [9], both of which aimed at accustomizing beginners to wheelchair operation.

2.2 Distance Reduction

To present an immersive virtual environment in a simple manner, a real-world space that is as large as the virtual space is needed. However, in recent years, the redirected walking (RDW) method has been proposed for walking simulations to compress the real-world space required to reproduce the virtual space [10]. This technique unconsciously manipulates the direction and moving distance of the user. Many techniques have been proposed to increase the effectiveness of RDW [11], and the conditions that produce RDW effects have been verified [12]. Moreover, it has been reported that the distance in the real space can be compressed by 14% [12].

A previous study has proposed a system that allows users to walk infinitely in a virtual space by exploiting the tactile sensations experienced while physically walking along a convex wall [13]. This system enhanced the immersive feeling by providing tactile feedback in addition to visual feedback and enhanced the effect of RDW. Moreover, methods that allow RDW to function in complex real-world spaces, including obstacles, have been proposed [14,15]. One method employs a system that guides the user in the direction opposite to the obstacle when he/she approaches the obstacle [14]. Furthermore, a system that guides the user to a large space without obstacles has been developed. In other method, the effects of RDW can be induced to users through auditory feedback [15]. The effects of the conventional method and RDW using only hearing induced to users have been reported to be almost the same. The use of RDW technology is often based on walking scenes, but it can also be applied for jumps [16]. Attempts to increase the number of people who can experience the same virtual space while using RDW have also been made, and a simulator that can be simultaneously used by at least eight users has been developed [17].

3 Research Goal

The simulators introduced in Sect. 2.1 involve a trade-off between cost and quality. A simulator that provides only visual feedback can be constructed with low-cost devices, such as PC displays and HMDs, but it is not realistic because it does not provide motion feedback to the user. Conversely, a simulator that provides visual and motion feedback can give the user a high sense of reality, but it requires expensive devices, such as a motion platform.

To deal with these tradeoffs, a VR-based wheelchair simulator using a combination of motion patterns attainable by an electric-powered wheelchair and vection-inducing videos displayed on an HMD was proposed [1]. However, this system requires real and virtual distances traveled by the electric-powered wheelchair to be the same.

To reduce the distance traveled in the wheelchair simulator in the real space, it is necessary to determine the relationship between the distances traveled by the wheelchair in the real world and the immersive VR. However, to the best of our knowledge, existing works did not focus on this relationship. Therefore, in this study, we clarify the relationship between the motion behavior of the electric-powered wheelchair in the real world and the motion distance perceived by the user in the virtual space.

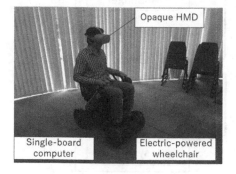

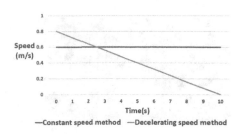

Fig. 1. Appearance of the simulator.   **Fig. 2.** Examples of the speed settings of the electric-powered wheelchair.

Table 1. Detailed list of the hardware.

Hardware	Product name
HMD	Oculus Go
SBC	Raspberry Pi3
Electric-powered wheelchair	WHILL Model-CR

4   Implementation

We implemented a VR-based wheelchair simulator, whose speed and distance in the real space can be freely changed. Our simulation system consists of an opaque HMD, HMD controller, single-board computer (SBC), and electric-powered wheelchair, as shown in Table 1. Figure 1 shows the appearance of the simulator. Two speed settings can be selected, namely, *constant speed* and *gradually decreasing speed*. Figure 2 shows plots of the sample speed settings of the wheelchair. Figure 3 shows the video displayed on the HMD. The video shows the perspective of a user moving along a corridor with the wheelchair. The video playback application on the HMD was implemented using Java, and the electric-powered wheelchair control application on the SBC was implemented using Python. Figure 4 describes the structure of the system. The user can select a simulation type and start the simulation using the HMD controller by selecting the start button displayed on the HMD. The HMD and SBC perform WebSocket communication wirelessly.

When the simulation starts, the HMD sends a simulation start signal to the SBC, which controls the wheelchair according to the simulation selected by the user. Then, the wheelchair starts driving in the video on the HMD and in the real space at the same time. At the end, the wheelchair on the video and in the real space stops.

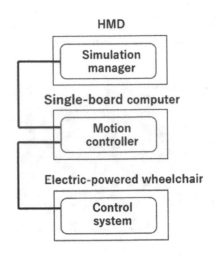

Fig. 3. Scene displayed on the HMD.

Fig. 4. Architecture of the simulation system.

5   Experiment

5.1   Purpose

The purpose of this experiment was to clarify the relationship between the motion behavior of the electric-powered wheelchair in the real world and the driving distance perceived by the user in the virtual space. As a first step, we conducted a simulation driving experiment on a flat ground.

5.2   Participants, Ethical Concerns and Environment

The participants were nine in lab students in their 20s. None of the authors of this paper were included as participants. Moreover, none of the participants had a motor disability or used a wheelchair in their daily lives. All the participants were informed that they could refuse to continue the experiment at any time without negative consequences. The participants wore earplugs during the simulation to avoid the influence of the sounds of the wheelchair's motor on their speed estimation. The experimenters checked whether the participant had motion sickness when they underwent the simulation. We built a driving course in a room of approximately $10 \, \text{m}^2$. The room had a flat floor and a carpet with short fibers. Figure 5 shows a schematic of the driving course, and Fig. 6 shows a photograph of the experimental environment. We did not allow outsiders in the room and ensured the safety of the participants.

5.3   Procedure

The experimenter, rather than the participant, performed each simulation first to ensure that external factors (e.g., operation mistakes) affecting the simulation experience were minimized. The video displayed on the HMD was recorded

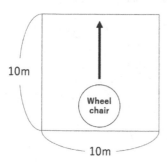

Fig. 5. Schematic of the driving course.

Fig. 6. Photograph of the experimental environment.

while using the wheelchair in the corridor for a distance of 8 m at a speed of 0.8 m/s, which took 10 s. The experimental conditions were determined based on the results of the preliminary experiments. The conditions are listed in Tables 2 and 3.

We prepared five 10-s constant-speed settings named C-1, C-2, C-3, C-4, and C-5 with speeds of 0.32, 0.40, 0.48, 0.56, and 0.64 m/s, which correspond to distances of 3.2, 4.0, 4.8, 5.6, and 6.4 m, respectively. These values were 60%, 50%, 40%, 30%, and 20% shorter than the driving distance on the displayed video clip, respectively. In addition, we prepared experimental conditions for the same constant speed as that of the video displayed on the HMD (0.8 m/s) and denoted it as N.

Similarly, we prepared five 10-s decreasing speed settings named D-1, D-2, D-3, D-4, and D-5 with an initial speed of 0.8 m/s and decelerations of 0.08, 0.064, 0.048, 0.032, and 0.016 m/s², which correspond to driving distances of 4.0, 4.8, 5.6, 6.4, and 7.2 m, respectively. These values were 50%, 40%, 30%, 20%, and 10% shorter than the driving distance on the displayed video clip, respectively.

The participants used the simulator for a driving distance of 8 m at a speed of 0.8 m/s before the start of each experimental setting. This method was performed to allow participants to experience the travel at the same driving speed and distance as that of the wheelchair displayed on the HMD. Each participant randomly underwent two trials for each simulation pattern. After the completion of each simulation, the wheelchair was returned to the starting position before removing the HMD so that the participants could not visually see the distance traveled. Every time they experienced a simulation pattern, they provided answers (Yes/No) to the following questions: Q1) Did the distance traveled with the wheelchair feel shorter than that on the video displayed on the HMD? Q2) Did the wheelchair speed feel the same as the speed of the video displayed on the HMD? The participants also responded to an open-ended questionnaire.

Table 2. Experimental conditions for constant speed.

Experimental conditions	Speed (m/s)	Distance (m)
C-1	0.32	3.2
C-2	0.40	4.0
C-3	0.48	4.8
C-4	0.56	5.6
C-5	0.64	6.4
N	0.80	8.0

Table 3. Experimental conditions for decelerating speed.

Experimental conditions	Initial speed (m/s)	Deceleration (m/s^2)	Distance (m)
D-1	0.8	0.080	4.0
D-2	0.8	0.064	4.8
D-3	0.8	0.048	5.6
D-4	0.8	0.032	6.4
D-5	0.8	0.016	7.2

6   Results

6.1   Perception of Distance

All participants answered "No" (i.e., the real distance did not seem shorter than the virtual distance) to Q1 for N. A binomial test at a significance level of 0.05 showed that the number of participants who answered "No" was significantly greater than that of participants who answered "Yes" (i.e., the real distance seemed shorter than the virtual distance).

Figure 7 shows the results of the answers to Q1 for the constant speed condition. The percentage of participants who answered "No" for C-1, C-2, C-3, C-4, and C-5 was 33%, 77%, 66%, 88%, and 100%, respectively. Binomial tests at a significance level of 0.05 showed that the number of participants who answered "No" was significantly greater than that of participants who answered "Yes" for C-4 and C-5.

Figure 8 shows the results of the answers to Q1 for the gradually decreasing speed condition. The percentage of the participants who answered "No" for D-1, D-2, D-3, D-4, and D-5 was 55%, 55%, 55%, 88%, and 88%, respectively. Binomial tests at a significance level of 0.05 showed that the number of people who answered "No" was significantly greater than that of participants who answered "Yes" for D-4 and D-5.

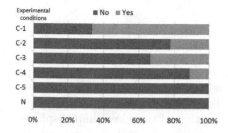

Fig. 7. Response distribution in Q1 for constant speed condition (N = 9).

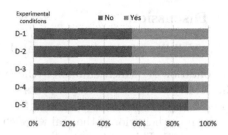

Fig. 8. Response distribution in Q1 for decreasing speed condition (N = 9).

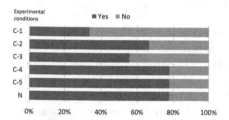

Fig. 9. Response distribution in Q2 for the constant speed condition (N = 9).

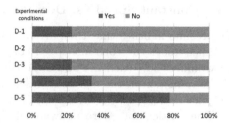

Fig. 10. Response distribution in Q2 for the decreasing speed condition (N = 9).

6.2 Perception of Speed

The percentage of participants who answered "Yes" (i.e., the real speed felt the same as the virtual speed) to Q2 for N was 77%. A binomial test with a significance level of 0.10 showed that there was a significant tendency for the number of participants who answered "Yes" to be higher than the number of participants who answered "No". (i.e., the real speed did not feel the same as the virtual speed).

Figure 9 shows the results of the answers to Q2 for the constant speed condition. The percentage of participants who answered "Yes" for C-1, C-2, C-3, C-4, and C-5 was 33%, 66%, 55%, 77%, and 77%, respectively. A binomial test with a significance level of 0.10 showed that there was a significant tendency for the number of participants who answered "Yes" to be higher than the number of participants who answered "No" for C-4 and C-5.

Figure 10 shows the result of the answers to Q2 for the gradually decreasing speed condition. The percentage of participants who answered "Yes" for D-1, D-2, D-3, D-4, and D-5 was 22%, 0%, 22%, 33%, and 77%, respectively. Binomial tests at a significance level of 0.05 showed that the number of people who answered "Yes" was significantly fewer than those who answered "No" for D-2. Also, a binomial test with a significance level of 0.10 showed that there was a significant tendency for the number of participants who answered "Yes" to be higher than the number of participants who answered "No" for D-5.

7 Discussion

7.1 Validity of the Experimental Environment

In condition N, which simulated the behavior of the wheelchair displayed on the HMD, 100% of the respondents answered "No" to Q1 and 77% answered "Yes" to Q2. This finding indicates that condition N did not yield inconsistency between the behavior of the real wheelchair and that of the wheelchair displayed on the HMD. This leads us to determine that the experimental environment was appropriate for the discussion in the next subsection.

7.2 Constant Speed vs. Decreasing Speed

The results indicate that the participants were unaware of the reduction in the distance under the constant speed condition when the distance decreased by a maximum of 30% (i.e., C-4 and C-5). By contrast, the participants were unaware of the reduction in the distance under the decreasing speed condition when the distance decreased by a maximum of 20% (i.e., D-4 and D-5).

The participants were unaware of the reduction in C-4 and were aware of the reduction in D-3, although the real distances traveled by the wheelchair were the same (0.56 m). This is probably because participants were aware of the incompatibility between the real and virtual speeds in D-3; the real speed changed, whereas the virtual speed was constant. In addition, 78% of the participants answered "No" to Q2 for D-3. One participant stated that he/she noticed a deceleration, which made him/her perceive a shorter distance. Other participants gave similar feedback.

7.3 Future Outlook

In this experiment, the distance can be reduced by 30% for constant speed velocity and 20% for decreasing speed. This knowledge can be used in the future to reduce the travel distance of wheelchair simulations on flat grounds.

However, this knowledge is limited only when driving on an indoor flat ground. In wheelchair simulators, simulations can also be conducted on terrain, such as slopes and flat grounds, so verification on flat grounds alone is not sufficient. Therefore, in the future, we plan to verify whether the distance can be reduced in wheelchair simulations, such as slopes and uneven roads.

In addition, because this experiment was performed for a relatively short distance of 8 m, the results may not be applicable to long distances. Therefore, in future studies, whether the same results can be obtained from simulations over long distances should be verified.

8 Conclusions

In this study, we clarified the relationship between the motion behavior of an electric-powered wheelchair in the real world and the driving distance perceived by the user in the virtual space. We aim to reduce the required real-world distance for wheelchair simulations. Accordingly, the experimental results showed that the required real-world distance can be reduced by 30% and 20% using the constant speed and decreasing speed approaches, respectively. The results of this study can contribute to the development of wheelchair simulators that require less space.

The main limitations of our study are as follows: First, we evaluated only short straight road scenes. Second, experiments were performed at a relatively short distance (8 m). Third, the number of participants was small. In future studies, we plan to verify whether the driving distance can be reduced in simulations on longer and more complex paths, such as paths with slopes and uneven roads, and to increase the number of participants.

Acknowledgements. This work was supported by JSPS KAKENHI Grant No. JP19H04160.

References

1. Miyata, A., Motooka, K., Go, K.: A wheelchair simulator using limited-motion patterns and vection-inducing movies. In: Proceedings of the 31st Australian Conference on Human-Computer-Interaction (OzCHI 2019), pp. 508–512 (2019)
2. Thomas, P., Tamar, W., Shimon, R., Evelyne, K.: Wheelchair simulators: a review. Technol. Disabil. **21**(1–2), 1–10 (2009)
3. Abellard, P., Randria, I., Abellard, A., Ben Khelifa, M.M., Ramanantsizehena, P.: Electric Wheelchair Navigation Simulators: Why, When, How? Mechatronic Systems Applications, pp. 161–186 (2010)
4. Desbonnet, M., Cox, S.L., Rahman, A.: Development and evaluation of a virtual reality based training system for disabled children. In: Proceedings of the ICD-VRAT 1998, pp. 177–182 (1998)
5. Rodriguez, N.: Development of a wheelchair simulator for children with multiple disabilities. In: Proceedings of the VAAT 2015, pp. 1–4 (2015)
6. Silva, Y.M., Simes, W., da Silva Tefilo, M.R., Naves, E.L.M.: Training environment for electric powered wheelchairs using teleoperation through a head mounted display. In: Proceedings of the ICCE 2018 (2018)
7. Stewart, D.: A platform with six degrees of freedom. In: Proceedings of the UK Institution of Mechanical Engineers, vol. 180, no. 1, pp. 371–386 (1965)
8. Sonar, A., Burdick, K.D., Begin, R.R., Carroll, J.J.: Development of a virtual reality-based power wheel chair simulator. In: Proceedings of the ICMA 2005, pp. 222–229 (2005)
9. Niniss, H., Inoue, T.: Electric wheelchair simulator for rehabilitation of persons with motor disability. In: Proceedings of the SVR 2006 (2006)
10. Razzaque, S., Kohn, Z., Whitton, M.C.: Redirected Walking. In: Eurographics 2001, vol. 9, pp. 105–106 (2001)
11. Bolling, L., Stein, N., Steinicke, F., Lappe, M.: Shrinking circles: adaptation to increased curvature gain in redirected walking. In: Proceedings of the IEEE VR 2019 (2019)
12. Steinicke, F., Bruder, G., Jerald, J., Frenz, H., Lappe, M.: Estimation of detection thresholds for redirected walking techniques. IEEE Trans. Visual. Comput. Graph. **16**(1), 17–27 (2010)

13. Matsumoto, K., Ban, Y., Narumi, T., Yanase, Y., Tanikawa, T., Hirose, M.: Unlimited corridor: redirected walking techniques using visuo haptic interaction. In: SIGGRAPH 2016 Emerging Technologies (2016)
14. Thomas, J., Rosenberg, E.S.: A general reactive algorithm for redirected walking using artificial potential functions. In: Proceedings of IEEE VR 2019 (2019)
15. Rewkowski, N., Rungta, A., Whitton, M., Lin, M.: Evaluating the effectiveness of redirected walking with auditory distractors for navigation in virtual environments. In: Proceedings of the IEEE VR 2019 (2019)
16. Hayashi, D., Fujita, K., Takashima, K., Lindeman, R.W., Kitamura, Y.: Redirected jumping: imperceptibly manipulating jump motions in virtual reality. In: Proceedings of the IEEE VR 2019 (2019)
17. Eric, R., Bachmann, E.H., Hoffbauer, C., Messinger, J.: Multi-user redirected walking and resetting using artificial potential fields. In: Proceedings of the IEEE VR 2019 (2019)

Ski for Squat: A Squat Exergame with Pneumatic Gel Muscle-Based Dynamic Difficulty Adjustment

Priyanka Ramasamy, Swagata Das$^{(\boxtimes)}$, and Yuichi Kurita

Graduate School of Advanced Science and Engineering, Hiroshima University,
Higashihiroshima, Japan
{priyankaramasamy,swagatadas,ykurita}@hiroshima-u.ac.jp

Abstract. We propose a safe design of squat exergame to maintain lower extremity strength that includes Dynamic Difficulty Adjustment (DDA). This is to optimise the game difficulty according to a Knee Shakiness (KS) parameter. We modulated two parameters to implement DDA namely, movement speed and Pneumatic Gel Muscle (PGM)-based assistance. The movement speed of the user relates to the frequency of squatting, and the PGM-based assistance was provided by pneumatic actuators called PGMs attached on the hip and knee joints of the lower extremity. We provided variable PGM-based assistance during the onset phase of the squat and a fixed PGM-based resistance during the end phase of the squat. We used collectible spherical objects in the exergame to maintain a good squat posture. The squat posture parameters, knee distance and squat depth showed improvement through the proposed design. Introducing DDA could also significantly reduce KS during the squats.

Keywords: Squat-exergame · Squat posture · Dynamic Difficulty Adjustment (DDA) · Virtual Reality (VR) · Lower extremity · Pneumatic Gel Muscles (PGMs)

1 Introduction

Promoting and sustaining proper health must be a priority regardless of our changing lifestyle. Lack of essential physical exercise could contribute to an increased toll of fatalities because of chronic illnesses such as heart conditions, cancer, and diabetes. Several new pieces of research led to the promotion of a robust physique through scientific innovations. These researches considered the requirements of both healthy people and individuals with motor disabilities caused by age or other adverse conditions. A broadly accepted technological advance to realise at-home physical exercise and rehabilitation is the concept of exergame that incorporates exercise and gaming collectively [1]. Integrating exercises with games is a reasonable way of dealing with health disorders which result from insufficient physical exercise such as obesity, stress, weakness

© Springer Nature Switzerland AG 2021
M. Antona and C. Stephanidis (Eds.): HCII 2021, LNCS 12769, pp. 449–467, 2021.
https://doi.org/10.1007/978-3-030-78095-1_33

and psychological ailments. Implementation of home-based exergame designs can prospectively help in conditioning the health both physically and mentally [2]. Simplified user-centred style of exergames can raise the immersion in users, which can induce increased health-promoting activities [3].

The basic squat is a prominent training exercise that strengthens several parts of our body such as back, core, and lower extremity [4]. Researchers advocated the benefits of the squat in several studies in the past. In this work, we adopt two-leg standing squat exercise as the assigned task in an exergame aimed at realising efficient training of the lower extremity. It is noteworthy that, if we do not adopt a good squat posture, the risk of injury may increase. Therefore, we constructed our exergame to attain a correct squat posture throughout the exercise session. Also, we added a Dynamic Difficulty Adjustment (DDA) module in the exergame. We adopted this module to optimise the game difficulty conforming to the player's performance and stability during the game. This raises the exergame's likeliness to motivate users of all age groups. Besides, it reinforces the demand of physical exercise in the game and restricts the possibility of injuries and falls because of extreme fatigue. We incorporated a soft actuator module that assists and resists the player according to the dynamic difficulty level. Hence, we developed a novel standing squat exergame by recognising the individual limitations and prerequisites of each user through a combination of the features of squat posture maintenance, regulation of difficulty and soft actuator-based assistance and resistance.

2   Related Research

Several pieces of research were conducted in the recent years to determine the prospects of exergame applications with dependence on expertise and difficulty levels. A few representative studies are introduced in this section. A simple exergame to promote muscle strength and balance in seniors was introduced in [5]. This study also reports the essential preferences of senior participants while playing commercial exergames. The relevance of dynamic difficulty is accurately reported in [6] with particular emphasis on the computational and design requirements. An exergame with optimised difficulty levels was presented in [7]. This research demonstrates that introducing dynamically adjusted difficulty factors in a game raises the overall enjoyment of the users. Another work showed that the levels of performance and attention using Electroencephalographic (EEG) assessment can optimise the challenge in a gaming environment [8]. An Evolutionary Algorithm (EA) was adopted to alter the difficulty level during playtime in a robotic rehabilitation system in [9]. Hocine et al. reported a gaming system with dynamic difficulty in terms of post-stroke therapeutic sessions, which is mainly directed to promote the functionality of the upper limb [10]. Kristan et al. used Artificial Intelligence (AI)-based DDA to raise the efficiency of two simulated computer-controlled players by building up the competitiveness and obtained ≥100% strength of the player. This work was conducted with a serious game called Transform@ aimed at promoting entrepreneurship skills [11].

We must meet certain standards to raise the stability of the lower extremity successfully. Squats have been utilised in several training regimes directed towards strengthening of the lower extremity. However, incorrect set repetitions and posture of squats would adversely influence the performance of lower limbs as summarised in [12]. A recent study examined the neuromuscular and functional adaptations after prolonged squat exercise in resistance-trained men. The research confirmed that full and parallel squats are prescribed to increase strength and functional performance in trained individuals. Also, the practice of half-squat was discouraged because of limitations in performance enhancements and increased pain and discomfort after the training [13]. Another research determines the Anterior Crucial Ligament (ACL) and Posterior Crucial Ligament (PCL) forces linked with various depths of the squat. This study advocates a wide stance (knee distance ≥ shoulder width) and unrestricted movement of the knees during squat [14]. Other researches have again established that extremely deep squats may contribute to increased strain on ACL and anterior displacement of the knees [15]. The effects of fatigue and decision making on ACL injury risk for the hip and knee joints of female athletes have also been stated in [16].

Mobility-based risks are prevalent among the people who rarely undertake physical exercises and show poor control of overall locomotion. Previous work implemented an Artificial Neural Network (ANN)-based offline evaluation of lower limb risk level [4] and a squat exergame with variable load using Pneumatic Gel Muscles (PGMs) [17]. The exergame in this work was designed by following the Stealth-Adaptive Exergame Design (SAED) technique proposed in [18].

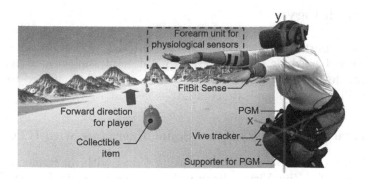

Fig. 1. A representative scene showing all components used for the study. The figure also shows the sagittal (x), transverse (y), and frontal axes (z) representation for data acquisition.

3 Purpose of This Work

This research focuses on the development of an exergame directed at the strengthening of the lower extremity through squat exercise. In this paper, we advocate some improvements in a previously proposed ski exergame by considering the posture and pace factors of the SAED framework [18]. We designed the exergame by recognising various aspects to encourage proper squat posture and reduce the risk of injury through dynamic adjustment of the game difficulty. Figure 1 illustrates a representative image revealing the components and measurement axes in the exergame. We used collectible items aligned to the participant's squatted head position to hold a good squat posture. We compared this approach with the formerly proposed squat exergame using gates [17]. The comparison results are presented in this paper. A DDA-based difficulty adjustment technique is also implemented in this paper to reduce the chances of injury during the exercise. We dynamically manipulate two parameters in the game according to the shakiness in the knees. The manipulated parameters are the moving speed and the degree of assistance provided by the PGMs to perform hip and knee flexion during the onset phase of a squat. PGMs are flexible and lightweight pneumatic actuators that can be operated using considerably low air pressure [19]. We control PGM assistance through a PWM valve that adjusts the force achieved by the PGM actuation.

We organise this paper as follows. After defining the purpose of this research in this section, we detail the different components used in the exergame in the next section named methodology. Then we include the experiment protocol section that summarises the methods adopted during the user study. The next section reveals the results obtained from the user study. Finally, we have the discussion, future work and conclusion sections of the paper.

4   Methodology

This section reports the various components utilised to develop the exergame. The components include sensors used to monitor physiological signals in the participants during game-play and the control system module used to optimise the game difficulty through soft actuators.

4.1   Virtual Reality (VR)-Based Squat Exergame with HTC Vive

We developed the proposed exergame using Unity with an immersive virtual environment. HTC Vive Virtual Reality (VR) headset was used for the VR user interface. We used Vive trackers for monitoring three points of the lower extremity namely, left knee (x_{lk}, y_{lk}, z_{lk}), right knee (x_{rk}, y_{rk}, z_{rk}) and torso (x_t, y_t, z_t). The position of the head mount display (x_h, y_h, z_h) was also used for classification of the phases of squat. Here, x, y, and z refer to the sagittal, transverse, and frontal axes, respectively. The left and right knee trackers were positioned just above the knee joints as shown in Fig. 1. The torso tracker was placed at the centre of the abdomen. The Vive trackers were used to calculate various parameters that were used to monitor the performance and stability of the user. Two kinds of game conditions were used for this study. The conditions were aimed at making the participants squat by using gates and collectible items in

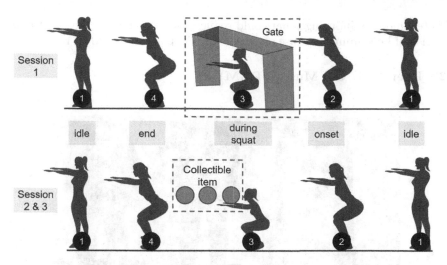

Fig. 2. Methods used in Unity exergame to induce squat. In session 1, we used ski gates which participants had to avoid colliding with (based on Ramin et al. [17]). In sessions 2 and 3, we used collectible items on the ski path. Users could collect these items only if they do a correct parallel squat. The figure also shows different phases of a squat, as detected by the Unity code.

the form of spheres. Figure 2 illustrates the two conditions. For both conditions, we developed an algorithm to detect the phases of squat through Unity-based code. The phases are defined as follows:

– Idle: User is standing and not attempting squat yet
– Onset: User is attempting squat
– During squat: User is squatting (parallel squat or deep squat)
– End: User is attempting to return to a standing upright position or idle phase.

Squat Exergame Using Gates. Since the user study is based on a ski scenario, ski gates are suitable game objects to be used for squat action. While using this game condition, the participants were instructed to avoid colliding with the gates by squatting as low as possible without falling. After the gate passed, they have to stand until the next gate arrives. The squat depth was not fixed and the frequency of squatting was constant. The height of the ski gates was adjusted according to the height of the participants through calibration. This condition was based on previous work by Sakoda et al. [17].

Squat Exergame Using Collectible Spheres. This is a new condition introduced in this paper that includes collectible game objects on the ski pathway of the user. The collectible items were reachable to the user if a parallel squat is done correctly. The height of the collectible items was adjusted according to the user's dimensions through a calibration process before each session.

This technique of inducing squat could reduce the variations in the squat depth. The risk of knee injury because of excessively deep squats could be reduced [15].

4.2 Pneumatic Gel Muscle (PGM)

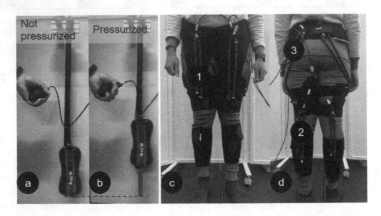

Fig. 3. Actuation of a PGM using a hand-held rubber pump: (a) not pressurised and (b) pressurised conditions of a 30 cm natural length PGM with 0.5 kg attached weight. (c) Anterior and (d) posterior positions of the PGMs attached to assist and resist during squat movements. PGM pair 1: assisting hip flexion positioned parallel to Rectus Femoris, PGM pair 2: assisting knee flexion positioned parallel to Biceps Femoris and PGM pair 3: resisting hip extension positioned parallel to Gluteus Maximus muscles.

PGMs are Pneumatic Artificial Muscles (PAMs) comprising a soft inner tube guarded by an outer mesh [19]. PGMs can be actuated using compressed air with air pressure ranging from 0.05 MPa to 0.3 MPa. By actuating, the length of the PGMs can be varied, which results in linear contraction force. PGMs are suitable for developing wearable motion-assist or resist suits because of their flexibility and soft structure. Apart from the flexible characteristic of PGMs, these artificial muscles can be actuated using considerably low air-pressure to generate acceptable levels of forces compared to other low-pressure artificial muscle counterparts [19]. If both ends of a PGM are attached to two sides of a joint, actuation and deflation of the PGM can provide a certain level of torque to that joint. The same concept is used to provide assistance and resistance to the lower extremity in this study. Figure 3 shows the actuated and deflated conditions of a standard length PGM with 0.5 kg attached weight. This is done through a hand-held rubber pump which generates very low air pressure. In this study, we use three separate sets of PGMs. Each set comprises 4 PGMs with 2 PGMs for each leg. The first set is of 37 cm stretched length and is attached parallel to Rectus Femoris muscle. The second set is of 30 cm stretched length and is attached parallel to the Biceps Femoris muscle. The third set is of 44 cm stretched length and is attached parallel to the Gluteus Maximus muscle. The attachment position of all PGMs can be seen in Fig. 3 in the same sequence as mentioned here.

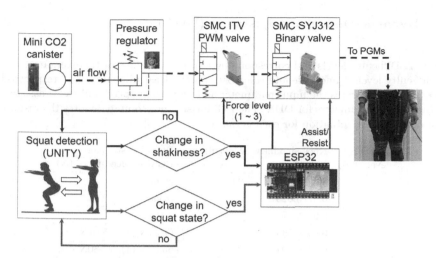

Fig. 4. Control flow diagram showing the components used to regulate the actuation of PGMs.

4.3   Control System

The PGMs are actuated using controlled compressed air through the components illustrated in Fig. 4. A mini CO_2 canister from NTG Ltd. Japan was used as a source of compressed air. The canister was attached with a coarse pressure regulator which is always set to 0.5 MPa. We used a PWM valve from SMC (ITV0031-2L) to optimise the level of air pressure required to actuate the artificial muscles. Besides, two binary valves were each assigned to control the assistance and resistance-associated PGMs. The PGMs attached to support the knee and hip flexion (1 and 2 in Fig. 3) were connected with the assist binary valve. The remaining PGMs (3 in Fig. 3) were attached to the resist binary valve to provide resistance during hip extension. The digital control signal to the valves was provided through an ESP32 microprocessor unit. Through online data streaming of knee Vive trackers, the Knee Shakiness (KS) was monitored. If the KS was found in a certain range (≥ 0.03 m/s), the PGM assistance was turned on and the level of air-pressure was changed through the PWM valve. PGM-based resistance was provided through the resist binary valve whenever the end of a squat phase was detected, irrespective of KS. The resultant force because of PGM actuation was calculated according to the linear polynomial equation denoted in [20].

4.4 Dynamic Difficulty Adjustment (DDA)

Table 1. Difficulty levels and corresponding parameter values in the exergame. Here, the difficulty levels 1 and 6 denote the most and the least difficult levels, respectively. Knee Shakiness (KS) is the input parameter and movement speed and PGM assistance are the output parameters for DDA. The PGM assistance column denotes the resultant force due to PGM actuation for each actuator.

Difficulty level (1–6)	Knee shakiness (m/s)	Movement speed (m/s)	PGM assistance or PGM induced force (N)
1	≤0.02	2.5	None
2	0.02–0.025	2.1	None
3	0.025–0.03	1.7	None
4	0.03–0.035	1.3	60.17N (1); 25.01N (2)
5	0.035–0.04	0.9	65.86N (1); 27.80N (2)
6	≥0.04	0.5	75.34N (1); 32.45N (2)

Adjusting the game difficulty according to the performance of the user enables the possibility of an increased motivation towards finishing the game task. A too low or too high difficulty for any individual can create a build-up of negative attitude leading to lost interest in the task. Therefore, it is crucial to adjust as many elements in the game as possible to enrich the gaming environment and make it optimum for each individual. In our study, we constantly monitored the average KS of the participant. According to this parameter, we optimised two elements in the game to adjust the difficulty level. The first element was the movement speed in the virtual environment. The frequency of squat could be adjusted through this speed. The second parameter was the level of assistive force (in Newtons) provided through the hip and knee flexion assistance PGMs. Table 1 lists the KS conditions used to define the 6 difficulty levels. The movement speed adopted for various difficulty levels is also listed. The ranges of KS used to define the difficulty levels were decided through pilot testing with 14 participants in an exergame session described in Sect. 5.1 as session 1. The assistance provided through PGMs was adjusted according to the difficulty levels from 4 to 6. However, a fixed resistance was provided throughout the gaming session. The force generated by a single resistance PGM was fixed at 90.51N.

4.5 Physiological Parameters

Monitoring physiological data gives us important information about the user's body functioning and fatigue levels during the exercise session. In this study, we recorded three types of physiological data namely, heart rate, Galvanic Skin Response (GSR) and skin temperature. Heart rate detection with wearable sensors is a standard measure of fatigue during training exercises used by researchers and therapists [21]. We used Fitbit Sense to log heart rate data. This module

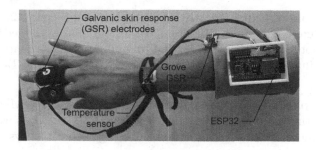

Fig. 5. The forearm attachment unit including Grove Galvanic Skin Response (GSR) sensor and a temperature sensor.

comprises an optical sensor which uses Photoplethysmography (PPG) signals to detect pulse rate in beats/min. GSR is an approach of measuring the electrical conductance of the skin. Characteristics of GSR have been studied to overcome cardiac problems by detecting the stress level in [22]. Work-related stress is a common prevailing problem with all age groups that was analysed in different forms of acute behaviours using GSR sensors [23]. Physical stress has also been measured with the help of GSR sensors in [24]. The parameter shows the level of emotional activity in humans while exposed to an overall stressful environment and physical workouts. The increase in sympathetic emotions and promotion of sweat glands results in high electrical conductivity. In our study, GSR was measured using Grove GSR sensor by attaching two electrodes on any two fingers of the right hand as shown in Fig. 5. The third parameter skin temperature was measured by a particle sensor (MAX30105). Skin temperature can reveal the intensity of acute stress [25]. Therefore, we monitored this parameter during our study. The temperature sensor was tied to the wrist using a soft cloth band as shown in Fig. 5.

5   User Study

We conducted this user study to identify various effects of introducing DDA and PGM-based assistance and resistance in a squat exergame. This section describes the details about the user study. The experimental procedure comprised three different sessions with the combination of two types of exergame models as shown in Fig. 2, DDA, and PGM-based assist and resist.

5.1   Exergame Sessions

Here we describe the conditions that defined each session during the user study.

Ski Gate Exergame Without DDA: Session 1. In this session, the exergame contained ski gates as shown in Fig. 2. The movement speed of the user was constant in the game. The ski gate condition was not tested with DDA and PGMs because Sakoda et al. had already undertaken similar work in [17].

Collectible Sphere Exergame with DDA (Speed): Session 2. This session comprised a different exergame condition, collectible spheres aligned to the user's direction of motion as shown in Fig. 2. Additionally, the movement speed in this session was adjusted according to the conditions of KS listed in Table 1.

Collectible Sphere Exergame with DDA (Speed and PGM): Session 3. Session 3 was the integration of session 2 and PGMs. The PGMs were actuated according to the values mentioned in Table 1 using the control system shown in Fig. 4.

All participants started with session 1 and the other two sessions were randomised in order. Participants started with session 1 because this session was used to determine the range of KS to establish the difficulty levels for sessions 2 and 3. The three training sessions were conducted for three consecutive weeks with one session per week. One proper deep squat or parallel squat takes approximately 6 or 7 s for completion. Each subject performed 6 sets comprising 15 squat repetitions per set for each training session. 3 min rest was provided after completion of each set. Therefore, the total time consumed for each training session was around 35 min comprising 90 squat encounters in total. This training protocol included the measurement of squat parameters through Vive trackers, and physiological data including heart rate, GSR and temperature. After each session, subjective feedback was also collected from the participants using a questionnaire. The questionnaire included queries about the exergame based on NASA Task Load Index (TLX) and also covered necessary information such as user's age, height, weight, sex and any recent motor complications. The experimental procedure was adopted from previous research [26].

5.2   Participants

11 male and 3 female participants were selected for the study. Their mean age was 25.6 ± 3.5 years. All subjects were university students who had no known musculoskeletal impairments or any other recent complications in their lower extremity. All subjects were healthy and considered fit to take part in all three sessions after a general evaluation. The general evaluation comprised 3 trial squats during which the participants identified themselves if they felt any discomfort, and the experimenter examined if they performed the squats with a correct posture. Also, the users were asked to sign an informed consent which was approved by an ethics committee ensuring that the experimental protocol was established under the ethical standards covered in the Declaration of Helsinki.

5.3 Experiment Protocol

Each training session started with a detailed explanation of the experimental protocol to the participant. A trial was provided for each session to get familiar with the gaming conditions. PGMs were attached to the lower extremity for session 3 only. Then the Vive trackers were secured to knee and torso positions. The forearm attachment for physiological sensors was also fixed to the participant's right forearm. The Fitbit tracker was then attached to the left wrist for heart rate logging. Then we asked the participants to stand at a pre-defined position (marked on the floor) and comfortably wear the VR headset. Next, after the Unity scene is played, a calibration period was notified to the user during which (s)he has to do 2 squats and then wait for the actual game to start. The calibration is used to identify the dimensions of the user and adjust the height of the gates and collectible spheres. Then the user squats in synchronisation with the approaching objects in the virtual environment. During the game, if the participant collides with an object because of insufficient squat depth or timing error, a pop-up is used to notify about the collision, which also leads to a reduced score. They can also view the number of remaining squats in a set. After finishing 15 squats, the participants can see their final score (which is also the number of correct squats). The sequence of activities were identical for all three sessions that comprised 6 sets each.

6 Parameters Studied and Their Results

This section briefs the parameters studied to identify the effects of introducing DDA and posture correction in the exergame. A summary of the evaluation of the parameters is also presented.

6.1 Data Acquired from Vive Trackers

Three parameters were calculated from the data acquired using Vive trackers. The parameters for three different sessions were compared using repeated-measures Analysis of Variance (ANOVA).

Knee Shakiness (KS): Squats induce shakiness in both knees. Excessive shakiness in the knees indicates weak lower extremity. We calculated the KS using the derivative of sagittal position data (velocity) of both knee position trackers.

$$KS = \frac{\Delta x_k}{\Delta t} \tag{1}$$

Here, x_k is the knee position (sagittal axis), t is the time. The average sagittal velocity of both knees was calculated and recorded during all sessions. Figure 6a shows the comparison results of average KS during different sessions. Session 3 showed the lowest KS, which was also significantly reduced as compared to both sessions 1 and 2.

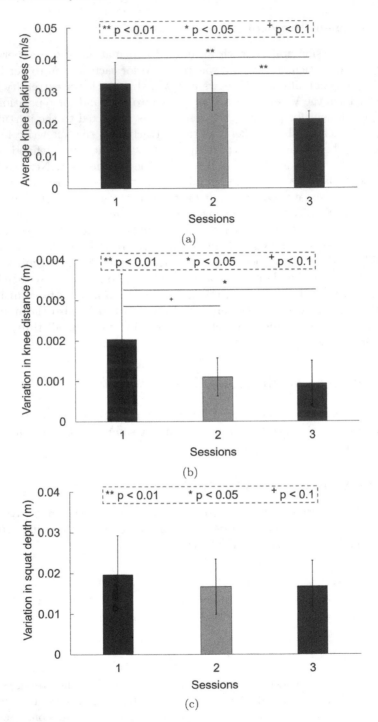

Fig. 6. Comparison of motion data for different sessions. (a) average knee shakiness relates to the fatigue level of the user (b) variation in knee distance and (c) variation in squat depth correspond to posture maintenance during squat.

Knee Distance (KD): The distance between the knees must be maintained to ensure proper posture during a squat. Therefore, we compared the level of variation in the knee distance for different sessions. The parameter was directly calculated by finding the difference between the left and right knee positions in the sagittal axis as follows.

$$KD = |x_{lk} - x_{rk}| \tag{2}$$

Here, x_{lk} is the left knee position (sagittal axis) and x_{rk} is the right knee position (sagittal axis). The knee distance variation was quite large during the first session and was significantly reduced in sessions 2 and 3 as shown in Fig. 6b.

Squat Depth (SD): This parameter was calculated using the transverse axis data of the torso tracker.

$$SD = |y_{t_3,peak} - y_{t_1}| \tag{3}$$

Here, $y_{t_3,peak}$ is the negative peak value of torso position (transverse axis) during squat and y_{t_1} is the torso position (transverse axis) during idle phase. The squat phases can be referred from Fig. 2. Similar to knee distance, the squat depth should also have less variation in consecutive squats. Previous research has suggested that muscle activation does not differ based on squat depth [14]. A deeper squat could increase the risk of anterior displacement of the knees and increased strain on the ACL and meniscus [15]. We observed from the squat depth data that, using gates to induce squats (session 1) made participants do deeper squats as compared to the other two sessions. The reason behind this was the absence of fixed squat depth constraint in the game for the first session. However, for the other two sessions, as we introduced collectible items instead of gates, the squat depth requirement was fixed throughout and the variation in the squat depth was reduced as shown in Fig. 6c.

6.2   Data Acquired from Physiological Parameters

Three physiological sensors were used to monitor the state of participants during the exercise sessions. The heart rate data was directly evaluated as beats/min. The GSR data was also directly evaluated without filtering. The skin temperature data was filtered using a median filter to remove the non-linear noise as seen in Fig. 7.

Heart Rate: The comparison of average heart rate during the three sessions is illustrated in Fig. 8. Sessions 2 and 3 showed reduced average heart rate as compared to session 1. However, the statistical significance in this reduction was only with 90% accuracy. The median value of average heart rate of all three sessions showed a very low variation.

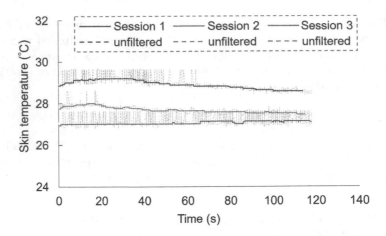

Fig. 7. Skin temperature of a representative participant during all sessions (raw and median-filtered data).

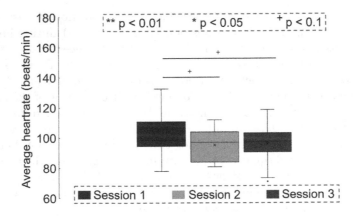

Fig. 8. Comparison of average heart rate for different sessions.

Galvanic Skin Response (GSR): The GSR levels were recorded during each session and linear curve-fitted. The slope of the fit was considered as the rate of change in the GSR level over the period of the exercise, which is compared in Fig. 9. The third session that included PGM-based assistance and resistance showed steady GSR levels as compared to the other two sessions. This shows that the stress levels of participants were significantly lower during session 3.

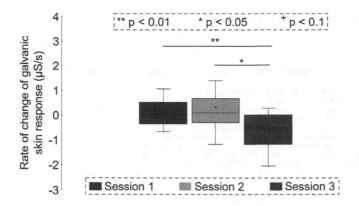

Fig. 9. Comparison of the rate of change of Galvanic Skin Response (GSR) data for different sessions. Lower value indicates low emotional stress with progression in the exercise session.

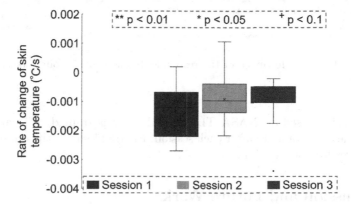

Fig. 10. Comparison of the rate of change of skin temperature for different sessions. Reduction in body temperature is commonly observed while exercising.

Skin Temperature: Similar to GSR data, the rate of change of skin temperature was found using linear curve fitting of the median-filtered skin temperature data. Figure 10 shows the comparison of the rate of change of skin temperature for all three sessions. A negative change is indicated during all three sessions. However, no significant difference was found for this data.

6.3   Questionnaire Data

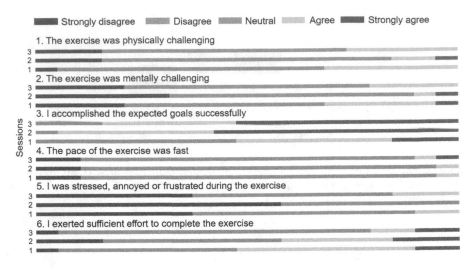

Fig. 11. Questionnaire feedback of the respondents based on 5 point Likert Scale for each session.

A questionnaire-based on NASA TLX postulates was framed. All participants answered the questionnaire after each session. Figure 11 shows the questions and the responses for each session.

7   Discussion and Future Work

We introduced DDA to adjust the difficulty level of a squat exergame. From the motion data as shown in Fig. 6, it can be observed that the KS during the exercise was significantly reduced by adding the DDA mechanism to the exergame. Besides, by changing the type of exergame object to induce squat, we could achieve lower variation in both knee distance and squat depth, which shows an improvement in the squat posture. As one purpose of this work was to maintain good squat posture with minimal chances of a knee injury, through the data in Fig. 6, we can say that we achieved this objective. According to the GSR data, we observed that the combination of PGM-based force feedback and DDA reduced emotional stress significantly. The average heart rate during the exercise was significantly less after introducing DDA. There was no significant difference in the rate of change of skin temperature for the three sessions. According to the questionnaire data, sessions 2 and 3 were not as challenging as session 1, both mentally and physically. However, more participants were satisfied with their performance during sessions 2 and 3 compared to session 1. Most participants did not have strong opinions about the pace of all three exercise sessions. More participants disagreed to being stressed, annoyed or frustrated during session 3 as compared to the other two sessions. Self-effort was more agreed to in sessions 1 and 2.

Future work of this research includes verifying the feasibility of this exergame for elderly users. We also plan to integrate additional parameters in the game that can increase the challenge level of the game. We should also make sure that the game is made compatible with the type of user from the beginning of playtime. We have to include a pre-evaluation of the user to implement this aspect, as suggested in [4]. We also plan to replace the supporters used for PGM attachment by a full body suit with PGMs attached to different DOFs that can be used as per requirement. The suit also needs to be tailored according to the dimension requirements of various users. Another issue we want to address in the future is the delay involved in PGM actuation. The PWM valves used in this research incur a considerable delay in actuating the PGMs. This delay can be reduced by using prediction algorithms. Also, we plan to incorporate a depth camera for body tracking and replace the Vive trackers to reduce disturbance to the user. We also plan to use AI to develop a significantly optimised exergame so that users can benefit to the most extent.

8   Conclusion

In this paper, we proposed a squat exergame with DDA using PGM-based assistance and resistance. We conducted a user study involving 14 participants to compare the proposed exergame with a previously published version. We observed that through the proposed configuration, proper squat posture could be maintained and GSR stress levels, and knee shakiness could be significantly reduced.

Acknowledgement. This work is a part of the project named 'Smart society for enjoying long healthy life - Developing AI smart coaching technology that facilitates voluntary skill-up for elderlies'. The project is commissioned by the New Energy and Industrial Technology Development Organization (NEDO), Japan.

References

1. Sween, J., Wallington, S.F., Sheppard, V., Taylor, T., Llanos, A.A., Adams-Campbell, L.L.: The role of exergaming in improving physical activity: a review. J. Phys. Activity Health **11**(4), 864–870 (2014)
2. Bolton, J., Lambert, M., Lirette, D., Unsworth, B.: PaperDude: a virtual reality cycling exergame. In: CHI 2014 Extended Abstracts on Human Factors in Computing Systems, pp. 475–478 (2014)
3. Hagen, K., Chorianopoulos, K., Wang, A.I., Jaccheri, L., Weie, S.: Gameplay as exercise. In: Proceedings of the 2016 CHI Conference Extended Abstracts on Human Factors in Computing Systems, pp. 1872–1878 (2016)
4. Tadayon, R., Vega Ramirez, A., Das, S., Kishishita, Y., Yamamoto, M., Kurita, Y.: Automatic exercise assistance for the elderly using real-time adaptation to performance and affect. In: Antona, M., Stephanidis, C. (eds.) HCII 2019. LNCS, vol. 11573, pp. 556–574. Springer, Cham (2019). https://doi.org/10.1007/978-3-030-23563-5_44

5. Nawaz, A., et al.: Designing simplified exergame for muscle and balance training in seniors: a concept of 'out in nature'. In: Proceedings of the 8th International Conference on Pervasive Computing Technologies for Healthcare, pp. 309–312 (2014)

6. Hunicke, R.: The case for dynamic difficulty adjustment in games. In: Proceedings of the 2005 ACM SIGCHI International Conference on Advances in Computer Entertainment Technology, pp. 429–433 (2005)

7. Colwell, A.M., Glavin, F.G.: Colwell's castle defence: a custom game using dynamic difficulty adjustment to increase player enjoyment. CoRR, abs/1806.04471 (2018)

8. Stein, A., Yotam, Y., Puzis, R., Shani, G., Taieb-Maimon, M.: EEG-triggered dynamic difficulty adjustment for multiplayer games. Entertainment Comput. **25**, 14–25 (2018)

9. Andrade, K.d.O., Pasqual, T.B., Caurin, G.A.P., Crocomo, M.K.: Dynamic difficulty adjustment with evolutionary algorithm in games for rehabilitation robotics. In: 2016 IEEE International Conference on Serious Games and Applications for Health (SeGAH), pp. 1–8 (2016)

10. Hocine, N., Gouaïch, A., Cerri, S.A., Mottet, D., Froger, J., Laffont, I.: Adaptation in serious games for upper-limb rehabilitation: an approach to improve training outcomes. User Model. User-Adapted Interact. **25**(1), 65–98 (2015)

11. Kristan, D., Bessa, P., Costa, R., de Carvalho, C.V.: Creating competitive opponents for serious games through dynamic difficulty adjustment. Information **11**(3), 156 (2020)

12. Myer, G.D., et al.: The back squat: a proposed assessment of functional deficits and technical factors that limit performance. Strength Condition. J. **36**(6), 4 (2014)

13. Pallarés, J.G., Cava, A.M., Courel-Ibáñez, J., González-Badillo, J.J., Morán-Navarro, R.: Full squat produces greater neuromuscular and functional adaptations and lower pain than partial squats after prolonged resistance training. Eur. J. Sport Sci. **20**(1), 115–124 (2020)

14. Comfort, P., Kasim, P.: Optimizing squat technique. Strength Condition. J. **29**(6), 10 (2007)

15. Escamilla, R.F.: Knee biomechanics of the dynamic squat exercise. Medicine Sci. Sports Exercise **33**(1), 127–141 (2001)

16. Borotikar, B.S., Newcomer, R., Koppes, R., McLean, S.G.: Combined effects of fatigue and decision making on female lower limb landing postures: central and peripheral contributions to ACL injury risk. Clin. Biomech. **23**(1), 81–92 (2008)

17. Sakoda, W., Tadayon, R., Kishishita, Y., Yamamoto, M., Kurita, Y.: SKI exergame for squat training to change load based on predicted locomotive risk level. In: 2020 IEEE/SICE International Symposium on System Integration (SII), pp. 289–294. IEEE (2020)

18. Tadayon, R., Sakoda, W., Kurita, Y.: Stealth-adaptive exergame design framework for elderly and rehabilitative users. In: Gao, Q., Zhou, J. (eds.) HCII 2020. LNCS, vol. 12208, pp. 419–434. Springer, Cham (2020). https://doi.org/10.1007/978-3-030-50249-2_30

19. Ogawa, K., Thakur, C., Ikeda, T., Tsuji, T., Kurita, Y.: Development of a pneumatic artificial muscle driven by low pressure and its application to the unplugged powered suit. Adv. Robot. **31**(21), 1135–1143 (2017)

20. Thakur, C., Ogawa, K., Kurita, Y.: Active passive nature of assistive wearable gait augment suit for enhanced mobility. J. Robot. Mechatron. **30**(5), 717–728 (2018)

21. Ahmad, I., Kim, J.-Y.: Assessment of whole body and local muscle fatigue using electromyography and a perceived exertion scale for squat lifting. Int. J. Environ. Res. Public Health **15**(4), 784 (2018)

22. Villarejo, M.V., Zapirain, B.G., Zorrilla, A.M.: A stress sensor based on galvanic skin response (GSR) controlled by ZigBee. Sensors **12**(5), 6075–6101 (2012)
23. Bakker, J., Pechenizkiy, M., Sidorova, N.: What's your current stress level? detection of stress patterns from GSR sensor data. In: 2011 IEEE 11th International Conference on Data Mining Workshops, pp. 573–580. IEEE (2011)
24. Fernandes, A., Helawar, R., Lokesh, R., Tari, T., Shahapurkar, A.V.: Determination of stress using blood pressure and galvanic skin response. In: 2014 International Conference on Communication and Network Technologies, pp. 165–168. IEEE (2014)
25. Herborn, K.A., et al.: Skin temperature reveals the intensity of acute stress. Physiology Behav. **152**, 225–230 (2015)
26. Dexheimer, J.D., Schroeder, E.T., Sawyer, B.J., Pettitt, R.W., Aguinaldo, A.L., Torrence, W.A.: Physiological performance measures as indicators of crossfit® performance. Sports **7**(4), 93 (2019)

Mobile Application for Determining the Concentration of Sulfonamides in Water Using Digital Image Colorimetry

Pedro Reis[1], Pedro H. Carvalho[1], Patrícia S. Peixoto[2] (ID),
Marcela A. Segundo[2] (ID), and Hélder P. Oliveira[1,3]([✉]) (ID)

[1] INESC TEC – Institute for Systems and Computer Engineering,
Technology and Science, Porto, Portugal
`helder.f.oliveira@inesctec.pt`
[2] LAQV – REQUIMTE, Faculty of Pharmacy, University of Porto, Porto, Portugal
[3] Faculty of Sciences, University of Porto, Porto, Portugal

Abstract. Antibiotics are widely applied for the treatment of humans and animals, being the Sulfonamides a special group. The presence of antibiotics in the aquatic environment causes the development antibiotic-resistant bacteria, which is related to the emerging of untreatable infectious diseases. One of the most common methods for determine it consists in high-performance liquid chromatography coupled with mass spectrometrym, which is not suitable for an in situ analysis strategy.

One important property of sulfonamides is how the compound reacts when added the colorimetric reagent p-dimethylaminocinnamaldehyde, opening the possibility of using colorimetry to measure the concentration. To allow an analysis on the field, the solution needs to be fully mobile and practical. In this context, we recently developed a new screening method based on a computational application running over a picture of the sample; however, despite this approach improving the analysis process when compared to traditional methods, it is still not fully mobile.

Smartphones' computational capabilities are increasing and more powerful than many laptops of older generations. Taking this into account, we developed a mobile analysis application that leverages the computing power and ease of use of a smartphone. The acquired picture will pass through a color correction algorithm to normalize the capture considering the environmental lighting. When the algorithm finishes processing the image, the app will return the estimated concentration of the sample. This approach enables in situ analysis, without requiring an Internet connection nor specific analysis equipment, and the ability to have a rather precise guess of the level of contamination of any water.

Keywords: Mobile applications · Colorimetry · Sulfonamides detection

This work is financed by the ERDF – European Regional Development Fund through the Operational Programme for Competitiveness and Internationalisation - COMPETE 2020 Programme and by National Funds through the Portuguese funding agency, FCT - Fundação para a Ciência e a Tecnologia within project POCI-01-0145-FEDER- 031756.

M. Antona and C. Stephanidis (Eds.): HCII 2021, LNCS 12769, pp. 468–484, 2021.
https://doi.org/10.1007/978-3-030-78095-1_34

1   Introduction

As modern medicine advances, more forms of combating diseases arise. Sulfonamides are an important group of antibiotics, and they are widely used not only to treat humans, but also farm animals [1]. Sulfonamides and their metabolites are frequently found in environmental water. They can reach this medium through different pathways, such as wastewater discharges, contaminated manure and slurry, and aquaculture. Their presence accelerates natural selection on bacteria colonies in the water, since sulfonamides kill the bacteria that cannot resist antibiotics, allowing the others to proliferate. It was also found that the aquatic medium is highly favorable to the transfer of genes [2], which lead to more bacteria acquiring the antibiotic resistant gene. This escalated into the global threat of antimicrobial resistance, hence the quantification of sulfonamides concentration in water is crucial to assess environmental risk and to establish health and environmental policies. Currently there are several strategies being used to quantify sulfonamides, but for most traditional methods, it has to collect a water sample to be tested and take it to a laboratory capable of doing this procedure. This approach is impractical, expensive, and not mobile.

Recently, Carvalho et al. [3] developed a new computational framework to detect sulfonamides in water. This approach is based on the colorimetric reaction between sulfonamides and the reagent p-dimethylaminocinnamaldehyde, after retention of these antibiotics in a solid support. It was observed that there exists a relation between the intensity of the color product to the concentration of sulfonamides in the sample. Knowing this, we developed an experimental study to understand if it could quantify sulfonamides in μg per liter using digital colorimetry. The investigation concluded that this approach was viable, and provided a more streamlined process to get an estimation of the degree of contamination in waters. However, despite being more practical and much less expensive, it requires the use of a personal computer to perform the processing, hinders the solution's mobility, or the sample be transported and later processed in a lab computer.

Mobile devices are not only becoming more prevalent, but also more computationally capable. A smartphone could handle taking the picture of the reaction, and after this there could have two possible solutions:

- Upload the captured photograph to a web server, and run the already finished algorithm on that capture. A simple approach, with potentially the best results in terms of performance, since the performance could be improved by upgrading hardware on the servers. It also enabled the algorithm to be used without needing any porting effort. However, this has two major disadvantages, which are the reliance on an Internet connection and the need for servers capable of processing the algorithms. The former is of critical importance, as there are use cases of analyzing waters in remote regions with no Internet access.
- Use the photograph and run a new, mobile-friendly version of algorithm to detect sulfonamides concentration locally. This would be the most complex

task, as it requires the porting of the algorithm, coupled with the need for performance optimizations, since smartphone hardware is not as powerful as a computer. Despite this, it has none of the major shortcomings of the already mentioned alternative. This makes all the difference if an area or device has connectivity issues.

Taken into account all this considerations, in this work, we decided to tackle running the algorithm locally, as its advantages far outweigh the disadvantages, mainly because it would be a fully mobile solution, despite being more challenging approach. Taken in consideration the algorithm developed in the past [3] and the requirements for this new mobile application, we defined the following objectives:

- **Fully migrate the algorithm to a mobile-friendly language**: The algorithm developed by Carvalho et al. [3] is reliant on *MATLAB*, which is a proprietary language that mobile devices cannot run. There is a version of *MATLAB* for Android (*MATLABMobile*), but it is reliant on an Internet connection for any processing. This would not be ideal, since some of the regions could be remote, and no Internet connection would be available; In order for the processing to take place in the device and take advantage of the work already done, the algorithm would have to be ported to a new language. This removes the limitation of working with proprietary software, allowing the team to be more in control of the entirety of the code;
- **Use manual input to assist the algorithm**: Using the touch capabilities of smartphones, we can give the user direct control on specific parts of the algorithm, if the automated version fails;
- **A high-performance application**: Despite the advances in mobile computing, it will never be as good at performing complex operations as a laptop or a desktop. For this reason, performance is a critical priority, so as to allow the quick analysis of multiple pictures. Ideally, the user could also tweak the level of precision to allow for faster analysis.

2   Literature Review

Appearing in 1968, sulfonamides are an important functional group of antibiotics that are very widely used. Some of it's common use cases revolve around the treatment of both urinary and upper respiratory tract infections [4]. The widespread consumption of this compound is understandable, since it is low cost, low toxicity (i.e. well tolerated by patients), and very effective against bacteria. However, the appeal of the consumption of antibiotics is promoting an overprescription of these compounds. To further complicate matters, these drugs have also been used for the treatment of livestock. These factors cause an increase in the appearance of sulfonamides in environmental water.

The presence of sulfonamides in water promotes the proliferation of bacteria colonies with antibiotic-resistant genes. To measure the concentration of these compounds, there are several methods, with the ones listed requiring a laboratory capable of performing these procedures:

- **High-performance liquid chromatography tandem mass spectrometry (HPLC-MS)**: This method essentially combines two different processes, where liquid chromatography separates the individual components of the sample, and mass spectrometry analyses the mass structure of each element [5]. This synergistic approach is extensively used, not only for the detection of sulfonamides, but also other classes of organic compounds composed by multiple molecules;
- **Capillary electrophoresis**: The previous method can sometimes be limited by low efficiency in the separation process, which is critical in residues analysis [6]. This method can be an alternative to that approach, by separating the components of a solution according to their charge and size. This is done by the use of a very small tube (capillary), in which the sample (injector) travels until reaching a destination vial. Smaller molecules are faster than larger ones, and in a point of the cable there is a detector (integrator or computer) that analyzes what is passing through the capillary;
- **Immunoassay**: Antibodies are highly specific molecules capable of binding to a particular target structure. In the context of the research done by Li et al. [7], an antibody was created that could bind to the structure of sulfonamides. This area of investigation started in 2000, when Muldoon et al. [9] produced a monoclonal antibody that detected eight sulfonamides. More recently, Korpimäki et al. [8] produced antibodies capable of detecting different sulfonamides under various levels of concentration;
- **Gas chromatography coupled with atomic emission detection**: Developed by Chiavarino et al. [10], it can analyse nine sulfonamides by initially separating the compounds using gas chromatography, and then using atomic emission detection for the determination of the sulfonamides.

Traditional methodologies for analyzing contaminated water for sulfonamides have limitations. They require a person to collect a sample in situ, transport it to a lab, and expensive and resource intensive processes. On top of that, in some remote regions of the world, getting the sample from the location to the lab can also be a costly and time consuming endeavour. Algorithms using digital image colorimetry can mitigate some of these limitations. For example, after collecting a sample, the investigator could later use software to process the image of the chemical reaction between the sulfonamides and the reagent. This would be less expensive, and generate less overhead to get an estimation of the contamination.

2.1 Colorimetry

Colorimetry is a methodology that quantifies physically the human color perception. Similar in nature to spectrophotometry, it is solely focused on the visible region of the electromagnetic spectrum. To perform colorimetry, a device capable of capturing the wavelengths of visible light is required. Traditional tools include:

- **Tristimulus colorimeter**: Also called a colorimeter, it is frequently used for display calibration. It works by analyzing the colors the screen emits using photodetectors, to establish a display profile that can be used for the calibration [11].

– **Spectrophotometer**: a device that can quantitatively measure the spectral reflectance, transmittance or irradiance of a color sample [12].

Although these devices are specialized in obtaining raw wavelength data, they are geared only for experienced users, like photographers or researchers, not the average consumer. For this reason, any function that might require an average user (like taking a picture to analyze a wound) becomes out of reach for most. A smartphone could be a more practical, common tool, that has most of the features required for this type of analysis, albeit with some issues.

2.2   Android and Mobile Cameras

Android is one of the largest current operating systems in the world, with over 70% market share as of June 2020. Developed by Android Inc. and later acquired by Google in 2005, it has grown massively since it's debut in 2007. It now amasses over 85% of the smartphone market share, totalling over 329 million devices as of the second quarter of 2018[1]. The first mobile camera appeared in 2000 with the J-Phone, featuring 0.11 megapixels. 6 years later, Sony released the Sony Ericsson, with a 3.2 MP camera. Not only was this a lot more powerful in terms of raw pixel count, it also featured more technologies such as image stabilization, auto-focus and a flash. Tech giants entered a race for megapixels, with again Sony releasing in 2009 the Sony Ericsson S006, featuring a 16 MP camera. Around that time, the smartphone industry started to boom, and devices with large cameras were becoming more inconvenient. Size and form factor started to carry more importance, and the previous model's cameras were quite bulky. For these reasons, camera development reached a standstill, since it was becoming more apparent that it was not only raw megapixel count that determined the quality of a picture.

Software was coming to the front stage, with companies starting to developing more and more features, such as HDR, panoramas, and more intelligent ways of capturing detail. Images were being processed with more advanced methods, some even featuring AI to enhance a photograph. This advancement in software features is a double-edged sword however, as two cameras with similar hardware specifications might produce completely different results. This presents a large problem with using colorimetry, since the accuracy of the color value is of the utmost importance for the final result.

2.3   Device and Lighting Variation

When the color of the image is critical to the result of the processing, it becomes vital to ensure that different devices under the same conditions can capture a very similar photograph. Unfortunately, this does not happen, as the vast majority of smartphones operates in the RGB color space, which is device dependent,

---

[1] https://www.statista.com/topics/876/android/.

i.e. changes in every equipment. To address this, before using the image, it needs to be processed from a device dependent color space like RGB, to a device independent color space like CIE L*a*b*, CIE XYZ or sRGB.

Color constancy is the perception of the same color appearing constant even in varying lighting scenarios [13]. Color correcting images to a device independent color space helps achieve constancy by approximating the hue of the colors to the real hue of the objects. There are multiple algorithms that can transform color spaces, such as:

- **Root-Polynomial Regression**: Mapping from a device dependent RGB color space to a device independent XYZ space using linear color correction (LCC) can often have a high amount of error. Polynomial color correction can have higher precision, but it is susceptible to changes in exposure. Root-polynomial regression was created to solve this problem. It is an extension of LCC with low complexity that enhances color correction performance [14]. An example of the color correction method can be seen in Fig. 1.

 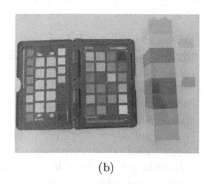

(a)   (b)

Fig. 1. Example of color correction algorithm using root-Polynomial regression. a) original photo, b) photo after correction

- **Simulated Annealing**: Standard camera calibrations use a color checker, which is a professional grade equipment featuring color patches, where the values are known beforehand by the manufacturer. This allows the application of a transformation matrix from each patch to its corresponding known value in the XYZ color space. A common methodology to do this is by using a least-squares regression, but there is an error associated caused by algorithm limitations and CCD dark currents (when unwanted free electrons are generated in a charged coupled device of a camera due to thermal energy) [15].

Machine learning was an avenue of exploration for color constancy. Bianco et al. [16] used a Convolutional Neural Network (CNN) to estimate the scene illumination using as input a RAW image. It uses a color checker to establish the ground truth, and utilizing a CNN combining feature learning and regression the results obtained were better than every state-of-the-art technique at the time. Around the same time, Lou et al. [17] was also exploring AI in the same field, more specifically Deep Neural Networks (DNN). By approaching color constancy as a DNN-based regression and using trained datasets with over a million images, they managed to outperform state-of-the-art implementations by 9%, while maintaining good performance throughout.

Dang et al. [18] also highlighted the importance of color correcting images when used for health purposes, more specifically a photoplethysmogram (PPG). This operation is used for detecting blood volume changes through illuminating the skin and measuring changes in light absorption [19]. Using different devices for capturing the photo results in errors that reduce the precision of the measurements. For this, they developed a color correction algorithm using a least squares estimation based method, and with this reduced the mean and standard deviation differences between devices.

In the context of sulfonamide analysis using digital image colorimetry, Carvalho et al. [3] compared the efficiency of different color correction methods. For all tests, they used a color checker as mentioned in the simulated annealing method. The current implementation of their algorithm tested out 5 different methodologies:

– **Weighted Gray Edge**: Different edge types exist in images: shadows, highlights, materials, etc. These different edges contribute differently to illuminant estimation. This algorithm classifies edges based on photometric properties, and then evaluates the edge-based color constancy according to the edge types. The research showed that using an iterative weighted Gray-Edge based on based on highlights reduces the median error by about 25%. In an uncontrolled scenario, it can offer improvements of up to 11% against regular edge-based color constancy [20].
– **Illuminant Estimation Using White Patch (White)**: Utilizes a white patch, and estimates the illuminant based on the difference of the value of the patch to absolute white, since any deviation is caused by illumination.
– **Illuminant Estimation Using Achromatic Patches (Neutral)**: Similar to the previous method, but uses the average of a 6 patch color set.
– **Color Correction Matrix RGB to RGB**: Used the 24 colors provided in a color checker, and compares the colors to the reference values provided by the manufacturer. Uses a least squares regression between the two sets of values.
– **Color Correction Matrix RGB to XYZ**: Similar to the previous method, but maps to the XYZ color space.

Comparisons were done between the standard deviations of all the previous methodologies in each color space, and in over 90% of them, the color correction matrix from RGB to XYZ yielded the best results [3].

2.4   Colorimetry Using Smartphones

Modern smartphones have many sensors that can be useful in assisting a medical diagnosis, such as microphones to record user input, heart beat monitors, or cameras. One example of the camera being used in medicine is for the analysis of diabetes wound healing. In the US, 7.8% of the population have diabetes, and over 5 million patients have chronic wounds that require frequent visits to the doctor. Agu et al. [21] designed an application called Sugar with the intention of helping the user track the progress of their wounds more easily.

Another example of a smartphone camera using colorimetry for a medical situation was the analysis of tongue images. Wang et al. [22] researched in the area of a traditional chinese medicine, where tongue images can indicate physiological differences on the body. The researchers faced the same adversities that we mentioned previously, namely the device variation arising from the RGB color space. Photographs captured in one device might contain different color values from another photograph taken in the same environment with another smartphone. Traditional methods to ensure color constancy like polynomial regression were not very successful due to the restricted range of colors of the tongue, so they needed to be further optimized. The color correction algorithm utilizes a color checker to calibrate the device for the scenario of the tongue images. After the algorithm was developed and applied, the researchers reached a difference of under 0.085% compared to the real value, with a high adaptability to different tongues and varying lighting conditions.

Jarujamrus et al. [23] developed an application for the analysis of mercury in water. A small amount of this element in water can produce massive damages to the entire ecosystem that depends on it. For this reason, they developed a way to use smartphones and colorimetry to assess the level of mercury contamination in water. Mercury does not have a visible representation, so in order to analyze a sample using colorimetry, there had to be a way to visually check the concentration. For this they created a reaction that produced a color that changed intensity according to the amount of mercury in the sample. To achieve this they used a microfluidic paper-based analytical device (μPAD) that was coated with synthetic silver nanoparticles (AgNPs). These particles disappeared from a deep yellow to a fainter yellow as the concentration of mercury increased.

In the work of Carvalho et al. [3], we developed a more inexpensive way to assess concentration of sulfonamides in water samples, in contrast to traditional methodologies, which are considered as impractical and resource expensive since as they required a sample to be sent to the laboratory to be analyzed. To solve this problem, we explored the use of digital image colorimetry. In this methodology, a chemical reagent was required (p-dimethylaminocinnamaldehyde), but the process was streamlined, and did not require any complex laboratory equipment for the analysis process. To analyze the reaction, all that was necessary was a smartphone camera to take a picture of the reaction, and a computer to run the algorithm. To test the algorithm, many pictures were taken, varying in sulfonamide concentration, and device that captured them. To make the concentration vary, samples were prepared in a laboratory to ensure the values of the concentration were known beforehand. This allowed the results of the analysis to be directly compared to the real values. Photographs were taken with different smartphones to determine the impact that device variation had on the final results. The experience consisted of taking a photo of the sample together with a color checker to help on the color correction (see Fig. 1). The first step of the algorithm consisted on the segmentation both of the sample and the color checker. Afterwards, and using the information contained in the color checker, we applied the algorithm from Akkaynak et al. [24], which demonstrated that the RGB to XYZ color space conversion resulted in a more independent-device result. Finally, the sulfonamide concentration value of the sample, was found by finding a linear correlation with the Hue component from the HSV color space.

3   Architecture

The key advantage of this application is that it enables the analysis of a sample on the field, without requiring any specific equipment for the task. With this use case in mind, several requirements arise and many architecture decisions have to be made.

3.1   Requirements

Several functional requirements were identified in the application planning, namely:

- The user needs to be able to load previously taken pictures, or take pictures from within the application to launch an analysis;
- During the acquisition of photos, the distance between the mobile device and the scene is not fixed. The only requirement is that color checker and sample must be visible in the photo;
- The user needs to be able to store samples, so that they could analyse them later;
- The user can intervene directly in the algorithm, with a manual implementation for each step, so a valid estimation could be achieved, even if the automatic version fails;
- The user can select a specific number of patches for the color checker, in order to have full control over the patches used;
- The user can select the level of precision of the algorithm, to allow control over the time it takes to get an analysis.

3.2   Key Architecture Decisions

The first major decision on creating this mobile application was the selection of the target devices. Our goal was to support the lowest possible Android version that did not undermine the requirements for the app, which ended up being version 4.0.3. The second major component regarding the architecture is the framework that was used to port the algorithm itself. Since *MATLAB* cannot run on Android devices, a capable alternative had to be found. For this purpose we investigated what image processing frameworks were available for Android that also allowed for an extremely high level of performance. We selected *OpenCV* based on the following advantages:

- Well supported, with a specific build for Android;
- Decently documented, expediting the development process;
- Comprehensive alternative to *MATLAB* that could run on Android device;
- Allows the code to be run without requiring any internet connection;
- Open-source and does not require any type of licenses;

4   Implementation

In Fig. 2 is presented an example a typical photo of the environment, in which the color checker is located left of the disk, with the color patches (the individual squares) on the right side.

Fig. 2. Example image of the environment.

4.1   Initial Menu

In order to begin analyzing a sample, the user would have to input some image, either by loading an already taken picture, or by launching the phone's camera application and capturing a photo. After that, the flow of information converges to the analysis setup screen. The interface for the analysis setup screen is presented in Fig. 3.

After selecting or acquiring a photo, the analysis setup interface is shown, where the user views the image that needs to be stored, and is required to provide a name to later help identify the sample. Whether the user selects to defer or to carry immediate analysis, the image is uploaded and stored in the application's external memory, saving the date of the upload as metadata.

Fig. 3. Sample menu screen.

4.2 Settings Menu

In the settings menu, the user has the possibility of selecting a specific set of color patches of the color checker to be used by the color correction algorithm. The original algorithm used exclusively all 24 patches for the color correction matrix, but more recently we discover that is possible to obtain similar or better results by selecting specific patches of the color checker, and not all the 24 (see Fig. 4).

One idea that was established to improve the usability of the application was a customizable level of precision. For this, we incorporated two customizable settings that can be controlled, namely the color checker finding precision and the overall quality (see Fig. 4).

4.3 Algorithm Implementation - Automatic Steps

The original algorithm [3] ported to the Android application, is based on the following steps:

1. Detection of the Color Checker: Identifies the corners of the part of the color checker that contains the color patches (see Fig. 5a);
2. Detection of the Patches: Identifies all the color patches on the color checker (see Fig. 5b);
3. Color Correction: Creates a color correction matrix that will be used in fixing the lighting variations on the images;
4. Detection of the Disk: Detects the disk in which the sample is located (see Fig. 5c);

Fig. 4. Settings menu screen.

5. Detection of the Sample: Identifies the parts of the disk that contain the sample after the reaction (see Fig. 5d).

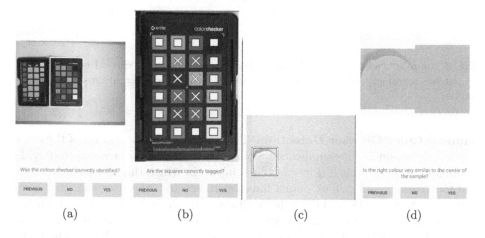

(a)   (b)   (c)   (d)

Fig. 5. Snapshots after running the algorithm automatically. a) color checker segmentation, b) patches segmentation, c) disk segmentation, d) sample segmentation.

4.4   Algorithm Implementation - Manual Steps

Even the algorithm runs automatically in all steps, since the start of the project, one of the major avenues for improvement was the utilization of user input as a backup plan in case the automatic detection fails in any step (see Fig. 6). This would boost the robustness of the application, allowing the extraction of results from a photo, even if it could not be done automatically. The automatic process could fail for various reasons, but the most reliably reproducible error is when the background of the photo has high contrast elements that influence the thresholding results. To achieve this, a chain of inputs and expected outputs for each stage was designed. This enables the user to intervene, regardless of which step the algorithm is in, and then seamlessly transition to the next stage, which will be performed automatically again. This shift back from manual to automatic increases accuracy, while prioritizing speed by removing the human input bottleneck whenever possible.

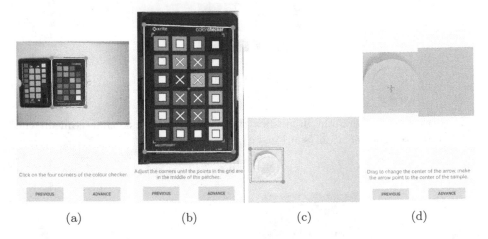

(a)   (b)   (c)   (d)

Fig. 6. Snapshots after running the algorithm manually. a) color checker segmentation, b) patches segmentation, c) disk segmentation, d) sample segmentation. (Color figure online)

Manual Color Checker Detection. The manual implementation of the color checker detection is not complex, since the only inputs the user needs to provide is the four corners. This is done via touch input, in which the user picks in order the four corners. After four points have been selected, the user can grab each one of the four points, and drag the position until all four points align with the corners. Although this technique worked well when testing with an emulator, when using an actual device, it was clear that dragging the point to where the user was touching was not practical, since the precise location was being occluded by the finger. For this reason we altered slightly the input scheme, and when the user clicks anywhere on the screen, the nearest point will be selected, and the difference from the current input is used to alter the point's position. This allows for a much higher degree of precision, while simultaneously increasing the user comfort when interacting in this mode. The interface of this step can be seen in Fig. 6a. The green handles represent the ways the user can interact with the selection, and these remain consistent throughout the entire application.

Manual Color Patches Identification. If the automatic detection fails on the patches segmentation, and the user wants to manually intervene, the user interface will change, showing to the user a grid of rectangles with a bounding white rectangle with green vertices. The user then drags the nearest selected point until the grid aligns well with the patches grid. When that happens, the user can select ADVANCE, and the application will calculate the averages of each grid rectangle, and store them in the required list of colors. The method of interacting with the corner handles is similar to the previous step, to maintain consistency in user input while also providing a forgiving experience, with a precise alignment being easy to perform (see Fig. 6b).

One advantage of this method, is that even in very extreme warping cases, the user can still correctly get a decent result, since the user can still alter the position of off-screen handles. A compilation of several cases can be seen in Fig. 7.

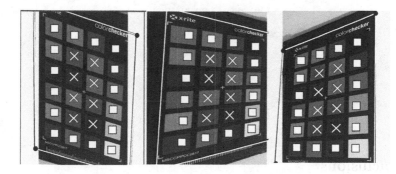

Fig. 7. Warping with manual patches detection.

Manual Disk Detection. In this manual procedure, the user first drags selecting the overall bounding box. If the selected region is not perfect, the user can then fine-tune the selection by dragging either the top-left or bottom-right handle. As before, the user does not need to touch the point itself, since the closest point will be automatically selected, and only the motion is used to change the point's position. When performing this, the rectangle will be resized, with no shape changing. When tested, this proved to be an efficient solution, capable of delivering fast and precise results (see Fig. 6c).

Manual Sample Detection. A new crosshair will appear on the center of the left side, which will be the user's way of input. By dragging around the screen, the crosshair will move according to the motion, and the new color will be the average of a small square around the currently selected point. The user will then hover the crosshair to the center of the sample, and ADVANCE (see Fig. 6d).

4.5   Extracting the Result for Sulfonamides Concentration

In order to extract the result for the Sulfonamides concentration, we used the same approach by Carvalho et al. [3] which determine it by using the Hue component from the HSV color space. Figure 8 shows a snapshot of the final activity screen containing the measured result.

Measured Concentration
Value:

2.98 µg/L

DISCARD   SAVE RESULTS

Fig. 8. Results screen.

5   Conclusions

Sulfonamides are an important antibiotic group to combat bacteria. It is low cost and low toxicity, which lead to it's widespread usage. This usage has lead to an increase in the presence of antibiotics in water compartments, which proliferates bacteria capable of resisting antibiotics. The impact of these bacteria is becoming a global threat, and analysis needs to be performed on waters to assess their level of contamination.

Current methods for determining sulfonamides concentration are expensive and impractical. They require resources and a laboratory setup. Colorimetry appears to be an interesting way forward, increasing practicality, but so far is still not fully mobile. Smartphones have already been used in the field for digital image colorimetry, with positive results. This work further proved the viability of smartphones for colorimetry tasks, providing adequate estimations of concentration of sulfonamides in a sample.

Some of the limitations of this work are somewhat similar to those found in the work by Carvalho et al. [3], namely:

1. Despite being limited after color correcting the image, lighting variations can still play a big role in the final concentration estimation;
2. Different smartphones may capture different photographs, with some camera applications processing the image irregularly to achieve more realistic or pleasing results, such as when using HDR. This presents a problem, since color correcting the image will be of reduced efficiency, if not worthless. This

could be mitigated by either creating an entire new custom camera application that followed a specific set of parameters, or by creating a new camera view within this application that handled that part. That way we could limit some features to ensure that the result is captured raw, without extra image processing.

References

1. Hruska, K., Fránek, M.: Sulfonamides in the environment: a review and a case report. Veterinarni Medicina **57** (2012)
2. Aydin, S., Ince, B., Ince, O.: Assessment of anaerobic bacterial diversity and its effects on anaerobic system stability and the occurrence of antibiotic resistance genes. Bioresour. Technol. **207**, 332–338 (2016)
3. Carvalho, P.H., Bessa, S., Silva, A.R.M., Peixoto, P.S., Segundo, M.A., Oliveira, H.P.: Estimation of sulfonamides concentration in water based on digital colourimetry. In: Morales, A., Fierrez, J., Sánchez, J.S., Ribeiro, B. (eds.) IbPRIA 2019. LNCS, vol. 11867, pp. 355–366. Springer, Cham (2019). https://doi.org/10.1007/978-3-030-31332-6_31
4. Connor, E.E.: Sulfonamide antibiotics. Prim. Care Update OB/GYNS **5**(1), 32–35 (1998)
5. Gbylik-Sikorska, M., Posyniak, A., Sniegocki, T., Zmudzki, J.: Liquid chromatography-tandem mass spectrometry multiclass method for the determination of antibiotics residues in water samples from water supply systems in food-producing animal farms. Chemosphere **119**, 8–15 (2015)
6. Hoff, R., Kist, T.: Analysis of sulfonamides by capillary electrophoresis. J. Sep. Sci. **32**, 854–66 (2009)
7. Li, C., et al.: A class-selective immunoassay for sulfonamides residue detection in milk using a superior polyclonal antibody with broad specificity and highly uniform affinity. Molecules **24**(3), 443 (2019)
8. Korpimki, T., Brockmann, E.-C., Kuronen, O., Saraste, M., Lamminmki, U., Tuomola, M.: Engineering of a broad specificity antibody for simultaneous detection of 13 sulfonamides at the maximum residue level. J. Agric. Food Chem. **52**(1), 40–47 (2004). PMID: 14709011
9. Muldoon, M.T., Holtzapple, C.K., Deshpande, S.S., Beier, R.C., Stanker, L.H.: Development of a monoclonal antibody-based cELISA for the analysis of sulfadimethoxine. 1. Development and characterization of monoclonal antibodies and molecular modeling studies of antibody recognition. J. Agric. Food Chem. **48**(2), 537–544 (2000)
10. Chiavarino, B., Crestoni, M.E., Di Marzio, A., Fornarini, S.: Determination of sulfonamide antibiotics by gas chromatography coupled with atomic emission detection. J. Chromatogr. B Biomed. Sci. Appl. **706**(2), 269–277 (1998)
11. Schanda, J., Eppeldauer, G., Sauter, G.: Tristimulus color measurement of self-luminous sources. In: Colorimetry, Understanding the CIE System, pp. 135–157 (2007)
12. Bunaciu, A.A., Hoang, V.D., Aboul-Enein, H.Y.: Applications of differential spectrophotometry in analytical chemistry. Crit. Rev. Anal. Chem. **43**(3), 125–130 (2013)
13. Foster, D.H.: Color constancy. Vis. Res. **51**(7), 674–700 (2011). Vision Research 50th Anniversary Issue: Part 1

14. Finlayson, G.D., Mackiewicz, M., Hurlbert, A.: Color correction using root-polynomial regression. IEEE Trans. Image Process. **24**(5), 1460–1470 (2015)
15. Yu, H., Cao, T., Li, B., Dong, R., Zhou, H.: A method for color calibration based on simulated annealing optimization. In: 3rd International Conference on Information Science and Control Engineering, pp. 54–58 (2016)
16. Bianco, S., Cusano, C., Schettini, R.: Color constancy using CNNs. In: IEEE Conference on Computer Vision and Pattern Recognition Workshops (2015)
17. Lou, Z., Gevers, T., Hu, N., Lucassen, M.P.: Color constancy by deep learning. In: Proceedings of the British Machine Vision Conference (2015)
18. Dang, D., Cho, C.H., Kim, D., Kwon, O.S., Chong, J.W.: Efficient color correction method for smartphone camera-based health monitoring application. In: 39th Annual International Conference of the IEEE Engineering in Medicine and Biology Society, pp. 799–802 (2017)
19. Alian, A., Shelley, K.: Photoplethysmography: analysis of the pulse oximeter waveform, pp. 165–178 (2014)
20. Gijsenij, A., Gevers, T., Weijer, J.: Improving color constancy by photometric edge weighting. IEEE Trans. Pattern Anal. Mach. Intell. **34**, 1 (2012)
21. Agu, E., et al.: The smartphone as a medical device: assessing enablers, benefits and challenges. In: IEEE International Conference on Sensing, Communications and Networking (2013)
22. Wang, X., Zhang, D.: An optimized tongue image color correction scheme. IEEE Trans. Inf Technol. Biomed. **14**(6), 1355–1364 (2010)
23. Jarujamrus, P., et al.: Use of a smartphone as a colorimetric analyzer in paper-based devices for sensitive and selective determination of mercury in water samples. Anal. Sci. **34**(1), 75–81 (2018)
24. Akkaynak, D., et al.: Use of commercial off-the-shelf digital cameras for scientific data acquisition and scene-specific color calibration. J. Opt. Soc. Am. A Opt. Image Sci. Vis. **31**(2), 312–321 (2014)

Making Parking Lot Accessible Through IoT

José Rafael Rojano-Cáceres[1]([⊠]) [iD], Jesús Antonio Rosas-Percastre[1],
Teresita Alvarez-Robles[2], and J. Andrés Sandoval-Bringas[2]

[1] Universidad Veracruzana, Xalapa, Veracruz, Mexico
rrojano@uv.mx, zS19020041@estudiantes.uv.mx
[2] Universidad Autónoma de Baja California Sur, La Paz, Baja California Sur, Mexico
{tj.alvarez,sandoval}@uabcs.mx

Abstract. When we think in accessibility in a parking lot we could consider aspects as adaptation of facilities as such as ramps or elevators, even accessible signage. But here we talk about the possibility to communicate the state of parking spots which allows better decision making for people visiting a specific facility. On the other hand we motivated the accessibility through the information conveyed in a mobile application for people who use the sign language as a natural tongue. Therefore to achieve such purposes we design and implement a system based on Internet of the Things to monitor parking status through computer vision, and a web service which publish updates about the availability.

Keywords: IoT · Accessibility · Inclusion · Smart parking

1 Introduction

According to the World Health Organization (WHO) around 1 billion people live with some disability, this represent about the 15% of the global population. However disability could be permanent or transitory whereby under this condition probably a bigger number of people will require accessibility in facilities. It is in this sense, not only living with some disability is a concern, but also the environment as well as personal factors [1] arise when facing particular situations as finding parking lot. Finding parking lot is also a mainstream for big cities or cities where the vehicle fleet is excessive for the size of the town because this generate pollution and traffic [2]. In Mexico, the estimation of vehicle fleet for 2019 was 50 million of vehicles circulating [3] for a population of almost 130 million people [4]. On the other hand, generate appropriate infrastructures for smart cities that support the parking lot problem in Mexico could be difficult because of corruption and poor attention to urban and accessibility problems. Therefore, a more appropriate scenario would be to look towards the local institutions in each city which also contribute to the problem, for example the universities. The big universities generally have campuses distributed around a city, also they generally offer services as Wi-Fi for students and academic population, but their parking lots are reduced, so it is common to find traffic around schools and universities, because of people waiting for a parking space. Also the problem can be generated within or outside the parking lot, for example

M. Antona and C. Stephanidis (Eds.): HCII 2021, LNCS 12769, pp. 485–493, 2021.
https://doi.org/10.1007/978-3-030-78095-1_35

people who makes double-side parking, or they are badly parked. Anyway, parking lots do not support the needs of people with or without disability, which in the second case can be more frustrating and limiting for who should park several blocks away from their destination. Therefore, in this article we propose a parking lot that provides better accessibility for any people with the support of Internet of the Things.

2 Internet of the Things

The Internet of the Things (IoT) has as a purpose monitoring and controlling things from around the world [5]. In this sense, one of the most colloquial examples for IoT could be remote light control or monitoring house events from cellphone. To achieve this goal IoT architecture require at least three layers called: perception layer, network layer and application layer. Perception layer is the lowest layer constituted by sensors and actuators. The middle layer is used for communication using different protocols as RFID, ZigBee, Wi-Fi, Bluetooth or any other supported by the device. Finally, the upper layer provide the necessary services to the final user. In the case of a parking lot the variety of technologies besides IoT includes RFID and CCTV [6], ultrasonic sensors [7], and PIR/IR sensors [8] to name some. Also, different Microcontroller units (MCU) architectures have been proposed to enable a smart parking for example Arduino or Raspberry. Lastly, the information acquired by the lower layer is transmitted through the MCU to the Internet to be processed by some API and then published to be consumed by some device.

2.1 Smart Parking

A smart parking is one of the elements that are part of a smart city. Thus, an smart parking can be conceived as a facility equipped with an IoT infrastructure, and whose purpose according to [9] and [10] can require different technologies to detect vehicles. Between such purposes we can find reservation, payment, guidance, or automated parking.

Therefore to implement such infrastructures we need to choose the appropriate elements according to our purpose. In a short review, we decide to identify which hardware elements are commonly used in lower and middle layer. In the Table 1 we observe a combination of sensors as RFID, PIR/IR, GSM, beacons, and cameras for lower layer, and for middle layer we found Arduino, ESP modules, Raspberry and Jetson. The application layer is barely described in the purpose column, because it is not the main purpose for our analysis.

2.2 Sensors

Sensing the presence of vehicles is fundamental for a smart parking. To achieve this task different sensors as PIR, IR, ultrasonic or cameras can be used. The physical approach consider factors as distance between object which are measured by devices as electromagnetic or sound waves, or infrared radiation. Instead, cameras use processing image to identify data about vehicles or available spots. Some of the papers reviewed use camera mainly as a part of a system to identify car plates in the context of security or parking fee

Table 1. Some related work and the hardware infrastructure used.

References	Hardware	Purpose
[8]	RFID, PIR & IR sensors, camera	Smart campus infrastructure proposal
[11]	Raspberry Pi 3, Raspberry Pi camera, Arduino Uno R3	Car plate recognition
[12]	Arduino Mega 2560, Ethernet shield Wiz5100, RFID	Finding parking slot
[13]	Arduino MKR NB 500, Arduino MKRFOX 1200, Arduino MKR Wan 1300	Review about sensors in the power consumption context
[14]	Arduino Mega, GSM module	Use of GPS to find nearer parking lot to the user
[15]	Logitech c920 pro HD, Funxwe Security camera, Nvidia Jetson Nano	Addressed the computer vision problem
[16]	Raspberry Pi, GA VX-800 camera, HD-3000 camera	Car plate recognition
[17]	Arduino Mega, Arduino Uno, Esp8266	Smart city and parking prototype
[18]	Libelium, MultiTech Conduit	Smart parking
[19]	IR Sensor, Espressif module, Raspberry Pi, RFID	Smart parking
[20]	Beacons	Smart parking
[21]	Raspberry Pi, Esp8266, IR	Car plate recognition for smart parking

[11, 16, 21]. In our review we found two approach for making a smart parking: DUY or use commercial products, most of the papers implemented the first approach. In Fig. 1 we appreciate the physical difference for each one. Also another point can be the cost of implementing each solution, in the DUY case for the sensors in item a, we estimate a budget around 50 dollars[1], while in the commercial approach the budget is around 167 dollars[2].

3   Design of Proposal

In the previous section we describe the elements to implement a sensing unit for the lower layer in a smart parking, also we estimate some cost according to the information provided in commercial web pages. Thus, such units generally works sensing one spot, so if we need to sense several places the cost increases according to the number of places required. In this regard, implementing an infrastructure based on image processing could

---

[1] Information computed from https://www.amazon.com.

[2] https://www.arrow.com/es-mx/products/sp-inst/libelium-comunicaciones-distribuidas-sl.

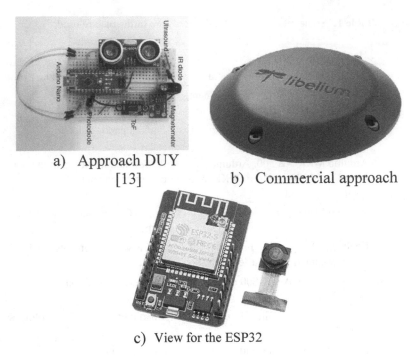

a) Approach DUY [13]   b) Commercial approach

c) View for the ESP32

Fig. 1. Example of sensors created with the approach a) Do it yourself, b) Commercial solution, and c) module ESP32. (Image from libelium's web page: https://www.libelium.com/iot-products/smart-parking/. Image taken from https://www.amazon.com.)

be preferred. Thus, our proposal implements computer vision through a low cost MCU based on ESP 32 with integrated camera. The general architecture is as follows in Fig. 2. Lower layer is composed by MCU/Camera which purpose is perceiving parking lot. Such information is send through WI-FI to a device which is capable of processing images to establish available spots, a web service (WS) is responsible of getting information about the spots for publishing in request to petitions, as well as it is capable to store information related with the parking lot availability or booking. Finally, the user can manipulate the information in the upper layer from a smart phone or any other client which can be capable of consuming the WS.

3.1 Design of Application

The application designed is very simple at this moment. It only presents information about the total space by section, which for our testing faculty has two section: teachers and students. Besides it display iconic information about the place for people with disability. Also in our design we propose the use of sign language in order to communicate specific information for deaf people. It is important because in our faculty are given sign language course where teachers are deaf. The proposed interface is shown in Fig. 3.

In such figure, the first screen display the welcome information where we use an avatar to give the information. The avatar was used only as a demonstration but it will

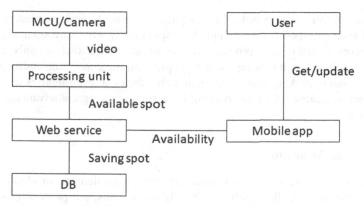

Fig. 2. General architecture for smart parking.

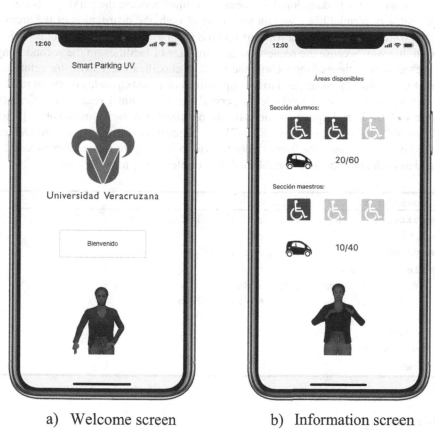

a) Welcome screen   b) Information screen

Fig. 3. Prototype application displaying information about parking lot availability. (Avatar model taken from https://skfb.ly/6SC6r. Car icon taken from https://thenounproject.com/term/small-car/1062422/.)

be used video information recorded for this purpose. In the b item, we present only the number of available spot, but we do not show specifically where are situated, it would be future work to tackle such problem. In this image we decided to apply a level of opacity to the place which is occupied. So, people with some motor disability problems can make a plan to parking near to the main entry their car, even there is not reserved place if there is a place within the parking lot it represents a great advantage for their displacement.

3.2 Processing Algorithms

In order to process the information from camera we implement an algorithm with OpenCV using the HAAR classifier with AdaBoost. Thus, the processing stage has two steps: for the first step we established in an assisted way the coordinated system of reference within the parking lot, this process is manual because the parking lot does not have visible referential lines, we can see in Fig. 4 both, the distribution of the areas of interest which one designed for teachers and the second one for students, but no strictly used in that way because the request exceeds the size of facilities, in the second image we see the view of the parking lot with the result of classification. Having the references point, the second step correspond to the application of a hard cascade algorithm to identify the presence or not of a vehicle. In general the Algorithm 1 receive an referential system with the Id and square positions for the parking lot as the following objet [{"id": "0", "points":"$x_1, y_1, x_2, y_2, x_3, y_3, x_4, y_4$"}, ...]. Then it is loaded the trained model, and iteratively are processed the frames from the video looking for the number of vehicles parked in each zone and then is published the counter through the web service.

```
Algorithm 1. Count vehicles
Requires: vector of referential points, vector = [{Ref₁, ...,
Refₙ}]
Requires: load classifier, classifier = HAAR
While video do
    For each frame in video do
      If classifier(frame) == true then
         Counter++
      End if
    Publish counter
End while
```

3.3 Results

We test the algorithm presented in the previous section taking video in different areas. As example we can see in Fig. 4b the results for detection vehicles in the teacher's area. Previously to the task of classification we mapped only 12 spots, and then with this vector we feed the video having a result a precision of 83% of classification. Visually we appreciate the result in such figure. It would be necessary to say that the video taken is

a)   Area of parking lot

b)   View for the teacher's area

Fig. 4. Parking lot sections in the faculty and results of processing algorithm.

not in the best position, it means it does not cover the interest areas as would be parking spots for people with disabilities. In this case the video is taken from the access control booth.

As a result we could propose for a university facility the implementation only in areas of interest as reserved spots, and to implement a general counter of vehicles to globally know the availability in the parking lot.

4 Conclusions

In this article we present a proposal to make a parking lot accessible through IoT, the sense of accessible has two intentions. On the one hand, it conveys the opportunity to attend a problem of mobility and pollution problems which are generated in crowd cities by vehicular fleet. On the other hand, it refers to the application used to present the information to the users.

As we previously stay it would be difficult to implement in many places a commercial infrastructure for a smart parking, but a reasonable option for institutions as universities is to follow a low cost proposals as discussed here. In this work we tackle a small parking lot with a capacity of 100 vehicles, and which area are divided in two sections (see Fig. 4a). In this scenery we pose the idea of paid attention to reserved spots, so it would be necessary only two devices for monitoring such specific areas. In Fig. 4a, we denoted the reserved areas with the International Symbol of Access (ISA) also named wheelchair symbol. So covering such specify areas we can send updates to the mobile application. That is the reason for which in Fig. 3b we only draw three ISA symbols for each section.

Also, as we stay in Sect. 3.1 Design of application, we have eventually courses of sign language where deaf people who also drives arrives to our faculty, so making the information accessible through sign language in the mobile application contributes to help to facilitate access and identification of available spaces.

References

1. OMS: Informe mundial sobre la discapacidad: Discapacidades, de Organización Mundial de la Salud (2011). http://www.who.int/disabilities/world_report/2011/es/
2. Rodić, L.D., Perković, T., Županović, T., Šolić, P.: Sensing occupancy through software: smart parking proof of concept. Electron. 9(12), 1–28 (2020)
3. INEGI: Parque vehicular (2020). https://www.inegi.org.mx/temas/vehiculos/#Informacion_general
4. World Bank: México: panorama general (2020). https://www.bancomundial.org/es/country/mexico/overview
5. Jabraeil Jamali, M.A., Bahrami, B., Heidari, A., Allahverdizadeh, P., Norouzi, F.: Towards the Internet of Things. EICC. Springer, Cham (2020). https://doi.org/10.1007/978-3-030-18468-1
6. Fraifer, M., Fernström, M.: Designing a Smart Car Parking System (PoC) prototype utilizing CCTV nodes: a vision of an IoT parking system via UCD process. Adv. Sci. Technol. Eng. Syst. 2(3), 755–764 (2017)
7. Lookmuang, R., Nambut, K., Usanavasin, S.: Smart parking using IoT technology. In: Proceedings of 2018 5th International Conference on Business and Industrial Research: Smart Technology for Next Generation of Information, Engineering, Business and Social Science, ICBIR 2018, pp. 1–6 (2018)
8. Pandey, J., Singh, A.V., Rana, A.: Roadmap to smart campus based on IoT. In: ICRITO 2020 - IEEE 8th International Conference on Reliability, Infocom Technologies and Optimization (Trends and Future Directions), pp. 909–913 (2020)
9. Fatima, Z., Bhargava, L., Kumar, A.: Smart infrastructures (2020)
10. Al-Turjman, F., Malekloo, A.: Smart parking in IoT-enabled cities: a survey. Sustain. Cities Soc. 49 (2019)

11. Bin Mohd Nazri, M.S., Long Alif Faiqal Bin Tengku Long Gaafar, T., Sofian, H., Bakar Sajak, A.A.: IoT parking apps with car plate recognition for smart city using node red. In: 2020 11th International Conference on Information and Communication Systems, ICICS 2020, pp. 324–330 (2020)
12. Patro, S.P., Patel, P., Senapaty, M.K., Padhy, N., Sah, R.D.: IoT based smart parking system: a proposed algorithm and model. In: 2020 International Conference on Computer Science, Engineering and Applications, ICCSEA 2020 (2020)
13. Perković, T., Šolić, P., Zargariasl, H., Čoko, D., Rodrigues, J.J.P.C.: Smart parking sensors: state of the art and performance evaluation. J. Clean. Prod. **262** (2020)
14. Tripathi, V.R.: Smart vehicle parking system using IoT. In: International Conference on Electrical and Electronics Engineering, ICE3 2020, pp. 285–290 (2020)
15. Sieck, N., Calpin, C., Almalag, M.: Machine vision smart parking using internet of things (IoTs) in a smart university. In: 2020 IEEE International Conference on Pervasive Computing and Communications Workshops, PerCom Workshops 2020 (2020)
16. Shabasy, N.E., Abdellatif, M.M.: IoT for smart parking. In: 2019 International Conference on Advances in the Emerging Computing Technologies, AECT 2019 (2020)
17. Kumari, S., Kulkarni, S., Patil, N., Deshpande, V.: An internet of things (IoT) based implementation of smart digital city prototype. In: Proceedings of the 3rd International Conference on Smart Systems and Inventive Technology, ICSSIT 2020, pp. 176–184 (2020)
18. Coulibaly, M., Errami, A., Belkhala, S., Medromi, H.: A live smart parking demonstrator: architecture, data flows and deployment. In: 2020 5th International Conference on Smart and Sustainable Technologies, SpliTech 2020 (2020)
19. Metilda Florence, S., Uma, M., Fancy, C., Saranya, G.:A study of remotely booking slot for vehicle using Internet of Things. Int. J. Electr. Comput. Eng. **10**(5), 5392–5399 (2020)
20. Mackey, A., Spachos, P., Plataniotis, K.N.: Smart parking system based on bluetooth low energy beacons with particle filtering. IEEE Syst. J. **14**(3), 3371–3382 (2020)
21. Swami, I., Suthar, A.: Smart vehicle tracker for parking system. Adv. Intell. Syst. Comput. **1189**, 455–462 (2021)

Blind-Badminton
A Working Prototype to Recognize Position of Flying Object for Visually Impaired Users

Masaaki Sadasue[✉], Daichi Tagami, Sayan Sarcar, and Yoichi Ochiai

University of Tsukuba, Tsukuba, Japan
sadaoooo@digitalnature.slis.tsukuba.ac.jp

Abstract. This paper proposes a system for recognizing flying objects during a ball game in blind sports. "Blind sports" is a term that refers to a sport for visually impaired people. There are various types of blind sports, and several of these sports, such as goalball and blind soccer, are registered in the Paralympic Games. This study specifically aimed at realizing games similar to badminton. Various user experiments were conducted to verify the requirements for playing sports that are similar to badminton without visual stimulus. Additionally, we developed a system that provides users with auxiliary information, including height, depth, left and right directions, and swing delay by adopting sound feedback via a binaural sound source, as well as haptic feedback via a handheld device. This study evaluated several conditions including that of a balloon owing to its slow falling speed and adopted a UAV drone that generates flight sounds on its own and adjusts its speed and trajectory during the course of the games. To evaluate playability, this study focused on three points: a questionnaire following the experiment, the error in the drone's traveling direction, and the racket's swing direction. From the play results and answers of the questionnaire, it was determined that the users were able to recognize the right and left directions, as well as the depth of the drone using the noise generated by the drone, and that this approach is playable in these situations.

Keywords: Visual-impaired · Blind sports · UAV drone · Motion capture

1 Introduction

There are approximately 20 billion visually impaired people in the world [17]. Blind sports refer to sports that are designed for visually impaired people. These sports have various types, and several sports among them, such as goalball and blind soccer, are registered events in the Paralympic Games. This paper focuses on the ball game for visually impaired people. Several ball games for visually impaired people have model sports. These ball sports are generated by changing the original rule as a sound source into a ball like a bell, and they have one thing in common: they all require bouncing. This is owing to the presence of a sound

© Springer Nature Switzerland AG 2021
M. Antona and C. Stephanidis (Eds.): HCII 2021, LNCS 12769, pp. 494–506, 2021.
https://doi.org/10.1007/978-3-030-78095-1_36

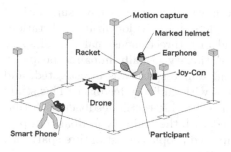 

Fig. 1. Blind badminton system outline. (Left) This is a diagram of the positional relationship between the player and the flying object. Diagram of face-to-face capture of player motion. (Right) Measures the positional relationship between the drone and the player.

source, which makes it possible to localize sound by bouncing. However, sports that do not require bouncing, such as badminton and volleyball, are challenging for visually impaired people to play. Therefore, this study speculated that the ability to recognize objects in flight could increase the variety of ball sports for the visually impaired. Accordingly, we created and evaluated a system for recognizing objects in flight using a feedback system with motion capture (Fig. 1). Based on the results obtained, the limitations and future potential of this system are discussed.

2   Related Work

2.1   Sound Localization for Visually Impairment People

Sound localization for visually impaired people There have been several studies on sound localization for visually impaired people. We know that visual information plays a crucial role in spatial understanding, and it should be acknowledged that people with visual impairments have severe disabilities in their lives [3]. It is also known that when a monaural sound source is adopted, sound localization is lower in people with low vision than in blind or sighted people [2]. In particular, several studies have measured the auditory localization of blind, low vision, and sighted people, and have also investigated the differences between them [8,9,20]. These studies have demonstrated that a blind person's auditory localization of sound sources is better than that of other people, provided the blind person is earlier. In addition, there is a significant difference between low vision and clear-eyed people. It is also possible to obtain cross-modal sensation in adults, and the cross-modal approach to the auditory and tactile vision considered in this study may be successful over a long period of time. Because visually impaired people are usually supported by sound assistive technology, voice assistive technology is very beneficial in this case [12]. There are also systems that enable navigation in virtual spaces via sound sources, and it can be stated that the efforts to help visually impaired people achieve their goals, solely via sound sources, are yielding significant results [6]. Furthermore, there have a few studies have summarized the results obtained from experiments that determine the localization of stationary visually impaired people in a ball and in a threedimensional virtual space [13]. In these studies, the localization of stationary visually impaired people in a sound-included ball or in a virtual sound source space was investigated, and the horizontal approach has been successful with auditory feedback. This study adopted auditory feedback and attempted to provide tactile feedback such that the vertical feedback would not be confused with the auditory feedback. In particular, support techniques for visually impaired people consist of three patterns: sound, touch, and cooperation from others [11].

2.2 Sports for Visually Impaired People

This research investigated stereotaxis in visually limited situations to create sports for the visually impaired. Physical exercise has been determined to be beneficial in boosting the self-esteem of visually impaired people [10]. In recent years, in the human-computer interaction field, assistive technologies for the visually impaired have been flourishing in the fields of sports, entertainment, and games [2,4,5]. Currently, there are several sports for the blind, such as goalball and spinning, as well as sports modified for visually impaired people [15]. There have been several sports-related studies for the visually impaired. Many of these studies are related to assisted locomotion in virtual space [7], and by conducting experiments on subjects, some of them have focused on creating a sports game for the visually impaired, such as the Wii sports event called exergame [14,18]. In these studies, exergames for visually impaired people have been investigated to increase the amount of physical activity available to visually impaired people. However, owing to the waiting time required between games and the limited amount of physical activity that can be performed in these games, it was inferred that the amount of physical activity provided by this game does not differ significantly from that of normal life.

2.3 Using Drone in the Sports Scene

This research also investigated the localization of drones under the conditions of limited vision. Several studies have been conducted on the use of drones to support the lives of visually impaired people. Many of these studies have adopted drones primarily for walking assistance [1,16]. In addition, the use of drones in sports has increased in recent years. Drones are mainly utilized to analyze the movement of athletes from a third party's perspective, or to analyze the movements of athletes during a match, which helps to determine future strategies and countermeasures for the match. There are also studies on the use of drones as sparring partners in boxing [19]. Furthermore, there a certain research adopted drones as a ball that does not readily consider the difference in ability between children and adults. This study conducted its initial research to measure the localization required for an approach that adopts drones in racket-based ball games.

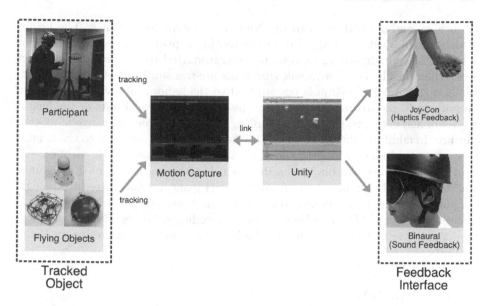

Fig. 2. System overview. This figure shows how the movements of the player and the flying object are feedback.

3   Implementation

In this study, badminton was selected as a model sport. There are three reasons for this choice. First, because badminton is an indoor sport, it is not influenced by the weather and about it is not limited by equipment issues. Second, because it is a one-on-one sport, it minimizes the risk of contact. Third, this sport model does not require bouncing. This study also investigated the localization of sound sources with eyes closed and blindfolded by sighted people. Therefore, motion capture[1,2] is adopted in Fig. 2 to obtain three-dimensional (3-D) information by attaching reflective markers to the flying object, such that the state of the flying object is understood. The markers adopted micron 14 mm, while the shuttlecock solely used 3 mm. In addition, this study proposes a method for providing feedback to the user via motion capture. To enable the subject recognize a flying object in 3-D, visually impaired people need to know the speed, height, and depth of the flying object. This study proposes a system that provides feedback to each of them. Therefore, this system is proposed to provide feedback for each of them. In addition to the white nylon shuttlecock, we adopt a slow balloon with a large volume, as well as drone[3], which has a flight sound with adjustable trajectory and speed. Regarding the height, Joy-Con was adopted because it has

---

[1] https://www.mocap.jp/optitrack/products/prime-41/ (last accessed: February, 5th, 2021).

[2] https://www.mocap.jp/optitrack/products/prime-17w/ (last accessed: February, 5th, 2021).

[3] https://www.ryzerobotics.com/jp/tello (last accessed: February, 5th, 2021).

vibrations, and it is attached to the Nintendo switch[4] as feedback. The height of the flying object is obtained from the motion capture, and when the object is significantly high, strong vibrations are transmitted to the participant; however, when the object is low, weak vibrations are transmitted to the participant. When a sine wave vibration is transmitted to the hand, sensitivity increases in proportion to the frequency; therefore, the upper and lower limits of the height are 1.7 m and 0.4 m, respectively, according to the measurement range of motion capture. In addition, the vibration in the meantime is proportional to the height, Frequency is altered to depth, and a binaural sound source with earphones is used. A 5kHz sinusoidal binaural sound, which varies according to the distance and direction of the flying object from the participant, is transmitted to the participant via wireless earphones. When the sound localization in the horizontal direction exceeds 4 kHz, a 5kHz sine wave exceeding 4 kHz is adopted to follow the azimuth well. The expression of the binaural sound adopts a Steam Audio for unity.

4 Experiments

This study investigates the source localization of each flying object when subjects are provided with tactile and auditory feedback based on the 3-D information of the flying object obtained using motion capture. This investigation was divided into two patterns. The first is an experiment that adopts the proposed system in a shuttlecock and balloon, and the second is an experiment that adopts this system in a drone.

This study was conducted in a room with dimensions a 240 cm × 180 cm × 238 cm. In addition, six motion captures were adopted, and the width between each of them was approximately 60 cm. Participants entered the room successively, and they were blindfolded after the experiment was explained to them. The distance between the thrower and the participant in a straight line is 2.5 m, and six OptiTracks (4 Prime 41, 2 Prime 17 W) were positioned around the pitcher. Furthermore, participants were asked to hold a racket in their dominant hand, localize a flying object, and hit it repeatedly. At this point, the subject was asked to determine the approximate location of the ball with the racket because hitting the drone too hard might cause damage and pose a danger to the subject. For each experiment, the person conducting the experiment was trained on how to conduct the experiment in a tutorial, the subject attempted this five times. In addition, the location of the flying object was randomly determined. Based on the participants' shoulders, the direction of flight for all the objects was determined to be right side up, left side up, right side down, and left side down.

---

[4] https://www.nintendo.co.jp/hardware/switch/accessories/ (last accessed: February, 5th, 2021).

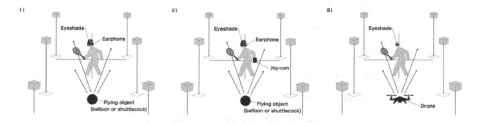

Fig. 3. Study 1's experiment design. (i) Using only earphone. (ii) Using earphone and Joy-Con. (iii) Using only drone.

4.1   Study 1: Using Shuttlecock, Balloon and Just Drone

In Study 1, experiments were conducted using the shuttlecock, balloons, and drones. First, unlike drones, shuttlecocks and balloons do not have flight sounds; therefore, when this these research experiments were conducted, a binaural sound source was employed and the participants were asked to conduct the experiments. In addition, this study adopted the Joy-Con to provide feedback on the vertical direction of the flying object. Subsequently, sound localization was investigated with the drone alone. In other words, the experiments were conducted in five patterns with: 1) balloons and binaural sound sources, 2) balloons, binaural sound sources, and Joy-Con, 3) shuttlecocks and binaural sound sources, 4) shuttlecocks, binaural sound sources, and JoyCon, and 5) drones (Fig. 3).

Participant. Five people (one female and four males), aged between 20 and 23 years, participated in the experiment. These participants also participated in the experiments presented in Sect. 4.2.

Procedure. The order of the experiments was randomized by the participants, and the experiments one and zero were conducted for each participant. First, before the experiment with earphones, participants were blindfolded and asked to wear earphones. Then, the participants were asked to throw the object to the subject using a voice signal, and as a tutorial, they were asked to practice hitting the object five times with the racket. Similarly, before the experiment with Joy-Con, the subjects were asked to confirm the vibration feedback of the flying object by moving it up and down while holding the Joy-Con, and as a tutorial, they were asked to practice hitting the object with the racket five times. In the experiment with the drone, the direction of the drone was decided and then it was given a voice signal before moving it forward.

Result. The average hit rate in Study 1 is presented in Fig. 4. In the shuttlecock case, the subjects could not hit the racket even once, regardless of whether they were provided with auditory or tactile feedback. In the case of the balloons, when the subjects were provided information on the height of the balloons by

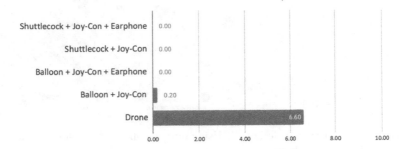

Fig. 4. Average number of hits in Study 1

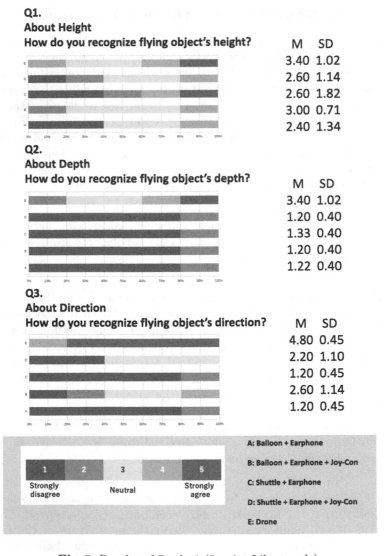

Fig. 5. Results of Study 1 (5-point Likert scale).

tactile feedback, they were able to hit the racket an average of 0.2 times, but were unable to reach the height once. In the free text of the questionnaire, a participant notes, *"shuttlecocks and balloons fall so fast that I couldn't catch the right timing to swing the racket"*. However, when using the drone, subjects were able to hit the target on an average of 6.6 times in 10 trials. This indicates that the sound localization by the drone sound is relatively complete compared to the case with the shuttle or balloon. Another factor is that the drone will not fall in this experiment. The figure also presents the results of obtained from a questionnaire, which evaluated the degree to which the subjects were able to recognize the height, depth, and direction of flying objects on a five-point scale in Fig. 5. For quantitative measurements in this questionnaire, subjects were asked to answer each item on a five-point scale of "strongly disagree, disagree, neutral, agree, and strongly agree." Via the analysis of variance using the F distribution with a significance level of 5% for each questionnaire result, it is determined that the average of the questionnaire results is different for depth and direction because the F value reaches the rejection area for depth and direction. In all cases, the numbers related to drones are high, and the survey results indicate the functionality of sound localization using the sounds emitted by drones. However, the results obtained from the questionnaire regarding height do not reach the rejection region for the F value, and it can be stated that no significant difference exists between any of the experiments. Furthermore, in the free text of the questionnaire, a participant notes that because you can grasp the direction and depth just by the operation of the drone's sound, it may be beneficial to be solely managed by the height. The localization of sound by the sound emitted by the drone was significant in the horizontal direction. However, it was less effective in the vertical direction. Therefore, this study decided to apply the sound and vibration feedback system adopted in Study 1 in the drone, and conduct an additional experiment as presented in Study 2.

4.2 Study 2: Using Drone Linked Joy-Con and Earphone

Most participants in Study 1 were unable to react and hit the racket because the shuttle and balloon were moving too fast. In contrast, participants were able to recognize the moving direction of the drone in the experiment conducted with the drone alone because the flight sound and speed of the drone were slower than the other two flying objects. However, many participants find it difficult to recognize the drone in its vertical direction. Therefore, in Study 2, this research applies the system to a drone to support sound source localization. Study 2 comprises two investigations: one using a drone, earphone, and JoyCon, and the other using a drone and Joy-Con (Fig. 6). Each experiment was conducted ten times.

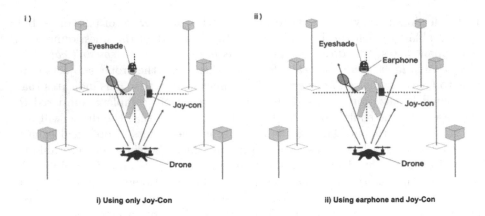

i) Using only Joy-Con   ii) Using earphone and Joy-Con

Fig. 6. Study 2's experiment design

Participant. Twelve participants (1 female and 11 males), aged between 19 and 23 years, were recruited to participate in the experiment.

Procedure. In Study 2, an experiment was conducted with this system applied to a drone. The order and number of experiments were randomized as in Study 1 and conducted 10 times each. In this study, for the earphone wearing study, the participants were first asked to put on the earphones and check the location of the moving drone with the marker. As a practice, five tutorials were provided to them. Similarly, in the survey using Joy-Con, the participants were asked to confirm the position of the drone moving up and down before the survey.

Result. The hit rate in Study 2 is presented in Fig. 7. When both the sound and haptic feedbacks were applied, the subjects could hit the drone 3.58 times on average. When haptic feedback was applied, the subjects could hit the drone 3.67 times on average. However, in the case of the drone alone, subjects were able to hit the target 6.6 times on average, as illustrated in Study 1, and the probability of hitting the target is higher in the case of the drone alone than in the case of providing each feedback. Based on this result and the comment in the free text of the questionnaire (*"My concentration was disturbed by the many sensations I had to concentrate on."*), it is significantly possible that the sound localization triggered by the drone's flight sound is disrupted by the other feedback.

The correlation between the drone's direction and the direction in which the participant actually swings the racket is illustrated in Fig. 8. When tactile and auditory feedbacks were applied, swinging errors were more frequent than when two feedbacks were not applied or when tactile feedback was provided. However, there were more errors in the vertical direction in both the experiment with the drone alone and the experiment with the haptic feedback, which indicates that the drone sound alone is insufficient for vertical sound localization. We also conducted t-tests for height, depth, and direction using the same questionnaire as in Study 1 at a significance level of 5%; however, there were no significant

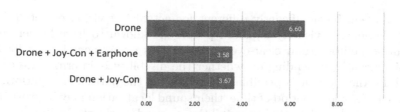

Fig. 7. Average number of hits in a experiment

Player's Swing Direction

		Upper Right	Under Right	Upper Left	Upper Right
	Upper Right	100	0	0	0
Drone's Direction	Under Right	30.8	69.2	0	0
	Upper Left	0	0	84.6	15.4
	Under Left	0	0	15.4	4.6

Player's Swing Direction

		Upper Right	Under Right	Upper Left	Upper Right
	Upper Right	75.9	24.1	0	0
Drone's Direction	Under Right	10.3	86.2	0	8.65
	Upper Left	0	0	86.1	13.9
	Under Left	0	0	26.9	73.1

Player's Swing Direction

		Upper Right	Under Right	Upper Left	Upper Right
	Upper Right	90.6	6.3	3.1	0
Drone's Direction	Under Right	41.9	48.4	6.5	3.2
	Upper Left	0	6.3	87.5	6.2
	Under Left	0	0	48	52

Fig. 8. Top) Percentage of participants hit the drone. Middle) Percentage of participants hit the drone with Joy-Con. Bottom) Percentage of participants hit the drone with Joy-Con and earphone.

differences in the population of any of the questionnaire results. These results indicate that the sound localization support using Joy-Con and earphones with binaural sound sources is not very significant at this point, and that humans can relatively estimate the depth and direction from the sound sources emitted from using drones alone. However, in the free description of the questionnaire, a participant notes, """ The experiment using Joy-Con became easier and easier to understand as I got used to it.. Repeating the exercise suggests that it is possible to predict the height of the drone based on the vibration sensations.

5   Disccusion and Future Work

In this study, an experiment was conducted with clear-eyed subjects that were asked to wear blindfolds with their eyes closed. However, it is very possible that the results will be significantly different for actual low vision or totally blind people. In general, visually impaired people are known to have higher spatial recognition abilities than clear-eyed people. This experiment is also likely to vary significantly, depending on whether the disability is intermediate or congenital. Furthermore, it is possible that by having the participants perform this experiment for a long period of time, their sound localization may improve owing to habituation. Based on these possibilities, to validate the study, it is necessary to conduct multiple experiments by preparing actual subjects and altering the duration and conditions. In addition, this study requires several motion captures and other equipment because 3-D information on the flying object is required to provide feedback to the user. However, these equipment are too expensive to install in actual sport venues. Because the purpose of this project is to expand the range of sports, this challenge is considerably a critical issue. Therefore, in this study, we developed several solutions to address this challenge. First, this study determines that the sound source localization is most accurate when the experiment is conducted with a single drone. Therefore, in this study, we should consider a system that can be solely completed by controlling the drone. To realize this, we also need to address the challenge of using a racket to hit the drone. Therefore, it would be beneficial to create a new sport in which the gut is removed and the drone is passed through the frame, or to develop a drone and protector that are not dangerous and do not disrupt the balance even if hit. Accordingly, it would be possible to create a sport that does not require installation costs and can be performed at a lower cost than this experiment with only a drone and a PC.

6   Conclusion

In this study, a system was developed to provide auditory and tactile feedback based on 3-D information, and the sound source localization of several objects, including drones, were investigated. Study 1 investigated the shuttlecock, balloon, and drone with the proposed system applied. Consequently, the drone without the system was able to localize the sound source better. However, it was impossible to localize the drone in the vertical direction; therefore, Study 2, which applied the proposed system to the drone, was conducted. The results obtained from Study 2 indicated that wearing earphones eliminated the drone's flight sound and made it difficult to localize the sound source. In addition, we inferred that the adoption of a vibration device would interfere with the investigation because it requires the simultaneous use of multiple senses. Furthermore, horizontal swinging errors did not occur even when the drone was used alone or with Joy-Con. This suggests that the drone's flight sound may be able to localize the sound source relatively, and this study attempted to investigate sound source localization under various conditions using a single drone. In addition, a system that can provide vertical support was developed in this study. In this study, a questionnaire using the Likert scale was adopted after the experiment. The results obtained from the questionnaire did not exhibit significant differences in any of the height, depth, and left-right recognition cases. However, the left/right positions and depth could be recognized by the sound of the drone. Because there are various types of visual impairments, future studies will conduct a long-term research and develop a practical system by grouping visually impaired people. In addition, long-term research will be conducted to develop a practical system. Furthermore, this study was conducted with blindfolded clear-eyed participants. Because previous studies have demonstrated that sound source localization is more substantial in blind people than in sighted people, it is possible that the results of the drone localization research revealed in this study may also be more substantial in blind people, and we would like to continue this investigation in the future.

Acknowledgement. This work was supported by JST, CREST Grant Number JPMJCR19F2, Japan.

References

1. Al Zayer, M., Tregillus, S., Bhandari, J., Feil-Seifer, D., Folmer, E.: Exploring the use of a drone to guide blind runners. In: Proceedings of the 18th International ACM SIGACCESS Conference on Computers and Accessibility, ASSETS 2016, pp. 263–264. Association for Computing Machinery, New York (2016). https://doi.org/10.1145/2982142.2982204

2. Archambault, D., Olivier, D.: How to make games for visually impaired children. In: Proceedings of the 2005 ACM SIGCHI International Conference on Advances in Computer Entertainment Technology, ACE 2005, pp. 450–453. Association for Computing Machinery, New York (2005). https://doi.org/10.1145/1178477.1178578

3. Axelrod, S.: Effects of Early Blindness. American Foundation for the Blind, New York (1959)

4. Hasegawa, S., Ishijima, S., Kato, F., Mitake, H., Sato, M.: Realtime sonification of the center of gravity for skiing. In: Proceedings of the 3rd Augmented Human International Conference. AH 2012, Association for Computing Machinery, New York (2012). https://doi.org/10.1145/2160125.2160136

5. Hermann, T., Höner, O., Ritter, H.: AcouMotion – an interactive sonification system for acoustic motion control. In: Gibet, S., Courty, N., Kamp, J.-F. (eds.) GW 2005. LNCS (LNAI), vol. 3881, pp. 312–323. Springer, Heidelberg (2006). https://doi.org/10.1007/11678816_35

6. Huggard, A., De Mel, A., Garner, J., Toprak, C.C., Chatham, A.D., Mueller, F.: Musical embrace: facilitating engaging play experiences through social awkwardness. In: CHI 2013 Extended Abstracts on Human Factors in Computing Systems, CHI EA 2013, pp. 3067–3070. Association for Computing Machinery, New York (2013). https://doi.org/10.1145/2468356.2479612

7. Kim, S., Lee, K.p., Nam, T.J.: Sonic-badminton: audio-augmented badminton game for blind people. In: Proceedings of the 2016 CHI Conference Extended Abstracts on Human Factors in Computing Systems, CHI EA 2016, pp. 1922–1929. Association for Computing Machinery, New York (2016). https://doi.org/10.1145/2851581.2892510

8. Kujala, T., Alho, K., Huotilainen, M., Ilmoniemi, R.J., Lehtokoski, A., Leinonen, A., Rinne, T., Salonen, O., Sinkkonen, J., Standertskjöld-Nordenstam, C.G., Näätänen, R.: Electrophysiological evidence for cross-modal plasticity in humans with early- and late-onset blindness. Psychophysiology **34**(2), 213–216 (1997). https://doi.org/10.1111/j.1469-8986.1997.tb02134.x

9. Lessard, N., Paré, M., Lepore, F., Lassonde, M.: Early-blind human subjects localize sound sources better than sighted subjects. Nature **395**(6699), 278–280 (1998). https://doi.org/10.1038/26228

10. Lieberman, L., Haegele, J., Columna, L., Conroy, P.: How students with visual impairments can learn components of the expanded core curriculum through physical education. J. Vis. Impairment Blindness **108**, 239–248 (2014). https://doi.org/10.1177/0145482X1410800307

11. Lieberman, L.J., Ponchillia, P.E., Ponchillia, S.V.: Physical education and sports for people with visual impairments and deafblindness: Foundations of instruction (2013)

12. Lumbreras, M., Sánchez, J.: Interactive 3D sound hyperstories for blind children. In: Proceedings of the SIGCHI Conference on Human Factors in Computing Systems, CHI 1999, pp. 318–325. Association for Computing Machinery, New York (1999). https://doi.org/10.1145/302979.303101

13. Mieda, T., Kokubu, M., Saito, M.: Rapid identification of sound direction in blind footballers. Exp. Brain Res. **237**(12), 3221–3231 (2019). https://doi.org/10.1007/s00221-019-05670-4

14. Morelli, T., Foley, J., Columna, L., Lieberman, L., Folmer, E.: Vi-Tennis: a vibrotactile/audio exergame for players who are visually impaired. In: Proceedings of the Fifth International Conference on the Foundations of Digital Games, FDG 2010, pp. 147–154. Association for Computing Machinery, New York (2010). https://doi.org/10.1145/1822348.1822368

15. Reid, G., Stanish, H.: Professional and disciplinary status of adapted physical activity. Adap. Phys. Activity Q. **20**(3), 213–229 (2003). https://doi.org/10.1123/apaq.20.3.213. https://journals.humankinetics.com/view/journals/apaq/20/3/article-p213.xml

16. Seuter, M., Macrillante, E.R., Bauer, G., Kray, C.: Running with drones: desired services and control gestures. In: Proceedings of the 30th Australian Conference on Computer-Human Interaction, OzCHI 2018, pp. 384–395. Association for Computing Machinery, New York (2018). https://doi.org/10.1145/3292147.3292156

17. World Health Organization: World report on vision. World Health Organization (2019). https://www.who.int/publications/i/item/world-report-on-vision. Accessed 8 Oct 2019

18. Yuan, B., Folmer, E.: Blind hero: enabling guitar hero for the visually impaired. In: Proceedings of the 10th International ACM SIGACCESS Conference on Computers and Accessibility, Assets 2008, pp. 169–176. Association for Computing Machinery, New York (2008). https://doi.org/10.1145/1414471.1414503

19. Zwaan, S.G., Barakova, E.I.: Boxing against drones: drones in sports education. In: Proceedings of the The 15th International Conference on Interaction Design and Children, IDC 2016, pp. 607–612. Association for Computing Machinery, New York (2016). https://doi.org/10.1145/2930674.2935991

20. Zwiers, M.P., Van Opstal, A.J., Cruysberg, J.R.M.: A spatial hearing deficit in early-blind humans. J. Neurosci. **21**(9), RC142–RC142 (2001). https://doi.org/10.1523/JNEUROSCI.21-09-j0002.2001. https://www.jneurosci.org/content/21/9/RC142

Framework for Controlling KNX Devices Based on Gestures

Jedid Santos[1](✉) ⓘ, Ivo Martins[2] ⓘ, and João M. F. Rodrigues[3] ⓘ

[1] Institute of Engineering (ISE), Universidade do Algarve, Faro, Portugal
[2] INESC-ID & ISE, Universidade do Algarve, Faro, Portugal
immartin@ualg.pt
[3] LARSyS & ISE, Universidade do Algarve, Faro, Portugal
jrodrig@ualg.pt

Abstract. The demand for comfort and versatility in the management of different types of devices in a home or office is exponentially increasing. More and more people want a comfortable environment for leisure or work, something practical, sustainable and safe. This includes, obviously, all the range in the target user population, including people with disabilities, and cultural differences. With all the above in mind, it is important to develop adaptive interfaces that can adjust on-the-fly to each user needs and conditions. This paper presents an initial framework that integrates human actions: gestures and/or poses in a way to activate and command devices using KNX standard. The pose detection algorithm is used to detect different gestures/poses, where each gesture or group of gestures integrated with KNX allows easy and universal communication with various types of existing automation devices. The initial results show that the framework is capable of commanding different devices effortlessly, with the ability to develop interfaces that adapt to each user needs.

Keywords: Gesture detection · Home automation · Smart systems · Ambient intelligence · KNX

1 Introduction

Universal Access can be defined as the global requirement to deal with diversity in a target user population, this includes people with disabilities, elders and population with cultural differences [1]. The scope and nature of tasks and technological platforms and the effects of its proliferation at home, business and social enterprises is one of the hot topics for research. Thus, special attention should be given to adaptive interfaces [2, 3], i.e., interfaces that can adapt on-the-fly for each user.

The above is related to the demand for comfort and versatility in the management of different types of devices mainly at home or office. More and more people want a comfortable environment for leisure or work, something practical, sustainable and safe. Achieving this level of automation today is a real challenge, as it involves more wiring, from sensors and actuators to control and monitoring centres. For professionals, this amount of wiring also means greater design and installation efforts, greater fire risk and

© Springer Nature Switzerland AG 2021
M. Antona and C. Stephanidis (Eds.): HCII 2021, LNCS 12769, pp. 507–518, 2021.
https://doi.org/10.1007/978-3-030-78095-1_37

rising costs. Several solutions exist to minimize this, one of them is the KNX protocol for communication with and between devices [4].

KNX is a technology for home and commercial building automation, that allows to control different devices, such as lighting, security, energy management, AVAC systems, etc. KNX is also the only open standard for home and building control and complies with EN 50090, EN 13321-1 and ISO/IEC 14543 [4]. With the use of KNX, we can exclude the use of isolated sensors and actuators, making it possible to communicate over the internet with all these devices. The protocol has a topology where it is possible to support up to 65.500 devices of about 500 manufacturers, enabling a wide range of automation applications [4].

In parallel, Ambient Intelligence (AmI) is a concept that is intrinsically and thoroughly connected with Artificial Intelligence (AI) [5–7]. AmI typically refers to electronic environments that are sensitive and responsive to the presence of people. Ambient intelligence would allow devices to work in concert to support people in carrying out their everyday life activities, tasks and rituals in an intuitive way using information and intelligence that is hidden in the network connecting these devices. The above also connects to Human-Machine Cooperation (HMC) which consists of developing autonomous machines that learn to cooperate with humans. Depending on its use, pre-developed cooperation arrangements and common sense mechanisms, HMC does not require absolute computational power. The ultimate goal is to develop conditions so that machines and humans can work together, making the task of both easier [8–10].

We can say that a "circle" is created, where adaptative interfaces that can adapt to each user on-the-fly as to be in line with HMC and at the same time, in the present case, allow to create without effort AmI environments. The paper focuses on the above circle, as it presents an initial prove-of-concept framework, which by recognizing a person's actions (movements) is also capable of controlling a large number of devices using the KNX standard, being the main contribution the connection between human gestures or poses and the way of communicating with automation equipment.

A real implementation where HMC is employed can be observed in Project WEL-SAFE.DV: Welcome Safety Device. It consists of a device that can be placed in a hotel, establishment, or event allowing automatic check-in without touching the customer/user, it includes the prediction of some basic body characteristics such as age. One further feature that can be integrated into the initial infrastructure is the touchless activation and control of devices, as presented in this paper.

The paper is structured as follows: The Introduction is presented in this Section. Section 2 presents a broad context and the state of the art. Section 3 describes the proposed method. Some experimental results are presented in Sect. 4. Conclusions and future work are drawn in Sect. 5.

2   Contextualization and Related Work

Home automation has been increasingly used to create intelligent environments where we can bring more comfort and safety to people's daily lives. For devices proper functioning, a reliable communication between sensors and actuators is essential. As presented by Sapundzhi [11] the KNX system can act on devices that can be monitored and controlled remotely, for instance to control lighting, heating and audio and video controls. The KNX can also be integrated together with small single board computers, such as Raspberry PI for use in home automation. In [12] the system controlled by the Raspberry enables the verification of temperature, humidity, presence sensor, CO_2 sensor and light control for a smart home solution. Moreover, KNX has already been tested and integrated with other types of systems, such as Natural Language Processing (NLP). For example in [13] a system was implemented in a classroom controlled by an intelligent device, allowing to perform actions in lights, printer and TV operation.

With the increase in automation systems and the challenge of improving the quality of life, KNX is being increasingly used to monitor and automate more and more the functioning of equipment, making the concept of intelligent environment to be used continuously. Currently, with the SARS-COV-2 pandemic and COVID-19 disease, this is even more important, that systems can be developed to act on devices and control them remotely, without touching any equipment or sensors.

This type of control can be implemented using video cameras (IP cameras), which are one of the cheapest sensors that allow us to replace a diversity of sensors, traditionally integrated into a home or office automation, such as motion detectors, touch sensors, light sensors and switches. By connecting Computer Vision (CV) with modern Machine Learning (ML) methods [14], including Deep Learning [15] it is possible to detect, define and quantify human movements and actions [16–18] as well as recognize persons by their gait [19] or by their face [20].

In the case of facial recognition, it can be used for assisted robots that collaborate with people, as described by Baltanas et al. [21], or in the case of Bellotto et al. [22] to help the elderly with Mild Cognitive Impairment (MCI). Both have in common the development of environments where it is possible to use these two technologies, Computer Vision and Domotics (sensor/actuator devices), to help/facilitate people's daily lives, especially the elderly, where they have the most needs.

There are more examples of smart environments, monitored only by a camera, like the one presented by Daher et al. [23], where they track and recognize the basic activities of an elderly person. In the same direction, Chen et al. [24] analyzes persons falls using OpenPose, where key points of the human skeleton and the speed of descent in the centre of the hip joint, angle of the body's central line with the ground and the width-height relationship of the rectangular external body is used to detect the fall. In Kavya et al. [25], on the other hand, a classifier is used to detect a person, and a combination of estimation of the fundamental point is used and calculates the rate of change of the angle between the tracked points to the ground, also to detect persons falls.

Computer vision is also used to detect specific gestures made by the person's hand to interact with devices [26]. Palsa et al. [27] uses a learning algorithm for the detection and recognition of gestures to interact with a virtual application, being able to navigate and select different types of equipment. In the same way, Hernández et al. [28] also uses gestures for interaction in a virtual environment, focusing on the detection and use of people's natural gestures to interact.

Thus, it is possible to develop touchless interfaces, allowing real-time wireless control of any device, and that can adapt on-the-fly to the natural actions of each user, that is, different users can turn a light on or off using different actions (movements). It is important to note that this technology can also allow the user to program actions in a specific environment, such as the office, and export the same action (movement) to a different environment, for example to the office, without the need to reprogram the same action for the same function.

3   Adaptive Control Devices Framework

Before introducing the Adaptive Control Devices Framework (ACDf), it is important to stress out the difference between *devices functionalities, actions* and *movements. Device functionalities*, are the functionalities that a device allows interaction. Using an example, a led lamp can have four functionalities: (i) turn-on, (ii) dimmer the illumination; (iii) change the colour (of the light) and (iv) turn-off. An *action* is the activation of specific device functionality. For instance turn-on the device. The same *action* can be applied to different devices, for example, turn-on the air-conditioned, or turn-on the TV. *Movement(s)*, corresponds to the movements done by any part of the user body or group of movements done by the user to achieve a specific action. For instance, raise the arm – *swipe-up*, turn the arm from right to left – *swipe-left*, rotate the head to the left side – *rotate-left*, stretch your arm to the left/right and hold still horizontally *n* seconds (s) – *lateral n*.

Finally, an *action* can be associated to a single body *movement*, example, the action *turn-on* can be associated to the movement *swipe-up,* or an *action* can be associated to a group of *movements,* for example, increase the illumination or increase the volume of the TV, can be done by the concatenation of two *movements: swipe-up lateral 3* (3 s) to select the *action* "increase", and after that a *swipe-left* once or several times to select the *action* "increment" the illumination/sound.

The ACDf is divided into five main modules, this paper addresses the first three:

(a)   Communication with devices (via KNX);
(b)   Detection of human *movements*;
(c)   Association between human *movements, actions* and *device functionalities*;
(d)   Learning personalized *actions* - development of the adaptative interface;
(e)   Store and share actions over the internet (cloud).

As mentioned in the Introduction, the paper objective is to present an initial prove-of-concept of a framework that by recognizing a person's *movements-actions-device functionalities* can control devices using KNX standard. This corresponds to modules a) to c). At this stage all *movements-actions* are predefined, and the number of *devices functionalities* are limited.

In a future paper (out of the focus of the present) modules c) to e) will be addressed. Module c), is going to be addressed again in a way to generalize the association between *movements-actions-devices functionalities,* so that any device *functionalities* integrated to the framework can be associated automatically to the existing *actions* (without any human supervision). The same way, a full range of *movements-actions* will be presented.

Module d) consists in the development of the adaptative interface, where each user can, if intended, teach to the system his/her *movement(s)* to associate to each *action.*

The idea is always to minimize and simplify to the maximum the number of *actions*. Module e), consists in storing in the cloud all correspondences of *movements – actions* and *actions – devices functionalities*, so in any place/environment the same user, after being recognized by the framework (for instance by facial recognition) can use the same set of *actions* (that he previously taught, for instance, the ones he felt most ergonomic) when he/she intend to command a device. This means that after a set of *action* has been learnt by the framework (in module d)) and associated to that user (in module c)), those actions can be used in any place or environment (in the world), without any kind of (extra) configuration.

Finally, it is important to reinforce that the *movements* that can be achieved by a "young" person, for instance, a *swipe-up*, cannot be, probably, done by an elderly person with mobility problems, in this case, the elderly can replace the *movement* by a *swipe-left* or a *rotate-left* or any other suitable. Once again, the framework will allow customizing easily the associations between *movements-actions*, by learning by mimic the user *movements* (out of the focus of the present paper).

3.1 Communication with Devices

As mentioned before, KNX was used for communicating with devices [4]. A simple installation of a KNX consists of a KNX power supply (DC 30 V), one sensor, such as a switch, one actuator and a single unshielded twisted-pair (UTP) cable, see Fig. 1 on the left. For the present framework, for interfacing to the KNX system was used KNXnet/IP Tunnelling, see Fig. 1 on the right.

In a KNX installation each KNX device has an *individual address* that must be unique, for the identification of the device within the installation. The communication between devices is carried out via *group addresses*. Each group address can be assigned to devices as required, allowing the communicating between several devices at the same time. However, while actuators can listen to several group addresses, sensors can only send one group address per telegram.

In the present framework, which aims to make communication with devices simpler, an open-source library was used [29]. This library was implemented in Python, where it is possible to connect over IP with KNX devices, specifying the IP address of the KNX IP Interface connected to the KNX system and sending the *action* that the KNX

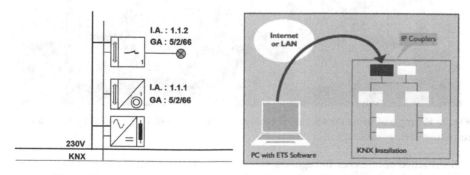

Fig. 1. Example of a simple connection of KNX devices, adapted from [4].

device(s) must perform, thus, it is possible to associate *device functionalities* with the *movements* (using the mentioned *actions*).

KNX Communication Library supports the following pipeline: (a) for its initialization, (a.1) inclusion of the IP that is associated with the KNX IP Interface and (a.2) inclusion of the individual(s) or group(s) addresses configured by the KNX software for the device(s) connected to this interface. (b) After initialization, (b.1) choose device or group of devices, (b.2) send information to perform the *action - functionality* according to the *movement* performed and (b.3) receive recognition of the functionality activated.

3.2   Detection of Human Movements

For *movements* detection it was used the GluonCV toolkit [30, 31], it is a deep learning tool for Computer Vision that works in Python. In this kit we can find classification algorithms, object detection, pose estimation, among others. It is composed of models already tested and pre-trained, ready to use.

In the GluonCV, we use for pose estimation the Simple Pose with a ResNet18 backbone [32] trained with an input size image of 128×96 pixels (px), being this choice a trade-off between accuracy and speed[1], once we intend to use in the framework any standard HD camera and laptop computer (see Sect. 4). This model returns a vector with the coordinates of the 17 key points, that represents the joints position on the person, as can be seen in Fig. 2. This Fig. 2 shows the detection of two persons and the respective percentage of average accuracy. The joints in these images are connected by lines to better demonstrate the user and joints detection.

3.3   Association Between Movements, Actions and Device Functionalities

As mentioned before, at this stage, prove-of-concept, the module c) - Association between human *movements*, *actions* and *device functionalities* were predefined and limited. As demonstrated in e.g. [27, 28] exists a group of *movements* that are already used

Fig. 2. Example of using the GluonCV estimator with its 17 joints, connected by lines, and the respective average accuracy.

---

[1] Visualization of inference throughputs vs. validation average precision of COCO pre-trained models can be seen in https://cv.gluon.ai/model_zoo/pose.html, accessed 2020/12/23.

for virtual environments, and these *movements* were used as the basis for the standard *movements* implemented in the framework project.

In the present stage of the framework, *actions* considered are (i) *start*, to start the interaction with devices, (ii) *next* and (iii) *previous* which allows, for instance, navigate between devices, when there is more than one being controlled. Activate or disconnect devices, (iv) *turn-on* and (v) *turn-of*, and if the device has the functionality of increasing or decreasing a certain parameter, the (vi) *increase* and (vii) *decrease* actions.

Table 1 shows the correspondence between *actions* and *movements*. The *movements* are coded in the following way: type + direction + body part + position + duration. Specifically, (a) type of movement: *static, swipe, rotation, walk*, etc.; (b) direction of movement: *up, down, left* and *right*; (c) body part that is going to do the movement, *arm-right, arm-left, head*, etc.; (d) position: *lateral, frontal, any*, and (e) duration (minimum) of the movement in *n* seconds.

In the case, *actions* with "*", means that they are complementary, the same movement does both actions, doing the negative of the action that is activated. In the case of movements with duration "0", means that there is no minimum time to do that *movement*.

For the detection of these movements, the matrix with the coordinates returned by the pose estimate is used, and through this, comparisons are made between a reference(s) joint(s) and the joint(s) that represent the occurred *movement*. For example, for detecting *swipe-up*, the user's *shoulder* joint is used as a reference, and the *wrist* joint is checked for the motion, i.e., is checked if the coordinates of the *wrist* is above or below the corresponding *shoulder* joint coordinates (reference point), thus detecting whether or not there was a predetermined movement (Fig. 3 top row). For each *action* defined is applied the KNX communication pipeline mentioned in Sect. 3.1.

Once again it is important to stress, if the user is an elderly person with motor limitations or someone that does not feel comfortable with these *movements* for the specific *action*, the framework can learn new movements, module d) – adaptative interface (out the focus of this paper). The most simple example that can be given is for instance *action increase*, where the default *movement* is "*swipe-right + arm-right + any + 0*", that is the usual movement done a right-handed person, left-handed ones typically will prefer "*swipe-left + arm-left + any + 0*". Also, it is important to stress that *actions* are

Table 1. Correspondence between *actions* and *movements*. *Movements* marked with (*) are the same *movement*, if applied, makes the negation of the previous one.

Action	Movements (brief explanation)
start	*static + arm-both + lateral* + 3 (both arm laterally during 3 s)
next	*swipe-up + arm-right + lateral* + 0 (raise the right arm laterally)
previous	*swipe-up + arm-left + lateral* + 0 (raise the left arm laterally)
turn-on*	*swipe-up + arm-right + any* + 0 (raise right arm vertically)
turn-off*	*swipe-up + arm-right + any* + 0 (raise right arm vertically)
increase	*swipe-left + arm-right + any* + 0 (right arm move from right to left)
decrease	*swipe-right + arm-right + any* + 0 (right arm move from left to right)

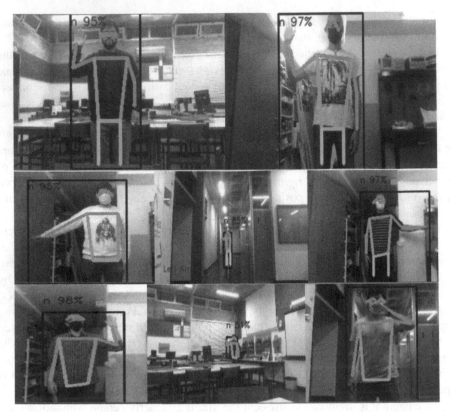

Fig. 3. Detection of several movements done by different users in different environments (see text for details).

"hard-coded" in the framework. What is changeable in the adaptative interface are the *movements*. The next section presents the results of some test scenarios.

4   Tests and Results

The tests were done by 6 different users in 3 different environments: laboratory, corridors and office. All with a different set of natural and artificial illumination and in different buildings. In all tests was used HD Webcams placed around 1 m above the floor level, and i5 Laptops, 5–8th generation Intel Processors, with SSD and 8 GB RAM. The tested KNX installation consists of a power supply 320 mA RMD, an universal dim actuator 1gang, 50–500 W/VA RMD and a KNX IP router RMD, together with the ETS5 software for programming the KNX installation (Fig. 4 top).

The presented test scenario consists in the activation and regulation of a lamp light intensity, shown in Fig. 4 bottom-right. The users can do all the *actions* in any order, but the *actions increase/decrease* are only valid with the device activated (*turn-on*).

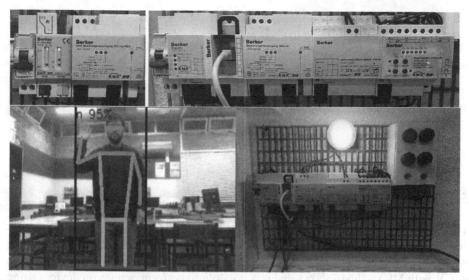

Fig. 4. Top row, detailed image of the KNX IP router (left) and devices (right). Bottom row, detection of a *swipe-up* (left), and the activation of the KNX device – lamp (right).

The 6 users were divided into 3 groups of 2, each group test one of the three environments, doing 5 repetitions for each of the *actions* presented in Table 2. The test scenarios consist in the users being more or less face forward to the camera, at a position approximately 0° (degrees) - frontal to the camera, and at distances of 1, 2, 3, 4 and 5 m (meters), do the respective *movements* to activate the mentioned *actions* (Table 2). Then the users change to a position around ±25° (degrees) to the right and the left and repeat the same distances. All users before performing the test were briefed with the *movements-actions* but were not induced to do it in a certain way, it was left to the user to perform the gesture as he considered the most correct way. Examples of users doing movements can be seen in Figs. 3 and 4.

The total number of test samples was 2.250, comprises: 3 environments × 2 users per environment × 5 repetitions per *action* × 5 *actions* × 3 positions × 5 distances. This means, that for each of the five *actions* has adquired 450 test samples. Table 2 shows the percentage of correct *actions* achieved by the framework.

Overall, the tests present satisfactory results, with an overall average correct *actions* of 73.3%. No major flaws were detected in the framework. The results had better accuracy when the user has at distances of 2 m because the pose estimator can detect the person full body and presented the joints with good precision, and consequently, the *movements* to *action* classification were done with more acurracy. No error was detected when an *action* is well defined and communicated to the KNX devices.

As expected, the few tests done with very low or no light (less than 1% of the overall tests) fail, the remaining of the fails were due to gestures done very quickly and gestures where the user is not doing the intended gesture for the intended *action*.

Table 2. Table with the percentages of correct answers obtained during the tests.

Action	Accuracy (%)
next	76,7
previous	80,0
on/off	83,3
increase	66,7
decrease	60,0

5 Conclusions

The framework was presented for the control of KNX devices through the use of computer vision, using a pose estimation algorithm, provided by the GluonCV library, and the use of an open-source library for communication between KNX devices. The integration of CV with ML methods, shows that it is possible to perform *actions* on devices using pre-configured body *movements*, that were detected and interpreted by the framework, as shown by the tests in different environments and scenarios.

Future developments consists in the implementation of modules d), e) and the optimization of module c), as already explained in the text. After this final implementations, two tests are mandatory, one with users with light motor disabilities, like elders, analyze the framework in term of user experience (UX) and technology acceptance, by applying a Technology Acceptance Model (TAM) to the specification and the expected personas that is going to use the framework.

Acknowledgements. This work was supported by the Portuguese Foundation for Science and Technology (FCT), project LARSyS - FCT Project UIDB/50009/2020, INESC-ID - FCT Project UIDB/50021/2020 and project WELSAFE.DV - Welcome Safety Device financed by Portugal2020, CRESC2020 and FEDER.

References

1. Stephanidis, C.: Adaptive techniques for universal access. User Model. User-adap. Interact. **11**(1–2), 159–179 (2001)
2. Rodrigues, J.M.F., et al.: Adaptive card design UI implementation for an augmented reality museum application. In: Antona, M., Stephanidis, C. (eds.) Universal Access in Human-Computer Interaction 2017, Part I, LNCS 10277, pp. 433–443 (2017). https://doi.org/10.1007/978-3-319-58706-6_35
3. Johnston, V., Black, M., Wallace, J., Mulvenna, M., Bond, R.: A framework for the development of a dynamic adaptive intelligent user interface to enhance the user experience. In: Proceedings of the 31st European Conference on Cognitive Ergonomics, pp. 32–35 (2019)
4. KNX: KNX Smart Home and Building Solutions. Global. Secure. https://www.knx.org/knx-en/for-your-home/. Accessed on 12 Nov 2020
5. Gams, M., Gu, I.Y.H., Härmä, A., Muñoz, A., Tam, V.: Artificial intelligence and ambient intelligence. J. Ambient Intell. Smart Environ. **11**(1), 71–86 (2019)

6. Hussain, M.Z., Ullah, Z., Hassan, T., Hasan, M.Z.: Ambient intelligence. In: LGURJCSIT, vol. 2, pp. 15–20 (2018)
7. Martín, A.A.S., Guerrero, E.G., Santamaría, L.E.B.: Prospective integration between Environmental Intelligence (AMI), Data Analytics (DA), and Internet of Things (IoT). In: Congreso Internacional de Innovación y Tendencias en Ingenieria (CONIITI), pp. 1–6, IEEE (2019)
8. Crandall, J.W., Oudah, M., Tennom, et al.: Cooperating with machines. Nat. Commun. **9**, 233 (2018). https://doi.org/10.1038/s41467-017-02597-8
9. Ishowo-Oloko, F., Bonnefon, J.F., Soroye, Z., Crandall, J., Rahwan, I., Rahwan, T.: Behavioural evidence for a transparency-efficiency tradeoff in human-machine cooperation. Nat. Mach. Intell. **1**(11), 517–521 (2019)
10. Pierr, M., Lemoine, P.: Human-machine cooperation: adaptability of shared functions between humans and machines - design and evaluation aspects. In Eng. Sciences. U. Polytechnique Hauts-de-France (2020). https://hal.archives-ouvertes.fr/tel-02959402
11. Sapundzhi, F.: A survey of KNX implementation in building automation. TEM J. **9**, 144–148 (2020)
12. Feki, E., Kassab, K., Mami, A.: Integration of the small board computers Rasp berry PI in home automation based on KNX protocol. In: IEEE 19th Mediterranean Microwave Symposium (MMS), pp. 1–4 (2019)
13. Yumang, A., Abando, M., Dios, E.: Far-field speech-controlled smart classroom with natural language processing built under KNX standard for appliance control. In: International Conference on Computer and Automation Engineering, pp. 219–223 (2020)
14. Alpaydin, E.: Introduction to Machine Learning. MIT Press (2020)
15. Sachan, A.: Human pose estimation using deep learning in OpenCV. https://cv-tricks.com/pose-estimation/using-deep-learning-in-opencv/. Accessed on 01 July 2020
16. Sawant, C.: Human activity recognition with openpose and Long Short-Term Memory on real time images (No. 2297). EasyChair (2020)
17. Yunus, A. P., Shirai, N.C., Morita, K., Wakabayashi, T.: Human Motion Prediction by 2D Human Pose Estimation using OpenPose (No. 2580). EasyChair (2020)
18. Cao, Z., Hidalgo, G., Simon, T., Wei, S.E., Sheikh, Y.: OpenPose: realtime multi-person 2D pose estimation using part affinity fields. IEEE Trans. PAMI **43**(1), 172–186 (2021). https://doi.org/10.1109/tpami.2019.2929257
19. Chikano, M., Tomiyasu, F., Awai, S., Hirai, Y., Konno, T.: Person matching technology using gait information of 2D pose estimation. In: 2020 IEEE 2nd Global Conf. on Life Sciences and Technologies (LifeTech), pp. 140–144. IEEE (2020)
20. Satake, H., Tani, R., Shigeno, H.: A task placement system for face recognition applications in edge computing. In: 2020 IEEE 17th Annual Consumer Communications & Networking Conference (CCNC), pp. 1–6. IEEE (2020)
21. Baltanas, S., Sarmiento, J., Jimenez, J.: A face recognition system for assistive robots. In: Proceedings of the 3rd International Conference on Applications of Intelligent Systems, Art. 29, pp. 1–6 (2020). https://doi.org/10.1145/3378184.3378225
22. Bellotto, N., Carmona, M., Cosar, S.: ENRICHME integration of ambient intelligence and robotics for AAL. In: Wellbeing AI: From Machine Learning to Subjectivity Oriented Computing, Technical Report SS-17–08 (2017)
23. Daher, M., Najjar, M., Diab, A., Khalil, M., Dib, A., Charpillet, F.: Ambient assistive living system using RGB-D camera. In 4th International Conference on Advances in Biomedical Engineering (ICABME), pp. 1–4 (2017)
24. Chen, W., Jiang, Z., Guo, H., Ni, X.: Fall detection based on key points of human-skeleton using OpenPose. Ing.: Symmetry **12**(5), 744 (2020). https://doi.org/10.3390/sym12050744
25. Kavya, T.S., Jang, Y.M., Tsogtbaatar, E., Cho, S.B.: Fall detection system for elderly people using vision-based analysis. Sci. Tech. **23**, 69–83 (2020)

26. Kim, S.H., Jang, S.W., Park, J.H.: Robust hand pose estimation using visual sensor in IoT environment. J. Supercomput. **76**, 5382–5401 (2020). https://doi.org/10.1007/s11227-019-03082-3

27. Palsa, J., Vokorokos, L., Bilanova., Z.: User interface of smart environment based on human body gestures. In: IEEE 18th World Symposium on Applied Machine Intelligence and Informatics (SAMI), pp. 165–170 (2020). https://doi.org/10.1007/s11227-019-03082-3

28. Hernández, D., Calleros J.M., García J., Vizzuett L.: Gesture-based interaction for virtual reality environments through user-defined commands. In: Human-Computer Interaction. HCI-COLLAB 2018. Communications in Computer and Information Science, vol. 847, pp. 143–157 (2019). https://doi.org/10.1007/978-3-030-05270-6_11

29. XKNX: Asynchronous Python Library for KNX. https://xknx.io/. Accessed on 12 Nov 2020

30. Guo, J., et al.: GluonCV and GluonNLP: Deep learning in computer vision and natural language processing. J. Mach. Learn. Res. **21**, 1–7 (2020)

31. GluonCV, State-of-the-art Deep Learning Algorithms in Computer Vision. https://cv.gluon.ai/. Accessed on 12 Nov 2020

32. Xiao, B., Wu, H., Wei, Y.: Simple baselines for human pose estimation and tracking. In: Proceedings of the European Conference on Computer Vision (ECCV), pp. 466–481 (2018)

Effect of Olfactory Stimulation with Vanilla Odor on Degree of Electrical Activity to Control Gastrointestinal Motility

Eiji Takai[1,2](✉), Takahiro Aoyagi[1], Keita Ichikawa[2], Yasuyuki Matsuura[2,3], Fumiya Kinoshita[4], and Hiroki Takada[2]

[1] Soda Aromatic Co., Ltd., Chiba 270-0233, Japan
Eiji_Takai@soda.toray.co.jp
[2] Graduate School of Engineering, University of Fukui, Fukui 910-8507, Japan
[3] Department of Cross Cultural Studies, Gifu City Women's College, Gifu 501-0192, Japan
[4] Faculty of Engineering, Toyama Prefectural University, Toyama 939-0398, Japan

Abstract. Sensory evaluation has been generally used to assess odors; however, attempts have also been made to evaluate odors based on physiological responses in vivo during olfactory stimulation. In this study, we conducted linear and non-linear analyses of the effects of vanilla odor at different concentrations on an electrogastrogram (EGG), as well as sensory evaluation of the odor. We also investigated the relationship between the concentration of vanilla and changes in the EGG to explore its potential as an odor evaluation method. Heart rate variability analysis was performed during odor presentation—to investigate the effect of olfactory stimulation by vanilla odor on autonomic nerve activity—after which a sensory evaluation was performed to ascertain which characteristics of the presented samples were affected by the increase in the translation error of the EGG during vanilla olfactory stimulation. The translation error itself was estimated using the Wayland algorithm for the EGG during odor presentation. The results showed a significant increase in the translation error in the order of control, low concentration vanilla (LV), and high concentration vanilla (HV), suggesting that the randomness of the EGG increased in proportion to the concentration of the presented sample. Correlation analysis between the translation error and the odor intensity showed that the stronger the odor, the greater the randomness of the EGG. These results suggest that the EGG can be used as an odor evaluation method.

Keywords: Electrogastrography · Non-linear analysis · Vanilla odor

1 Introduction

Sensory evaluation has been generally used to assess odors; however, attempts have been made to evaluate odors based on physiological responses in vivo during olfactory stimulation [1].

© Springer Nature Switzerland AG 2021
M. Antona and C. Stephanidis (Eds.): HCII 2021, LNCS 12769, pp. 519–530, 2021.
https://doi.org/10.1007/978-3-030-78095-1_38

Regarding food, the aroma is a crucial factors determining preference and appetite, making it essential to evaluate. It is also possible that food aroma affects digestive activity. For example, olfactory stimulation by grated carrots has been reported that suppressed gastric motility in rabbits and then accelerated it [2]. Gastric motility is controlled by the parasympathetic nervous system. Moreover, researchers have reported that the gastric vagus nerve in mice could be activated by olfactory stimulation by lavender essential oil [3], ginger [4], fermented milk [5], and whiskey [6], and inhibited by grapefruit essential oil [7]. Consequently, olfactory stimulation is thought to affect gastric motility and gastric vagal activity. However, a few reports exist on the effects of olfactory stimulation on gastric electrical activity in humans.

Transcutaneous electrogastrography is a noninvasive and simple method for measuring gastric myoelectrical activity. Electrogastrography measures the electrical activity that controls the peristalsis of the stomach using electrodes attached to the abdominal surface around the stomach [8]. Electrogastrography has not been completely studied because it is easily affected by diaphragmatic myoelectrical activity associated with breathing and cardiac electrical activity. However, recent improvements in measurement technology allow this technique to measure gastric functions and autonomic nerve activity.

The electrogastrogram (EGG) of a healthy individual shows a waveform of approximately three cycles per minute (cpm) [9]. Therefore, frequency analysis such as a fast Fourier transform (FFT) algorithm is used to analyze EGGs. It has also been confirmed by numerical analysis that the mathematical model considered for generating an EGG in healthy individuals has nonlinearity, described by a stochastic resonance model [10]. Specifically, it is represented by a stochastic differential equation that adds the electrical activity of the intestinal tract and other organs to the gastric electrical activity. Therefore, nonlinear analysis can be a useful analysis technique in addition to linear analysis techniques using FFTs. Analyses using the maximum Lyapunov exponent [11] and the Wayland algorithm [12] have also been attempted.

Conversely, odors are known to change their note depending on their concentration. Indole (C_8H_7N), which is an aromatic compound, smells like jasmine at low concentrations but smells like feces at high concentrations [13]. This is thought to be due to a change in the response pattern of olfactory receptors between low and high concentrations [13], and differences have also been observed in the physiological response to olfactory stimulation. For example, it has been reported that the effects on autonomic nerve activity differed in heart rate variability analysis when different intensities of jasmine tea odor were presented and that this was related to odor preferences [14]. Therefore, in this study, we set two levels of odor concentration and conducted a sensory evaluation of the presented odor to investigate which characteristics of the odor affected the EGG.

In this study, we conducted linear and non-linear analyses of the effects of vanilla odor at different concentrations on the EGG, as well as a sensory evaluation of the odor. Subsequently, we investigated the relationship with the changes in EGGs to explore their potential as an odor evaluation method.

This paper was written based on the papers cited [15].

2 Methods

2.1 Experimental Method

The experiment participants were eight healthy young males (mean age ± standard deviation: 23.25 ± 0.78 years). The participants were fully briefed on the experiment beforehand, and their written approval was obtained. In addition, this experiment was approved by the Ethics Committee of the School of Engineering, University of Fukui (H2019001). The participants did not have gastrointestinal diseases, hypertension, chronic respiratory diseases, metabolic diseases such as diabetes, or neurological diseases such as Parkinson's disease.

In the experiment, electrocardiograms (ECGs) and EGGs were taken in the supine position in a sound-insulated laboratory for 20 min at rest and 20 min during the odor presentation. After completing the ECG and EGG measurements, the participants performed a sensory evaluation of the odor. Five evaluation items were used: odor intensity, preference, familiarity, appetite, and pleasantness. Moreover, scores were assigned using the visual analog scale (VAS). Measurements were obtained at least two h after meals to reduce the influence of eating and at the same time of day for each subject to account for circadian rhythms.

Disposable electrocardiography electrodes (Vitrode Bs, Nihon Kohden) were used for the EGGs and ECGs, and the electrodes were affixed in the positions shown in Fig. 1. The electrodes were applied after the skin resistance was sufficiently lowered using Nihon Kohden's Skin Pure gel. Measurements were performed by monopolar induction, and data were captured at a sampling frequency of 1 kHz using a Biotop mini (East Medic Corporation).

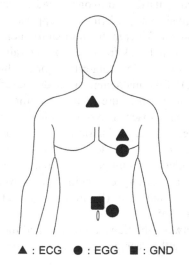

▲ : ECG   ● : EGG   ■ : GND

Fig. 1. Electrode attachment positions

Odor presentation was performed by placing a 30-mm diameter cotton ball impregnated with 1 g of odorant in a 30 mL glass bottle and fixing the glass bottle 5 cm from the subject's nose with a clamp. The samples were odorant blends with a vanilla note (Soda Aromatic Co., Ltd.) and comprised a high concentration vanilla odorant (HV) prepared at 1) a concentration six times higher than that of ordinary vanilla odorant, 2) a low concentration vanilla odorant (LV) prepared by diluting HV 100 times using a solvent (triethyl citrate), and 3) a control sample using only solvent (Control). The samples were presented randomly to account for order effects.

2.2 Analysis Method

The ECG was A/D converted at a sampling frequency of 1 kHz, and heart rate variability analysis was performed for approximately 17 min—from 3 min to 20 min—after the start of the odor presentation. First, the ECG time series was obtained by A/D conversion at 1 kHz, from which the R-R interval was extracted. The extracted R-R interval was resampled at equal time intervals of 1 s, and the power spectral density (PSD) was calculated by FFT. A range of 0.04–0.15 Hz was defined as the low frequency (LF) band and 0.15–0.4 Hz as the high frequency (HF) band. The LF and HF components were calculated by determining the PSD integral values for each [16]. The mean heart rate was calculated from the R-R interval. The HF component represents parasympathetic activity, and the LF component represents sympathetic and parasympathetic activity. In addition, an increase in the mean heart rate indicates sympathetic dominance, while a decrease indicates parasympathetic dominance.

The EGGs were A/D converted at a sampling frequency of 1 kHz and then resampled at 1 Hz. A band-pass filter with a cutoff frequency of 0.015–0.15 Hz was applied to remove any noise introduced by the electromyogram and surrounding electronic devices. As with the ECG, FFT analysis was performed for approximately 17 min during odor presentation. We focused on 2.4–3.7 cpm, the normal frequency band of EGGs [9], and calculated the peak frequency and peak frequency power value in this band (Fig. 2).

Subsequently, we used the Wayland algorithm for nonlinear analysis to estimate the translation error (E_{trans}) of the mathematical model describing the EGG [17]. The translation error is a quantitative measure of the smoothness of the trajectory of an attractor embedded in the phase space. The translation error has a non-negative value. The closer the value is to zero, the more deterministic the mathematical model, and the larger the value is, the more it can be considered to be random. The translation error was also calculated for approximately 17 min during the odor presentation.

The calculated values and sensory evaluation scores were statistically compared using the Wilcoxon signed rank test (Bonferroni correction). In this study, the significance level was set at 0.05.

Correlation analysis between the translation error and the sensory evaluation score was performed by calculating the Pearson correlation coefficient.

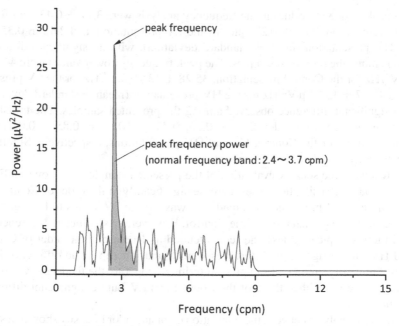

Fig. 2. Typical example of an EGG power spectrum graph

3 Results

Heart rate variability analysis and the calculation of the mean heart rate were performed on the ECG for approximately 17 min during the odor presentation (Fig. 3). The HF component, which is an index of parasympathetic nerve activity, was 0.23 ± 0.02 ms^2 for the Control presentation, 0.25 ± 0.03 ms^2 for the LV presentation, and 0.23 ± 0.03 ms^2 for the HV presentation (mean $\pm$ standard deviation), with no difference observed among the presented samples. The values of the LF component, which is an index of the sympathetic and parasympathetic activity, were 0.20 ± 0.02 ms^2 for the Control presentation, 0.25 ± 0.05 ms^2 for the LV presentation, and 0.21 ± 0.01 ms^2 for the HV presentation (mean $\pm$ standard deviation), with no difference observed among the presented samples. The mean heart rate was 57.39 ± 3.91 bpm for the Control presentation, 56.52 ± 5.22 bpm for the LV presentation, and 61.74 ± 5.22 bpm for the HV presentation (mean $\pm$ standard deviation), with no difference observed among the presented samples.

The EGG was also subjected to FFT frequency analysis and the estimation of translation error by the Wayland algorithm for approximately 17 min during the odor presentation (Fig. 4). In addition, Fig. 5 shows a typical example of an EGG measured and recorded for two min from five min after the start of the odor presentation.

The peak frequency values in the frequency analysis were 3.17 ± 0.43 cpm for the Control presentation, 2.82 ± 0.23 cpm for the LV presentation, and 2.82 ± 0.35 cpm for the HV presentation (mean ± standard deviation), with no significant difference observed among the presented samples. The peak frequency power values were 44.01 ± 5.96 μV^2/Hz for the Control presentation, 35.28 ± 13.48 μV^2/Hz for the LV presentation, and 49.27 ± 15.03 μV^2/Hz for the HV presentation (mean ± standard deviation), with no significant difference observed among the presented samples. The translation errors were, in ascending order, 0.58 ± 0.06, 0.75 ± 0.01, and 0.85 ± 0.02 (mean ± standard error) for the Control, LV, and HV presentations, respectively. Significant differences were found among all the samples.

The results of the sensory evaluation of the presented samples are shown in Fig. 6. In terms of odor intensity, the scores increase significantly in the order of Control, LV, and HV. In terms of preference, the tendency was for the LV scores to be higher and HV scores to be lower than those of the Control. However, no significant difference was found. In terms of pleasantness, the scores tended to decrease in the order of Control, LV, and HV, but no significant differences were found. There was no difference in the score for familiarity among all samples. In terms of appetite, the tendency was for the HV scores to be lower than those of the Control and LV, but no significant difference was found.

Correlation analysis between the translation error and odor intensity showed a strong positive correlation of r = 0.777 (Fig. 7).

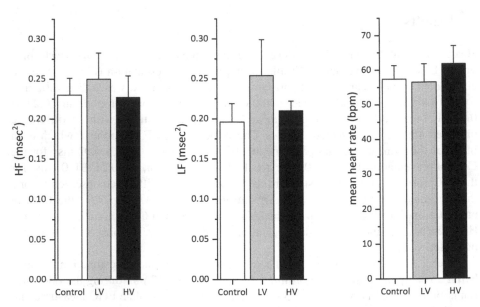

Fig. 3. Heart rate variability analysis and heart rate during aroma presentation

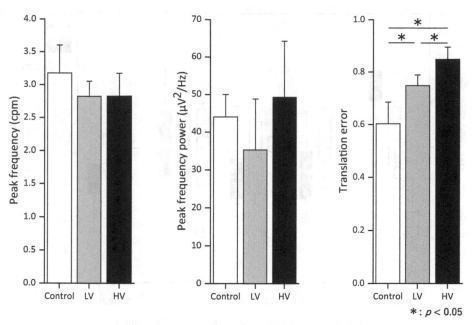

Fig. 4. Frequency analysis and translation error of the EGG during the presentation of odor

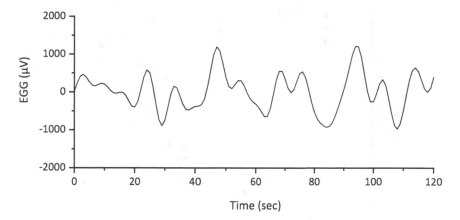

Fig. 5. Typical example of an EGG

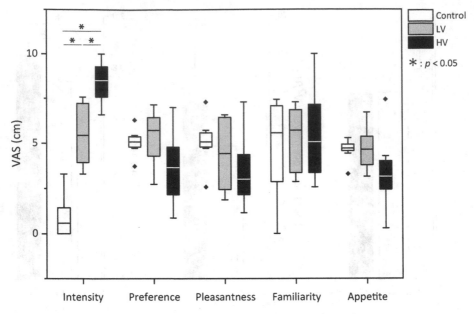

Fig. 6. Sensory evaluation of the presented samples

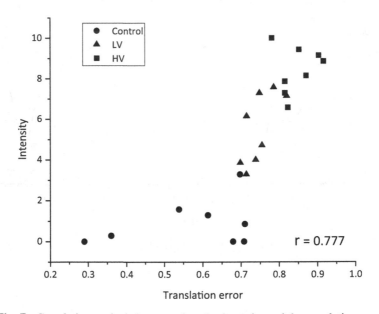

Fig. 7. Correlation analysis between the odor intensity and the translation error

4 Discussion

In this study, the effects of olfactory stimulation on EGGs were investigated using different concentrations of vanilla odors. First, heart rate variability analysis was performed during odor presentation to investigate the effect of olfactory stimulation by vanilla odor on autonomic nerve activity. As a result, there was no difference in the value of the HF component, which is an index of the parasympathetic nerve activity, or the value of the LF component, which is an index of the sympathetic nerve activity and parasympathetic nerve activity, when any of the samples were presented. Previous studies have reported that unpleasant odors predominate the sympathetic nervous system [18], while highly preferable odors predominate the parasympathetic nervous system [19]. In this study, there were no significant differences between the presented samples in terms of the degree of preference or pleasantness in the sensory evaluation, which may be a reason for the lack of change in autonomic activity. In addition, there was no difference in the mean heart rate between the presented samples, which is consistent with the report that vanilla olfactory stimulation does not alter the R-R interval in healthy individuals [20].

In the frequency analysis of the EGG, there was no difference between the presented samples in terms of both peak frequency and peak frequency power values. A previous study found a correlation between power values at approximately 3 cpm in the EGG and HF values in heart rate variability analysis [21]. The present results are consistent with this report. In the frequency analysis of the EGG during gustatory stimulation, which is the same chemical sense as that of smell, it was reported that the percentage of normal waves increased during sweet or salty flavor presentation more than during bitter flavor presentation [22]. Jin et al. [22] stated that sweet and salty flavors stimulate the parasympathetic nervous system and promote gastric myoelectrical activity because they are pleasant flavors, while bitter flavors stimulate the sympathetic nervous system and suppress gastric myoelectrical activity because they are unpleasant flavors. Although a difference between the senses of taste and smell is present, it is conceivable that the preference and comfort of the presented stimuli may be reflected in the gastric myoelectrical activity. No difference in these scores was observed for the samples used in this study, suggesting that there may have been no change in the EGG frequency analysis.

The translation error was estimated using the Wayland algorithm for the EGG during odor presentation. The results showed a significant increase in the translation error in the order of Control, LV, and HV, suggesting that the randomness of the EGG increased in proportion to the concentration of the presented sample. It has been reported that the mathematical model of the EGG represents the relationship between gastric and intestinal electrical activity [10]. Therefore, vanilla olfactory stimulation may have altered the association with gastrointestinal electrical activity and increased randomness.

Next, a sensory evaluation was performed to ascertain which characteristics of the presented samples were affected by the increase in the EGG translation error during vanilla olfactory stimulation. As for the odor intensity, the scores increased significantly in a concentration-dependent manner, suggesting that the participants were able to discriminate the odor intensity of the samples. In terms of preference, pleasantness, and appetite, HV tended to score lower than Control and LV. Although the vanilla odor was reported to be highly preferred in a previous study [23], in this study, the concentration of the HV could be substantially high and caused the participants to have a negative impression of HV, thereby showing a tendency to lower their scores. As there was no difference in the scores for familiarity among all samples, it can be assumed that none of the samples were a novel odor to the participants. This result suggests that the randomness of the EGG may be affected by odor intensity.

Because the translation error of the EGG and the odor intensity score increased with the concentration of the odor sample, we conducted a correlation analysis on the translation error and the odor intensity score for each participant. A strong positive correlation was observed, suggesting that the randomness of the EGG was higher when the participants strongly sensed the odor. The lack of significant changes in the heart rate variability analysis or the EGG frequency analysis suggests that some changes in the relationship with gastrointestinal electrical activity, rather than changes in autonomic activity, may have occurred. When vanillin ($C_8H_8O_3$), the main odor component of vanilla, was inhaled by mice, food intake increased [24], suggesting that olfactory stimulation by vanillin may have affected the hypothalamus or feeding center. Since the gastric myoelectrical activity is modulated by the hypothalamus [9], the olfactory information of vanilla may influence the relationship with gastrointestinal electrical activity via the hypothalamus. This study focused on the effect of olfactory stimulation on gastric myoelectrical activity; thus, only ECG and EGG measurements were performed. The mechanism by which olfactory stimulation influences gastrointestinal electrical activity is unclear; however, brain measurements conducted simultaneously with the electrogastrogram may clarify this mechanism.

5 Conclusions

In this study, we used frequency analysis and nonlinear analysis to clarify the effects of olfactory stimuli on the EGG and investigated which characteristics of the presented odors affect the EGG by comparison with sensory evaluation. The results showed that olfactory stimulation by vanilla odor increased the randomness of the EGG based on the value of the translation error. Correlation analysis between the translation error and the odor intensity showed that the stronger the odor, the higher the randomness of the EGG. These results suggest that the EGG can be used as an odor evaluation method.

As this study was conducted only with vanilla odor, the obtained results may be were a phenomenon specific to vanilla odor. In the future, we plan to clarify the effects of olfactory stimulation by odors other than vanilla on the EGG.

References

1. Miyazaki, Y.: The relationship between subjective evaluation and physiological response. Jpn. J. Sens. Eval. 1(1), 37–42 (1997). (in Japanese)
2. Sumikama, T.: The relation between the stimulation of smell and the gastric movements. J. Physiol. Soc. Jpn. 21, 70–81 (1959). (in Japanese)
3. Shen, J., Niijima, A., Tanida, M., Horii, Y., Maeda, K., Nagai, K.: Olfactory stimulation with scent of lavender oil affects autonomic nerves, lipolysis and appetite in rats. Neurosci. Lett. 383(1–2), 188–193 (2005)

4. Niijima, A., Hashimoto, K., Sakakibara, I., Amagaya, S., Aburada, M.: Effects of olfactory and gustatory stimulation of Zingiberis rhizome on the efferent nerve activity of the gastric branch of the vagus nerve and adrenal branch of the sympathetic nerve. Jpn. J. Taste Smell Res. **10**(1), 97–102 (2013). (in Japanese)

5. Kawaguchi, K., Kotani, M., Nagai, K.: Effect of the odor of fermented milk on autonomic nerve activity and behavior. Aroma Res. **15**(4), 340–345 (2014). (in Japanese)

6. Niijima, A., Koda, H., Kiso, Y., Nagai, K.: Modulation of autonomic nerve activity by whiskey aroma. Aroma Res. **10**(3), 256–259 (2009). (in Japanese)

7. Shen, J., Niijima, A., Tanida, M., Horii, Y., Maeda, K., Nagai, K.: Olfactory stimulation with scent of grapefruit oil affects autonomic nerves, lipolysis and appetite in rats. Neurosci. Lett. **380**(3), 289–294 (2005)

8. Alvarez, W.C.: The electrogastrogram and what it shows. J. Am. Med. Assoc. **78**, 1116–1118 (1922)

9. Yamanaka, Y., Asahina, M.: Electrogastrogram test. In: Japan Society of Neurovegetative Research. Autonomic Function Test, 5th edn. Bunkodo, Tokyo, pp. 361–364 (2007). (in Japanese)

10. Takada, H., Matsuura, Y., Yokoyama, K.: A study of stochastic resonance as a mathematical model of electrogastrography during supine position. Bull. Gifu Univ. Med. Sci. **3**, 119–123 (2009)

11. Matsuura, Y., Takada, H., Yokoyama, K.: Dependence of Lyapunov exponent on embedding delay in electrogastrography analysis. IEEJ Trans. EIS **129**(12), 2243–2244 (2009). (in Japanese)

12. Matsuura, Y., Takada, H., Yokoyama, K., Shimada, K.: An example of multi-channel electrography analyzed by Wayland algorithm. Jpn. J. Ergon. **43**(4), 228–232 (2007). (in Japanese)

13. Kato, A.: Receptor pharmacology and specificity. In: Touhara, K. (ed.) Science of Chemoreception, pp. 120–133. Kagakudojin, Kyoto (2012). (in Japanese)

14. Inoue, N., Kuroda, K., Sugimoto, A., Kakuda, T., Fushiki, T.: Autonomic nervous responses according to preference for the odor of jasmine tea. Biosci. Biotechnol. Biochem. **67**(6), 1206–1214 (2003)

15. Takai, E., Aoyagi, T., Ichikawa, K., Matsuura, Y., Kinoshita, F., Takada, H.: Effect of olfactory stimulation with vanilla odor on degree of gastric myoelectrical activity. Jpn. J., Hyg (2021). in Press)

16. Murase, C., Kawamoto, R., Sugimoto, S.: Changing of emotions by the stimulation of visual and auditory senses - an analysis of heart rate variability (HRV). J. UOEH **26**(4), 461–471 (2004). (in Japanese)

17. Matsumoto, T., Tokunaga, R., Miyano, T., Tokuda, I.: Chaos and time series, pp. 54–64, Baifukan, Tokyo (2002). (in Japanese)

18. Kanai, H., Tsuji, H., Asanomi, M., Ishizawa, H., Nishimatsu, T., Miyasaka, H.: Influence on heart rate variability and neuronal activity by inhalation of fragrance with different preference. J. Jpn. Soc. Kansei Eng. **7**(3), 469–476 (2008). (in Japanese)

19. Moritaki, N., Inoue, K., Yamazaki, H.: Effect of Japanese dashi on autonomic nervous system activity and mental fatigue in humans. J. Jpn. Soc. Nutr. Food Sci. **71**(3), 133–139 (2018). (in Japanese)

20. Hilz, M.J., Wang, R., Liu, M., Muresanu, D., Flanagan, S., Winder, K., Hösl, K., Hummel, T.: Emotional and autonomic processing of olfactory stimuli is compromised in patients with a history of mild traumatic brain injury. J. Neurotrauma **37**(1), 125–138 (2020)

21. Takada, H., Matsuura, Y., Yokoyama, K.: Analysis of the relationship between electrogastrography and R-R interval time series. Bull. Gifu Univ. Med. Sci. **1**, 27–30 (2007). (in Japanese)

22. Jin, X., Katsuura, T., Iwanaga, K., Shimomura, Y., Inoie, M.: The influence of taste stimuli and illumination on electrogastrogram measurements. J. Physiol. Anthropol. **26**(2), 191–195 (2007)
23. Iwasa, A., Aoki, T.: Physiological and psychological effects by combination of smell and color. Bull. Grad. School Hum. Dev. Env. Kobe Univ. **4**(1), 203–210 (2010). (in Japanese)
24. Ogawa, K., Tashima, A., Sadakata, M., Morinaga, O.: Appetite-enhancing effects of vanilla flavours such as vanillin. J. Nat. Med. **72**(3), 798–802 (2018)

Continual Learning for Object Classification: A Modular Approach

Daniel Turner⊙, Pedro J. S. Cardoso⊙, and João M. F. Rodrigues$^{(\boxtimes)}$ ⊙

LARSyS & ISE, Universidade do Algarve, Faro, Portugal
{pcardoso,jrodrig}@ualg.pt

Abstract. A Human can immediately add new items to its set of known objects, whereas a computer, using traditional computer vision algorithms, would typically have to go almost back to the start and re-learn the all collection of objects (classes) from scratch. The reason the network must be re-trained is due to a phenomenon named Catastrophic Forgetting, where the changes made to the system during the acquisition of new knowledge brings about the loss of previous knowledge. In this paper, we explore the Continual Learning problem by proposing a way to deal with Catastrophic Forgetting. Our proposal includes a framework capable of learning new information without having to start from scratch and even "improve" its knowledge on what it already knows. With the above in mind, we present the Modular Dynamic Neural Network (MDNN), a network primarily made up of modular sub-networks that progressively grows in a tree shape and re-arranges itself as it learns continuously. The network is divided into two main blocks: (a) the feature extraction block, which is based on a ResNet50; and (b) the modular dynamic classification block, which is made up of sub-networks structured in such a way that its internal components function independently from one another. This structure allows that when new information is learned only specific sub-networks are altered in a way that old information is not forgotten. Tests show promising results with a set of ImageNet classes and also with a set of our own classes.

Keywords: Neural Networks · Continual Learning · Catastrophic Forgetting

1 Introduction

McCarthy in 1960 [1] said: *"Our ultimate objective is to make programs that learn from experience as effectively as humans do. It may not be realized how far we are presently from this objective"*. These words are still true, despite the enormous advances in the Artificial Intelligence (AI) field that have occurred since then. This reasoning can easily be extended in terms of Universal Access in Human-Computer Interaction (HCI) as we are still in the process of designing computer technology that produces experiences as effective as humans can transmit.

This paper focusses on the application of this concept to object classification, with the intention to create a framework capable of learning new classes of objects without forgetting previously learned ones. The current state-of-the-art shows that the methods

© Springer Nature Switzerland AG 2021
M. Antona and C. Stephanidis (Eds.): HCII 2021, LNCS 12769, pp. 531–547, 2021.
https://doi.org/10.1007/978-3-030-78095-1_39

most effectively used for object classification are neural network-based. While very effective and widely used, if we decided to add new classes to the previous learned ones, and therefore continued the learning process from where we had left off, this would cause *Catastrophic Forgetting* [2]. This means that after training new classes, the network's ability to recognize old/known classes would be severely reduced.

The usual approach for avoiding this problem when adding a new class would be to simply retrain the (complete) network from scratch, using all the classes that we want the network to recognize. The problem here is that the training process is usually very time consuming, even with powerful machines. While this may not be a problem for some situations, it is if we want to be able to add new classes constantly and consistently. Given that with currently accessible hardware the training process can take anywhere between hours and days, it is impossible for networks to learn multiple classes per day when using this approach. This type of learning problem is referred to as Continual Learning (CL) [3], where a few other names are also commonly used, such as Lifelong Learning [2], Sequential Learning [4] and Incremental Learning [5], all with slight and unclear differences.

The main contribution of the paper is an initial framework that learns new classes without needing to retrain its entire network of classifiers, while coping with the scalability problems that come with expanding architectures.

In this context, project *WELSAFE.DV: Welcome Safety Device* consists of a device that can be placed in a hotel, establishment, or event allowing automatic check-in without touching of the customer/user, including the prediction of some basic body characteristics, such as age. One further feature, that will be integrated into the infrastructure, is the automatic recognition of new objects that are presented on-the-fly to the device, taking advantage of the framework presented in this paper.

The present section introduced the reader to the context and goals of the paper and Sect. 2 includes a state of the art for Continual Learning and some background concepts. Section 3 addresses the architecture, tests and results of the implemented CL framework and, finally, the conclusion and future work is presented in Sect. 4.

2   Related Work

Neural Networks (NN) are currently receiving vast amounts of attention and being applied to all kinds of real-world problems. They are currently the natural choice for dealing with images when it comes to detection, recognition and classification of persons, objects or scenes. Many studies about Continual Learning use humans as an ideal example of continual learners [2, 4, 6, 7]. The reason for this is that, as is the case with NN, many of the ideas behind CL are inspired by how investigators presume our brains work.

In this context, Continual Learning, means being able to update the prediction model for new tasks while still being able to reuse and retain knowledge from previous tasks. CL problems assume an incremental setting, where tasks are received one at a time and, most studies on the matter, also consider the non-storage of data to be an essential characteristic of a continual learner. Lomonaco *et al.* [8] proposed CORe50, a dataset and benchmark that is more appropriate for testing CL methods when compared with normal image datasets. CORe50 takes different factors into account, like the image capture order and different levels of illumination and occlusion. She *et al.* [7] then tested a variety of CL methods on this dataset to get an idea of their behavior in real-world environments and concluded that the current algorithms are far from ready to face such complex problems.

Requeima *et al.* [9] approach multi-task classification using *Conditional Neural Adaptive Processes*, and while this may not directly be considered a CL method, it can be applied to CL scenarios. De Lange *et al.* [6] studied a variety of CL methods and organized them in the form of a tree diagram, where they sorted 29 different methods into categories and sub-categories. The authors concluded that iCaRL [10] was the leading performer for replay-based methods, MAS [4] was the leading performer for regularization-based methods, and PackNet [11] was the leading performer for parameter isolation methods. However, all the methods featured their advantages and limitations with regards to each other, e.g., PackNet showed the most promising accuracy but, although it can learn a large number of tasks, it does have a limit based on the size of the model. For a detailed explanation of each method please see [6].

Van de Ven *et al.* [12] apply a range of CL methods to three different scenarios of increasing difficulty, as a way of comparing their performance in different situations. In the first scenario, the models are informed about the identity of the task to be performed, meaning that the model can choose to use specific components to perform the task at hand. In the second scenario, the identity of the task is no longer available, but the model is only required to solve the given task and not necessarily identify what task it has performed. In the third scenario, the model must be able to solve a given task and identify what task it was presented with. Parisi *et al.* [2] also discussed three different approaches to CL (they refer to it as lifelong learning). The first approach they introduce is based on retraining the entire network with regularization, meaning that they deal with Catastrophic Forgetting by applying constraints to the update of the neural network weights. The second approach selectively trains sections of the network and expands it as needed, acting as a type of dynamic architecture that adds new neurons dedicated to new information. And the third approach consists of methods that model complementary learning systems for memory consolidation, where they distinguish between learning and memorizing.

Pellegrini *et al.* [13] present latent replay for real-time CL. In their work, the authors divide the low-level feature extraction and high-level feature extraction. Furthermore, they control the rate at which each one of the levels are trained in such a way that, when trained on new data, the low-level feature extraction is altered very little or not at all. This strategy makes possible for them to store intermediate data to be retrained alongside new data when new classes are learned, without having to re-perform low-level feature extraction to the stored data.

While there are mentions of CL as early as the 1990s, where concepts and ideas are mentioned, almost all research with practical testing and applications has only been made very recently. The fact that many of the researched papers use different terms for CL, and the fact that there are no standard categorizations for CL methods or consistent descriptions of CL are indicators of just how new this area of study is in terms of practical applications. The state-of-the-art shows, especially the most recent papers, that there are many existing CL methodological approaches with many differences between them. They vary to such an extent that it is hard to find a situation where they could all be applied, which would allow us to easily compare them. Nevertheless, some of the papers mentioned show similarities to the framework that will be proposed, and we will discuss this along the paper.

3 Modular Dynamic Neural Network

Our proposal, the *Modular Dynamic Neural Network* (MDNN), is a network primarily made up of modular sub-networks that progressively grows and re-arranges itself as it learns continuously. The network is structured in such a way that its internal components function independently from one another. This structure allows that when new information is learned only specific sub-networks are altered, in such a way that old information is not forgotten. The network is divided into two main blocks: (a) *feature extraction* and (b) *modular dynamic classification.*

For the first part of the network, (a) *feature extraction*, we used a pre-trained ResNet50 [14] as a backbone, which has been shown to yield exceptional results in image classification, e.g. see [15]. This feature extraction block is used only to extract generic "low-level" features, while class-specific features will be extracted by much smaller and simpler (modular) networks in the dynamic classification block. The feature extraction part of our network is the only part which is never altered when learning new classes, because the components in the next block depend on it to be consistent.

The second part of the network, the (b) *modular dynamic classification* block, is comprised of multiple small modules. These modules are responsible for classifying specific classes or groups of classes that, as new information is learned, are automatically divided into groups of modules and sub-modules based on their class's similarities. Figure 1 shows how the sub-modules fit into the proposed architecture: the modules containing information inside brackets are modules that contain sub-modules (e.g., $[X_1, X_2, \ldots, X_{n_x}]$) or groups of sub-modules in the case of nested brackets (e.g., $[[X_1, X_2, \ldots, X_{n_x}], \ldots])$, where X_1 to X_{n_x} are modules with no children and n_x is the number of sub-modules belonging to their parent. The modules which contain their own sub-modules are designated as *node modules* and they contain one binary classifier for each direct child module. The modules with no children are designated as *endpoint modules* and contain only data obtained during the training process.

When the network is learning new information, the data obtained by the feature extraction component is stored within the *endpoint modules* for later use, specifically for when some classifiers have to be retrained to avoid confusion with a new class. It is important to emphasize that the data preserved from each class is not the class data in its raw format, but the features extracted from the inputs, which should have a smaller dimension. In the case of the adopted ResNet50, after being re-sized using nearest-neighbor interpolation, each sample image with a dimension of 224×224 pixels (px) and 3 colour channels ($224 \times 224 \times 3$) is reduced to a 1×2048 vector.

This module-based structure allows our network to have a dynamic growth that fits well with our objective of coping with the scalability problems, that normally accompany this type of approach. This is achieved because our modular structure makes it possible to make classifications without using the entire network. Ensuring that certain sections of the network can work independently from one another makes, it possible to alter or add modules without affecting others. This means that by treating sections of the network as modules, where each one is responsible for a given class or group of classes, we can safely add, remove or alter parts of our networks' knowledge base without affecting the rest.

Finally, it is important to stress that there are other viable options that could substitute the selected feature extraction backbone (ResNet50), such as VGG16, Inception, or EfficientNet [17–19]. In the future, comparative tests will be done using feature extraction sections from different networks.

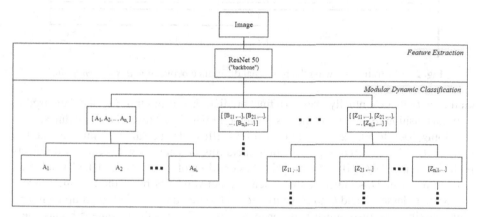

Fig. 1. Modular Dynamic Neural Network architecture.

3.1 Modular Dynamic Classification

As mentioned, the modules present in our network are of two different types: (a) *endpoints,* which are responsible for the storage of the feature data extracted from a single class during training, and (b) *nodes,* which contain references to two or more sub-modules and a *binary classifier* for each one of those sub-modules. Each of these sub-modules can then also be *endpoints* or *nodes.* Figure 2 top illustrates the difference between *nodes* and *endpoints* with a basic demonstration of a possible network with three classes.

Each module of the *node* type has its own set of binary classifiers, which, in this case, are NN that output two values: a confidence value for "true" and a confidence value for "false" (both between 0 and 1), where the definition of what is true and what is false depends on the *node* and its position in the network. Each binary classifier represents one of a nodes' sub-modules. In the first case we have the ones that represent *endpoints,* which define "true" as the one and only class they are responsible for, and "false" as the classes present in all the other modules and sub-modules in parallel with that *endpoint.* In the second case we have the classifiers that represent *nodes,* which consider all their own sub-module classes as "true" and all the classes present in the other parallel modules and sub-module as "false". During classification, these binary classifiers are used to determine which sub-module to continue through and define a

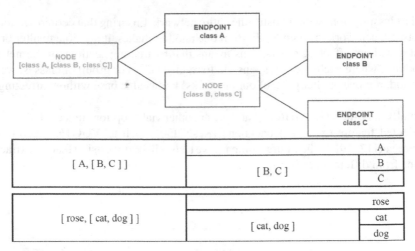

Fig. 2. Illustration showing the positional difference between *nodes* and *endpoints*.

kind of path that eventually leads to a final prediction. During training, they are used in a similar fashion to determine the best location in which to "insert" new modules.

Going back to Fig. 2 the bottom two rows illustrate the same example as the top figure but with a different representation, including an analogy with real world objects in the last one. Classes B and C are joined as children of a *node* (*node* [B, C]) and class A is on its own. This indicates that when this network was built, the training process considered classes B and C to be similar to each other, and decided to group them and train classifiers to distinguish between A and B ∪ C. And then, some sub-classifiers were trained to specialize in distinguishing between classes B and C. To clarify, in the example, there are 4 binary classifiers, namely to distinguish: A (against [B, C]), [B, C] (against A), B (against C), and C (against B).

Going into more detail, each *Binary Classifier* (BC) present in the network has the exact same structure, but of course different trained weights. In other words, the number of layers, the number of neurons in each layer, the connections, the activation functions etc. are all the same, and the only difference between them is their trained weights. The main reason for this is to maintain consistency and give all the classifiers an equal chance of success and to avoid "favoritism". This is important because there are points during classification and training processes where comparisons are made between the predictions of the different classifiers.

The structure used for the binary classifiers consists of six fully connected layers with the following numbers of neurons: 128, 64, 64, 32, 32 and 2 respectively. The final layers' activation function is a Sigmoid function.

Figure 3 shows the full MDNN architecture in more detail: the top row shows a simplified representation of the ResNet50 feature extraction and the bottom shows how the network's structure is extremely flexible and how there is no limit to how many sub-modules a *node* can have or to how many sub-modules those sub-modules can have. The figure's bottom also shows how the maximum is used to decide which submodule to continue the process with. For our network to meet its purpose of distinguishing classes from other classes, the minimum number of classes the network can initialize with is two. Therefore, the root module will always be a *node,* as *endpoints* only ever represent one class and *nodes* are the only modules which can contain more modules.

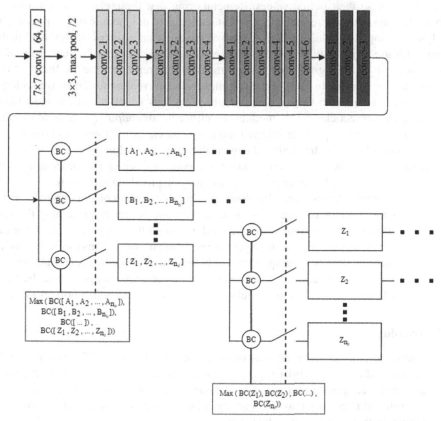

Fig. 3. MDNN architecture: at the top, ResNet50 architecture [20] – feature extraction block; at the bottom, the modular dynamic classification block (using a simplified notation of Fig. 1).

It is important to remember that every time we call upon a binary classifier, no matter where it is located in the network, the input values are always the same feature values which were extracted once from the data sample being classified. The positioning of modules within other modules is simply used to decide if and which other modules should be used, but the feature data itself is never altered. It is important to clarify this because, when thinking of a tree-like structure that uses NN one might easily confuse it with a single network in a tree format, like that which is seen in [21] where everything is backward-dependent. Therefore, it must be noted that our "tree" is merely a representation of the order in which things are done and which data is used by each binary classifier. All in all, the data is not transformed intermediately, i.e., the input data for the last modules is the same as it was for the first modules.

Because of the way our dynamic network is structured, the classification process can be recursive, because when it is applied to different *nodes* of the network, those results will determine whether it should be re-applied to certain *sub-nodes,* i.e., the classification process is (i) first applied to the root *node* and then, possibly, (ii) recursively applied to other *nodes* depending on the results.

So, the first step is to apply the extracted features to all the classifiers in the current *node* and analyse their output values. Remembering that these classifiers tell us how certain they are that the presented sample data belongs to the module they represent, by applying our input sample's features to each of the binary classifiers (represented in the figure with the formula $BC(X) \in [0, 1]$), we will obtain a group of values between 0 and 1 (because of the sigmoid activation function) that represent the likeliness of our input sample belonging to each of the modules in the current *node*. Then, we seek out the maximum value from these results, which will tell us which module is most likely to include the correct class. This module can either be an *endpoint* or a *node* and that will dictate the next step. If the selected module is an *endpoint*, then the classification process is complete, and the predicted class is the class that belongs to that *endpoint*. If the selected module is a *node* then we enter that *node* and repeat this process until the selected module is eventually an *endpoint* resulting in a final classification.

This implementation is something that makes us able to meet one of our main objectives where we aim to avoid scalability issues. We manage this because only the sub-classifiers in the highest-scoring *nodes* are used, meaning that, in a lot of cases, we can make classifications using only a small percentage of the network. This means that as the network grows our classification speed will only be slowed down for similar classes that get grouped together, because a bit more time is required to make distinctions between them. In the future, we will explore solutions to optimize the classification process.

3.2 Training

The addition of a new class begins with the network being fed a set of data samples and a label, and with this, the network can: (i) process the data samples, (ii) decide where best to place the new endpoint, (iii) make any necessary adjustments to the existing modules, and (iv) train the necessary classifiers so that when the network is presented with data of the same class in future it can identify it.

Figure 4 right side depicts an example of how the network can change as new classes are added. Here it starts off able to classify three classes, A-rose, B-cat, and C-dog, where B and C are grouped together. Then four more classes are added one at a time (D-tree, E-fish, F-bush, and G-frog) making it able to classify a total of seven classes. The position in which new classes are placed in the network is not random. There are several processes involved in calculating the optimal position for a new class, some of which can be recursive. When we want our network to learn a new class, we are essentially asking it to be able to tell the new class apart from the ones which have already been learned. This brings us to the most important priority of our class placement process: avoiding conflict/confusion between classes. The best way, we propose, to avoid confusion between classes is to group them by their similarities and then focus on their differences. This concept of grouping classes refers to the placement of modules in parallel within a node, as seen in Fig. 4, where, for example, in the first state of the network class B is grouped with class C.

To find similarities between a new class and existing classes, we make use of the binary classifiers placed within the nodes. The process of identifying similar classes is

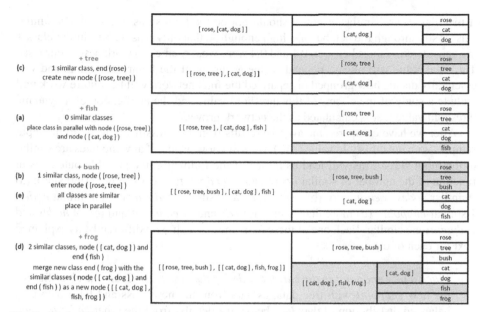

Fig. 4. Right side, the demonstration of how the network can grow progressively by adding and joining modules. The modules highlighted in green are new modules and the modules highlighted in blue are pre-existing modules that had to be retrained either to avoid confusion or to ensure that the parent nodes are aware of the new class. Left side, a description of the intermediate steps taken for the addition of each class.

relatively similar to the classification process, but instead of only searching for the single most similar class, here we are searching for any number of partially similar classes. I.e., we are looking for somewhere to place our new class. When we enter a *node*, we are faced with *n* possible routes to follow which can be a mix of *endpoints* and/or *nodes* and the idea is that any of our *node* or *endpoint* classifiers that might accidentally mistake the new class for their own should be grouped with the new class and retrained, so that when presented with samples of the new class in the future they do not make the same mistake again. To achieve this, we must first see which *nodes/endpoints* are at all similar to our new class. Thus, the first thing we do is classify all the samples of our new class with all the classifiers in the current node, and then we can use these results to decide on how best to proceed.

Once we have all the current *node's* classifier results from all the new samples, we move on to calculate the average certainty per classifier, which gives us a single value for each one, representing how likely it is to mistake the new class for its own class (or classes if it represents a *node*). We should notice that, the use of the average was the first natural choice for an initial proof-of-concept, but in the future, we will be looking for other solutions, to achieve better classes discrimination.

These average values can now be easily analyzed to see which classes are the most like our new class. By establishing a threshold value AV_c to compare these values with (in the initial case, AV_c was empirically set to 0.3), we can use that comparison to make a final decision on whether a class is similar or not. As this threshold value is what decides if two classes are similar or not, it should not be too high so as to not let any similar classes slip through the net, but also high enough so that only reasonably similar classes are considered. Values between 0.1 and 0.4 were what seemed to work best in our tests. The ideal value will always depend on the accuracy of the binary classifiers and will essentially decide how grouped or separated the final network will be. Future work will include a study of the effects of this threshold value and the application of a dynamic threshold value that is calculated as the network grows.

After we have compared the average results from the classifications of all the input samples with the threshold value (AV_c), we will know which, if any, modules are similar to the input class. This will lead us to one of the following five possible outcomes in function of the number of similar *nodes* and/or *endpoints*, see also Fig. 4 (left side): (a) 0 similar *nodes* or *endpoints*; (b) 1 similar *node*, 0 similar *endpoints*; (c) 0 similar *nodes*, 1 similar *endpoint*; (d) more than 1 similar *node* and/or *endpoint* and (e) all *nodes* and *endpoints* are similar. Each one of these outcomes is dealt with differently, as explained next for each of the cases:

(a) *Place a new endpoint in the current node for the new class.* Train the classifier for the new *endpoint* with true data, as data from the new class and false data as a balanced distribution of data (see below for details) from the other *endpoints* and *nodes* present within in the current node.

(b) *Enter that similar node and repeat the positioning process over the subtree.*

(c) *Create a new node and place inside it a new endpoint for the new class as well as the endpoint that was matched with the new class.* Train the classifier for the new *endpoint* with true data as data from the new class and false data as data from the class it was matched with. Retrain the classifier for the pre-existing *endpoint* that was moved into the new *node* with its true data as the data it was stored with and false data as data from the new class.

(d) *Create a new node and place inside it a new endpoint for the new class as well as all the endpoints/nodes that were matched with the new class.* Train the classifier for the new *endpoint* with true data as data from the new class and false data as a balanced distribution of the data from all the other *nodes/endpoints* it was matched with. Retrain the classifiers for all the pre-existing *nodes* and *endpoints* which were moved into the new *node* using balanced distributions of their own data as true data and balanced distributions of their sibling's data as false data. The children modules of the *nodes* that were moved into the new *node* do not need to be touched as they are not backward dependent and only relate to each other.

(e) *Place a new endpoint in the current node for the new class.* Train the classifier for the new *endpoint* with true data as data from the new class and false data as a balanced distribution of data from the other *endpoints* and *nodes* present in the current *node*. Retrain the classifiers for all the pre-existing *nodes* and *endpoints* in the current *node* using balanced distributions of their data as true data and balanced distributions of their sibling's data as false data.

Of the above processes, case (ii) is the only one which does not involve placing the new class or training any networks, but it does repeat the entire process applied to an identified sub-node and eventually, there will be a point where there are no more sub-nodes and case (ii) will no longer be an option so, the new class is guaranteed to eventually be placed somewhere in the network.

Once the new class has been placed within the network, it is necessary to retrain the parent *node* to also consider the new class as true data so as to increase the chance of success of the classification process, by increasing the chance that future samples of the new class will reach their respective endpoint. This retraining of the parent *node* must then be applied to the parent of the parent, and the parent of the parent of the parent, and so on and so forth, until reaching the root node of the network. This process helps to guarantee that, when presented with samples of the new class in the future, the initial *nodes* will be more likely to send the data down the correct path.

As we are using the same classifiers for the training process that we use for the classification of new data, when we retrain/correct the most problematic parts of the network, we are immediately making drastic improvements to the classification process. This is due to the fact that we are predicting and correcting the modules that will cause the most errors after adding the new class before they even become a problem.

3.3 Balanced Training Data

Neural networks are proven to have higher success rates when trained on balanced data [22], meaning that they should, in principle, be trained with approximately the same number of samples per class. And, as we are dealing with binary classifiers (deciding between two classes: true and false), this means that we should, in principle, aim for an equal number of true and false samples leaving us to tackle the problem of what to do when we have a different number of each.

The algorithm implemented for selecting training samples calculates the maximum possible number of samples per class that can maintain an optimal distribution based on their positions in the network. In our situation, where we have various groups of classes with their own sub-groups, an optimal distribution does not mean using the same number of samples for each class. It means that the same number of samples should be used from each of a *nodes'* children, i.e., if one of these children is an *endpoint* and one is a *node* then the same number of samples will be used from each, where the *nodes'* samples will be a mix of its children's samples and so on. For example (recall Fig. 2), if we were training a classifier to recognize an *endpoint* A as true and a *node* [B, C] as false, and A, B and C all had n samples each, a balanced distribution for this classifier would be n samples of A and n samples of [B, C]. Then, to maintain an equal distribution, the n samples of [B, C] would consist of $n/2$ samples of B and $n/2$ samples of C.

This example makes the problem seem quite straightforward, but when we have different numbers of samples per class and a more complex network, with various nested modules on both the true and the false side, it is necessary to have an algorithm that can calculate the optimal distribution for any situation and still make use of as many samples as possible. Maintaining this equal distribution signifies that, alongside with the network's depth, the classes with fewer samples will dictate how many samples can be used from the classes with more samples. So, it is recommended to establish a *minimum number of samples (MNS)* to use when a class is added to the network to reduce this effect (MNS as set equal to 175 in our case). More tests will be done in the future to determine the best *MNS* value.

There are two main steps to this process: (i) The first one is to calculate the largest possible number of samples that permits us to use the distribution we just explained. To do this, we multiply the number of sub-modules in the *node* by the number of samples of the sub-module with the smallest number of samples. The number of samples to be used from the sub-modules which are also *nodes* are calculated the same way. This means the process is applied recursively until all the sub-modules that belong to the *node* we are calculating have also been calculated. When this process finishes, we end up with the maximum number of samples that lets us maintain an equal distribution for the *node* requested.

So, let M_p be the maximum possible number of samples that lets us maintain an equal distribution for the *node* being calculated, and $M_{p,i}$ represents the maximum number of samples that can be used by one of the node's sub-modules, with p representing the path created by the indexations that lead to the location of the *node* in question. E.g., in the final state of the network shown in Fig. 4, the path to reach the *node* "[cat, dog]" would be the second sub-module of the root *node* and then the first sub-module of that *node*. Meaning that for the *node* "[cat, dog]", the indexations represented by p would be "2,1", and the number of samples present in the *endpoint* "dog" would be "$M_{2,1,2}$". The value of n_p represents the number of sub-modules present in the node being calculated, and M the number of samples which is computed as follows:

$$M = n_p \times \min(M_{p,1}, M_{p,2}, \ldots, M_{p,n_p}). \tag{1}$$

(ii) The second step is to recursively divide this number by the number of children in a *node* until all the *endpoints* are reached, leaving us with a number of samples to use per class. For that we use the value obtained from the first step (the maximum possible number of samples that lets us maintain an equal distribution) and progressively divide it throughout our network. The *node* being calculated distributes its number evenly between its children. The children that are also *nodes* then do the same thing with their values to their own children, resulting in sub-divided values. This is repeated until all sub-modules of the initial *node* are reached and eventually results in a final number of samples to be used for each class (E_p). With the value of M_p calculated in part one, it is possible to compute $E_{p,i}$, which is essentially the value of M_p evenly distributed between each of the node's sub-modules.

While in step one the values of the parents depended on the values of the children, in step two the values of the children depend on the values of the parents. To initialize the process, the *node* being calculated has its value set with $E_p = M_p$ and then its sub-module's values are calculated as $E_{p,1} = E_{p,2} = \ldots = E_{p,n_p} = E_p/n_p$. Then, each sub-modules' are calculated the same way until all the *endpoints* that are descendants of the *node* being calculated are reached, which will eventually result in a series of final numbers of samples to be used from each *endpoint*.

4   Tests and Results

Continual Learning networks do not have many well-known and reputable datasets for their validation. While some do exist, they do not hold the same reputation as popular datasets like ImageNet [16]. One of the datasets we mentioned in the state-of-the-art,

Core50 [8], while created for the purpose of CL validation, is structured in such a way that is not compatible with how our network learns. In Core50, data samples from already known classes are also presented as training data, to attempt improve the knowledge of previously known classes, but our architecture currently learns one class at a time. While it is included in our future work to develop ways to perform that type of learning as well, due to time constraints, we decided to perform our tests on ImageNet and some classes from our own dataset.

Because our network learns over time, we decided to re-calculate the accuracy values every time we added another class, to show how the accuracy evolved over time/new class additions. We demonstrate the accuracy per class as well as the global accuracy, and we also show the evolution of the modular network over time. We performed one test using some random classes (11) from the ImageNet dataset. The ImageNet dataset consists of 1,000 classes with a different number of samples per class and images of different sizes. The reason we did not perform a full set of tests with the ImageNet dataset is the training and classification processes are very costly in terms of processing power, nevertheless, this is intended to be done as future work.

All ImageNet tests were performed using 400 images from each class (300 for training and 100 for testing). The network's final structure for the test with 11 classes can be seen in Fig. 5 top/middle, and Fig. 5 bottom shows how the accuracy behaves when we classify more/different classes, with accuracy being defined by the number of correct predictions divided by the total number of predictions.

We start with two classes, "airplane propeller" and "almond tree", and after that, as each new class is learned, we present the accuracy result for the new class as well as for the already known classes. It is important to stress that this result shows only "*1 run*", which means that there was no selection of best or worst results, but just one random run. The column labelled as "11" shows the final accuracy of the framework *per* class. Of the 11 classes, 2 (~18%) of the classes (marked in red) present very poor results, 4 classes (~36%) present accuracy between 0.70 and 0.90 (marked in yellow), and 5 (~45%) present accuracy results above 0.90 (marked in green). The overall mean accuracy is 0.81. Looking at the last line in Fig. 5 bottom row, it appears, that as more classes are added to the network, the overall accuracy is more or less stable except for two significant decreases in columns 3 and 8. These two decreases happened when the two lowest scoring classes were added to the network ("alyssum" and "astilbe"). These classes are somewhat similar as they are both plants and, although they were grouped together, it appears that the binary classifiers responsible for specializing in distinguishing between the two classes did not do a good enough job in this case.

The other test consists of image samples acquired using a regular HD webcam in a "natural" environment with no additional illumination or any other special care. Two classes of object were used: "teacup" and "glass bottle". For that, video data was acquired by filming different objects of those classes with different view angles. Images to train our network with were then extracted as frames from the final videos in intervals of 0.5 s and then fed to the network to perform the learning process. New objects were filmed to generate the test data. These new objects were from the two classes that were learned but they were not present in the training videos. This was to make sure the resulting network was not generalized to the specific objects present in the training videos. For

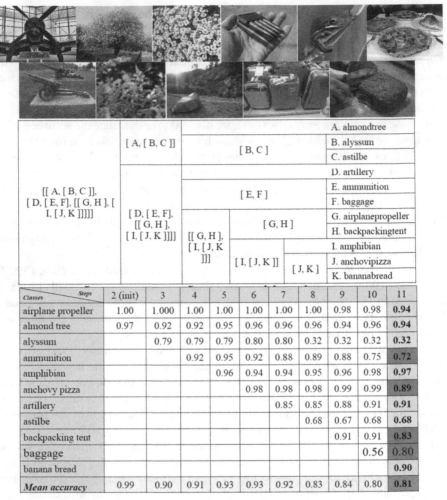

					A. almondtree
	[A, [B, C]]		[B, C]		B. alyssum
					C. astilbe
[[A, [B, C]], [D, [E, F], [[G, H], [I, [J, K]]]]]					D. artillery
	[D, [E, F], [[G, H], [I, [J, K]]]]	[E, F]			E. ammunition
					F. baggage
				[G, H]	G. airplanepropeller
		[[G, H], [I, [J, K]]]			H. backpackingtent
			[I, [J, K]]		I. amphibian
				[J, K]	J. anchovipizza
					K. bananabread

Classes \ Steps	2 (init)	3	4	5	6	7	8	9	10	11
airplane propeller	1.00	1.000	1.00	1.00	1.00	1.00	1.00	0.98	0.98	**0.94**
almond tree	0.97	0.92	0.92	0.95	0.96	0.96	0.96	0.94	0.96	**0.94**
alyssum		0.79	0.79	0.79	0.80	0.80	0.32	0.32	0.32	**0.32**
ammunition			0.92	0.95	0.92	0.88	0.89	0.88	0.75	**0.72**
amphibian				0.96	0.94	0.94	0.95	0.96	0.98	**0.97**
anchovy pizza					0.98	0.98	0.98	0.99	0.99	**0.89**
artillery						0.85	0.85	0.88	0.91	**0.91**
astilbe							0.68	0.67	0.68	**0.68**
backpacking tent								0.91	0.91	**0.83**
baggage									0.56	0.80
banana bread										**0.90**
Mean accuracy	0.99	0.90	0.91	0.93	0.93	0.92	0.83	0.84	0.80	**0.81**

Fig. 5. Top, representation of the resulting network structure of a test performed using 11 classes from ImageNet. Bottom, the accuracy per step/class addition. (Color figure online)

each of new class 390 frames were used to train the network and 130 were used to test its performance.

In Fig. 6, the top two rows show examples of images of the two new classes, "teacup" and "glass bottle", that were added to the existing network (from the ImageNet test with 11 classes). The third row shows how the original network structure (shown in Fig. 5 middle row) grew to learn the two new classes, which naturally resulted in a slightly larger network (right). Figure 6 bottom shows how the two new classes affected the accuracy results for each of the 11 previously learned ImageNet classes. It also presents the new, overall, accuracy of the network (0.82). The final accuracies for "glass bottle" and "teacup" were 0.89 and 0.99 respectively. The final accuracies for all the classes learned by the network are presented in the last column ("13"). Out of the 13 classes, 2

(~15%) (marked in red) presented very poor results, 6 (~46%) presented results between 0.70 and 0.90 (marked in yellow), and 5 (~38%) presented accuracy results above 0.90 (marked in green).

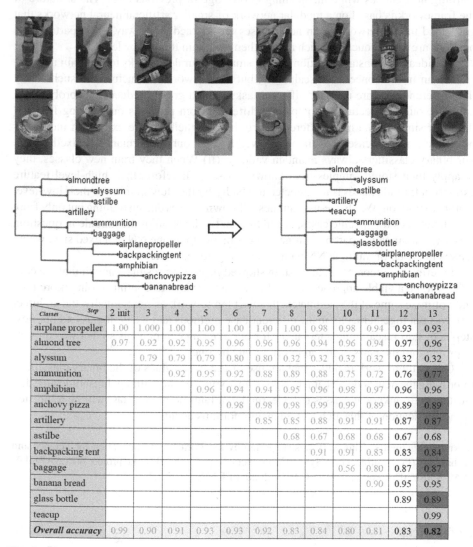

Classes \ Step	2 init	3	4	5	6	7	8	9	10	11	12	13
airplane propeller	1.00	1.000	1.00	1.00	1.00	1.00	1.00	0.98	0.98	0.94	0.93	0.93
almond tree	0.97	0.92	0.92	0.95	0.96	0.96	0.96	0.94	0.96	0.94	0.97	0.96
alyssum		0.79	0.79	0.79	0.80	0.80	0.32	0.32	0.32	0.32	0.32	0.32
ammunition			0.92	0.95	0.92	0.88	0.89	0.88	0.75	0.72	0.76	0.77
amphibian				0.96	0.94	0.94	0.95	0.96	0.98	0.97	0.96	0.96
anchovy pizza					0.98	0.98	0.98	0.99	0.99	0.89	0.89	0.89
artillery						0.85	0.85	0.88	0.91	0.91	0.87	0.87
astilbe							0.68	0.67	0.68	0.68	0.67	0.68
backpacking tent								0.91	0.91	0.83	0.83	0.84
baggage									0.56	0.80	0.87	0.87
banana bread										0.90	0.95	0.95
glass bottle											0.89	0.89
teacup												0.99
Overall accuracy	0.99	0.90	0.91	0.93	0.93	0.92	0.83	0.84	0.80	0.81	0.83	0.82

Fig. 6. The top two rows are images of the two new classes that were added the network, those classes being "glass bottle" and "teacup" respectively. The third row shows the transition between the network from the ImageNet test with 11 classes (left, from Fig. 5 top row) and the same network after the addition of two new classes (right). Bottom row, accuracy over time/class - addition of 2 new classes obtained from video footage to the network previously created using 11 ImageNet classes shown in Fig. 5 bottom row. (Color figure online)

5 Conclusions

We have presented a proof-of-concept of an image classification framework, capable of learning new classes while maintaining knowledge of previous ones. The structure of the framework is based on a modular network of smaller artificial neural networks that get added to the network when new classes are learned. This way, other parts of the network are left untouched which allows them to retain their knowledge.

The idea of a constant addition of new smaller neural networks to the main network creates an initial concern for scalability, but the network is structured in such a way that different parts are used for different tasks, which greatly reduces this problem. In addition, our architecture is completely different from previous ones, being LR [13] the most similar. The main differences are that: (i) their feature extraction method is not static (in some cases it is trained slowly), where ours is permanently fixed so that our binary classifiers always maintain validity. (ii) When they train new classes, they re-apply their stored samples from known classes. Therefore, their high-level feature extraction for old classes is not affected too badly by the slow training of their low-level feature extraction. We also re-use samples of known classes during training but only from specific classes for specific cases, depending on the location of the module in question. (iii) The classification part of their network is made up of one NN of a fixed size, where ours is made up of multiple NN with more being added as needed.

In terms of outcomes, initial testing showed promising results, enough that we consider it to be a viable approach to CL, but we are anxious to continue doing more tests and optimize some of the parameters that we plan to work on next. Finally, the architecture was put together using many different base methods and technologies and our next step is to start researching alternatives for our existing components so that we can start improving all the parts of the architecture one by one.

Other future work includes making use of the false values of the binary classifiers, improving the new node placement algorithm, exploring the training threshold value and clustering of unknown classes to be learned at a later point. The last will be a big step in the application of this architecture in autonomous agents.

Acknowledgements. This work was supported by the Portuguese Foundation for Science and Technology (FCT), project LARSyS - FCT Project UIDB/50009/2020 and project WELSAFE.DV (AAC 15/SI/2020) Portugal 2020, CRESC 2020, FEDER.

References

1. McCarthy, J.: Programs with common sense. In: RLE and MIT Computation Center (1960). http://jmc.stanford.edu/articles/mcc59.html. Accessed 30 Nov 2020
2. Parisi, G.I., Kemker, R., Part, J.L., Kanan, C., Wermter, S.: Continual lifelong learning with neural networks: a review. Neural Netw. **113**, 54–71 (2019)
3. Ebrahimi, S., Meier, F., Calandra, R., Darrell, T., Rohrbach, M.: Adversarial continual learning. In: Vedaldi, A., Bischof, H., Brox, T., Frahm, J.-M. (eds.) ECCV 2020. LNCS, vol. 12356, pp. 386–402. Springer, Cham (2020). https://doi.org/10.1007/978-3-030-58621-8_23

4. Aljundi, R., Rohrbach, M., Tuytelaars, T.: Selfless sequential learning. In: Proceedings of 7th International Conference on Learning Representations, arXiv preprint arXiv:1806.05421 (2019)

5. Chen, C.P., Liu, Z.: Broad learning system: an effective and efficient incremental learning system without the need for deep architecture. IEEE Trans Neural Netw. Learn. Syst. **29**(1), 10–24 (2017)

6. De Lange, M., et al.: Continual learning: a comparative study on how to defy forgetting in classification tasks. arXiv preprint arXiv:1909.08383 (2019)

7. She, Q., et al.: OpenLORIS-Object: a dataset and benchmark towards lifelong object recognition. In: Proceedings of International Conference on Robotics and Automation, pp. 4767–4773 (2020)

8. Lomonaco, V., Maltoni, D.: CORe50: a new dataset and benchmark for continuous object recognition. In: Proceedings of 1st Conference on Robot Learning, in PMLR, vol. 78, pp. 17–26 (2017)

9. Requeima, J., Gordon, J., Bronskill, J., Nowozin, S., Turner, R.E.: Fast and flexible multi-task classification using conditional neural adaptive processes. Adv. Neural Inf. Process. Syst. **33**, 7957–7968 (2019)

10. Rebuffi, S.A., Kolesnikov, A., Sperl, G., Lampert, C.H.: iCaRL: incremental classifier and representation learning. In: Proceedings of IEEE Conference on Computer Vision and Pattern Recognition, pp. 2001–2010 (2017)

11. Mallya, A., Lazebnik, S.: PackNet: adding multiple tasks to a single network by iterative pruning. In: Proceedings of IEEE Conference on Computer Vision and Pattern Recognition, pp. 7765–7773 (2018)

12. van de Ven, G.M., Tolias, A.S.: Three continual learning scenarios and a case for generative replay In: Proceedings of 7th International Conference on Learning Representations, arXiv preprint arXiv:1904.07734 (2019)

13. Pellegrini, L., Graffieti, G., Lomonaco, V., Maltoni, D.: Latent replay for real-time continual learning. In: Proceedings of IEEE/RSJ International Conference on Intelligent Robots and Systems, arXiv preprint arXiv:1912.01100 (2020)

14. He, K., Zhang, X., Ren, S., Sun, J.: Deep residual learning for image recognition. In: Proceedings of IEEE Conference on Computer Vision and Pattern Recognition, pp. 770–778 (2016)

15. Sharma, N., Jain, V., Mishra, A.: An analysis of convolutional neural networks for image classification. Procedia Comput. Sci. **132**, 377–384 (2018)

16. Deng, J., Dong, W., Socher, R., Li, L. J., Li, K., Fei-Fei, L.:. ImageNet: a large-scale hierarchical image database. In: Proceedings of IEEE Conference on Computer Vision and Pattern Recognition, pp. 248–255 (2009)

17. Simonyan, K., Zisserman, A.: Very deep convolutional networks for large-scale image recognition. In: Proceedings of International Conference on Learning Representations arXiv preprint arXiv:1409.1556 (2015)

18. Szegedy, C., Vanhoucke, V., Ioffe, S., Shlens, J., Wojna, Z.: Rethinking the inception architecture for computer vision. In: Proceedings of IEEE Conference on Computer Vision and Pattern Recognition, pp. 2818–2826 (2016)

19. Tan, M., Le, Q.V.: EfficientNet: rethinking model scaling for convolutional neural networks. In: Proceedings of 26th International Conference on Machine Learning, arXiv preprint arXiv: 1905.11946 (2019)

20. Fang, W., et al.: Recognizing global reservoirs from landsat 8 images: a deep learning approach. IEEE J. Sel. Top. Appl. Earth Obser. Remote Sens. **12**(9), 3168–3177 (2019)

21. Wan, A., et al.: NBDT: neural-backed decision trees. arXiv preprint arXiv:2004.00221 (2020)

22. Hensman, P., Masko, D.: The impact of imbalanced training data for convolutional neural networks. Degree Project in Computer Science, KTH Royal Institute of Technology (2015)

Author Index

Actis-Grosso, Rossana I-3
Alexander, Andrew I-639
Almeida, Leonelo Dell Anhol I-166
Altieri, Alex I-521
Alvarez-Robles, Teresita II-485
Alvarez Rodríguez, Francisco II-3
Alves, Joana I-136
Amat, Ashwaq Zaini I-339
Ametoglou, Gkioulan II-72
Amin, Akhter Al II-189, II-202
Anceaux, Françoise I-71
Andriamahery-Ranjalahy, Ken H. II-12
Antonaci, Francesca Giada I-599
Antunes, D. R. II-25, II-167
Aoyagi, Takahiro II-519
Apedo, Kodzo I-418
Arbore, Andrea II-358

Baird, Alice I-617
Batselé, Elise I-418
Berget, Gerd II-221
Bernabé, Rocío II-241
Berquez, Léa II-12
Bong, Way Kiat I-116
Boutiflat, Mathilde I-418
Brahmankar, Yugeshwari I-444
Breen, Michael I-339, I-533
Bruce, Carrie I-89
Buchet, Elise I-418
Bueno, Juliana I-461, II-82, II-167
Bühler, Christian II-328
Burzagli, Laura II-347
Byrnes, Nathan I-339

Calmels, Charline I-21
Canal, M. C. II-167
Canteri, R. II-167
Capellini, Roberta I-3
Cardoso, Pedro J. S. II-531
Carreño, Mónica II-3
Carvalho, Pedro H. II-468
Casado, Johanna I-326
Cavallo, Piero II-241
Ceccacci, Silvia I-521

Chacón-Rivas, Mario I-349
Chapman, Richard II-95, II-109
Chatzilari, Elisavet II-385
Chávez, Romelia II-3
Cheng, Irene I-630, II-400
Chinnici, Marta II-358
Choudhry, Shatabdi I-639
Conneely, Fiona I-639
Correia, Tiago I-136
Cox, Daniel J. I-339
Cruz, Ana Paula I-429
Czarnecki, Steven I-339

da Rocha, Victor Hazin I-405
Dankwa, Nana Kesewaa I-39
Darmawaskita, Nicole II-41
Das, Meenakshi II-52
Das, Swagata II-449
de la Vega, Gonzalo I-326
de Oliveira, Káthia Marçal I-418
Dehon, Loïc I-418
Delcroix, Véronique I-418
Delgado-Cedeño, Daniel I-349
Dery-Pinna, Anne-Marie I-369
Di Gregorio, Marianna II-62
Díaz-Merced, Wanda I-326
Dozio, Nicolò I-599
Draude, Claude I-39
Dutra, Taynara Cerigueli I-53

Efthimiou, Eleni II-72
Eide, Signe Aanderaa I-186
Eirinaki, Magdalini I-444
Emiliani, Pier Luigi II-347
Eusébio, Celeste I-136
Ezzedine, Houcine I-418

Fabian, Claudia M. I-326
Fagernes, Siri II-221
Farzidayeri, Jamshid I-533
Felipe, Daniel I-53
Felipe, Tanya Amara II-82, II-167
Ferreira, João I-482

Ferreira, Marta Angélica Montiel   II-82, II-167
Ferrise, Francesco   I-599
Figliolia, Amanda Coelho   I-153
Fioriti, Vincenzo   II-358
Flouda, Christina   II-72
Fotinea, Stavroula-Evita   II-72
Fragoso, Olivia   II-3
Fresno, Nazaret   II-255
Fuglerud, Kristin Skeide   I-116
Fujikake, Kazuhiro   I-545
Fülber, Heleno   I-482
Furnell, Steven   I-197

Galvão, L.   II-167
Garcia, Beatriz   I-326
García, Laura Sánchez   II-82, II-167
Gasparini, Isabela   I-53
Georgiadis, Kostas   II-385
Geurts, Hélène   I-418
Ghedin, Francesco   I-3
Giannoumis, G. Anthony   I-213
Giboin, Alain   I-369
Giraldi, Luca   I-521
Gjøsæter, Terje   I-213, I-232
Glasser, Abraham   II-189
Gonçalves, D. A.   II-167
Gonzalez Clavijo, Claudio Camilo   I-473
Goulas, Theodor   II-72
Grandi, Fabio   I-280, I-294
Große, Ulrike   I-99
Guedes, A. P.   II-167
Guedira, Youssef   II-367
Guerreiro, Joel   II-154
Guerrier, Yohan   I-71, I-418
Gupta, Nandita   I-89
Gupta, Suraj   I-213

Haelewyck, Marie-Claire   I-418
Hajari, Nasim   I-630, II-400
Hasan, Sayed Kamrul   I-232
Hassan, Saad   II-202
Heitplatz, Vanessa N.   II-328
Helkala, Kirsi   I-197
Ho, Chester   II-400
Howard, Ayanna   II-52
Huang, Weilun   I-384
Huenerfauth, Matt   II-189, II-202
Hunt, Spencer   I-339

Iatskiu, C. E.   II-167
Ibarra-Manzano, Mario-Alberta   I-630
Ibarra-Manzano, Oscar   II-400
Ichikawa, Keita   I-589, II-519
Iijima, Ryo   II-412

Jamshidi, Fatemeh   II-95
Jaramillo Alvarez, Gloria Patricia   I-473
Jariwala, Abhishek   II-109
Jessel, Nadine   II-12
Johnson, Ronan   I-639
Ju, Yunran   I-384
Juiter, Chalakorn   I-555
Jura, Nicolas   I-418
Justice, Cameron L.   I-339

Kalaganis, Fotis P.   II-385
Keates, Simeon   I-567
Kennedy, Deven A.   I-339
Khaliq, Yousaf   I-339
Kinch, Martin   I-567
Kinoshita, Fumiya   I-394, II-519
Klinghoffer, Sydney   I-639
Kolski, Christophe   I-71, I-418
Kompatsiaris, Ioannis   II-385
Kon, Satoe   II-138
Korman, Alex   I-580
Kristensen, Josefin   I-250
Krömker, Heidi   I-99
Kurita, Yuichi   II-449
Kuroiwa, Jousuke   II-267
Kushalnagar, Raja   II-189
Kuwano, Sakura   II-138

Langley, Caleb   I-533
Lastre-Dominguez, Carlos   II-400
Leite Ribeiro Okimoto, Maria Lucia   I-461
Leite, Patricia da Silva   I-166
Leopardi, Alma   I-521
Lepreux, Sophie   I-418
Lindblom, Jessica   I-250
Liu, Miao   II-118
Liu, Shuo   I-617
Lotivio, Tristan C.   I-339
Lu, Jun-Li   II-412

Maia Bisneto, Alvaro Boa Vista   I-405
Mandala, Mahender   II-52
Mangiron, Carme   I-269
Maragos, Petros   II-277

Marcolin, Federica   I-599
Marghitu, Daniela   II-52, II-95, II-109
Martins, Ivo   II-507
Maschio, Eleandro   I-53
Mata, Omar   II-424
Matsuura, Shu   II-138
Matsuura, Yasuyuki   I-589, II-519
McClarty, James   I-533
McDaniel, Troy   I-429, II-41, II-424
McDonald, John   I-639
McGee, Hunter K.   I-339
Medola, Fausto Orsi   I-153
Meier, Alan   I-429
Méndez, Juana Isabel   I-429, II-424
Mengoni, Maura   I-521
Mercadier, Caroline   I-21
Merlin, Bruno   I-482
Migkotzidis, Panagiotis   II-385
Migovich, Miroslava   I-580
Milling, Manuel   I-617
Miranda, Othoniel   I-429
Miyata, Akihiro   II-438
Molina, Arturo   I-429, II-424
Moncrief, Robyn   I-639
Motooka, Kousuke   II-438

Nakane, Kohki   I-589
Nakayama, Shota   II-267
Naveteur, Janick   I-71
Nikolopoulos, Spiros   II-385
Nonis, Francesca   I-599

Ochiai, Yoichi   II-412, II-494
Odaka, Tomohiro   II-267
Okawara, Takumi   II-438
Okuno, Honoka   I-394
Oliveira, Hélder P.   II-468
Ono, Rentaro   I-545, I-589
Opolz, Suellym Fernanda   II-82
Osone, Hiroyuki   II-412

Pachodiwale, Zeeshan Ahmed   I-444
Papadimitriou, Katerina   II-72, II-277
Parada-Cabaleiro, Emilia   I-617
Parakh, Neha   I-444
Parelli, Maria   II-277
Patel, Dhruvil   I-444
Pavlakos, Georgios   II-277
Peffer, Therese   I-429, II-424
Peixoto, Patrícia S.   II-468

Pereira, Luis   II-154
Pérez, Citlaly   I-429
Peruzzini, Margherita   I-280, I-294
Picelli Sanches, Emilia Christie   I-461
Poljac, Ana-Maria   I-186
Ponce, Pedro   I-429, II-424
Potamianos, Gerasimos   II-72, II-277
Pozzi, Simone   I-280
Prati, Elisa   I-280, I-294
Pudlo, Philippe   I-418

Qian, Zhenyu Cheryl   I-384

Ramasamy, Priyanka   II-449
Ramos, Célia M. Q.   I-312
Reckers, Derrick M.   I-339
Reis, Pedro   II-468
Rekik, Yosra   I-418
Renevier-Gonin, Philippe   I-369
Rodrigues, Janaine Daiane   II-25
Rodrigues, João M. F.   I-312, II-507, II-531
Rodrigues, L.   II-167
Rojano-Cáceres, José Rafael   II-485
Romero-Fresco, Pablo   II-291
Rosas-Percastre, Jesús Antonio   II-485
Roselli, Ivan   II-358
Rouillard, José   II-367
Ryskeldiev, Bektur   II-412

Sadasue, Masaaki   II-494
Saenz, Maria   I-639
Sanchez Alvarez, Jhon Fernando   I-473
Sandnes, Frode Eika   I-153, I-186
Sandoval-Bringas, J. Andrés   II-485
Santos, Jedid   II-507
Sapountzaki, Galini   II-72, II-277
Sarcar, Sayan   II-412, II-494
Sarkar, Medha   I-339, I-533
Sarkar, Nilanjan   I-339, I-533, I-580
Schöne, Cathleen   I-99
Schuller, Björn W.   I-617
Schulz, Trenton   I-116
Sebillo, Monica   II-62
Segundo, Marcela A.   II-468
Serpa, Antonio   I-21
Shitara, Akihisa   II-412
Sigismondi, Nicola   II-358
Silva, A. M. C.   II-167
Silva, Diogo   I-405
Silva, Samuel   I-136

Simon-Liedtke, Joschua Thomas   I-116
Soler Gallego, Silvia   II-308
Song, Meishu   I-617
Sturr, Ben   I-639
Suwa, Izumi   II-267
Swenson, Brandon   I-533

Tagami, Daichi   II-494
Takada, Hiroki   I-394, I-545, I-589, II-519
Takai, Eiji   II-519
Talipu, Abudukaiyoumu   I-521
Tassistro, Francesca   I-3
Teixeira, António   I-136
Teixeira, Leonor   I-136
Teixeira, Pedro   I-136
Todt, E.   II-167
Touyama, Hideaki   I-394
Trevethan, Kyle   I-533
Trindade, D. de F. G.   II-167
Truillet, Philippe   I-21, II-12
Turner, Daniel   II-531

Ulrich, Luca   I-599
Unterfrauner, Elisabeth   I-326

Vella, Frédéric   I-21
Veras, Allan   I-482
Vezzetti, Enrico   I-599
Vigouroux, Nadine   I-21
Vitiello, Giuliana   II-62
Vivar-Estudillo, Guillermina   I-630
Vogler, Christian   II-189

Wade, Joshua   I-533, I-580
Wade, Justin W.   I-339
Wang, Yingjie   II-118
Wilkens, Leevke   II-328
Wilson, Devon   I-339
Wolfe, Rosalee   I-639
Wölfel, Alexander   I-99
Woods, Naomi   I-197
Wu, Ko-Chiu   I-555

Yamato, Yuki   II-438
Yang, Zijiang   I-617

Zamprogno, Leonardo Zani   I-482
Zhang, Xinyong   I-499

Printed in the United States
by Baker & Taylor Publisher Services

Printed in the United States
by Baker & Taylor Publisher Services